Wissenschaftliche Untersuchungen
zum Neuen Testament

Herausgeber/Editor
Jörg Frey

Mitherausgeber/Associate Editors
Friedrich Avemarie · Judith Gundry-Volf
Martin Hengel · Otfried Hofius · Hans-Josef Klauck

190

Clare K. Rothschild

Baptist Traditions and Q

Mohr Siebeck

Clare K. Rothschild, born 1964; 1986 B.A. University of California, Berkeley; 1992 M.T.S. Harvard University; 2003 Ph.D. University of Chicago; currently Assistant Professor of Theology at Lewis University, Romeoville, IL.

ISBN 3-16-148791-5

ISSN 0512-1604 (Wissenschaftliche Untersuchungen zum Neuen Testament)

Die Deutsche Bibliothek lists this publication in the Deutsche Nationalbibliographie; detailed bibliographic data is available in the Internet at *http://dnb.ddb.de*.

The book was typeset by Martin Fischer in Tübingen, printed by Gulde-Druck in Tübingen on non-aging paper and bound by Großbuchbinderei Spinner in Ottersweier.

Printed in Germany.

For my grandfather:
Alexander Bernard Komoroske
1912–2005

The dove descending breaks the air
With flame of incandescent terror
Of which the tongues declare
The one discharge from sin and error.
The only hope, or else despair
Lies in the choice of pyre or pyre –
To be redeemed from fire by fire.

T. S. Eliot, "Little Gidding,"
Four Quartets

Acknowledgments

The foundational idea for this book arose in a three-and-a-half hour conversation on a car ride from Grand Rapids, MI to Chicago, IL in February, 2003. Good friend and colleague, James A. Kelhoffer and I were headed home from the Midwest Society of Biblical Literature meeting. For the meeting Jim had prepared a presentation on John the Baptist's diet of "locusts and wild honey" (Mk 1:6/Mt 3:4). I presented a topic, spinning off of my dissertation research, on two literary themes – charismatic and didactic – in Luke-Acts. These two themes, I argued, represent the author's explanation for the rapid growth of the Jesus movement, one of the dilemmas his second *logos* sets out to resolve. As Arthur Darby Nock argued in the early part of the 20th century, these motifs addressed different audiences for different purposes: the didactic (e.g., speeches) addressed audiences stirred by appeals to the intellect, while the charismatic (e.g., miracles) addressed audiences persuaded by appeals to the sensational (*Conversion: The Old and the New in Religion from Alexander the Great to Augustine of Hippo* [Oxford: Claredon, 1933] 254–56). They are artificially brought together in Acts (cf. Philostratus' *Vita Apollonii*) to portray early Christian missionary work as ubiquitous – affecting everyone. During this long car ride discussion with Jim, I began to think about this division between didactic and charismatic as it was played out elsewhere in the NT – in terms, for example, of John the Baptist, Jim's topic at the conference, and Jesus. Thus I trace the question of literary divisions between traditions associated with these two historical personages to that day.

This book was written under the generous supervision of Hans-Josef Klauck at the University of Chicago who read the entire manuscript and provided excellent critical feedback. I have also received numerous critical comments from Hans Dieter Betz with profit. I wish to express gratitude to Dr. Henning Ziebritzki at Mohr Siebeck in Tübingen for his interest in the manuscript and to Dr. Jörg Frey of the Evangelisch-Theologische Fakultät, University of Munich for his careful observations about the thesis and prompt recommendation of the manuscript to the WUNT series. I also wish to thank Tanja Mix, Jana Trispel and all others at Mohr Siebeck who assisted in the production of this work.

Many colleagues have provided assistance on aspects of the manuscript, in particular James A. Kelhoffer, Johann Thom, Chris Mount, Karina Martin Hogan, Matthew Goff, and participants of the various societies of which I am a member, including the Society of Biblical Literature, the Midwest Society of

Biblical Literature, the Chicago Society of Biblical Research, and the Association of Chicago Theological Schools (New Testament). Also helpful were the
critical comments of the anonymous editors of the *Journal of Religion* and the
Journal of Biblical Literature. Presentations of various segments of the book
have elicited valuable feedback. In particular, I wish to thank Margaret M.
Mitchell for the opportunity to present part of Chapter 4 to the Early Christian
Studies Workshop at the University of Chicago in November 2004.

I also express gratitude to Annette Bourland Huizenga who ably assisted in all
aspects of editing not to mention the production of indices and to the students
of Saint Mary's College (IN) and Lewis University (IL) for dialogue on aspects
of the thesis.

Finally, I thank my parents, Judith R. and Alex B. Komoroske Jr. and sisters,
Kirsten A. Komoroske and Jessica K. Solomon for their enthusiastic support of
iconoclastic approaches to religious ideas and life, and my husband, Douglas
and our children, Maxwell and Luke, who have each, in their varying capaci-
ties, rallied nobly for the cause of higher learning. The book is dedicated to my
grandfather who died in the course of its completion.

Table of Contents

Abbreviations and References

The Greek New Testament is cited from the *Novum Testamentum Graece*, Nestle-Aland 27ᵗʰ edition. Abbreviations correspond to The SBL Handbook of Style (1999); the *Oxford Classical Dictionary* (³1996); Liddell, Scott and Jones, *A Greek-English Lexicon*; and G. W. Lampe, *A Patristic Greek Lexicon*, including the following:

1 En.	*1 Enoch*
AB	*Anchor Bible*
ABD	D. N. Freedman (ed.), *Anchor Bible Dictionary*
AJP	*American Journal of Philology*
AJT	*American Journal of Theology*
AnBib	Analecta biblica
ANF	Ante-Nicene Fathers
ANRW	Aufstieg und Niedergang der römischen Welt
Apoc. Zeph.	*Apocalypse of Zephaniah*
Apul., *Met.*	Apuleius, *Metamorphoses*
As. Mos.	*Assumption of Moses*
ASTI	*Annual of the Swedish Theological Institute*
ATANT	Abhandlungen zur Theologie des Alten und Neuen Testaments
AthR	*Anglican Theological Review*
b.	born
BBR	*Bulletin for Biblical Research*
BDAG	W. Bauer, F. W. Danker, W. F. Arndt and F. W. Gingrich, *A Greek-English Lexicon of the New Testament and Other Early Christian Literature* (³2000)
BDF	F. Blass, A. Debrunner and R. W. Funk, *A Greek Grammar of the New Testament and Other Early Christian Literature*
BETL	Bibliotheca ephemeridum theologicarum lovaniensium
BHS	Biblia Hebraica Stuttgartensia
Bib	*Biblica*
BJRL	*The Bulletin of the John Rylands Library of Manchester*
BN	*Biblische Notizen*
BR	*Biblical Research*
BSac	*Bibliotheca sacra*
BT	*The Bible Translator*
BWA(N)T	Beiträge zur Wissenschaft vom Alten (und Neuen) Testament
BZ	*Biblische Zeitschrift*
BZNW	Beihefte zur Zeitschrift für die neutestamentliche Wissenschaft und die Kunde der älteren Kirche

c.	century
ca.	circa
CBQ	Catholic Biblical Quarterly
CBQMS	*Catholic Biblical Quarterly Monograph Series*
CCSL	Corpus Christianorum, Series Latina
CD	Damascus Document
Cic., *Rep.*	Cicero, *De republica*
CJRT	Canadian Journal of Religious Thought
CH	*Church History*
Corp. Herm.	*Corpus Hermeticum*
CSEL	Corpus scriptorum ecclesiasticorum latinorum
CurTM	Currents in Theology and Mission
DDD	K. van der Toorn et al. (eds.) *Dictionary of Deities and Demon* (^{2}1999)
Did.	*Didache*
Dion. Hal.	Dionysius of Halicarnassus
Diss.	Dissertation
DNP	H. Cancik and H. Schneider (eds.), *Der Neue Pauly: Enzyklopädie der Antike*
DSD	Dead Sea Discoveries
DUJ	*Durham University Journal*
Ébib	Études bibliques
EKKNT	Evangelisch-katholischer Kommentar zum Neuen Testament
Epiph.	Epiphanius
EpRev	*Epworth Review*
EstBib	Estudios bíblicos
ET	English translation
Euseb., *Hist. eccl.*	Eusebius of Caesarea, *Historia ecclesiastica* (*Church History*)
Euseb., *Praep. evang.*	Eusebius of Caesarea, *Praeparatio evangelica* (*Preparation for the Gospel*)
ETR	*Etudes théologiques et religieuses*
EvQ	*Evangelical Quarterly*
ExpTim	*Expository Times*
FC	The Fathers of the Church
FRLANT	Forschungen zur Religion und Literatur des Alten und Neuen Testaments
FS	Festschrift
Gk.	Greek
Gos. Eb.	*Gospel of the Ebionites*
Gos. Naz.	*Gospel of the Nazarenes*
Gos. Thom.	*Gospel of Thomas*
HDR	Harvard Dissertations in Religion
Heb.	Hebrew

Herod.	Herodotus
HKNT	Handkommentar zum Neuen Testament
HNT	Handbuch zum Neuen Testament
HNTC	Harper's New Testament Commentaries
Hom., *Od.*	Homer, *Odyssey*
HTKNT	Herders theologischer Kommentar zum Neuen Testament
HTR	Harvard Theological Review
HUT	Hermeneutische Untersuchungen zur Theologie
ICC	International Critical Commentary
IDB	G. A. Buttrick (ed.), *Interpreter's Dictionary of the Bible*
Int	*Interpretation*
IQP	International Q Project
ITQ	*Irish Theological Quarterly*
JBL	*Journal of Biblical Literature*
JECS	*Journal of Early Christian Studies*
JETS	*Journal of the Evangelical Theological Society*
JHS	*Journal of Hellenic Studies*
Jos., *Ant.*	Josephus, *Antiquitates Judaicae* (*Jewish Antiquities*)
Jos., *B.J.*	Josephus, *Bellum judaicum* (*Jewish War*)
Jos., *Vita*	Josephus, *Vita* (*The Life*)
JQR	*Jewish Quarterly Review*
JR	*Journal of Religion*
JSNT	*Journal for the Study of the New Testament*
JSNTSup	Journal for the Study of the New Testament: Supplement Series
JSOT	*Journal for the Study of the Old Testament*
JSOTSup	Journal for the Study of the Old Testament Supplement Series
JTS	*Journal of Theological Studies*
Jub.	*Jubilees*
Justin, *Dial.*	Justin Martyr, *Dialogus cum Tryphone (Dialogue with Trypho)*
KEK	Kritisch-exegetischer Kommentar über das Neue Testament (Meyer-Kommentar)
Lat.	Latin
LCL	Loeb Classical Library
LE	The "Longer Ending" of the Gospel of Mark (Mk 16:9–20)
LSJ	Liddell, Scott and Jones, *A Greek-English Lexicon*
Luc., *Alex.*	Lucian of Samosata, *Alexander* (*Pseudomantis*) (*Alexander the False Prophet*)
LXX	Septuagint
Mart. Ascen. Isa.	*Martyrdom and Ascension of Isaiah*
ms(s)	manuscript(s)
MT	Masoretic Text
NA[27]	Aland, K., et al rev. and ed. *Novum Testamentum Graece*. 27th ed.

NeoT	*Neotestamentica*
NHL	J. M. Robinson (ed.), *The Nag Hammadi Library*, Revised Edition
NHS	Nag Hammadi Studies
NICNT	New International Commentary on the New Testament
NIGTC	New International Greek Testament Commentary
NovT	*Novum Testamentum*
NovTSup	Novum Testamentum, Supplements
NPNF	Nicene and Post-Nicene Fathers
NRSV	New Revised Standard Version
NT	New Testament
NTAbh	Neutestamentliche Abhandlungen
NTApo	W. Schneemelcher (ed.), *New Testament Apocrypha*, Revised Edition
NTS	*New Testament Studies*

OCD	Hornblower and Spawforth (eds.), *Oxford Classical Dictionary*, (^{3}1996)
OTP	J. H. Charlesworth (ed.), *The Old Testament Pseudepigrapha*
Ovid, *Fast.*	Ovid, *Fasti*

par.	parallel(s)
PG	J. Migne (ed.), *Patrologia graeca*
Philo, *Abr.*	*De Abrahamo* (*On the Life of Abraham*)
Philo, *Mos.*	*De vita Mosis* (*On the Life of Moses*)
Philo, *Prob.*	*Quod omnis probus liber sit* (*That Every Good Man Is Free*)
Philo, *Spec.*	*De specialibus legibus* (*On the Special Laws*)
Philo, *Virt.*	Philo, *De virtutibus* (*On the Virtues*)
PL	J. Migne (ed.), *Patrologia Latina*
Pl., *Apol.*	Plato, *Apologia*
Plut., *Num.*	Plutarch, *Numa*
Plut., *Rom.*	Plutarch, *Romulus*
Plut., *Thes.*	Plutarch, *Theseus*
Ps.-Clem.	*Pseudo-Clementines*
PTS	Paderborner Theologische Studien
PW	Pauly-Wissowa, *Real-Encyclopädie der classischen Altertumswissenschaft*

RAC	T. Klauser (ed.), *Reallexicon für Antike und Christentum*
RB	Revue Biblique
RGG^4	Religion in Geschichte und Gegenwart, 4th ed.
RHPR	Revue d'histoire et de philosophie religieuses

SANT	Studien zum Alten und Neuen Testaments
SBB	Stuttgarter biblische Beiträge
SBLDS	Society of Biblical Literature Dissertation Series
SBLMS	Society of Biblical Literature Monograph Series
SBLSP	SBL Seminar Papers

SBT	Studies in Biblical Theology
SC	Sources chrétiennes
SE	*Studia evangelica*
Sib. Or.	*Sibylline Oracles*
SNTSMS	Society for New Testament Studies Monograph Series
SNTSU	Studien zum Neuen Testament under seiner Umwelt
SP	Sacrina pagina
SPCK	Society for Promoting Christian Knowledge
ST	Studia Theologica
STDJ	Studies on the Texts of the Desert of Judah
StPatr	Studia patristica
StudBT	Studia Biblica et Theologica
StudLit	*Studia Liturgica*
TCGNT	B. M. Metzger, *A Textual Commentary on the Greek New Testament*
TDNT	G. Kittel and G. Friedrich (eds.), *Theological Dictionary of the New Testament*
T. Job	*Testament of Job*
TLZ	*Theologische Literaturzeitung*
TNTC	Tyndale New Testament Commentaries
TPI	Trinity Press International
TRev	Theologische Revue
TSK	*Theologische Studien und Kritiken*
TU	Texte und Untersuchungen zur Geschichte der altchristlichen Literatur
TynBul	*Tyndale Bulletin*
TZ	*Theologische Zeitschrift*
VC	*Vigiliae Christianae*
VT	*Vetus Testamentum*
VTSup	Vetus Testamentum Supplements
Vulg.	Vulgate
WBC	Word Biblical Commentary
WC	Westminster Commentaries
WMANT	Wissenschaftliche Monographien zum Alten und Neuen Testament
WUNT	Wissenschaftliche Untersuchungen zum Neuen Testament
ZAW	*Zeitschrift für die Alttestamentliche Wissenschaft*
ZKG	*Zeitschrift für Kirchengeschichte*
ZNW	*Zeitschrift für die Neutestamentliche Wissenschaft*
ZTK	*Zeitschrift für Theologie und Kirche*

Chapter One

New Testament Baptist Traditions

> To obtain a valid and vivid picture of the Baptist what we need is
> not more new evidence but a better understanding of the way to
> read the available New Testament sources.[1]

1.1 Introduction

Most scholarly attention paid to John the Baptist focuses on what can be known
of the life of the historical Baptist – his baptizing in the Jordan River and
maintaining a wilderness 'ascetic' lifestyle.[2] Significantly less consideration,

---

[1] C. H. Kraeling, *John the Baptist*, 6.

[2] Standard works on this topic include E. Bammel, "The Baptist in Early Christian Tradi-
tion," *NTS* 18 (1971–72) 95–128; J. Becker, *Johannes der Täufer und Jesus von Nazareth*
(Neukirchen-Vluyn: Neukirchener Verlag, 1972); Jean Daniélou, *The Work of John the Baptist*
(Baltimore: Helicon, 1966); M. Dibelius, *Die urchristliche Überlieferung von Johannes dem
Täufer* (Göttingen: Vandenhoeck & Ruprecht, 1911); J. Ernst, *Johannes der Täufer: Interpre-
tation, Geschichte, Wirkungsgeschichte* (BZNW 53; Berlin: de Gruyter, 1989); A. S. Geyser,
"The Youth of John the Baptist: A Deduction from the Break in the Parallel Account of the
Lucan Infancy Story," *NovT* 1 (1956) 70–75; M. Goguel, *Au seuil de l'évangile: Jean-Baptiste*
(Paris: Payot, 1928); P. W. Hollenbach, "Social Aspects of John the Baptist's Preaching Mis-
sion in the Contexts of Palestinian Judaism," *ANRW*, II.19.1, 850–75; C. H. Kraeling, *John the
Baptist* (New York: Scribner, 1951); H. Lichtenberger, "Reflections on the History of John the
Baptist's Communities," *FolOr* 25 (1988) 45–9; E. Lohmeyer, *Das Urchristentum 1: Johan-
nes der Täufer* (Göttingen: Vandenhoeck & Ruprecht, 1932); E. Lupieri, *Giovanni Battista
fra Storia e Leggenda* (Brescia: Paideia, 1988); J. P. Meier, *A Marginal Jew: Rethinking the
Historical Jesus. Volume Two: Mentor, Message, and Miracles* (New York: Doubleday, 1994)
19–223; idem, "John the Baptist in Matthew's Gospel," *JBL* 99/3 (1980) 383–405; J. Murphy-
O'Connor, "John the Baptist and Jesus: History and Hypothesis," *NTS* 36 (1990) 359–74;
Heinrich Peter, *Johannes der Täufer in der urchristlichen Überlieferung* (Marburg: H. Bauer,
1911); J. Reumann, "The Quest for the Historical Baptist," in *Understanding the Sacred Text:
Essays in Honor of Morton S. Enslin on the Hebrew Bible and Christian Beginnings*, ed.
J. Reumann (Valley Forge, PA: Judson, 1972) 181–99; J. Schütz, *Johannes der Täufer* (Zürich:
Zwingli, 1967); C. H. H. Scobie, *John the Baptist* (London: SCM, 1964); J. Steinmann, *Saint
John the Baptist and the Desert Tradition* (New York: Harper, 1958); W. B. Tatum, *John the
Baptist and Jesus: A Report of the Jesus Seminar* (Sonoma, CA Polebridge, 1994); W. Trilling,
"Die Täufertradition bei Matthäus," *BZ* (1959) 271–89; R. L. Webb, *John the Baptizer and
Prophet: A Socio-Historical Study* (Sheffield: JSOT Press, 1991); idem, "John the Baptist and
his Relationship to Jesus," in *Studying the Historical Jesus: Evaluations of the Current State of
Current Research*, ed. B. D. Chilton and C. A. Evans (Leiden: Brill, 1994) 179–229; idem, "The
Activity of John the Baptist's Expected Figure at the Threshing Floor (Matthew 3.12 – Luke
3.17)," *JSNT* 43 (1991) 103–11; W. Wink, *John the Baptist in the Gospel Tradition* (Cambridge:

however, has been given to the precise nature of the literary evidence and the relationship of this evidence to the corpus of narrative and teaching materials attributed to Jesus in the NT and related documents. With a few minor exceptions, most studies of Baptist traditions rely on the canonical gospels and Josephus, *Ant.* 18.116–19 uncritically. In particular, the coherence of the Synoptic witnesses is taken for granted, despite frequently ambiguous, implausible, and even, contradictory qualities. Regarding historical John research, Walter Wink once commented that where historical Jesus research has its "messengers of defeat," research on the historical John has none.[3] Today, however, the John quest likewise faces defeat and rightly so. Nevertheless, the traditions in his name represent not just a neglected niche of the study of early Christian literature, but an area with much to offer modern understandings of the NT.[4] The present examination brings together two traditionally separate specializations of NT studies: the historical Baptist and Q research. Specifically, this work addresses the perplexing relationship of NT Baptist traditions to their most reliable and ancient witness, Q.[5] To my knowledge, no such monograph-length study scrutinizing the intersection of these two separate divisions of NT studies has, as of yet, been undertaken.

Cambridge University Press, 1968); idem, "Jesus' Reply to John: Matt. 11:2–6/Luke: 7:18–23," *Forum* 5 (1989) 121–28; A. Yarbro Collins, "The Origin of Christian Baptism," *StudLit* 19 (1989) 28–46.

These studies usually also treat Josephus, *Ant.* 18.116–19. They also often exclude apocryphal, gnostic, patristic and Mandaean evidence. For systematic examinations of all of the evidence, see J. Ernst, *Johannes der Täufer*; W. Wink, *Gospel Tradition*; E. Bammel, "The Baptist in Early Christian Tradition"; R. Webb, *John the Baptizer and Prophet*; E. Lupieri, *Giovanni Battista*. About the later traditions, specialist E. Bammel writes, "Although these legends are meant to fill gaps, this task is not performed by adding or inventing stories, but mainly by embellishing those traits which are envisaged already in canonical tradition" ("John Did No Miracle," in *Miracles: Cambridge Studies in Their Philosophy and History* [London: A. R. Mowbray, 1965] 186). J. Massyngberde Ford's argument that parts of the book of Revelation can be traced to the historical Baptist are dismissed (*Revelation: Introduction, Translation, Commentary*, AB 38 [Garden City, NY: Doubleday, 1975] 28–37). Webb has a useful table of texts referring to John in the first two centuries C.E. ("John the Baptist and his Relationship to Jesus," 185–86).

[3] *John the Baptist*, x.

[4] The recent "discovery" of "the cave of John the Baptist" provided a small but welcome surge of interest in John the Baptist. It is, however, otherwise unrelated to this literary-critical study of the canonical texts. The present author is not qualified to judge the conclusions of Shimon Gibson in his documentation of the findings: *The Cave of John the Baptist* (New York: Doubleday, 2004).

[5] This study assumes the Two Document Hypothesis (2DH) with some qualification of Matthean and Lukan so-called "*Sondergut*" materials in the second half of the discussion. For a thorough, recent, persuasive explanation of this position with chart, see John S. Kloppenborg, *Excavating Q: The History and Setting of the Sayings Gospel* (Fortress: Minneapolis, 2000) 31–33.

Emphasizing its distance from historical John research, the present literary discussion refers to NT traditions about John the Baptist as "Baptist."[6] In this valuation no conclusion is drawn as to what extent these traditions reflect the historical teacher. 'Baptist' traditions are here defined as what various diverse Christian voices of the four gospels are willing to submit about (descriptions) or attribute to (sayings) John the Baptist. 'Baptist' traditions represent what early Christians transmit about John.

That said, NT interpretation overwhelmingly supports classification of these traditions as redaction and, as such, unreliable.[7] This thesis regards such a classification as a premise in need proof. In contrast, the present thesis views the burden of proof for the origin of these traditions on any wishing to claim derivation other than among the followers of John. Specifically, this study tests the assumption that their origin is among John's followers, arriving in Christian documents as unmodified forms. The present investigation aims to show that most Baptist traditions, in fact, make more sense when interpreted in this way.

While acknowledging Christian transmission, if the canonical 'Baptist' traditions were passed down to the four evangelists as forms then they were probably not originally 'Christian' fragments, but 'Baptist.' They were not, however, 'Baptist' in the sense of the historical Baptist, but in the sense of unknown representatives (comparable to the also unknown NT evangelists) associating themselves with his name or movement.[8] In this study, NT Baptist traditions

---

[6] In line with scholarly convention, the English adjective, "Baptist" is used throughout this work to refer to those traditions, individuals, or groups considering themselves associated in whatever close or distant way with John the Baptist. So-called 'Baptist' traditions do not, however, necessarily imply 'Baptist' communities before, at the time of, or after the time of Jesus or as the necessary purveyors of these traditions. For the arguments for and against the existence of Baptist communities in the first and early second century, see below n. 8. Although most assume John's ministry preceded Jesus', Baptist traditions are not necessarily earlier than Jesus' or other NT traditions.

[7] John Reumann makes this point: "What catches the eye particularly is that in example after example key verses ... are labeled 'redactional' by recent critics, i.e., editorial additions by the evangelist, *not from any earlier source*" ("The Quest for the Historical Baptist," 192; emphasis original).

[8] Outside the four gospels, evidence of disciples of the Baptist persisting in the period of early Christianity includes Acts 18–19, Justin Martyr, *Dial.* 80 and *Ps.-Clem.* Rec. 1.54, 60; Hom. 2.23–4. Cf. also references to "Hemerobaptists," appearing in *Ps.-Clem.* Hom. 2.23–4; Hegesippus (Eusebius, *Hist. eccl.* 4.22.7); and Epiphanius, *Pan.* 17; *Apos. Con.* 6.6.5. Ephraem of Syria too possesses a parallel report to *Ps.-Clem* Rec. 1.60 possibly based on a common source (J. Thomas, *Le mouvement baptiste,* 116 ff.). Because, however, no evidence positively connects John's followers with this group, J. Thomas denies any link (*Le Mouvement Baptiste,* 36). Also, most scholars deny any real connection between Baptist followers and the rise of Mandaeanism. Kurt Rudolph writes: "*Johannes der Täufer und seine Jüngerschaft haben nach dem Befund der uns zugänglichen Quellen keine Beziehung zu den Mandäern gehabt*" (*Die Mandäer* [Göttingen: Vandenhoeck & Ruprecht, 1960] 1.80; emphasis original). Although the twelve disciples in Acts 19 know only the "baptism of John," they are referred to as "disciples" (v. 1: μαθητάς) and "believers" (v. 2: πιστεύσαντες), assignations used exclusively for Jesus'

are compared to other NT traditions about Jesus, in particular those in Q. As an eclectic group, the NT Baptist traditions, nonetheless, generate a roughly uni-

---

followers in Luke-Acts. The discrepancy may reflect competition between Baptists and Paul (baptism by water [John] or by the spirit [Paul]) – rather than John and Jesus. Spirit baptism is later imputed to Jesus, probably by Paulinists and, no less, via Baptist traditions in which John predicted a coming one baptizing with the spirit (e.g., Q 3:16b, Mk 1:8)! On Acts 19:1–7, without any additional explanation, Helmut Koester asserts: "Acts 19:1–7 does not itself prove the continuing existence of the Baptist sect … because it is constructed entirely on the basis of Luke's theory of the mediation of the holy spirit" (*Introduction to the New Testament*, Vol. 2, "History and Literature of Early Christianity" [New York/Berlin: de Gruyter, 1982] 73). W. Brandt, too, dismissed any evidence of followers of the Baptist in Acts (*Die jüdischen Baptismen*, 122). W. Baldensperger, however, points out that χριστιανοί (Acts 11:26) meant simply "messianists" and could have been applied to either group: "Non-Pauline Christianity in the Orient ca. the year 100 of our era must have resembled a Baptist Jewish sect" (*Der Prolog des vierten Evangeliums. Sein polemisch-apologetischer Zweck* [Freiburg: J. C. B. Mohr (Paul Siebeck), 1898] 106). The most cogent assimilation of the historical evidence on early Baptist communities is presented by E. Käsemann in "The Disciples of John the Baptist in Ephesus," in *Essays on New Testament Themes* (Philadephia: Fortress, 1982) 136–48. Characterizing past scholarship on the topic rather brutally as a "barely conceivable variety of naïveté, defeatism and fertile imagination …. from the extremely ingenuous on the one hand to the extremely arbitrary on the other," Käsemann concludes that, despite Luke's depiction of these twelve Ephesian disciples as "immature Christians …. it is disciples of the Baptist who are the subject of the passage; *the Gospels themselves presuppose the existence of a Baptist community in competition with the young Church.* These disciples have naturally no contact with the Christian fellowship, know nothing of the Spirit which has been bestowed on Christendom and therefore have to be enlightened about the place of the Baptist as the forerunner of Jesus and be subjected to re-baptism, which incorporates them into the Church and imparts to them the Spirit. This gives us a consistent and historically intelligible situation at which, on any other hypothesis, we cannot arrive" (140–42; emphasis added). In response to the question of why Luke obscured his presentation of John's disciples, Käsemann replies, "The answer is simple: the existence of a community owing allegiance to the Baptist could not be admitted without endangering gravely the Church's view of his function. For such a community would be bound to put John in the place which Jesus occupied in Christendom, making him Messiah and Kyrios and thus the rival of Jesus; it would thus run counter, in the most concrete and thoroughgoing fashion, to the Church's tradition of the forerunner of Jesus…. Neither can we overlook the fact that this construction has a polemic intention – the refutation of the claims of the Baptist community. Jesus himself had been baptized by John and had in some sense appealed to his authority; parts of very early Christendom had sprung from the circle around the Baptist …. Our Gospels, like the tradition underlying them, have escaped from the dilemma by presenting the claims of the Baptist community as a misunderstanding of the Baptist's message and by depicting John himself as pointing forward to the Christ who should follow him …. *As his tradition made John into the herald of Jesus, so Luke has gone on to make John's disciples into an odd species of Christian and thus he has radically eliminated any suggestion of real rivalry.* Such a presentation can certainly only be possible if Luke knew of the existence of a Baptist community by hearsay alone and was not obliged to attach to it any real significance because, for him at least, it belonged to a past already remote" (141–43; emphasis added). The location of this Baptist community in Ephesus may reflect the author's intention to place them where Apollos was known to have worked (148). Other than Ephesus, there is no evidence for Baptist communities outside of Palestine and Syria. *Ex hypothesi*, the Baptist community was, however, not remote for the author of the Gospel of Mark; see Ch. 4. W. Baldensberger was the first to present the conclusion of a vital Baptist community during and impacting the earliest phase of the Christian movement (*Der Prolog des vierten Evangeliums. Sein polemisch-apologetischer*

fied representation of John and his message. The present discussion contrasts elements of this rough unanimity with a variety of other canonical Gospel traditions, pointing, in particular, to Q's affinity with elements of the NT's collective portrayal of the John the Baptist.

The question can be anticipated: Of what value is Josephus' account of John the Baptist (*Ant.* 18.116–19) to this investigation? The answer to this question is, quite simply, its value is limited. Not only is Josephus' presentation of John tainted by his own biases and predilections diminishing its reliability as fact, but even if his account could be verified, the connection between the historical Baptist and NT Baptist traditions is unclear. The *bruta facta* of the historical Baptist are only of value to the study of Baptist traditions if one is attempting to demonstrate continuity between the teacher and his tradition. This study possesses no such aim. Granted themes of NT Baptist traditions occasionally

---

Zweck. His argument was severely criticized by Wilhelm Brandt in *Die jüdischen Baptismen, oder das religiöse Waschen und Baden im Judentum mit Einschluß des Judenchristentums* (Beihefte zur ZATW 18; Giessen: Verlag von Alfred Töpelmann, 1910) 81–82, 146. Brandt, rather, argues (with F. Overbeck) that the Ephesian Baptists of Acts 18–19 are a fiction of the author (81). Clayton R. Bowen, however, defends Baldensberger's position in "John the Baptist in the New Testament," 49–76. In addition to the evidence summoned by Baldensperger, Bowen makes some of his own observations such as that, although not previously mentioned or described as a named group in this Gospel, Mk 2:18 uses μαθηταὶ Ἰωάννου as a group with which the readers are supposed to be familiar (46). Depicting the followers of the Baptist as the "most dangerous rival of the early Church" (the citation is from O. Cullmann, "Ὁ ὀπίσω μου ἐρχόμενος," in *The Early Church: Studies in Early Christian History and Theology,* ed. A. J. B. Higgins [Philadelphia, Westminister, 1956] 177), see M. Dibelius, *Die urchristliche Überlieferung von Johannes dem Täufer.* Also acknowledging the unexplored possibilities of the influence of Baptist and his movement on early Christianity is Ernest W. Parsons, "The Significance of John the Baptist for the Beginnings of Christianity," in *Environmental Factors in Christian History,* eds. John Thomas McNeill, Matthew Spinka and Harold R. Willoughby (Chicago: IL: The University of Chicago Press, 1939) and Michael Wolter, "Apollos und die ephesinischen Johannesjünger," *ZNW* (1987) 49–73. Parsons argues the two dominant themes that emerge from the fragmentary and casual evidence on the Baptist in the NT: "the imminence of the kingdom of God and the ethical preparation for participation in it" have a "definite influence" on the message of Jesus (3, 2). Parsons goes so far as to claim: "The early message of Jesus was essentially that of John" (3). Parsons' interpretation even includes NT passages illustrating these two originally Baptist themes (e.g., Acts 2:38; 3:19–20; 8:12; 11:15–18; 1 Thess 1:9–10; Gal 1:4; 1 Cor 1:7–8; Phil 4:5; Heb 10:36–39; 2 Pet 3:1–13). See also Colin Brown, "What Was John the Baptist Doing?" *BBR* (1997) 49 and T. W. Manson, "John the Baptist," *BJRL* (1953–54) 395–412. Some denials of the existence of Baptist communities arise in reaction to frequent assumptions of competition between the two groups. The mistake of this reaction is to "throw out the baby with the bath water," that is, to deny existence of the groups instead of just their rivalry. Rejecting the idea of a Baptist sect is J. A. T. Robinson, "Elijah, John and Jesus: An Essay in Detection," *NTS* (1958) 279 n. 2. Robinson correctly points out, however, that attempts to use Mandaean literature to prove the existence of a first-century Baptist sect are anachronistic. Interestingly, John the Baptist is the only saint whose feast day, like Jesus', is the day of his birth; Paul's celebrates the day of his conversion and all the others celebrate the day of the saint's death. John's feast day (June 24), attested in the sermons of Augustine, was apparently established by the year 400.

coincide with Josephus' account about John and, in the course of the present argument, these coincidences are pointed out. About them, however, little more is said. Furthermore, although this investigation includes a brief discussion of the chronological relationship of John's and Jesus' ministries, no literary arguments are construed on the basis of an imagined tradition-historical trajectory. Christian traditions may predate, in certain cases, Baptist ones. In either case, the point is irrelevant to this synchronic, comparative thesis. The focus of this investigation is the Baptist traditions themselves and what they successfully convey about early Christian literature, its processes and aims.

1.2 John the Baptist in Q

Although Q's pronounced Baptist *Tendenz* is widely recognized, most studies on the Baptist neglect Q as a source in its own right about John's life and work. Even specialists on Baptist traditions frequently overlook Q in their work on the topic.[9] For example, in the opening to his *ANRW* article, "John the Baptist in NT Traditions and History," Edmondo F. Lupieri comments,

> For the historical reconstruction of the figure of John the Baptist we can look to five written sources. Four of them are Christian texts: the Gospel of Mark, the work of Luke (Gospel and Acts), the Gospel of Matthew, and the Fourth Gospel. The fifth text is a relatively short section in the historical production of the greatest Judeo-Hellenistic historian: Flavius Josephus. All these five works were written during the second part of the first century A. D., which means roughly between 30 and 70 years after the death of the Baptist, and have different degrees of significance for the modern historian.[10]

Against Lupieri, the present examination argues that Q be regarded as a sixth, separate and important written witness for investigations of Baptist traditions.

Pointing to the significance of John in Q, Christopher Tuckett writes:

---

[9] Walter Wink is an exception: *John the Baptist*, 18–26. Wink's view of Q is, however, debatable on a few points. Wink writes: "The validity of analyzing Q as a literary unit is not self-evident. Even if its order and content could be agreed upon, there would still be the question of the legitimacy of a *redaktionsgeschichtliche* approach, since Q is not so much a 'redaction' as a collection, a miscellany of logia without sufficiently clear or extensive editorial data (in most cases) to allow us to speak of its viewpoint with any degree of thoroughness. Nevertheless it is necessary that the Q material be treated, not only as a prolegomenon to the study of John's role in Matthew and Luke, but also as a source for Jesus' own view of John, which serves in turn as a control for assessing the church's subsequent modifications of the John-traditions" (18 n. 1). Josef Ernst is also an important exception: *Johannes der Täufer: Interpretation, Geschichte, Wirkungsgeschichte* (BZNW 53; Berlin: de Gruyter, 1989) 39–8; and, Michael Tilly dedicates a chapter to "Johannes der Täufer in der Logienquelle Q": *Johannes der Täufer und die Biographie der Propheten: Die synoptische Täuferüberlieferung und das jüdische Prophetenbild zur Zeit des Täufers* (BWANT 7/17; Stuttgart: W. Kohlhammer, 1994) 69–104.

[10] *ANRW* 2/26/1 (1993) 430.

One of the more surprising features of Q is the amount of space devoted to John the Baptist. John's preaching is set out in detail in Q 3:7–9 and in 3:16 f., and a long section a little later in Q (7:18–35) discusses the position of John in some detail. So too John's ministry is evidently given a significant place in the saying Q 16:16. ... The reasons for devoting so much space to John are not clear. Much of this material probably had a complex prehistory behind it before it ever reached Q. ... Nevertheless, despite possible reservations about the status of John at one level, it seems clear that there is also in Q wholehearted support for John's teaching and a willingness to incorporate the tradition of his teaching into Q itself with no hint that John's message had been superseded, or rendered in any way invalid, by the ministry of Jesus himself.[11]

---

[11] Christopher Tuckett, *Q and the History of Early Christianity: Studies on Q* (Edinburgh: T & T Clark; and Peabody, MA: Hendrickson, 1996) 108–9. B. H. Streeter once described Q as a "prophetic book," specifying: "The relatively large amount of space given to John the Baptist ... suggest that Q was composed *at a time and place where the prestige of John was very considerable*" (*The Four Gospels* [London: Macmillan, 1926] 291–92; emphasis added). On John's prominence in Q, C. Scobie acknowledges, "John figures prominently in Q" (*John the Baptist*, 13). Also, "From all these considerations, it would appear that the Q source is the most reliable: it is the earliest, it contains the greatest proportion of material concerning John, it has the highest estimate of John, and it contains the clearest evidence of Semitisms" (C. Scobie, *John the Baptist*, 17); and, "... Q, which is the earliest and most reliable source for the reconstruction of John's message" (C. Scobie, *John the Baptist*, 70; cf. also 201). On Q 7:18–35, David R. Catchpole writes: "From Q 7:18–35 it is evident that the Q community maintained a lively interest in John the Baptist. ... The natural *Sitz im Leben* of all this editorial activity would arguably be a Christian community which is, at one or more stages in its own development (depending on how many editorial strata are discernible in Q 7:18–35), *in direct contact with the continuing Baptist movement*" (*The Quest for Q* [Edinburgh: T. & T. Clark, 1993] 61–62; emphasis added). J. P. Meier comments, "The criterion of discontinuity, as well as confirmation at times from Mark, John, or Josephus, makes the core of the Q tradition on the Baptist fairly reliable" (*A Marginal Jew*, 2.28). And, "This is one reason why we started with the Q material to give ourselves a better basic orientation. Now that we have some initial grasp of the historical Baptist, we can search for elements in the Marcan narrative that cohere with or supplement our preliminary sketch" (42–43). John Meier also notes the Q passages on John "demonstrate some of the closest word-for-word correspondence between Matthew and Luke that we find in the Q material (see especially Matt 3:7–10 ‖ Luke 3:7–9)" (*A Marginal Jew*, 28). Meier concludes that the close agreement may indicate that this material was fixed early on. Cf. also E. Bammel, "The comparatively large amount of space in Q given to the Baptist has puzzled scholars a good deal. It is even more surprising that a document that is supposed to consist merely of sayings of Jesus starts with sections dealing with John" ("The Baptist in Early Christian Tradition," 99). Also, John H. Hughes writes, "This material [Q] serves as an important check to the presentation of the ministry of John the Baptist by the Gospel writers. It is not that the information about John in Q must be accepted as an infallible record, but rather that the picture which emerges of him there is often so far removed from what E. W. Parsons describes as 'the traditional and conventional view that John was the conscious forerunner of Jesus' as to demand consideration both of its possible accuracy and of its compatibility with the apparently contradictory judgment on John accepted by the early church" ("John the Baptist: The Forerunner of God Himself," 194–95). Arland D. Jacobson is also in agreement: "The basic difference is that in Q John appears as a prophet in his own right but in Mark he has been subordinated to Jesus. ... But in Q, John is independent, a preacher of repentance before the imminent judgment of Yahweh" ("The Literary Unity of Q," *JBL* 101 [1982] 107). Cf. also J. Taylor, "Both Matthew and Luke may have felt that the Q Baptist block was a little long and too enthusiastic about John. Abbreviations and relocations of material lessened its force without

Building on Tuckett's assessment of John's position in Q, the present investigation argues that *current models of Q suggest that, at some early stage in its undoubtedly complex pre-history, Q existed as a source containing Baptist traditions exclusively.* This argument is constructed, primarily, on the following literary observations: (1) double attribution or the attribution of certain sayings to John in Q, but to Jesus elsewhere;[12] (2) contradictions between Jesus' sayings in and outside of Q,[13] (e.g., fasting/feasting,[14] afamilial/familial, itinerant/urban,[15]

---

necessarily lessening its tone" (*The Immerser: John the Baptist within Second Temple Judaism* [Grand Rapids, MI: Eerdmans, 1997] 300). J. Taylor also warns that "It is possible that Q linked Jesus and John together as belonging to the era of the kingdom of God, though it is not quite clear" (*The Immerser*, 310). J. P. Meier points out that in the Gospel of Matthew, "the prophetic figure of the Baptist stands in the time of fulfillment alongside of Jesus" ("John the Baptist in Matthew's Gospel," 396). Standard works on Q also consulted include: David R. Catchpole, "The Beginning of Q: A Proposal," *NTS* 38 (1992) 205–21; J. S. Kloppenborg, *The Formation of Q: Trajectories in Ancient Wisdom Collections* (Philadelphia: Fortress, 1987) esp. 317–28; idem, *Q Parallels: Synopsis, Critical Notes, and Concordance.* Foundations and Facets: New Testament (Sonoma, CA: Polebridge, 1988); idem, ed. *The Shape of Q: Signal Essays on the Sayings Gospel* (Minneapolis: Fortress, 1994); John S. Kloppenborg Verbin, *Excavating Q: The History and Setting of the Sayings Gospel*; Andreas Lindemann, ed. *The Sayings Source Q and the Historical Jesus* (BETL 158; Leuven: Leuven University Press and Peeters, 2001); James M. Robinson, Paul Hoffmann and John S. Kloppenborg, ed. *The Critical Edition of Q* (Minneapolis: Fortress Press, 2000); Risto Uro, ed. *Symbols and Strata: Essays on the Sayings Gospel Q* (Suomen Eksegeettisen Seuran Julkaisuja; Publications of the Finnish Exegetical Society 65; Helsinki: Finnish Exegetical Society; and Göttingen: Vandenhoeck & Ruprecht, 1996). With Tuckett's statement (cited above), J. Taylor also agrees. Taylor writes: "It is impossible, given the evidence we have, to make a definitive distinction between what must have been John's teaching concerning basic righteousness and what must have been exclusively Jesus' own .... However, thematically, John and Jesus appear to have shared a significant amount of teaching material" (*The Immerser*, 151). Cf. also W. Wink, *Gospel Tradition*, 18–26; E. Bammel, "The Baptist in Early Christian Tradition," 99–101; J. Kloppenborg, *The Formation of Q*, 322–25. Here the present author presses the question of the relationship of materials attributed to John and Jesus. Of interest also (see below), the claim that Luke's infancy narrative of John is based on written sources from a Baptist movement has been made. See P. Winter, "The Cultural Background for the Narratives in Luke I–II," *JQR* 45 (1954) 159–67, 230–42, 287; idem, "The Proto-Source of Luke 1," *NovT* 1 (1956) 184–99. Rejecting this claim is S. Ferris, *The Hymns of Luke's Infancy Narratives: Their Origin, Meaning and Significance* (Sheffield: JSOT Press, 1985) 86–98 and E. Bammel, "The Baptist in Early Christian Tradition," 96. Cf. also W. Wink, *John the Baptist in the Gospel Tradition*, 58–81.

[12] Although probably correct to conclude that John and Jesus both taught a need for repentance and righteous living in light of eschatological expectations, C. Scobie cites examples of double attribution as mere points of agreement between Jesus and John (*John the Baptist*, 161). C. Kraeling describes the relationship between the two in this way: "From their Baptist brethren they received John's Infancy narrative...and above all a goodly number of the words of John. The words of John apparently came to the knowledge of the Christian group at a very early date, for some of the more striking of them, like the word about the 'generation of vipers' and the word about the 'two baptism' were so deeply imbedded in the tradition that they came to be regarded as words of Jesus himself..." (*John the Baptist*, 175).

[13] According to C. Kraeling the contradictions are: John fasted, Jesus rejected fasting; John practiced baptism, Jesus did not; John found the final eschatological judgment cause for fear, Jesus did not; John demanded exemplary conduct in adherence to the Law, Jesus waived the letter of the Law; John insisted on a wrathful God prepared to execute imminent judgment;

didactic/charismatic,[16] spiritual-moral/physical, traditional [stressing obedience to the Law, including purification]/iconoclastic [flouting Law on certain points, denying efficacy of purification rites, including dietary (Mk 7:1–23, 7:14)],[17]

Jesus emphasized God's mercy and his patience in seeking and saving the lost; John awaited the day of judgment; for Jesus, the kingdom, while in the future was also in a sense already present (*John the Baptist*, 146–47). C. Scobie's list of contradictions adds that "John's ethical teaching was typically Jewish, but Jesus demanded a much more radical ethic" and "John's teaching implies that by the performance of certain acts man can earn the right of entry into the Kingdom; but Jesus taught that whatever men do, they are still 'unprofitable servants' in the sight of God" (*John the Baptist*, 160). Another contradiction proposed by Scobie is the point of rewards. According to Scobie, John offers no reward for righteousness emphasizing, rather, the coming crisis. With eschatological fulfillment, however, Jesus emphasizes rewards (e.g., Mt 5:3–13) (Scobie, *John the Baptist*, 210). J. P. Meier, however, interprets Mt 3:11–12 as (alternately with punishments) John's enunciation of rewards (*A Marginal Jew*, 2.39).

[14] J. Taylor, *The Immerser*, 204–7, 210. Although Jesus rejected fasting it soon became a regular feature of Christian piety (*Did.* 8:1; much earlier in Mk 2:20). The practice may have entered as a result of assimilation of Baptist elements into Christian circles (C. Kraeling, *John the Baptist*, 174). Baptism, too, followed this trend. For example, for John, baptism was necessary for salvation; for Jesus, not so, but later followers accommodated John's followers in this way. C. Scobie notes that Jesus did not fast – a practice that often served as an outward expression of repentance and humility in traditional Judaism (*John the Baptist*, 134).

[15] C. Scobie notes that Jesus went to people, whereas John expected people to come to him (*John the Baptist*, 156).

[16] The Fourth Gospel argues John performed no signs (Jn 10:41). Although it is possible to distinguish between didactic/charismatic for John/Jesus in NT traditions, this polemical assertion in the Fourth Gospel drives a suspicion that John, too, performed miracles (*contra* J. Taylor, *The Immerser*, 218, 319). The Gospels provide accounts that some people were, however, disappointed and left unconvinced by John because he did no sign (Mt 11:7–19; Lk 7:24–35). Perhaps John performed miracles, insisting, however, that they indicate the coming, and not instantiation, of the kingdom. Josephus overlooks them as he overlooks the miraculous deeds of other prophets in his rationalizing version of Jewish origins. Similarly, Josephus eliminates eschatological elements. H. Koester comments: "Josephus suppresses the eschatological component of John's teaching, however, and says that the reason for his execution was Antipas' fear of a popular insurrection" (*Introduction to the New Testament*, Vol. 2, "History and Literature of Early Christianity" [New York/Berlin: de Gruyter, 1982] 71). Moreover, according to Josephus, claims were made by messianic pretenders that signs would accompany them (Theudas promises that the waters of the Jordan will divide [*Ant.* 20.5.1]; and the Egyptian assures that at his command the walls of Jerusalem will fall [*Ant.* 20.8.6/*Bell.* 2.13.5]). Furthermore, that John performed signs is a better explanation for how he attracted great crowds of tax-collectors, prostitutes, and soldiers and why Herod Antipas would have demanded his imprisonment and execution. The idea that Antipas was personally affronted by John's moral teaching about divorce is historically unlikely. Rudolf K. Bultmann, *The History of the Synoptic Tradition* (Oxford: Blackwell, [2]1968 [[2]1931]) 24: "That stories of John's miracles were in circulation is in itself quite credible; for the assertion that he performed none (John 10:41) is obviously a piece of polemic. And does not Mark 6:14 imply that reports of the Baptist's miracles were current?" J. Murphy-O'Connor does not acknowledge this reference: "Neither the Gospels nor Josephus depict John as a miracle-worker" ("John the Baptist and Jesus: History and Hypotheses," 372). C. Kraeling, however, observes that the idea that John's disembodied spirit served Jesus as the means by which he performed works of power [Mk 6:14–16] is "no small concession to John's power" (*John the Baptist*, 160).

[17] The discussion over purity between Jesus and John in Jn 3:25 suggests Jesus and his disciples were not strict enough for John (cf. Mk 7:1–23) (Scobie, *John the Baptist*, 155).

and expectant/fulfillment eschatology);[18] and (3) thematic continuities between Q sayings and Baptist traditions.[19]

1.3 The Corpus of Baptist Traditions

Close examination of the literary evidence beginning with Q, but ultimately including all NT gospel traditions, suggests more remains of John's teaching than previously recognized. In the past, nearly every study on John the Baptist laments a dearth of evidence. Expressing this disappointment, in the opening to the third chapter of her study, *The Immerser*, Joan Taylor asserts,

> We have no independent body of material, or list of John's sayings, collected by any Jewish group … But the New Testament writings consistently avoid John's teaching.[20]

Charles Scobie echoes the sentiment:

> We saw that although he [John] probably spoke of the coming Kingdom, *he declined to go into details*. There is no hint in John's message of an elaborate blueprint of the future. Not for him the apocalyptic arithmetic of Daniel, or the conducted tours of Enoch, or the

---

[18] John works within a framework of expectation; Jesus, of fulfillment (J. Murphy-O'Connor, "John the Baptist and Jesus: History and Hypotheses," 372 n. 54). Also, "Many students of the New Testament conclude that Jesus' eschatology was more orientated to the present time of fulfillment than to the future consummation" (A. Y. Collins, "The Origin of Christian Baptism," 36). Cf. also Collins' conclusion: "Christian and rabbinic baptism both have their ultimate roots in the ritual washings of Leviticus. Both came to function as rituals of initiation. The major difference is the relation of this ritual to eschatology. Both expect a fulfillment but the two communities place themselves on different sides of the turning point between the two ages" ("The Origin of Christian Baptism," 42). Enslin views as another contradiction that John, with "the earlier prophets," foresees "the Day of the Lord as an awful curse, a *dies irae*"; whereas Jesus "saw it as good news" (Morton S. Enslin, "John and Jesus" *ZNW* 66 [1975] 16). "Good news," however, seems also to have been an expression John used (e.g., Lk 3:18). Whether he saw the coming judgment, therefore, as "good" relies on normative interpretations of this word.

[19] For example, the proclamation of judgment by John, the future outpouring of the spirit, the demand for repentance, righteous living and social justice are not just themes of Baptist traditions in Q, but themes of Q overall. See also C. Scobie, *John the Baptist*, 208, 210.

[20] *The Immerser*, 101–2. Cf. also: "Our information concerning John is extremely abbreviated" (110). At many points throughout her book, in arguments about John, Taylor recommends comparisons with sayings of Jesus to make the point. For example, in her examination of the word שוב, she writes, "People who so turn around can count themselves among the righteous who will be spared destruction at the end. As Jesus is recorded as saying, 'Enter by the narrow gate…'" (108). Cf. also 83–84, 117, 122, 123 ("John hardly demanded less than what Jesus was to ask of 'the rich young man' [Matt. 19:16–30; Mark 10:17–31; Luke 18:18–30]"), 126, 127, 130, 135–36 (comparison of Jesus' teachings and *Targum Pseudo-Jonathan*) 148, 150 ("There are certainly striking similarities between the teaching of John and Jesus"). At one point, however, Taylor does express my view that "Christians may have quarried recollections of John's teaching and placed profound *logia* on the lips of Jesus" (150) and at another, "It seems likely that much more of John's message has remained than has hitherto been recognized and that it is embedded in the heart of the Christian ethos" (153; cf. also conclusion on 154).

military strategy for the war against Gog and Magog; his was a simple message of punishment for evil and reward for righteousness.[21]

Similarly, in his book, *John the Baptist in the Gospel Tradition*, Walter Wink remarks:

We have found no evidence in the Gospels, however, that written documents or 'Gospels' about John existed or were employed by the Evangelists.[22]

And John Meier concurs:

John and his immediate followers produced no literature … . in a sense he [John] resumes the purely oral preaching of Elijah and other OT prophets.[23]

Meier continues,

There is no arguing with John, because *he presents no arguments to establish his position.* There is no explicit argument from Scripture, no invocation of a previous rabbinic teacher, not even the prophetic legitimation, "The word of the Lord came to me, saying …" John knows the end is near, he knows the conditions for escaping destruction, and that is the end of the matter.[24]

These perspectives well reflect the most popular position about John in the NT gospels, namely that he appeared in the desert clothed like a prophet offering a baptism for the remission of sins with the simple and concise message that the end is near. These perspectives contradict, however, testimony in the Gospel of Luke that "with *many other* exhortations he [John] preached good news to the people (πολλὰ μὲν οὖν καὶ ἕτερα παρακαλῶν εὐηγγελίζετο τὸν λαόν)" (3:18). Likewise, they conflict with Josephus' testimony that John delivered rousing "sermons" (*Ant.* 18.118). Only Carl H. Kraeling accounts for these contradictions among witnesses:

That there may have been a Baptist 'literature' in the period of the early Church is entirely possible, but the specific suggestions of its use by the Evangelists are unconvincing or rest on the most tenuous hypotheses. The chances are that whatever the New Testament writers knew about John came by word of mouth into the tradition which their informants handed on to them.[25]

---

[21] C. Scobie, *John the Baptist*, 74; emphasis added.

[22] W. Wink, *John the Baptist*, 110.

[23] J. P. Meier, *A Marginal Jew*, 2.31.

[24] J. P. Meier, *A Marginal Jew*, 2.40; emphasis added. The argument that the component of imminent eschatology (bordering on the apocalyptic) among Jewish and Christian prophets implies lack of commitment to ethical exhortation, let alone to amassing records of any kind, is false. As many have observed (J. P. Meier himself included on 41), prophecy and apocalypticism, despite their interests in coming judgments, are literary genres. Most groups that upheld eschatological beliefs maintained simultaneous commitments to both moral exhortation and books. This may be related to the role of scribes in the development of apocalypticism.

[25] C. Kraeling, *John the Baptist*, 5; emphasis added.

The present thesis builds on Kraeling's position of the existence of John's teachings within the early church, going beyond Kraeling, however, by developing the hypothesis that such teachings were handed down to the evangelists *in written form*. The contention here is a significant quantity of John's teachings was preserved in Q attributed only later to Jesus by the evangelists and/or their sources.[26]

1.4 Synoptic 'Special Materials'

The present examination focuses on NT materials about John and Q. Important, therefore, to this discussion, are methodological issues germane to Q studies. One of the less thoroughly examined presuppositions of modern Q research concerns Q's relationship to Matthean and Lukan *Sondergut*. Nominating diverse *Sondergut* fragments for inclusion in Q is, of course, common. For at least a century of Q research, scholars have acknowledged that reconstructions of Q based on the mechanical selection of non-Markan Matthean and Lukan parallels alone are overly rigid. B. H. Streeter's inability to fathom Q's inclusion of any but double tradition material is, today, not so much famous as infamous.[27] Yet even as Streeter was rigorously attacked during the last century for his position, the *Critical Edition of Q* holds, rather dogmatically, to this same stance.[28] Nonetheless, it is conceivable that the authors of the Gospels of Matthew and Luke dealt with their Q source(s) in much the same way as their Markan one(s). That is, on the one hand, the author of the Gospel of Matthew was reluctant to omit material from Mark. Whereas, on the other hand, the author of the Gospel of Luke cut materials from Mark with relative liberty, utilizing less of this important source.[29] This observation alone suggests that certain "Special M" passages originated in Q.

Past research (prior to Harnack) on the topic of including *Sondergut* in Q arose as part of the trend exalting Q as the most ancient written report about the movement following Jesus' death and as the crucial, missing link between oral traditions of an 'original' band of Jesus' followers and written documents.[30] This

---

[26] *Contra* M. S. Enslin, "John and Jesus," 5–6; C. Scobie, *John the Baptist*, 16.

[27] Streeter eventually recanted this position. He also held to the idea that "M" and "L" were written documents (*The Four Gospels*, 223–70; also chart on 150). Most today take these designations to refer to unknown sources.

[28] *The Critical Edition of Q* is not actually a "critical edition," as this expression is applied in the field of Classics. It is, rather, a "text and translation."

[29] Material from Markan source(s) used by Matthew, but omitted by Luke includes: Mk 4:33–34; 6:17–19; 6:45–8:21 ("The Great Omission"); 9:9–13; 9:43–8; 10:1–12; 11:12–14; 11:20–25; 14:3–9; 15:16–20.

[30] Adolf von Harnack, *Sayings of Jesus: The Second Source of St. Matthew and St. Luke*, trans. J. R. Wilkinson (London: Williams & Norgate/New York: G. P. Putnam's Sons, 1908) 250–51.

trend, characterized by an uneasiness with a 'sayings' tradition exhibited interest in appending biographical details to Q's sayings to justify its qualification as a gospel or proto-gospel, a more comfortable early Christian generic designation. To this end, certain scholars wrestled with Lukan and Matthean *Sondergut*. In contrast, this study possesses a different determination. While past commentators hypothesized that, for example, the "Special L" section of Lk 3:1–20 on John's teaching belonged to Q,[31] this study broadens the spectrum considerably by viewing a wide variety of *Sondergut* materials from the perspective of other Baptist traditions. Matthean and Lukan *Sondergut* are now addressed in turn.

---

[31] See Heinz Schürmann, *Das Lukasevangelium* (HTKNT 3; Freiburg/Basel/Vienna: Herder, 1969) 1.169. See J. Ernst, *Johannes der Täufer*, 93–98, 312–13 for a summary of the positions. J. C. Todd claims Lk 3:1–20 represents a source-document of the Baptist's teaching: "From all this we may conclude that we have here an original document from the school of the Baptist, and this is of importance not only for itself but for the criticism of Q (the *Logia* of Jesus). As restored by Harnack, Q begins with the words of the Baptist, a section which is quite in place in a Gospel but hardly in a collection of Sayings of the Lord. This comes into Q simply by the mechanical process of selecting the non-Marcan material common to St. Matthew and St. Luke. If the arguments given above are sound, we restore this section to its context in St. Luke's Gospel and show that the 'Logia of John' probably antedated and possibly suggested the 'Logia of Jesus'" ("Logia of John," *ExpTim* [1910] 174). For J. P. Meier, "...there is no convincing reason why Matthew, an evangelist intent on moral catechesis, should have omitted this moral sermon from his Gospel" (*A Marginal Jew*, 2.42). Cf. also Paul Wernle, *Die synoptische Frage* (Freiburg i. Br.: Mohr, 1899). On the authenticity of Lk 3:1–20, scholarly opinion is divided. J. Wellhausen first argued that the passage was Lukan on account of its "characteristically Greek expressions" (*Das Evangelium Lucae* [Berlin: Reimer, 1904] 5). E. Bammel and others, however, argue a connection to or inclusion in Q ("The Baptist in Early Christian Tradition," *NTS* 18 (1971–72) 105–6; also I. Howard Marshall, *The Gospel of Luke* (Grand Rapids: Eerdmans, 1978) 142. J. Kloppenborg points out that two components of Lk 3:1–20, vv. 7–9 and 16–17, are parts of the double tradition with parallels at Mt 3:7–10 and 3:11–12 respectively (*The Formation of Q* [Philadelphia: Fortress, 1987] 74). Lk 3:10–14 is excluded from Q because it is not a part of the double tradition. In John Meier's opinion, "The sayings in Matt 3:7–12 par. and Luke 3:10–14 could just as easily stand in some Jewish report on the Baptist, so lacking are they in specifically Christian content" (*A Marginal Jew*, 2.42). The inclusion concerning John's priestly (Aaronic) lineage in Lk 1 is also interesting. An Aaronic or priestly Messiah was among those (with a Davidic messiah, the angel Michael and the Danielic Son of Man) expected to play a role in the eschatological events at the end (R. Webb, *John the Baptizer and Prophet*, 219–60). C. R. Bowen, "John the Baptist in the New Testament," in *Studies in the New Testament: Collected Papers of Dr. Clayton R. Bowen*, ed. Robert J. Hutcheon (Chicago, IL: University of Chicago, 1936) 51, 58–60, following D. Völter (*Theologisch Tijdschrift* 30 [1896] 244–69), believes that Luke 3:1–20 derives from an independent Baptist source. So also Harald Sahlin, *Studien zum dritten Kapitel des Lukasevangeliums* (Uppsala: Lundequistska, 1949). Of course, one can argue that as an outgrowth of the Baptist movement, these traditions belonged to what become 'Christian' all along, but this does not change the fact that certain texts were, at some point, not understood in terms of a life of Jesus, in some cases altering dramatically their meaning. On the infancy narrative, Kraeling argues that it is best to regard it not necessarily as a historical source concerning the Baptist, but as a "record of the piety of the Baptist circles that created it" (*John the Baptist*, 20).

1.4.1 *Matthean* Sondergut: *The Sermon on the Mount*

An important, initial catalyst for the present thesis on Matthean *Sondergut*, Baptist traditions and Q was provided by Hans Dieter Betz's exposition of a compositionally-balanced and comprehensive pre-Matthean Sermon on the Mount (SM).[32] The fundamental difficulty for source-critical analyses of the SM is that while it gleans a majority of its material from Q it also incorporates seminal information from both Mark and "Special M." Because the SM, as Betz demonstrates, impresses, in its final form in Matthew, as an all-inclusive, literary whole, scholars typically conclude that the author of Matthew composed the sermon on the basis of his three or more sources. In contrast, however, Betz argues that the SM was *handed down* to a final redactor of the Gospel of Matthew in a version of Q Betz designates: "Q[Matt]."[33] According to Betz, passages from Mark and "Special M" were built into the SM not by Matthew, but by a pre-Matthean redactor of Q.

Scholarly response to Betz's source hypothesis on this point is, in at least one case, unfavorable.[34] This resistance to his theory may be characterized by Ockham's razor: namely, whether it is *necessary* to posit an otherwise unknown pre-Matthean redactor of Q as conjoining the same sources with which we already believe an author/redactor of Matthew to have worked. Critics counter that it is more plausible to think of the SM as simply composed by "Matthew." Critics also question whether hypotheses regarding redactions of Q, such as Q[Matt] and Q[Luke], too glibly dismiss Q's general definition as non-Markan verbatim agreements between Matthew and Luke.[35]

The possibility remains, however, that both Betz *and* his critics are correct if the so-called "Special M" materials, and possibly even those from Mark, were at some stage originally incorporated in Q. Such a claim cannot, however, be made on the basis of Betz's demonstration of the SM's compositional unity alone. Stylistic (including rhetorical) and theological connections between non-Q "Special M" and Markan SM materials must also be demonstrated for such a claim to be convincing. The present position is that stylistic and theological continuities, associated with Baptist traditions, have been overlooked in comparisons of Q, Mark and *Sondergut* by past investigations and that a careful study of this type avails new insights into the question of the relationship between these groups of materials. Of course, to be cogent, each argument for the inclusion of other materials in Q encompasses both stylistic (e.g., Aramaisms, lack of Christol-

---

[32] H. D. Betz, *The Sermon on the Mount* (Minneapolis: Fortress, 1995).

[33] H. D. Betz, *The Sermon on the Mount*, 24–44.

[34] See Dale Allison, *JBL* 117/1 (1998) 136–38.

[35] This was a problem for B. H. Streeter who described the dilemma of selecting between Q and Q[Matt] and Q[Luke] as a dilemma of selecting between Q and non-Q (*The Four Gospels*, 238; see 224 [synopsis], 235–38).

ogy, and other distinguishing characteristics of Q) *with* various thematic (e.g., Baptist) connections. When such continuities are demonstrated, however, Betz's argument for the compositional integrity of the SM is the coup de grâce on the dependable conclusion that Q and/or Q^{Matt} included a wider array of materials.

Also, Betz's argument that the SM originally existed as an ancient epitome of sayings too suggests a relationship between the SM and Q. As a collection of sayings – even an abridgement of only the most important sayings assembled to facilitate, perhaps, memorization – Betz's SM is highly compatible with current ideas about and reconstructions of Q. This profound 'generic' similarity, added to actual material overlaps, demand scholarly attention on an order not previously paid. Thus, as one element of the investigation, this project takes up the question of connections between Q, Matthean and Lukan *Sondergut*, and Markan traditions vis-à-vis Baptist traditions.

If the proposal that SM *Sondergut* and/or certain Markan traditions originated in Q does not solve all of the source-critical problems of the SM, it may provide a more plausible, less rigid understanding of Q. As surely as Q was at one time a written document, it was probably also regarded, at least by the authors of Matthew and Luke, in the same way as they viewed another of their written sources, the Gospel of Mark: *valuable enough to merit serious rewriting*. The idea that Q was too precious to edit, containing only the most reliable, ancient, authentic sayings of Jesus – not a single one of which would ever be omitted from a record about his life – reflects modern, unproven assumptions about Q's content and value.

Admittedly complicated to prove, the implications of this aspect of my hypothesis that certain Matthean *Sondergut* sayings are traceable to Q, if correct, are far-reaching. While the list of candidates for inclusion in Q in this thesis is not long, it does consist of certain "Special M" contributions to the SM with a substantial effect on the history of interpretation, not to mention Western civilization in general. Well known parables, such as the wheat and tares (13:24–30, 36–43), the dragnet (13:47–50), the sheep and the goats (25:31–46) and the marriage feast (22:11–14) are each investigated in the course of this study for connections to Q and to traditions regarding the Baptist.[36] Additional Q candidates

---

[36] T. W. Manson also connects various "Special M" passages to the known teachings of John: "The other peculiarity of M which excites notice is the close connection of much of the teaching in it with that of John the Baptist. This again holds of both thought and expression. In the Sermon on the Mount, Mt. vii. 19, 'Every tree which does not produce good fruit is cut down and cast into the fire,' is a reproduction of the saying of John in Mt. iii. 10 = Lk. iii. 9. Again the parables of the Wheat and the Tares (Mt. xiii. 24–40, 36–43), of the Dragnet (xiii. 47–50), of the Sheep and Goats (xxv. 31–46), and perhaps also of the Ten Virgins (xxv. 1–13) and of the Marriage Feast (xxii. 11–14) are all of them just variations, more or less elaborate, on the theme of John the Baptist – wheat and chaff (Mt. iii. 12 = Lk. iii. 17)" (*The Teaching of Jesus: Studies of Its Form and Content*, 2nd ed. [Cambridge University Press, 1943] 37).

from "Special M" proposed in the course of this examination include: 6:1–18;[37] 11:11; 13:52 (v. 51?); 19:16–17; and 21:28–32.[38]

1.4.2 Lukan Sondergut

In terms of the Gospel of Luke, scholarship of the 1950s once categorized large sections of the Lukan infancy narratives as Baptist in origin.[39] While such conclusions are largely outdated today, the favorable depiction of John the Baptist in these passages remains baffling. For example, in Luke 1–2:

> (1) John is the one who "will turn many of the sons of Israel to the Lord their God" (1:16) and "will go before the Lord (ἐνώπιον κυρίου, not messiah) to prepare his ways" (1:76b);[40]

---

[37] On Mt 6:16–18 Joan Taylor writes: "Obviously there is the problem of authenticity here. The Matthean saying may not come from Jesus" (*The Immerser*, 206). Taylor also notes E. P. Sanders, *Jesus and Judaism* (Philadelphia: Fortress, 1985) 402 n. 24. Sanders writes: "Those who regard the passage as authentic will be constrained to defend it against the accusation of being pettifogging, and they may say that its author intended to encourage the right attitude in fasting. Will the same defence be allowed others in Judaism who passed rules?" Cf. *Jesus and Judaism*, 274. This position was also held by Paul Wernle (*Die synoptische Frage*, 224–33).

[38] See J. Taylor, *The Immerser*, 306.

[39] See W. Wink, *John the Baptist*, 60–82. Although Wink sides against the conclusion of so many scholars concerning a Baptist source behind the Lukan infancy narratives, his presentation of the arguments is reliable. The theory of a Baptist source behind the infancy narratives relies on a variety of observations including: (1) absence of the widespread Gospel tendency to subordinate John to Jesus in these two chapters; (2) exalted view of John including, perhaps, references to John as the Davidic Messiah (Lk 1:69b); (3) Semitisms, colloquialisms, and a generally Israel-focused (non-Gentile) perspective; (4) several north Italian Latin versions that ascribe the Magnificat to Elizabeth (cf. W. Wink, *John the Baptist*, 60 n. 2; (5) interpretations of the Benedictus (1:68–79) as a Baptist hymn (cf. discussions of the passage by M. Dibelius, *Die urchristliche Überlieferung von Johannes dem Täufer*; C. Kraeling, *John the Baptist*, 166–71; P. Winter, "Magnificat and Benedictus – Maccabean Hymns?" *Bulletin of the John Rylands Library*, xxxvii (1954) 328–47; M. Goguel, *Jean-Baptiste*, 74; and P. Vielhauer, "Das Benedictus des Zacharias," *ZThK*, xlix [1952] 255–72). This theory is, at least, one hundred years old. W. Wink traces its first proposal to D. Völter. It was subsequently developed by numerous other scholars, including W. Baldensperger, J. R. Wilkinson, M. Dibelius, C. R. Bowen, E. Norden, R. Eisler, M. Goguel, R. Bultmann, E. Lohmeyer, W. Bauer, C. Kraeling, P. Vielhauer and P. Winter (Wink, *John the Baptist*, 60 n. 1). C. Kraeling writes: "The autonomy and significance of John in the Infancy Narrative demands that the story arose in Baptist circles, and as an early Baptist narrative it requires careful consideration in any discussion of John's antecedents" (*John the Baptist*, 18). For corroborating views on the Lukan infancy narratives, see C. Scobie, *John the Baptist*, 49–59. On the lack of Christian elements in these chapters see H. L. MacNeill: "Everything in these two chapters, on the contrary, is definitely, positively, patriotically, and enthusiastically Jewish" ("The *Sitz im Leben* of Lk 1.5–2.20," *JBL* [1946] 126, 127). Finally, the infancy narratives of John served as a model for those of Jesus just as the narratives of Jesus' deeds and words from Mk and Q in the Third Gospel served as a model for the portraits of Peter and Paul in Acts.

[40] The reference to John as "the dawn from on high" is derived from Lk 1:76–79. The aorist form of the verb, ἐπεσκέψατο is selected here on the argument that ancient mss with the future

(2) John is the one whose birth indicates that the day of redemption has come (1:69);

(3) John is selected to deliver the message of salvation to God's people (1:77);

(4) John is called μέγας either in the sense of a Hellenistic divine man, or Jewish Son of God, or both (Lk 1:32; cf. Acts 8:10); and,

(5) John is described as the "horn of salvation" (κέρας σωτηρίας, 1:69a) or Davidic messiah[41] expected to bring political liberation to the Jewish people (Lk 1:71–5; cf. also Lk 3:15 and Jn 1:19 ff.)[42]

The 'Magnificat' offers another case in point. Not based on arguments reconstructing Aramaic etymological origins, but on its literary context in Luke, prior

form, ἐπισκέψεται reflect early Church interests. For a brief survey of the difficulty, refer to J. Taylor, *The Immerser*, 107 n. 7 who also favors the aorist reading.

[41] During the Hellenistic and early Roman periods, both Levitical and Davidic messiahships could be envisioned. (See M. de Jonge, "The Word 'Anointed' in the Time of Jesus," *NovT* [1966] 132–48.) In Sir 45:6–26; 49:4–5, for example, Levi is exalted over the royal line of David. Most deny the originality of the reference to the *Davidic* line of John the Baptist by John's *priestly* father in Lk 1:69. (See Ernest W. Parsons, "The Significance of John the Baptist for the Beginnings of Christianity," 12.) However, like other messianic expectations, opposing traits of two different individuals (Levitical *or* Davidic; priest *or* king; Elijah *or* Messiah; baptizing with water *or* spirit/fire) could be merged in a new conception of a single, anticipated figure. The motivation for such a convergence of traditions in the identification of a single individual may have been to satisfy the expectations of the widest possible set of converts/adherents. Like Jesus' lineage (e.g., Mt 1:1–17; Heb 4:14–5:10), John's dual levitical (Lk 1:5) *and* Davidic descents in Lk 1–2 (cf. not only Lk 1:69, but the Lukan genealogy as well [Lk 3:23–38]) may provide an example. And, the question might be posed: Would the second half of the Benedictus celebrate John (vv. 76–79) and the first half, Jesus (vv. 68–75)? Moreover, Luke's genealogy emphasizes Jesus' priestly and prophetic over his kingly [Matthew's genealogy] descent. As Clayton Bowen points out, not only does Luke deemphasize David's position in his genealogy and trace Jesus through *Nathan* to David (rather than, as in Matthew's genealogy, through Solomon to David), but after Jesus and Joseph, Luke's genealogy begins with Eli, a priestly name. Also, twice this author includes Levi, the ultimate progenitor of the priestly line, and both Amos and Nahum are mentioned ("John the Baptist in the New Testament," 66–67). In the Gospel of Luke, the author insists from the very beginning that John the Baptist descends from the line of Aaron (1:5), Jesus, from the line of David (1:27, 32; 2:4). Jesus even summons the example of David to defend why he and disciples pick and *eat* on the Sabbath (Mk 2:23–28/Mt 12:1–8/Lk 6:3–4). In Lk 1:73 (also Lk 1:55), however, the promise that John the Baptist picks up is not the one to David, but to Abraham. This may be related to John's insistence that nationality alone does not qualify one as a recipient of Abraham's promise (Lk 3:8). Cf. "daughter of Abraham" in Lk 13:16 and "son of Abraham" in Lk 19:9 and 13:28. Finally, some have argued that Q 17:37, about a "corpse," points to priestly concerns. This interpretation may point to Baptist traditions rather than anti-Christian, empty tomb polemic.

[42] Cf. *Ps.-Cl.* Rec. 1.60: "And, behold, one of the disciples of John asserted that John was the Christ, and not Jesus, inasmuch as Jesus Himself declared that John was greater than all men and all prophets. 'If then,' said he, 'he be greater than all, he must be held to be greater than Moses, and than Jesus himself. But if he be the greatest of all, *then must he be the Christ*'" (ET: ANF, 8.93 [*PG* 1240b – c]). Cf. also Rec. 1.54: "Yea, some even of the disciples of John, who seemed to be great ones, have separated themselves from the people, and proclaimed their own master as Christ" (ANF 8.92 [*PG* 1237b–1238a]). Ephraem of Syria has a parallel version; see Joseph Thomas, *Le Mouvement Baptiste*, 116 where the two texts are reproduced side by side. Also Hom. II, 8, 17, 23–4; III, 22; cf. Rec. III, 61. J. Thomas concludes that the polemic against John in the Clementine literature attests the continued existence of a Baptist sect.

to its attribution to Mary, various manuscript evidence preserves[43] that this hymn of praise was attributed to John's mother, Elizabeth.[44] As scholars have observed, the prevalence of Semitisms and the evidence of dual christologies in Lk 1–2 may suggest Baptist origins.[45] Of course, Baptist origins do not necessarily connote a relationship to Q. Connections if present must be demonstrated. The details of these narratives, however, beg fresh examination with up-to-date comparative materials and interpretive tools. Outside the infancy narratives, additional candidates for Q from the Lukan *Sondergut* under investigation in this study include: Lk 7:16b–18, 29–30; 9:40; 18:9, 18–19; 19:10–14; and 20:49–51.

In conclusion, whether or not *Sondergut* traditions are persuasively connected through Baptist traditions to Q, at the very least, this examination of certain passages of Matthean and Lukan *Sondergut* vis-à-vis Q pries open long-held assumptions regarding these texts, pointing to ever-present, yet habitually overlooked, Baptist traditions as important sources for comparison.

1.5 Methodological Considerations

Too frequently academic scholarship on John the Baptist navigates right over methodological dilemmas, ignoring obvious concerns and emphasizing, rather, the interest value of ready-at-hand conjecture. New reconstructions of the life of the historical John denounce forerunners for tailoring the evidence to suit their arguments, while acting very quickly to commit the selfsame error. In the 1950s and 60s some of the best historical examinations of John (e.g., C. H. Kraeling, C. Scobie) were eclectic in method organizing their interpretations topically and selecting from the evidence at will and without explanation. Soon thereafter, mainstream preoccupation with redaction-criticism insisted that the different theological dispositions of the individual evangelists be taken into greater account. The excellent examinations by Walter Wink and Ernst Bammel are, for example, organized on a gospel-by-gospel ("source-by-source") basis.

Emphasis on redaction-critical interpretation has today, however, subsumed other approaches to the detriment of accurate interpretations of the materials. It now takes place at the cost of any perceived historical value of the texts. In the case of the Baptist fragments, a subjugating disposition toward John is supposed for all four evangelists. The conviction among scholars of this disposition is so

---

[43] Some ancient authorities read "Elizabeth" for "Mary" in Lk 1:46. Cf. Lk 1:46 (Elizabeth has been the speaker to that point) with 1:56: "And Mary remained with her (ἔμεινεν δὲ Μαριὰμ σὺν αὐτῇ)." See Bruce M. Metzger, *A Textual Commentary on the Greek New Testament* (Stuttgart: Deutsche Bibelgesellschaft, [2]1994) 109.

[44] Cf. W. Wink, *John the Baptist*, 60 n. 2; F. C. Burkitt, "Who Spoke the Magnificat?" *JTS* (1905–6) 220–7. Also, n. 39 above.

[45] Cf. R. Laurentin, *Structure et théologie de Luc I–II* (Paris: Gabalda, 1957) 111–16; also W. Wink, *John the Baptist*, 72–79.

fervent it has been allowed to completely overtake any ability of the traditions to speak for themselves. Contrary to majority opinion, the assumption of the present study is that *polemic does not control every piece of the evidence*. Specifically, the present thesis argues that Rudolf Bultmann overemphasized the polemical quality of Synoptic passages about the Baptist, basing his interpretations of the material about John on a projected *Sitz im Leben* of competition between the disciples of Jesus and John.[46] Taking just one example, interpretations of the Baptist saying in Jn 3:30, "He must increase, but I must decrease,"[47] in its context in the Fourth Gospel, reflect overwhelming agreement: the fragment is not tradition, but redaction – here the author radically subjugates John to Jesus. Most fail, however, to recognize that in this passage *in its context* only John is qualified to subjugate himself to Jesus and *apart from this context*, in a context, for example, of Baptist references to a coming Elijah or Messiah figure, Yahweh himself, or some combination of the three, the statement might simply reflect, not competition, but genuine humility: that when the expected figure arrives naturally he will increase and I will decrease. Here I do not wish to deny some level of competition between the movements as represented in, for example, the Fourth Gospel. I am only interested in momentarily liberating the Baptist fragments from this totalitarian interpretational scheme to compare findings.

Some commentators do acknowledge the significant degree of respect paid to John by the canonical evangelists (e.g., W. Wink, J. P. Meier and others).[48] With this, a few commentators, such as Tuckett (above), even acknowledge Q as a primary source of John's respect.

As Walter Wink has correctly pointed out, the fact that John the Baptist is included in *all* Gospel traditions is curious:

Polemic does not explain John's presence in the gospels; it supplies but a piece of the puzzle.[49]

Wink continues with the following list of questions:

Why is John the Baptist accorded such a prominent place in the Gospel tradition? Why, for that matter, is he mentioned at all? Why did Jesus lavish on John words of such high praise that the church would later find them a source of profound embarrassment? And

---

[46] Before Bultmann: W. Baldensperger (*Der Prolog des vierten Evangeliums: Sein polemisch-apologetischer Zweck*. R. Bultmann relegates much to rivalry between the church and the disciples of John. Such a contention is, however, frequently inaccurate (*The History of the Synoptic Tradition*, 246 ff.). See above n. 8. See also W. Wink, *John the Baptist*, 12 n. 1, and 98–110.

[47] On predictive use of δεῖ – meaning "it is necessary" – in this saying, see my earlier work, *Luke-Acts and the Rhetoric of History* (WUNT 2/175; Tübingen: Mohr Siebeck, 2004) 185–212.

[48] Wink writes of John's "negative judgement before his positive value is acknowledged" (*John the Baptist*, 97).

[49] W. Wink, *John the Baptist*, 110.

why, in spite of this, did the church include John in the Christian proclamation, and assert what they could have left unsaid: that John marked the turning point in the history of salvation?[50]

Commentators like Wink pay lip service to John's prominence in NT traditions, yet permit their interpretations of Baptist fragments to be controlled by the assumption that the canonical evangelists propagandistically subjugated these traditions to those of Jesus. This contradiction is largely responsible for the halt in progress on the meaning and significance of NT Baptist traditions. How can John's prominence *and* subjugation in the NT be understood?[51]

Apropos of Wink's questions, this study attempts to correct the assumption regarding subjugation of Baptist to Christian traditions in the NT, demonstrating that this supposition derives from a myopic focus on the context of the fragment (redaction), as opposed to the fragment itself. In contrast, this thesis sets forth that, *when examined apart from their immediate literary contexts in accounts about Jesus, the fragments devoted to John tell a different story.*[52] Furthermore, the present thesis adds to Tuckett's assertion of the prominence of John the Baptist in Q, that, not just Q, but the Gospel of Mark too accords astonishing authority to John, suggested by observations explored further in Ch. 4, such as: (1) John is not subordinated at Jesus' baptism (Mk 1:9–11); (2) Jesus is depicted as the successor of John (1:14–15; 9:2–8); (3) Herod takes the displays of the miraculous by Jesus and his disciples (6:13) as evidence that Jesus represents John *redivivus* (6:16); (4) John performs miracles (6:14); and (5) Jesus defines his own authority with respect to John's (11:30–2).[53] As we will see, only infrequently does a literary tradition about John seem to reflect the deleterious hand of the early Christians.

The motivation for the recontextualization of Baptist traditions by Christians (an impulse the canonical gospels share) was primarily Christological:[54] although John was an undeniably reputable prophetic figure frequently mistaken for the Christ, he was not, according to the four evangelists, the Christ. Of course, the necessity for such a strong position against John as Christ points to a pressing reality of this contention.

---

[50] W. Wink, *John the Baptist*, x.

[51] C. Scobie asks the related question, "How could Jesus think so highly of John, and yet differ so widely from him?" (*John the Baptist*, 145).

[52] The author of the Gospel of Matthew, who (among the four evangelists) might have found it least customary/acceptable for a student to usurp his teacher, acknowledges (albeit unwillingly) John's baptism of Jesus (Mt 3:13–17). The Gospel of John goes to great lengths to ensure Jesus, *as John's disciple* (1:27, 3:22 ff.), is in some ultimate sense prior to John (Jn 1:1, 15, 30). Similarly, the Lukan infancy narratives make the claim that "precedence is not determined chronologically" (C. Kraeling, 177). The Lukan and Matthean genealogies provide still other answers. Jesus' baptism by John is a part of the problem. It is addressed by each evangelist differently.

[53] W. Wink, *John the Baptist*, 13.

[54] W. Wink, *John the Baptist*, 103.

1.5.1 Redactional Biases

Walter Wink provides an example of how a predetermined understanding of a single evangelist's bias incorrectly determines conclusions concerning Baptist traditions. The theory of Mark's secret of a suffering Messiah, not itself objectionable begets, however, on Wink's reading of Markan redaction, an accompanying, less convincing interpretation of a secret concerning John as a suffering Elijah-like figure.[55]

A second example from Wink concerns Luke-Acts. Accepting Conzelmann's scheme of salvation history, Wink apprehends every Baptist fragment in Luke in terms of John's role between Conzelmann's first and second aeons.[56] In doing so, however, Wink misses the highly nuanced program for Baptist traditions devised by this author.[57] An understanding of the redaction of the pieces is pertinent when sources are known – as in Matthean and Lukan redaction of the Markan source(s). However, as Dibelius first observed about Acts, when sources are not so effortlessly identified, source-, form-, and redaction-criticism must be enhanced by *Stilkritik*[58] – an investigation of, not only syntactic and semantic observations, but a full range of stylistic qualities, including elements of diction, key words and themes. The unknown derivation of many NT Baptist fragments makes the admonition to apply the full range of critical methods to these passages never more pertinent.

In sum, the present analysis attempts to balance redaction- with source-, form- and other critical methods as means of attaining more coherent interpretations of Baptist traditions. The method is primarily literary: synchronic and comparative. As such, it avoids doubtful dichotomies of interpretation emerging from tradition-historical approaches in which speculative chronological ordering

---

[55] For the full development of this parallel theology, see W. Wink, *John the Baptist*, 13–17. "No non-Christian tradition known to us speaks of the sufferings of Elijah" (W. Wink, *John the Baptist*, 14 n. 1 for a list). The position of this project on the Gospel of Mark and in particular the transfiguration event, is not far from Wink's. The present argument is, however, not derived from a theological idea (mysterious necessity of suffering), but on the basis of literary observations. See Ch. 4.

[56] W. Wink is only one of many scholars who, taking a gospel-by-gospel approach to the Baptist materials, falls victim to this error. Cf. also E. Bammel "The Baptist in Early Christian Tradition," 95–128 and J. P. Meier in "John the Baptist in Matthew's Gospel," 383–405.

[57] E.g., the author of the Gospel of Luke omits (1) Jesus' baptism by John and John's arrest and beheading (Mk 6:17–29/Mt 14:3–12; Lk 3:19–20); (2) reference to John as Elijah (Mk 9:9–13/Mt 17:9–13; cf. also Mt 11:12–13/Lk 16:16); and (3) references to John's clothing and diet (Mk 1:6/Mt 3:4) which he may have felt recalled Elijah (2 Kgs 1:8; Zech 13:4). For a recent assessment of Baptist traditions in the Gospel of Luke (in particular Luke's omission of Mk 1:6), see James A. Kelhoffer, *The Diet of John the Baptist: "Locusts and Wild Honey" in Synoptic and Patristic Tradition* (WUNT 176; Tübingen: Mohr Siebeck [2005]) 129–32.

[58] M. Dibelius, "Style Criticism of the Book of Acts," in *Studies in the Acts of the Apostles*, ed. Heinrich Greeven, trans. Mary Ling (London: SCM, ¹1956; Mifflintown, PA: Sigler, 1999) 4; German: *Aufsätze zur Apostelgeschichte* (Göttingen: Vandenhoeck & Ruprecht, 1951).

of sources is permitted to determine interpretative decisions (e.g., Q vis-à-vis Mark). Although this study makes a case for revival of the use of form-criticism, no single critical method dominates its interpretation.

1.5.2 Irregularity of Baptist Tradition Occurrences

Summarizing, redaction-dependent, gospel-by-gospel treatments of NT Baptist traditions currently hold sway. Such an overuse of any single critical method alone warrants scholarly attention (Reason #1). The incorrect assumption that a negative redactional disposition toward Baptist traditions determines their meaning and diminishes their value, however, intensifies the necessity of renewed study (Reason #2). And, NT Baptist traditions merit our additional study for yet a third and final, infrequently acknowledged reason: the enigmatic irregularity of their occurrences (Reason #3).

To this day no persuasive explanation exists for the arbitrary distribution of materials about John throughout the NT Gospels.[59] Particularly challenging is the sporadic insertion of the narrative of John's death in Mk 6:14–29.[60] Also puzzling, however, are the insertions at Lk 3:1–20, Lk 5:33–39/Mt 9:14–17, Lk 7:18–35/Mt 11:2–19 and Jn 1:6–8 and 15. The erratic appearances of Baptist traditions within the NT suggest an existence prior to their present context and thus recommend, with reasons one and two listed above, that each pericope be examined, at least initially as a form,[61] apart from predetermined understandings of the bias of a single evangelist.[62]

1.5.3 Final Points of Method

In terms of the organization of primary materials, past approaches divide the data into the following three categories: (1) sayings of John; (2) sayings of

---

[59] On the dispersion of Q material about the Baptist in Matthew and Luke, J. Taylor argues: "Both Matthew and Luke may have felt that the Q Baptist block was a little long and too enthusiastic about John. Abbreviations and relocations of material lessened its force without necessarily lessening its tone" (*The Immerser*, 300).

[60] Perhaps because Mk 6:14–16 assumes John is dead, the author of the Gospel of Mark considers it necessary at this point (Mk 6:17–29) to narrate his death (W. Wink, *John the Baptist*, 11). Concerning John's death in Mark, Wink also comments: "The account bears all the marks of bazaar-gossip" (*John the Baptist*, 28).

[61] Even before developing his most famous work on form criticism (*Die Formgeschichte des Evangeliums* [Tübingen: Mohr (Siebeck) ²1933 (1919)]; ET: *From Tradition to Gospel* [SL 124; New York: Scribner, 1965]), Martin Dibelius applied form-criticism to NT Baptist traditions in *Die urchristliche Überlieferung von Johannes dem Täufer* (FRLANT 15; Göttingen: Vandenhoeck & Ruprecht, 1911) 48.

[62] Irregularity of the occurrences of Baptist traditions in the NT gospels also suggests the possibility that source materials originally about John, including, but not restricted to modern reconstructions of Q, were being attributed to Jesus.

Jesus about John; and (3) statements by the evangelists about John.[63] This study, however, attempts to move beyond these categories because the categories themselves reflect assumptions about the primary material this thesis wishes to challenge, (e.g., a saying by Jesus about John may actually reflect a saying of John's attributed to Jesus).[64] In contrast, the categories applied in this study emerge from literary observations of these traditions including, but not limited to, their current narrative contexts.

Furthermore, this investigation accepts the following general assumptions regarding Q put forth by John Kloppenborg and/or the IQP: (1) Q was a written document; (2) Q was composed in Greek; (3) Q's order is generally better preserved by the Gospel of Luke than the Gospel of Matthew; (4) a significant portion of Q is preserved in the double tradition, however, certain sayings, were preserved only by Matthew or Luke; (5) Q contains no account of Jesus' 'passion'; and (6) Q may have had no account of Jesus' baptism.[65] Despite discussions here of Q's inclusion of certain *Sondergut* materials, in the present investigation, Q is not treated as a random collection. Rather this study deals with Q as a coherent literary unity, reliant upon the many sound arguments that demonstrate this theory.[66]

Differently, however, the present method of investigation does not correspond to any particular model suggested for Q's formation.[67] Whether Q demonstrates stratigraphic lines is, according to the present argument, disputable. In keeping with the so-called "principle of parsimony," a question posed too infrequently is whether a majority of Q can be conceived as a single stage of tradition. The position reflected here is that this premise must be fully debunked before proposals concerning layers and stages can be persuasively set forth.[68] Up to the present, Q scholarship has omitted this step, erroneously assuming, for example, that wisdom and apocalyptic sayings cannot exist side by side in a single layer of tradition. This assumption warrants the charge of *multiplicanda argumentum*. The present thesis, in the main, treats Q as a single stage of tradition, indicating where contrasting proposals fall short.

---

[63] Differently, John Meier bases his organization on the exegetical principle of prioritizing the oldest, most reliable source which he takes to be the Q document. Meier refers to the prioritization of Q over Mark as a "well-known academic prejudice" (38). Although contradicting this prioritization of Q, Meier's argument for the authenticity of Mk 1:8 over Q 3:16b is strong (*A Marginal Jew*, 2.36–38).

[64] See Ch. 6 on the kingdom of God sayings in Q.

[65] See J. S. Kloppenborg, *Q Parallels*, 16 (positions for/against baptism); see also: 20 (positions for/against temptation).

[66] See, in particular, "The Literary Unity of Q," *JBL* 101 (1982) 365–89; repr. in: John S. Kloppenborg, *The Shape of Q*, 98–115.

[67] J. Kloppenborg, *Excavating Q*, 112–65.

[68] See Adela Yarbro Collins' review of John Kloppenborg's *The Formation of Q* (*CBQ* 50 [1988] 722).

Finally, a high percentage of Q scholarship consists of ingenious explanations, all consequents of the unproven assumption that Q's sayings originally derived from Jesus or his followers. A provenance with Baptist followers, I hope to show, precludes these solutions by negating the questions first attracting them.

1.6 Summation

Building on past scholarship, this project endeavors to understand Q in terms of its widely acknowledged and pervasive emphasis on John the Baptist. Although the present investigation is literary, focusing on the remaining written traditions, much of the previous work on these traditions is categorized as "historical John research." Chapter 2, therefore, begins the study with an evaluation of the *status quaestionis* of the quest for the historical John. The bulk of this past research limits itself to the evidence of the NT gospels and Josephus' *Antiquitates Judaicae*. The present investigation is not different, although some consideration is paid in the notes to extra-canonical evidence, such as the Gospel of the Ebionites, the Gospel of the Nazarenes, the Pseudo-Clementines, and the encomium attributed to John Chrysostom, too hastily dismissed by commentators.[69]

Chapter 2 also assays questions regarding the historical John, such as: to what extent did John and Jesus work together in their ministries, if indeed they had any interaction at all?[70] If Jesus accepted John's baptism, did he accept John's message? If Jesus accepted John's baptism and message, did he follow after John as a disciple for any length of time? Did Jesus form a similar movement himself? Was Jesus motivated to engage in John's or his own similar movement – including baptizing others – when/because John was murdered by Herod Antipas?[71] Did Jesus once embrace John's baptism/message only to move beyond it later, establishing a rival sect with or without a rite of baptism? Were the eschatological outlooks of the two men identical?[72]

The third chapter compares Q with other canonical, particularly Synoptic, texts regarding John the Baptist. The first part of Chapter 3 focuses on dual attestation: canonical sayings attributed to both John and Jesus, such as the expression "brood of vipers" (Mt 3:7 / Lk 3:7; Mt 12:34; 23:33) and the message

---

[69] Cf. C. Scobie, *John the Baptist*, 203; J. Taylor, *The Immerser*, 8.

[70] Morton Enslin argues that the two never met ("John and Jesus," 9–10).

[71] Morton Enslin argues Jesus was inspired to take up John's ministry when John was murdered ("John and Jesus," 16–18).

[72] J. P. Meier comments: "If Jesus accepted John's message and baptism, presumably he affirmed John's basic eschatological outlook. To be sure, Jesus may have developed or even moved away from John's eschatology later on. But a totally un-eschatological Jesus trips over the very stumbling-stone early Christianity found so difficult: John the Baptist, the independent Jewish prophet of fiery imminent eschatology, to whom Jesus himself adhered" (*A Marginal Jew*, 2.32).

concerning the nearness of the kingdom (4:17/3:2).[73] The implications of dual attestation for understanding Q are considered.

The second part of Chapter 3 enhances the comparison of John and Jesus traditions of the first section. Certain contradictions within the relatively large corpus of Jesus materials suggest some canonical sayings are falsely attributed to Jesus, making more sense as traditions about John. The investigation of contradictory traditions is undertaken through a comparison of traditions inside and outside Q.

The third section of this chapter enhances the proposed separation of traditions regarding John and Jesus in and outside Q through an investigation of thematic continuities between Q sayings and Baptist traditions. Here themes such as announcement of a coming kingdom, eschatological warnings and pronouncement of punishment on "this generation" and its leaders demonstrate clear connections between Baptist traditions and Q.

The fourth and final section of Chapter 3 examines the potential origination in Q of certain "Special M" or "Special L" pericopes. Here *Sondergut* passages are read with a hermeneutic of suspicion for stylistic and thematic continuity with Baptist traditions and Q. The goal of this final section is to systematize and offer a control for past arguments on Q's inclusion of *Sondergut* material, as well as to expand and improve upon them, by introducing comparisons with Baptist traditions.

Regarding Q's Baptist *Tendenz*, the question of to what extent it should be allowed to dictate interpretation is also addressed in Chapter 3. The results of studies that appropriate some fad, ideological or other approach at the outset by which they in turn interpret a given literary opus or corpus possess obvious limitations. Q's pronounced Baptist *Tendenz* should not, therefore, be permitted to dictate interpretations of Q. Nevertheless, Q's widely-acknowledged and pervasive Baptist slant has, up until now, been neglected as a basis on which to evaluate the individual sayings and source overall. Few, if any, would argue Q has no Baptist *Tendenz* and few if any would argue that Q has been sufficiently studied with an eye to the implications of this leaning, either for its own interpretation, or for the Synoptic corpus over all. Thus, while no single generic, thematic or other authorial predilection determines the contents and meaning of any given NT source or text (or even passage!), neglect of Q's Baptist bias makes it an important unresolved avenue of investigation today.

---

[73] Cf. comment by W. Wink: "The extent to which Matthew carries out this assimilation is seen in the manner in which he freely exchanges the Baptist and Jesus traditions one with another. Words of Jesus are placed in the mouth of John and vice versa" (*John the Baptist*, 33). Examples of the dual attestation of traditions *about* John and Jesus include: the charge of a demon (9:34; 12:24; 10:25; "Because there were demons there [in the wilderness] it could be said he had a demon at his beck and call" [C. Kraeling, *John the Baptist*, 29]; cf. also Jn 8:48–49; 10:20–21); the claim that wisdom is served by both John and Jesus (11:19c); the claim that both John and Jesus exemplify righteousness (3:15; 21:32); and the claim that John and Jesus are each (metaphorically) lights that have, in some sense, "dawned" (Lk 1:76/Mt 4:16).

A second question anticipated by Chapter 3 concerns the ethics of historiography (recording John's sayings as Jesus'). The end of this chapter, therefore, addresses such issues, including bases in ancient Jewish and Graeco-Roman literature for the compilation of a master's sayings (John) under the rubric of his student (Jesus). The present thesis takes for granted that the authors of the canonical Gospels compiled what they considered to be reliable sources in the composition of their narratives. The idea that one or more of their sources originally preserved traditions about John is, historically-speaking, irrelevant, not only because it can never be proven whether a given evangelist knew a source was about John instead of Jesus (assuming unknown layers of pre-Synoptic redaction), but because the practice of compiling *related* sources in the composition of an ancient history of origins was common historiographical practice. Furthermore, with specific regard to sayings, numerous precedents exist for the practice of combining diverse sources under the rubric of a single school or teacher in both Jewish prophetic and Greek philosophical literature. This topic is treated at the end of Chapter 3.

Chapter 4 takes up the role of Baptist traditions in the Gospel of Mark. This chapter argues that this gospel writer's *a priori* understanding of John the Baptist as Elijah pervades his work. Although the view is common that an Elijah typology determines Mark's presentation of John in the beginning of his gospel, in this chapter I propose that this characterization is brought to a climax in the center of the Second Gospel at Jesus' transfiguration, and even recurs elsewhere (Mk 6:15; 8:28; 9:11), including, perhaps, Jesus' enigmatic cry to Elijah in Mk 15:35. These references to the Baptist as Elijah in the beginning, middle and end of this gospel function as a sub-structure over which the ministry of the Markan Jesus is superimposed. On one hand, the phase of Jesus' ministry based predominantly on *healings and miraculous displays* is inserted between John's baptism of Jesus and John's "resurrection" on the 'mountain of transfiguration' in Mark 9. On the other hand, the phase of Jesus' ministry based predominantly on *teaching* is inserted between John's "resurrection" in Mark 9 and Jesus' resurrection in Mark 16. John's baptism, backed by the message of the divine voice, provides the esteemed imprimatur on Jesus' healing ministry; John's "resurrection," also backed by the message of a divine voice, provides the same for Jesus' teaching ministry, offering official sanction of Jesus as John's successor.

Chapters 5 and 6 address the difficult 'Son of Man' and 'Kingdom of God' expressions (respectively) prevalent in Q.[74] Specifically, these chapters argue that the NT offers convincing proofs that both expressions originated with John.[75]

---

[74] In terms of the well-argued distinctions between wisdom, prophecy and apocalyptic literary genres, figures like John the Baptist should not be understood solely on the basis of the stereotypes provided by the Hebrew canon. Sapiential and prophetic (even apocalyptic) reflect generic categories that ancient Jewish authors used to collect, order, and organize their traditions. They should not drive us to exclude that in real life Jeremiah, Amos, Malachi or

Chapter 7 contains a summation of the arguments of the book with questions for further research.

---

another Hebrew prophet might have also played the role of sage espousing the very wisdom of Proverbs, likewise Job or Qoheleth, the role of prophet with words of warning for their generation. The shift from oral to written always entails a reconfiguration of the traditions. When it comes to John and Jesus, therefore, we can not assume on the basis of OT *book* paradigms that the historical figures themselves can be so stereotyped. In the new preface to the second edition Kloppenborg's *The Formation of Q*, Kloppenborg denies having made the claim of separating wisdom and apocalyptic in his strata theory of Q. He cites John J. Collins as chief among those to have *misread* his argument with one footnote alleging Collins' error and another footnote enumerating those who "tediously repeat Collins' misunderstanding" (*The Formation of Q*, xii nn. 6, 7). Kloppenborg insists: "...the assertion that 'wisdom' and 'apocalyptic' are found together in such documents as the *Wisdom of Solomon* or *1 Enoch* or the *Didache* hardly implies either that such elements belong to the same compositional stratum of those documents, or that just because wisdom and apocalyptic cohere in some documents, they must cohere in all. On the contrary, a case must be made, based on an analysis of the *actual literary deployment* of Q's sayings, noting continuities, aporiae, abrupt disjunction, changes in rhetorical and argumentative mode. Such a case must depend on *literary* factors, not on vague arguments from analogy. Analogies may be adduced on all sides of the debate. The question is not whether wisdom and apocalyptic, or wisdom and prophecy, can subsist in the same document; of course they can and do in various documents. The question is, when diverse elements subsist in a document, how does one understand the literary and generic relationship among the various elements" (emphases original). Important secondary literature on this topic includes: John J. Collins, "Wisdom, Apocalypticism, and Generic Compatibility," in *In Search of Wisdom: Essays in Memory of John G. Gammie*, ed. Leo G. Perdue, Bernard B. Scott and William J. Wiseman (Louisville: Westminster John Knox Press, 1993) 165–66, 181–85; Hans-Peter Müller, "Mantische Weisheit und Apokalyptik," in *Congress Volume:Uppsala, 1971*, VTS 22 (Leiden: E.J. Brill, 1972), 268–93; James C. VanderKam, "The Prophetic-Sapiential Origins of Apocalyptic Thought," in *A Word in Season: Essays in Honor of William McKane*, JSOTSS 42, ed. J. D. Martin and P. R. Davies (Sheffield: JSOT Press, 1986), 163–76; idem, *Enoch and the Growth of an Apocalyptic Tradition*, CBQMS 16 (Washington, DC: The Catholic Biblical Association of America, 1984), esp. 52–75; Michael Fishbane, *Biblical Interpretation in Ancient Israel* (Oxford: Clarendon Press, 1985), 443–505; J. G. Gammie, "Spatial and Ethical Dualism in Jewish Wisdom and Apocalyptic Literature," *JBL* 93 (1974) 356–85; M. E. Stone, "Lists of Revealed Things in the Apocalyptic Literature," in *Magnalia Dei: The Mighty Acts of God*, ed. F. M. Cross, W. E. Lemke and P. D. Miller (Garden City, NY: Doubleday, 1976), 414–54; John J. Collins, "Cosmos and Salvation: Jewish Wisdom and Apocalyptic in the Hellenistic Age," *History of Religions* 17 (1977) 121–42; M. A. Knibb, "Apocalyptic and Wisdom in 4 Ezra," *Journal for the Study of Judaism in the Persian, Hellenistic and Roman Periods* 13 (1982) 56–74; Frederick J. Murphy, "Sapiential Elements in the Syriac Apocalypse of Baruch," *Jewish Quarterly Review* 76 (1986) 311–27; G. W. E. Nickelsburg, "Wisdom and Apocalypticism in Early Judaism: Some Points for Discussion," in *SBLSP 1994* (Atlanta: Scholars Press, 1994), 715–32; idem, *1 Enoch 1: A Commentary on the Book of 1 Enoch, Chapters 1–36, 81–108*, Hermeneia Series (Minneapolis: Fortress Press, 2001) esp. 50–54, 337–44, 454–56; Shannon Burkes, "Wisdom and Apocalypticism in the Wisdom of Solomon," *HTR* 95 (2002) 21–44. Other influential essays include H. D. Betz, "On the Problem of the Religio-Historical Understanding of Apocalypticism," *Journal for Theology and the Church* 6 (1969) 146–54 and J. Z. Smith, "Wisdom and Apocalyptic," in *Religious Syncretism in Antiquity*, ed. B. Pearson (Missoula, MT: Scholars Press, 1975), 131–56. On 4Q Instruction, see Matthew J. Goff, *The Worldly and Heavenly Wisdom of 4Q Instruction: Studies on the Texts of the Desert of Judah* (Leiden: Brill, 2003).

[75] W. Wink concludes that the fact that John material was inevitably attributed to Jesus (particularly by the author of the Gospel of Matthew) is only natural; the sources only ever be-

Admittedly, the quantity of primary materials occupying the focus of this study is vast. As Baptist traditions are scattered throughout the four gospels and Q, the scope is broad and the task, difficult. Furthermore, because, prior to this study, no monograph-length study on Baptist traditions and Q existed, such a project involves diverse secondary literature. Q scholarship, the Gospel of Mark, 'Son of Man' sayings, and 'Kingdom of God' sayings, not to mention historical John research, have each, for more than a century, commanded their own area of investigation. Each of these trajectories of interpretation informs the present argument. I, however, do not possess prolonged expertise in any one of these important fields. Nevertheless, I am convinced that Baptist traditions have a new and valid perspective to lend to these important areas of research and have tried to make this case to my readers. It was not possible to do justice to each topic on its own terms in the space of a single monograph while maintaining a focus on the specific intersection of Baptist traditions and Q. Over time I hope that the most convincing ideas presented here will attract the more exacting work they deserve.

Finally, in accordance with current conventions of Q research, Q texts are cited according to Lukan versification (e.g., Q 3:16b–17 = Lk 3:16b–17). Unless specified otherwise, assumptions regarding Q's contents conform to *The Critical Edition of Q*, eds. James M. Robinson, Paul Hoffmann, John S. Kloppenborg (Minneapolis: Fortress, 2000). It is difficult to discuss a text the contents of which are disputed. It is, nonetheless, a valid and necessary task. To do so, therefore, one must continually resist the temptation to indulge questions of content: Was this pericope in Q? What was its exact wording in Q? Where was it located with respect to other Q materials? Questions of this type threatened to overtake my project. The aim of this study, I reminded myself regularly, is to take seriously the International Q Project's (IQP) construction of the Q text, viewing it both on its own (apart from Matthew and Luke) and as an entirety (posing limited questions about *Sondergut*). A few of the IQP's decisions about Q's contents are disputed in the footnotes. Based on the IQP's reconstruction of the Greek text, unless noted, the English translations of Q are my own.

---

longed to one group of people and one movement: "Both Baptists and Christians belonged to the heretical sectarian Baptist movement, and both paid allegiance to John" (*John the Baptist*, 105). Also, "These syncretistic Jewish sects, though fiercely independent, share one thing in common: the centrality of baths or baptism in lieu of sacrifice. As a broad movement of protest against contemporary piety, these groups were heterodox, schismatic, highly individualistic, quick to shift to the latest 'revelation,' and capable of borrowing from one another without establishing relationships of dependency" (108); and "…the church stood at the center of John's movement from the very beginning and became its one truly great survivor and heir" (110).

Chapter Two

The *status quaestionis* of the Quest of the Historical John

> Many of those in higher places regarded him as dangerous, a de-
> monic force disturbing men's minds and retarding the wheels of
> progress. Many of the common people of his day found him not only
> provocative but compelling, so much so that for almost a decade
> after his violent death the question of his vindication was a popular
> issue. For some centuries the rite he performed was bartered about
> and imitated in sundry syncretistic religious communities of the
> Near East, and in Christianity and in one non-Christian, non-Jewish
> sect he has played a continuous role down to the present day. This
> makes him a person of significance in his own right and an excellent
> medium for the study of the period to which he belonged.[1]

2.1 Introduction

Although interest in the historical John has flourished since the early second
century, a majority of these treatments are pious, seeking to explain John's life
in order to better understand 'the real Jesus'[2] or to better imitate John's purported
model of 'asceticism.'[3] Over the past hundred years, however, certain scholars,

---

[1] Carl H. Kraeling, *John the Baptist*, 3.

[2] I borrow this expression from Luke Timothy Johnson, *The Real Jesus: The Misguided
Quest for the Historical Jesus and the Truth of the Traditional Gospels* (San Francisco: HarperSanFrancisco, 1996).

[3] An unexplored paradox of the church father's interest in John the Baptist (his diet and
clothing, in particular) is why they sought to imitate John on issues of lifestyle where John
evidently conflicted with Jesus. The apparent early resumption of both fasting and baptism after
Jesus' death is a conundrum early Christian studies has yet to work out. James A. Kelhoffer
explains the problem in terms of Christian *paideia*; see *The Diet of John the Baptist,* 203–4).
Hartwig Thyen refers to John's "asceticism" as one of three *"differentiae"* between John and
Jesus ("ΒΑΠΤΙΣΜΑ ΜΕΤΑΝΟΙΑΣ ΕΙΣ ΑΦΕΣΙΝ ΑΜΑΡΤΙΩΝ," in *The Future of Our
Religious Past: Essays in Honour of Rudolf Bultmann*, ed. James M. Robinson, trans. Charles E.
Carlston and Robert P. Scharlemann [New York: Harper & Row, 1971] 144). On the importance
of John the Baptist in the development of monasticism and other ascetic movements, E. F. Lupieri comments, "Even if the figure of Jesus Christ has obviously always been the first and most
important model to be imitated by every Christian, the figure of John the Baptist became, from
the very beginning of monasticism, the special model, the favored example of the true master to
be followed by every monk" ("John the Baptist: The First Monk. A Contribution to the History
of the Figure of John the Baptist in the Early Monastic World," in *Monasticism: A Historical
Overview* [Word and Spirit 6; Still River, MA: St. Bede, 1984] 11). Lupieri also notes, however,
that following John's, as over and against Jesus', model was a source of concern: "From the

in particular, Dibelius (1911), Lohmeyer (1932), Kraeling (1951), Schlatter (1956), Scobie (1964), Schütz (1967), Wink (1968), Ernst (1989), and most recently Taylor (1999) have sought to address the fragmented remaining sources (primarily the NT gospels and Jos. *Ant.* 18.116–19) about John from a historical viewpoint.[4] Despite the progress of these treatments, they still largely presume the historicity of the evidence, formulating individual historical reconstructions on the basis of ostensibly reliable pieces.[5]

Added to this is the fact that, as John Reumann observes, "'Life-of-John study' lacks a chronicler like Albert Schweitzer or the many surveys of *Leben Jesu* books."[6] One might be inclined to think of Joan Taylor's recent *magnum opus* on John, *The Immerser: John the Baptist within Second Temple Judaism,* as somehow bridging Reumann's gap. The title, after all, suggests an investigation of the historical John. In her introduction, however, Taylor emphatically denies any such association: "This study," she writes, "is not a 'life of John.'"[7] In line

---

beginning of monastic history, monks were accused by their opponents of not following the true teaching of Jesus. This problem was real and caused preoccupation among some of the monastic writers" ("John the Baptist: The First Monk," 16; cf. also 14).

[4] M. Dibelius, *Die urchristliche Überlieferung von Johannes dem Täufer*; E. Lohmeyer, *Das Urchristentum 1: Johannes der Täufer*; C. H. Kraeling, *John the Baptist*; A. Schlatter, *Johannes der Täufer* (Basel: Verlag Friedrich Reinhardt AG, 1956); C. H. H. Scobie, *John the Baptist*; J. Schütz, *Johannes der Täufer*; W. Wink, *John the Baptist*; J. Ernst, *Johannes der Täufer*; and Joan E. Taylor, *The Immerser*. At the beginning of the 20th century, Theodor Innitzer (*Johannes der Täufer. Nach der Heiligen Schrift und der Tradition dargestellt ... Preisgekrönte Schrift* [Wien: Mayer & Co., 1908]) and Robert Eisler (*The Messiah Jesus and John the Baptist according to Flavius Josephus' Recently Rediscovered 'Capture of Jerusalem' and the Other Jewish and Christian Sources* [London: Methuen, 1931]) also treated this problem. One might also include Jürgen Becker's study, *Johannes der Täufer und Jesus von Nazareth* and Michael Tilly's work, *Johannes der Täufer und die Biographie der Propheten: Die synoptische Täuferüberlieferung und das jüdische Prophetenbild zur Zeit des Täufers* (BWANT 7/17; Stuttgart/Berlin/Köln: W. Kohlhammer, 1994). A methodological problem of this chapter arising out of a desire to be in dialogue with past commentators on John the Baptist is continual references in the studies to John and Jesus as historical personages. In order to circumvent any problem of the present author's perception and project the following caveat is necessary: in the body or notes of this paper, wherever a commentator refers to "John" as a historical individual, in no case does the present author accept such a conclusion. Rather I regard references to "John" or "Jesus" as implying later communities upholding and preserving traditions associated with either of these two men.

[5] With the notable exception of the new treatment by James A. Kelhoffer (*The Diet of John the Baptist*), the historicity of Baptist traditions such as baptizing, fasting, and wilderness-dwelling are virtually undisputed in scholarship. The most important scholarly treatments of Baptist traditions, including those of C. H. Scobie, Paul W. Hollenbach, Josef Ernst, Walter Wink, and more recently, Joan E. Taylor, all endorse the reliability of the ancient evidence on these points. Thus, while it is not understood precisely what is meant by traditions associated with John such as "baptizing in the river Jordan" (Mk 1:5 par.), "fasting," (Mk 2:18 par.) "eating locusts and wild honey" (Mk 1:6 par.) or being "clothed with camel's hair" (Mk 1:6 par.), no scholar yet rejects the historical value of these ancient testimonies.

[6] John Reumann, "The Quest for the Historical Baptist," 184. Cf. also Gösta Lindeskog, "Johannes der Täufer: Einige Randbemerkungen zum heutigen Stand der Forschung," *ASTI* 12 (1983) 55–83.

[7] J. Taylor, *The Immerser*, 9.

with this claim, Taylor avoids any sequential and/or methodological treatment of John's many *Lives*. Rather, her work focuses on the context of Second Temple Judaism for understanding NT traditions about John. Taylor's conclusions demonstrate, like others before her, reliance on the evidence of the four gospels and Josephus as historical.

Although surveys such as Schweitzer's on the historical Jesus offer little to understandings of the historical personage, they are extremely useful in moving scholarship forward on a topic by exposing trends of past treatments. That the historical John quest has no such chronicle points directly to its arrested development. Today even historical study of his context in Second Temple Judaism has evolved only slightly beyond its state in the early 20th century. The shocking contribution of Taylor's study, which downplays connections between the Dead Sea Scrolls and John the Baptist, is how little even an archaeological discovery of this magnitude offers to our study of this topic. Thus, Reumann's assessment (issued in 1972) remains valid, even for the most recent studies.

In his brief survey of John's *Lives*, Reumann also describes progress on the historical Baptist as "something of a chimera."[8] He explains:

All the hazards of the quest for the historical Jesus exist in the search for the history of John, and then some: conflicting sources, canonical and beyond; tendentiousness in sources; the unsettling role of form and redaction criticism; problems of *religionsgeschichtlich* background; the theology of the early Christian church; *plus the fact that*, if we take seriously the possibility of the Baptist provenance for some of the materials (as many scholars named above do), what we have in the New Testament is *separated* from historical actuality *both by Christian usage and by (earlier) Baptist use*. It is as if we were trying to recover the historical Jesus from traditions filtered through a second, later disciple community of another faith, say Islam (save that the separation in time from the event is shorter). If in the Gospels, to use R. H. Lightfoot's oft misunderstood phrase, we hear, in the case of Jesus 'little more than a whisper of his voice,' then in the case of the Baptist we have only an echo (or echoes) of his whisper. In short, there is more diversity in modern studies about the Baptist than assumed, more optimism than warranted about recovering knowledge of him historically, and more reason to suspect we cannot throw real light on him than even in the case of Jesus.[9]

While a number of Reumann's claims here are disputable, such as whether the Baptist movement or its traditions were earlier than Jesus' or whether Baptist belief ('faith') was as different from Christian belief as Christian belief is from Islam, his conclusions regarding not only the *status quaestionis* of the quest for the historical John, but also possibilities for progress of historical research are probably accurate: prospects for break-throughs are few.

One may ponder, however, whether all is lost. I would agree with Reumann that the roles of form- and redaction-criticism are "unsettling." And, as Reumann

---

[8] J. Reumann, "The Quest for the Historical Baptist," 184.
[9] J. Reumann, "Quest for the Historical Baptist," 187; emphases original.

correctly points out, the most reliable evidence about John from the canonical gospels and Josephus *is* inherently flawed. According to Reumann, however, the flaws of the evidence result from radical distortion by the "theology of the early church," "Christian usage," and "Baptist use" and are so severe as to make even Lightfoot's 'whisper' of Jesus an impossibility for John.[10] Is Reumann also correct in this supporting explanation of the condition of the evidence?

In contrast to Reumann's position, the present view is that Christian "distortions" are unproven and stem from the false assumption that all NT Baptist traditions are propagandistically subjugated to NT Jesus traditions. This chapter argues, rather, that *resulting from neglect of a chronicle such as Schweitzer's on Jesus, historical studies of John proceed with far too little awareness both of the extent to which the sources have been reworked and of the assumptions guiding interpretations of the sources.* Sharp picks and maps in hand, interpreters plunge forward like nineteenth century archaeologists: the goal, not to excavate and document with painstaking care, both material culture and its context ultimately *leaving it where it was found*, but to recover and bring 'West' rare charms and ruins. Like these early archaeologists research on the historical John is carried out with insufficient attention to method, both in technique and documentation.

Joan Taylor's approach is careful, although she alternates, like many before her, between accepting the data of the gospels at face value (historical) *versus* negotiating their meaning in terms of redaction, without ever stepping outside the exegesis to explain her strategy.[11] She, like many others, utilizes the modern interpreters' *carte blanche* to sift the remaining fragments on John for historicity without any methodological justification other than a general commitment to a pan-critical approach. Possible pitfalls in this *ad hoc* process are numerous. To claim, for example, a given Baptist fragment represents an author's editorial work ('redaction') does not necessarily imply the datum is 'propaganda' (i.e., 'fiction?') *as opposed to* 'history.' The broader question (one the present chapter seeks to pose) is: What hermeneutic applies critical methods consciously and judiciously, governs approaches to *all* remaining Baptist fragments, and can

---

[10] R. H. Lightfoot, *History and Interpretation in the Gospels* (London: Hodder & Stoughton, 1935) 255.

[11] In only two sentences Taylor accepts the historical value of all of the NT and Josephus' traditions about John. She writes: "In terms of the scope of this study, I will not repeat the systematic examinations of John the Baptist in the literature (New Testament, Josephus, apocryphal and Gnostic writings, Mandaean material, and patristic texts); these have been undertaken by Josef Ernst, Walter Wink, Ernst Bammel, Robert Webb, and Edmondo Lupieri. *The basic conclusions of these excellent studies of the Baptist tradition-history suggest that only the New Testament material and the evidence of Josephus (excluding the Slavonic version) are historically valuable*" (*The Immerser*, 8; emphasis added). In the only section of her book dedicated to method (1–13), Taylor is silent on her own strategy, apart from an indirect reference to her work as a "historical reconstruction" which she then qualifies as "at best good guesswork based on the data at our disposal" (13).

posit a plausible *Sitz im Leben* to explain why Baptist fragments in the canonical gospels are accessible through such an approach?

Although Reumann may be correct regarding the hopelessness of progress for historical John studies, I believe there is room for more work. Specifically: Reumann's declaration of hopelessness may be true for the historical John, but this position does not apply to the traditions in his name. What is more, Reumann's declaration cannot be held with certainty even about the historical personage until all critical methods and assumptions guiding the history of interpretation are subjected to elevated levels of scrutiny. Every presupposition of research must be inspected on the chance that hundred-, sometimes even thousand-year-old theories are misguided.

The purpose of this chapter is to assess the *status quaestionis* of the quest of the historical John and, on the basis of this assessment, to provide my own interpretations of key components of John's life. Through an analysis of both primary and secondary sources, positions on the historical John are offered here for the heuristic purpose of exposing three faulty methodological assumptions in scholarship. These assumptions are: (1) unqualified reliance on the canonical gospels and Josephus, *Ant.* 18.116–19 as historical about the Baptist; (2) assumption of a subjugating *Tendenz* (redaction) on the part of the canonical evangelists with regard to Baptist traditions, the Fourth Gospel, in particular; (3) principle propounded in historical-critical studies that Baptist traditions were radically distorted by the evangelists and other leaders of the early church; (4) conviction of hopelessness with regard to Baptist traditions.

2.2 Constituencies of Baptists among Early Christians

Taking Reumann's thesis as a starting point, we first observe that his pessimism is anchored in at least one incorrect assumption. Undoubtedly accurate that groups eventually labeled Christian "filtered" traditions of groups eventually labeled 'Baptist' (those who identified themselves primarily with the baptism of John as portrayed, for example, in Acts 18:3–4, and also appearing in extra-canonical traditions),[12] the derivative assumption that so-called 'Christians' deliberately obfuscated or expunged 'Baptist' traditions requires validation. If the Gospel of John is reliable on this point,[13] then at least some first- and early second-century followers of Jesus, (excluding, for the moment, John's discipleship of Jesus himself [e.g., Mk 1:9 par.]), were former (Jn 1:35–36, 40–42), perhaps concurrent (Acts 18–19), followers of the Baptist. The possibility even exists that, at

---

[12] E.g., Justin Martyr, *Dial.* 80; *Ps.-Clem.* Rec. 1.54, 60. See above 3–5 n. 8.

[13] The reliability of Baptist traditions in the Fourth Gospel is explored further in section 2.5.

some point, 'Baptists' comprised a larger segment of the 'Jesus movement' than 'Christians.'[14] In any case, if even the smallest measure of 'Baptist' participation in early 'Christianity' is admitted, the NT gospels may have been collected, organized, even composed with, not exclusively 'Christian,' but, 'Baptist' interests in mind. For such a Baptist contingency, it is conceivable that the evangelists would have imputed to John real credit and authority, in particular, where John is the topic of discussion – even to the extent of compromising (however slightly) otherwise thorough-going 'Christian' theologies.[15] Any presence of John's followers within Christian circles would, at the very least, have acted as a natural delimitation of the evangelists' claims about John, if not actually determining aspects of their content. In the event of Baptist participation in Christian audiences, it is unlikely the evangelists would have radically misrepresented or distorted John's important legacy. John's mere presence in the canonical gospels proves that the NT gospels were devoted, not to simply Jesus, but to the documentation of his movement. In short, Reumann's premise that Christian authors altered Baptist traditions requires clarification and substantiation.

If followers of John the Baptist comprised any part of one or more of the four evangelists' audiences, which it is likely they did, the question of research becomes, not how strenuously a hermeneutic of suspicion can be pressed against the fragile, remaining Baptist fragments embedded in the NT gospels (even say, to the point of absolute pessimism à la Reumann). Rather, we should ask: What methodological approach or combination of approaches responsibly and effectively frees Baptist traditions to convey their meaning and historical context?

2.3 Critical Methods and Quests for the Historical John

In order to fully comprehend the problem of methodological approaches to John's quest, a clearer appreciation of what propels Reumann's pessimism is necessary. Reumann's pessimism derives, in part, from an emphasis on redac-

---

[14] On the existence of Baptist communities in the late first century, see 3–5 n. 8.

[15] The question of course arises of how different the two (Jesus vs. John) theologies would have been. Cf. the view of John H. Hughes: "It is clear from the prominent and honoured place of John the Baptist in the Gospel record that the early Christians must have accepted the intimation of Jesus that his own ministry was decisively related to the fulfilment of the coming eschatological drama proclaimed by John. There is evidence to suggest that many of John's disciples also came to recognize that their master's prophecy of the coming of the Lord Yahweh and the future Kingdom had been fulfilled in a way only glimpsed by John himself .... Some support for this suggestion is provided by the incidence of baptism, prayer and fasting in the early Church, for this could indicate the incorporation of many Johannite practices into the life of the Church as a consequence of former followers of John having come to recognize that Jesus had fulfilled the expectations of their old master" ("John the Baptist: The Forerunner of God," 214).

tion criticism far outweighing what pioneers of this method ever imagined. As cited above, Reumann describes the perilous state of John's quest in redaction's terms: "conflict" (the most classic), "tendentiousness," "theology," and "Christian usage."[16] As originally conceived, redaction criticism *complemented* other important critical methods such as source- and form-criticism, for the most part, using the language of form-criticism to do so. With precisely this point, Willi Marxsen once advocated that, *in addition* to the *Sitze im Leben* of the historical Jesus and the early church, a third existed, that of the evangelists.[17] Redaction criticism represents the necessary inclusion of a third important criterion in the study of the texts, that of the author's voice. This method was, however, generated, defined in terms of, and intended, not as an alternative to, but as an extension of form-criticism, considered, at this time in the first half of the twentieth-century, the most dependable critical method.

Now at the beginning of the twenty-first century, however, rather than an examination focusing on an ancient author's comments, summaries and other insertions, redaction-criticism has become an examination of a perceived totality – a given author's 'theological' argument and overall outlook, increasingly taken as programmatic for the presentation of all forms and sources. *And* form-criticism offers no complementary approach, but is considered out of vogue. Localized meanings of forms and sources within the four gospels are scrutinized in favor of the purportedly more prudent assumption that redaction has modified not just the contexts, but the traditions beyond recognition.[18] For studies of the historical Baptist, this naïve overexertion of redaction-criticism has resulted in paralysis ("hopelessness") on the part of interpreters. However, it is not simply an inability to rely on Baptist fragments as historical, as Reumann maintains, but also to decipher their value and meaning as authentic traditions.

For example, today interpreters insist on dealing with Baptist fragments in Mark only in terms of their own individual construals of Markan 'theology.' The problem of this approach is that it neglects that both Matthew and Luke subsume many of the same fragments, virtually unchanged, into their works as well. While true that a given evangelist's deployment of a tradition implies its endorsement by that author, use of virtually identical traditions by a few different authors should prioritize the study of the fragment as form over its examination as an element of each new context. The *Zeitgeist* of the field of Biblical Studies today, however, dictates that rather than imagine a given gospel *context* is constructed around a Baptist fragment as a historical 'form' or 'tradition' (as in

---

[16] J. Reumann, "Quest for the Historical Baptist," 187.

[17] W. Marxsen, *Mark the Evangelist: Studies on the Redaction History of the Gospel* (Nashville: Abingdon, 1969 [1956, ²1959]) 23. Marxsen's study provides an example of such a methodological focus.

[18] Modeling this approach is E. Bammel, "The Baptist in Early Christian Tradition," *NTS* 18 (1971–72).

the older sense of redaction-criticism), one assumes that where, for example, John radically subordinates himself to Jesus, John's words are accessible only in terms of each individual evangelist's presumed theological disposition. The former position, viewing fragments as forms, held by pioneer form critics, is judged hopelessly inexpert – even literalistic. Therefore, scant attention is paid to what we will see are, in the case of Baptist traditions, often obvious avenues of interpretation.

For example, the possibility remains, (if seldom broached), that statements such as the Baptist's subjugating remarks in the Gospel of John are authentic, only not in their given context.[19] John's (and/or his followers') self-subjugation may represent a rhetorical strategy – a rhetoric of modesty or false modesty.[20] John may have used subjugating language to subordinate himself to Moses, Elijah, the Messiah, the "coming one," the Son of Man or some combination of these figures. Redactional considerations should *supplement not override* other possible interpretive solutions about Baptist traditions such as these. Redaction criticism is but one of a panoply of critical techniques, *less effective individually than as a group.*

More than the difficulties posed by the repetition of a single tradition in multiple NT gospels, the fragmented nature of the remaining evidence on the Baptist makes source- and form- more valuable than redaction-criticism for evaluating meaning and significance. Both fragmented and highly sporadic (e.g., Mk 6:14–29; Jn 1:6–8, 15) qualities of NT Baptist traditions, like the repetition of traditions, demand analyses free from preconceptions regarding any single author's theological position.[21] In order to substantiate real gains in critical studies of Baptist traditions, research should first consider a Baptist fragment apart from any of its present literary contexts and in a plausible *Sitz im Leben,* such as among first-century followers of John.

2.4 Redaction Criticism: Propagandistic Subjugation of John

According to this critical re-examination of quest for the historical John methodologies, not only is the narrow emphasis on redaction criticism *in lieu of other*

---

[19] E.g., Jn 3:30. Of Jn 1:6–8, only v. 8 specifies John's subordinate position to Jesus. In v. 6 John receives the esteemed designation as "a man sent from God" and in v. 7 his importance is scarcely reduced by the identification as "witness to testify to the light in order that *all might believe through him.*"

[20] Cf. Greek rhetorical strategy of εἰρωνεία: Anaximen. Lampsac. *Rh.* 21 and Aristotle, *Rh.* 3.19.5.

[21] E.g., the very common assumption that the Gospel of John, in particular, cannot, from a historical viewpoint, be trusted. On this question, see Hans-Josef Klauck, "Die Sakramente und der historische Jesus," in *Gemeinde, Amt, Sakrament: Neutestamentliche Perspektiven* (Würzberg: Echter, 1989) 274–76.

methods in need of limitation, but the significance of a given author's Christology for redaction also demands restraint. As argued above, redaction criticism has developed today into the examination of an author's total 'theological' program. For the four canonical gospels, the central component of such a perceived agenda is often taken to be Christological. With regard to this supposition, it must first be acknowledged that any perceived program of a single evangelist is always hypothetical. In contrast, the weight of the evidence – inconsistencies, complexities, and outright contradictions (the preoccupation of much of modern biblical scholarship) – favors the *absence* of a single determinative theology for any of the NT gospels. Nevertheless, in terms of such a Christological component, the most widespread assumption for Baptist traditions is, as above, that they have been propagandistically subjugated to Jesus traditions. The heart of this hermeneutical premise is, of course, Jesus-centered (as opposed to Baptist-centered) and in need of corroborating proofs. Not only does this assumption reduce to a single deduction what should be a much more complex approach to the remaining evidence on these two important historical figures, it is also, I hope to show, incorrect.

Although many commentators acknowledge that John is held in a position of relative respect in the NT, the guiding assumption of research on the historical John is that each of the four evangelists reflects in his redaction a blanket determination to subordinate John to Jesus, distorting to varying extents every remaining piece of evidence about him. Many of the world's finest scholars maintain this position. Charles Scobie, for example, writes:

The Gospels have no interest in John (or in anyone else for that matter) for his own sake; they are concerned with him only in so far as he is connected with Jesus.[22]

Similarly, John Meier remarks: "All four gospels have to struggle to 'make John safe' for Christianity."[23] Meier continues,

This incredible diversity, not to say conflict, of interpretations in the Four Gospels is due to a simple fact. Right at the beginning of the ministry of Jesus stands the independent ministry of the independent Baptist, a Jewish prophet who started his ministry before and apart from Jesus, who won great popularity and reverence apart from Jesus, who also won the reverence and submission of Jesus to his baptism of repentance for the forgiveness of sins, and who left behind a religious group that continued to exist apart from Christianity. The Baptist constituted a stone of stumbling right at the beginning of Christianity's story of Jesus, a stone too well known to be ignored or denied, a stone that each evangelist had to come to terms with as best he could. The embarrassment of the evangelists as well as the diverse, not to say contradictory, ways in which *they try to bend the independent Baptist to a dependent position within the story of Jesus* argues well for his historical existence.

---

[22] C. Scobie, *John the Baptist*, 11. Although Scobie later adds, "Then again, the excessive stress on the subordination of John gives rise to suspicion. We are constantly being reminded of his [John's] inferiority to Jesus" (15).

[23] J. P. Meier, *A Marginal Jew*, 2.21.

The evangelists (and their sources before them) did not go out of their way to create a monumental problem for their own theologies by creating John the Baptist.[24]

Meier develops his conclusions from certain tenuous assumptions based on redaction criticism. According to Meier, a subjugating *Tendenz* on the part of the evangelists is so sure that the criterion of embarrassment (embarrassment by 'Christians' of the Baptist) becomes the secure means by which to ascertain the historical authenticity of the fragments.[25] The links in Meier's chain of reasoning are, however, more delicate than he is willing to acknowledge. If redaction-criticism first, and the subjugating assumption on the part of the evangelists second, are not permitted interpretative hegemony over all Baptist traditions, the possibility emerges that the fragments reveal a John with whom early Christians longed for association, making the criterion of embarrassment moot. That the evangelists incorporate Baptist traditions at all, let alone a relatively large group of these traditions, is an immediate indication of John's importance to these writers. That said, the upcoming analysis will modify and include the criterion of embarrassment – positing embarrassment to Christians and Baptists alike – to demonstrate how the Baptist traditions actually reflect an affinity for John the Baptist on the part of the evangelists.

Likewise, Joan Taylor presupposes a similar situation:

A central issue for Christian theologians has been not the implication of Jesus' baptism by John and Jesus' acceptance of John's teaching, but the general problem of Jesus' subordination to John – at least during some period of Jesus' life. *The Gospel writers were certainly at pains to reverse this subordination.*[26]

Only Walter Wink leaves open the possibility that, at times in the NT, John is depicted for his own sake. Wink submits the following question:

But even if, as we shall see, the church did on occasion find itself polemically engaged with John's disciples, is it valid to generalize from these localized instances and interpret the entire body of tradition about John as polemically inspired?[27]

This chapter picks up on Wink's point, arguing that his contention has been bypassed by scholars to the detriment of progress in this niche of our field. Here I attempt to demonstrate through analysis of the Baptist fragments that, irrespective of their value for understanding the historical John, the canonical gospels' inclusion and treatment of Baptist traditions is predominantly positive. Efforts to subjugate John pale in comparison to attempts to demonstrate an association

---

[24] J. P. Meier, *A Marginal Jew*, 2.22; emphasis added.

[25] For example, John's baptism of Jesus would have been a cause of early Christian embarrassment, making the event's historical authenticity certain (*A Marginal Jew*, 2.100–5, esp. 102–3).

[26] J. Taylor, *The Immerser*, 7; emphasis added.

[27] W. Wink, *John the Baptist*, xi.

with his power and prestige. Furthermore, many Baptist fragments, when viewed apart from present contexts, make clear sense in terms of other known Baptist traditions, thus casting doubt on arguments of tampering by Christian tradents. In this chapter I put forth a limited number of proposals regarding the historical Baptist stemming from my analysis. The purpose of these propositions is purely heuristic: to view results of the application of the proposed method. In some cases, more than one possible interpretation is set forth.

2.4.1 The Presupposition of John as Forerunner

At the root of the assumption of John's blanket subjugation to Jesus in the NT gospels is John's position as forerunner to Jesus as Christ, beginning with the Gospel of Mark. Mark's view of John as forerunner is generally interpreted in one of two ways: (1) John/Baptist tradition considered John forerunner to Jesus (literal); (2) Mark subjugates John to Jesus by means of a forerunner-perfecter (literary/historical) model, but for John/Baptists, John was no forerunner. Describing the literary-historical model (#2) is Ernst Bammel:

As the historiography of antiquity was largely influenced and directed by schemes that were at the disposal of the respective authors, it is likely that devices of this kind exercised their influence on the shaping of the material. A *scheme* like that of forerunner and perfecter or of saviour figure and perverter or of a pair of companions was readily at hand to an author of these days. Indeed, the prominence of at least two of these devices in old Christian literature is more than obvious.[28]

Bammel's point is well taken. The forerunner-perfecter model was one available scheme by which the evangelists organized sources. That said, this conclusion, 'forerunner (John) – perfecter (Jesus)' results from an outlook presupposing that Jesus' superiority to John guided the redaction of every gospel pericope – an assumption in need of proof. Tabling this assumption – not so much the overall Christological position on Jesus by Mark or the other three NT evangelists, but the extent to which such a position can be said to distort Baptist traditions – offers new possibilities for envisaging the overworked fragmentary evidence on John. Checked here, rather by a criterion of embarrassment[29] that, *with respect to Baptist sources, keeps embarrassment to 'Christians' as well as to 'Baptists'*

---

[28] E. Bammel, "The Baptist in Early Christian Tradition," 96; emphasis added. Rudolf Bultmann played a key role in developing this line of interpretation. By his insistence on the rivalry of the Baptist and Christian movements, Bultmann pioneered the trail of suspicion regarding the Baptist and Baptist communities. See *The History of the Synoptic Tradition*, 20, 23–24, 164–66, 246–47, and 302.

[29] See J. P. Meier, *A Marginal Jew*, 1.168–71. With regard to assessing the Baptist fragments of the NT from a historical-critical viewpoint, Meier writes, "Just as important is the criterion of embarrassment, for the Baptist is a 'wild card' in the Gospel tradition" (*A Marginal Jew*, 2.21).

in mind, a new perspective on sources about John comes into view.[30] Balancing redaction- with form- and source-criticism permits Baptist fragments to be studied separate from any given evangelist's Christological or other concern. Thus, either of the above positions is adopted by interpreters to the exclusion of the possibility that the historical John considered *himself* "forerunner," even exploiting Isa 40:3 (3–5?) and/or Mal 3:1, 4:5–6 to this end, simply not forerunner to Jesus.[31] John may very well have considered himself a forerunner, even

---

[30] The criterion of embarrassment is one of many historical-critical criteria by which scholars evaluate the historicity of a given form. The question this criterion asks is whether x or y form is historical on the basis of embarrassment to authors and/or redactors of the NT gospel traditions. Like Jesus traditions, the criterion is (it is thought, reliably) applied to Baptist traditions to determine historicity. References to the criterion in this chapter have two purposes: (1) to provide background on past interpretations of a given tradition or traditions; and (2) to subject to scrutiny exactly what 'embarrassment' to 'early Christians' meant. The present chapter proposes that today the criterion of embarrassment implies a homogenous group of early followers of Jesus the concerns of which are known from traditional readings of the gospels. Such a group, however, is purely fictional. This chapter proposes that one plausible modification of this group in the direction of diversity is Baptist followers among those embarrassed by gospel traditions. The concern of this chapter is not with authenticity (what this criterion sets out to demonstrate). Rather it seeks to broaden understandings of the Baptist traditions, by viewing a variety of past interpretations, some based on the criterion of embarrassment.

[31] Jeffrey A. Trumbower writes: "Of course, later Christians used Malachi and many other texts to interpret and justify John's role in salvation history, but I will attempt to demonstrate that this hermeneutical process began with the Baptist himself" ("The Role of Malachi in the Career of John the Baptist," in *The Gospels and the Scriptures of Israel*, eds., C. A. Evans and W. R. Stegner [JSNTSup 104; Sheffield: Sheffield Academic, 1994] 29). Also, John H. Hughes, "John the Baptist: The Forerunner of God Himself," 191–218. Similarly, for Isa 40:3, James Dunn argues: "… Jn 1.23 does have the Baptist using Isa. 40.3 in self-testimony, and this evidence cannot be lightly dismissed since it is precisely in its Baptist traditions that the Fourth Gospel seems to have strong historical roots and to have been able to draw on traditions unknown to or unused by the Synoptics. It is quite likely, then, that the association of Isa. 40.3 with the Baptist came down to the first Christians in different forms and that its use by Mark as Christian evaluation of the Baptist is simply the result of Christian editing of earlier tradition. It is possible to deduce, therefore, that the Baptist had himself been influenced by Isa. 40.3 … We may further hypothesize that this fact was sufficiently well known in his immediate circle and from them it fed directly into Christian evaluation of the Baptist" ("John the Baptist's Use of Scripture," in *The Gospels and the Scriptures of Israel*, eds., C. A. Evans and W. R. Stegner [JSNTSup 104; Sheffield: Sheffield Academic, 1994] 45–46). Dunn also demonstrates parallels between Baptist traditions and other parts of Isaiah, such as 30:27–28 (51). In addition to Isa 30:27–28 and 40:3, Dunn lists Isa 4:4; 10:15–19; 10:33–11:4; 34:10 (fire); 51:1–3; 52:14–15 and 66:24 (fire) (53–54). However, Dunn interprets the prevalence of copies of Isaiah discovered at Qumran (19) and literary parallels between Baptist traditions and Isaiah as a "correlation between the Baptist and Qumran … strengthening the likelihood of some *influence* on the Baptist stemming from or mediated through the Qumran community" (54; emphasis added). Nb. insertion of ἱερεῖς as the first word of Isa 40:2 (LXX). Klyne R. Snodgrass connects this address to Mal 2:7 – in which a priest is described as "a *messenger of the Lord* of hosts (διότι ἄγγελος κυρίου παντοκράτορός ἐστιν)" ("Streams of Tradition Emerging from Isaiah 40:1–5 and Their Adaptation in the New Testament," *JSNT* [1980] 26). Cf. ἰδοὺ ἀποστέλλω τὸν ἄγγελόν μου πρὸ προσώπου σου (Mk 1:2).

predicting a "perfecter," "mightier" and/or "coming one," messiah, Elijah, Yahweh, or some other figure or conflation of figures. Such a tradition, preserved, perhaps by John's followers, is later integrated by Christians with other materials *without, however, significant modification* to the statement. John forecast one to come. Whomever John identified as that figure (and, in all likelihood, as a good prophet, the prediction was deliberately ambiguous),[32] Christians identified the figure as Jesus. As we will see, a crack in the sturdy presupposition of John's role as forerunner creates new opportunities for the interpretation of the other NT Baptist traditions.

2.4.2 John on Trial

Returning to Reumann, in the conclusion to his article, he restates his position on historical John studies summarizing it in forensic terms:

> It is only here and there, I think, that we can, with much confidence, put our finger on a 'fact' and label it 'history,' less often, perhaps, than in the case of Jesus, for the quest of the historical Baptist proceeds in double jeopardy.[33]

Reumann's utilization of the legal analogy of 'double jeopardy' for research on the historical Baptist[34] nicely summarizes modern reticence on the part of NT scholarship to push forward on this question indeed on historical questions in general where 'jeopardy' is often considered – to stretch the analogy – more than doubled! Such a reticence is, in part, warranted. It is not, however, an excuse for failing to clarify or correct past methodological dilemmas, where we see them, or bypassing historical questions altogether. Post-modernism did not obviate historical questions; it simply redefined them. Since the radical historicism of the late 19th – early 20th centuries, biblical scholars still seek to understand so-called 'traditions,' even when a presumed originating point of the tradition postdates its current context (e.g., for Baptist traditions, when an originating point among *Baptists*, as opposed to the historical John, is presumed). Whether a Baptist tradition is traceable to the historical John is unknowable and irrelevant. When, therefore, in the course of this chapter, Baptist traditions are evaluated against a redefined criterion of embarrassment, it is not as a means of verifying

---

[32] Regarding Lk 7:19 James Dunn writes, "So a search for particular scriptural precedents at this point may be wrong-headed in assuming that 'the one coming' was more clearly delineated in the Baptist's mind" ("John the Baptist's Use of Scripture," 50).

[33] J. Reumann, "The Quest for the Historical Baptist," 194.

[34] Reumann has somewhat misused the term "double jeopardy." He seems to mean that, for various reasons (cited above), the quest for the historical John is doubly difficult. This usage is not strictly legal. "Double jeopardy" in a legal sense would mean that if John were tried on one premise and found innocent, he could not be tried again on a second premise. For modern criminal justice, this principle is, of course, a good thing: one cannot be tried twice for the same crime. Above I simply interpret what I think Reumann intends by his use of the analogy.

historicity (the traditional goal of the traditional understanding of this criterion), but as a means of testing and demonstrating correspondences between different evaluating techniques.

Thus, the present examination proceeds optimistically, demonstrating that provisional suspension of long-held scholarly assumptions that (1) redaction-criticism overrides insights from other critical methods and (2) John is systematically and in every case subjugated to Jesus in the remaining NT fragments about him – reveals interpretations of Baptist traditions not formerly apparent. Whether these new explanations correspond to history "wie es eigentlich gewesen"[35] is immaterial. That they expose and correct past methodological errors, however, gives them interpretative hegemony until, of course, something better comes along.

Pressing the legal analogy, if the foundational premise for Reumann's allegation of double jeopardy for Baptist traditions is inherently flawed (i.e., if these fragments are historically trustworthy apart from their present NT context), then no subsequent evidence meets the criteria for double jeopardy. If neither preliminary nor subsequent evidence mounted is valid, then John is not being held for offenses, is not "on trial," and faces no "jeopardy" whatsoever. Reumann's dilemma of double jeopardy as applied to research on Baptist traditions in the NT is eradicated by the fact that foundational, let alone any subsequent, premises are ultimately unfounded.

In closing the introductory section of this chapter, progress on the Baptist quest has ground to a halt. Cessation is so decisive that the most recent academic studies about John by historians explicitly deny any association with his quest. The fact remains that the Baptist fragments have not been given a fair appraisal. They have suffered at the hands of interpreters *overusing* one critical method and at the same time *overassigning* one narrow Christological perspective to the authors and audiences of the texts incorporating these traditions. Given the fragmentary nature of the evidence, the multiple attestations of these fragments and the plausible hypothesis that followers of John the Baptist constituted members of the evangelists' original audiences, Baptist traditions merit renewed attention and investigation.[36]

The specific aim of the following analysis is, therefore, largely negative: to correct, by means of an examination of the primary evidence, the faulty assump-

---

[35] L. von Ranke, *Sämmtliche Werke*, bds. 33–34 (Leipzig: Duncker & Humblot, 1874) vii.

[36] Existence of a group(s) of John's followers ("Baptists") in the period from roughly 30 to 90 C.E. is as plausible as the existence of Pharisees: the evidence (pre-rabbinic) for each is the same (NT gospels and Josephus, *Ant.* 18 [passages in *B.J.* are parallel to three in *Ant.*; a few additional references are located in *Ant.* 13.171–73, 288–98]; cf. also *Vita* 10, 12). Qumran provides background, but is not a source for either group. If, however, one denies the existence of such a group of John's followers, the hermeneutical exercise of positing such a group, nevertheless, broadens our discussion of the texts.

tion that redaction colors the interpretation of every Baptist fragment. Positively, this investigation seeks to broaden the discussion to include source-, form-, and other critical concerns by its insistence on examining the extant remains as fragments. It will be shown that Baptist and Christian traditions are mixed in the NT (as in, for example, the double attribution of phrases to John *and* Jesus [e.g., Q 3:9b//Mt 3:10; Mt 7:19]) *without modern concerns for uniformity and as if constituents of both 'Christian' and 'Baptist' groups are in mind.* While concluding observations do not offer a new and improved historical John, they do, I hope, expand current views of the history and meaning of these traditions.

The balance of the present chapter is devoted to analytical reconsideration of Baptist fragments grouped according to key issues of historical John research. The following components of John's life and ministry are treated in order:

(1) *Relationship between the Overall Ministries of John and Jesus*: Did John and Jesus minister at the same time? Was John's ministry chronologically and otherwise prior to Jesus' ministry?

(2) *Disciples*: Did John and Jesus share disciples? Did any of these disciples maintain a double loyalty?

(3) *Message*: What was John's message? What was the relationship of his message to his practice of immersion?

(4) *Practice of Immersion*: Was John a 'baptizer' and, if so, what did baptizing entail? Did John immerse others in water or simply exhort others to immerse themselves? What were the risks/rewards associated with baptism by John? Was Jesus baptized by John? If so, what did Jesus' baptism by John imply about his relationship with John? Did Jesus baptize others?

(5) *Audience/Locale*: Who was John's audience? Where did John minister?

In the analysis, near exclusive attention is given to the evidence of the NT gospels and Josephus, *Ant.*, although care is taken to avoid preferential treatment of any single source.

For ease of reference, a catalogue of all NT references to John is provided in the chart below.[37] Passages from Q, a decisively underestimated source of Baptist materials, are conveniently indicated in bold type under the columns of both "Matthew" and "Luke."[38]

---

[37] Robert L. Webb has a more thorough chart tracking all primary sources in the first two centuries. Other texts include: *Prot. Jas.* 8:3; 12:2–3; 22:3; 23:1–24; PCair. § 2; *Gos. Eb.* § 2, 3; *Gos. Naz.* § 2; *Gos. Heb.* § 2; *Gos. Thom.* § 46 ("John the Baptist and His Relationship to Jesus," 185–86). Michael Tilly also includes a helpful chart specifying Q passages (*Johannes der Täufer*, 145).

[38] For a list of all NT *logia* of John (Greek with ET), see Appendix I.

Chart I.

THEME	MATTHEW	MARK	LUKE-ACTS	JOHN	JOSEPHUS, *ANT.*
John Provides Witness to the Light				1:6–8	
Prediction of "Coming One"	3:11–12; 11:3	1:7–8	Lk 3:15–18; 7:20 Acts 13:25	1:15, 24–28	
John's Birth Narrative			Lk 1:5–25		
Announcement to Mary of Elizabeth's Pregnancy			1:36		
Mary's Visit to Elizabeth			1:39–45		
Birth of John and John's Childhood			1:57–80		
Wilderness/Practice of Immersion	3:1–6 **(Q)**	1:2–6	3:1–6 **(Q)**		
Announcement of Judgment	3:7–10 **(Q)**		3:7–9 **(Q)**		
Ethical Teaching			3:10–14		
Jesus' Baptism	3:13–17	1:9–11	3:21–22	1:30–34	
John's Statement about Himself				1:19–23	
John's Disciples Switch Allegiance to Jesus				1:35–40	
John Imprisoned	4:12	1:14			
Jesus Baptizes near John				3:22–24	
Questions about Fasting	9:15	2:19	5:34	3:25–30	

THEME	MATTHEW	MARK	LUKE-ACTS	JOHN	JOSEPHUS, *ANT.*
Jesus Baptizes More Disciples than John				4:1–3	
Samaritan Ministry				4:38	
Question of Fasting	9:14–17	2:18–22	5:33–39	3:29	
John's Question from Prison	11:2–6 **(Q)**		7:18–23 **(Q)**		
Jesus on John as Prophet	11:7–15 **(Q)**		7:24–30 **(Q)**	1:21	
Children in Marketplace	11:16–19 **(Q)**		7:31–35 **(Q)**		
Jesus as John Raised from the Dead	14:1–2	6:14–16	9:7–9		
Death of the Baptist	14:3–12	6:17–29	3:19–20		
Declaration about the Son of Man	16:13–14	8:27–28	9:18–19		
John's Prayer			11:1		
John as Elijah	17:9–13	9:9–13			
Law Until John	11:12–13 **(Q)**		16:16–17 **(Q)**		
John's Baptism: Heavenly or Human	21:23–27	11:27–33	20:1–8		
Parable of Two Sons	21:28–32 **(Q)**		7:29–30 **(Q)**		
John as Lamp				5:33–36	
Where John Baptized				10:40–42	
Water/Spirit Baptism			Acts 1:5; 11:16		

THEME	MATTHEW	MARK	LUKE-ACTS	JOHN	JOSEPHUS, *ANT.*
Apostles from John's Time			Acts 1:21–22		
Good News after John's Baptism			Acts 10:37–38		
Apollos Knows Only John's Baptism			Acts 18:24–26		
Disciples Know Only John's Baptism			Acts 19:1–7		
John's Life/Ministry and Death					*Ant.* 18.116–19

2.5 Analysis

2.5.1 Chronological Relationship of the Ministries of John and Jesus

The assumption that John is systematically subjugated to Jesus in all four gospels, particularly the Gospel of John, misleads on the topic of the relationship between these two 'kingdom' movements.[39] This section argues that the data favor an interpretation of John's ministry as proximate, both chronologically and otherwise, to Jesus'.

As many acknowledge, the first few chapters of the Gospel of John imply that the ministries of John the Baptist and Jesus were concurrent, taking place between approximately 28 C.E. and, at the latest, 36 C.E. Both ministries were

---

[39] It is Jane Schaberg's proposal that Mary Magdalene was such a leader (*The Resurrection of Mary Magdalene: Legends, Apocrypha, and the Christian Testament* [New York/London: Continuum, 2003] 260–76). Schaberg defines the movement is this way: "This was an emancipatory movement, resisting the domination of Roman and probably Temple establishments, focused on intertwined political, economic, social and theological issues, revolutionary in Segal's sense. It can be reconstructed as a particular form of the diverse *basileia tou theou* (Kingdom of God) movement in Second Temple Judaism. John the Baptist's movement, the Therapeutae, sporadic Zealot-type groups, apocalyptic conventicles, Pharisaic *havuroth*, and perhaps the Qumran community may be considered other forms" (*The Resurrection of Mary Magdalene,* 261–62). For directing scholarly focus to Jesus' *movement* as opposed to his historical person, Schaberg cites Elisabeth Schüssler Fiorenza (*Jesus and the Politics of Interpretation* [New York/London: Continuum, 2000] 20–25; *Jesus: Miriam's Child, Sophia's Prophet: Critical Issues in Feminist Christology* [New York: Continuum, 1994] 131).

concentrated in the regions of Judea, Samaria, and Galilee.[40] On one hand, some past arguments, rooted in a traditional Christocentric hermeneutic, claim that because the Gospel of John is the most blatantly anti-Baptist of the four gospels, divulgence of the simultaneity of John's and Jesus' ministries, transparent in the first five chapters of this gospel, (e.g., Jn 1:15, 19–40, 3:23–30; 4:1–3, 38; 5:31–36; 10:40–42), must (on the criterion of embarrassment) be historical. On the other hand, separate similarly rooted arguments allege that the simultaneity of the two ministries merely represents a subjugating device of the author: to bring the two individuals into confrontation in order that Jesus' ministry can be publicly declared champion (redaction-critical method).[41] The conclusion of the latter proposal denies the historical simultaneity of the two ministries.

The view that both Christian *and* Baptist concerns preoccupied this author, however, offers new possibilities for the interpretation of the opening section of the Fourth Gospel. Although John's statements of self-subordination in John 1–5

---

[40] On the theory of overlapping ministries, see J. P. Meier, *A Marginal Jew*, 2.19; J. Taylor, *The Immerser*, 55–59, 255–58, 294; and C. H. Kraeling, *John the Baptist*, 93–94. Against the simultaneity of the two ministries, Wink argues that "Mark 6:14 shows conclusively that the activities of Jesus and John were both chronologically and spatially separated. Jesus is taken for John the Baptist raised from the dead. Those who expressed this opinion could not have seen the two of them working together, or known of Jesus' baptism by John or even of a period of Jesus' discipleship under John" (*John the Baptist*, 9). Also, "John is dead. Jesus appears, and his behavior so strikingly resembles John's that people leap to the conclusion that he is John risen from the dead. The belief expressed here is not that John has been resurrected (ἀναστάσις) but that he has been physically resuscitated (ἐγήγερται – 6:14): raised from the grave, not brought back from heaven (as, i.e., Elijah, who never died)" (W. Wink, *John the Baptist*, 10). Wink, however, is not correct about the implications of these events. Jesus and John could have worked simultaneously for years until Herod Antipas attempts to squelch the movement(s) by hauling off the more notorious (John). Reporting back whether John's death, in fact, brought a halt to the potential insurrection, the reply could have been, unfortunately, the movement persists virtually uninterrupted by a similar leader (Jesus). To this report, the plausible reaction, particularly because John was recently murdered, is: it is as if the new leader is the old leader risen from the dead. In contrast to Wink, regarding Jn 3:26, J. Murphy-O'Connor argues that "baptizing was Jesus' habitual ministry while in Judaea at this period …. In Judaea, therefore, Jesus exercised a ministry which was both contemporary with, and identical to, that of John the Baptist" ("John the Baptist and Jesus," 363); and, "At that stage [earliest days of Jesus' public ministry] he was but an extension of the ministry of the Baptist" (366; cf. also 372). Morton Enslin argues that Jesus' and John's paths did not cross – rather that John is incorporated into the Christian picture later ("John and Jesus," 7). Interestingly, in the Gospel of John, John's response to his disciples over Jesus' successful baptizing ministry is: "No one can receive anything except what has been given from heaven" (Jn 3:27). This response is picked up a few verses later in Jn 3:32–36 when Jesus replies, "He [John] testifies to what he has seen and heard, yet no one accepts his testimony. Whoever has accepted his testimony has certified this, that God is true. He whom God has sent [i.e., John; cf. Jn 1:6] speaks the words of God, for he [God] gives the Spirit without measure. The Father loves the Son and has placed all things in his hands. Whoever believes in the Son has eternal life; whoever disobeys the Son will not see life, but must endure God's wrath." In this passage, as elsewhere (cf. Mk 9:12), "God's Son" may be construed as John the Baptist.

[41] W. Wink, *John the Baptist*, 91–92.

(1:15, 20–23, 26–27, 30–31, 33; 3:28–30) doubtlessly represent John's inferior position to Jesus in this context, John's authority in these chapters is never questioned. That the majority of subjugating comments about John in the Gospel of John *are spoken by John* suggests, not Jesus' authority, but John's. *John is the only person authorized to qualify his position.*[42] Indeed, in these chapters, John and his disciples have an important distinction: they are the *only* individuals capable of recognizing divinity (Jn 1:38, 41, 45, 49, 51).

Furthermore, concerning John's self-deprecating remarks, as noted above, they may be historical, even if their present context is contrived. For example, the historical John may have observed, "The one upon whom you see the Spirit descend and remain, this is the one baptizing with the Holy Spirit (ἐφ᾽ ὃν ἂν ἴδῃς τὸ πνεῦμα καταβαῖνον καὶ μένον ἐπ᾽ αὐτόν, οὗτός ἐστιν ὁ βαπτίζων ἐν πνεύματι ἁγίῳ)" (Jn 1:33); "Behold, the lamb of God who takes away the sin of the world (ἴδε ὁ ἀμνὸς τοῦ θεοῦ ὁ αἴρων τὴν ἁμαρτίαν τοῦ κόσμου)!" (1:29; cf. also 1:36);[43] "This was he of whom I said, 'The one coming after me became before me, because he was before me' (οὗτος ἦν ὃν εἶπον, ὁ ὀπίσω μου ἐρχόμενος ἔμπροσθέν μου γέγονεν, ὅτι πρῶτός μου ἦν)" (Jn 1:15; cf. 1:30); and, "that one must increase, but I must decrease (ἐκεῖνον δεῖ αὐξάνειν, ἐμὲ δὲ ἐλαττοῦσθαι)" (Jn 3:30), referring, not to Jesus as in the present context, but to a coming Son of Man, Messiah, or possibly even himself.[44] John may have de-

---

[42] Compare, also, Oscar Cullman's observation that the polemic against the Baptist in the Fourth Gospel is directed, not against John himself, but against those who regard the Baptist as the Messiah ("Ὁ ὀπισω μου ἐρχόμενος," 178).

[43] Reference to the phrase: ἴδε ὁ ἀμνὸς τοῦ θεοῦ twice in the Fourth Gospel may indicate it was – or was one of – John's signature exclamations.

[44] See D. Brent Sandy, "John the Baptist's 'Lamb of God' Affirmation in its Canonical and Apocalyptic Milieu," *JETS* 34/4 (1991) 447–60 in which Sandy argues (assuming the historicity of the proclamation) that John the Baptist's "Lamb of God" logion does not refer to Jesus' substitutionary atonement. Rather, on the basis of a variety of parallels, "lamb" refers to a messianic deliverer and "taking away the sin of the world" refers to the Messiah's cleansing the world of sin (458). Sandy summarizes: "'Behold the Lamb of God' was a seminal statement, both for John the Baptist and his listeners and for John the Evangelist and his readers. But in the Evangelist's discourse the meaning was clearly enriched by the events that occurred between the spoken and written versions of the statement. Therefore to understand what John the Baptist intended by his affirmation in light of what it would have meant after Jesus' death and resurrection is both anachronistic and superficial. But to understand the Baptist's statement in light of its OT and apocalyptic milieu is to move closer to the intent of the speaker and to the perception of the initial hearers" (459). Sandy's argument shares its conclusions with the earlier article of Raymond E. Brown, "Three Quotations from John the Baptist in the Gospel of John," *CBQ* (1960) 292–98. Cf. also the view of John H. Hughes, based on his interpretation of Mal 3–4, that John may have viewed *himself* as the eschatological prophet preparing Israel through his preaching of a coming kingdom *and thus as the Messiah*: "The evidence provided in Malachi and also in Ecclus. xlviii 9–10 for the expectation of Elijah as the precursor of Yahweh strengthens the claim that before and during the time of Jesus the role of Elijah was *not* thought to be that of the Messiah's forerunner. The implication of these passages is that the eschatological Prophet, far from being expected as the forerunner of the Messiah, was *himself* regarded as a messianic figure, if not

clared, "Behold, the Lamb of God…" (Jn 1:36) with reference to, not a *present*, but *future* (coming) messiah. Such a saying might have been celebrated, or at least memorable, for its enigmatic and/or innovative blend of the two ideas of a sin sacrifice (typically, bull, goat or sheep [Lev 4–5]) with a Passover lamb (not for sacrifice). That John once stated, "I myself am not the Christ (ἐγὼ οὐκ εἰμὶ ὁ Χριστός)" (Jn 1:20), implies neither that John thought Jesus was the Messiah, nor that John never issued such a denial. Furthermore, bringing John and Jesus together in order to depict *John* acclaiming Jesus' ministry as superior, renouncing his own ministry, and redirecting his disciples to Jesus (e.g., Jn 1:20–34, 35–42; 3:28–30) does not degrade John, but upholds his position as principal teacher of the *basileia* movement(s).[45]

The problem of interpretation might be described as a case of missing the forest for the trees. The attempts (such as Jn 1:8) littered throughout the first five chapters of the Fourth Gospel to curtail John's prominence and power are not here denied.[46] They are, however, of secondary importance and incapable of dampening John's profound authority in this text. Indeed, this point applies to all four of the canonical gospels. John is only subordinated to Jesus in minor redactional alterations of received traditions. In the more significant choices of composition, for example, the selection to include John in one's narrative in the first place, let alone permitting him to introduce one's account or to qualify his own authority, the evangelists demonstrate a collective desire to depict the Jesus movement in close association with John. Subjugating statements by John such as those in Jn 1–5 reflect only trivial departures from a position of overwhelming dedication to John's authority and importance. A 'criterion of embarrassment' *to later Christians and Baptists* handily corroborates this reading of the role of the Baptist in the first five chapters of the Fourth Gospel: against the embarrassing

---

the Messiah …. Since both the eschatological Prophet and the Messiah were thought of as appearing at the end of days to directly prepare the way for God's Kingdom, it can be appreciated that their roles were more or less identical. The Messianic status of the eschatological Prophet is confirmed by the accounts given by Josephus of two men who claimed to be prophets. The reaction of both the civil authorities and the general population to the claims made by the two men shows that they were regarded as Messianic pretenders" ("John the Baptist: The Forerunner of God Himself," 13; emphasis added). On Jewish expectation of an eschatological prophet, see O. Cullman, *The Christology of the New Testament* (London: SCM, 1959) 44 and F. W. Young, "Jesus the Prophet: A Re-examination," *JBL* (1949) 285–99. On a surface reading, Jn 1:20 appears to contradict the view that John considered himself the Messiah (cf. also Jn 1:25 and Acts 13:25). Hughes' interpretation makes clearer sense of the few times in the Gospels in which the questions regarding identity as the Messiah or Elijah are posed consecutively (Jn 1:20–21, 25; Mt 16:14–16). Hughes adds that Jn 6:14 is evidence that correlation between the Messiah and a coming eschatological prophet was popular during Jesus' lifetime (194).

[45] See n. 39.

[46] Of the roughly thirty-seven Baptist traditions in the NT and Jos. *Ant.* (see Chart I), only six of the traditions (four in the Gospel of John [1:6–8; 1:19–23; 1:35–40; 4:1–3] and two in Acts [18:24–26; 19:1–7]) trivialize John in a direct way. These slights are best explained in terms of redaction.

charge that the Jesus movement possessed no dignified origin (and while qualifying from a religio-philosophical standpoint that although younger than John,
Jesus is, as *logos*, ultimately prior [Jn 1:1–16]), this gospel counters that, on the
contrary, it commenced under the powerful aegis of the august and venerable
John the Baptist.[47]

Another observation from the *context* of the first chapters of the Gospel of
John supports this interpretation of the concurrent prominence of John's and
Jesus' ministries in the four gospels. In John 1, John the Baptist sees Jesus and
announces, "Behold the Lamb of God who takes away the sin of the world"
(Jn 1:29). After this point in the narrative, however, the author offers no indication that John ceases, or even slows or curtails, his own ministry in any way (e.g.,
Jn 3:23, 26) – not even after some of his own (key?) disciples defect (v. 37). Unless the author implies by the defection of certain disciples, John's demise, then,
in this discrepancy, the author of the Gospel of John tips his hat to the Baptists,
acknowledging that John's popular ministry of baptism for the remission of sins,
for awhile at least, continued alongside the ministry of his former student, Jesus
of Nazareth. In other words, John's ministry offered a valid alternative to Jesus'
ministry while both men were alive. This explanation does not, however, resolve
the conflict between the pronouncement that *Jesus* as "Lamb of God" "takes
away the *sin of the world*" (Jn 1:29) and the fact that, despite the universality of
the claim about Jesus, John's program of baptism still persists.[48] The proximity
of the ministries of these two first century Jewish individuals and their dual
prominence is also deduced from Jesus' insistence to John (attempting to prevent
his own baptism) in the Gospel of Matthew: "For, in this way, it is proper for
us to fulfill all righteousness (οὕτως γὰρ πρέπον ἐστὶν ἡμῖν πληρῶσαι πᾶσαν
δικαιοσύνην)" (Mt 3:15).

The simultaneity of the ministries is negatively corroborated by Mk 1:14 and
Lk 3:20 – traditions notorious for their tendentious imprisonment of John before
any narration of Jesus' ministry can begin. In Mark, Jesus is not permitted to un-
leash *his* message of the kingdom of God until John is securely locked up – left
for dead (Mk 1:14–15). Mark's restriction of the kingdom message to Jesus is

---

[47] Pierson Parker argues that although John and Jesus may have disagreed on issues, Jesus'
sole mission was to avenge John's death to Herod Antipas. According to Parker, Jesus' geographical movements, in particular, prove this point: "From the beginning Jesus had aligned
himself with the Baptist. When Antipas jailed John, Jesus moved at once into Antipas' land.
There he confronted Antipas' people, and increasingly antagonized the tetrarch himself, who
clearly perceived the links to John the Baptist" ("Jesus, John the Baptist, and the Herods," *PRS*
[1981] 11).

[48] Nb. the purpose of John's baptism in the Fourth Gospel is never specified. John 3:25 may
imply the rite was related to issues of purification (περὶ καθαρισμοῦ). Joan Taylor discusses the
question of multiple baptisms. Taylor writes: "Absolutely nothing in our sources gives us any
reason to presume that John's immersion invalidated any other subsequent form of immersion
or ablution, sprinkling or anything else that removed ritual impurity as prescribed in the Law.
We are left pondering the distinctive purpose of John's immersion" (*The Immerser*, 64).

probably related to his protocol for succession among teachers, a topic addressed by the author in Mark 9 (and by the present study in Chapter 4). One might even infer from Mark's unambiguous limitation of news of a coming kingdom to Jesus (Mk 1:14) – a tenet breached by Matthew (Mt 3:2) – that John was actually first to predict this new reign. Such an announcement would, of course, provide a much-needed explanation for John's death.[49] For the author of Luke-Acts, Jesus could not even be baptized until John's imprisonment (Lk 3:20), specifying that Jesus is baptized, not by any human "baptizer," but by the Holy Spirit (Lk 3:21–22). In both of these passages the prevalent redactional assumption that Baptist traditions are being subjugated to Christian ones *is* helpful. Careful positioning of traditions clearly indicates a desire to rein in John's authority with respect to Jesus. Like the Gospel of John, however, these moves are subtle as compared to the overall trend indulged by all four evangelists of lauding John and prizing an association with him.[50] On top of this, of course, is that any curtailing of John's influence too reflects his strength.

In summary, scholarly consideration of the relationship between John's and Jesus' ministries is impeded by stressing subjugation of Baptist to Christian traditions in every case. Although true in a few cases, such a disposition toward Baptist traditions misses cues to John's authority which indicate a solution to the question of his historical relationship to Jesus. Momentarily suspending this assumption, the present analysis reveals the prominence accorded to John in the canonical gospels and, not just a willingness, but frequently, desire on the part of the evangelists to closely associate the ministries of these two men. The Gospel of John *together with* the other Synoptic accounts attaches a certain cachet to John and his ministry that was probably in some measure historical.

The present analysis argues that, like the Synoptics, the Gospel of John is useful as a historical source when its Baptist fragments are dealt with as forms to which the evangelist allocated new contexts. These sayings encounter difficulties for interpretation only in later contexts in which Jesus is claimed as their referent while retaining references to John as speaker.[51] Wresting John's well-known subordinating statements from their secondary (tertiary?) NT contexts alleviates the contradiction of John's simultaneous prominence and subjugation in the Fourth, in particular, and (*mutatis mutandis*) the Synoptic gospels. John is a prominent figure whose celebrity is not tainted, let alone shattered, by self-subjugating statements. Comparison of the Synoptics with the Gospel of John demonstrates, not just the trap of wholesale dismissal of the Gospel of John in the quest for the historical Baptist,[52] but that related approaches of tribute are

---

[49] This question merits a full-length discussion and is, therefore, taken up in Chapter 6.

[50] The importance of John the Baptist in the Gospel of Mark is explored in Chapter 4.

[51] See also below (210–12).

[52] In his article on John's connection to the Qumran documents, W. H. Brownlee writes, "The most astonishing result of all is the validation of the Fourth Gospel as an authentic source

held by all four evangelists to their Baptist traditions. These positions probably sprung from rhetorical situations not conforming to modern concerns about coherency and contradiction *and involving Baptists.*[53]

The dates of the respective deaths of both men should also have fallen between 28 and 36 C.E., probably John's before Jesus'.[54] The claim in Mk 6:14 that Herod understood Jesus as John *redivivus* probably indicates John died first. It does not, however, with Wink, "show conclusively that the activities of Jesus and John were both chronologically and spatially separated."[55] Indeed Herod Antipas or Pilate may have summoned this argument only days after John's execution as the very basis upon which to also arrest and execute Jesus.[56]

2.5.2 John's Disciples

The categorical assumption that John is systematically subjugated to Jesus in all four gospels, particularly the Gospel of John, also misleads on the topic of John's disciples. Building on the argument of the previous section on John's concurrent activity and prominence with Jesus in the NT, this section shows that discipleship by John was, at the level of tradition if not always redaction, a

---

concerning the Baptist" ("John the Baptist in the New Light of Ancient Scrolls," in *The Scrolls and the New Testament*, ed. Krister Stendahl [New York: Harper, 1957] 52).

[53] On the viability of such a group, see 3–5 n. 8.

[54] On John's and Jesus' respective deaths, see Ch. 4. In Josephus' *Ant.*, the section on Jesus (*'Testimonium Flavianum'*) precedes that on John (18.63–64 vs. 116–19). T. W. Manson points out that the argument *against* "older is better" in the Pseudo-Clementine literature, (this argument opposes, for example, the absolute priority of the pre-existent *Logos* in the Gospel of John), would *not* have arisen unless John's ministry actually preceded Jesus ("John the Baptist," 398). John probably died in prison at Machaerus. The explanation of his death in Mark is fabricated. According to J. Taylor, "For Mark, John was Elijah (Mark 9:11–13); it was fitting that he too should be in conflict with a cunning Jezebel and a weak Ahab" (1 Kgs 21:17–24). Other parallels informing Mark's narrative may include Nathan before David (2 Sam 12:1–12) and King Ahasuerus' banquet promise to Esther and King Esther's indictment of Haman (Esther 5–7) (J. Taylor, *The Immerser*, 246). Bultmann did not think this story was originally in Mark (*History of the Synoptic Tradition*, 301). Others, however, believe Mark's account of John's death was original to the gospel (e.g., E. Schweizer, *The Good News according to Mark*, trans. Donald H. Madvig [Atlanta: John Knox, 1970] 135; Morna D. Hooker, *The Gospel according to Saint Mark* [BNTC; London: A & C Black/Peabody, MA: Hendrickson, 1991] 158). One might think the episode of John's death was omitted from Luke as a consequence of the author having already mentioned John's imprisonment at 3:19–20. Such a view of Lukan redaction is, however, overly simplistic. Luke was certainly capable of such overlaps and inconsistencies. More likely it was omitted from Luke on the basis of the connections it draws between John and Elijah – a relationship the Lukan author trims back, rather favoring connections between Jesus and Elijah.

[55] W. Wink, "John the Baptist," 9.

[56] As above, the evidence suggests Jesus' ministry commenced before John was arrested and killed. Furthermore, no text denies the possibility that John's and Jesus' ministries lasted only in the range of three and a half years *together* and that both men were executed within a matter of weeks or even days.

desirable pedigree, shared by Jesus and other prominent members of the early 'Christian' movement.[57]

According to all witnesses, John was popular, drawing large crowds through his powers of speech. Jesus, too, according to the remaining witnesses, attracted throngs.[58] Despite these multitudes of enthusiasts, in terms of disciples, it seems that John and Jesus shared. For example, according to the Gospel of John, Andrew, the brother of Simon Peter initially follows John, before switching allegiance to Jesus (Jn 1:40).[59] In Jn 1:41–51, an interesting concatenation of followers are subsequently linked to Jesus, and/or John, through Andrew. They include the seminal, historical figures: (1) Peter, Andrew's brother (1:41); (2) Philip ("from Bethsaida, the city of Andrew and Peter," 1:44); and, (3) Nathanael (found by Philip, 1:45). However, if, as above, one infers that the author of the Gospel of John contrives a direct confrontation between the Jesus and John movements for the purpose of championing Jesus, then Jn 1:40, depicting Andrew's defection (Jn 1:40), reflects a specific dispute on the point of discipleship. On this line of reasoning, Jn 1:35–51, as an artifice, represents the rare occurrence in Jewish,

---

[57] For NT witnesses regarding John's many "disciples," compare Mk 2:18; 6:28; Mt 9:14; 11:2; 14:12; Lk 5:33; 7:18; Jn 1:22, 32, 35, 37; 3:25, 27. Although traditions sometimes conflict, the Clementine accounts (*Ps.-Clem.* Rec. 1.54, 60; Hom. 2.23–4) testify to the presence of disciples of John. According to H. Lichtenberger, "...we already have in the New Testament itself mention of a 'diaspora' of John's disciples – in Ephesus" ("Reflections on the History of John the Baptist's Communities," *FO* [1988] 47). This point is, however, disputed (see above 3–5 n. 8). See also Michael Wolter, "Apollos und die ephesinischen Johannesjünger," *ZNW* (1987) 49–73. Tension between followers of the Baptist and followers of Jesus should have been greatest pre-70 C. E. However, as Lichtenberger correctly points out, "contrary to what we would expect, the polemic against Baptist circles increases in the later gospels" ("Reflections on the History of John the Baptist's Communities," 49). In terms of the history of tradition, Acts records that Simon Magus entered the 'Christian' movement with only water baptism by Philip. Was this the baptism of John? Cf. Acts 8:13, 16; cf. 19:2–3. Furthermore, in the Simonian *Apophasis Megale,* John's words concerning the ax and the tree are appropriated for Simonian theology (C. Kraeling, *John the Baptist,* 182). The Church Fathers say very little about John with the exception of their fascination with his diet, construing it ascetically. With regard to the limited attention given to John by the Fathers, Carl Kraeling asks whether he was "exploited too effectively by the 'heretics' to make him an attractive subject of Christian thought and speculation" (*John the Baptist,* 183). According to Kraeling, it was not until after the "Gnostic crisis" had passed that John "suddenly became again for the Church a very important person" (184). In the opinion of Clayton R. Bowen, John was a rival messiah or ἀντίχριστος ("John the Baptist in the New Testament" in *Studies in the New Testament: Collected Papers of Dr. Clayton R Bowen,* ed. Robert J. Hutcheon [Chicago, IL: University of Chicago, 1936] 75).

[58] The propensity to state/overstate crowds in the Gospel of Luke and Acts is a feature of this author's style. See my own work: *Luke-Acts and the Rhetoric of History.*

[59] According to the Gospel of John, Andrew was a disciple of *both* John and Jesus (Jn 1:35–40) – John, first and Jesus, second. Simon (Cephas/Peter), Philip and Nathanael may also have had dual allegiance (Jn 1:35–51). Cf. the claim of N. A. Dahl and G. Bornkamm that the disciples of John represent "the closest analogy" to the disciples of Jesus (Nils Alstrup Dahl, *Das Volk Gottes: Eine Untersuchung zum Kirchenbewusstsein des Urchristentums* [Oslo: J. Dybwad, 1941, repr. 1963] 161; G. Bornkamm, *Jesus of Nazareth,* trans. Irene and Fraser McLuskey with James M. Robinson [London: Hodder and Stoughton, 1960] 145).

even ancient, literature of a great teacher in his prime, publicly relinquishing his role, disbanding his school, and charging his students to go elsewhere.

Rather assuming that the Johannine author balances Christian with Baptist priorities, the possibility presents itself that, not just Jesus,[60] but his disciples too originated in the movement begun by John – *a valuable pedigree among followers of Jesus*.[61] From a Baptist perspective, not only is John authoritative here because only he is the only one qualified to redirect his disciples to Jesus, but he is the highly respected one with whom later tradition wishes to trace the training of Jesus (Jn 1:29–34) and certain of his key disciples (cf. also Jn 1:6–8, 15). What is more, as prophet, redirection of his disciples to Jesus may simply represent John's cryptic, yet accurate prediction of his own imminent imprisonment and death.[62]

Interestingly, here, for precisely the opposite reason, the criterion of embarrassment to Christians corroborates our reading. The criterion argues that the early church would not have invented a tradition in which Jesus, unable to at-

---

[60] See Kendrick Grobel, "He That Cometh after Me," *JBL* (1941) 397–401. Grobel's short article about Mk 1:7 and parallels attempts to demonstrate a difference between the two expressions: ὁ ἐρχόμενος and ὁ ὀπίσω μου ἐρχόμενος. The "one coming after me" refers to any one of John's disciples (Grobel thinks Jesus), if ὀπίσω is taken in the spatial sense of following behind (technical rabbinic terminology for discipleship). Insofar as ὁ ὀπίσω μου ἐρχόμενος refers to one of John's disciples, *it does not,* therefore, refer to the Messiah, the Greek expression for which would rather be simply ὁ ἐρχόμενος, its Hebrew equivalent, הבא. In sum, Grobel understands Mk 1:7 as an original saying of John's referring to Jesus, however, *not* as Messiah as student. It is the simple acknowledgment by a teacher of his student's "potentially greater capacity" (399). This interpretation, Grobel argues, helps to make sense of John's question from prison in which the prepositional phrase ὀπίσω μου is absent leaving only: σὺ εἶ ὁ ἐρχόμενος ἢ ἄλλον προσδοκῶμεν; On Grobel's reading, however, it is also possible that John's original saying was about a coming, messianic figure and, thus, like Lk 3:16 and Q 7:19 excluded the prepositional phrase. Nb. *The Critical Edition of Q* specifies ὀπίσω μου in Q 3:16b as "Matthew's" (14–15). If Q 3:16b and 7:19 are parallel, it is more likely Q omitted the prepositional phrase and Matthew added it on the basis of Mark and his own comfort level in exposing Jesus as originally John's disciple. Furthermore, according to Grobel, the author of the Gospel of Luke reveals his awareness of this tradition by his omission of ὀπίσω from 3:16 (Luke resisted somewhat Jesus' assignation as John's disciple; cf. also Lk 3:20–22). The argument of this book coincides with Grobel's that certain Baptist fragments are valued as historical forms (sayings) if not of the historical Baptist, then of his followers. These sayings are given updated meanings by their new contexts in the canonical gospels, but in and of themselves apart from these contexts, reflect largely unadulterated Baptist teachings.

[61] It is possible that behind Peter's name change from "Simon" to "Peter" (Mk 3:16 par.) is a switch of allegiance from one teacher to another. Peter may originally have been a disciple of John the Baptist who transferred allegiance, like his brother, Andrew (Jn 1:40), to become a disciple of Jesus. Paul, too, at some point experienced a name change (from "Saul" to "Paul" [Acts 13:9]) and apparently switched teachers from Gamaliel to (the risen) Jesus. Paul's name change, however, may merely represent the Roman form of "Saul," a switch coinciding at this point of the Acts' narrative with the growing popularity of the mission to the Gentiles.

[62] Cf. Deut 31:7 in which Moses, anticipating his own death, directs all Israel to new leadership under Joshua.

tract his own disciples, was thereby forced to appropriate those of his teacher.[63] For the criterion, the problem is not merely that Jesus is not *primus inter pares* – there is after all no shame in different teachers attracting different disciples, but that Jesus attracted his *teacher's* disciples, *his former peers*. This fact, the criterion reasons, must certainly have posed tactical difficulties for early Christians. Here, however, the assumption that Christians would be embarrassed of an originating association with John is both unproven and unlikely. Evidence of John as key witness, if not teacher, to Jesus in the beginnings of and throughout all four gospels undercuts this point leaving scholarship with the familiar contradiction of John's simultaneous prominence and subjugation. Furthermore, embarrassment to Baptists is here neglected. Suspending, however, both John's subjugation and Christian embarrassment, that Jesus and at least one of his disciples were originally followed John is a mark of status. For the evangelists, one might imagine a context in which deference was being paid to 'Baptists' as a part of their incorporation into a 'Christian' context. Such an acknowledgment of shared 'sectarian' lineages, even at the level of origins, would undoubtedly have helped to foster full merger and identity as a new hybrid entity.

Added to these observations on the Fourth Gospel is a final one on the Third. According to Lk 5:10, prior to their association with Jesus, Simon Peter and Andrew had business interactions with the sons of Zebedee, James and John. If this passage informed the background to Jn 1:40, it suggests that, through Andrew, at one time James and John, too, shared a loyalty to the Baptist.[64] This link impresses as outrageously tenuous, if not for Acts 1:22 which corroborates the point in its testimony that *Simon Peter and all those gathered to hear his speech* in Acts 1:15 were parts of the movement ἀρξάμενος ἀπὸ τοῦ βαπτίσματος Ἰωάννου.[65]

---

[63] Cf. the tendentious note on which Mk 2:15 ends: ἦσαν γὰρ πολλοὶ καὶ ἠκολούθουν αὐτῷ. Use of the word κύριος in a secular sense to refer to a human master or teacher is characteristic of Q occurring at least ten times: Q 6:46; 9:59; 12:42, 43, 46; 13:25; 14:21; 19:16, 18, 20. About this reference, in his very slim and handy booklet, *The Sayings of Jesus: The Sayings Gospel Q in English,* James M. Robinson writes, "Of course such human designations acquired progressively a higher implication, when referring to *or even just implying* Jesus" (James M. Robinson, ed., [Minneapolis: Fortress, 2002] xiv; emphasis added).

[64] Whether disciples were intended to simultaneously uphold their normal jobs while following John or Jesus is impossible to know. J. Taylor's argument that disciples were intended to return to their normal jobs is conjectural based on Lk 3:10–14 (*The Immerser*, 102, 117–19, 149). Disciples did not, however, necessarily form sects (αἵρεσεις). They may not even have formed cohesive groups, but this does not necessarily imply they returned to their normal jobs.

[65] W. Wink states: "It is *a priori* quite probable that a number of Jesus' first disciples were followers of John (cf. Acts 1:22)" (*John the Baptist,* 91). W. Wink also argues that Acts 1:22 ("beginning from the baptism of John") indicates "the whole central period of salvation": beginning, "not with 'the baptism of Jesus' or 'Jesus' baptism by John,' but with the baptizing ministry of John." "Luke may reflect here," Wink continues, "the same tradition preserved in the Fourth Gospel, that Jesus' disciples were originally disciples of John" (*John the Baptist,* 54).

In summary, when use of redaction criticism is negotiated judiciously with other historical-critical methods and John's subjugation to Jesus in all four gospels is not a blanket assumption of every Baptist tradition and when the criterion of embarrassment includes embarrassment to 'Baptists' as well as 'Christians' and others, the NT favors the bold view of Jesus and his disciples as proudly originating in the movement of John.

2.5.3 Teachings

The assumption that Baptist traditions were irreversibly distorted by the early church also deceives on the topic of John's teaching. This section argues that the message, perhaps even, "good news" of μετανοίας εἰς ἄφεσιν ἁμαρτιῶν (Mk 1:4) originated with the Baptist, accompanying his rite of immersion.

Joan Taylor points out that distinctive interpretations of the Law were essential to every Jewish teacher.[66] According to the Gospel of Mark, John proclaims, βάπτισμα μετανοίας εἰς ἄφεσιν ἁμαρτιῶν.[67] In Mark, once John is arrested, on arriving in Galilee Jesus' proclamation also speaks of repentance: "The time is fulfilled and the kingdom of God is near. *Repent, and believe in the good news* (πεπλήρωται ὁ καιρὸς καὶ ἤγγικεν ἡ βασιλεία τοῦ θεοῦ· μετανοεῖτε καὶ πιστεύετε ἐν τῷ εὐαγγελίῳ)" (Mk 1:15).[68] An important difference between the two messages is not only Jesus' exclusion of baptism, but Jesus' exclusion of John's qualification of repentance as "for the remission of sins."[69] Jesus' command to repent (μετανοεῖτε), without this qualification, appears hollow.

Based on Mk 1:15, Matthew's version of Jesus' message in Mt 4:17 also excludes the "remission of sins" from Jesus' proclamation, abbreviating, however,

---

[66] J. Taylor writes, "Individual teachers prescribed individual interpretations of Scripture that defined righteousness for their own disciples in particular ways. We know this from the various *halakhot* of rabbinic literature, which are rulings by individual teachers given to their disciples .... To define a set of particular teachings on righteousness for one's disciples did not mean that one was forming an exclusive sect, though a sect could grow out of the interpretations and ideas of a particular teacher, as we know from the early Nazarene 'sect,' αἵρεσις, the disciples of Jesus" (*The Immerser*, 105). Cf. E. Lupieri, "'The Law and the Prophets Were until John': John the Baptist between Jewish Halakhot and Christian History of Salvation," *Neotestamentica* 35 (2001) 49–56. Cf. also Qumran's "teacher of righteousness" in 4QMMT.

[67] See entire article on the topic by H. Thyen, "ΒΑΠΤΙΣΜΑ ΜΕΤΑΝΟΙΑΣ ΕΙΣ ΑΦΕΣΙΝ ΑΜΑΡΤΙΩΝ," 131–68.

[68] Knox Chamblin comments, "I am inclined to believe that Mk. 1:15 would be appropriate on the Baptist's lips" ("Gospel and Judgment in the Preaching of John the Baptist," 15).

[69] H. Koester refers to Jesus' message ("a call for repentance and the proclamation of the coming of God and his rule") as "analogous" to John's (*Introduction to the New Testament*, 2.73). C. H. Dodd believes this announcement was wrongly attributed to John (*The Parables of the Kingdom*, 33 n. 1). At least Dodd took double attribution of the message seriously. About the similarity of the messages, Knox Chamblin reflects, "...it may be inferred that at this point John's preaching has helped to determine Jesus' own message" ("John the Baptist and the Kingdom of God," 12). On this point, Chamblin refers to a Tyndale Biblical Theology Lecture, entitled, "John the Baptist and Jesus," delivered July 15, 1964 by E. A. Russell (12 n. 14).

the whole and swapping Mark's declaration of "good news" with his earlier proclamation of the nearness of the "kingdom" (Mk 1:15), in Matthew's case, "of heaven." Thus, Matthew 4:17 states only: "Repent, for the kingdom of heaven has come near." Interestingly, however, Mt 3:2 also excludes "remission of sins" *from John's message.* Here John's message is identical to Jesus' in Mt 4:17: "Repent, for the kingdom of heaven has come near" (cf. Lk 4:15). Not only is it noteworthy that these two summary messages of different Jewish teachers share verbatim agreement in Matthew, but it is further significant that the "remission of sins" (εἰς ἄφεσιν ἁμαρτιῶν) component of John's message in Mk 1:4 *never appears in Matthew in association with John.*[70] It is allocated, rather, to Jesus in Mt 1:21; 6:12, 14–15; 9:6/Mk 2:10; 18:21–35; 26:28.

These alterations by the author of Matthew are not coincidental. Quite clearly, they are intended to correct the possibility left open by Mk 1:4 that apart from Jesus – his ministry, let alone death – John offered an efficacious means of the remission of sins.[71] Matthew's revisions appear to us as dissembling on the part of the author or redactor with regard to the nature of John's offer of repentance; on the traditional *criterion of embarrassment* reading, it is an interpretation the early church would have been unlikely to contrive: the message of repentance, in particular, μετανοίας εἰς ἄφεσιν ἁμαρτιῶν originated with John the Baptist. As we will see, a close and original connection between John and a message of repentance has implications for the hypothesis that Q was originally a Baptist source, as repentance is an important and recurring theme in Q (cf. e.g., 3:8; 10:13; 11:32; 15:7, 10; 17:3).

For the NT evangelists μετανοίας εἰς ἄφεσιν ἁμαρτιῶν probably functioned as a thumbnail sketch or even summary motto of John's diverse teachings, derived from, or otherwise related to, his appellation, "the Baptist" or "the Baptizer" (ὁ βαπτιστής: e.g., Mk 8:28/Mt 16:14/Lk 9:19; Jos. *Ant.* 18.116 and ὁ βαπτίζων: e.g., Mk 1:4; 6:14, 24) – both Greek epithets the Synoptics apparently derived from Mark because *Q never uses it.*[72] The teachings behind this

---

[70] J. Lambrecht evaluates John's messages in Mark and Q: "When one compares Mark's picture of John with that of Q the most striking feature undoubtedly is the complete absence in Mark of judgment and threat. Of course, just as in Q the Baptist in Mark also preaches repentance, but he does not use the reproachful, insulting address 'vipers' brood,' he does not refer to Abraham their father and to God who can make children out of these stones, he does not mention the wrath to come, the axe laid to the trees and the tree cut down and thrown on the fire, nor the winnowing-shovel and the fire that can never be put out. No judgment, but forgiveness of sins. Mark's presentation of the Baptist is concentrated on the preparatory baptism of repentance and the announcement of the coming of an ἰσχυρότερος" ("John the Baptist and Jesus in Mark 1.1–15: Markan Redaction of Q?" *NTS* 38 [1992] 382).

[71] Mk 2:10 (part of an insertion?) and Mk 10:38 may represent attempts to consolidate the position of this gospel on "remission of sins": specifically that Jesus' death accomplished the task. Also, see M. Enslin, "John and Jesus," 3.

[72] The epithet appears in Lk 7:20 and 33, but is omitted in Matthean parallels (Mt 11:3, 18). It is also present in Mt 3:1, 11:11, 12, but omitted in Lukan parallels (Lk 3:2, 7:28, 16:16).

motto are neither completely lost, nor immediately apparent.[73] Inevitably they incorporated diverse legal interpretations (Lk 3:18), focusing perhaps on ethical prerequisites for baptism (Lk 3:18; Jos. *Ant.* 18.117).[74] John's exhortation to repent was certainly an insistence on righteous intentions to be demonstrated by righteous acts, such as almsgiving, prayer and fasting first, and later by baptism. The tone, if not the worldview, of John's broader message was probably apocalyptic. That John's only proclamation was "a baptism of repentance for the forgiveness of sins" (e.g., Mk 1:4) or that his many exhortations can be reduced to this phrase, however, is historically implausible. Josephus' omission of John's message of repentance confirms only that John's message was bigger than this single exhortation, presenting the possibility that the motto was Mark's: his fabricated or favorite summary of John's instruction.[75] Maybe Mark thought it captured perfectly John's two-pronged approach: moral with cultic atonement. Josephus prefers to highlight the more positive themes of "justice (δικαιοσύνη)" and "piety (εὐσεβεία)" of John's teaching (*Ant.* 18.117).

A similar set of circumstances surrounds references to both Jesus' and John's teachings as "good news." Although in the NT the verb, εὐαγγελίζειν typically applies to the teaching and message of Jesus, twice in the Gospel of Luke (Lk 3:18; 16:16) the verb refers to the teaching of John.[76] Stock interpretations of εὐαγγελίζειν referring to John's proclamation maintain that, by this expression, John is made to appear as the first Christian preacher.[77] A criterion of embar-

---

Thus the IQP omits John's epithet from Q. Like the Fourth Gospel (but for different reasons), John is not "baptizer" in Q.

[73] Cf. Joan Taylor's comment, "John's teaching was tremendously influential in the formation of Christianity. Precisely how much of John's teaching passed to Jesus, to his disciples or directly into the Christian tradition is impossible to determine, but the impact of John's teaching should not be underestimated" (*The Immerser*, 153). On what may have constituted Baptist teachings, see Ch. 3.

[74] On moral intentions preceding ethical acts, cf. also Mk 7:14–23 par. Josephus has at least two widely-acknowledged biases: he avoided Jewish eschatology and presented Jewish concepts rationally, often in Graeco-Roman philosophical terms. See Adela Yarbro Collins, "The Origin of Christian Baptism," 29; cf. also H. Koester, *Introduction to the New Testament*, 2.71 and J. P. Meier, *A Marginal Jew*, 2.20–1. Part of a small minority, C. Scobie argues the testimony of Josephus cannot be trusted with respect to the Baptist (*John the Baptist*, 111). Scobie's suspicion may, however, be warranted in the case of Josephus' omission of John's rite/ritual of baptism. Judaism, according to Josephus, should not be seen as a brand of mystery cult or, perhaps, in terms of developing Christian sacraments. Thanks to Hans-Josef Klauck for assistance on this point.

[75] Contrast Lk 3:18: "With *many other exhortations* he [John] preached good news to the people" (emphasis added).

[76] See E. Lupieri, "'The Law and the Prophets were until John:' John the Baptist between Jewish Halakhot and Christian History of Salvation," 49–56. Also, John's announcement of "good news" presents an exception to Hans Conzelmann's famous association of John with the period of Israel (*Die Mitte der Zeit* [Tübingen: Mohr/Siebeck, 2nd ed., 1957 (1953)]; ET: *The Theology of St. Luke* [New York: Harper & Row, 1960]).

[77] For example, C. Scobie, *John the Baptist*, 16. Cf., however, J. Taylor's comment: "One may wonder if these versions (Lk 3:18; Mt 3:2) are both preserving in different form some

rassment to Christians, however, favors an original association of the verb with John: the early church is unlikely to have attributed Jesus' distinctive "gospel" or "good news" proclamation to John. A criterion of embarrassment to Baptists corroborates this view: a Baptist contingency would have undoubtedly preferred mutual ascription of the good news message to John and Jesus over its complete appropriation for Jesus.

In summary, John probably delivered bold and various teachings, reflecting a life dedicated to expert elucidation of the Scriptures.[78] That the NT permits that John was a prophet at all – let alone "more than a prophet" as in Q 7:26 – implies,[79] with Joan Taylor, that he had his own authoritative interpretations of the Law. The teaching attributed to John in Lk 3:10–14 suggests such a vision and interest. Like other prophets before him, John's teaching seems to reflect passionate commitment to the salvation of Israel (e.g., Q 3:8–9). No evidence, however, proves his message represented a call to conversion or initiation in some formal sense.[80]

2.5.3.1 John's Perception of His Own Role

It is possible that, as one element of his teaching, John spoke about his own role. He may have considered himself a forerunner of the messiah (perhaps on the basis of interpretations of Isa 40:3 and Mal 3:1). He may even have considered his call to repentance preparation for a coming messiah/messianic kingdom.[81] As noted above, John's ignorance, ambivalence, or even rejection of Jesus' assignation as messiah, (cf. Q 7:18–23), does not preclude his consideration of himself as forerunner, even forerunner of a particular coming one.[82]

---

line in Q that described John as telling the good news that the kingdom was revealed" (*The Immerser*, 138).

[78] See James D. G. Dunn, "John the Baptist's Use of Scripture," 42–54; Jeffrey A. Trumbower, "The Role of Malachi in the Career of John the Baptist," 28–41. According to J. P. Meier: "… there is no reason to doubt *a priori* that John would have given moral directions to those who came for baptism" and "the natural impression is created that John too was something of a teacher of concrete morality" (*A Marginal Jew*, 2.41).

[79] The depiction of John in Q, according to John Kloppenborg, reflects deuteronomistic ideals for the role of prophet (*The Formation of Q*, 104–5.) Cf. also Q 3:7b; 7:24–26. See discussion below.

[80] A single immersion symbolizing a life dedicated to good deeds in the face of a rapidly approaching eschatological judgment may, however, be viewed as initiatory in some vague and informal sense. See J. Taylor, *The Immerser*, 64–72, 100 and A. Yarbro Collins, "The Origin of Christian Baptism," 33–34.

[81] As M. Enslin put it, "Their emphasis upon the coming kingdom could not fail to seem to entail a king" ("John and Jesus," 14).

[82] Cf. Jn 3:28 in which John describes himself as: ἀπεσταλμένος (cf. also Jn 1:6: Ἐγένετο ἄνθρωπος ἀπεσταλμένος παρὰ θεοῦ, ὄνομα αὐτῷ Ἰωάννης). As argued throughout, as often as the evangelists appropriate words of John as words of Jesus (see Ch. 3), they also give John his own words, but by means of artificial literary contexts, impart to them new meaning. There is, for example, no sound reason to doubt that John cited Isa 40:3. It is unlikely, however, that

In the role of forerunner, the Gospels of Mark and Matthew (following Mark) portray John as a figure like Elijah.[83] These witnesses imply neither that John considered himself Elijah,[84] nor that Jesus qualified, in John's mind, as the messiah and/or a "stronger/mightier"[85] or "coming" one.[86] John's Elijah-like

---

he did so with reference to Jesus (see above). And, the evangelists' manipulations of traditions can get much more complex. In Ch. 6 it is argued that Lk 7:28 is an example of a saying of John's attributed to Jesus about John.

[83] Cf. R. Bultmann, *History of the Synoptic Tradition*, 124–25. H. Koester refers to the NT's description of John as Elijah on the basis of his "activity in the desert," and "his 'social teaching' (Luke 3:10–14)" both of which Koester identifies as "Christian features" (*Introduction to the New Testament*, 2.71). See also Robert Macina, "Jean le Baptist étail-il Élie?: Examen de la tradition néotestamentaire," *Proche Orient chrétien* (Jerusalem) 34 (1984) 209–32; Georg Richter, "'Bist du Elias?' (Joh. 1,21)," *BZ* n.s. 6 (1962) 79–92, 238–56.

[84] So also John A. T. Robinson, "Elijah, John and Jesus: An Essay in Detection," *NTS* (1958) 263–81; repr. in *Twelve New Testament Studies* (London: SCM, 1962) 28–52 and Raymond E. Brown, "Three Quotations from John the Baptist in the Gospel of John," 292–98. Brown writes: "John the Baptist gives no indication of ever having thought of himself as playing the role of Elias. Jesus identified him as Elias (Mt 11,3–14), and this identification has naturally become traditional; but there is no reason to believe that John was aware of it" (297).

[85] Without further elaboration, H. Koester declares that the "stronger one" John's message announced was "originally God" (*Introduction to the New Testament*, 2.71). The three most common objections to this interpretation are summarized: (1) John would not have compared himself with God; (2) John would not have described God as merely "mightier"; and (3) God would not be described as wearing sandals. John H. Hughes, however, lays all three objections to rest *and* provides proof positive of John's announcement of Yahweh's imminent arrival, relying primarily on evidence from Q as less biased about John and the relationship between John's "mightier/coming one" and God ("John the Baptist: The Forerunner of God," 195–201).

[86] "As does Q, Luke pictures John as the forerunner of the messiah, the preparer of the way, the messenger before the Lord, the preacher of judgment and repentance; and as in Q, John is not identified with Elijah nor does he bring about the restoration of all things. In these last two respects Luke shows greater dependence on the conceptions of Q than on those of Mark" (W. Wink, *John the Baptist*, 57–58). Against Wink, by its citation of Mal 3:1 (itself associated with Elijah by way of Mal 4:5), Q 7: 27 suggests an association *in Q and Luke* between John and Elijah (cf. also Lk 1:76 in which Mal 3:1 is connected to John the Baptist). Wink adds, "Luke goes beyond both Mark and Q when he portrays John as an itinerant evangelist (3:3, 18) and a teacher of prayer (11: 1; 5:33) and ethics (3:10–14); but these motifs are latent in the representation of John as a prophet already developed by Q (7:26; 3:8) and betray Luke's special tendencies" (*John the Baptist*, 58). In response to C. Scobie's view that John's prediction of a "coming one" was deliberately vague, P. G. Bretscher and J. Knox argue John's reference is to Yahweh; see P. G. Bretscher, "'Whose Sandals?' (Matt. 3:11)," *JBL* (1967) 81–87 and J. Knox, "The 'Prophet' in the New Testament Christology," in *Lux in Lumine: Essays to Honor W. Norman Pittenger*, ed. R. A. Norris (New York: Seabury, 1966) 23–24. Before Bretscher and Knox, the same view was held by A. Loisy, *The Birth of the Christian Religion* (London: G. Allen & Unwin, 1948) 64–67. It also appears in W. R. Farmer, "John the Baptist," *Interpreter's Dictionary of the Bible* 2 (New York: Abingdon, 1962) 956 and E. Käsemann, "The Disciples of John," 142. John H. Hughes too takes this position ("John the Baptist: The Forerunner of God Himself," 191–218). J. A. T. Robinson suggests John may have identified the coming one (baptizing with *fire* 2 Kgs 1:10, 12, not water) as Elijah ("Elijah, John and Jesus: An Essay in Detection," 265). Although John P. Meier argues cogently against it, in favor of the view that John announced the Coming One's baptism by fire only (not the Holy Spirit) is that the Coming One is also said to cut down trees and cast them into fire and separate wheat and chaff and burn

qualities in Mark and Matthew (e.g., diet and clothing; see below Ch. 4) imply only that Mark (Matthew building on Mark) and/or Mark's audience accepted *a priori* that Elijah's return would precede that of a messiah whom Mark takes to be Jesus (e.g., Mk 9:12).[87] They might also, as above, suggest that Elijah's relationship with Elisha provided a useful pattern on which to model an affiliation between John and Jesus.[88] In contrast, the Gospel of Luke reserves many of Elijah's traits for Jesus.[89] The author of Luke's recourse to the Elijah *topos* for

---

the chaff with fire (*A Marginal Jew*, 2.37–40). See T. W. Manson, "John the Baptist," 404 and Harry Fleddermann, "John and the Coming One (Matt. 3:11–12//Luke 3:16–17)," in *SBL 1984 Seminar Papers*, Kent Harold Richards, ed. (Chico: Scholars, 1984). Cf. also the curious affliction of the epileptic boy in Mt 17:15 who is said to fall often into the *fire* and the *water*.

[87] They perhaps knew of John's use of Mal 3:1–5 and connected his use to Second Temple interpretations of the passage claiming it referred to Elijah's return. See J. Taylor, *The Immerser*, 283. On other expectations of Elijah's return see John J. Collins, *The Scepter and the Star: The Messiahs of the Dead Sea Scrolls and Other Ancient Literature* (ABRL; New York: Doubleday, 1995) 116.

[88] Of importance here is the interpretation provided by Sir 48:1–16.

[89] For a recent defense of this position with new insights, see James A. Kelhoffer, *The Diet of John the Baptist*, 129–32; see also summary (133). Robert J. Miller argues against a "Jesus-Elijah typology" (619) in the Gospel of Luke ("Elijah, John, and Jesus in the Gospel of Luke," *NTS* 34 [1988] 611–22). The author of Luke-Acts deletes five of Mark's nine references to Elijah, but adds three of his own: 1:17; 4:25, 26. For Luke, Jesus, not John, is Elijah, the prophet *par excellence* (W. Wink, *John the Baptist*, 42). On the parallels in the Third Gospel between Jesus and Elijah from the Books of Kings, see P. Dabeck, "Siehe, es erschienen Moses und Elias," *Biblica* (1942) 175–89; T. L. Brodie, "The Accusing and Stoning of Naboth (1 Kgs 21:8–13) as One Component of the Stephen Text (Acts 6:9–14; 7:58a)," *CBQ* 45 (1983) 417–32; ibid., "Luke 7,36–50 as an Internalization of 2 Kings 4,1–37: A Study in Luke's Use of Rhetorical Imitation," *Bib* 64 (1983) 457–85; ibid., "Towards Unraveling the Rhetorical Imitation of Sources in Acts: 2 Kings 5 as One Component of Acts 8:9–40," *Biblica* 67 (1986) 41–67; ibid., "Towards Unraveling Luke's Use of the Old Testament: Luke 7.11–17 as an *Imitatio* of 1 Kings 17.17–24," *NTS* 32 (1986) 247–67; ibid., "The Departure for Jerusalem (Luke 9:51–56) as a Rhetorical Imitation of Elijah's Departure for the Jordan (2 Kgs 1, 1–2, 6)," *Bib* 70 (1989) 96–109; ibid., *The Crucial Bridge: The Elijah-Elisha Narrative as an Interpretive Synthesis of Genesis-Kings and a Literary Model for the Gospels* (Collegeville, MN: Liturgical Press, 2000). A. Schweitzer holds that John did not regard himself as Elijah, but that Jesus was the first to give him this designation (*The Quest of the Historical Jesus* (London: A. & C. Black, 1910) 371–74. On Jesus' depiction as Elijah in the Gospel of John, see J. Louis Martyn, "We Have Found Elijah," in *Jews, Greeks and Christians: Religious Cultures in Late Antiquity. Essays in Honor of William David Davies*, eds. Robert Hamerton-Kelly and Robin Scroggs (Leiden: Brill, 1976) 181–219. In a complex source-critical analysis, Martyn argues that Jesus' explicit identification as Elijah was a part of the author's Signs Source, suppressed slightly in the Gospel due to the potentially offensive idea that "the logos experienced successive incarnations" (218): "the Elijah Christology of the source had to give way to the Christology of eternal pre-existence" (218). The Source's implicit identification of Jesus as Elijah is, however, maintained in the Gospel of John and is observable in at least the following three features: (1) John the Baptist's denial he is Elijah (implying Jesus plays that role); (2) proposed literary allusions to 1 and 2 Kgs (e.g., Jn 4:50; 6:9; 9:7); and, (3) parallels to the miracles done by Elijah and Elisha (e.g., Jn 6, 11). See also Robert Fortna, *The Gospel of Signs: A Reconstruction of the Narrative Source Underlying the Fourth Gospel* (SNTSMS 11; London: Cambridge, 1970) 232.

his portrait of Jesus is probably related to his views of the recurrence of history, prophets in general, and Jesus as a prophet *par excellence*.[90]

Barring the possibility that John wore prophetic clothing and inhabited the wilderness near the Jordan in deliberate imitation of Elijah (Mk 1:6ab/Mt 3:4ab) and apart from his possible use of Mal 3:1–5, (one of the two messengers [the first?] in Mal 3:1 is frequently considered to be Elijah on the basis of Mal 4:5–6 [cf. Lk 1:76; 7:27]), none of the other remaining evidence necessarily implies John considered himself Elijah.[91] If John either considered himself, or expected another as, Elijah, the forerunner to the messiah, his prophecies on this point were, as all good prophecies, deliberately vague.[92] That said, it seems possible he did and that Jesus (and his disciples?) later turned John's expectation *of* Elijah into John's expectation *as* Elijah of a messiah, identified, in turn, as Jesus (e.g., Mk 9:12–13).[93]

With respect to John's anticipation of a "stronger one" (ὁ ἰσχυρότερος [Mk 1:7]) or "coming one" (ὁ ἐρχόμενος [Mt 3:11]), given the multiple NT attestations of this prediction (Mk 1:7/Mt 3:11/Lk = Q 3:16/Acts 13:25/Jn 1:27), the burden of proof is probably on those wishing to deny its authenticity as a Baptist saying.[94] While it may not – as portrayed by the four evangelists – have been among his most central sayings, there is no reason to doubt that John proclaimed a "coming" and/or "stronger one," likely on the basis of or related to his understanding of Isa 40:3 and other texts, such as Mal 3:1 and Exod 23:20.[95] John or

---

[90] See my own work, *Luke-Acts and the Rhetoric of History*, Ch. 4.

[91] See John H. Hughes, "John the Baptist: The Forerunner of God Himself," 191–218.

[92] Similarly, C. H. Scobie, *John the Baptist*, 60–86, 208–10 and J. P. Meier, *A Marginal Jew*, 2.35.

[93] Cf. the following comment by J. Taylor also cited above, "For much of the early Church, John was Elijah *redivivus* (see, e.g., Mark 9:11–13; Matt. 11:14; 17:10–12; Luke 1:17). It seems quite possible that Jesus thought so too" (*The Immerser*, 281). If John H. Hughes is correct regarding the messianic status of the eschatological prophet, it is possible Mark divided what was generally considered a single referent, in two: "eschatological Prophet" (John) and "Messiah" (Jesus) ("John the Baptist: The Forerunner of God Himself," 193). It is also possible, however, as Hughes argues, that Jesus himself is responsible for the innovation: acknowledging John's self-designation as Elijah and viewing his own role as similar, yet different, either perpetuating the preparation for Yahweh's arrival or, as Messiah, somehow initiating that arrival (212). As both John Hughes and Knox Chamblin ("Gospel and Judgement in the Preaching of John the Baptist," *Tyndale Bulletin* 13 [1963] 11 n. 13) point out, the two primary scriptural passages associated with John the Baptist, Isa 40:3 and Mal 3:1 (at least second reference in Mal 3:1 to a "messenger of the covenant"), both refer, in their original contexts, to Yahweh. John may have kept them in this context. Jesus, even, may have kept them in this context when referring to John's message. Only once the view of Jesus as "lord" is concretized do these references double (while remaining John's sayings) as references to Jesus (John J. Hughes, "John the Baptist: The Forerunner of God," 216–17).

[94] This phrase occurs in seven forms in the NT: Mk 1:17; Mt 3:11; Lk 3:16; Acts 13:25; Jn 1:15, 27, 30; each is different. See C. Kraeling, *John the Baptist*, 53. J. P. Meier has an excellent and thorough examination of this passage (*A Marginal Jew*, 2.32–40).

[95] It is unclear whether John used Mal 3:1–2 to refer to Elijah as in Mal 4:5.

his followers may have conceptualized this individual in eschatological terms such as the Son of Man figure in Dan 7.[96] Later Christians, however, specify Jesus as the one predicted.[97] Fulfillment of John's prophecy by Jesus is not, as one might think, an obvious source of offense to Baptists. Recall that without some kind of fulfillment, the prediction is false, and so is the prophet.

In conclusion, the assumption on the part of scholars that the early church changed, falsified or otherwise misrepresented Baptist traditions, permanently obstructing John's teachings, poses an obstacle to research on this topic. Although John's message is dramatically curtailed in the four gospels, what is left, if often erroneously recontextualized, impresses as historical. A central piece of his message, such as his baptism "of repentance for the remission of sins," is equivocated over by the author of Matthew and supported by criteria of embarrassment, both supporting its authenticity. This section concludes, therefore, that John's message of μετανοίας εἰς ἄφεσιν ἁμαρτιῶν represents a reliable summary of what were inevitably diverse teachings accompanying John's rite of immersion. With this, John's prediction of a "coming one" in Mk 1:7–8 par. is consistent over the four gospels and Acts, making it among the most reliable of NT traditions and also, therefore, reliable. Careful examination of these traditions, balancing methods and taking into account a Baptist contingency within early 'Christian' audiences, all four evangelists' tendency to subjugate John manifests itself, not in tampering with the traditions *per se*, only in appropriating them for a new and unifying *causa prima*.

Excursus: 2 Sam 23:1–7 (2 Kgdms 23:1–7 LXX) and Baptist Traditions

Connections between 2 Sam 23:1–7 (2 Kgdms 23:1–7 LXX) and Baptist traditions are often overlooked in scholarship. This possibly very archaic poem (10th c. B.C.E.?) contains the so-called "last words of David." The LXX version varies slightly from the Masoretic text. The present interpretation, focusing on its relevance for the NT, considers only the Greek version.

The poem opens with an ascription notice stating that the oracles contained in this section come from David:

Καὶ οὗτοι οἱ λόγοι Δαυιδ οἱ ἔσχατοι, Πιστὸς Δαυιδ υἱὸς Ιεσσαι, καὶ πιστὸς ἀνήρ, ὃν ἀνέστησεν κύριος ἐπὶ χριστὸν θεοῦ Ιακωβ, καὶ εὐπρεπεῖς ψαλμοὶ Ισραηλ.

---

[96] See Ch. 5.

[97] Acts 19:4 demonstrates this point well: "Paul said, 'John baptized with a baptism of repentance, telling the people to believe in the one coming after him, *that is, in Jesus* (τοῦτ' ἔστιν εἰς τὸν Ἰησοῦν).'" As others have argued, one goal of the Second Gospel seems to be to make sense of a bewildering morass of expected figures (Son of Man, Son of God, Christ/Messiah, Elijah, etc.) by using them in a narrative to separate and define the roles of John and Jesus. No small confusion arises for us, however, when the expected figures integrated in the messages of John and Jesus simultaneously function as *the models* upon which the evangelists narrate the lives of John and Jesus.

In the opening verse, King David is referred to as a πιστὸς ἀνήρ that "the Lord raised up (ἀνέστησεν)" and as the "anointed one of the God of Jacob (χριστὸν θεοῦ Ιακωβ)." In v. 2, David, as a prophet, claims divine inspiration for his final oracles: "The spirit of the Lord spoke by me and his word was on my tongue. The God of Israel says (πνεῦμα κυρίου ἐλάλησεν ἐν ἐμοί, καὶ ὁ λόγος αὐτοῦ ἐπὶ γλώσσης μου· λέγει ὁ θεὸς Ισραηλ)..." The oracles follow. The LXX Greek provides challenges to interpreters. An English translation is, nevertheless, attempted:

λέγει ὁ θεὸς Ισραηλ ἐμοὶ ἐλάλησεν φύλαξ Ισραηλ, παραβολὴν εἰπόν ἐν ἀνθρώπῳ πῶς κραταιώσητε φόβον θεοῦ; καὶ ἐν θεῷ φωτὶ πρωίας ἀνατείλαι ἥλιος, τὸ πρωὶ οὐ παρῆλθεν ἐκ φέγγους καὶ ὡς ἐξ ὑετοῦ χλόης ἀπὸ γῆς, οὐ γὰρ οὕτως ὁ οἶκός μου μετὰ ἰσχυροῦ· διαθήκην γὰρ αἰώνιον ἔθετό μοι, ἑτοίμην ἐν παντὶ καιρῷ πεφυλαγμένην, ὅτι πᾶσα σωτηρία μου καὶ πᾶν θέλημα, ὅτι οὐ μὴ βλαστήσῃ ὁ παράνομος. ὥσπερ ἄκανθα ἐξωσμένη πάντες αὐτοί, ὅτι οὐ χειρὶ λημφθήσονται, καὶ ἀνὴρ οὐ κοπιάσει ἐν αὐτοῖς, καὶ πλῆρες σιδήρου καὶ ξύλον δόρατος, καὶ ἐν πυρὶ καύσει καυθήσονται αἰσχύνῃ αὐτῶν.

A guard from Israel told me a parable. I replied among men: How will you strengthen the fear of the anointed one? And, in the morning light of God, let the sun rise early – from the lights which the Lord passed on, so also from the dew of the grass on the earth. For my house is not in such a way with the Mighty One: for he has made an everlasting covenant with me, prepared to honor it in every season; for my complete salvation and will is that the lawless one shall not flourish. They are all like thorns[98] pulled out, for they shall not be touched with the hand, and a man shall not work among them; replete with iron and the staff of a spear, he will ignite them with fire and they shall be burned in their shame. (2 Kgdms 23:3–7 [LXX])

Given the resonances with Christian traditions, it is mystifying why the evangelists or other early Christians evidently did not exploit this passage. Even more puzzling are the numerous links between this passage and Baptist traditions. Compare the following five examples: (1) the reference to David as the man whom the Lord raised up in v. 1 (πιστὸς Δαυὶδ υἱὸς Ἰεσσαὶ, καὶ πιστὸς ἀνὴρ ὅν ἀνέστησε Κύριος; cf. Lk 1:69: καὶ ἤγειρεν κέρας σωτηρίας ἡμῖν ἐν οἴκω Δαυὶδ παιδὸς αὐτοῦ); (2) the reference to the "sunrise" in v. 4 (ἀνατείλαι ἥλιος; cf. Lk 1:78: ἀνατολὴ ἐξ ὕψους); (3) the reference to the "Mighty One" in v. 5 (μετὰ ἰσχυροῦ; cf. Q 3:16b: ὁ ἰσχυρότερός); (4) the reference to the "covenant" also in v. 5 (διαθήκην γὰρ αἰώνιον ἔθετό μοι; cf. Lk 1:72: καὶ μνησθῆναι διαθήκης ἁγίας αὐτοῦ); (5) the reference to "salvation" also in v. 5 (πᾶσα σωτηρία μου; cf. Lk 1:77: τοῦ δοῦναι γνῶσιν σωτηρίας τῶ λαῶ αὐτοῦ ἐν ἀφέσει ἁμαρτιῶν αὐτῶν); and (6) the reference to the burning of shameful ones in a consuming fire in v. 7 (ἐν πυρὶ καύσει καυθήσονται αἰσχύνη αὐτῶν; cf. Q 3:17: τὸ δὲ ἄχυρον κατακαύσει πυρὶ ἀσβέστω).

---

[98] Cf. also references to thorns in Lk 6:44; 8:7, 14. Luke 6:44, in particular, is attached to Lk 6:43 which is closely related to the Baptist saying in Lk/Q 3:9b, and can be plausibly attributed to the Baptist.

These connections may indicate that David's "last words" (οἱ λόγοι Δαυιδ οἱ ἔσχατοι) informed teachings passed down to us as Baptist.

2.5.4 Practice of Immersion

This section argues that numerous inconsistencies on the point of baptism in the NT Gospels and Acts (let alone the rest of the NT) render impossible a clear picture of the historical circumstances surrounding John's purported ministry of baptizing. It puts forth that reliance on the four gospels and Josephus, *Ant.* 18.116–19 as historical on this point convey positions on this practice that should not be harmonized.

Six observations, described in turn below, make this case: (1) eschatology may have been a distinctive element of John's baptism, but this fact neither denies John also taught moral lessons, nor implies his moral lessons were only tertiary to a more primary baptism with eschatological warnings; (2) the crowds that appear in the canonical gospels and Josephus, *Ant.* as witnesses to John's ministry, if in any part historical, suggest John's baptism was not merely external, but possessed a moral/internal façet; (3) that, according to the NT, John "preached" his baptism also suggests it was more than an external ritual performance; (4) the brevity of information in the NT dissembles little: the brief phrase μετανοίας εἰς ἄφεσιν ἁμαρτιῶν, in particular, demonstrates John was more than a messianic wilderness fanatic; (5) Josephus' known penchant for Hellenizing notwithstanding, *Ant.* 18.117–18 too claims that John's baptism was secondary to his insistence, through persuasive teachings, on ethical behavior; and (6) a majority of NT gospel traditions depict Jesus as the more external/physically- and less internal/morally-oriented of the two teachers. Not only does Jesus spend most of his time in urban centers with family, friends and others, dining and entertaining, he is known for powers addressing visceral needs, such as healing, multiplying food, and controlling nature.

We begin with John's epithet, "baptizer." According to all sources, immersion was a key part of John's ministry, yet the appellation, "baptizer" has no precedents in Second Temple Judaism.[99] As Joan Taylor points out, in the *Bellum* and

---

[99] J. Taylor, *The Immerser*, 49–50. Taylor writes: "The title, 'the Immerser' may refer to someone who immerses himself often, but it is generally understood to mean that he immersed others. Mark quotes John as saying: 'I immerse you with [or 'in'] water...' (Mark 1:8a) which suggests that John was understood to be the agent of immersion. He is active, and those whom he immerses are to some extent passive" (*The Immerser*, 50). Cf. A. Schlatter's comment: "...der alle Welt 'ins Wasser steckt'" (*Johannes der Täufer*, 61). Whether "Baptist" functioned as John's surname, as "Christ" came to function for Jesus, is unknown. On John as the "one baptizing" vs. the "Baptist," see also C. R. Bowen, "Prolegomena to a New Study of John the Baptist" and "John the Baptist in the New Testament," in *Studies in the New Testament: Collected Papers of Dr. Clayton R Bowen*, ed. Robert J. Hutcheon (Chicago: University of Chicago, 1936) 30–76, esp. 33–48.

the *Antiquitates*, Josephus uses the verb, βαπτίζειν only in the sense of drowning, as in the example of Herod's agents who "baptize" the last Hasmonean priest, Aristobulus III (*B.J.* 1.437; *Ant.* 15.55).[100]

That said, Joseph Thomas's well-known study demonstrates that any alleged baptizing by John can and should be viewed in the context of a trend of baptizing movements in and around the region of the Jordan during the 1st century B.C.E. and 1st century C.E.[101] While different communities reflect individual adaptations of the practice, immersion itself, according to Thomas, warrants no special explanation. What may have been characteristic of John's immersion is an insistence on 'righteousness,' interpreted as pureness of intention in acts of virtue prior to immersion.[102] Such an insistence of John's cannot, however, be considered unique.[103] An emphasis on *eschatological implications* of 'righteousness' with immersion may correctly interpret a distinctiveness of John's baptism.[104] But even if John emphasized certain eschatological implications of his prescribed way of life, these implications should not be allowed, as in the canonical gospels, to subsume what was an undoubtedly rich ethical content of his teachings.[105] After all, the canonical depiction of John as one dressed in prophetic garb, dwelling by the Jordan, eating only (Mt 3:4)[106] locusts and wild honey and immersing individuals among the crowds he attracted, warning them to repent before an impending final cataclysmic judgment is implausible. John's scathing insult, "Generation of vipers!" (Q 3:7), alone implies a lengthy set of diverse and persuasive teachings to back it up.

---

[100] J. Taylor, *The Immerser*, 49–50.

[101] J. Thomas, *Le mouvement baptiste*. Some scholars believe the popularity of ablutions increased during the late Hellenistic and early Roman periods and were used in place of sacrifice. See, for example, C. Scobie, *John the Baptist*, 107 and A. Y. Collins, "The Origin of Christian Baptism," 36.

[102] Cf. like emphasis in Mt 5:8, 21–48.

[103] The insistence on ethical standards accompanying rites of sacrifice and/or ablutions is a theme of many earlier Jewish prophets (e.g., Isa 1:16–17; Ezek 36:25–28; Amos 5:18–24).

[104] The view that eschatological implications of righteousness were characteristic of John's baptism is, however, open to the possibility that it interprets, anachronistically, John's movement on Christian terms, imputing to John what became theologically problematic Christian claims regarding the nearness/delay of the end (J. Taylor, *The Immerser*, 70).

[105] J. Taylor, *The Immerser*, 101–2, 217–22. Cf. also J. P. Meier's comment: "While Josephus' depiction of the Baptist as a moral preacher concerned with virtue owes a great deal to the author's accommodation to his Greco-Roman milieu, it must be granted that Josephus agrees to a certain extent with Luke's special material on the Baptist (Luke 3:10–14)" (*A Marginal Jew*, 2.61). With respect to John the Baptist, H. Thyen argues that Lk 3:10–14 is spurious because the ethical content could never have been the teaching of the person who issued Q 3:7–9, 16b–17 and expected an imminent eschatological judgment ("ΒΑΠΤΙΣΜΑ ΜΕΤΑΝΟΙΑΣ ΕΙΣ ΑΦΕΣΙΝ ΑΜΑΡΤΙΩΝ," 136).

[106] See J. Kelhoffer, *The Diet of John the Baptist*, 4–7, 124–28.

Moreover, while purification rites were widespread and various in first-century Palestine, they were, as Joan Taylor points out, primarily autonomous acts.[107] Indeed the idea of *assisting* in 'self-immersion' for purification, if not simply unachievable, would probably have been considered abhorrent, as a purified person could not maintain purity while facilitating purification of another (cf. *Miqw.* 8:5).[108] The question, therefore, becomes: Would John himself have practiced repeated self-immersion due to his own contact with impure pre-catechants?[109] As above, by omitting from John's moral message "forgiveness of sins," Matthew's gospel focuses for the job of "baptizer" on removal of outward impurity alone, thereby minimizing the importance of John's ministry. "There is nothing morally sinful," writes Joan Taylor, "about being impure."[110] Such a depiction of John is often thought to reflect his subordination to Jesus as mere custodian of bodies, bathing away sinfulness in preparation for eschatological judgment without recourse to a school, philosophy, or even corpus of supporting doctrine. Here again, however, the evangelists' determination to subordinate John hides very little. As in the case of John's teachings, the summaries in the four gospels regarding John's baptizing large crowds reveal as much as they conceal. If large crowds flocked to John, he almost certainly did more than immerse them. Would threats of apocalyptic damnation have provided an adequate incentive? They probably would not. Among other strategies, speeches of the type John never delivers in the NT, but Josephus alleges John gave (οἱ λόγοι, *Ant.* 18.118), might have motivated Jews, such as Jesus, to renew their commitment to righteous living, in the way that John defined it. Josephus records that John was a famous teacher, attracting large crowds on account of his persuasive speeches, emphasizing improved ethical behavior that, once demonstrated, could be symbolized by immersion.[111] Josephus reports:

[John] exhorted the Jews to lead righteous lives, to practice justice towards their fellows and piety towards God, and so doing to join in baptism. In his view this was a necessary preliminary if baptism was to be acceptable to God. They must not employ it to gain pardon for whatever sins they committed, but as a consecration of the body *implying that the soul was already thoroughly cleansed by right behavior.*[112]

---

[107] J. Taylor, *The Immerser*, 51.

[108] J. Taylor, *The Immerser*, 51. See also, much earlier, C. R. Bowen, "Prolegomena to a New Study of John the Baptist," 30–48.

[109] M. Dibelius, too, argues that, in addition to repentance, John insisted only on a convert's self-immersion *in John's presence*: "Er sollte sich auf Geheiß des Meisters und in dessen Gegenwart im Wasser untertauchen" (*Johannes dem Täufer*, 135). The evidence is also unclear as to whether the immersion prescribed by John was a single or repeated ritual.

[110] J. Taylor, *The Immerser*, 58.

[111] According to Josephus, John's speeches were so convincing that, years later, Herod's military defeat by Aretas was ultimately attributed to the untimely murder of this popular and well-respected prophet (*Ant.* 18.116–19).

[112] *Ant.* 18.117–18; ET: Louis Feldman; emphasis added. On the ET of this passage, see John P. Meier, "John the Baptist in Josephus: Philology and Exegesis," *JBL* 111/2 (1992) 233.

Although, in part, reflecting Josephus' bias for philosophical over ritual religious practice, here baptism is merely an outward consecration; however, Josephus specifies, for John's baptism, without righteous deeds, one need not apply.

That John's speeches appear lost does not imply they did not exist. Added to the evidence above is the testimony of the Gospel of Luke: "With many other exhortations he preached good news to the people" (Lk 3:18). Furthermore, that John's speeches were accompanied by some act or acts of immersion[113] and that, therefore, John became known as "immerser" should not promote immersion to a more primary position than teaching in our understanding of his life and ministry. Recall that the Synoptics refer to the baptism "which John *preached*" or *"proclaimed"* (κηρύσσειν) as opposed to performed (Mk 1:4; Lk 3:3; Acts 10:37, 13:24). Eleven separate references to "the baptism of John" (βάπτισμα Ἰωάννου)[114] in the Synoptics and Acts are also best read in this same manner: a baptism John *taught*.[115]

Scant evidence of John's ministry alone implies (on a criterion of embarrassment to Christians), not that John's ministry focused on simple outward purification unsupported by and without recourse to presuppositions and teachings of a religious and/or philosophical nature, but that John's ministry was *primarily religious/philosophical*, featuring an insistence on inner (moral) transformation as a prerequisite to a single, symbolic immersion. As the NT evangelists' (Mark's) reductionistic motto of John's message μετανοίας εἰς ἄφεσιν ἁμαρτιῶν too suggests, there was more to John's ministry than immersion in expectation of imminent eschatological doom.[116] Rather what little the NT reveals about John's baptism denotes a sophisticated rite. Although even John may have referred to his baptism as one of "repentance for the remission of sins," *given this message*, he could not have permitted the outward sign of baptism alone to constitute full consecration of an individual facing judgment. In fact, John probably reserved his harsh chastisement, "Brood of vipers!" for those flocking to him for baptism with this very deception in mind. Although more generously exemplified in Q (cf. Q 3:7–9, 16b–17), the Gospel of Mark condenses John's message of purification through right behavior to one brief phrase. The concession to Baptists was pride of place at the beginning of this, as well as the other three NT gospels.[117]

---

[113] John's act of baptizing might also be interpreted in terms of the symbolic acts of well-known Jewish prophets, e.g., Ezek 9:1–11, 36:25–27.

[114] Mk 11:30; Mt 21:25; Lk 7:29; 20:4; Acts 1:22; 10:37; 13:24; 18:25; 19:3, 4.

[115] C. R. Bowen, "Prolegomena to a New Study of John the Baptist," in *Studies in the New Testament: Collected Papers of Dr. Clayton R Bowen*, 40–41.

[116] Compare here the bold assertion of H. Thyen: "…the formulation βάπτισμα μετανοίας εἰς ἄφεσιν ἁμαρτιῶν, which Mark apparently took over from the tradition, shows clearly that he is no mere preacher of repentance…" ("ΒΑΠΤΙΣΜΑ ΜΕΤΑΝΟΙΑΣ ΕΙΣ ΑΦΕΣΙΝ ΑΜΑΡΤΙΩΝ," 132–33).

[117] On the importance of John the Baptist for early Christianity, Clayton R. Bowen writes, "Though not a Christian, John the Baptist is clearly the fourth most important person in the New

What is more, *in contrast to* John's teachings, a majority of NT gospel traditions portray Jesus' as the more *corporeal* of the two ministries. Jesus is the "doctor" for "sinners," bringing physical healing through the restoration of abilities such as seeing, hearing, speaking, walking, and normal patterns of menstruation. Jesus multiplies food, drink, and even fish for one's livelihood.[118] In short, although Mark abridges John's work to mere baptizing and his teaching to an encapsulated message of repentance for the forgiveness of sins in preparation for an impending judgment equipped with eschatological leader, much ritual and religio-philosophical discourse is implied behind each of these two epitomic reductions. Although it is possible to read the gospel depictions of John's water baptism as superficial (shallow!) in comparison with the more profound healing and teaching legacy of Jesus and his followers, the condensed evidence suggests the opposite. The sparse records about John imply both a positive and philosophic view of John's work.

Finally, in terms of *baptism types*, the two evidently offered by John and Jesus (and their followers), by water and by the spirit, are neither mutually exclusive, nor diametrically opposed. While possible, as above, that connecting John's immersion with water and Jesus' with the spirit is a subjugating strategy on the part of evangelists,[119] even in the NT, Jesus' baptism with the spirit provides neither a clear alternative, nor a clear supplement to baptism with water. Indeed Jesus, when baptized by John with water, receives the spirit (Q 3:21–22; Mk 1:10)![120] Jesus himself never baptizes with the spirit unless baptism is allowed to refer, metaphysically, to his whole ministry (cf. Jn 20:22).

Also, the Gospel of John claims that Jesus, *almost as opposed to* John (e.g., Jn 3:23, as an afterthought: "John, *too*, was baptizing in Aenon near Salim because

---

Testament, looming in the consciousness of the Christian writers" ("Prolegomena to a Study of John the Baptist," 33). See, further, Ch. 3 where the argument is made that many NT traditions attributed to Jesus were originally those of John.

[118] While the Gospel of Mark's emphasis on Jesus' healing ministry is well known, the preoccupation with healing in the Gospel of Luke is equally strong, if not stronger. For example, just before the important *teachings* of the Sermon on the Plain (emphasizing Jesus' role as teacher) Luke spares a moment to summarize, emphasizing (three times) Jesus' capacity as effective *healer*: "They had come to hear him and (1) to be healed from their diseases. (2) And those troubled by unclean spirits were healed, (3) and the whole crowd sought to touch him, because power came out from him and healed all of them" (Lk 6:18–19). Also, in the Gospel of Luke, Jesus' "good news" is inseparably linked to healing in Lk 9:2, 6, 11 and 10:9.

[119] Observe the neat polarity between baptism by John in cold water and baptism by Jesus in a tongue of hot fire/spirit (Acts 2). Although Acts represents a confusion of traditions on the point of baptism, the development seems to have moved from water baptism (John and Jesus) to spirit baptism (Paul) with many parties combining both (e.g., water then spirit [Acts 19:3–7]). The development of Christian baptism during the second century exhibits the influence of Hellenistic mystery cults.

[120] M. Enslin, "John and Jesus," 3. See also Hans-Josef Klauck, *Vorspiel im Himmel? Erzähltechnik und Theologie im Markusprolog* (BTS 32; Neukirchen-Vluyn: Neukirchener, 1997) 88–89.

much water was there"), baptized with water, and through this practice attracted, at some point, even more followers than John.[121] If again we suspend the traditional assumption that the Fourth Gospel cannot be trusted,[122] a criterion of embarrassment to Christians favors that Jesus, like John, baptized others with water.[123] And, for Baptists such a claim posed no problems: as John's successor Jesus would undoubtedly have adopted this rite. Similar to Q, however, in the Fourth Gospel, John is never called 'Baptist' and never baptizes anyone.[124] What is more, in its context, by John's declaration in Jn 1:29 (cf. Jn 1:36) regarding Jesus: "Behold, the Lamb of God who takes away the sin of the world," John nullifies any potential exonerative value of a baptismal message of repentance Jesus may have had. It is also significant that John, in this context in the Fourth Gospel, is the only figure authorized to declare a shift from his own offer of forgiveness to Jesus'.[125]

That Jesus too was a kind of 'immerser,'[126] nicely disperses the otherwise anomalous later Christian practice of immersing others from a single individual to two and from a single group of followers to two.[127] It also helps to explain the prominence of the rite of baptism in Mt 28:19. Joan Taylor summarizes,

---

[121] With Joan Taylor, that Jesus did not baptize (e.g., Jn 4:2) leaves a "curious hiatus of the procedure" (*The Immerser*, 297). The miracle of the wedding at Cana may contain a veiled reference (in addition to veiled references to Jesus' passion) to the usurpation of John's baptism by Jesus' baptism: the water of John's movement/baptism (1:31, 33) is replaced by the wine of Jesus' movement/death and resurrection. See W. Wink, *John the Baptist*, 93; M. Dibelius, *Johannes der Täufer*, 112. See n. 140.

[122] J. Murphy-O'Connor agrees the Fourth Gospel has historical value ("John the Baptist and Jesus," esp. 366).

[123] Many commentators acknowledge this possibility. See J. Taylor, *The Immerser*, 296; J. Murphy-O'Connor, "John the Baptist and Jesus," 363.

[124] In Jn 3:23 John is said to baptize, but no specific individual(s) is named. The locations of both Aenon and Salim are unknown.

[125] Against H. Thyen who writes: "The Fourth Gospel goes far beyond Matthew in the depreciation of John and his baptism. Here, in fact, one can truly say that the baby has been thrown out with the bath water" ("ΒΑΠΤΙΣΜΑ ΜΕΤΑΝΟΙΑΣ ΕΙΣ ΑΦΕΣΙΝ ΑΜΑΡΤΙΩΝ," 140). Much of this article is misleading.

[126] E.g., A. Y. Collins, "The Origin of Christian Baptism," 36. Ernest W. Parsons argues Jesus did not baptize with water ("The Significance of John the Baptist for the Beginnings of Christianity," in *Environmental Factors in Christian History*, eds. John Thomas McNeill, Matthew Spinka and Harold R. Willoughby [Chicago: The University of Chicago Press, 1939] 14–15). This is also the position of Hans-Josef Klauck in "Die Sakramente und der historische Jesus," in *Gemeinde, Amt, Sakrament: Neutestamentliche Perspektiven* (Würzberg: Echter, 1989) 274–76. As some commentators point out, a remaining, intermediate option is that Jesus baptized with water early in his ministry, forgoing the practice later. Compare also the view of J. Murphy-O'Connor: "In Acts 19:1–7 Paul meets around twelve disciples in Ephesus who claim not to have heard of the Holy Spirit and to have been baptized into the baptism of John. Jesus, however, may have administered this baptism" (J. Murphy-O'Connor, "John the Baptist and Jesus," 367). Related to the practice of baptizing in the NT is the ritual immersion that preceded eating. Curiously, in Lk 11:38 a Pharisee who has invited Jesus to dine with him is "astonished" (θαυμάζω) to find that Jesus does not "immerse" (βαπτίζω) before eating. In Mark and Matthew, however, Pharisees and scribes raise this objection against, not Jesus, but his disciples.

[127] The Fourth Gospel maintains some ambivalence (Jn 4:2) on the topic.

The issue for the writer of the Fourth Gospel – as opposed to the editor who added the comment in 4:2 about Jesus not baptizing – was *when* Jesus baptized, not whether he did so or not.[128]

Following Taylor, the question elicited by the two "Lamb of God" exclamations (Jn 1:29, 36) is only: If Jesus baptized others with water, did he, in *this* or another (death/resurrection) way, remove "the sin of the world?" To this question, the author provides no solution increasing the likelihood that this saying of John's originated in a different context.

A final complicating element is that baptism 'by the spirit,' although foretold by John the Baptist and spoken about in Jesus' lifetime, was not possible, at least on Lukan terms, (apart from Jesus' receiving of the spirit from John through baptism with water),[129] until the bestowal of the spirit in Acts 2 following Jesus' ascension. Furthermore, according to Acts, once the spirit *is* bequeathed, believers continue to take part in water baptism as carried out by followers such as Philip and Apollos. This undoubtedly reflects persistent and heterogeneous admixing of the two rites among different groups within the movement(s).

2.5.4.1 *Jesus' Baptism by John*

Jesus' baptism is, for the NT, a special case of John's practice of immersion and it is one incident for which interpreters generally deemphasize the evangelists' subjugating disposition toward John in favor of a straightforward historical reading of the account. As John P. Meier writes,

> *...one of the most certain things we know about Jesus is that he voluntarily submitted himself to John's baptism for the remission of sins, an embarrassing event each evangelist tries to neutralize in his own way.* But the Baptist is not so easily neutralized. For all the differences between John and Jesus, some key elements of John's preaching and praxis flowed into Jesus' ministry like so much baptismal water. Hence, not to understand the Baptist is not to understand Jesus – a dictum borne out in the work of some recent scholars.[130]

Ignoring its record of supernatural intervention by a divine voice from heaven, Jesus' baptism by John is upheld, in the opinion of a majority of scholars, as one of the most historically likely events documented in the canonical gospels.[131]

---

[128] J. Taylor, *The Immerser*, 296; emphasis original.

[129] See below where a sub-section of this argument is devoted to the special case of Jesus' baptism by John.

[130] J. P. Meier, *A Marginal Jew*, 2.7; emphasis added.

[131] Most notably Rudolf Bultmann, *The History of the Synoptic Tradition*, 47; E. P. Sanders, *Jesus and Judaism* (Philadelphia: Fortress, 1985) 11; idem, *The Historical Figure of Jesus* (London: Penguin, 1993) 92–94. Cf. also H. Koester's comment, "That Jesus was baptized by John – this report should not be doubted – proves that Jesus was a disciple of John" (*Introduction to the New Testament*, 2.73). Also, Paul W. Hollenbach writes, "There can be no more certain fact of Jesus' life than his baptism by John," also referring to Jesus' baptism as "the bedrock fact of the beginning of Jesus' public career" ("The Conversion of Jesus: From Jesus the

While most believe the accounts preserved by Matthew and Luke were enhanced to accommodate the individual theological tolerances of these authors, the traditional criterion of embarrassment strongly suggests – scholars insist – the authenticity of, at the very least, Mark's unabashed single verse:

And it happened that in those days Jesus came from Nazareth of Galilee and was baptized in the Jordan by John (καὶ ἐγένετο ἐν ἐκείναις ταῖς ἡμέραις ἦλθεν Ἰησοῦς ἀπὸ Ναζαρὲτ τῆς Γαλιλαίας καὶ ἐβαπτίσθη εἰς τὸν Ἰορδάνην ὑπὸ Ἰωάννου). (Mk 1:9)[132]

In the words of Joachim Jeremias, such a "scandalizing piece of information" would not have been invented.[133]

Taking scholarly consensus a step further, however, the most plausible explanation of Jesus' baptism by John deduced via the criterion of embarrassment is that at some point in his life Jesus considered himself *in need of* John's baptism perhaps on the basis of an eschatological conviction. Whether by accepting John's baptism Jesus became John's disciple is difficult to prove.[134] If, however,

---

Baptizer to Jesus the Healer," *ANRW* 2.25.1, 198–99). Against this consensus are E. Haenchen, M. Enslin, and others.

[132] Whether a Q version of Jesus' baptism ever existed is debated. See J. S. Kloppenborg, *Q Parallels*, 16; J. P. Meier, *A Marginal Jew*, 2.103–4, 183–84; H. Schürmann, *Das Lukas Evangelium*, 1.197, 218. The author of the Gospel of Luke, in particular, has almost no use for water baptism, but nevertheless retains it from his sources as an important relic from the past. Arguments to the contrary can be found in Hans-Josef Klauck, *Vorspiel im Himmel? Erzähltechnik und Theologie im Markusprolog*, 71 n. 122.

[133] J. Jeremias, *New Testament Theology: The Proclamation of Jesus* (London: SCM, 1971) 45.

[134] While many scholars agree Jesus was John's disciple, it remains to define in what sense this discipleship can be understood. See Jürgen Becker, *Johannes der Täufer*, 12–15, 105; J. Ernst, *Johannes der Täufer*, 338–39; idem, "War Jesus ein Schüler Johannes' des Täufers?" *Vom Urchristentum zu Jesus. Joachim Gnilka Festschrift*, ed. Hubert Frankenmölle and Karl Kertelge (Freiburg/Basel/Vienna: Herder, 1989) 13–33; J. Gnilka, *Jesus von Nazaret: Botschaft und Geschichte* (HTKNT; Freiburg: Herder, 1993) 84–85; Paul Hollenbach, "The Conversion of Jesus," 203–4; C. Kraeling, *John the Baptist*, 162; C. Scobie, *John the Baptist*, 153–56. For a summary of the arguments, see J. Meier, *A Marginal Jew*, 2.116–130. Meier's own cogent view of this problem is worth citing in full: "In my opinion, Jesus' being baptized by John is one of the most historically certain events ascertainable by any reconstruction of the historical Jesus. The criterion of embarrassment strongly argues in favor of it; though less sturdy, the criterion of multiple attestation probably does as well. To a certain degree, even the criterion of discontinuity adds its voice. While it is more difficult to discern exactly what his being baptized meant to Jesus, it (alone with the events surrounding it) certainly involved a basic break with his past life, his confession that he was a member of a sinful Israel that had turned away from its God, his turning or 'conversion' to a life fully dedicated to Israel's religious heritage and destiny, his acknowledgment of John as an eschatological prophet, his embrace of John's message of imminent eschatology, and his submission to the special ritual washing John alone administered and considered part of the way to salvation. So strong was the impact of John on Jesus that, *for a short period, Jesus stayed with John as his disciple* and, when he struck out on his own, he continued the practice of baptizing disciples. While these two last points are not as certain as the fact of Jesus' being baptized, I think the criterion of embarrassment, applied to the Fourth Gospel, makes them fairly probable, especially since they are supported by the

Josephus is correct about the nature of John's rite, then we should understand about Jesus from this event that, acting on some unknown conviction, Jesus first demonstrated acts of personal piety which he later complemented by ablutions in the Jordan or some neighboring river such as "Aenon near Salim" (Jn 3:23).[135]

This position is, however, not without dissenters. Morton Enslin finds the idea of Jesus' baptism by John a "most natural surmise or invention" of the early Church:

> By the time the gospels were written baptism had become a universal practice. Farther and farther back it was read, as is invariably the case in a religion which takes itself seriously as one of revelation. What is now under God's blessing must always so have been. ... As Jesus unqualifiedly commanded it in the Great Commission, so he had commended and consecrated it for all time by his own example.[136]

Enslin's position, if nothing else, attempts to account for the fact that while little of the remaining evidence depicts Jesus' baptizing others, the practice is thoroughly integrated in traditions following his death,[137] a fact that is, indeed, difficult to explain.

A final possible interpretation of Jesus' baptism by John is simply that it preserves a tradition of John's authority as an eminent Jewish teacher. To have been baptized by John – perhaps even associated with him in any way – was a mark of esteem (if not quite the esteem Jesus eventually accrued). In this case the author of the Gospel of Mark, for example, viewed the datum of John's baptism of Jesus as a favorable association for Jesus in the sense of a preliminary sign of his potential, irrespective of John's, Jesus' or the church's eventual understanding or practice of the rite. Beginning his life of Jesus, the author of Mark proclaims boldly: the subject of his study has no ignominious origins. On the contrary, Jesus was associated with the venerable wilderness prophet John. This tack is, of course, reversed by the authors of Matthew and Luke who argue it is Jesus' ignominious origins that establish his credibility despite – or perhaps because of – their inclusion of this Markan pericope.[138]

Summarizing, scholarly consideration of John's and Jesus' practice of baptizing and the special case of Jesus' baptism by John have, more than for other

---

criterion of coherence as well" (129; emphasis added). I will say more on the question of Jesus' discipleship by John in Ch. 4.

[135] Cf. *Gos. Naz.* in *NTApo I: Gospels and Related Writings*, ed. W. Schneemelcher; ET. ed. R. McL. Wilson (Cambridge: Clarke, 1991) 160, frag. 2 (Jerome, *Adv. Pelag.* III.2). See P. W. Hollenbach, "The Conversion of Jesus, 196–219; J. Taylor, *The Immerser*, 321. *Contra* J. P. Meier, *A Marginal Jew*, 2.108–9.

[136] M. Enslin, "John and Jesus," 9. J. P. Meier, whose work on the passages is otherwise thorough and persuasive, here neglects the possibility of an apologetic dimension (*A Marginal Jew*, 2.40).

[137] Cf. *Did.* 7:1–4.

[138] In Luke's version (Lk 3:21–22) Jesus is not baptized by John, (who is in prison [Lk 3:20]), but by the Holy Spirit.

Baptist traditions, dodged misleading assumptions. The numerous variations on the point of baptism in the NT gospels and Acts, however, pose insurmountable challenges to a clear understanding of the historical circumstances under which either John or Jesus practiced such a rite.[139] The only point of which we can be moderately certain is that practices of baptism varied among different groupings of followers.[140] Whatever the nature of John's immersing, certainly Charles Scobie is correct that "[John's] baptism could not be understood, and had no significance apart from the preaching of the [John's] message."[141] In Scobie's opinion, John's baptism simply "acted out the message like Jeremiah's broken earthenware vessels."[142] For this reason, it is likely that the divine voice at Jesus' baptism in Mk 1:11/Q 3:22 (Mt 3:17)/Jn 1:33 supplants John's teachings in our texts. Like the limited number and compression of Baptist traditions in the NT overall, John's silence in all versions of this event (Mt 3:14 notwithstanding: ὁ δὲ Ἰωάννης διεκώλυεν αὐτὸν λέγων, Ἐγὼ χρείαν ἔχω ὑπὸ σοῦ βαπτισθῆναι, καὶ σὺ ἔρχῃ πρός με;) is implausible.[143]

Even if, *in the NT,* John's role of baptizing eclipses any message he may have delivered, the existence and profundity of such a message is, from the perspective of NT traditions, undeniable. As it happens, Josephus corroborates this view. Without such a message, the spare traditions regarding John's baptism do not make sense. Without such a message, no basis exists for John's authority as

---

[139] A. Y. Collins posits four possibilities for Christian baptism: "Some have hypothesized that the early Christians reverted to the baptism of John and reinterpreted it. Others have argued that the metaphor of baptism in the spirit in the teaching of John gave rise to a baptismal ritual associated with the gift of the spirit. Many have taken the position that the early Church simply borrowed the ritual of proselyte baptism from the Jews. Another possibility is that there was an unbroken continuity from the baptism of John through the baptism associated with the activity of Jesus to the baptism practiced by the early Christians" ("The Origin of Christian Baptism," 37), although, Collins concludes for this trajectory that the "operative symbol has shifted from cleansing that leads to a pure and holy life to death that leads to new life" (41).

[140] Is it coincidental that whereas Jesus dominated water (e.g., stilled water [Mk 4:35–41/ Mt 8:23–27/Lk 8:22–25]; walked on water [Mk 6:45–52/Mt 14:22–33/Lk 6:16–21]; and transubstantiated water into wine [Jn 2:1–11]), John is consigned to a life immersed by it? Cf. 1 Jn 5:6: Οὗτός ἐστιν ὁ ἐλθὼν δι᾽ ὕδατος καὶ αἵματος, Ἰησοῦς Χριστός, οὐκ ἐν τῷ ὕδατι μόνον ἀλλ᾽ ἐν τῷ ὕδατι καὶ ἐν τῷ αἵματι. Cf. also Jn 19:34. Neither figure, however, has much to do with fire (only John's expected "coming one" and Pentecost).

[141] C. Scobie, *John the Baptist,* 113.

[142] C. Scobie, *John the Baptist,* 113. Scobie also claims that John's moniker suggests that baptizing was his primary ministry, whereas actually preaching was (*John the Baptist,* 209).

[143] I would not hastily relegate even this verse ("I need to be baptized by you; and do you come to me?" [Mt 3:14]) to redaction. It is entirely plausible John or his followers contrived such a statement in discussions of the relationship between John's baptizing and the baptism John predicted by the holy spirit (and fire?) of "the coming one." In both style and content this verse matches well John's prediction of "the coming one" which, in the Gospel of Matthew, arises in the few verses immediately preceding Jesus' baptism: "I baptize you with water for repentance, but the one mightier than I is coming after me. I am not worthy to carry his sandals. He will baptize you with the Holy Spirit and fire" (Mt 3:11). In both cases the rhetoric is self-deprecating and the topic correlates two different baptisms.

prophet, teacher, predecessor or witness to anyone, let alone, Jesus. This authority is, after all, the basis upon which all four evangelists include John in their
accounts in the first place.

2.5.5 Audience and Locale

Finally, a subjugating Baptist *Tendenz* on the part of the canonical evangelists
also leaves an incorrect impression of John's audience and locale. This section
presents the view that John's audience was probably comprised of a variety of
different types of Jews, perhaps even so-called 'God-fearers.'

Determining the historical accuracy of singling out Pharisees (and Sadducees) as those flocking to hear John's message (e.g., Mt 3:7), as well as the
description of John's audience as tax collectors, soldiers, and prostitutes (Lk
3:10–14; 7:29; Mt 21:32), is not possible. It is, however, notable that the latter
three groups are remarkable for their similarity to evidence concerning Jesus'
audiences (Lk 5:27–32; 7:2–10, 29, 34; 15:1; 18:9–14). Regarding an audience
of Pharisees, Joan Taylor is probably correct that, of the Jewish 'sects' of this
period, John was probably closest to the Pharisees, perhaps, at one time, number-
ing himself among them.[144] As Taylor points out, within the Synoptics, the two
groups – followers of John and Pharisees – are depicted as allies on the topic of
fasting (e.g., Mk 2:18 par.). Also, John's personal religious journey resembles
what Josephus tells us of himself (*Vita* 11–12) that: *while a Pharisee*, he traveled
for a time to the wilderness to investigate an 'ascetic' way of life.[145] In the wilderness, Josephus claims to have followed a teacher named Bannus who himself
could have served as an apprentice to John, conveying to a young Josephus the
highly favorable impression of John Josephus later records in *Ant.* 18.[146]

Just as Josephus ultimately returned to urban life (*Vita* 12), John too, after
exhorting followers in the wilderness, probably charged them to return to their

---

[144] J. Taylor, *The Immerser*, 211. Cf. also, C. Scobie: "John may have felt more sympathy
towards the Pharisees, with whose general outlook and whose eschatology he had much in
common" (*John the Baptist*, 33).

[145] ἐσθῆτι μὲν ἀπὸ δένδρων χρώμενον, τροφὴν δὲ τὴν αὐτομάτως φυομένην
προσφερόμενον (*Vita* 11).

[146] Bannus was not, at least according to Josephus, an Essene. Josephus claims he thoroughly investigated the three "sects" of his "nation" – Pharisees, Sadducees, and Essenes.
Unsatisfied by this investigation, he *then* sought Bannus – implying that Bannus represents yet
a fourth approach (*Vita* 9–12). H. Lichtenberger claims that Josephus' depiction of John's immersion resembles that of the Essenes ("The Dead Sea Scrolls and John the Baptist: Reflections
on Josephus' Account of John the Baptist," in *The Dead Sea Scrolls: Forty Years of Research*,
ed. D. Dimant and U. Rappaport [Leiden: Brill, 1992] 340–46). Even if Lichtenberger is correct, this depiction is not necessarily historical, but may reflect Josephus' own propagandistic
interests. However, as C. Scobie observes, εὐσέβεια, δικαιοσύνη, ἀρετή and ἁγνεία are
characteristics of *both* John and the Essenes in the Josephan corpus (*John the Baptist*, 140;
emphasis added).

work.[147] However, no firm reason exists for insisting John remained in the wilderness either from his youth[148] or throughout his adulthood without interruption.[149] Josephus does not place John's ministry ἐν τῇ ἐρήμῳ at all. He never specifies where crowds gathered to hear John teach. Although Josephus acknowledges John's practice of baptizing, he does not stipulate whether the water John used was running or still.

In terms of John's dwelling ἐν τῇ ἐρήμῳ, three explanations are popular. First, many assume a wilderness habitat was contrived solely for the purpose of subordinating John (crude, frenzied, uncultured) to Jesus (civilized). The NT does not, however, specify how long John remains in the desert. A mere stint in "the wilderness"[150] may have been sufficient for accomplishing the narrative goal of

---

[147] J. Taylor, *The Immerser*, 28.

[148] For the idea that Luke expunged and compressed the story of John's youth (Lk 1:80), see A. S. Geyser, "The Youth of John the Baptist, 70–75. Geyser's idea is that what was suppressed is John's adoption and formation in his youth by the Essenes (75). While this thesis is highly speculative, Geyser's observation that the parallels between John and Jesus in Lk 1–2 drop off with the narration of Jesus in the Temple as a twelve-year old boy (2:41–52) is suggestive. For John, the author supplies only the solitary summary verse: "The child grew and became strong in spirit and was in the wilderness until the day he appeared to Israel" (Lk 1:80).

[149] According to C. Scobie: "It must not be supposed that John remained anchored to one spot" (*John the Baptist*, 43). For this argument, Scobie summons Lk 1:80 where the plural form, "deserts" (ἐν ταῖς ἐρήμοις) is used. On Scobie's reading, this implies "free movement." Insofar as the evidence allows, although John worked in the 'desert' near the Jordan, nothing suggests he was a hermit or proto-monastic. According to J. Murphy-O'Connor, however, John chose a place for his ministry that was "virtually inaccessible during the one season in the year when he could expect people to come to him, namely, the relatively cool winter months" ("John the Baptist and Jesus: History and Hypotheses," 359). Compare Murphy-O'Connor's observations: "The Jordan flows in a trench well below the level of the valley. The sides are of unstable marl, which becomes impassable when wet. The sides are lined with trees which grow closely together. Some of the great masses of reeds rise to a height of five metres. The dense undergrowth harbours the deadly Palestinian viper and the vicious wild boar" ("John the Baptist and Jesus," 359 n. 2). Furthermore, if Jesus' return from the wilderness was a reaction to John's imprisonment (Mk 1:14), then, it seems, "wilderness" experiences were not hermetically secluding. On this, C. Kraeling argues John did not remain in the desert, "immobilize[d] in anchorite fashion … John's wilderness sojourn did not have eremitic seclusion as its sole or dominant purpose. Even in the wilderness John permitted, and even encouraged, people to find him" (*John the Baptist*, 10).

[150] The author of the Gospel of Luke seems to understand the "wilderness" as separate from the region of the Jordan (cf. Lk 3:2 ff. and 4:1) although elsewhere they are "identical" (W. Wink, *John the Baptist*, 5). On John's ministry in the "wilderness," see also R. W. Funk, "The Wilderness," *JBL* (1959) 205–14 and C. C. McCown, "The Scene of John's Ministry," *JBL* (1940) 113–31. Cf. also Lk 15:4 – the wilderness as a place to pasture sheep and Mk 6:35 – the wilderness as a place in which a miracle is required to supply food for crowds. Paul W. Hollenbach views the wilderness in which John dwelt both "real and symbolic" ("The Conversion of Jesus: From Jesus the Baptizer to Jesus the Healer," 197–98). Furthermore, in the Gospel of Luke much is made of John's hill country origin. This may reflect the same interest as his wilderness habitat. Unlike the others, however, the Third Gospel admits John was not continually in the "wilderness" (Lk 1:80; 3:3). On a related point, there is an emphasis in Luke on Jesus' ministry in cities (i.e., 4:43; 5:12; 8:39; 9:10). The Third Gospel's sources, however, also share this aim.

authenticating John's ministry, in the way the temptation authenticates the ministry of Jesus.[151] Furthermore, the depiction of teachers of virtue avoiding cities is a contemporary stereotype.[152] Thus, John's wilderness setting might actually reflect precisely the opposite point most understand from the four gospels. Corroborating Josephus' testimony (*Ant.* 18.116–19) of John as a celebrated (to the point of stereotypical) Jewish philosophical teacher-prophet, it may demonstrate the evangelists' commendation, not minimization, of the Baptist.

Second, the NT depiction of John as wilderness-dweller,[153] is also explained, purely on a literary level, by a historian's need to disentangle two similar and simultaneous portraits. John's ministry is relegated to a desert locus, whereas Jesus' ministry is assigned to urban spheres (including, of course, neighboring hillsides and bodies of water).[154] This argument might also explain differences in the traditions regarding their diets: John 'fasted,' while Jesus flouted dietary restrictions (Mk 2:18; 7:18–23), even teaching in symposia-like settings.[155] If the two ministries were proximate to the extent that they shared disciples, ritual practices and locales then the author of Mark, like Plutarch in his *Lives*, could have deliberately juxtaposed the paradigms of wilderness 'ascetic' and urban socialite as a means of sorting and organizing overlapping sources with the goal of a complementary and cogent story of origins. This hypothesis will be taken up in greater length in the examination of Baptist traditions in the next chapter.

A final assumption, equally fallacious, but not yet mentioned in the course of this chapter, is the famous notion that John, as (life-long?) wilderness-dweller, possessed a relationship to the community or communities behind the cache of

---

[151] Mark's placement of Jesus' brief wilderness sojourn (1:12–13) immediately after Jesus' baptism (1:9–11) is probably based on the logic that Jesus had to receive the Spirit first to subsequently be driven out "by the spirit" (v. 12) into the wilderness. It is, however, more plausible that Jesus was out in the wilderness for his baptism having selected to participate in the baptism of the notable teacher, John. The "Satan," "wild beasts," and "angels" Jesus faces in the wilderness in Mark, may function, like John's diet of "locusts and wild honey" (1:6), to vivify the author's description of the wilderness. See J. A. Kelhoffer, *The Diet of John the Baptist.* Furthermore, it cannot be determined where in the "wilderness" John actually went. If he was in the Jordan valley around Samaria and Perea, north of the Dead Sea and Qumran, then Herod brought him south to the prison at Machaerus. Resolve on the part of the author of Mark to place John in the historic location of Joshua's crossing or Elijah's ascension may have determined this location. See J. Taylor, *The Immerser*, 42–48; J. P. Meier, *A Marginal Jew*, 2.26–27.

[152] *Prob.* 63; *Abr.* 22–23; *Spec.* 2.44; *Mos.* 2.34 (J. Taylor, *The Immerser*, 41). Also, on cities as sources of defilement, Jerusalem is often an exception (2 Macc 5:27; cf. 10:6). Cf. also 11QTᵃ.

[153] E.g., Mk 1:4, 2nd aor., ἐγένετο. Cf. however Lk 3:3: καὶ ἦλθεν εἰς πᾶσαν [τὴν] περίχωρον τοῦ Ἰορδάνου κηρύσσων βάπτισμα μετανοίας εἰς ἄφεσιν ἁμαρτιῶν.

[154] The warning in Mt 24:26: "So, if they say to you, 'Look! He is in the wilderness,' do not go out. If they say, 'Look! He is in the inner rooms,' do not believe it" may represent a stereotype against typical insurrectionists gathering followers in remote regions away from cities; cf. Acts 21:38.

[155] Cf. J. P. Meier's comment: "The interpretation aims at neutralizing the Baptist's independence to make him safe for Christianity" ("John the Baptist in Matthew's Gospel," 384).

documents known as the Dead Sea Scrolls. One can agree that John probably shared certain practices in common with this group(s); naming only a few: dietary concerns, ablutions, priestly lineage, the sharing of property, and an exegetical interest in Isa 40:3a.[156] These associations, however, must neither be overstated, nor overlooked.[157] Making too much or too little of purported links between John and the Qumran documents has won commentators on both sides due criticism.[158] Many questions hinder progress on this topic, not least of which is whether the canonical evangelists could have intentionally depicted John as an Essene, 'ascetic,' and/or inhabitant of the Qumran settlement. In his research on John's diet, James A. Kelhoffer argues that the Gospel of Mark allocates for John a dietary intake of "locusts and wild honey (ἀκρίδας καὶ μέλι ἄγριον)"[159] as elements of John's caricature as a wilderness-dweller.[160] This portrayal is, according to Kelhoffer, at least in part, utilized by Mark and adapted by Matthew

---

[156] J. Taylor, *The Immerser*, 22. Cf. A. Y. Collins' list of similarities between John's baptism and ritual washings at Qumran: "Both involved withdrawal to the desert to await the Lord; both were linked to an ascetic lifestyle; both included total immersion in water; and both had an eschatological context. These features, however, were not unique to John and the community at Qumran. The differences are at least equally striking: a priestly, exclusive community versus the activity of a prophetic, charismatic leader in a public situation; a ritual practiced at least once daily versus an apparently once and for all ritual; and a self-enacted ritual versus a ritual administered by John" ("The Origin of Christian Baptism," 32). J. P. Meier has a different list: "Both of them [John and the Qumranites] rejected ordinary lifestyles (urban or rural), stood in tension to the contemporary form of temple priesthood and worship, were active in or around the wilderness of Judea, had a sense that the definitive intervention of God in history was imminent, looked to Isa 40:3 as a prophecy of their work in the desert preparing for that intervention, called true Israelites to repentance in view of the approaching end of present history, predicted salvation or doom for Israelites depending on their response to the warning proclaimed to them, and practiced some water ritual or rituals as a sign of interior cleansing" (*A Marginal Jew*, 2.25). According to C. Scobie, John had in common with Essenes (as known from sources including the DSS) punishment by a river of fire, eschatological baptism conditional on repentance, and expectation of the Moses-like prophet. Different from the Essene movement was John's public ministry. These types of observations prompt Scobie's conclusion that John was an "evangelistic Essene" (*John the Baptist*, 207).

[157] Most recently J. Taylor criticizes those who make Essene/Qumran connections with John. She has received both praise and criticism on this point. Cf. the following reviews: Mark A. Powell, *CBQ* (1999) 171–72; J. K. Elliott, *NovT* (1999) 198–99; Brenda Shaver, *JR* (2000) 306–7. Powell summarizes in his review: "Taylor finds no good reason to link John and the Essenes, despite interesting parallels (asceticism, practice of baptism, appeals to Isaiah 40:3a)" (171). See also Hermann Lichtenberger, "Reflections on the History of John the Baptist's Communities," 45–49.

[158] See James H. Charlesworth, "John the Baptizer and Qumran Barriers in Light of the *Rule of the Community*," in *The Provo International Conference on the Dead Sea Scrolls*, D. W. Parry and E. Ulrich, eds. (STDJ 30; Leiden: Brill, 1999) 353–75. Critique of Charlesworth's position on John's diet vis-à-vis CD 12:14–15 in J. A. Kelhoffer, *The Diet of John the Baptist*, 53–54.

[159] J. A. Kelhoffer points out that in Mark this allocation is not sole and restrictive; in Matthew, however, it is. According to Kelhoffer's analysis, Matthew's account strains the limits of plausibility. See *The Diet of John the Baptist*, 121–28.

[160] J. A. Kelhoffer, *The Diet of John the Baptist*, 121–23.

to align John's ministry of baptizing with a long tradition of important Jewish wilderness events (e.g., death of Moses placed near the Jordan [Deut. 34:1–6]; location of Joshua's crossing into the land [Josh 3:16]; site of Elijah's translation [2 Kgs 2:1–12]). With an eye to the Qumran community, John's wilderness habitat may also have been calculated to categorize John with *current* Jewish wilderness events (e.g., Acts 5:36–37; Jos. *Ant.* 20.97–98). It is, however, impossible to confirm such a theory.

In conclusion, redaction-critical assumptions regarding NT Baptist traditions on the topics of John's audience and locale must be carefully negotiated with concerns derived from other critical methods, including a *Sitz im Leben* incorporating Baptists. The historical accuracy of singling out Pharisees and/or Sadducees as well as tax collectors, soldiers and prostitutes as John's audience cannot be ascertained. Audiences of Jews, or Jews *and* Gentiles, and a desert locus may make sense as literary strategies of the evangelists. Such strategies do not, however, preclude the historical veracity of these suppositions.

2.6 Summation

The above analysis seeks to correct scholarly prioritization of redaction- over the methods of source- and form- criticism and, in particular, the assumption of subjugating editorial treatment of NT Baptist traditions by each of the canonical evangelists. Such an assumption accepts *a priori* that Jesus' superiority to John in the narratives distorts beyond recognition all remaining traditions about John – a premise lacking proof. Diagnoses of the quest for the historical John are, to this day, pessimistic because they are plagued by the error of this defective presupposition.

Positing, in contrast, a historical context in which Christians and Baptists were forced (or relieved?) to combine efforts (possibly because the Baptists were theologically and/or otherwise defeated or because both groups recognized safety in numbers), perhaps, in the wake of the Jewish war with Rome (66–70 CE), this chapter argues that the four evangelists aspired not simply to harness, but as much to exploit John's influence within their circles.[161] Adopting materials

---

[161] In light of these distinctions between John and Jesus, a few brief observations can be made regarding the complete silence in the authentic letters of Paul on John the Baptist. Paul seems to have understood himself as taking up Jesus' charismatic ministry (Gal 6:17). To this end, he understated his rhetorical capabilities and emphasized (overstated?) his charismata (1 Thess 1:5; Gal 3:1–5; 1 Cor 1:17; 2:4–5; 12:9–10, 28–30; 2 Cor 10:10; 11:6; 12:11–12 [satirical?]; Rom 15:18–19). Also to this end he apparently relaxed (breached?) dietary laws and, perhaps, other traditional expressions of Jewish piety – highlighting, rather, displays of the miraculous. A comparison is provided by the figure of Apollos in Acts 18. Reputed to have carried on John's ministry by introducing or, at least, taking it to Hellenistic territory, Apollos is described as "eloquent (ἀνὴρ λόγιος)," "powerful in knowledge/exposition of the scriptures

not just from 'Christian,' but also 'Baptist' sources,[162] the NT evangelists present a surprisingly positive portrait of John – one that even, at times, *dangerously detracts from the presentations of Jesus.* Propagandistic minimization of all NT Baptist traditions represents scholarly overuse of redaction. It is an attempt to rescue the Baptist – a misplaced, if well-intended motivation.[163]

Suspension of the claim that John is systematically subjugated to Jesus in each of the four gospels reveals that slights against John in the gospels are trifling as compared with his overall endorsement. This approval of John is particularly clear once his statements of self-subordination in the NT are liberated from their present context to be understood as John's rhetorical style when referring to the coming judgment (e.g., rhetoric of humility). Borrowing a metaphor, John's subjugation to Jesus is a single tree in a great forest of his authentication in the four Gospels. The evangelists exhibit reverence toward John – a tactic playing into the hand of not just Baptists or Baptist followers of Jesus, but of any Jew who held John in respect. Repeatedly, as I have argued, the criterion of embarrassment – expanded to include embarrassment to Baptists and other kingdom-informed Jews – provides one benchmark against which to view conclusions derived from this new approach.

In conclusion, the present appraisal of Baptist traditions, in its attempt to balance the methods of redaction-, source- and form-criticism, reconstructs that John the Baptist was a Jewish prophet who assumed responsibilities of teaching (sapiential/eschatological) – a role confirmed by the presence in the sources, not just of crowds, but of disciples. After John's death – most likely brought about by his message (good news) of a coming 'kingdom'[164] – those espousing messianic convictions about Jesus construed many of the most memorable of John's teachings, such as his explanation of Isa 40:3 (open to multiple interpretations on account of its antiquity and ambiguity) as prophetic *about Jesus.* Perhaps on

---

(δυνατὸς ὢν ἐν ταῖς γραφαῖς)," speaking in a way that was "burning with respect to the spirit (ζέων τῷ πνεύματι ἐλάλει)," "teaching accurately (ἐδίδασκεν ἀκριβῶς)," however "believing/acknowledging only the baptism of John (ἐπιστάμενος μόνον τὸ βάπτισμα Ἰωάννου)" (Acts 18:24–25) with no mention of miracles. C. Scobie, however, does not agree that Apollos should be regarded as John's disciple (*John the Baptist*, 189). *Contra* Scobie, the question may be whether Apollos was to John as Paul was to Jesus. Paul W. Hollenbach argues that Jesus is a disciple of John's before he turns away to "pursue his own distinctly different movement" ("The Conversion of Jesus: From Jesus the Baptizer to Jesus the Healer," 198). Jesus is, according to Hollenbach, "converted" from a "baptizer," along the lines of John the Baptist, to a "healer" (197–219).

[162] Nb. a significant proportion of the canonical fragments about John derive from Q. For a presentation of the argument see Ch. 3.

[163] Background for such a motivation is provided by H. Thyen: "Because of the special affinity created by the historical situation between the Christian community and the Baptist sect the early church was threatened from the outset by a dangerous Baptist sub-movement against which it had to provide clear and decisive defences" ("ΒΑΠΤΙΣΜΑ ΜΕΤΑΝΟΙΑΣ ΕΙΣ ΑΦΕΣΙΝ ΑΜΑΡΤΙΩΝ," 167).

[164] See Ch. 6.

this basis alone, because he predicted a coming, eschatological figure, John was embraced as a prophet in Christian circles – for some, a prophet like Moses, for others, Elijah, for still others, a hybrid of these and other models. More likely, however, John was welcomed as a prophet on the basis of *many* predictions taken to be fulfilled in their time, and on account of compromises struck between 'Christians' and 'Baptists,' as two groups struggling, along with Pharisees and other Jews, to find meaning and recover their roots in the wake of political domination and destruction.

Thus, the present chapter submits that eliminating predetermined scholarly biases sheds light on Baptist traditions and on the short epoch Baptists shared with other leaders of the '*basileia* movement(s).'[165] The chapter's conclusions are summarized. First, according to NT traditions, John's ministry overlapped, to an unknown extent, with the ministry of Jesus. Second, Jesus adopted John's disciples, a reflection of the authority associated with John's 'sectarian' pedigree. Taking over John's disciples reflects either Jesus' inability or unwillingness (no need?) to win followers of his own. Third, John preached (originated?) a 'good news' message of repentance with first inward (moral/deeds of righteousness), then outward (cultic/baptism) manifestations; and probably, at least in part, on the basis of his interpretation of Isa 40:3, considered his own work preparatory for a coming messiah/messianic kingdom (to which "good news" messages are attached via Isa 40:9). In all likelihood, not different from Jesus, it was John's message of a coming kingdom that resulted in his death by Herod Antipas.[166] Fourth, the practice of immersion associated with John symbolized a commitment to a way of life based on teachings – a corpus of ethics-centered legal interpretations that probably corresponded on points with contemporary Pharisaism while also capturing views now associated with the Dead Sea Scrolls. Fifth, although his diet and clothing, according to Mark and Matthew, reflect, a conflation of stereotypes and other concerns (such as the desire to depict John, not as *predicting*, but *as* fulfillment of Isa 40:3 and Mal 3:1), no reason exists to doubt John spent some time in the wilderness fasting – even if neither of these practices (wilderness-dwelling and fasting) are yet fully understood. The connection between John's wilderness location and the idea of a new 'exodus' and/ or impending time of liberation was probably, on some level, deliberate on the part of the evangelists. It should not, therefore, rule out that John occasionally visited urban centers, dined on foodstuffs other than "locusts and wild honey," or even, every once in a while, neglected or rejected a fast.[167]

---

[165] Jane Schaberg uses this reference in *The Resurrection of Mary Magdalene*, 260–76. See above n. 39.

[166] See Ch. 6.

[167] The finite verb in the phrase, ἡ δὲ τροφὴ ἦν αὐτοῦ (Mt 3:4) suggests John subsisted solely on "locusts and wild honey." It represents a modification of the claim in Mk 1:6 and is implausible. See J. A. Kelhoffer, *The Diet of John the Baptist*, 4–7, 117–18.

These conclusions ultimately derive from the conviction that the NT gospels were devoted, not just to Jesus, but to the documentation of his movement. They are submitted, not in the hopeless spirit of an examination dedicated to a historical personage subject to double jeopardy, but hopefully, in the belief that the past has left traditions worth investigating and that history redefined is still an enterprise with profit.

Chapter Three

Baptist Traditions and Q

> In thus reducing to a minimum the relation between Jesus and
> John the aim of the Synoptic Gospels was to prevent people from
> thinking that Jesus owed the substance of his teaching to John.[1]

3.1 Introduction

As noted above, although many studies have undertaken to explain Baptist
traditions within the NT, most rely on the Gospel narratives uncritically. In
particular, the coherence of Baptist traditions within Synoptic witnesses is taken
for granted.[2] Furthermore, the overwhelming majority of treatments of Baptist
traditions arise in articles, monographs and books devoted to the historical
Baptist. This study shares no such aim. In contrast, this project focuses on the
Baptist traditions themselves: how narrative fragments concerning John the
Baptist are utilized by the canonical evangelists to document Christian origins
and what, if anything, their treatment indicates about the traditions, their meaning and origin.

Specifically, this chapter addresses the relationship between Baptist traditions
and the arguably most reliable and most ancient witness to the Baptist, Q.[3] Here
I argue that, on the basis of (1) *double attribution* or the attribution of certain
sayings to John in Q, to Jesus elsewhere in the Synoptics; (2) *contradictions*
between Jesus' sayings in and outside of Q; and (3) *thematic continuity* between
Q sayings and Baptist traditions, current models of Q suggest that, at some early
stage in its undoubtedly complex pre-history, *Q existed as a source containing
Baptist traditions exclusively.*

3.2 Double Attribution of Sayings

Although liturgical material could have been shared by successive teachers
within a single school or tradition, as Joan Taylor points out, "individual teachers

---

[1] M. Goguel, *The Life of Jesus*, trans. Olive Wyon (New York: Macmillan, 1944) 271.
[2] See above: Ch. 2.
[3] On John's prominence in Q, see 7–8 n. 11.

prescribed individual interpretations of Scripture."[4] Therefore, when John and
Jesus issue the exact same teaching to their disciples, particularly on a matter as
crucial as what constitutes righteous behavior, a historical problem arises.

Q 3:9b provides the first of three examples. It is a well-known saying concerning righteousness attributed to John in Q (cf. Mt 3:10), but to Jesus elsewhere
(Mt 7:19): "Every tree that does not bear good fruit is cut down and thrown into
the fire (πᾶν οὖν δένδρον μὴ ποιοῦν καρπὸν καλὸν ἐκκόπτεται καὶ εἰς πῦρ
βάλλεται)."[5] The only interruption in the otherwise verbatim agreement between
Matthew's version of this saying in the SM (Jesus) and Q (John) is the omission
of οὖν from Mt 7:19 in a majority of the manuscripts.[6]

The expression, γεννήματα ἐχιδνῶν ("brood of vipers") is also doubly attributed – to John in Q 3:7 (cf. Mt 3:7), but to Jesus in Mt 12:34 and 23:33. In
his commentary on Mt 3:7, Ulrich Luz refers to this expression as "key,"[7] arguing that Jesus takes it up from John later in the Gospel.[8] Notably, 'vipers' as an
epithet, is unknown in the OT, Josephus, or rabbinical writings.[9] The two ideas
"generation" and "snakes" of this epithet, however, occur together in Moses' valedictory canticle in Deut 32: "a crooked and perverse generation (γενεὰ σκολιὰ
καὶ διεστραμμένη)" (32:5; cf. 32:20) and "the anger of serpents, the incurable
anger of asps (θυμὸς δρακόντων ... καὶ θυμὸς ἀσπίδων ἀνίατος)" (32:33; cf.
32:24).[10] The word γεννήματα, too, occurs twice in this LXX passage. Both

---

[4] J. Taylor, *The Immerser*, 105. Cf. also E. Lupieri, "'The Law and the Prophets Were until
John:' John the Baptist between Jewish Halakhot and Christian History of Salvation," 49–56.

[5] On "fruit(s)," cf. Lk 3:8 (pl.)/Mt 3:8 (sg.). Some have argued, in light of Mt 3:11, that
the "fruit" in Mt 3:8 is John's immersion itself (Helmut Merklein, "Die Umkehrpredigt bei
Johannes dem Täufer," *BZ* 25/1 [1981] 36–7). The Gospel of Luke's version ("fruits") may
reflect redaction coordinated to the good deeds mentioned in vv. 10–14. Another example, also
pertaining to righteous behavior, is Lk 3:11: "Whoever has two coats must share with the one
having none (ὁ ἔχων δύο χιτῶνας μεταδότω τῷ μὴ ἔχοντι)." In Lk 3:11 the saying is attributed
to John. However, it closely resembles Jesus' saying in the SM: "And if anyone wants to sue
you and take your coat, give him the cloak also (καὶ τῷ θέλοντί σοι κριθῆναι καὶ τὸν χιτῶνά
σου λαβεῖν, ἄφες αὐτῷ καὶ τὸ ἱμάτιον)" (Mt 5:40). Cf. also Lk 9:3: μήτε [ἀνὰ] δύο χιτῶνας
ἔχειν attributed to Jesus. Emphasis on the practice of almsgiving in the *Didache* may be relevant
to this discussion. Cf. *Did.* 1.1–6; 4.5, 7–8; 11:12; 13:7.

[6] Surprisingly, R. Bultmann argues this saying originated with Jesus, later appropriated for
the Baptist: "That these sayings [Mt 3:7–10/Lk 3:7–9] are ascribed to the Baptist in Q does
not, of course, prove that he actually spoke them. The supposition is hardly likely to be wrong
that the sayings were in circulation in the Christian tradition, and were ascribed to the Baptist
out of a desire to have some record of his preaching of repentance" (*History of the Synoptic
Tradition*, 117).

[7] Luz explains the adjective "key" as: the author of the Gospel of Matthew is "vitally
concerned about the proclamation of judgment" (*Matthew 1–7*, 169).

[8] *Matthew 1–7*, 169.

[9] See Joseph A. Fitzmyer, *The Gospel According to Luke (I–IX)* (AB 28; Garden City:
Doubleday, 1981) 467.

[10] Cf. Ps 140:3; Phil 2:15. The section from Deut 27–30 with its focus on "abuse of covenant
privilege" may also inform Baptist traditions (James D. G. Dunn, "John the Baptist's Use of

references suggest fruits/produce that God provided for his people from the land (32:13b): (1) "He fed them the fruits of the fields (γεννήματα ἀγρῶν)" (32:13b); and (2) "Because a fire has been kindled from my anger, it will burn as far as Hades below; and it will devour the land, and its fruits (καταφάγεται γῆν καὶ τὰ γεννήματα αὐτῆς); it shall ignite the mountain's foundations" (32:22). The second, however, is open to a figurative interpretation ("devour the land, and its inhabitants/offspring") given that the proceeding five verses (32:23–27) specify near extinction of all Israelites by this fiery, divine wrath. The many connections between Q and Deuteronomy demonstrated by Arland Jacobson provide a background for understanding these connections.[11]

Parallels with Deuteronomy notwithstanding, it remains enigmatic that John refers to his followers/audiences with such a caustic address. Although this expression parallels somewhat vituperation in the CD 8:7–13 against enemies, in John P. Meier's words: "It is remarkable that John would use similar language not of the open enemies of God's people in high places, but rather of apparently pious Jews who come out to him for baptism."[12] From the perspective of the present position, if it is remarkable that John uses this language, how much more so that Jesus finds himself in a position to do so too.

John Meier also points out the close similarity of John's entire phrase "Brood of vipers, who revealed to you that you must flee from the coming wrath?" (γεννήματα ἐχιδνῶν, τίς ὑπέδειξεν ὑμῖν φυγεῖν ἀπὸ τῆς μελλούσης ὀργῆς;) (Mt 3:7) and Jesus' phrase "Snakes, brood of vipers, how shall you flee from the judgment of Gehenna?" (ὄφεις, γεννήματα ἐχιδνῶν, πῶς φύγητε ἀπὸ τῆς κρίσεως τῆς γεέννης;) (Mt 23:33).[13] Indeed, Meier concludes that because the phrase, "brood of vipers" in Mt 12:34 and 23:33 has no Synoptic parallels, it was probably imported from the Q sermon of the Baptist.[14] The expression oc-

---

Scripture," 49). Despite significant thematic and literary correlations, the last words of David are also ignored as a source of comparison for Baptist traditions. See above (63–65). A literary *topos* of "last words" may merit further investigation, particularly, in terms of apocalyptic writing.

[11] "The Literary Unity of Q," 365–89. As Dale Allison points out, against J. Kloppenborg, Q's Deuteronomistic theology is pervasive: "A final problem with Kloppenborg's view is that the assigning of the Deuteronomistic theology to the second stage seems artificial when the first stage is so full of the theme of rejection" (*The Jesus Tradition in Q* [Harrisburg, PA: TPI, 1997] 7.

[12] *A Marginal Jew*, 2.72 n. 41.

[13] "John the Baptist in Matthew's Gospel," 390.

[14] "John the Baptist in Matthew's Gospel," 389. A vitriolic tone may have been more characteristic of Baptist than Jesus traditions. The Gospel of Mark attributes only two woes to Jesus (Mk 13:17; 14:21). Numerous such exclamations can be found, however, in Q (10:13 [2X]; 11:42, 43, 44, 46, 47, 52; 17:1). Many have observed a pervasive sense of crisis in Q; see T. W. Manson, *The Sayings of Jesus* (London: SCM, 1949) 16; W. D. Davies, *The Setting of the Sermon on the Mount* (Cambridge: Cambridge University, 1966) 382–86; Howard Clark Kee, *Jesus in History: An Approach to the Study of the Gospels*, 2nd ed. (New York: Harcourt Brace Jovanovich, 1977) 84–117. On the background in both prophetic and sapiential literature of the

curs only once in the Gospel of Luke (3:7), attributed to the Baptist, and does not occur in Mark. Interestingly, 23:33 ("Special M" material) is integrated into Mt 23:2–39, a section predominantly Q in origin (e.g., Q 11:39a, 42, 39b, 41, 43–44; 11:46b, 52, 47–48; 11:49–51; 13:34–35). All four occurrences of this expression in the NT demonstrate verbatim agreement.[15]

As others have noted, Matthean redaction might suffice to explain these two examples,[16] if the author of the Gospel of Luke's introduction to the *Pater Noster* did not provide a third instance of a similar type of editorial modification. Although H. D. Betz dismisses the proposal, Eduard Meyer and others since have argued that the enigmatic request by Jesus' disciples preceding the Q version of the Lord's prayer in Luke: "Lord, teach us to pray, *just as, also, John taught his disciples* (Κύριε, δίδαξον ἡμᾶς προσεύχεσθαι, καθὼς καὶ Ἰωάννης ἐδίδαξεν τοὺς μαθητὰς αὐτοῦ)" (Lk 11:1) suggests that this prayer was originally composed by John.[17] On this point, Joan Taylor writes,

---

woe and corresponding macarism, see John J. Collins, *Seers, Sibyls and Sages in Hellenistic-Roman Judaism* (Boston/Leiden: Brill, 2001) 395–97.

[15] Cf. also snake with scorpion in Lk 11:11: τίνα δὲ ἐξ ὑμῶν τὸν πατέρα αἰτήσει ὁ υἱὸς ἰχθύν, καὶ ἀντὶ ἰχθύος ὄφιν αὐτῷ ἐπιδώσει;

[16] On Matthew's treatment of the Baptist, see also James L. Jones, "References to John the Baptist in the Gospel according to St. Matthew," *AThR* 41 (1959) 298–302 and Edgar Krentz, "None Greater among Those Born from Women: John the Baptist in the Gospel of Matthew," *CurTM* 10 (Dec. 1983) 333–38.

[17] The Greek word, καθώς is ambiguous. It may refer generally to the act of praying or specifically to a certain prayer. However, of seventeen occurrences of this word in the Third Gospel and eleven in Acts, ten out of twenty-eight (6 = Luke [1:2, 55, 70; 2:23; 5:14; 11:1]; 4 = Acts [7:42, 44, 48; 15:15]) link verbs of passing information (e.g., λαλέω [Lk 1:55, 70], παραδίδωμι [Lk 1:2], γράφω [Lk 2:23; Acts 7:42; 15:15], προστάσσω [Lk 5:14], διατάσσω [Acts 7:44]) with an object of *specific written* information. For example, in Lk 1:2 καθώς refers to Mark and other written sources of information used by the author in the construction of his narrative. Similarly, in Lk 1:55 καθώς refers to the promise made to Abraham and his descendants in Gen 17:6–8; 18:18; and 22:17. In Lk 1:70 καθώς refers to 2 Sam 7:11–16 (cf. also Ps 132). In Lk 2:23 καθώς designates Exod 13:2. In Lk 5:14 καθώς refers to Lev 13:2–8; 14:2–3. In Acts 7:42, καθώς refers to Amos 5:25–27, in Acts 7:44, καθώς refers to Exod 33:7; 25:8–9, and in Acts 7:48, καθώς refers to Isa 66:1–2. Lk 11:1 is another example of this paradigm. In Lk 11:1, the verb of passing information, διδάσκω is linked by καθώς with specific, written information: John's prayer. Contrast BDAG which classifies occurrences in five categories failing to acknowledge the grouping demonstrated here: (1) "of comparison" in which is noted "as a formula κ. γέγραπται *as it is written*," citing from Luke-Acts only Lk 2:23 and Acts 15:15 (493); here the entry also suggests a comparison with "κ. διδάσκω *as I teach*" in 1 Cor 4:17; (2) "of extent or degree to which"; (3) "of cause"; (4) "of temporality"; and (5) "After verbs of saying it introduces indirect discourse," citing Acts 15:14 (493–94). Also see Eduard Meyer, *Ursprung und Anfänge des Christentums*, 2 vols.; 4th and 5th ed. (Stuttgart: Cotta, 1924, 1.90–91). Meyer is influenced by the petition of forgiveness of sins in the prayer: "…und das Lukas 11, 1 auf die Bitte der Jünger zurückführt, sie ein Gebet zu lehren, wie Johannes das seinen Jüngern getan hat, das Vaterunser, in dem denn auch die ἄφεσις ἁμαρτιῶν wie bei Johannes im Mittelpunkt steht" (91). Nb. the wording of the forgiveness petition is slightly different in Matthew and Luke perhaps the influence of independent liturgical transmission. J. Taylor accepts that John may be responsible for the composition of this prayer (*The Immerser*,

It is hard to imagine why Luke might have invented such a peculiar introduction, so that Jesus is apparently copying John, prompted by his disciples.[18]

In the Gospel of Matthew, the prayer is attributed to Jesus in the SM (Mt 6:9–13). In Q, it is an isolated saying (Q 11:2b–4) the attribution of which, *like all Q sayings*, is unspecified.[19]

Most explanations of the double attribution of sayings in the Synoptics conclude that these two eschatological prophets, John and Jesus, simply shared the same message – perhaps Jesus as a disciple of John.[20] Charles Scobie cites examples of double attribution as points of agreement between Jesus and John.[21] In the context of her discussion of John's and Jesus' teachings in the Gospel of Matthew, Joan Taylor explains closely related sayings by "a policy [of the evangelist's] of assigning doubtful traditions to Jesus rather than to John, *to be on the safe side*."[22] Although confining his comment to the Gospel of Matthew, only Walter Wink takes seriously the implications of this phenomenon:

The extent to which Matthew carries out this assimilation is seen in the manner in which he freely exchanges the Baptist and Jesus traditions one with another. Words of Jesus are placed in the mouth of John and vice versa.[23]

151–53). Cf. John K. Elliott, "Did the Lord's Prayer Originate with John the Baptist?" *ThZ* 29 (1973) 215. H. D. Betz writes, "It is interesting, as Josef Ernst (*Johannes der Täufer: Interpretation, Geschichte, Wirkungsgeschichte* [BZNW 53; Berlin: de Gruyter 1989] 106) has pointed out, that some later manuscripts have 'reconstructed' the prayer of John the Baptist" (*Sermon on the Mount*, 349 n. 143). Nb. also comment by R. Webb, "… But Jesus had not taught his disciples to pray as John did, *until asked*" ("John the Baptist and his Relationship to Jesus," 227; emphasis added). Presumably Jesus' disciples knew how to pray, favoring the interpretation of Lk 11:1 as a request by one disciple to learn a specific prayer taught to Jesus by John (whether or not John composed it).

[18] J. Taylor, *The Immerser*, 152.

[19] In contrast, sayings in the *Gospel of Thomas* are frequently attributed to Jesus (e.g., *Gos. Thom.* § 2–7, 9–19, 22, 23, 25, 26, 28–31, 32–42, 44–50, 54–59, 61–64, 66–71, 73, 75–78, 80–90, *et al.*

[20] This position rests, in part, on the meaning of the phrase, ὀπίσω μου. See J. P. Meier, *A Marginal Jew*, 2.118, 192–3 nn. 61–2. In favor of understanding ἔρχεται ὀπίσω μου as implying discipleship is E. Lohmeyer, *Das Evangelium des Markus* (KEK; Göttingen: Vandenhoeck & Ruprecht, 1967) 18. See also K. Grobel, "He That Cometh After Me," 397–401; O. Cullman, "Ὁ ὀπίσω μου ἐρχόμενος," 177–82.

[21] C. Scobie, *John the Baptist*, 161.

[22] J. Taylor, *The Immerser*, 150. What Taylor means by "the safe side" is unclear; cf. J. P. Meier's use of "safe" also to refer to Matthew's adaptation of Baptist traditions ("John the Baptist in Matthew's Gospel," 384). Taylor writes: "If Jesus was once a disciple of John, he may have followed themes in John's teaching so closely in his own teaching that disciples of Jesus may have had difficulty in determining which saying belonged to John and which to Jesus" (150). Although she argues that individual Jewish teachers had their own signature interpretations of the scriptures, she claims it is not possible within the canonical gospels to identify distinctions between the two teachings of John and of Jesus. She does posit, however, that Jesus taught "much more widely" and "in connection with a healing mission" (151).

[23] W. Wink, *John The Baptist*, 33. As noted above, all three examples of double attribution occur in the Gospel of Matthew. It is an open point why this author attributes Baptist sayings

A further point not mentioned by Wink, however, concerns Q: *in every case, sayings of John are not attributed to Jesus arbitrarily throughout Jesus traditions; rather sayings of John in Q are attributed to Jesus in Synoptic materials outside of Q.*[24]

3.3 Contradictions Among "Jesus" Traditions

Also highlighting the ambiguity and complexity of the appropriation of Q traditions is the observation that certain alleged Jesus traditions in Q contradict well-known Jesus traditions outside of Q.[25] Not only do Jesus traditions in Q

---

to Jesus more easily than the author of the Gospel of Luke. The comment before the Lord's Prayer in Luke, perhaps implying it was originally taught or composed by John (Lk 11:1), is surprisingly direct and must be viewed in connection with other Lukan traditions such as John's imprisonment *before* Jesus' baptism (3:20) and the application of Elijah traditions to Jesus, not John (e.g., Luke's omission of Mk 1:6/Mt 3:4). Taking these observations together, it is difficult to construct a coherent disposition toward John for Luke. See 61 n. 89.

[24] Variations of double attribution can also be found outside Q in the following passages emphasizing general similarities between John and Jesus: the message concerning the nearness of the kingdom (Mt 3:2; 4:17/Lk 3:9); the charge of a demon (Mt 9:34; 11:18; 12:24; 10:25); the claim that wisdom is served by both individuals (Mt 11:19c); the claim that both John and Jesus exemplify righteousness (Mt 3:15; 21:32); and the metaphorical description of both John and Jesus as light that has dawned (Lk 1:76/Mt 4:16). The message of the nearness of the kingdom is doubly attributed to John and Jesus in two "Special M" passages. In Mt 3:2, John's entire proclamation is encapsulated in the saying, "The kingdom of heaven has come near (ἤγγικεν γὰρ ἡ βασιλεία τῶν οὐρανῶν)." In Mt 4:17, Jesus' entire proclamation is encapsulated by the same saying with the exception of its omission of the postpositive conjunction, γάρ. Inclusion of γάρ as conjuction in Mt 3:2 is probably connected to the imperative, μετανοεῖτε, preceding the saying in this verse: μετανοεῖτε· ἤγγικεν γὰρ ἡ βασιλεία τῶν οὐρανῶν. On Mt 3:2 and 4:17, Joan Taylor comments, "One may wonder if these versions are both preserving in different form some line in Q that described John as telling the good news that the kingdom was revealed" (*The Immerser*, 138). Omission of Jesus' call to repentance in parallel passages in Mark (6:8–11) and Luke (9:2–5) is consistent with portrayals of Jesus' ministry in the Synoptics. John's call to repentance is, however, intact in Mk (1:4).

[25] According to C. Kraeling the contradictions are: John fasted, Jesus rejected fasting; John practiced baptism, Jesus did not; John found the final eschatological judgment cause for fear, Jesus, "an occasion for joy"; John demanded "exemplary conduct" in adherence to the Law, Jesus "waived the letter of the Law" (e.g., "Be perfect as your father in heaven is perfect" [Mt 5:48] contradicts the "my burden is light" [Mt 11:30] saying); John insisted on a wrathful God prepared to execute imminent judgment whereas Jesus emphasized God's mercy and his patience in seeking and saving the lost (cf. Jn 12:47); John awaited the day of judgment whereas for Jesus, the kingdom, while future, was in some sense already present (*John the Baptist*, 146–47). Scobie's list of contradictions adds the following point: "John's ethical teaching was typically Jewish, but Jesus demanded a much more radical ethic"; and "John's teaching implies that by the performance of certain acts man can earn the right of entry into the Kingdom; but Jesus taught that whatever men do, they are still 'unprofitable servants' in the sight of God" (*John the Baptist*, 160). Another contradiction proposed by Scobie is on the point of rewards. According to Scobie, John offers no reward for righteousness emphasizing, rather, the coming crisis. Nb., Q's crisis boasts neither signs predicting its arrival (contrast Q

contradict Jesus traditions outside of Q, *but the former coincide, to varying extents, with Baptist traditions both in and outside of Q.* For example, outside of Q Jesus is known to feast (Mt 9:10–13/Mk 2:15–17/Lk 5:29–32;[26] Mt 9:14–15/ Mk 2:18–22/Lk 5:33–39;[27] Mt 11:19; Lk 15:2; Jn 2:1–11).[28] John is known to fast (e.g., Mk 1:6/Mt 3:4; Mk 2:18/Mt 9:14–17/Lk 5:33–39).[29] *In Q, however,*

17:23–24 and Mk 13), nor guarantees of vindication, even for the righteous. In terms of eschatological fulfillment, however, Jesus emphasizes rewards (e.g, Mt 5:3–13) (*John the Baptist*, 210). In contrast to Scobie's reading, J. P. Meier interprets Mt 3:11–12 as John's enunciation of rewards (*A Marginal Jew*, 2.39). Pointing to Q's de-emphasis of eschatological fulfillment and rewards, Kloppenborg makes the following comment in the context of his discussion of Q's apocalypticism: "Perhaps most surprising of all is Q's restraint when describing the 'positive' outcome of eschatological intervention. While there is a virtual avalanche of images concerning the judgment and destruction of the impenitent, there is no mention at all of the resurrection, and only passing reference to the motifs of cosmic transformation, re-creation, restoration, and the like. This is surprising because of the high frequency with which the motif of cosmic transformation (and to a lesser extent, resurrection) occurs in Jewish apocalypses" ("Symbolic Eschatology and the Apocalypticism of Q," *HTR* 80/3 [1987] 299–300).

[26] In terms of Mk 2:15–17, the emphasis may have been as much on the absurdity of Jesus' eating (i.e., "Why does he *eat* with tax collectors and sinners?" as on the absurdity of those with whom he ate, even if the author, by Jesus' response, chooses to stress the latter. That this passage is positioned *immediately before the people's question about fasting* (Mk 2:18–20) should not be neglected. Cf. also J. Taylor, *The Immerser*, 204–7, 210. Although Jesus rejected fasting it soon became a regular feature of Christian piety (*Did.* 8:1; much earlier in Mk 2:20; also Rom 6:1–4; Acts 2:41). This practice may have entered as a result of assimilation of Baptist elements into Christian circles (C. Kraeling, *John the Baptist*, 174). The practice of baptism too seems to have followed this trend: for John, it seems, his baptism was necessary for salvation; for Jesus, not so, but later followers accommodated John's followers in this way. Scobie notes that Jesus did not fast, a practice which often served as an outward expression of repentance and humility in traditional Judaism. Such traits, it seems, Jesus did not demand (C. Scobie, John the Baptist, 134). Rejecting this view, John Reumann denounces Maurice Goguel as maverick for his interpretation of Jn 3:25 that John and Jesus experienced a dispute the former emphasizing works of repentance, the latter, free forgiveness. This dispute, Goguel argued, erupted in John's view of Jesus as a renegade ("The Quest for the Historical Baptist," 186). See M. Goguel, *Au seuil de l'Évangile, Jean-Baptiste* ([Paris: Éditions Payot, 1928] 257–71, 74; cf. *Jesus and the Origins of Christianity* [New York: Harper Torchbooks 1960] 2.264–79). Compare also the position of H. Boers in *Theology out of the Ghetto: A New Testament Exegetical Study concerning Religious Exclusiveness* (Leiden: Brill, 1971) 45–56.

[27] With E. P. Sanders, *Jesus and Judaism*, 92; Michael Tilly, *Johannes der Täufer*, 49 and James A. Kelhoffer, *The Diet of John the Baptist*, 8. Unlike Mark and Matthew, Luke's version of this passage is particularly evocative of the point: "Then they said to him, 'John's disciples frequently fast and offer prayers just as the disciples of the Pharisees, but your disciples eat and drink' (οἱ μαθηταὶ Ἰωάννου νηστεύουσιν πυκνὰ καὶ δεήσεις ποιοῦνται ὁμοίως καὶ οἱ τῶν Φαρισαίων, οἱ δὲ σοὶ ἐσθίουσιν καὶ πίνουσιν)" (Lk 5:33). In the version of this saying from Mk 2:18–22 (cf. Mt 9:14–17) Jesus appears to refer to the disciples of John (and the Pharisees) as an "old cloak" and "old wineskins."

[28] E. F. Lupieri comments: "... in the New Testament he [John the Baptist] is the only figure who can be considered a model for ascetic life ... In fact, Jesus Christ ate and drank even with sinners, and the only time he fasted he did not join God afterwards but the Devil" ("John the Baptist: The First Monk," 16).

[29] Cf. the comment by H. D. Betz: "His [Jesus'] attitude toward fasting may have been one of the major differences between Jesus and John the Baptist, but if so we do not know the rea-

Jesus fasts and exhorts others to do the same (Q 4:2; 6:21a; 11:3; 12:22b–24, 29, 45–46).[30] Q even goes so far as to claim that Jesus' *opponents* "eat" and "drink" such that in the final judgment they will not be recognized (Q 13:26–7; 17:26–7, 28–9, 30).[31]

For this hypothesis, it is neither necessary to accept that John was a radical "ascetic," fasting continually, nor that he ate only "locusts and wild honey."[32] Some passages, such as Q 11:3, may simply imply dependence on God for a minimal level of subsistence. Minimal subsistence is, however, one definition of fasting.[33] Furthermore, the present conclusion also does not preclude that John

---

sons why they differed" (*The Sermon on the Mount*, 418). W. H. Brownlee remarks that John's diet may have represented "a repudiation of civilization as corrupting" ("John the Baptist in the New Light of Ancient Scrolls," 33).

[30] Nb. in the Markan wilderness (Mk 1:12–13), Jesus does not fast (cf. Mt 4:2/Lk 4:2).

[31] Cf. *Gos. Thom.* § 13: "Jesus said: I am not your master, for you have drunk, you have become drunk from the bubbling spring which I have caused to gush forth (?)" (*NTApo* 1.119; ET: Beate Blatz); also: *Did.* 1.3; 7.4; 8.1; 10:3; 11:6, 9; 12:3; and 13:1–3. Moreover, the end of Q may have included the theme of eating and drinking; Lk 22:30 is "Special L": "So that you may *eat and drink* at my table in my kingdom" (cf. Q 22:28, 30). Finally, Q 12:42 has the interesting reference to food "on time (ἐν καιρῷ)" indicating, with other uses of this expression in Q (e.g., 12:56), the postponement of eating/drinking until the completion of the eschatological judgment (cf. also the analogy in Q 13:21 between the kingdom and a loaf of bread). Q 13:29, too, describes "reclining/eating" (ἀνακλιθήσονται) (with Abraham, Isaac and Jacob) as an activity for the saved, subsequent to the eschatological judgment.

[32] James A. Kelhoffer correctly points out that the witnesses in Matthew and Mark concerning John's clothing and diet are not in agreement and should not be harmonized. Moreover, as above (78 n. 159), that John subsisted solely (as in Mt 3:4: ἡ δὲ τροφὴ ἦν αὐτοῦ ἀκρίδες καὶ μέλι ἄγριον) on some species of grasshopper and honey, dates or figs for an extended period of time is not plausible (*The Diet of John the Baptist*, 108–20). Kelhoffer also warns that John, like other Judaeans, could have survived in the wilderness on grasshoppers and honey water without being considered an ascetic, let alone, as later tradition interpreted, a radical ascetic. References to bread and wine may simply have symbolized urban locations; locusts and honey, rural spaces. Cf. also that John apparently wore rougher less comfortable clothing (camel hair); Jesus probably wore something more comfortable like wool ("sheep's clothing," Mt 7:15). See Eve-Marie Becker, "'KAMELHAARE… UND WILDER HONIG': Der historische Wert und die theologische Bedeutung der biographischen Täufer-Notiz (Mk 1,6)" 13–28, in *Die Bleibende Gegenwart des Evangeliums. Festschrift für Otto Merk*, eds., Roland Gebauer, Martin Meiser (Marburg: N. G. Elwert, 2003). The separate question of how crowds of Jews found John and traveled to see him, however, is a valid one.

[33] The practice of fasting (religiously-motivated, temporary abstention from food) in Hellenistic Judaism and the early church is not fully understood. As we know it, fasting could be undertaken annually as well as on specific occasions; see Lev 16:29; Zech 7:5–6; Ezra 8:21–23; Jon 3:7–9. Part of the point of fasting seems to be to bring one's body into a state of physical dependence on God for sustenance. The fasting in Ezra 8:21–23 "Then I proclaimed a fast there, at the river Ahava, that we might deny ourselves before our God, to seek from him a safe journey for ourselves, our children, and all our possessions," specifies dependence on God for sustenance in a wilderness setting and may recall Isa 40:3. Lk 18:12 indicates that some Jews practiced fasting bi-weekly. NT expressions, such as "to eat and/or drink nothing" or "to eat no bread," (cf. Lk 7:33) are periphrastic alternatives to "fasting" (νηστεύειν). Precedents can be found in 1 Sam 28:20: "Immediately Saul fell full length on the ground, filled with fear because of the words of Samuel; and there was no strength in him, for he had eaten nothing all day and

may have been critical of fasting or any other ritualistic purification done *without first* cleansing oneself inwardly and demonstrating this consecration in the ethical behavior of good works.[34] Finally, it is possible that not all of the above traditions refer to ritual fasting rather suggesting "eating" and/or "drinking" as a socio-ethical critique of the rich, gluttonous or otherwise excessive. Such a critique, however, also fits a Baptist milieu of wilderness "ascetics" (cf. 4QInstruction) better than a Christian setting in which disciples make the celebration of meals, even after and in commemoration of an execution, their custom.[35]

Finally, it is also not necessary, for this thesis, to accept that Jesus never fasted.[36] Indeed, no characterization of John or Jesus in this chapter should be embraced in its absolute sense. In the absence of complete clarity regarding, for example, John's and Jesus' fasting practices, the present argument will be plausible as long as its claims permit limited freedom of interpretation. In sum,

---

all night" (NRSV) and Zech 7:5–6: "Say to all the people of the land and the priests: When you fasted (צֹמ) and lamented in the fifth month and in the seventh, for these seventy years, was it for me that you fasted? And when you eat (אָכֹל) and when you drink (שָׁתֹה), do you not eat and drink only for yourselves." (NRSV) The latter are lines embedded in a passage of known importance to early Christians. See John Muddiman, "Fast, Fasting," *ABD* 2.773–76.

[34] John's idea was that the blessed should wait to "eat" (suspend all fasting) until the coming of the kingdom (e.g., Lk 12:37; 17:8). "Blessed are you who hunger" (Q 6:21) and "Woe to you who are full now" (Lk 6:25).

[35] Contrast the view of H. D. Betz on Q 6:21a who compares the mere physical quality of Q 6:21a with the ethical orientation of Mt 5:6 (*The Sermon on the Mount*, 129–32).

[36] It is, however, interesting that even the risen Jesus in his appearances likes to eat (e.g., Lk 24:41; cf. Jn 21:9–14). The traditional interpretation of the risen Jesus' consumption of food is anti-docetic. It could, however, simply suggest continuity with Jesus' pre-Easter behavior. The Jesus that the disciples knew loved to eat. Therefore, the risen Jesus eats. A comparison between Jn 3:25–30 and Mk 2:19–20 is instructive. In John, bridal imagery is preceded in 3:25 with a purported dispute between disciples of John the Baptist and Jesus "over purification (περὶ καθαρισμοῦ)." In Mark, however, related bridal imagery is preceded by a dispute between disciples of John the Baptist and Jesus over "fasting," suggesting a connection between the two. According to John W. Pryor, "The tradition [Jn 3:25] dealt with some kind of dispute between John's followers located in Judaea who were disturbed by what they considered to reflect a departure on the part of Jesus from the rigour of John on some question(s) of purity. The result is somehow linked to great success by Jesus in attracting crowds and converts. All of this is perhaps a foreshadowing of the greater success of Jesus later in Galilee, whose behaviour in matters of the Law was quite shocking and yet who proved to be so popular with the crowds" ("John the Baptist and Jesus: Tradition and Text in John 3.25," *JSNT* 66 [1997] 24). Pryor's insistence (19, 22, 24) on the Gospel of John's consistently harmonious depiction of Jesus' and John's movements is, however, disputable. Moreover, Q 7:34, also about eating (fasting?) habits, does not specify Jesus, but the Son of Man. Q 7:33–34 which reflects on two ministries – that of John the Baptist and that of the Son of Man – may be an interpolation in the saying, 7:31–32, 35. If the "Son of Man" refers to Jesus here, then the interpolation reflects non-Q (Markan) traditions of Jesus' eating and drinking more closely than Q's emphasis on a rigorous style of living. Also, the depiction of the "one to come" in the earlier part of this narrative block on the Baptist (Q 7:19) differs from the Q tradition on the "coming one" in 3:16b–17. In favor of interpreting the Son of Man in Q 7:34 as a reference to John the Baptist is not only the parallelism of vv. 33 and 34, but the absence of any, let alone a contrasting, conjunction.

the present section simply shows that exhortations in Q to fast cohere better with traditions regarding John than Jesus.[37]

Also, outside of Q, Jesus is known to minister in urban centers such as Galilee (Mk 1:39; Lk 4:44; Mt 4:23), Capernaum (Mk 1:21–22; Lk 4:31–32), Nazareth (Mk 6:1–6a; Lk 4:16–30; Mt 13:53–58), and Jerusalem.[38] With a few exceptions, he is depicted as a townsperson with an urban lifestyle.[39] John, however, according to the canonical witnesses, spends his life in more remote locations such as the Judaean wilderness somewhere near the Jordan River and/or Aenon near Salim (Jn 3:23), subsisting on "locusts and wild honey" (e.g., Mk 1:2–6; Lk 3:1–6; Mt 3:1–6). *In Q, however, Jesus waxes eloquently on life outside of cities* (Q 9:58; 10:3, 4, 5–9;[40] 12:22b–31, 33–34, 54–56; 14:27[41]; 15:4–5a,

---

[37] Cf. also theme of hunger in Magnificat (Lk 1:46–55) attributed in some ancient manuscripts to Elizabeth (Lk 1:53).

[38] Cf. Mt 11:1. As a basis for the claim that Jesus made his home in Nazareth, Mt 2:23 cites the unknown Jewish scripture: "He will be called a Nazorean (Ναζωραῖος κληθήσεται)." "Nazorean" here may refer to a messianic branch of David (Isa 11:1; Zech 3:8; 6:12) or to a Nazirite – one vowing to abstain from haircuts and wine (Num 6; Judg 13:5–7; Acts 18:18; 21:17–26). John the Baptist may be depicted as a Nazirite in Lk 1:15.

[39] Cf. Mk 1:12, 35, 45; 6:31, 46. Jesus' facile bouncing between so-called "deserted" loci and urban centers in Mark, however, suggests redaction as it seems to promote the author's theme of secrecy, as well as the themes of hostile masses and individuals persistently searching for Jesus (3:6, 32; 8:11; 11:18; 12:12; 14:1, 11, 55; cf. also 16:1). In their erraticism, they do not seem to reflect real retreats by Jesus to truly remote locations. Observe, for example, the author's comment at Mk 1:45 that Jesus "could *no longer enter into a town* openly, but ἔξω ἐπ' ἐρήμοις τόποις ἦν," (impf. form [ἦν] implies progressive/repeated aspect). When in the very next verse (2:1) he states, "When he returned again to Capernaum, after *a few days* (δι' ἡμερῶν), it was heard that he was *at home* (ἐν οἴκῳ)." In Lk 9:10 Jesus is said to *withdraw privately* to a *city* (Bethsaida) (NRSV)! The Greek text is: καὶ παραλαβὼν αὐτοὺς ὑπεχώρησεν κατ' ἰδίαν εἰς πόλιν καλουμένην Βηθσαϊδά.

[40] Q 10:5–9, 10–12, the saying on how to behave in houses and towns, including the recommendation on whether to eat and/or drink, suggests that the disciples addressed needed such advice. Presumably, if they lived in houses and towns, such counsel would be redundant. One can imagine the question from a disciple of John's: May we ever enter houses and towns and if so, may we eat and drink? Q 10:4 also advises to "greet no one" in contrast to other advice, such as, the parable of the good Samaritan (Lk 10:25–37). Q 12:2–3, 12:8–9, and warnings of persecution (e.g., Q 12:4–5) too take for granted that certain listeners, at some point in the future, will enter cities. Furthermore, not every piece of John's teaching was necessarily directed at his disciples. When he taught soldiers and tax collectors, he addressed urban issues they faced (e.g., Q 6:29, 29–30/Mt 5:41, 30; Q 6:34). An additional example is provided by Q 6:47–49. According to H. D. Betz, in Mt 7:24–27, the house pictured suffers flash-flooding, including heavy rain and high winds. Such a house is proverbial and may have been located anywhere. The house imagined in the SP, however, envisions the "high water of *one river*, with no mention of rains or winds" (*The Sermon on the Mount*, 559; emphasis added). The latter, "one river," may suggest a domicile by the Jordan and thus a connection to Baptist traditions. *The Critical Edition of Q*, in contrast, reconstructs this pericope from Matthew (98–101).

[41] The exhortation to "take up a cross" may not presuppose traditions regarding Jesus' death. Rather, with Bultmann, the idiom may be a "traditional figure for suffering and sacrifice" (*History of the Synoptic Tradition*, 161 n. 1). Although the interpretation may be slightly anachronistic (importing to *circa* 30 C. E. what is only documented for *circa* 60 C. E.), Bultmann cites

7; 17:1–2, 23–24, 37).[42] Q even preserves a severe warning against the cities of Chorazin and Bethsaida (Q 10:13).[43] Capernaum, a base for Jesus' healing ministry in Mark (Mk 1:21–28; 2:1–12), provides the hated culmination of this curse (Q 10:15).[44]

Anticipating the objection that an ancient philosopher, prophet or wise person does not have to dwell in the wilderness to allude to nature in writing (e.g., a *topos* of pastorality), the present argument points not simply to Q's pro-wilderness, but to its contrasting anti-urban rhetoric. Not only does the Jesus of Q advocate life outside the city, *in Q important urban establishments receive decisively negative portrayals.* John Kloppenborg observes: "Q treats the urban institutions and landmarks – the marketplace (ἀγορά; 7:3[2] *sic*; 11:43), the law courts and prisons (φυλαχή; 12:58–9), and the streets (πλατεῖα; 10:10?; 13:26) – negatively, as places where Q's opponents may be found."[45]

Here I stress that the argument is cumulative: no single Q saying reflecting rural or anti-urban rhetoric can be isolated as Baptist in origin. However, a case can be made for the relevance of the general emphasis on rural/anti-urban rhetoric in Q, in contrast to more urban-centered healing narratives about Jesus in, for example, the Gospel of Mark, for understanding the position of Q among traditions inherited by early Christians.

Also, outside of Q, Jesus, on one hand, is known to enjoy the company of family and other close filial relations: his mother, siblings, a small band of fisherman previously in business together, even one of the fisherman's mothers-in-law

---

A. Schlatter (*Der Evangelist Matthäus: seine Sprache, seine Ziel, seine Selbstständigkeit: ein Kommentar zum ersten Evangelium* [Stuttgart: Calwer Verlag, ³1948] 350–51) who conjectures a Zealot background – other agitators facing the possibility of crucifixion. Like Q 14:26, the saying both challenges respect for parents and shows how highly the teaching office could be held. A teacher was far more than a dispenser of wisdom, but one to whom disciples owed their lives. Contrast Mt 11:28–30 where Jesus describes his discipleship as "easy" and Mk 15:21 in which Jesus does not "carry his cross" himself, rather, permits it to be carried by the passerby, Simon of Cyrene. Against David Seeley who argues Q 14:27 is the earliest interpretation of the death of Jesus in Q ("Interpretations of Jesus' Death in Q," *Semeia* 55 [1991] 131–46).

[42] Along with this distinction is another from C. Scobie that Jesus went to others whereas John expected people to come to him (*John the Baptist*, 156). On this point, John A. T. Robinson comments, "Indeed, the great difference between John and Jesus lay in the fact that John remained in the desert and that men must come out to him: he refused to go to them…" ("The Baptism of John and the Qumran Community," in *Twelve New Testament Studies* [London: SCM, 1962] 13). Also, the discussion over purity in Jn 3:25 between Jesus and John may suggest that Jesus and his disciples were not strict enough for John (cf. Mk 7:1–23; C. Scobie, *John the Baptist*, 155).

[43] As well as lament over the largest and most powerful city, Jerusalem (Q 13:34–35).

[44] In light of arguments below concerning anti-Jesus polemic in Q, "Capernaum" – the nucleus of Jesus' ministry – here may represent metonymy for Jesus. On numerous occasions in all four gospels, Jesus is associated with Capernaum: Mk 1:21; 2:1; Mt 4:13; Lk 4:23; Jn 2:12; 6:24, 59.

[45] *Excavating Q*, 258.

(e.g., Lk 5:10; Mk 1:29–31; 3:21, 31–35;[46] 6:3; Jn 19:26–27).[47] On the other hand, John leaves family and other filial connections and exhorts others to do so too (e.g., Mk 1:2–6; Lk 3:1–6; Mt 3:1–6). *In Q, however, Jesus encourages the dismantling of familial ties* (e.g., Q 9:57–60; 12:53; 14:26–27; 17:33).

Furthermore, outside of Q, in NT teachings on divorce attributed to Jesus, such as Mt 5:31–32 and 19:3–9, divorce is permitted in cases of unchastity.[48] Q's teaching on divorce (Q 16:18; cf. Mk 10:11–12),[49] however, makes no such exception, rather assuming divorce necessarily leads to remarriage, and thus, adultery. Q proclaims:

Anyone who divorces his wife [and marries another] commits adultery, and whoever marries a woman being divorced commits adultery.[50]

Even with the comparatively little information about John in the NT, this Q teaching coincides with the tradition of John's castigation of Herod for marrying his brother Philip's wife, Herodias (Mk 6:17): "It is not permissible for you to have your brother's wife" (Mk 6:18; cf. Mk 6:17–20; Mt 14:3–12; Lk 3:19–20).[51]

Q's polemic against those who seek signs (e.g., Q 11:29) also contradicts the prevailing emphasis on Jesus' display of the miraculous outside of Q, but

---

[46] In this passage Jesus does not reject his biological family, he simply redefines the community of his followers as mothers, brothers and sisters, *reinforcing* his commitment to them and to familial structures in general. In Mk 1:20 the fishermen do indeed leave their father, but the brothers remain together as with Simon and Andrew (1:29). Cf. also Mk 6:4. On the issue of family language in Mark, see Stephen P. Ahearne-Kroll, "'Who Are My Mother and My Brothers?' Family Relations and Family Language in the Gospel of Mark," *JR* (2001) 1–25. Cf. also Arland D. Jacobson, "Divided Families and Christian Origins," in *The Gospel Behind the Gospels. Current Studies on Q*, ed., R. A. Piper (NTSuppl. 85; Leiden: Brill, 1995) 361–63; idem, "Jesus against the Family: The Dissolution of Family Ties in the Gospel Tradition," in *From Quest to Q: Festschrift James M. Robinson,* eds. Jon Ma. Asgeirsson, Kristin De Troyer, Marvin W. Meyer (Leuven: Leuven University, 2000) 189–218.

[47] Cf. also Mt 20:20–23.

[48] The unchastity clause may reflect the school of Shammai's interpretation of "something objectionable" (Deut 24:1). In 1 Cor 7:10–11 Paul relaxes the divorce law provided that neither individual remarries. In Mt 19:8–9 the teaching on divorce subordinates Moses' teaching to its own which purports to take into account what God himself intended from the beginning: "but from the beginning it was not this way (ἀπ᾽ ἀρχῆς δὲ οὐ γέγονεν οὕτως)" (v. 8). Cf. also Mt 5:31–32.

[49] The version of the prohibition in Mk 10:12 also includes no exception clause. It is different from the Q version, however, in that it reflects the Roman law permitting a woman to initiate divorce. The Q version – tied neatly to Herod Antipas – mentions only the husband's right.

[50] See *The Critical Edition of Q*, 470.

[51] Although Matthew's version of the Q saying (Mt 19:9) includes the exception clause (μὴ ἐπὶ πορνείᾳ) and Mt 5:31–2 includes it as well (however the wording is different: παρεκτὸς λόγου πορνείας), it was not original to either. Against the majority (see U. Luz, *Matthew*, 1.304–6), H. D. Betz disagrees, taking the exception as original to the SM (*The Sermon on the Mount*, 249–50).

coincides with near absence of data on John's performance of signs.[52] Indeed, the only miracle that does occur in Q is noteworthy for its lack of the marvelous.[53]

[52] Cf. Jn 5:36; 10:25, 37–8, 41. With regard to the meaning and historicity of Jn 10:41 (Ἰωάννης μὲν σημεῖον ἐποίησεν οὐδέν), E. Bammel argues that indeed the historical John did no miracles. As Bammel points out, however, the following observations suggest that Jn 10:41 is anti-Baptist polemic and that the historical Baptist *did* once perform miracles: (1) "the life of Jesus is surrounded by miracles and, according to the Acts, even more those of his apostles. Why not that of his forerunner and main witness too?" Within the canonical gospels and Acts, not to mention the non-canonical Acts ("'wonderbooks' *par excellence*") even false prophets perform miracles; (2) "the divination of an eminent man is expressed in extraordinary circumstances which accompany his birth and *surround his public activity*"; indeed such signs are a "feature of the Augustan age" (emphasis added); (3) "sages and prophets are divine persons (θεῖοι ἀνέρες) more than anybody else … the Jewish world is no exception to this"; and (4) miraculous deeds are anticipated for John by Lk 1:15, 17 and 76 (183–84). On the basis of his own interpretation of NT Baptist traditions, Josephus and later Christian traditions from Syria and Egypt, Bammel argues that, "the theory of some scholars, that the verse [Jn 10:41] is to be understood solely as a tendentious polemic against the truth and that a wonder-working activity of the Baptist can be deduced from this (*e negativo*), does not really match the facts. On the other hand, it is much more likely that the lack of signs became an embarrassment within the Baptist communities, and it may even be that statements palliating the lack of signs circulated in these communities, which had not yet moved to the Gnostic habit of disregarding and even despising miracles" ("John Did No Miracle," 187). Later Bammel adds, "The fact, that John was not reputed to have done miracles may have been used as a charge against the Christians, who claimed the Baptist as a witness for their Messiah" (200). Exceptions Bammel discusses include Mk 6:14, 8:12, as well as possibly 11:27–30. The basis for Herod's conclusion that Jesus is John *redivivus* is given in Mk 6:14 and Mt 14:2 (cf. Lk 9:7) as Jesus' miracles. Bammel concludes, however, that these exceptions suggest only that "such ideas may have been entertained"; about them, he summarizes: "Their relevance is of such a small degree that it seems unreasonable to suppose that this may have influenced the wording of John 10:41" (187). Thus, a thorough evaluation of all of the evidence suggests to Bammel that Jn 10:41 is historical. Against Bammel, the Fourth Gospel's claim is John performed no sign (σημεῖον), *not* no miracle. R. Bultmann's comments are also noteworthy: "In discussions between Jesus' disciples and those of John the messianic character of the ἔργα, i.e., the miracles performed by Jesus, was denied. The disciples of Jesus replied that messianic prophecy was being fulfilled in their master's miracles. Whether it is possible to go further and assume that the prophecy of Isa. 35:5 f. had already been applied by John's disciples to the Baptist must remain open to doubt. That stories of John's miracles were in circulation is in itself quite credible; for the assertion that he performed none (Jn. 10:41) is obviously a piece of polemic. And does not Mk. 6:14 imply that reports of the Baptist's miracles were current?" (*History of the Synoptic Tradition*, 24). On this passage in Mark, see also J. Murphy-O'Connor, "John the Baptist and Jesus," 372. Finally, Sir 48:12–14 reflects a tradition in which Elisha is thought to have performed "twice as many signs" as Elijah. The obvious deduction is that Elijah performed signs, if only a limited number. As in the case of fasting where this thesis admits the possibility that Jesus may have, in some capacity, fasted, it is also within this project's scope to imagine that John performed some healings, miracles or exorcisms. Herod's assumption, on the basis of the healing activities of Jesus and his disciples, that the beheaded John the Baptist has been raised from the dead in Mk 6:14 certainly suggests this possibility. If associated with John, then the healing of the centurion's son (Q 7:1, 3, 6b–9, 10), the exhortation to "cure the sick" (Q 10:9) and the first verse of the Beelzebul accusation (Q 11:14) in which a dumb demoniac is "healed" provide additional examples. In terms of the Beelzebul accusation, however, the fact that a controversy is stirred up around the exorcism is noteworthy. The hyperbole of Q 17:6 is rhetorical and does not imply miraculous signs.

[53] If Lk 11:14 belongs in Q, it too (or alone) may qualify as a display of the miraculous.

In Q 7:1, 3, 6b–9 and 10, Jesus replies to the centurion seeking healing for his son, "Am I, by coming, to heal him (ἐγὼ ἐλθὼν θεραπεύσ[ω] αὐτόν)?" (Q 7:3; cf. Mt 8:7)[54] The centurion then asks that by Jesus' "speech" (εἰπὲ λόγῳ [Q 7:7]) the boy be healed.[55] In his *Antiquitates*,[56] Josephus hails John for his powers of speech[57] – in Feldman's ET: crowds "were aroused to the highest degree by his sermons (καὶ γὰρ ἤρθησαν ἐπὶ πλεῖστον τῇ ἀκροάσει τῶν λόγων)" for he possessed an "eloquence that had so great an effect on mankind (τὸ ἐπὶ τοσόνδε πιθανὸν αὐτοῦ τοῖς ἀνθρώποις)" (*Ant.* 18.118); in John Meier's: it was a "powerful ability to persuade people."[58] If Josephus is correct that John's ministry attracted crowds by means of compelling teachings, and if subsequent followers

---

See J. Kloppenborg, *Q Parallels*, 90–93. Q 17:6 does not necessarily imply miraculous signs. This conclusion counters that of G. Theissen, "Wanderradikalismus, Literatursoziologische Aspekte der Überlieferung von Worten Jesu im Urchristentum," in *Studien zur Soziologie des Urchristentums*, 2nd ed. (Tübingen: Mohr Siebeck, 1983) esp. 79–105; ET: *The Sociology of Early Palestinian Christianity* (Philadelphia: Fortress, 1978).

[54] ET: *The Critical Edition of Q*, 106–7; cf. Jn 4:46–54.

[55] *The Critical Edition of Q*, 110–11.

[56] Unlike the so-called *Testimonium Flavianum* (*Ant.* 18.63–64), the authenticity of this pericope (*Ant.* 18.116–19) is generally not disputed.

[57] This passage appears in all manuscripts without any significant variant and was known to Eusebius (*Eccl. Hist.*, 1.2.4–6; *Dem. evang.*, 9.5.15) and Origen (*Cont. Celsum*, 1.47). On the reliability of *Ant.* 18.5.2 § 116–19 (as compared to the unreliability of the *Testimonium Flavianum* 18.3.3 § 63–4), see John P. Meier, *A Marginal Jew*, 2.19–23. Cf. also J. Kloppenborg's conclusion regarding Q that: "The dominant mode of address is sapiential, not prophetic …. the mode of persuasion is not prophetic – by appeal to the authority of God – but sapiential, by rhetorical question and appeal to observation of nature and of ordinary human relations …. And there are no indications that Q represented itself to its intended audience as oracles of the Exalted Lord" (*The Formation of Q*, 321–22). Kloppenborg concludes that the two dominant modes (sapiential and prophetic) represent two different strata of tradition. Behind this point lies the discussion of the complex relationship between wisdom and apocalyptic in the late Hellenistic and early Roman Periods. For background on this debate, see H. D. Betz, "On the Problem of the Religio-Historical Understanding of Apocalypticism"; J. Z. Smith, "Wisdom and Apocalyptic"; John J. Collins, "Wisdom, Apocalypticism, and Generic Compatibility"; James C. VanderKam, "The Prophetic-Sapiential Origins of Apocalyptic Thought"; and, Shannon Burkes, "Wisdom and Apocalypticism in the Wisdom of Solomon". The present author's assessment of primary sources, not just within the NT, but including *4 Ezra* and *2 Baruch,* is that Kloppenborg's conclusion is overly facile. During the late Hellenistic and early Roman periods, wisdom and apocalyptic explanations for life's difficulties overlapped. Traditional creation theologies offered more rational (apocalyptic theologies, less rational) solutions. See Karina Martin Hogan, "Theologies in Conflict in 4 Ezra: Wisdom Debate and Apocalyptic Solution," Ph.D. Diss., University of Chicago, 2002. Kloppenborg emphatically *agrees* that the two theologies existed together, claiming only that Q clearly demonstrates a *literary* separation of the two (e.g., *Formation*, xii). Even on the basis of literary shifts from "wisdom" to "apocalyptic" among sayings and clusters of sayings in Q, however, the argument that these shifts derive from two strata, if plausible, is not necessary (*multiplicanda argumentum*); and, an abiding concern is the attempt to rescue "Jesus" from an ultimately fallacious apocalyptic message.

[58] *Josephus, Jewish Antiquities*, Books XVIII-XIV, trans. Louis H. Feldman (LCL; Cambridge, MA: Harvard University Press, repr. 1996); cf. also J. P. Meier, *A Marginal Jew*, 2.20; idem, "John the Baptist in Josephus: Philology and Exegesis," *JBL* 111/2 (1992) 225–37.

of John maintained this emphasis, this healing account reflects John's ministry well. Moreover, for Q's account the question remains: Was the centurion's son ever healed?[59]

Furthermore, the appearance of a ἑκατοντάρχης *at all* prompts an important question. Although, in the canonical gospels, this is the only member of the Roman military to interact with Jesus before his crucifixion,[60] Lk 3:14 attests that John interacted with soldiers regularly directing certain of his teachings specifically to them: ἐπηρώτων δὲ αὐτὸν καὶ στρατευόμενοι λέγοντες, Τί ποιήσωμεν καὶ ἡμεῖς; καὶ εἶπεν αὐτοῖς, Μηδένα διασείσητε μηδὲ συκοφαντήσητε καὶ ἀρκεῖσθε τοῖς ὀψωνίοις ὑμῶν. What is more, Matthew's version of the healing of the centurion's servant includes a saying of Q invective linked to Baptist traditions by both style and content: "But I tell you: Many will come from east and west and recline with Abraham, Isaac, and Jacob in the kingdom of heaven, but the sons of the kingdom will be thrown out into the outer darkness; weeping and gnashing of teeth will be there" (Mt 8:11//Q 13:29, 28; cf. Q 3:7–9, 16b–17).[61]

Finally, not only does Q's great temptation scene exhibit key features of Baptist traditions, such as its setting away from urban centers and its depiction of Jesus' fasting,[62] *and* stand out as a rare section of narrative in Q (of which there are only five[63] *all except the temptation and the healing of the centurion's son explicitly connected to John*),[64] but in it, *he refuses to perform miracles three times.* Indeed in this passage miracles are portrayed as "temptations" from "Satan" (Mk 1:13; Mt 4:3: the "tempter" [ὁ πειράζων]). Apart from Q, however, in all four canonical gospels, Jesus is renowned for his willingness and ability to perform miracles.[65]

---

[59] Both Matthew and Luke amplify the story of the centurion's son (Mt 8:6, παῖς; Lk 7:2, δοῦλος) to assuage concerns over whether the (servant?) boy/slave was actually healed. Cf. the last sentence of each account: Lk 7:10: "When those who had been sent returned to the house, they found the slave being in good health"; and Mt 8:13b: "And the son was healed in that hour." Cf. also Jn 4:51–54.

[60] Jesus' audience probably also included fishermen, tax collectors, and many who were sick and demon-possessed.

[61] With a different purpose in mind, J. Kloppenborg describes the centurion's son episode as "closely associated with the second complex of Baptist-related sayings" (*The Formation of Q*, 117).

[62] Nb. in Mark's version of Jesus' temptation in the wilderness, Jesus does not fast (Mk 1:12–13). Picking up the point again in Mk 2:18–20, the author seems fairly adamant that Jesus did not fast. A. D. Jacobson argues for the temptation narrative's "lateness" (*The First Gospel: An Introduction to Q* (Sonoma, CA: Polebridge, 1992) 90–91.

[63] The five sections are: (1) Q 3:7–9, 16b–17; (2) Q 4:1–4, 9–12, 5–8, 13; (3) Q 7:1, 3, 6b–9, 10; (4) Q 7:18–19, 22–23, 24–28, 29–30, 31–35; (5) Q 11:14–15, 17–20.

[64] Apart from the baptism narrative (1 occurrence: 3:21) and temptation narrative (4 occurrences: 4:1, 4, 12, 8), Jesus' name occurs only twice in Q at 7:9 and 9:58. Against this maximum of seven, John's name occurs a total of eight times. See 127 n. 188. For a list of those against inclusion of Jesus' baptism in Q, see J. Kloppenborg, *Q Parallels*, 16. Nb. "Not in Q" group includes J. Kloppenborg (1987).

[65] Healing and exorcism is Jesus' primary work in Mark (e.g., 1:23–26, 30–31, 32–34, 39, 40–45; 2:1–5, 11–12; 3:1–5, *et al.*). The expressions, ὁ ἰσχότερος (Mk 1:7) and ἐξουσία

Naturally, the gospel amplifying the significance of Jesus' miracles most by referring to these acts of power as "signs" omits his wilderness temptation.[66]

The principal interpretations of these contradictions are two-fold: (1) either Jesus' characterization in Q as fasting, wilderness-dwelling, rejecting familial ties, offering no allowances for divorce, not even in the case of a Herod, and refusing to perform miracles is appropriated by the Synoptic authors for their characterizations of John, (otherwise characterizing Jesus as feasting, city-dwelling, familial, offering certain allowances for divorce, and performing miracles); or (2) these passages in Q were originally about John.[67]

3.4 Thematic Continuity: Baptist Traditions and Q

Despite the paucity of evidence in the NT about John, *all of the major themes of Q can be connected to his few traditions.* These thematic correlations include: (1) the announcement of a coming kingdom (e.g., Q 6:20; 7:28; 10:9; 11:2b, 20, 52; 12:31; 13:18; 16:16; 17:20–21; cf. Mt 3:2); (2) eschatological warnings (Q 3:7–9; 3:16b–17); (3) pronouncement of punishment on this generation and its leaders (e.g., Q 7:31; 11:29, 30, 31, 32, 50, 51; cf. Mt 3:7);[68] (4) rejection of traditional family structures (e.g., Q 9:59–60; 12:49, 51, 53; 14:26; cf. Lk 1:80); (5) the rigors of an itinerant, wilderness lifestyle (e.g., Q 9:58; 10:4; 12:22b–31, 33–34; 14:27; 16:13; cf. Mk 1:6/Mt 3:4); (6) warnings of persecution (e.g., Q 6:22–23; 12:4–5, 8–12; 17:33; cf. Mk 6:17–29/Mt 14:3–12/Lk 3:19–20); and (7) wisdom sayings (e.g., Q 3:9, 11, 13, 14, 18; cf. Lk 3:10–14, 18).[69] Furthermore,

---

(e.g., Mk 3:15; cf. also 1:22; 2:10; 11:28–9) refer to this work. Δυνάμεις in Mk 6:2, 5 too includes miracles. Cf. Lk 24:19 which implies that the role of prophet includes displays of the miraculous.

[66] Cf. Jn 1:51.

[67] Other Q ideals/teachings that comport better with Synoptic depictions of John than Jesus include that Q advocates non-violence, rejects traditional means of prosecution through courts and exhorts disciples to forgo retaliation against enemies (Q 6:27–30), whereas Jesus does not (Lk 22:36; Mk 14:47/Mt 26:51/Lk 22:49–50). John Kloppenborg lists these among other characteristics of Q in "Symbolic Eschatology and the Apocalypticism of Q," 305.

[68] Interestingly, the Greek word in the first half of Q 7:28, γεννητοί of the expression, γεννητοὶ γυναικῶν is not only an Aramaism, but a NT *hapax legomenon* from Q (Lk 7:28/Mt 11:11) with close semantic connections to another *hapax legomenon* from Q – the Greek word, γεννήματα, from the expression γεννήματα ἐχιδνῶν. The latter, of course, first appears in the NT as an expression of John's (Q 3:7). Cf. also Mt 12:34 and 23:33 in which John's expression is applied to Jesus; and, εἰς γενεὰς καὶ γενεὰς in the Magnificat attributed to Elizabeth in several north Italian Latin ms versions (Lk 1:50) (see 16 n. 39). Finally, note close semantic relationship between the word, γεννήματα from the expression, γεννήματα ἐχιδνῶν ("brood of vipers") and the numerous castigations in Q against ἡ γενεά or this "generation" (e.g., Q 7:31; 11:29, 30, 31, 32, 50, 51). "This generation" referred to in Q becomes the Pharisees in the Gospel of Mark (A. Jacobson, "The Literary Unity of Q," 382).

[69] Burton Mack picks up on many of these ideas, but considers them Cynic qualities of

thematic images in NT Baptist traditions also occur in Q, including wheat/chaff (Q 10:2; cf. Q 3:17),[70] snakes (Q 11:12; cf. Q 3:7),[71] trees (Q 6:43–45; cf. Q 3:9), fruit (Q 6:43–45; cf. Q 3:9), fire (Q 12:49; cf. Q 3:17), children (τὰ τέκνα, Q 3:8; 7:35; 11:13; 13:34; cf. also τὸ παιδίον, Q 7:32 and ὁ νήπιος, Q 10:21),[72] and stones or rocks (Q 4:3, 11; 11:11; cf. Q 3:8).[73] For Baptist traditions, these themes and images complement John's sum exhortation to repent.[74] About Q, too, John Kloppenborg states, its "main concern is with impenitence."[75]

The best argument about thematic connections between Q and Baptist traditions is also provided by John Kloppenborg.[76] In his discussion of recurring motifs in Q, Kloppenborg mentions first the Lot cycle. Q begins, Kloppenborg points out, by placing John "in the region of the Jordan" (πᾶσαν ἡ [τὴν] περίχωρος[ν] τοῦ Ἰορδάνου) (3:2b–3a). This phrase parallels passages in the Tanakh (e.g., Gen 13:10–12 [LXX]: πᾶσαν τὴν περίχωρον τοῦ Ἰορδάνου; cf. also 19:17, 25, 28) in the story of Lot.[77] With Kloppenborg, this observation might not hold much significance if John's message appearing next in Q that "*warns* against reliance on kinship to Abraham, *threatens* a fiery destruction, and *inverts* the story of Lot's wife by declaring God's ability to fashion people out of stones or pillars" did not provide a group of further allusions to the Lot cycle

---

the Jesus' followers who comprised the Q social group (*The Lost Gospel: The Book of Q and Christian Origins* [San Francisco, CA: HarperSanFrancisco, 1993]).

[70] Within NT traditions, harvest language for the judgment is first attributed to John (Q 3:16b–17); cf. Lukan *Sondergut* material: "Satan has demanded to sift you as the wheat (ὁ Σατανᾶς ἐξῃτήσατο ὑμᾶς τοῦ σινιάσαι ὡς τὸν σῖτον)," harvest language of judgment (Lk 22:31). Furthermore, v. 32 is interesting for its inclusion of the verb, ἐπιστρέφειν: "But I have prayed for you that your faith will not fail; and when you have turned again, strengthen your brothers." Also, mill (17:34–35) and millstone (17:1–2) sayings may be connected to John's exhortations on wheat and chaff and the threshing floor (Q 3:17).

[71] Cf. also references to "snake" (ὄφις) in Mt 10:16 and Lk 10:19. To these examples, if one adds every occurrence of the expression, "brood of vipers" and Mk 16:18 (Longer Ending), all Synoptic references to snakes are exhausted. Interestingly, Mt 10:16 shares two images associated with the Baptist: both "snakes" and "doves." For the history-of-religions background on snakes as it pertains to the "Longer Ending" of Mark, see James A. Kelhoffer, *Miracle and Mission: The Authentication of Missionaries and Their Message in the Longer Ending of Mark* (WUNT II/112; Tübingen: Mohr Siebeck, 2000) Ch. 6.

[72] The prevalent theme of children is traced in Q to John (3:8).

[73] Images of stones and fire also appear together in *Gos. Thom.* § 13.

[74] About the Baptist's use of images, James Dunn writes, "This was a man for whom the environment was a book which spoke about God as much as did the oracles of the prophets" ("John the Baptist's Use of Scripture," 54).

[75] J. Kloppenborg, "Symbolic Eschatology and the Apocalypticism of Q," *HTR* 80/3 (1987) 303–304. Cf. also Arland D. Jacobson's comment: "In Q, even miracles are understood in the context of repentance (cf. 10:13; 11:14–20; 10:5–12; and cf. 11:20; par. to 10:9)" ("The Literary Unity of Q," 385).

[76] J. Kloppenborg Verbin, *Excavating Q*, 118–21, 163.

[77] J. Kloppenborg Verbin, *Excavating Q*, 118–19.

in Genesis.[78] Moreover, in the middle of Q, a second allusion to the destruction of Sodom occurs in 10:12, "I say to you, it will be more tolerable for Sodom on that day than for that town." *And,* at the end of Q, the cycle resurfaces again: "Similarly, just as it was in the days of Lot: they were eating, drinking, buying, selling, planting, building, but on the day Lot left Sodom, fire and sulfur rained from heaven and destroyed everything. The day on which the Son of Man is revealed will be like this" (17:28–30)[79] and "I tell you, there will be two; one is taken and the other is left. Two women will be grinding at the mill; one is taken and the other is left" (17:34–35).[80] As Kloppenborg points out, the connection between Lk 17:34–35 and the Lot cycle is unimpeachable as the two verbs of the last phrase (v. 35), ἀφίεται (spared) and παραλαμβάνεται (swept away) appear in Gen 18:26 and 19:17 (LXX) respectively, with reference to "the sparing of Lot's family" and "the destruction of the wicked."[81]

Although as Kloppenborg explains, Q's *use* of the Lot cycle is not unique[82] and Q's *explanation* of the coming judgment is not confined to allusions to this cycle, (including, for example, allusions to Ezekiel as well),[83] the cycle, nonetheless, has special significance with respect to Q's framework precisely because it surfaces in the beginning, middle and end.[84] Kloppenborg writes:

This implies that the allusions to the Lot cycle are not simply an accident of the heterogeneous traditions absorbed in the collection but derive from purposeful editing at a stage near the main redaction of Q.[85]

What is compelling about this observation from the perspective of the present thesis is *the explicit connection between Q's framework and entirety – "at a stage near the main redaction of Q" – and John the Baptist.* Recall that in Q 3:2b–3a *John,* not Jesus, is the figure like Lot who is found "in the region of the Jordan."[86]

---

[78] J. Kloppenborg Verbin, *Excavating Q*, 119; emphasis added. On the claim in Hasmonean literature to Abrahamic descent as a basis for political power, see Richard A. Horsley, *Whoever Hears You Hears Me: Prophets, Performance, and Tradition in Q* (Harrisburg, PA: Trinity Press International, 1999) 118.

[79] The inclusion of Lk 17:28–29 is disputed; see *The Critical Edition of Q*, 516–17; *Q Parallels*, 192–95.

[80] J. Kloppenborg Verbin, *Excavating Q*, 119. Cf. also Lk 17:32–33: "Remember Lot's wife. Those who try to make their life secure will lose it, but those who lose their life will keep it."

[81] J. Kloppenborg Verbin, *Excavating Q*, 119.

[82] J. Kloppenborg Verbin, *Excavating Q*, 119: "First, the Lot story already had a long history of exegetical use in the Tanak and the literature of Second Temple Judaism, being employed as the archetype of a divine judgment that was total, sudden, and enduring, and which occurred without human instrumentality."

[83] J. Kloppenborg Verbin, *Excavating Q*, 120.

[84] J. Kloppenborg Verbin, *Excavating Q*, 120–21.

[85] J. Kloppenborg Verbin, *Excavating Q*, 120–21.

[86] No Lot-cycle passage explicitly specifies a connection to Jesus.

3.5 *Sondergut* and Q: Introduction

Implicated in this discussion is the Matthean and Lukan *Sondergut*.[87] It is, how-ever, difficult to say with certainty what material from the so-called *Sondergut* may have been included in Q. Most arguments for the inclusion of *Sondergut* in Q are speculative, relying on prior ideas of Q, its form and content, and how a passage of *Sondergut* fits this scheme.[88] The present approach seeks to avoid this pitfall by not simply matching form and content between the individual citations of the IQP's proposed contents of Q and select passages from the *Sondergut*, but taking into account source-, form-, redaction- and rhetorical-critical issues of both Q and the "Special Materials" in assessing the plausibility of *Sondergut* inclusions.[89]

The next section on Matthean and Lukan *Sondergut* assays the relationship between Q and certain passages from the "Special Materials."

3.5.1 *Matthean* Sondergut

If the author of Luke-Acts cut as much from Q as he did from Mark (of which he uses roughly only one-third),[90] a significant portion of the material now rel-

---

[87] B. H. Streeter held to the idea that "M" and "L" were actual written documents (*The Four Gospels,* 223–70; also chart on 150). Most today take these designations to refer to unknown sources.

[88] E.g., H. Schürmann, *Traditionsgeschichtliche Untersuchungen zu den synoptischen Evangelien* (Düsseldorf: Patmos Verlag, 1968).

[89] Petros Vassiliadis argues that *Sondergut* passages can be admitted to Q on the basis of, among other things, theological and stylistic agreement with the rest of Q. With regard to Vassiliadis' thesis, J. Kloppenborg comments: "These are sound and responsible criteria" (Petros Vassiliadis, "The Nature and Extent of the Q Document," *NovT* 20 [1978)] 49–73; John Kloppenborg, *The Formation of Q,* 84). Cf. also J. Kloppenborg Verbin, *Excavating Q,* 95–6; Athanasius Polag, *Die Christologie der Logienquelle* (WMANT 45; Neukirchen-Vluyn: Neukirchener, 1979).

[90] The present author does not, however, wish to make too much of statistical studies of Q's content – in particular those by A. M. Honoré ("A Statistical Study of the Synoptic Problem," *NovT* 10 [1968] 95–147), Charles E. Carlston and Dennis Norlin ("Once More – Statistics and Q," *HTR* 64 [1971] 59–78), Petros Vassiliadis ("The Nature and Extent of the Q Document," 49–73), and Frans Neirynck ("Q," *IDBSup* [1976] 715–16). Regarding this type of data John Kloppenborg summarizes: "Statistics are very imprecise and potentially misleading indicators of the extent of Q" (*The Formation of Q,* 82). Also, in Kloppenborg's words: "...we must reckon with the possibility that parts of Q are now irretrievably lost, and further, that some Matthaean and Lucan *Sondergut* may in fact derive from Q" (*The Formation of Q,* 82). With regard to the possibility that "Special M" consists of passages the author of Luke-Acts omitted from Q, compare our reliance on the Lukan order of Q based, in part, on the way the author of Luke-Acts retained Markan order. If the argument about Luke's use of Mark is determinative for under-standing the order of Q it is also a valid premise on which to build arguments of the inclusion of "Special M" materials in Q (J. Kloppenborg Verbin, *Excavating Q,* 88, 95) See above 12.

egated to "Special M" may have originated in Q.[91] For this reason, sections from
Matthean *Sondergut* warrant evaluation first. The working hypothesis of this
section is that a Baptist *Tendenz* proves useful in negotiating certain *Sondergut*
candidates for Q, in particular, "Special M" sections of the Sermon on the Mount
(SM). In the following discussion a comparison is made between the following
five Baptist traditions and "Special M" passages: (1) Mt 6:16–18; (2) Mt 6:1–18;
(3) Mt 7:13–23; (4) Mt 5:3–12; and (5) Mt 25:31–46.[92]

Mt 6:16–18

Continuity is discernible between Baptist traditions and the third of the three
components of the SM section on cultic instruction:[93]

> And whenever you fast, do not look downcast, as the hypocrites, for they hide their faces
> in order to reveal to people that they are fasting. Amen, I tell you, they have received their
> reward! But when you fast, anoint your head and wash your face, so you do not reveal to
> people you are fasting, but to your Father who is in secret; and your Father the one seeing
> in secret will reward you. (Mt 6:16–18)

As noted above, according to Synoptic passages outside of Q, including two in
the Gospel of Matthew, (Mt 9:14–15; 11:18–19; cf. Mk 2:18–20; Lk 5:33), *in
contrast to John's disciples who fast,*[94] *Jesus and his disciples do not fast*. Why
then Jesus' instruction on fasting?[95] This discrepancy is heightened in view of
sayings in P. Oxy. 654 and *Gospel of Thomas* 104 in which Jesus is said to reject
fasting:

> His [Jesus'] disciples asked him and said: "How shall we fast, and how shall we pray, and
> how shall we give alms, and what shall we observe when we eat?" Jesus said, "Do not lie,
> and what you hate do not do! For all things will be full of truth before heaven. For nothing
> is hidden that will not be made manifest. *Blessed is he who does not do these things*. For
> all things will be made manifest to the Father who is in the heavens." (P. Oxy. 654)[96]

---

[91] G. D. Kilpatrick argues that the only persuasive explanation for Q's disappearance is its
absorption into Matthew and Luke ("The Disappearance of Q," *JTS* 42 [1941] 182–84). In line
with the present argument, however, Q's mysterious disappearance might be said to coincide
with the mysterious disappearance of the disciples of John the Baptist; both are, in a sense,
absorbed into Matthean and Lukan communities of tradition.

[92] A few additional candidates for inclusion in Q from among the Matthean *Sondergut* come
up in the context of the discussions of Ch. 6.

[93] For an outline ("*conspectus*") of the whole SM with explanation, see H. D. Betz, *The
Sermon on the Mount*, 50–66.

[94] According to J. Kelhoffer, that John's disciples fast is one of a few different positions on
John's diet represented by the Synoptic texts (*The Diet of John the Baptist,* 7–8).

[95] A further question is whether fasting is connoted by the perplexing phrase: τὸν ἄρτον
ἡμῶν τὸν ἐπιούσιον δίδου ἡμῖν τὸ καθ᾽ ἡμέραν of the Lord's prayer (Q 11:3). See 90–91
n. 33.

[96] Greek text taken from K. Aland, *Synopsis*, 85; ET: H. D. Betz, *The Sermon on the Mount*,
336. Cf. *Gos. Thom.* § 6.

They said [to him]: "Come, let us pray today and fast." Jesus said: "What then is the sin that I have done, or in what have I been overcome? But when the bridegroom comes out [departs] from the bridal chamber, then let them fast and pray." (*Gos. Thom.* § 104)[97]

The argument that Jesus and his disciples feasted before his death only to resume fasting after it – thus necessitating a teaching on fasting – is a justification, not an explanation for this contradiction.[98] Although *P. Oxy.* and *Gos. Thom.* may represent later traditions arising as objections to Christians adopting fasting practices in spite of certain Jesus traditions' rejection of them, these two texts, nevertheless, provide additional support for traditions in the Gospel of Mark (Mk 2:18–20) and elsewhere, claiming Jesus rejected fasting.

Background for such a discrepancy between the SM and other NT traditions can be sought in critical discussions of sources. According to H. D. Betz's argument, the SM was handed down to the author of the Gospel of Matthew in its entirety from a version of Q that Betz refers to as Q[Matt].[99] Betz's critics, however, contend that the author of Matthew had a hand in the SM's composition. The argument turns, in part, on the question of *Sondergut.* Why, critics ask, is it necessary to postulate that a person other than the author of Matthew had access to Matthew's exact same sources?[100] Betz argues that the author of the Gospel of Matthew is less likely than another to have composed the SM because, among other things such as the SM's lack of christological recognition, let alone appreciation, of Jesus' salvific death and resurrection, passages in the SM exhibit "tension" with materials included in other parts of this gospel.[101] The Gentile mission, for example, is opposed by the SM.[102] Dale Allison, in his review of Betz's work, points out, however, that Matthew 10, too, opposes the Gentile mission making inner-Matthean "tension" a poor guide for conclusions about sources.[103]

---

[97] *NTApo*, 1.129; ET: Beate Blatz. Cf. also *Gos. Thom.* § 14, 27, 102.

[98] The "Special L" passage, Lk 14:15: "Blessed is the one who *will eat* (future) bread in the kingdom of God" where eating is a future, not present, eschatological act also contributes to the discussion. As above, even the risen Jesus likes to eat (e.g., Lk 24:41; cf. Jn 21:9–14).

[99] For a summary of the arguments as well as a description of his position, see H. D. Betz, *The Sermon on the Mount*, 42–44.

[100] See review by Dale Allison, *JBL* 117/1 (1998) 136–37: "The SM features dozens of words .... as well as phrases and constructions .... characteristic of Matthew. It also includes emphases .... and uses compositional techniques .... typical of the rest of the Gospel. The SM looks very Matthean, and it is not clear that Betz has an effective rebuttal to this simple observation, which was first made years ago in review of his earlier work."

[101] H. D. Betz, *The Sermon on the Mount*, 44.

[102] H. D. Betz, *The Sermon on the Mount*, 320, 566–67.

[103] D. Allison continues: "Jesus is not 'Son of man' in Matthew 1–4, nor is there a single Christological title in the speech in cha 18. In cha 10 Jesus is once 'the Son of man' but never 'Lord,' 'Christ,' or 'Son of David,' or 'Son of God.' 'Son of David' is missing from every single major discourse, 'Son (of God)' from every discourse save chaps. 24–25. And references to Jesus' salvific death and resurrection are very few and far between in the first half of the Gospel" (D. Allison, *JBL* 117/1 [1998] 137).

If, however, "Special M" material, such as this passage on fasting, originated in Q, as suggested by its contradiction of other Jesus traditions *and* its continuity with Q and traditions concerning the Baptist, *and* its thorough integration into the highly organized, deliberately-crafted, and largely-Q SM, the arguments of both Betz and his critics are moot. No middle person in possession of the same sources as the author of the Gospel of Matthew needs to be postulated for an understanding of how this pericope made its way into the SM. To be sure, arguments for the inclusion of certain *Sondergut* passages in reconstructions of Q must not be based solely on a perceived Baptist *Tendenz* of Q, but also on the inclusion of Aramaisms, lack of Christology, and other distinguishing characteristics of Q. The problem confounding this otherwise sound methodological approach is, however, *most of Q's distinguishing characteristics are shared by the SM.*[104] Careful negotiation of connections to John the Baptist, therefore, have a heretofore unappreciated importance in the discussion.[105] Mt 6:16–18 "on fasting" is a single example. A few additional examples help to demonstrate the point.

Mt 6:1–18

Indeed a reevaluation of the SM's entire cultic section (Mt 6:1–18) is warranted for yet another reason. Three arguments for the inclusion of "Special M" passage 6:1–18 in Q are presented in this section. First, all three parts of the instruction emphasize that the recommended duties – almsgiving, prayer and fasting – be fulfilled in private:[106] for example, Mt 6:6: "… pray to your Father who is in se-

---

[104] An important exception is absence of Son of Man sayings in the SM. The concept does, however, appear in SP/Lk 6:22 (cf. SM/Mt 5:11); see Betz, *The Sermon on the Mount*, 148–49.

[105] Lack of Christology in the SM (according to the disputed argument of Betz) coincides with this established characteristic of Q, drawing the two into close connection (*The Sermon on the Mount*, 145; idem, "The Problem of Christology in the Sermon on the Mount," in Theodore W. Jennings Jr., ed., *Text and Logos: The Humanistic Interpretation of the New Testament* [FS for Hendrikus W. Boers] [Atlanta: Scholars, 1990] 191–209; repr. in idem, *Synoptische Studien*, 230–48). On Q, John Kloppenborg writes: "… it is clear that Q represents an important and distinctive moment in early Christian theologizing – in particular, because there is no evidence that Q had developed a view that found particular salvific meaning in the death of Jesus himself. In its appeal to the Deuteronomistic view of the prophets – as ignored, persecuted, and even killed – one can see an instance of one set of Jesus' followers *availing themselves of resources from the tradition* in order to render intelligible their own experience …" (*Excavating Q*, 164; emphasis added). Also, cf. the following comment by James M. Robinson: "For Easter does not fall here, or at the beginning or end of Q, or anywhere in Q. Q has the timelessness of eternal truth, or at least of wisdom literature" ("Jesus – From Easter to Valentinus [or to the Apostles' Creed]," *JBL* 101 [1982] 23).

[106] As H. D. Betz points out, emphasis in this section of the SM (6:1–18) resides, by privilege of position, with the giving of alms (6: 1–4) (*The Sermon on the Mount*, 353–61). This emphasis may coincide with the intention of Q 7:29–30 ("For John came to you … the tax collectors and … [responded positively] [but the religious authorities rejected him]") (ET: *The Critical Edition of Q*, 138–39) as well as John's teaching in Lk 3:10–14. In the latter passage, three different groups of people request that John explain the appropriate response to baptism.

cret and your Father, seeing in secret, will reward you (πρόσευξαι τῷ πατρί σου τῷ ἐν τῷ κρυπτῷ· καὶ ὁ πατήρ σου ὁ βλέπων ἐν τῷ κρυπτῷ ἀποδώσει σοι)"

To two of the three groups John replies that the appropriate response is honest management of finances. Interestingly, as Dennis Hamm has argued, the type of conversion exhorted in this passage by John (turning to a righteous management of finances) is demonstrated perfectly in the "Special L" repentance of Zacchaeus ("Zacchaeus Revisited Once More: A Story of Vindication or Conversion?" *Bib* 72 [1991] 249–52). Furthermore, in the conclusion to the Zacchaeus story, Jesus pronounces Zacchaeus "a son of Abraham." This assertion echoes John's teaching that "God is able from these stones to raise up children to Abraham" (Lk 3:8/Mt 3:9). John's teaching to the soldiers that they should be content with their wages (Lk 3:14) also aptly summarizes the theme of the "Special M" parable of the laborers in the vineyard (Mt 20:1–16). The verb of lending, δανίζειν is a NT *hapax legomenon*, occurring only in Q 6:34–35 and resembling the point of Lk 3:10–14. Also, like the Baptist teaching in Lk 3:10–14, the parable of the Good Samaritan curiously advertises the theme of fair remittance for services (Lk 10:35). Cf. also "Special L" warning against avarice, Lk 12:13–15. Alms are a Lukan interpolation in Q 11:41 and Lk 12:33. See *The Critical Edition of Q*, 272 n. 3; *Q Parallels*, 112. Cf. the "Special L" parable of the dishonest manager in Lk 16:1–12, 14–15, with its themes of the dangers of wealth and sound financial management, to the parable of the Pharisee and the tax collector (18:9–14), where the theme of the intention behind almsgiving and prayer (as in the SM) is portrayed. Q's inclusion of Lk 16:13, 16–18 may suggest Lk 16:1–12, 14–15 also belonged to Q. The inclusion of the related parable in Q 19:12–13, 15–24, 26 is perhaps the best argument for such an addition. Also, 17:1–2, 3–4, 6 suggest the same possibility for the parable of the rich man and Lazarus in Lk 16:9–31 ("Special L"), the theme of which is also financial management, but incorporates other important Baptist tradition themes such as Abraham (16:22, 23, 24, 25, 29, 30), a negative disposition toward feasting (16:19, 21), burning flames (16:24), warning/punishment (16:28), and repentance (16:30). This passage reflects a doubtful and negative approach to the idea of *post mortem* appearances. Finally, the unusual "Special L" teaching from Lk 14:28–33 about building a tower and waging a war resembles 3:10–14 about calculating the cost of discipleship – sensible themes on which to expound a message for soldiers. Whether, according to E. Lupieri, John's "wild" food exempted him from tithing is irrelevant to the question of whether John exhorted his audience(s) to tithe. In any case, the present author agrees with Lupieri that John's behavior may have represented John's own and more strict *halakhah* ("'The Law and the Prophets Were until John': John the Baptist between Jewish Halakhot and Christian History of Salvation," 53–54). Also interesting is the question of paying taxes. From the emphasis on sound financial decisions in Lk 3:10–14 it seems plausible to deduce that John (and followers) paid taxes and exhorted others to do so as well. The recurring question of whether Jesus (and followers) paid taxes and exhorted others to do so remains unanswered. Mt 22:15–22 and 17:24–27 may suggest Jesus did not and that this was an issue on which the two men were divided. Cf. also the behavior of Judas the Galilean who exhorted his followers not to pay tribute to the pagan state and called those who did cowards (Josephus, *Ant.* 18.4–10, 23–25; ἀποτίμησις in *Ant.* 18.4). Pierson Parker agrees that Jesus' reply to conspirators regarding Roman taxation (Lk 20:22–26) recalls the words of John the Baptist in Lk 3:13–14: "Extort no more taxes than the amount prescribed…"; tax no one wrongly with "threats and false accusations." That this issue was raised at Jesus' trial ("Special L" insertion in Lk 23:2: "We found this man perverting our nation, forbidding us to pay taxes to the emperor…") again may imply Jesus differed from John on the issue of taxes. Whereas John exhorted followers to pay no more than you must, Jesus may have heightened the demand exhorting followers to pay no more ("Jesus, John the Baptist, and the Herods," 4–11). Finally, key Baptist themes of repentance or destruction constitute the clear warning of the "Special L" examples of the Galileans "whose blood Pilate mingled with their sacrifices" or the eighteen upon whom the tower of Siloam fell (Lk 13:1–5), as well as "Special L" parable of the fig tree planted in the vineyard, requiring a final chance to bear fruit before it is cut down (Lk 13:6–9).

(cf. 6:4, 18). Betz argues, and the present author agrees, that this privacy clause may suggest a critique of public worship.[107] The question, therefore, arises whether such a theological doctrine of "inconspicuous piety,"[108] as Betz refers to it, more likely originated in traditions following an urban ministry emphasizing public performances of healing and exorcism or a wilderness ministry emphasizing inner repentance demonstrated in acts of piety followed by baptism.[109]

Second, Mt 6:6 specifies that in order to pray "in secret" one should: "go into your room (εἴσελθε εἰς τὸ ταμεῖόν σου)." Q 17:23 juxtaposes this same word "room (ταμεῖον)" with "wilderness (ἔρημος)" in its recommendation that in neither place should one search for the Son of Man because when he comes his appearance will be like lightning (Q 17:24). The saying assumes that "room" and "wilderness" are the two natural choices to expect the Son of Man.

The word is taken into Q here on the basis of Mt 24:26[110] because its Lukan parallel (Lk 17:23–24) excludes it. The word ταμεῖον does occur, however, in Luke's version of two other Q sayings: Lk 12:3 (Mt 10:27) and Lk 12:24 (Mt 6:26 [SM]), but *The Critical Edition of Q* omits this word from its reconstruction of these verses because it is absent from parallels in Mt 10:27 and 6:26.[111] The curious fact is that Mt 6:6 and 24:26 and Lk 12:3 and 12:24 are the only NT occurrences of this word. To be consistent, therefore, either the word should be omitted from Q 17:23 (it is not in Luke) or Q 12:3 and 12:24 should include the word, "indoors," confining all NT occurrences of this word to Q except Mt 6:6 which then, as a "Special M" passage, might be considered Q partly on this basis.

Furthermore, the "room" in which the disciples are exhorted to pray in Mt 6:6 is contrasted with "synagogues" and "street corners" where "hypocrites" are said to pray. In light of the other NT applications of the word, ταμεῖον, this contrast suggests, not just a critique of *public* (with Betz), but *city* cult and worship. According to Ulrich Luz, ταμεῖον in Mt 6:6 refers to "the storage room which was always present in the Palestinian farmhouse,"[112] rendering the translation: "And whenever you pray, do not be like the hypocrites, for they love to pray

---

[107] H. D. Betz, *The Sermon on the Mount,* 360. Cf. also Q 13:26 where teaching "on the streets," similar to eating and drinking (disposing of the fast) before the appropriate time, results in damnation.

[108] H. D. Betz, *The Sermon on the Mount,* 343–46.

[109] H. D. Betz does discuss the difficulty of the doctrine (*The Sermon on the Mount,* 339, 343, 347). Cf. C. Kraeling, *John the Baptist,* 152–54; Paul W. Hollenbach, "Conversion of Jesus: From Jesus the Baptizer to Jesus the Healer," 196–219.

[110] In Mt 24:26 the plural form is used: ἐν τοῖς ταμείοις. Cf. also the uncontracted form: τὸ ταμεῖον.

[111] *The Critical Edition of Q,* 292–93, 338–39.

[112] Ulrich Luz, *Matthew 1–7,* trans. Wilhelm C. Linss (Minneapolis: Fortress, 1989) 359; German edition, *Das Evangelium nach Matthäus* (EKKNT; Zurich/Einsiedeln/Cologne: Benziger and Neukirchen-Vluyn: Neukirchener, 1985).

standing in the synagogues and at the street corners .... But whenever you pray, go into your storage room...." Such rooms were an architectural feature of houses in rural areas where harvesting took place. A connection to John and his imagery for the impending judgment is plain.[113] A paraphrase of the message of Q 17:23–24 might read: Do not search for the Son of Man anywhere, in either the wilderness where we dwell or in the storehouses where we expect him to arise and clear his threshing floor. Do not search for him at all because the *location* of his first appearance, like lightning, cannot be anticipated.

A third and final observation about Mt 6:1–18 concerns occurrences of the word ὑποκριτής. All three of the cultic institutions recommended by the SM (almsgiving, prayer and fasting) are linked to each other by their comparisons with the purported behavior of "hypocrites" (often associated with Pharisees in Matthew): (1) Mt 6:2: "Then whenever you give alms do not sound a trumpet before yourself, as the hypocrites do in the synagogues[114] and in the lanes, so that they may be glorified by people"; (2) Mt 6:5: "And whenever you pray, do not be like the hypocrites; for they love to pray standing in the synagogues and at the street corners, so they may be seen by people"; and (3) Mt 6:16: "And whenever you fast, do not look downcast, like the hypocrites, for they hide their faces so as to reveal to people that they are fasting." Citing Ulrich Wilckens' *TDNT* article and others, H. D. Betz argues the references here are not merely slanderous, rather all three suggest an original meaning of "hypocrites" as "playactors."

The "hypocrite" here is not primarily one who is simply morally dishonest or a dissembler and faker, but the "typical" religious practitioner whose external performance sharply conflicts with fundamental religious and moral principles. The reason for the discrepancy is not hard to guess. Besides the usual ignorance and folly, it is selfishness and arrogance. People of such character, it is assumed, love to "perform" (ποιεῖν) "in the synagogue and in the streets" (ἐν ταῖς συναγωγαῖς καὶ ἐν ταῖς ῥύμαις).[115]

To better understand "hypocrites" in the SM, occurrences of the expression in Matthew 23 offer a comparison. The SM and Matthew 23 share a curious integration of primarily "Special M" and Q materials. They are, however, further related by their references to "hypocrites." The address, "hypocrites" occurs three times in the SM (above) and six times in Matthew 23 (below):[116]

(1) Mt 23:13: Οὐαὶ δὲ ὑμῖν, γραμματεῖς καὶ Φαρισαῖοι ὑποκριταί, ὅτι κλείετε τὴν βασιλείαν τῶν οὐρανῶν ἔμπροσθεν τῶν ἀνθρώπων· ὑμεῖς γὰρ οὐκ εἰσέρχεσθε οὐδὲ τοὺς εἰσερχομένους ἀφίετε εἰσελθεῖν.

---

[113] Cf. also the "Special L" insertion in Lk 6:38: "A good measure – pressed, shaken and overflowing – will be placed in your lap." This curious saying possesses the Baptist theme of the coming judgment (e.g., Lk 6:37) as a harvest.

[114] Cf. συναγωγή, Q 12:11.

[115] *The Sermon on the Mount*, 356–57, 361, 419–21; cf. *Did.* 8:1. Ulrich Wilckens, "ὑποκρίνομαι," *TDNT* 8.559–71.

[116] Cf. also 23:28, ὑποκρίσεῶς.

Woe to you, scribes and Pharisees, hypocrites! You block the kingdom of heaven before people. For you do not enter, and you prohibit those coming to enter.

(2) Mt 23:15: Οὐαὶ ὑμῖν, γραμματεῖς καὶ Φαρισαῖοι ὑποκριταί, ὅτι περιάγετε τὴν θάλασσαν καὶ τὴν ξηρὰν ποιῆσαι ἕνα προσήλυτον, καὶ ὅταν γένηται ποιεῖτε αὐτὸν υἱὸν γεέννης διπλότερον ὑμῶν.

Woe to you scribes and Pharisees, hypocrites! You cross the sea and the land to make one proselyte, and then you make him twice a son of hell as yourselves.[117]

(3) Mt 23:23: Οὐαὶ ὑμῖν, γραμματεῖς καὶ Φαρισαῖοι ὑποκριταί, ὅτι ἀποδεκατοῦτε τὸ ἡδύοσμον καὶ τὸ ἄνηθον καὶ τὸ κύμινον καὶ ἀφήκατε τὰ βαρύτερα τοῦ νόμου, τὴν κρίσιν καὶ τὸ ἔλεος καὶ τὴν πίστιν· ταῦτα [δὲ] ἔδει ποιῆσαι κἀκεῖνα μὴ ἀφιέναι.

Woe to you, scribes and Pharisees, hypocrites! You tithe mint and dill and cumin and have neglected the weightier matters of the law: justice and mercy and faith. It is necessary to do these things also not neglecting those things.

(4) Mt 23:25: Οὐαὶ ὑμῖν, γραμματεῖς καὶ Φαρισαῖοι ὑποκριταί, ὅτι καθαρίζετε τὸ ἔξωθεν τοῦ ποτηρίου καὶ τῆς παροψίδος, ἔσωθεν δὲ γέμουσιν ἐξ ἁρπαγῆς καὶ ἀκρασίας.

Woe to you, scribes and Pharisees, hypocrites! You clean the outside of the cup and the plate, but inside they are full of greed and intemperance.

(5) Mt 23:27: Οὐαὶ ὑμῖν, γραμματεῖς καὶ Φαρισαῖοι ὑποκριταί, ὅτι παρομοιάζετε τάφοις κεκονιαμένοις, οἵτινες ἔξωθεν μὲν φαίνονται ὡραῖοι, ἔσωθεν δὲ γέμουσιν ὀστέων νεκρῶν καὶ πάσης ἀκαθαρσίας.

Woe to you, scribes and Pharisees, hypocrites! You are like whitewashed tombs, which on the outside appear beautiful, but on the inside are full of dead bones and all kinds of uncleanness.

(6) Mt 23:29: Οὐαὶ ὑμῖν, γραμματεῖς καὶ Φαρισαῖοι ὑποκριταί, ὅτι οἰκοδομεῖτε τοὺς τάφους τῶν προφητῶν καὶ κοσμεῖτε τὰ μνημεῖα τῶν δικαίων, καὶ λέγετε, Εἰ ἤμεθα ἐν ταῖς ἡμέραις τῶν πατέρων ἡμῶν, οὐκ ἂν ἤμεθα αὐτῶν κοινωνοὶ ἐν τῷ αἵματι τῶν προφητῶν.

Woe to you, scribes and Pharisees, hypocrites! You build the tombs of the prophets and decorate the graves of the righteous, and you say, "If we had lived in the days of our fathers, we would not have played a part with them in the blood of the prophets."

---

[117] A similar case might be made for the word, γέεννα which occurs in Mt 5:22 and 29 as well as 23:15, 33, providing another link between these passages. The severity of the language, the emphasis on condemnation in judgment and punishment in all four cases, as well as in Mt 18:9/Mk 9:43, 45, 47, are connections to Baptist traditions. The relevant passage in Q is 12:5. The only other NT occurrence of this word is Jas 3:6. A similar case can be made for the word, θησαυρός in Q 12:33–34/Mt 6:19–20 and Q 6:45/Mt 12:35. Baptist connections can be identified with occurrences in Mt 13:44, 52 and even the parable of the rich man (Mk 10:21/ Mt 19:21/Lk 18:22). The three remaining NT examples are: 2 Cor 4:7, Col 2:3, and Heb 11:26. The verb, θησαυρίζειν is likewise rare; appearing in Mt 6:19–20 and Lk 12:21, it too may be relevant in this argument.

In these passages, as in the SM, not only is the word "hypocrite" used to refer to the purported audience, but it reflects an overall tone of condemnation and punishment. Such a tone matches both Baptist traditions and Q. What is more, these six passages from Mt 23 provide direct thematic and literary connections to Baptist traditions and Q. Q citations can be identified at Mt 23:4, 6–7, 13, 23, 25–26, 27–28, 29–31 and 34–36. Five other literary connections include (1) the woe form (Mt 23:13, 16, 23, 25, 27, 29, 37–39);[118] (2) the expression, "father," (Mt 23:9);[119] (3) a reference to the "sending" of the prophets (Mt 23:34/Q 11:49), and to their death, specifically the spilling of their blood (Mt 23: 29–31, 35/Q 11:49–51); (4) a reference to the kingdom of God, a probable reference to repentance preceding baptism (Mt 23:26); (5) and most importantly, John's signature address to his crowds, "Snakes, generation of vipers!" (Mt 23:33/Q 3:7a)

Furthermore, although Mt 6:2, 5, and 16 are not included in modern reconstructions of Q, two SM passages containing "hypocrite" do occur in Q (in total: SM – 3; Mt 23–6; Q – 2): (1) Q 6:42 (a probable reference to disciples): "Hypocrite (ὑποκριτά), first cast out from your eye the beam and then you will see to cast out the speck from your brother's eye"; and, (2) Q 12:56, "Hypocrites (ὑποκριταί)! You know how to interpret the appearance of the earth and sky, why do you not know how to interpret the present time?" Although present in the first passage (6:42), *The Critical Edition of Q* excludes ὑποκριταί in its reconstruction of the latter passage (12:56), designating it "Luke's."[120] For Luke, however, the only occurrence of the expression, other than these two, is 13:15, the "Special L" narrative of the healing of a crippled woman. To the synagogue leaders who dispute Jesus' healing on the Sabbath, Jesus replies, "You hypocrites! Does not each of you on the Sabbath let loose his ox or donkey from the manger, and lead it to drink (ὑποκριταί, ἕκαστος ὑμῶν τῷ σαββάτῳ οὐ λύει τὸν βοῦν αὐτοῦ ἢ τὸν ὄνον ἀπὸ τῆς φάτνης καὶ ἀπαγαγὼν ποτίζει)?" Curiously, this exclamation is followed by another with, as others have shown, clear links to Baptist traditions: "And ought this woman, a *daughter of Abraham,* whom Satan bound for eighteen years, not be loosed from this chain on the Sabbath day (ταύτην δὲ θυγατέρα Ἀβραὰμ οὖσαν, ἣν ἔδησεν ὁ σατανᾶς ἰδοὺ δέκα καὶ ὀκτὼ ἔτη, οὐκ ἔδει λυθῆναι ἀπὸ τοῦ δεσμοῦ τούτου τῇ ἡμέρᾳ τοῦ σαββάτου)?" (v. 16; cf. Q 3:8, 13:28/Mt 3:9)[121]

A final, relevant occurrence of the word "hypocrite" is found in the Matthean version of the parable of the faithful and unfaithful servants (Mt 24:51). This parable provides a challenge for source critics. Versions of it arise in Matthew,

---

[118] The Sermon on the Plain's woes ("Special L") resound with the Baptist theme of future despair for those eating and, therefore, "full" now (too soon) (Lk 6:25).

[119] If John composed the *Pater Noster* then use of the expression "father" to refer to God in the four gospels may have originated with him.

[120] *The Critical Edition of Q*, 390–91, n. 1.

[121] Cf. υἱὸς Ἀβραάμ, Lk 19:9.

Mark and Luke. That said, the consensus of the International Q Project is that it originated in Q (12:42–46). Only the Matthean version, however, includes the expression, "hypocrites:" καὶ διχοτομήσει αὐτὸν καὶ τὸ μέρος αὐτοῦ μετὰ τῶν ὑποκριτῶν θήσει· ἐκεῖ ἔσται ὁ κλαυθμὸς καὶ ὁ βρυγμὸς τῶν ὀδόντων (v. 51). Interestingly, Baptist elements such as the theme of condemnation and punishment pervade Q's version of the parable.[122] Moreover, Q's version relates that when the unfaithful servant errantly places faith in the notion that "My master (ὁ κύριός μου) is delayed," he "begins to beat his fellow slaves, and eats and drinks with the drunken" (Q 12:45). Such an advisory against "eating and drinking with those being drunk" (ἐσθίῃ δὲ καὶ πίνῃ μετὰ τῶν μεθυόντων) resonates with passages indicting Jesus and his followers for offensive meal fellowship, failure to observe fasting regulations, and drunkenness (e.g., Lk 5:27–32; 11:37–38; 14:12–24; 15:2; Mk 2:18–22; Q 7:34?; Acts 2:13, 15). If followers of the Baptist originally taught this parable of Q 12:35–48, then the "delay of the Master" that resulted in lapsing of responsibilities might represent a Baptist polemic against Christians.[123] To restate the parable: Jesus, thinking the Master is delayed, begins to eat and drink with those being drunk. In other words, Luke's delay of the *parousia* (à la Conzelmann) might, originally, have been Jesus' or his followers' – a reaction to the postponement of John's message of an imminent eschatological end.

Other than the examples discussed above, the designation, "hypocrites" occurs only three other times in the NT[124] in Mk 7:6/Mt 15:7 (question about hand-washing before eating) and Mt 22:18 (question about paying taxes; cf. ὑπόκρισις in Mk 12:15/Lk 12:1).[125] All examples demonstrate literary links between Baptist traditions and Q.

Thus the argument of this section is three-fold. First, Betz's observation of the SM theme of "inconspicuous piety" more likely originated in a wilderness ministry emphasizing inner repentance demonstrated in acts of piety followed by baptism than an urban ministry emphasizing public performances of healing and exorcism, recommending Baptist connections for the "Special M" passages in the SM where this exhortation occurs (Mt 6:4; 6; and 18). Second, occurrence of the word ταμεῖον in Mt 6:6 also suggests this passage originated in Q. And,

---

[122] The macarism in v. 46 may also provide a link to Baptist traditions.

[123] We often reserve our most heated criticisms for family or other close partners. Luke's proposed familial relationship between John and Jesus (Lk 1:36) might provide background for these circumstances between John and Jesus. While the two share numerous points in common, even minor differences can prove sources of great resentment.

[124] In the NT gospels ὑπόκρισις is virtually interchangeable with ὑποκριτής. The three occurrences of the former are treated in my argument (cf. Mt 23:28; Mk 12:15/Lk 12:1). Three additional examples of ὑπόκρισις occur in Gal 2:13; 1 Tim 4:2; 1 Pet 2:1.

[125] Lk 12:1 is excluded from Q, whereas Lk 12:2–3 is not. See *The Critical Edition of Q*, 290–95.

third, occurrences of the word ὑποκριταί (Mt 6:2, 5 and 16) share significant links with both Baptist traditions and Q.

Mt 7:13–23

Yet another question arises with respect to the SM section on eschatological warnings (7:13–23). As Betz shows, this section is comprised of three parts. In the first part (7:13–14), the "Special M" "two ways" tradition, two opposing lifestyles are outlined by means of two metaphors, not neatly complementary: (1) the narrow gate/hard road leading to "life"; and (2) the wide gate/easy road leading to "destruction." Presumably, Jesus' teaching is the difficult "way" leading to life. According to another saying in Mt 11:28–30, however, Jesus' way is not difficult: "Come to me all those tired and burdened …. For my yoke is easy, my load is light" (Δεῦτε πρός με πάντες οἱ κοπιῶντες καὶ πεφορτισμένοι …. γὰρ ζυγός μου χρηστὸς καὶ τὸ φορτίον μου ἐλαφρόν ἐστιν).[126] With Betz, this SM pericope evokes a context in which two opposing teachings are contrasted: a narrow gate and hard road with a wide gate and easy road.[127] The context for such a saying (Mt 7:13–14) is best evaluated in light of the other two pieces of this section on eschatological warnings (Mt 7:15–20; 7:21–23).

First in order of appearance is the "Special M" counsel: "Beware of false prophets, who come to you in sheep's clothing (ἐν ἐνδύμασιν προβάτων) but inside are rapacious (ἅρπαγες) wolves" (Mt 7:15).[128] According to Matthew and Mark, John dwells in the wilderness, "clothed with camel hair and a leather belt around his waist" and eating "locusts and wild honey"(Mk 1:6/Mt 3:4). Jesus, however, as an urban-dwelling prophet, wore, according to Ulrich Luz, a mantle or pelt of sheep.[129] If John fasted and Jesus did not, the polemic of this verse too may be directed against Christians – a polemic extended by the phrase: "but inside are rapacious wolves" (Mt 7:15), in which "wolves" is a metaphor for urban lives of predatory voracity and gluttony, forming a second prong of attack.[130] As

---

[126] *Did.* 6.2.

[127] I would agree with H. D. Betz that the "difficult road" *is* the SM, differing only in that much, if not all, of the SM's teaching was John's (*The Sermon on the Mount*, 521–27).

[128] On ψευδοπροφῆται in the Gospel of Matthew, cf. also Mt 24:11–14.

[129] Cf. Mt 3:4//Mk 1:6 in which John is clothed in "camel's hair" (τρίχας καμήλου). Cf. also Q 7:24–25; *Gos. Thom.* § 78. This interpretation is possible whether or not sheepskin was the traditional garb of a prophet (1 Kgs 19:13, 19; 2 Kgs 2:8, 13; Zech 13:4; Josephus, *Vi.* 2; and 1 Clem 17:1). See U. Luz, *Matthew 1–7*, 442 n. 24; H. D. Betz, *The Sermon on the Mount*, 535.

[130] "Wolves" is additionally ironic in that wolves are extremely menacing in cities. Cf. also Paul Hoffman's view that the image of God's lamb, Israel, among Gentile wolves is inverted here (*Studien zur Theologie der Logienquelle*, NTAbh n.s., 8 [Münster: Aschendorff, 1972; 2nd ed., 1975; 3rd ed., 1980] 294–95). Such an inversion demonstrates thematic connection to John's statement in Q 3:8 that God can produce children of Abraham from rocks. Q 13:28–29 should be interpreted in the same manner as Q 3:8 (God's ability to make children of Abraham from rocks); neither implies a Gentile mission. Similarly, that many will come from sunrise and sunset and recline with Abraham, Isaac and Jacob in the kingdom does not imply that

part of Q, these verses would be connected to the disciples' commission: "Run along! Look, I send you as sheep (ἄρνας) among wolves" (Q 10:3) in which John's disciples are not wolves disguised as sheep, but actual sheep.[131]

The third and final section of the SM's eschatological warnings (also "Special M") further characterizes these false prophets as prophesying, exorcising demons, and performing miracles (Mt 7:22). Various opponents have been proposed to identify these false prophets. Citing H. D. Betz:

> Modern scholars have been more than ready to propose identifications: Zealots, Pharisees, Essenes, rigoristic Jewish Christians, followers of the apostle Paul, or Hellenistic antinomians.[132]

Betz, thinking of an author of the SM in the 50s,[133] favors Paul as the original opponent of this "Special M" tradition.[134] In line with the present argument, however, this passage may be traced to even earlier (?) layers of tradition and directed against an opponent not hitherto identified: Jesus, known for all three indictments – prophecy, exorcism, and miracles. This passage coheres well with Q's anti-miraculous stance noted above.

Taking up, then, the unanswered question above concerning the context of the first warning against the wide gate and easy road, if the second and third of the three eschatological warnings represent anti-Christian polemic, the first

---

those coming are Gentiles. It simply suggests that Jewish parentage, apart from the bearing of good fruit and John's baptism, is no guarantee of entrance into God's kingdom. Only Jewish heritage, *with* the bearing of good fruit and John's baptism, can provide such a guarantee. As R. Bultmann writes, "It is not that Q had a universalist perspective. One should perhaps even consider whether the saying of Matthew that restricts the mission to the Jews derived from Q (Matt 10:5–6) ("What the Saying Source Reveals about the Early Church," in J. Kloppenborg, *The Shape of Q*, 32). The Roman centurion, people of Tyre and Sidon, men of Nineveh and the Queen of Sheba are all Gentiles who put the Jews to shame in Q (Dieter Lührmann, "Q in the History of Early Christianity," in J. Kloppenborg, *The Shape of Q*, 61). Q is interested in judgment against the Jews. The Gentiles provide the foil for Jewish obstinacy and the resulting judgments throughout history. As James Dunn points out, God's wrath was frequently directed against Israel for flouting covenant obligations. Dunn cites Exod 32:10–12; Num 25:1–4; Deut 29:16–28; 2 Chr 24:18; Isa 9:18–10:5; Jer 7:16–20; 25:6; Ezek 22; Mic 5:10–15; *Jub.* 15:34; 36:10; 1QS 2:15; 5:12)" ("John the Baptist's Use of Scripture," 47–48). Finally, Judaism of this period may have included Gentiles (Dieter Georgi, *The Opponents of Paul in Second Corinthians* [Philadelphia: Fortress, 1986] 83–117).

[131] Cf. *Did.* 16.3; Jn 10:16, 18, 26–30. Commonly identified as Gentiles, the "other sheep" of Jn 10:16 make as much sense as followers of the Baptist: "But I have sheep which are not from this farmyard (καὶ ἄλλα πρόβατα ἔχω ἃ οὐκ ἔστιν ἐκ τῆς αὐλῆς ταύτης)." R. Bultmann takes v. 16 as an interruption signifying some "ecclesial interest" (*The Gospel of John*, trans. G. R. Beasley-Murray, R. W. N. Hoare, and J. K. Riches [Philadelphia: Westminster, 1971] 383–84). Also, as above, the version of the saying in Matthew (Mt 10:16) shares two images associated with the Baptist: both "snakes" and "doves": "See, I am sending you out like sheep into the midst of wolves; so be wise as serpents and innocent as doves."

[132] H. D. Betz, *The Sermon on the Mount*, 534, references in nn. 130–35.

[133] H. D. Betz, *The Sermon on the Mount*, 88.

[134] H. D. Betz, *The Sermon on the Mount*, 527–31, 534–36.

may too, making Q the most plausible original context of the first warning, too. The interpretation of this verse then becomes: Jesus' gate is wide, his way, easy whereas John's gate is narrow, *his* way, difficult. This entire section fits Oscar Cullmann's interpretation of Jn 10:7–10, a pericope that incorporates the elements of both "sheep" and "gate":

Ἀμὴν ἀμὴν λέγω ὑμῖν ὅτι ἐγώ εἰμι ἡ θύρα τῶν προβάτων. πάντες ὅσοι ἦλθον [πρὸ ἐμοῦ] κλέπται εἰσὶν καὶ λῃσταί, ἀλλ᾽ οὐκ ἤκουσαν αὐτῶν τὰ πρόβατα. ἐγώ εἰμι ἡ θύρα· δι᾽ ἐμοῦ ἐάν τις εἰσέλθῃ σωθήσεται καὶ εἰσελεύσεται καὶ ἐξελεύσεται καὶ νομὴν εὑρήσει. ὁ κλέπτης οὐκ ἔρχεται εἰ μὴ ἵνα κλέψῃ καὶ θύσῃ καὶ ἀπολέσῃ· ἐγὼ ἦλθον ἵνα ζωὴν ἔχωσιν καὶ περισσὸν ἔχωσιν.

Amen, amen, I tell you, I am the sheep's gate. All those who came before me are robbers and rogues; but the sheep did not listen to them. I am the gate. Whoever enters through me will be saved and will move about freely and find a grazing field. The robber does not come except to steal and slaughter and ruin. I came that they may have life, and have it abundantly.

Oscar Cullmann argues that in this passage, similar to Jn 1:16 and 3:31, πάντες includes John the Baptist and represents polemic against those arguing John's messiahship on the basis of chronological priority.[135] Interestingly, nestled in this section in Matthew, as the second half of the second eschatological teaching (7:16–20), is the teaching on "fruits," mentioned above, *attributed to John in Q 3:9b, but to Jesus in Mt 7:19.*

Mt 5:3–12, 25:31–46

Two final notes complete this investigation of candidates for Q from the Matthean *Sondergut*. First, H. D. Betz posits that pronouncement of Jesus' beatitudes may have first occurred in a ritual setting such as baptism.[136] If H. D. Betz is correct that the *Sitz im Leben* of the SM's macarisms (Mt 5:3–12) is one of multiple baptisms, then, although Betz has in mind the baptismal activity of the early church, their *origination*, too, (part Q [Q 6:20–23,]/part *Sondergut*) is more consistent with traditions concerning John.[137]

---

[135] O. Cullman, "Ὁ ὀπίσω μου ἐρχόμενος," 181–82. One thinks here also of the servant/ disciple not greater than his master/teacher sayings of Mt 10:24–25; Jn 13:16 and 15:20 which also seem to indicate competition between Jesus and John – more specifically an unfavorable disposition of John toward Jesus. The following Q saying is also relevant: "Nobody can serve two masters (κυρίοις); for a person will either hate the one and love the other, or be devoted to the one and despise the other" (Q 16:13a).

[136] Betz qualifies that the question "cannot be answered with any certainty" (*The Sermon on the Mount*, 95). He also notes that the declaration, "You are my beloved son with whom I am well pleased" in Jesus' baptism (Mt 3:17) comes "close to a beatitude, but the literary form is different" (95).

[137] H. D. Betz cites Tomas Arvedson as sharing his view of the original setting of the Beatitudes as ritual (*Das Mysterium Christi: Eine Studie zu Mt 11,25–30* [Arbeiten und Mitteilungen aus dem neutestamentlichen Seminar zu Uppsala 7; Leipzig: Lorentz; Uppsala: Lundeqvistska

Second, outside the SM, Mt 25:31–46, a "Special M" passage of great importance for the history of Christian tradition, possesses ties to Baptist traditions.
This famous so-called "Judgment against the Gentiles" teaching includes seminal Baptist themes, such as judgment (e.g., Q 3:7–9), the kingdom (e.g., Mt 3:2),
reference to God as "Father," (e.g., Lk 11:1–2), eternal punishment (e.g., Q 3:7),

---

Boekhandlen, 1937] 94–104). Although a tradition of Jesus' baptizing exists (Jn 3:22 and 4:1;
cf. Jn 4:2); John's is the more secure (with NT and Josephus, *Ant.* 18.116–17), making his the
more likely setting for the composition of macarisms. Q has a surplus of macarisms – at least
eight scattered throughout the collection; cf. Q 6:20–23; 7:23; 15:9b; 10:23–24; 12:43, 13:35.
H. D. Betz, *The Sermon on the Mount*, 92–105. The Gospel of Mark, in contrast, has only two
macarisms (Mk 11:9–10). Also, Q uses μακάριος (except 13:35) whereas Mark uses εὐλογέω.
Cf. the comment by A. D. Jacobson, "What is striking, then, i[s] (*sic*) the relative abundance
of macarisms in Q and their scarcity in Mark ("The Literary Unity of Q," 373). Jacobson
enumerates other contrasts between the Gospel of Mark and Q, including the many woes in Q
contrasted with only two (Jacobson, however, incorrectly finds none, "The Literary Unity of
Q," 101) in Mark; the presence of four "eschatological correlatives" in Q (11:30; 17:24, 26, 29,
30), contrasted with none in Mark (see Richard A. Edwards, "The Eschatological Correlative as
Gattung in the New Testament," *ZNW* 60 [1969] 9–20); the propensity for sayings concerning
judgment in Q, contrasted with none in Mark ("The Literary Unity of Q," 102); association
between the "day" and the Son of Man in Q, not evident in Mark ("The Literary Unity of Q,"
103); the rarity of both conflict and miracle stories in Q, with eleven in Mark ("The Literary
Unity of Q," 103); use of metaphor and comparison in Q less common in Mark ("The Literary
Unity of Q," 104); the eschatological setting of most parables in Q different from their setting in
normal daily life in Mark ("The Literary Unity of Q," 104); and the parabolic sayings beginning
with τίς ἐξ ὑμων ("who among you") (Q 12:25; 11:11; 15:4), absent from Mark ("The Literary Unity of Q," 104). Jacobson concludes that because Mark and Q comprise different forms
(miracles and conflict stories vs. macarisms, woes, eschatological correlatives and prophetic
threats), they represent independent traditions (105). Finally, positioned after the Q block on
the theme of anxiety (Q 12:22b–31) and before two Q pericopes regarding the judgment (Q
12:49, 51, 53, 54–56), the parable of the watchful slaves in Q 12:42–46 includes a macarism
(12:43) together with other Baptist themes such as a comment on the proper allocation of food
and drink (12:42, 45) and emphasis on punishment for disobedience (12:47–48). In adition to
continuity of form (macarism) between the SM and Q, content also coincides. Taking just one
example, traditionally the difference between Lk 6:20b ("Blessed are you poor [μακάριοι οἱ
πτωχοί]…") and Mt 5:3 ("Blessed are the poor in spirit [μακάριοι οἱ πτωχοὶ τῷ πνεύματι]…")
is explained as a kind of spiritual or moralistic improvement by the Matthean author or redactor.
David L. Balch, treating Lk 6:20b, argues against H. D. Betz, (Balch, however, errantly disagrees with Betz on Mt 5:3 not Lk 6:20b; granted Betz argues the SM and SP are not different on
the point, stating the SM "simply spells out what the SP suggests" [*The Sermon on the Mount*,
575–76]), that the saying describes "*la condition humaine*" (ancient topos = *condicio humana*;
The Sermon on the Mount, 114–15) claiming rather that the words bless "Cynic mendicancy"
and possess "an irreducible economic element" ("Philodemus, 'On Wealth' and 'On Household
Management': Naturally Wealthy Epicureans against Poor Cynics," in *Philodemus and the
New Testament World*, eds., John T. Fitzgerald, Dirk Obbink, Glenn S. Holland [NovTSup 111;
Leiden: Brill, 2004] 177). Balch specifies that Jesus' words in Lk 6:20b bless the mendicant
lifestyle that Jesus himself lives out (177, 194) and compares Lk 16:19–31. The assumption of
Jesus as mendicant, however, ignores numerous traditions to the contrary; see above: 89–92.
Also, on Baptist themes of the "Special L" pericope, the rich man and Lazarus (Lk 16:19–31),
see above: 104–5 n. 106. By way of clarification, the expression "multiple baptisms" here is
meant to imply a quantity of different people baptized once as opposed to a quantity of baptisms
(over a period of time) for a single individual as at Qumran.

hunger/thirst (e.g., Mt 11:18; Mk 1:6 par.), strangers (e.g., Q 3:8, Lk 3:10–14), a lack of clothing (e.g., Mk 1:6 par.), and prison (e.g., Mk 1:14; 6:17; Lk 3:20; Mt 14:3).[138] This teaching also touches on the Baptist theme of purification through good works ("fruit"), as opposed to recourse to nationality (Q 3:8). That v. 32 ("all of the nations will be gathered before him [the Son of Man in his glory]") implies the key theme of Gentile judgment is neither proven nor likely.

3.5.2 *Lukan* Sondergut

It should come as no surprise that connections between Lukan *Sondergut* and Q are less convincing than connections between Matthean *Sondergut* and Q. Although "Special L" shares with Q an interest both in the Baptist and in teaching materials,[139] unlike Q, the majority of "Special L" Baptist traditions are narratives *about* John, rather than sayings *of* John. The "Special L" Infancy Narratives about Jesus are, for example, also about John. Famously, "Special L," includes the promise of John's birth (1:5–25), Mary's visit to Elizabeth (1:39–56), the birth of John the Baptist (1:57–80), and examples of John's ethical teaching (3:10–14). If Matthew's use of Mark establishes a precedent, there is no reason to believe Matthew omitted significant quantities of Q, thus establishing a place for these traditions in Q. Nevertheless, a few connections are brought out below regarding the following three passages: (1) Lk 3:23–28; (2) Lk 1:68–79; and, (3) Lk 12:50.

Lk 3:23–38

The genealogies in both "Special L" and "Special M" possess interesting connections to the Baptist. Because "Special L" and "Special M" have versions of Jesus' genealogy and because the genealogical connections established between Adam and Joseph in Luke and Abraham and Joseph in Matthew are both immediately contradicted in the accounts by traditions about a virgin giving birth, the question arises whether an early version of these genealogies originated in Q tracing the lineage of John.[140] Genealogies, after all, were a tradition of Jewish

---

[138] *Ex hypothesi*, "sheep" – also present in this passage (vv. 32, 33) – is a Baptist theme.

[139] These two interests of the Lukan *Sondergut* – the Baptist and teaching materials – come together in Luke's record of Baptist teachings in Lk 3:11, 13 and 14. "Special L," however, prefers parabolic teaching to sayings. Q also does not share the "Special L" interest in healings.

[140] Defending this position on the Lukan genealogy almost one hundred years ago is Clayton R. Bowen, "John the Baptist in the New Testament," 51, 57–71. Bowen argues that Lk 3:1 provides an initial clue to the origin of this section in a Baptist community: "The first verses of chapter 3 give an elaborately calculated date. By a series of synchronisms the year (apparently 29 A. D.) is established in which – the word of God came unto John the son of Zacharias in the wilderness! Every reader is conscious of a start of surprise; the careful dating creates the expectation that the long-delayed principal clause is to offer a statement about Jesus. On the contrary its statement is about John, as is the entire lengthy passage to vs. 20, which brings the Baptist's story down to the point where he rests in Herod's prison .... It [the third chapter] gives a date for the

priests and John's father, at least according to Lk 1:5, belonged to the priestly order of Abijah (cf. Ex 40:12–15). His mother, too, is said to have been a descendant of Aaron[141] and she, not Mary, carries the significance of a woman, like Sarah, advanced in age and unable to bear children (Lk 1:7). If a barren woman gives birth, the child may attract a genealogy; if a virgin gives birth, a story of divine origins *sans généalogie* is appropriate. Against the majority of interpreters, Ulrich Luz agrees that the Matthean genealogy, at least, was *not* the product of the author of Matthew. Luz points, in particular, to the break in the genealogy at Mt 1:16 on its mention of Mary.[142] In the Gospel of Luke, the genealogy is just one of many fascinating traditions in chapters 1–2 with strong connections to John the Baptist, including the Magnificat, commonly referred to, during the 1950's and 60's, as a Baptist tradition.[143] Sharing the *topic* of John the Baptist,

---

beginning of his work, though none for the beginning of Jesus' work… In other words, the whole passage 3:1–20 belongs to a narrative dealing with John which originally had nothing in it about Jesus" (50–51). Bowen also notes that when Jesus does appear in vs. 21 his introduction is "indirect and abrupt:" "Jesus having been baptized…" (50). Similarly, Joan Taylor writes, "Luke's special material (L) – which may not have been homogeneous – may well have contained a body of historically authentic traditions about John the Baptist. After all, one of the most important passages for the dating of the events connected with Jesus (Cf. Luke 2:1–2) is found in Luke alone in relation to John, *not* Jesus" (*The Immerser*, 114; emphasis original).

[141] Cf. *Gos. Eb.* § 2. The Davidic qualities of the lineage should be compared to the Davidic line in Zechariah's prediction about his son, John the Baptist (Lk 1:69b). Consider also Mk 12:35–37: the question about David's son. This passage has long posed theological difficulty to scholars for its questioning of Jesus' Davidic lineage. One clear motivation for the author or redactor of the Gospel of Matthew to rewrite Mark was the latter's rejection in this passage of Jesus' Davidic lineage. For this reason, the author of Matthew placed a Davidic-centered genealogy (along with other supporting data) at the beginning of his book (cf. Mt 1:1–17). Surprisingly, however, the author of Matthew also duplicates Mk 12:35–37 in Mt 22:41–46. On the other hand, in Lk 1:68–79, Zechariah's prophecy about his son imputes Davidic lineage to John: "He has raised up a mighty savior for us, in the house of his servant, David." Interestingly, however, earlier in Luke's Infancy Narrative John's lineage is given as priestly: his father is a priest in the line of Abijah and his mother a descendant of Aaron. Given the similarity of numerous traditions about John and Jesus in the Synoptics, it should come as no surprise that attributions of Davidic lineage were claimed for both teachers; cf. Sir 48:15 ff. This passage challenging Jesus' Davidic messiahship may, therefore, reflect a historical *Sitz im Leben* of dispute between followers of John and Jesus over this issue.

[142] U. Luz, *Matthew 1–7*, 1.107.

[143] Cf. the comment by H. Thyen, "It has long been recognized and may be taken as established that here Christian tradition is intermingled with fragments which come from the Baptist sects" ("ΒΑΠΤΙΣΜΑ ΜΕΤΑΝΟΙΑΣ ΕΙΣ ΑΦΕΣΙΝ ΑΜΑΡΤΙΩΝ," 154). As above, some ancient mss (versions) preserve "Elizabeth" for Mary at Lk 1:46. The pronoun "her" in the first half of Lk 1:56, "And Mary remained with *her* about three months …" only makes sense if vv. 46b–55 had been spoken by Elizabeth. Cf. also C. Scobie, *John the Baptist*, 54–55. Although not a popular topic today, the origin of the Lukan infancy narratives commanded much scholarly attention in the past. For a summary of the Magnificat alone, see Stephen Benko, "The Magnificat, a History of the Controversy," *JBL* 86 (1967). Rejecting the idea of Baptist sources in Lk 1–2 is P. Benoit, "L'Enfance de Jean-Baptiste selon Luc I," *NTS* (1957) 169–94 and J. A. T. Robinson, "Elijah, John and Jesus: An Essay in Detection," 279 n. 2. An interesting, if highly speculative,

however, is not a sufficient basis on which to argue connections between Q and "Special L." Such a temptation should be resisted. If in fact, the hypothesis is correct that Q existed as a source containing Baptist traditions exclusively, it is likely other written Baptist sources existed alongside it. Baptist traditions in the Lukan *Sondergut* not only represent an evangelist's *access* to such traditions but, more importantly, *willingness* to take advantage of such traditions for a reconstruction of Christian origins.

Lk 1:68–79

In terms of Lukan *Sondergut*, another example should be included. Zechariah's prediction about his son John, in the "Special L" passage of Lk 1:68–79, shares a few indirect affinities with Q. In this prediction, the verb, ἐπισκέπτεσθαι refers to John twice. The first occurrence is in 1:68: "Blessed is the Lord God of Israel, for he *has visited* and redeemed his people (Εὐλογητὸς κύριος ὁ θεὸς τοῦ Ἰσραήλ, ὅτι ἐπεσκέψατο καὶ ἐποίησεν λύτρωσιν τῷ λαῷ αὐτοῦ)."[144] The verb appears again in 1:78: "By the tender mercy of our God, the dawn from on high *has visited* us (διὰ σπλάγχνα ἐλέους θεοῦ ἡμῶν, ἐν οἷς ἐπεσκέψατο ἡμᾶς ἀνατολὴ ἐξ ὕψους)…"[145] Just as Jesus is described in Mt 4:16 as "light" that has "dawned," here in Lk 1:78 John is referred to as a "dawn from on high."[146] Interestingly the verb, ἐπισκέπτεσθαι occurs only one other time in the Gospel of Luke. In Lk 7:16, in another "Special L" section, after Jesus raises the widow's son at Nain, the widow exclaims about Jesus, "A great prophet has arisen among us!"[147] and "God *has visited* his people! (Προφήτης μέγας ἠγέρθη ἐν ἡμῖν καὶ ὅτι Ἐπεσκέψατο ὁ θεὸς τὸν λαὸν αὐτοῦ)." After this exclamation, in v. 17, the author generalizes that "This word about *him* [Jesus?] spread in all of Judea and all the surrounding region (καὶ ἐξῆλθεν ὁ λόγος οὗτος ἐν ὅλῃ τῇ Ἰουδαίᾳ περὶ αὐτοῦ καὶ πάσῃ τῇ περιχώρῳ)." This summary remark is followed by a statement in v. 18 *specifying a connection to John*: "And *his* disciples reported all these things to *John*." The two previous associations of God's "visitation" with John (Lk 1:68, 78) may suggest a connection to John for this exclamation in Lk 7:16.[148]

---

thesis comes from J. Massyngberde Ford who argues Lk 1–2 reveals that John and his family were Zealots ("Zealotism and the Lukan Infancy Narratives," *NovT* [1976] 280–92). For her thesis, much is made of the word, στρατία in Lk 2:13 and Acts 7:42 (287–88). For the Benedictus as a militant hymn, see Paul Winter, "Magnificat and Benedictus – Maccabean Psalms?" 328–47.

[144] Cf. Lk 1:25: ἐφοράω and Lk 1:48: ἐπιβλέπω.

[145] For a defense of the aorist form (ἐπεσκέψατο) as original, see Joan Taylor, *The Immerser*, 107 n. 7.

[146] Cf. also Jn 5:35 in which Jesus refers to John the Baptist as a "lamp (ὁ λύχνος)."

[147] In Lk 1:76 John is referred to as "the prophet of the Most High."

[148] Moreover, in Lk 19:44 the related form ἐπισκοπή occurs. In this "Special L" addition to the Markan apocalyptic discourse in Luke, Jesus admonishes: "They will crush you, both

Furthermore, Wink's argument that Lk 1:69, another verse from Zechariah's prophecy about John, originally referred to the resurrection of Jesus (on the basis of Acts 2:24, 32; 3:15, 22, 26; 4:10; 5:30; 13:30, 34, 37) is less persuasive than the observation that the verb ἐγείρειν (ἤγειρεν), used in v. 69 in the sense of "appearing" or "arriving on the scene as a leader," *with* the verb ἐπισκέπτεσθαι, used in the sense of divine visitation in v. 68, together have a parallel in the verse, mentioned above, Lk 7:16: "Fear seized all of them; and they glorified God, saying, 'A great prophet has a*risen* among us!'[149] and 'God has visited his people!'"[150] Moreover, the verb ἐγείρειν is also used in the sense of "coming on the scene" in Q 7:28 (Mt 11:11; cf. Lk 7:28) where it refers to John: "Among those born of women there has not arisen (ἐγήγερται) anyone greater than John the Baptist."[151] Thus, both exclamations of Lk 7:16: "A great prophet has arisen among us!" and "God has visited his people!" possess rather significant lexical ties to Baptist traditions.

Finally, this passage (Lk 7:11–17) is situated in the Gospel of Luke between two Q blocks: the healing of the centurion servant (Lk 7:2–10) and the messengers from John inquiring about the one to come (Lk 7:18–35). In it, Jesus' name does not occur. And, this miracle possesses a clear parallel to Elijah in 1 Kgs 17, a figure Mark, Q and Matthew all correlate with John the Baptist, but the author of Luke-Acts, famously, associates with Jesus.

Lk 12:50

Comparison with Baptist traditions also favors the inclusion of Lk 12:50 in Q. This verse forms a doublet with Q 12:49, a saying that, while omitted from Matthew,[152] *is included* in modern reconstructions of Q.[153] Lk 12:50, however, exhibits clear literary parallelism with 12:49. It possesses the particle, δὲ evinc-

---

your children and you, and they will not leave stone upon stone among you; because you did not recognize the season of your visitation (καὶ ἐδαφιοῦσίν σε καὶ τὰ τέκνα σου ἐν σοί, καὶ οὐκ ἀφήσουσιν λίθον ἐπὶ λίθον ἐν σοί, ἀνθ' ὧν οὐκ ἔγνως τὸν καιρὸν τῆς ἐπισκοπῆς σου)." The word does not occur in Mark. The only place it occurs in Matthew is "Special M" passage 25:31–46: the description of criteria upon which the sheep and goats will be separated at judgment day (γυμνὸς καὶ περιεβάλετέ με, ἠσθένησα καὶ ἐπεσκέψασθέ με, ἐν φυλακῇ ἤμην καὶ ἤλθατε πρός με [v. 36] and ξένος ἤμην καὶ οὐ συνηγάγετέ με, γυμνὸς καὶ οὐ περιεβάλετέ με, ἀσθενὴς καὶ ἐν φυλακῇ καὶ οὐκ ἐπεσκέψασθέ με [v. 43]). By their references to spare (no?) clothing, weakness (fasting?) and imprisonment, these two passages share clear connections to Baptist traditions.

[149] Cf. Lk 19:44; Acts 1:20.

[150] The verb, ἐγείρειν suggests the superlative and refers to a prophet; cf. Lk 7:16; Jn 7:52; and Mk 11:32.

[151] W. Wink, *John the Baptist*, 67. Cf. also Jn 7:52 where "the prophet," said not to "arise from Galilee" (cf. Deut. 18:15, although LXX uses ἀνίστημι) is not specified.

[152] Mt 10:34 may be its reminiscence.

[153] *The Critical Edition of Q*, 376–77; *Q Parallels*, 142–43. J. Jeremias, *Die Sprache des Lukasevangeliums* (Göttingen: Vandenhoeck & Ruprecht, 1980) 223; more recently, C. P. März,

ing a relationship with the previous verse and is thematically linked to Q by its reference to baptism (cf. Q 3:7, 16b and 21). Finally, the verse immediately following Lk 12:50 (12:51), like the verse immediately before it (12:49), is included by the *IQP* in Q.

Beyond these strictly literary relationships, connections to Baptist traditions for both v. 49 and v. 50 are, one might think, self-evident:

Fire I came to hurl upon the earth and how I wish it was already ablaze (Πῦρ ἦλθον βαλεῖν ἐπὶ τὴν γῆν, καὶ τί θέλω εἰ ἤδη ἀνήφθη) (Q 12:49);

I have a baptism with which to baptize and how I am constrained until it is completed (βάπτισμα δὲ ἔχω βαπτισθῆναι, καὶ πῶς συνέχομαι ἕως ὅτου τελεσθῇ) (Lk 12:50).

With its themes of imminent judgment and fire, the first resembles the two well-known Baptist sayings:

And already the ax lies at the root of the trees. So every tree not bearing good fruit will be chopped down and thrown into the fire (Q 3:9); and,

I baptize you with water, but the one coming after me is more powerful than I .... His pitchfork is in his hand and he will clear his threshing floor and gather the wheat into his barn, but the chaff he will burn with unquenchable fire (Q 3:16b–17).[154]

As a saying of John's, Q 12:49 does not contradict Q 3:17. The person exclaiming v. 49 does not proclaim *himself* the one to come who will burn the trees not bearing good fruit (Q 3:9) and the chaff (Q 3:17). That the "fire" is not yet "ablaze" (ἀνάπτω; cf. ET's "kindled" and "lit") suggests that the person making the statement only "ushers" or prepares for a "fire" *expected soon*. Both vv. 49 and 50 reflect the speaker's impatience for the commencement of judgment being pronounced.

Connections of the second saying (Lk 12:50) to John are, however, more complex. Neither John P. Meier nor Joan Taylor mention Lk 12:50 in their studies.[155] Charles Scobie mentions it only to claim that the meaning of βαπτίζειν appears here in the metaphorical sense of "overwhelm" as in Mk 10:38, 39. John Kloppenborg (in a footnote)[156] and Christopher Tuckett[157] mention the verse, arguing similarly, it is a rewriting of Mk 10:38: "But Jesus said to them, 'You do not know what you ask. Are you able to drink the cup that I drink, or to be baptized with the baptism with which I will be baptized?'" By this interpretation, both

---

"'Feuer auf die Erde zu werfen, bin ich gekommen ...' Zum Verständnis und zur Entstehung von Lk 12, 49," in *A Cause de l'Evangile:* Études sur les Synoptiques et les Actes (FS J. Dupont; Paris: Cerf, 1985) 479–511, esp. 480–85; cf. also J. Kloppenborg, *The Formation of Q*, 152.

[154] C. Tuckett acknowledges that Q 3:16 "ties in well" with 12:49, dismissing, however, any connection to Lk 12:50 (*Q and the History of Early Christianity*, 157).

[155] For a list of scholars for and against inclusion of Lk 12:50 in Q, see J. Kloppenborg, *Q Parallels*, 142.

[156] *The Formation of Q*, 151 n. 213; also idem, *Q Parallels*, 142.

[157] *Q and the History of Early Christianity*, 157.

Kloppenborg and Tuckett tie Lk 12:50, not to the final judgment of v. 49, but to Jesus' death. Citing an analogy with Lk 17:25, Kloppenborg further claims about Lk 12:50 that it "alerts the reader to the necessity of Jesus' suffering."[158]

In fact, Lk 12:50 is ambiguous. Some conclude that the verb ἔχω, with complementary infinitive βαπτισθῆναι, results in a translation, "I have a baptism with which [I am] to be baptized" or "There is a baptism by which I must be baptized." In these translations, the object, βάπτισμα is treated as a kind of special case cognate accusative with the passive infinitive. Joan Taylor explains, however, that in Hellenistic Greek the active and passive meanings of the verb βαπτίζειν were somewhat blended.[159] According to Taylor, the only ancient parallel text for someone actively dunking or immersing someone else is Josephus, *B.J.* 1.437/*Ant.* 15.55 in which Aristobulus III is drowned by agents of Herod. Normally people immersed themselves. Taylor writes,

> There is no clear parallel in any current Jewish immersion rite for someone acting as an immerser alongside the person who is being immersed in the water. In Jewish immersion rites, the person goes down into the water and immerses himself or herself. No one pushes the person underwater.[160]

In Mk 1:9–10, although Jesus "was baptized" (ἐβαπτίσθη [passive]) by John, he evidently "comes up" out of the water himself (ἀναβαίνων [active]).[161] Would John have dunked Jesus only to have Jesus then emerge from the water on his own strength? Is it conceivable that John both submerged and pulled Jesus out of the water, with Jesus "coming out of the water" only in the sense of conveying himself to the land? As Taylor points out, in terms of John's hands-on involvement the question remains as to whether John would have, by actively dunking those coming to him, continually exposed himself to their perceived impurities. Were they, however, already consecrated by prerequisite good deeds?[162] At the close of her thorough investigation of this question Joan Taylor concludes with some reservation: "He [John] may well have held on to them."[163]

Returning to βάπτισμα δὲ ἔχω βαπτισθῆναι, another, yet untested, possibility is to read this enigmatic phrase in light of Lk 3:21–22. In this passage the author of Luke-Acts famously fails to specify by whom Jesus is baptized. The most common interpretation of this passage is that the two passive forms of the verb βαπτίζειν in v. 21 (βαπτισθῆναι and βαπτισθέντος) represent divine passives: Ἐγένετο δὲ ἐν τῷ βαπτισθῆναι ἅπαντα τὸν λαὸν καὶ Ἰησοῦ βαπτισθέντος καὶ προσευχομένου ἀνεωχθῆναι τὸν οὐρανὸν.[164] In other words, Jesus is bap-

---

[158] J. Kloppenborg, *The Formation of Q*, 151 n. 213.
[159] J. Taylor, *The Immerser*, 51–2.
[160] J. Taylor, *The Immerser*, 50.
[161] J. Taylor, *The Immerser*, 51.
[162] See discussion of John's baptism in Ch. 2.
[163] J. Taylor, *The Immerser*, 51.
[164] Nb., ἀνεωχθῆναι, too, may qualify as a divine passive.

tized *by God* who then exclaims in v. 22, "You are my beloved Son with whom I am pleased (Σὺ εἶ ὁ υἱός μου ὁ ἀγαπητός, ἐν σοὶ εὐδόκησα)."[165] John's agency in the baptism is so irrelevant for (denied by?) the author of Luke-Acts John is said to be secured in prison (Lk 3:19) before Jesus even arrives on the scene at the Jordan for his immersion.

Given Lk 3:21–22, βαπτισθῆναι of Lk 12:50 may also represent a divine passive. In this case, Lk 12:50 would assert that although John "*has* a baptism (βάπτισμα δὲ ἔχω),"[166] it is, in point of fact, a baptism from God in that those who experience it are purified not by any human individual but by the deity. An English translation might read: "I have a baptism for [many] to be baptized [by God]." The passive infinitive is then epexegetical. At this point it may be helpful to recall that, at least according to Mk 11:30 (Lk 20:4), the origin of John's baptism was a point of contention. The question is posed by Jesus to the Jerusalem authorities in Mk 11:30: τὸ βάπτισμα τὸ Ἰωάννου ἐξ οὐρανοῦ ἦν ἢ ἐξ ἀνθρώπων; Lk 12:50 offers a fitting response to this inquiry.

Reading βαπτισθῆναι of Lk 12:50 with Lk 3:21–22 as a divine passive offers an interpretive solution to the verse that takes seriously its accusative object, βάπτισμα. It also avoids arbitrarily importing to Luke the Pauline interpretation reflected in Mk 10:38, rather prioritizing connections to other passages in the same gospel. On this reading, Lk 12:50 makes most sense as originally a saying of John's, particularly for the Synoptics in which Jesus is never said to baptize.[167] This interpretation is also easily accessible by means of its literary parallel with v. 49: Πῦρ ἦλθον βαλεῖν and βάπτισμα [δὲ] ἔχω βαπτισθῆναι as both *deriving* from Q and *reflecting* John's impatience with his own role in the impending judgment.

In answer to Kloppenborg's observation that the verb τελέω in Lk 12:50 represents Lukan redaction are its seven occurrences in the Gospel of Matthew – five of which (Mt 7:28; 11:1; 13:53; 19:1; 26:1) can be found in the formulaic conclusions to Jesus' great speeches – as certain redaction as any of Kloppenborg's examples from Luke (Lk 2:39; 12:50; 18:31; 22:37/Acts 13:29).[168] This comparison with Matthew seriously debilitates the argument that the verb, τελέω is a special indicator of Lukan redaction. Furthermore, its use by the author of Luke-Acts to refer to the Lukan theme of fulfillment of a divine plan, acknowledged by Kloppenborg, does not affect its connection to the previous v. 49, the following v. 51, or to Q in general. Luke 7:29–30, a passage adopted in most

---

[165] Cf. J. Fitzmyer, *The Gospel according to Luke I–IX*, 480–82. Fitzmyer does not specify divine passive, but does mention an implication of the agency of God. On the meaning of ἀγαπητός here as one destined to die, see J. P. Meier, *A Marginal Jew*, 2.188 n. 26.

[166] Main verb + accusative direct object; cf. Lk 14:18, "I have a need, going out, to see it (ἔχω ἀνάγκην ἐξελθὼν ἰδεῖν αὐτόν)."

[167] Contrast Jn 3:22 and 4:1.

[168] *The Formation of Q*, 151 n. 213.

reconstructions of Q,[169] provides a precedent in Q for the idea that God's divine plan (esp. ἡ βουλή τοῦ θεοῦ in v. 30) is fulfilled by John (cf. Mk 11:30–33/ Lk 20:1–8/Mt 21:23–27). Interestingly, Lk 7:29–30 also provides a parallel for the rare and enigmatic βάπτισμα + βαπτισθῆναι equation of this verse.[170]

What is more, the divine passive interpretation may also apply to Mk 10:38. This passage is, however, as interpreters acknowledge, most likely connected to Paul's understanding of baptism (Rom 6:3–4) – one façet of both authors' (Paul's and Mark's) arguments about the necessity of suffering. In Rom 6:3–5 Paul makes use of the divine passive to redefine Christian baptism, explaining Jesus' martyrdom as a type of baptism from God. While Mk 10:38, Rom 6:3–5, and Lk 12:50 all espouse divine agency in baptism, Lk 12:50 stands alone in its failure to support an explicit interest in Jesus' suffering and believers' imitation of this suffering through persecution.

In summary, arguments favoring Lk 12:50's inclusion in Q include the following: (1) inclusion of Lk 12:49 (other half of doublet) in Q despite its omission from Matthew; (2) literary parallelism of Lk 12:50 with Lk 12:49: "I have come … and how I wish …" and "I have a baptism … and how I am constrained …";[171] (3) presence of the particle, δέ in Lk 12:50; (4) inclusion of Lk 12:51 in Q; (5) connection to Q 3:7, 16b, and 21 by virtue of its reference to baptism; and (6) connection to Baptist traditions through an interpretation of divine agency in baptism.[172]

3.6 Summation

The above observations aim to provide some background for Tuckett's assertion that Q's pre-history was undoubtedly complex.[173] While it may exceed

---

[169] J. Kloppenborg, *Q Parallels*, 58.

[170] J. Kloppenborg, *Q Parallels*, 142; *The Formation of Q*, 151 n. 213.

[171] In the argument of C. E. Carlston, an inordinate quantity of Q material appears as wisdom, not *Gattung*, but tradition; and, literary parallelism is one hallmark of sapiential style ("Wisdom and Eschatology," in *Logia: Les Paroles de Jésus – The Sayings of Jesus. Memorial Joseph Coppens*, Joël Delobel, ed. [Leuven: University Press, 1982] 111–12).

[172] Other possible connections to this verse are provided by Mt 3:15 and Lk 7:29–30. In Mt 3:15, (also Matthean redaction) Jesus claims "all righteousness" is "completed" (πληροῦν) in Jesus' baptism.

[173] B. H. Streeter and T. W. Manson understand Q as a paranetic supplement to early Christian kerygma (B. H. Streeter, "The Literary Evolution of the Gospels," *Oxford Studies in the Synoptic Problem* [Oxford: Clarendon, 1911] 209–27; T. W. Manson, *The Sayings of Jesus* [London, SCM, 1949] 9). Their argument was against Adolf von Harnack who understood Q as Jesus' *ipsissima verba* (*The Sayings of Jesus*; trans. J. R. Wilkinson [New York: Putnam's Sons; London: Williams & Norgate, 1908] 171). In *The History of the Synoptic Tradition*, R. Bultmann too argues Q was primarily ethical instruction, however, expanded by the early church which both created its own sayings and co-opted others from popular culture. For Bultmann, this instruction, nevertheless, presupposed Christian kerygma (368). In *Theology of the*

the evidence to assume Q was originally John's "Spruchevangelium," modern reconstructions of Q suggest that at some point in its pre-history, Q existed as a collection of sayings attributed to John, either together with sayings of Jesus, or alone. If the four canonical gospels and Josephus, *Ant.* 18.116–19 are at all reliable on the historical Baptist then the traditions of Q simply cohere more closely with John than Jesus. If, however, it is impossible to accord to the four Gospels and Josephus any degree of historical reliability, it can at least be said that *the rules according to which the authors of the four Gospels sorted traditions about John and Jesus place Q in greater continuity with the side of John.* This dichotomy is not *imposed upon*, but *emerges from* the extant witnesses.

One historical explanation for this hypothesis, not new,[174] is that John's most persuasive, articulate and well-known sayings were deliberately assimilated under the rubric of 'Jesus' during some phase of early Christianity.[175] As many have shown, in response to, among other causes, loss of their earliest witnesses and perhaps the destruction of the Temple and/or the Jewish war with Rome in the late 60s and early 70s C.E. *at about the time when the Synoptic Gospels were written*, the Christian and Baptist movements united.[176] The unification

---

New Testament (trans. K. Grobel, 2 vols. [New York: Charles Scribner's Sons, 1951–55] 1.3), however, Bultmann emends his view, arguing Q is not simply the church's expanded collection of Jesus sayings, but rather represents the non-messianic preaching of Jesus, a transitional stage before the development of the *kerygma* (although he understands the impending eschatological event forecast in Q as the arrival of the risen Lord). In contrast, Siegfried Schulz seeks to understand Q without reference to Jesus' passion. Schulz argues Q represents a "pharisaic-nomistic and apocalyptic structure of thought," in comparison with *Pirke Avot*. For Schulz, salvation in Q comes, not by Jesus' death and resurrection, but by the "messianic Torah, his [Jesus'] prophetic-apocalyptic proclamation and his priestly instruction" ("Die Bedeutung des Markus für die Theologiegeschichte des Urchristentums," *Studia Evangelica* 2; Texte und Untersuchungen 87 [Berlin: Akademie Verlag, 1964] 138). The present author agrees with Schulz, arguing, however, on the principle, *causae non sunt multiplicandae praeter necessitatem*, that this means of salvation fits more easily what is known of John's, not Jesus', message.

[174] C. H. Kraeling, *John the Baptist*, 158–87; J. A. T. Robinson, "Elijah, John and Jesus: An Essay in Detection," 278–81.

[175] James Dunn writes: "Given the widespread use of Greek within Palestine at the time and the fact that there were not a few Jews (in Jerusalem at least) whose principal language was Greek (Acts 6.1), it is likely that Greek versions of the Baptist traditions were soon circulating in Greek-speaking circles within Palestine, *perhaps already within the period of Jesus' ministry*" (James D. G. Dunn, "John the Baptist's Use of Scripture," 44; emphasis added).

[176] C. H. Kraeling, *John the Baptist*, 128–31, 158–87. Walter Wink comments: "These syncretistic Jewish sects, though fiercely independent, share one thing in common: the centrality of baths or baptism in lieu of sacrifice. As a broad movement of protest against contemporary piety, these groups were heterodox, schismatic, highly individualistic, quick to shift to the latest 'revelation,' and capable of borrowing from one another without establishing relationships of dependency" (*John the Baptist*, 108). And, "… the church stood at the center of John's movement from the very beginning and became its one truly great survivor and heir" (W. Wink, *John the Baptist*, 110). Cf. also J. Kloppenborg Verbin's comment that the "supporting social networks" of the Q document "apparently disappeared in the wake of the First Revolt" (*Excavating Q*, 445).

process of these movements undoubtedly entailed a pooling of resources for the documentation of origins. The chronological simultaneity of these two Jewish individuals, the geographic proximity of their ministries, the similarity of their audiences,[177] the likeness of their eschatological convictions (if not the messages derived from these convictions)[178] – and, if the Gospel of Luke can be trusted (Lk 1:36), their blood relation – made it a matter of course for historically-minded authors fifty or more years later to conflate limited traditions. Even competitive anti-Jesus polemic would have been included in the interest of preserving all authoritative 'kingdom movement' traditions. NT parallels for preserving, even canonizing, polemic are too numerous to count. Contradictions appear within Paul's letters themselves, let alone between Paul's letters and the Pauline school, or Paul's letters and other letters, such as the Epistle of James.[179]

Many precedents in both Jewish and Graeco-Roman texts exist for this type of assimilation of traditions. For example, the sayings of important philosophical teachers were regularly recorded by their students. Among Jewish texts, Moses is an example of a prophet under whom numerous diverse traditions – narratives, not just sayings – were collected. Another prominent example from the Hebrew scriptures is the prophet Isaiah under whose name an impressive array of later prophecies is recorded. Similar arguments about the accretion of traditions under the name of a single prophet have been made about the prophetic books of Jeremiah, Ezekiel and Zechariah.[180]

Such amalgamations of sayings under the names of Jewish prophets, how-ever, reverse the direction of the John/Jesus collection. Generally-speaking, in the case of the prophets, the sayings of later prophets are collected under the names of earlier ones, perhaps because the later prophets are considered, in some sense, of the same "school." The apocryphal books of Baruch, however,

---

[177] John's audience may have included fishermen (Jn 1:40), tax collectors, soldiers (Lk 3:12, 14) and perhaps prostitutes (Mt 21:31–32). With Joan Taylor, John probably also addressed Pharisees (*The Immerser*, 155–211). Although Mark includes women among those addressed by Jesus' ministry (Paul also later incorporates women), Q does not.

[178] Ultimately, at least in Markan traditions, in his own ministry Jesus carried out neither John's requirement for baptism nor his requirement for repentance. These requirements became unnecessary once the "coming one" (who is, for Mark, Jesus, but who was, for John, Yahweh or the Son of Man [?]) appeared. With this appearance, complete restoration is begun and the arrival of the kingdom is hailed. The Synoptics may even allude to Jesus' condemnation of John's practice of baptizing in Mk 7:1–15; Mt 15:1–11. It is doubtful whether John agreed that Jesus' public exhibitions of the miraculous were tantamount to the arrival of the kingdom; his apparent question from prison (Q 7:20) with Jesus' reply may, in fact, have suggested the opposite (see 208–11). The two sayings in Mk 2:21–22 may allude to this difference in their messages. See E. P. Sanders, *Jesus and Judaism*, 108–13. Like John, Q insists on repentance and is tacit on promises of salvation.

[179] See e.g., Matt A. Jackson-McCabe, *Logos and Law in the Letter of James: The Law of Nature, The Law of Moses, and The Law of Freedom* (NovTSup 100; Leiden: Brill, 2001).

[180] The question of the composition/assimilation of individual prophetic books is extremely difficult, hinging in part on an understanding of prophetic "schools."

provide a parallel to the proposed view of how Q was appropriated by Matthew and Luke. In the books of Baruch, the appropriation flows in the same direction as Q to Matthew and Q to Luke in that Jeremiah's sayings are what his disciple and scribe, Baruch records in books of his own name (although the books could not have been written by the historical Baruch). In these two cases, more recent traditions are not filed under an older prophet's name/school/movement. Rather, older traditions are filed under a more recent name/school/movement. In the case of Q, Jesus, the follower turned teacher, did not write down the traditions of his teacher, John. Rather, a different, much later, anonymous student of one or both movements – valuing, like the author/compiler of the *Gospel of Thomas,* a sayings collection – took up this work.[181]

Among later Jewish writings, the *Pirke Avot* is a compilation of the sayings of numerous unknown sages attributed to R. Yohanon, his students and others, as a means of garnering authority for the teachings by establishing connections through schools and traditions – a priority among certain Pharisees.[182] In the *Pirke Avot,* Rabbi Yohanan ben Zakkai is mentioned, followed by a list of five of his pupils. Under each student's name is a list of sayings. Although the question is not settled as to the origin of any individual saying, (indeed the sayings may not belong to any of the teachers listed, merely to tradition), they are attributed in *Pirke Avot* to Rabbi Yohanan's school as a means of guaranteeing their authentication and preservation.

All Greek and Roman examples are variations of the Socratic tradition in which great masters taught (Socrates), but did not write. Students, (including much later students of the tradition), recorded the teachings (e.g., Plato, Xenophon). Because intellectual property rights were shared within this type of philosophical school community, whether a master's teaching was recorded in his or his student's name was a less important question than that it was recorded at all. Among Greek examples roughly contemporary with the four gospels is Arrian who, although known today as a historian, was revered in his own time as a philosopher for compiling the doctrines of Epictetus who apparently did not write anything down.

---

[181] See above: Ch. 2.

[182] Jacob Neusner, *Introduction to Rabbinic Literature* (New York: Doubleday, 1994) 547–608; Louis Finkelstein, "Introductory Study to Pirke Aboth," *JBL* 57 (1938) 13–50; repr. *Pharisaism in the Making* (New York: KTAV, 1972) 121–58. A. Saldarini, "The End of the Rabbinic Chain," *JBL* 93 (1974) 97–106; E. Bickerman, "La Chaîne de la tradition pharisienne," *RB* 59 (1952) 44–54; repr. *Studies in Jewish and Christian History Part II*; AGJU 9 (Leiden: E. J. Brill, 1980) 256–69. Furthermore, in Jewish tradition, in contrast to Classical prophets beginning with Amos, earlier prophets such as Elijah and Elisha, did not write, but spoke. The death of a prophet, it seems, provided the impetus for recording the prophecies. Moreover, during the postexilic period the forms of prophetic expression shifted such that: "postexilic prophets often expressed their oracles as additions to existing collections, rather than speaking in their own persons as earlier prophets had done" (John Barton, "Prophecy [Postexilic Hebrew]," *ABD* 5.495).

In every case, the work of writing down and/or attributing sayings was not intentionally misleading or deceptive.[183] Rather, followers of Jesus, such as the authors of the gospels of Matthew and Luke, acted as redactors of a variety of reliable sources and labored in an endeavor of historiography, consolidating traditions in the interest of preserving the collective origins of both groups.[184]

Influenced by the conclusions of Carl Kraeling, Walter Wink concludes that the fact that John's teachings were inevitably attributed to Jesus (particularly by the author of the Gospel of Matthew) was only natural; the sources, he argues, only ever belonged to one group of people and one movement:

> Both Baptists and Christians belonged to the heretical sectarian Baptist movement, and both paid allegiance to John.[185]

On a practical level, combining traditions ensured that ancient authors had sufficient sources for persuasive accounts of origins. In terms of traditions about Jesus, however, this assimilation of sources may have been additionally motivated. A difficulty of the traditions about Jesus was that his purported acts of power did little for his image.[186] As Acts attests miracles were performed

---

[183] As J. Kloppenborg points out, examples of double attribution are also found in Diogenes Laertius. "Friends share in common" is attributed to both Bion (4.53) and Pythagoras (8.10); "Nothing too much," to both Thales and Solon (1.41, 63). See *The Formation of Q*, 292 n. 97.

[184] J. Kloppenborg explains that named collections were preferable to unnamed collections: "In most cases, the instruction is ascribed to a figure of some distinction and authority: a king ... vizier ... priest ... scribe ... or other figure of authority" (*The Formation of Q*, 265). In the Pharisaic-rabbinic tradition, according to J. Neusner, preference was shown to living authorities ("Types and Forms of Ancient Jewish Literature: Some Comparisons," *HR* 11 [1971–72] 367). In the case of Q, apparently Jesus best provided such an authority. Cf. also R. O. P. Taylor, *Groundwork of the Gospels* (Oxford: Blackwell, 1946) 81; J. D. Crossan, *In Fragments: The Aphorisms of Jesus* (San Francisco: Harper and Row, 1983) 229. Because some pericopes of Q are *chriae*, as opposed to *gnomai*, at least some of the sayings in Q were probably, in their original context, ascribed to a certain person (*The Formation of Q*, 291–92). Despite H. Koester's view that Q circulated anonymously at first ("Apocryphal and Canonical Gospels," *HTR* 73 [1980] 105–30), Q was probably not, at any time, completely anonymous. Also, in the words of J. Kloppenborg: "... although some sayings are transmitted anonymously as general folk wisdom, there was a strong pressure to attach sayings to concrete historical figures" (*The Formation of Q*, 292 n. 97); and, "One could surmise that the competition of religious, philosophical and ethical systems which characterized the Hellenistic and imperial periods reinforced the already strong pressure to attach sayings to an authoritative figure. The chriic form, for which attribution is an intrinsic part, was ideally suited to the combination of caustic wit, pointed polemic and radical ethical command which Cynics popularized. In this case, anonymous pronouncements were scarcely an option; the radical comportment of the teaching dictated the necessity of attachment to a historical figure" (*The Formation of Q*, 294).

[185] W. Wink, *John the Baptist*, 105; cf. also 23.

[186] Although frequently on the basis of later evidence (both in Christian and rabbinic traditions), E. Bammel, nevertheless, makes the point that some type of miraculous display customarily accompanied the message of θεῖοι ἀνέρες. Bammel writes, "Disbelief in particular miracles is not unheard of, but to state that someone did no miracle is, as far as I know, unique"; and "The praise of a man of God who did *not* perform miracles was completely unknown in Jewish sources" ("John Did No Miracle," 181, 191, respectively; emphasis original).

regularly by charlatans, magicians, even demons (e.g., 8:9–24; 16:16–18). Authentication of a Jewish prophet required not miraculous displays (although they might accompany), but authoritative interpretations of the Law. Assimilating Baptist traditions with descriptions of Jesus' displays of healing and other acts of power could have served to enhance Jesus' portrait with this necessary, authenticating component.[187]

It might at this point behoove us to recall that scholarly consensus regarding Q's opening verse (apart from the possibility of the single word, Ἰησοῦ [Q 3:0!]), is that it begins with John.[188] In *The Critical Edition of Q*'s reconstruction:[189]

(…) Ἰωάννη (…) πᾶσα [] η [] περί {χωρ} ο [()] τοῦ Ἰορδάνου

(…) John (…) all the region of the Jordan (…) (Q 3:2b–3a)

What type of an ancient document, it should be asked, would announce John followed by a list of sayings of Jesus?[190] The canonical gospels do, of course. This fact, however, suggests what we should all, in the legacy of important scholars such as Helmut Koester and others, be loathe to admit: *that the canonical framework dictates our constructions and interpretations of Q.*

If correct, this hypothesis has the potential to illuminate various conundrums of NT studies. For example, the Gospel of Mark excluded much of the material of Q because the author – and even perhaps his audience – acknowledged it as a collection of Baptist materials.[191] Paul excluded virtually any reference to Jesus'

---

[187] Cf. also the paucity of Jesus' sayings in both the Gospel of Mark and the Pauline corpus.

[188] Furthermore, as different from *Gos. Thom.*, quotation formulae are largely absent from Q. Apart from the disputed baptism (Q 3:21) and temptation segments (Q 4:1, 4 [in Luke only], 12; 5:8), Q possesses only two explicit occurrences of the name, Jesus: (1) Q 7:9, in the centurion narrative; and, (2) Q 9:58, in a quotation formula for which the verbs of speaking (the second of only three components of these formulae) *vary* in Matthew (λέγει) and Luke (εἶπεν). The name of John, however, occurs a total of eight times in Q: 3:2b; 7:18, 22, 24, 28, 29, 33; 16:16.

[189] *The Critical Edition of Q*, 4–7.

[190] Ulrich B. Müller observes: "Diese Spruchquelle beginnt also mit Worten des Johannes des Täufers, ansonsten konzentriert sie sich allerdings auf Jesusworte" (*Johannes der Täufer: Jüdischer Prophet und Wegbereiter Jesu* [Leipzig: Evangelische Verlagsanstalt, 2002] 103). Surprisingly, E. Bammel argues that the Z (Signs) Source, first proposed by A. Faure ("Die alttestamentliche Zitate im 4. Evangelium u.d. Quellenscheidungshypothese," *ZNW* [1922] 107 ff.) and later developed by R. Bultmann, (*Das Evangelium des Johannes* [Göttingen: Vandenhoeck & Ruprecht, 1978 (1941)] 78 ff., 541), too, began with the Baptist ("John Did No Miracle," 195, 198–99).

[191] See below: Ch. 4. Cf. the comment by J. Kloppenborg Verbin: "Thus Mark's relationship to prior oral tradition is highly ambivalent. He is extraordinarily sparing in placing sayings on Jesus' lips…" and "… Mark's Jesus, by contrast, is not only absent; he is silent too" (*Excavating Q*, 355). Here Kloppenborg Verbin cites the work of W. Kelber, *The Oral and the Written Gospel: The Hermeneutics of Speaking and Writing in the Synoptic Tradition, Mark, Paul, and Q* (Philadelphia: Fortress, 1983) 196, 207–11. For a brief summary of past arguments for and against Mark's prior knowledge of Q, see J. Lambrecht, "Q and Mark 8,34–9,1," in *Logia. Les*

teaching in his letters because he understood Jesus' significance, not on the basis of any teaching, but on the basis of his displays of the miraculous, in particular his resurrection (e.g., 1 Cor 15:12–19). Interestingly, Paul frequently downplays his own (obvious) rhetorical strengths (1 Cor 1:17; 2 Cor 10:10; 11:6) insisting, rather, on his ability to perform miracles (2 Cor 12:11–12 [satirical?]; Gal 3:1–5; Rom 15:18–19; 1 Thes 1:5; 1 Cor 2:4–5; and 1 Cor 12:9–10, 28–30).[192] Paul never mentions the Baptist.[193]

If an ancient proof-text is required for the existence of a much broader array of Baptist sayings, it can, of course, be found without difficulty. In Lk 3:18 the author summarizes:

So, with *many other exhortations*, he [John] preached good news to the people (Πολλὰ μὲν οὖν καὶ ἕτερα παρακαλῶν εὐηγγελίζετο τὸν λαόν).[194]

Paroles de Jésus – The Sayings of Jesus. Mémorial Joseph Coppens, Joël Delobel, ed. (Leuven: Leuven University Press, 1982) 277–304.

[192] James A. Kelhoffer, "The Apostle Paul and Justin Martyr on the Miraculous: A Comparison of Appeals to Authority," *GRBS* 42 (2001) 163–84.

[193] Cf., however, Acts 13:24–25 in which Paul even cites the Baptist (a novel combination of elements resembling Jn 1:20 and Mk 1:7/Jn 1:26–27). Although 1 Cor 1:10–17 does not specify John in its list of rivals (Paul, Apollos, Cephas), 1 Cor 1:17 is, nevertheless, interesting as possible anti-Baptist polemic in its two-pronged attack on the very attributes for which the Baptist was hailed: baptizing (βαπτίζειν) and persuasive speech (ἐν σοφίᾳ λόγου). Cf. Josephus, *Ant.* 18.116–19. An interesting question is posed by Rom 1:3–4: "…the gospel concerning his Son, who was descended from David according to the flesh and was declared to be Son of God with power according to the spirit of holiness *by resurrection from the dead*…." (NRSV). Here Paul evidently rejects Jesus' assignation as "Son" at his baptism by John or at the transfiguration as, for example, recorded in the Gospel of Mark. Also of interest is 1 Cor 10:1–2 which brings together themes associated with the Baptist including cloud, sea, Moses and baptism.

[194] Nb., emphasis, by its sentence position, on the Greek word πολλά.

Chapter Four

Q, Baptist Traditions and the Gospel of Mark

> It is always the mark of the later (and often less skillful) hand to try to make explicit what the earlier master had been content to leave implicit. ... Mark lays demands on his readers which they have frequently been unable to meet.[1]

> For much of the early Church, John was Elijah *redivivus* ...
> It seems quite possible that Jesus thought so too.[2]

4.1 Introduction

The Gospel of Mark is replete with information about John the Baptist.[3] Historically, the Second Gospel is first of the Synoptics to commence the "good news of Jesus Christ" (Mk 1:1) with the proclamation of the Baptist. The Second Gospel is also first to associate John with Mal 3 and Isa 40 (Mk 1:2–3)[4] and to describe John after Elijah as one "clothed in camel hair and a leather belt around

---

[1] Morton Enslin, "The Artistry of Mark," *JBL* (1947) 394–95.

[2] Joan E. Taylor, *The Immerser*, 281.

[3] Clayton R. Bowen tabulates: "Save Jesus, Peter, and Paul, he [John the Baptist] is by far the most frequently named person in the New Testament, and this though he was neither a companion nor a follower of Jesus. His name, according to Moulton and Geden, occurs sixteen times in Mark, twenty-three times in Matthew, twenty-four times in Luke, nine times in Acts, or seventy-two times in the synoptic writers combined. ... Besides, the Baptist is mentioned nineteen times in the Fourth Gospel .... Thus the New Testament names the Baptist ninety-one times..." ("Prolegomena to a New Study of John the Baptist," 32–33). Mark alone applies the term ὁ βαπτίζων to John. He is apparently not afraid to emphasize that John baptized – if, perhaps, more insistent that he *preached* a baptism of repentance (1:4). However, as Bowen also points out, eleven of the sixteen occurrences of John's name omit his epithet or any descriptive phrase referring to baptism about which Bowen concludes that John is simply "too well known... to need further specification" (46). However, that neither Q, nor the Gospel of John include John's epithet may indicate he was *more than* mere "baptist/baptizer" to them. See also Eberhard W. Güting, "The Relevance of Literary Criticism for the Text of the New Testament: A Study of Mark's Traditions on John the Baptist," in: *Studies in the Early Text of the Gospels and Acts: The Papers of the First Birmingham Colloquium on the Textual Criticism of the New Testament*, D. G. K. Taylor, ed. (Text-critical Studies 1; Atlanta: Society of Biblical Literature, 1999) 142–67.

[4] Apart from Lk 1:76, Luke does not associate John the Baptist with the prediction from Mal 3:1 until Lk 7:27. His introduction to John in Lk 3:1–6 employs only Isa 40 (vv. 3–5). In contrast, Mark uses both Mal 3:1 and Isa 40:3 to introduce John in Mk 1:2–3. The problem for Luke may have been an association between Mal 3:1 and Elijah.

his waist (ἐνδεδυμένος τρίχας καμήλου καὶ ζώνην δερματίνην περὶ τὴν ὀσφὺν αὐτοῦ)" and as a prophet "in the wilderness (ἐν τῇ ἐρήμῳ)" (Mk 1:4), "eating grasshoppers and wild honey (ἐσθίων ἀκρίδας καὶ μέλι ἄγριον)" (1:6).[5] The Second Gospel introduces that John baptized Jesus (1:9–11), that John's disciples, with the Pharisees, observed certain unknown fasting regulations

---

[5] The similarities between the depiction of John in Mark and Elijah in 2 Kgs should not, however, be overstated. In 2 Kgs 1:8, Elijah is described simply as "a hairy man with a leather belt around his waist" (LXX). Cf. also Zech 13:4. John's location by the Jordan is, perhaps, more relevant (2 Kgs 2:8, 14). The Jordan is significant in the Elijah-Elisha cycle. Elisha's authentication as successor to Elijah is effected in his crossing of the Jordan (2 Kgs 2:13–14; cf. 1 Kgs 17:3, 5; 2 Kgs 2:8). Colin Brown takes the Synoptic portrayal of John's location at the Jordan historically. Accepting J. Murphy-O'Connor's observation of the geographical difficulties of John's Jordan location and rejecting John's baptism as ritual purification, Brown understands the historical John's work along the lines of other messianic imposters, concluding: "John was organizing a symbolic exodus from Jerusalem and Judea as a preliminary to recrossing the Jordan as a penitent, consecrated Israel in order to reclaim the land in a quasi-reenactment of the return from Babylonian exile. ... In short, John waded across, and baptism was effected by heeding John's call to leave the land and follow him in penitence into the Jordan and return as consecrated members of a renewed Israel" ("What Was John the Baptist Doing?" *BBR* [1997] 45). The present author disagrees that Brown accurately represents the actions of the historical John. Brown's interpretation makes too much of the act of baptizing which may reflect Christian emphasis. That John "*proclaimed* a baptism" (Mk 1:4/Mt 3:1/Lk 3:3/Acts 10:37), suggests John's primary occupation, also reflected by Josephus (*Ant.* 18.117–18), is teaching not baptizing. The present author, therefore, accepts Brown's portrayal of the historical John as background the author of Mark intended. Not cited by Brown, but sharing many of the same conclusions is Clayton R. Bowen, "Prolegomena to a New Study of John the Baptist," 30–48. Bowen, in turn, acknowledges many earlier scholars such as Matthias Schneckenberger, Wilhelm Brandt, Julius Wellhausen, Martin Dibelius and Edward I. Bosworth – as adumbrating his position. Also, although generally inaccurate regarding the "pre-Christian" background of Elijah traditions, see J. Jeremias, "Ἠλ(ε)ίας," *TDNT*, Gerhard Kittel, trans. and ed. G. W. Bromiley (Grand Rapids, Michigan: Eerdmans, 1964) II.928–41. Jeremias neglects, that *Sib. Or.* 2:187–89, the Coptic *Apoc. El.* and the Hebrew *Book of Elijah* all indicate Christian editing. Critical of Jeremias are Morris M. Faierstein, "Why do the Scribes Say that Elijah Must Come First?" *JBL* (1981) 76; Dale C. Allison, Jr., Critical Note on Faierstein's "Elijah Must Come First," *JBL* (1984) 256–58; Georg Molin, "Elijahu: Der Prophet und sein Weiterleben in den Hoffnungen des Judentums und der Christenheit," *Judaica* 8 (1952) 65–94 and Brenda J. Shaver, "The Prophet Elijah in the Literature of the Second Temple Period: The Growth of a Tradition," Ph.D. Diss., University of Chicago, 2001, 5–7. M. Faierstein argues that Mk 9:11 implies no relationship between Elijah as forerunner to the Messiah in Mal 3:23–24: "The disciples ask Jesus, 'Why do the scribes say,' when they might have used one of the formulae indicating reference to a biblical text or even cited these verses if they understood the idea of Elijah as forerunner to be biblical in origin. Considering the extensive citation of biblical texts, particularly in Matthew, it would be surprising that they did not cite this text, if they understood it in this way. Instead they refer to the authority of 'the scribes'" ("Elijah Must Come First?" 77). Qumran fragments incorporate an expectation of Elijah: 4Q558 (explicit) and 4Q521 (an "Elijah-like eschatological prophet") (John J. Collins, *The Scepter and the Star: The Messiahs of the Dead Sea Scrolls and Other Ancient Literature*, 116–17). See also idem, *Apocalypticism in the Dead Sea Scrolls* (New York: Routledge, 1997). Also, qualifying John's diet as a depiction of Elijah, see the excellent new study by James A. Kelhoffer, *The Diet of John the Baptist*, 129–32, 133. Kelhoffer argues John's diet emphasizes *where* (in the wilderness), not *who* (Elijah-like figure) John is. Mark's use of the LXX version

(2:18), and that John was beheaded by Herod Antipas, son of Herod the Great and tetrarch of Galilee and Perea (4 B.C.E.–39 C.E.) (6:14–29). Other less publicized facts about John also introduced by the Gospel of Mark include that Herod misapprehended Jesus as the Baptist *redivivus* on account of the "powers at work in him" (6:14; cf also 8:28),[6] that Jesus refers to John as Elijah *and* the Son of Man (9:12–13), and that Jesus explains his own authority on the basis of the authority accorded to John's baptism by the chief priests, scribes and elders (11:27–33). Paul Achtemeier summarizes the Second Gospel's attention to John the Baptist well:

> By beginning the story of Jesus' Galilean ministry with John the Baptist, Mark announces his importance for understanding that mission, a point again confirmed by Jesus when he identifies the ability to understand the significance of John the Baptist with the ability to understand his own: to fail to understand the one necessarily leads to failure in understanding the other (11:27–33). Both Jesus and John share the same God-given authority.[7]

Thus, while Q's interest in John is notoriously profound,[8] Mark's attention to the Baptist is also substantial.

Although relatively little ink has been spilt on the topic of the Baptist and Baptist traditions in Mark, a few theses warrant mention.[9] Paul Achtemeier, for

---

of Isa 40:3 emphasizes this point. Whereas the Hebrew text describes a voice with a message to prepare the way of the Lord in the wilderness, the Greek text and Mark *locate the voice* in the wilderness (*The Diet of John the Baptist*, 129–33). Cf. Elijah's sustenance in the wilderness (1 Kgs 17:2–6; 19:5–7). On the legendary qualities of the Elijah stories in the Books of Kings, see H. Gunkel, *Elias, Jahve und Baal* (Tübingen: Mohr, 1906). Finally, in Lk 4:25, 26, Elijah and Elisha represent the theme of judgment on Israel through their demonstration of miracles among the nations. More than Mark, Luke appropriates Elijah's traits for his depiction of Jesus. Discussion of the scribes' question that Elijah must come first is omitted in Luke. In Luke, after Jesus' transfiguration, instead of conversing with his disciples about the coming of Elijah, the author abbreviates Mark with the following summary: "After the voice, Jesus was found alone. And they remained silent and in those days reported to no one what they had seen" (Lk 9:36). The next morning, Jesus heals a boy with a demon. In Luke, all Markan references to the Baptist as Elijah (e.g., Mk 1:6, 6:14–29, 9:11–13, 15:34–36) are removed. Predominantly, Jesus is Elijah in Luke (esp. 7:11–17; 9:54 [although this teaching is rejected by Jesus in v. 55]; 24:51 – all three "Special L" passages *not in Mark*). In Luke, John is likened to Elijah in Zechariah's prayer (1:16–17). See also W. Wink, *John the Baptist*, 42.

[6] If, for Mk 6:14, NA[27] is followed, ἔλεγον, meaning "many [or "people"] were saying," implies that the view of John as Elijah *redivivus* was not limited to Herod, but was widely held. Cf. Mt 27:64 in which "the first" may refer to beliefs that John was risen from the dead. See Bruce M. Metzger, *A Textual Commentary on the New Testament*, 2nd ed. (New York: American Bible Society, 1994) 76. Into Mk 8:28 "...and others one of the prophets," Mt 16:14 inserts "Jeremiah or": "and others Jeremiah or one of the prophets." The origin of such a speculation is unknown; cf. Jesus ben Ananias who apparently understood himself as a new Jeremiah (*B.J.* 6.300–309). Ascension with subsequent appearances is documented for the prophet Jeremiah.

[7] "Mark, Gospel of," *ABD* 4.548 .

[8] Christopher M. Tuckett, *Q and the History of Early Christianity: Studies on Q*, 108–9.

[9] In addition to the commentaries, literature on the historical John treats this topic. In particular, (most full citations can be found in Ch. 2), E. Bammel, "The Baptist in Early Christian

example, argues that Baptist traditions are organized, like the author's various other unknown sources, to further his theological point that "the passion of Jesus is the interpretative key to his career and its meaning."[10] Ernst Bammel describes Baptist traditions in Mark as "singularly disproportionate,"[11] referring to the brevity of the author's attention to John's *message* (Mk 1:7–8; 2 verses) as compared to the narrative about John's *death* (6:14–29; 16 verses). And, Walter Wink emphasizes "John's sufferings as Elijah-incognito," claiming John's persecution represents its own Elijianic secret, preparing "the way for the fate of Jesus."[12] The present hypothesis builds on all three of these positions arguing that Mark's *a priori* understanding of John the Baptist as Elijah governs his entire narrative,[13] in particular the events of chapters 6–13. As we will see, this argument

---

Tradition"; J. Becker, *Johannes der Täufer und Jesus von Nazareth*; M. Dibelius, *Die urchristliche Überlieferung von Johannes dem Täufer*; J. Ernst, *Johannes der Täufer*, 4–38; M. Goguel, *Au seuil de l'évangile: Jean-Baptiste*; P. W. Hollenbach, "Social Aspects of John the Baptist's Preaching Mission in the Contexts of Palestinian Judaism"; Hans-Josef Klauck, *Vorspiel im Himmel? Erzähltechnik und Theologie im Markusprolog*; C. H. Kraeling, *John the Baptist*; H. Lichtenberger, "Reflections on the History of John the Baptist's Communities"; E. Lohmeyer, *Das Urchristentum 1: Johannes der Täufer*; E. Lupieri, *Giovanni Battista fra Storia e Leggenda*; J. Meier, *A Marginal Jew,* 19–223; idem, "John the Baptist in Matthew's Gospel"; J. Murphy-O'Connor, "John the Baptist and Jesus: History and Hypothesis"; J. Reumann, "The Quest for the Historical Baptist"; J. Schütz, *Johannes der Täufer*; C. H. H. Scobie, *John the Baptist*; J. Steinmann, *Saint John the Baptist and the Desert Tradition*; W. B. Tatum, *John the Baptist and Jesus: A Report of the Jesus Seminar*; W. Trilling, "Die Täufertradition bei Matthäus"; W. Wink, *John the Baptist in the Gospel Tradition*; idem, "Jesus' Reply to John: Matt. 11:2–6/Luke: 7:18–23"; R. L. Webb, *John the Baptizer and Prophet: A Socio-Historical Study*; idem, "John the Baptist and his Relationship to Jesus"; idem, "The Activity of John the Baptist's Expected Figure at the Threshing Floor (Matthew 3.12 – Luke 3.17)"; A. Yarbro Collins, "The Origin of Christian Baptism."

[10] "Gospel of Mark," *ABD* 4.548. This citation represents Achtemeier's conclusion about the role of the disciples in Mark. However, regarding John the Baptist, Achtemeier reiterates, "Mark shows again how he makes his points by the arrangement of his traditions. In this instance, Mark made clear that Jesus' death was a necessary, indeed inevitable, climax to his career, just as it had been for his forerunner" (4.549). On the theological quality of Mark's narrative vis-à-vis its value as history, see Morton S. Enslin, "The Artistry of Mark," 385–99.

[11] "The Baptist in Early Christian Tradition," 96.

[12] W. Wink, *John the Baptist*, 15–17; cf. also, J. Lambrecht, "John the Baptist and Jesus in Mark 1.1–15: Markan Redaction of Q?" *NTS* 38 (1992) 383; and E. Lupieri, "Johannes der Täufer," *RGG*⁴, 516. Walter Wink argues that the author of Mark customizes a version of the "messianic secret" for John, creating what Wink refers to as "the secret of John's Elijahship" (*John the Baptist*, 15). Wink writes, "Since it is immediately after the transfiguration scene that Jesus identifies Elijah with John, Mark probably intends to indicate that Jesus discovered this 'mystery' on the mount" (15). Wink denies, however, any connection between his hypothesis and the numerous resurrection theories of the transfiguration scene: "The belief expressed here is not that John has been resurrected ... but that he has been physically resuscitated ... raised from the grave, not brought back from heaven (as, i.e., Elijah, who never died)" (*John the Baptist*, 10).

[13] The present chapter's insistence on the importance of Elijah in Mark is shared by Silvia Pellegrini, *Elija: Wegbereiter des Gottessohnes: Eine textsemiotische Untersuchung im Markusevangelium* (HBS 26; Freiburg/New York: Herder, 2000). Cf. also the certainty of

regarding Baptist traditions in Mark provides a critical piece of the overall thesis of this book regarding NT Baptist traditions. The following analysis attempts to demonstrate this claim.

4.2 The Meaning and Significance of the Markan Transfiguration

In Mk 8:22–26, immediately after the healing of the blind man at Bethsaida, the Markan narrative commences with Jesus' question: "Who do people say that I am (Τίνα με λέγουσιν οἱ ἄνθρωποι εἶναι)?" (8:27). To this question, the disciples volunteer, "John the Baptist," "Elijah," and "one of the prophets (οἱ δὲ εἶπαν αὐτῷ λέγοντες [ὅτι] Ἰωάννην τὸν βαπτιστήν, καὶ ἄλλοι, Ἡλίαν, ἄλλοι δὲ ὅτι εἷς τῶν προφητῶν)."[14] Jesus then asks them who they consider him to be. Peter responds that Jesus is the "Christ" (Σὺ εἶ ὁ Χριστός [8:29]). This response is then followed by Jesus' foretelling of his death and resurrection, including three sayings with parallels in Q. Although it is not immediately apparent why (and individual interpretations vary), it seems clear this passage is intended as a clue to understanding the rest of the book.

Jesus' transfiguration (Mk 9:2–8) immediately follows these sayings. Often linked to Peter's response that Jesus be considered the Messiah (8:29), the transfiguration is variously understood as (1) a misplaced account of Jesus'

J. Lambrecht's conviction: "For Mark John the Baptist is above all the forerunner of Jesus Christ, the Elijah who returns for his eschatological task … In the Markan gospel, already in 1.1–15, there can be no misunderstanding about the identity and function of the Baptist" ("John the Baptist and Jesus in Mark 1.1–15: Markan Redaction of Q?" 382).

[14] About this passage, Paul Achtemeier comments, "Not only was John the precursor of Jesus in his preaching of repentance (cf. 1:4 with 1:15), he was also Jesus' precursor in his final fate. That point is made in the traditions that Mark assembled in 6:14–29. In one tradition (6:14–16), there is a discussion about the way in which Jesus was perceived by the public. Several possibilities are listed: Jesus is Elijah, he is another of the prophets. The major identification, however, is with John the Baptist. That is the official view, since that is also the identification Herod makes (6:16)" ("Mark, Gospel of," *ABD* 4.548). I argue that all three possibilities put forward about Jesus ("John the Baptist," "Elijah," and "one of the prophets"), identify John. On the development in the Second Temple Period – when "prophecy had ceased" and "the prophetic spirit had withdrawn" (286) – of the title "prophet" into an eschatological term exclusively, see Franklin W. Young, "Jesus The Prophet: A Re-Examination," 285–99. In any age, a longing for the return of the prophet Elijah is logical because Elijah never died (S. Mowinckel, *He That Cometh*, trans. G. W. Anderson [New York: Abingdon, 1954] 299). Similarly, Brenda Shaver explains that Elijah's ascension captured the attention of so many because as one who never died, he lives on among the heavenly beings poised to return to earth, if necessary, to help people ("The Prophet Elijah in the Literature of the Second Temple Period," 54); also, C. Houtman, "Elijah," *DDD*, 283. For background on ascension traditions, see Alan Segal, "Heavenly Ascent in Hellenistic Judaism, Early Christianity and their Environment," *ANRW* 2.23.2, 1333–94.

resurrection;[15] (2) a forecast of Jesus' *parousia*;[16] (3) an adumbration of Jesus' enthronement in heaven and/or ascension;[17] and (4) a "visio-literary metamorphosis of the genre of *bat qôl*" (daughter of a voice).[18] With no clear consensus of interpretation, apart from clear links to Exod 24:15–18 in which Moses encounters the glory of God on the mountain, both form and content of the transfiguration continue to baffle scholars today.[19] Nonetheless, on one point scholars are unanimous: partly on the basis of its placement *after* Peter's avowal of Jesus as Christ (8:29) and *between* two Markan passion predictions (8:31; 9:31), *this theophany is taken to reflect Christological concerns exclusively.*[20] The question posed here is whether this argument is indisputable.

---

[15] R. H. Stein, "Is the Transfiguration (Mark 9:2–8) a Misplaced Resurrection Account?" *JBL* (1976) 79–96.

[16] G. H. Boobyer, "St Mark and the Transfiguration," *JTS* (1940) 119–40. Boobyer argues that the understanding of the transfiguration in Mark is the same as *Apoc. Pet.* – as the *parousia* of Christ. His argument falters, particularly, on the point that *doxa* as a description of Jesus' metamorphosis occurs in Luke (9:32), but not Mark (128). Although providing persuasive parallels for the expectation of prophets such as Moses and at the *parousia*, Boobyer fails to explain why Elijah, not Jesus, is said to "appear" in Mk 9:4. Against E. Lohmeyer, Boobyer argues the transfiguration is best understood in the light of Christian, not Jewish eschatology.

[17] H. Riesenfeld, *Jésus Transfiguré* (Copenhagen: E. Munksgaard, 1947).

[18] This citation is Bruce Chilton's summary (in "Transfiguration," *ABD* 6.641) of his explanation of the transfiguration in "The Transfiguration: Dominical Assurance and Apostolic Vision," *NTS* 27 (1980) 115–24. Cf. also F. R. McCurley, "And After Six Days" (Mark 9.2): A Semitic Literary Device," *JBL* (1974) 67–81.

[19] The majority of scholars maintain that the transfiguration is a misplaced resurrection account. G. Volkmar was first to espouse it (see H. Baltensweiler [*Die Verklärung Jesu* (Zürich: Zwingli, 1959) 91]), followed by J. Wellhausen (*Das Evangelium Marci* [Berlin: G. Reimer, 1909] 71) and K. G. Goetz (*Petrüs als Grunder und Oberhaupt der Kirche und Schauer von Gesichten nach den altchristlichen Berichten und Legenden: eine exegetisch-geschichtliche Untersuchung* [Leipzig: Hinrichs, 1927]). J. Blinzler lists six important advocates of this view (*Die neutestamentlichen Berichte über die Verklärung Jesu* [Münster: Aschendorff, 1937]). W. Schmithals adds at least ten more, including R. Bultmann, W. Bousset, M Goguel, M. S. Enslin, P. Vielhauer, H. Koester and J. M. Robinson ("Der Markusschluss, die Verklärungsgeschichte und die Aussendung der Zwölf," *ZTK* [1972] 384 n. 13). Robert H. Stein adds to these: A. Loisy, E. Käsemann, H. D. Betz, T. J. Weeden, F. W. Beare, F. R. McCurley, W. Schmithals, and M. J. Thrall ("Is the Transfiguration [Mark 9:2–8] a Misplaced Resurrection-Account?" 79 n. 2). This hypothesis receives criticism, however, from J. Blinzler, H. Baltensweiler, C. H. Dodd (C. H. Dodd, "The Appearances of the Risen Christ: An Essay in Form-Criticism of the Gospels," in *Studies in the Gospels*, eds. G. H. Boobyer and R. H. Stein [Oxford: Blackwell, 1955]). Johannes M. Nützel also has a thorough history of scholarship treating this problem in *Die Verklärungserzählung im Markusevangelium: Eine redaktionsgeschichtliche Untersuchung* (Würzberg: Echter Verlag, 1973) 10–86. Still a different view is held by J. B. Bernardin. On the basis of parallels, such as 1 En 46:1 ff, 48:6, 105:2; *Sib. Or.* 5:414; and 2 Bar 29:3, Bernardin holds that Jesus' transfiguration is a momentary demonstration of his preexistent glory (as the Messiah) ("The Transfiguration," *JBL* [1933] 181). Cf. also John Knox's reference to the transfiguration as "the invasion of memory by faith" (*On the Meaning of Christ* [New York: C. Scribner's Sons, 1947] 72).

[20] For an explanation of the different types of Christological models in the NT and an exploration of the θεῖος ἀνήρ type, see Hans Dieter Betz, "Jesus as Divine Man," in *Synoptische Studien* (Tübingen: Mohr Siebeck, 1992) 18–34. Also, on the wider religious context of

The transfiguration narrative takes place on an unspecified high mountaintop. There Jesus, Peter, James and John are said to witness the appearance of "Elijah *with* Moses (ὤφθη αὐτοῖς Ἠλίας σὺν Μωϋσει)" (vv. 2–8).[21] Immediately after his transfiguration, in vv. 9–10, Jesus commands the disciples not to reveal what they had just seen "until after the Son of Man had risen (ἀναστῇ) from the dead" (9:9).[22] Although the disciples do not understand this command, they are described as keeping their questions to themselves (9:10).

Next, a discussion takes place between Jesus and these disciples *about Elijah* – specifically, why the scribes say that Elijah must come first (9:11). Jesus responds that indeed *Elijah has already come*: "But I tell you: Elijah has come, and they did to him whatever they wished just as it is written about him (ἀλλὰ λέγω ὑμῖν ὅτι καὶ Ἠλίας ἐλήλυθεν,[23] καὶ ἐποίησαν αὐτῷ ὅσα ἤθελον, καθὼς γέγραπται ἐπ᾽ αὐτόν)" (9:13).[24] Reflected not only in the scholarly consensus on this passage, but also in the clarifying interpolation in Matthew's version of this account (Mt 17:13), in Jesus' reply to the question by his disciples, Jesus utilizes "Elijah" as a code reference for John the Baptist. Matthew 17:13 explains: τότε συνῆκαν οἱ μαθηταὶ ὅτι περὶ Ἰωάννου τοῦ βαπτιστοῦ εἶπεν αὐτοῖς ("Then the disciples understood that he was speaking to them about John the Baptist").[25] A similar point is explicit in Mt 11:13–14: "For all the

---

"divinized human beings," see Hans-Josef Klauck, *The Religious Context of Early Christianity* (Minneapolis: Fortress, 2003) 250–330.

[21] R. Bultmann argues the two figures were not originally specified as Elijah and Moses, but were "anonymous holy ones" (*History of the Synoptic Tradition*, 260, 309). With or without the chronological order of the two names in Mk 9:4 (reversed in Mk 9:5), there is no evidence they represent, for the author of Mark, the law and the prophets.

[22] The verb ἀναστῇ is an intransitive second aorist subjunctive appearing as part of reported speech and referring to an event to take place in the future.

[23] The second perfect form of the Greek verb, ἔρχομαι here denotes an action completed in the past the results of which have continuing importance in the present. Cf. the second perfect feminine participle in Mk 9:1: ἐληλυθυῖαν.

[24] In 9:12, before Jesus declares that Elijah has already come, he affirms the scribe's teaching cited by his disciples that Elijah will come first and adds that Elijah's role in coming will be "to restore all things (ἀποκαθιστάνει πάντα)." John Bowman draws a connection between the word "restore" (ἀποκαθίστημι, Mk 9:12) and שׁוב in Mal 4:6, thus linking this word in Mark specifically to the idea of Elijah's return (*The Gospel of Mark: The New Christian Jewish Passover Haggadah* [Leiden: Brill, 1965] 345). The words "as it is written of him" in Mk 9:13 pose a difficulty. Nowhere is the martyrdom of Elijah *redivivus* predicted in Scriptures, although this fact has not deterred scholars from suggesting possibilities, such as 1 Kgs 19:2, 10 or Rev 11:6. See C. G. Montefiore, *The Synoptic Gospels*, 2nd ed. rev. (London: Macmillan, 1927) 1.209. John Bowman suggests the phrase refers to the story of John's death in Mk 6:17–29 (*The Gospel of Mark: The New Christian Jewish Passover Haggadah*, 198).

[25] The disciples' understanding reflects their own election. Cf. *Corp. Herm.* 13.1 in which a mountaintop is a place of revelation and descending the mountaintop results in election: "My father, you spoke indistinctly and in riddles when talking about divinity in the *General Discourses* … But after you talked with me coming down from the mountain, I became your suppliant" (ET: Brian P. Copenhaver; *Hermetica: The Greek* Corpus Hermeticum *and the* Latin

prophets and the law prophesied until John; and if you are willing to accept it, he is Elijah the one being about to come (πάντες γὰρ οἱ προφῆται καὶ ὁ νόμος ἕως Ἰωάννου ἐπροφήτευσαν· καὶ εἰ θέλετε δέξασθαι, αὐτός ἐστιν Ἠλίας ὁ μέλλων ἔρχεσθαι)."[26]

If this second section (Mk 9:9–13), "the coming of Elijah,"[27] is read as an editorial comment on the first section, the "transfiguration" (Mk 9:2–8), and if, thus, the use of "Elijah" as a code word for John the Baptist in the second passage is intended to elucidate Elijah's identity in the first, *and* if the verb ὤφθη used of Elijah in the first passage is, as many scholars agree, a *terminus technicus* denoting a resurrection appearance (see discussion below),[28] then – suspending

---

Asclepius *in A New English Translation with Notes and Introduction* [Cambridge: Cambridge University, 1992] 49).

[26] Emphasizing that the author of the Gospel of Mark considered John the Baptist's identification as Elijah as *a reliable teaching of Jesus against a variety of opponents* who rejected this teaching as false, Étienne Trocmé writes, "Lastly, the opposition between Jesus and scribes, in Mark, is sometimes set in the context of eschatological and messianic expectation. In these passages too we see the Evangelist's hostility rebound from the Jewish doctors on to certain Christian circles he abhorred. This transfer is not obvious in 9.11–13, where Jesus, in reply to a question by Peter, James, and John referring to a doctrine taught by the scribes, identifies, in rather mysterious terms, John the Baptist with Elijah *redivivus* as announced in Mal 4.5–6 (LXX 3.23–4). It is nevertheless present in this text if we can trust to two indications. The first concerns the identification of John the Baptist with Elijah. The view of the Christians of the day on this point were indeed far from being unanimous: 'Johannine' circles were categorically opposed to this identification (cf. John 1.21); in the church for which Matthew was written the idea was favoured, although not imposed on those who did not accept it; elsewhere certain people, among whom there may have been disciples of Jesus, preferred to reserve for him the honour of being Elijah *redivivus*. By introducing a *logion* where Jesus identifies John the Baptist with this eschatological personage, Mark is thus contradicting certain Christians as well as criticizing the spiritual blindness of the scribes, whose thinking is imprisoned in a too rigid apocalyptic framework. There would perhaps be no cause for comparing the two groups the Evangelist is opposing here, were it not for second indication that encourages us to do so. Mark puts the doctrine of the scribes concerning Elijah *redivivus* into the mouths of Peter, James, and John, whose inability to understand Jesus' teaching he has just stressed (9.10; cf. 8.32 and 9.5–6), and suggests that the three disciples had sought in Jewish speculations an argument with which to contradict their Master. It is as though the author of the Gospel of Mark wished to insinuate that in paying too much attention to the ideas of the γραμματεῖς, certain Christians were deviating from the real teaching of Jesus" (*The Formation of the Gospel according to Mark*, trans. Pamela Gaughan [Philadelphia: Westminster, repr. 1975 (1963)] 116–17).

[27] This section is omitted from Luke as a part of that author's program of inventing Jesus as Elijah.

[28] The form is 3rd person singular aorist passive of ὁράω. Here it is intransitive, used thus with the dative. Cf. Lk 24:34; Acts 9:17; 13:31; 26:16; 1 Cor 15:5. Whereas the idea of heavenly appearances is popular in Luke-Acts, the transfiguration scene is the only such occurrence in the Gospel of Mark. In Mark, Jesus himself is never said to "appear," only to "have been raised (ἠγέρθη)" (Mk 16:6). While it is difficult to be sure exactly what type of "seeing" is suggested by ὤφθη, a few observations can be made: (1) Acts 2:3 indicates sudden manifestation of something previously not visible; (2) in Lk 9:31, the disciples are explicitly *not* asleep, but awake for the vision; and, (3) the 3rd person singular form used by the voice from the cloud ("This is my son, the beloved; listen to him!" [Mk 9:7]), in contrast with the 2nd person singular in the

momentarily the assumption that the transfiguration represents Christological concerns exclusively – the most logical explanation of the transfiguration is that it represents *Jesus'* brief "transformation" (μετεμορφώθη [Mk 9:2/Mt 17:2])[29] on witnessing *John's resurrection from the dead.* Can this hypothesis be demonstrated?

As Margaret Thrall has pointed out, "There is...some explicit or implicit allusion to Elijah and Moses in five of the seven verses of the Marcan narrative. In some sense *they are the figures upon whom the whole story turns.*"[30] To be sure, the unusual description of Jesus and his disciples meeting "Elijah *with* Moses (Ἠλίας σὺν Μωϋσεῖ)," suggests that Elijah, if not Moses, plays a key role in this short narrative.[31] If "Elijah" designates John the Baptist in 9:4, as it does in 9:13, then Elijah's appearance in the transfiguration scene suggests, that although dead (beheaded only two chapters earlier [6:14–29]), John appears from heaven – *with* Moses to back him – to ratify what apparently could not be disclosed to Jesus before John was arrested and killed, namely, Jesus' position as his successor – specifically, John's approval of Jesus' interpretations of the Law.[32] Parallel to

---

baptism ("You are my son, the beloved; with you I am well pleased," Mk 1:11), indicates that the importance of what is seen is not for Jesus, but his disciples. Although the Gospel of Mark possesses no other occurrence of the aorist passive of ὁράω, it is possible to deduce the author's intention by the following observations. If ὤφθη does not suggest resurrection, it must represent a heavenly "presence" of some other kind. Mark, however, rejects other types of appearances, as witnessed by (1) his exclusion of the many traditions of angelophanies known to the author of Luke-Acts; (2) his exclusion of post-resurrection appearances known to Paul (1 Cor 15:5–8) and the other evangelists; and (3) his clarification that Jairus' daughter, who is also "raised," but after being raised resumes her normal pre-raised state, was not dead, but sleeping (Mk 5:39). We know from Mk 12:24–27 and 16:6, however, that the author accepts resurrection from the dead. It is therefore likely that if the author of Mark implies by "Elijah," John the Baptist, then John's "appearance" is a resurrection appearance.

[29] Cf. 2 Cor 3:18 and Rom 12:2. See J. Behm, "μεταμορφόω," *TNDT*, 4.762–67; E. Lohmeyer, "Die Verklärung Jesu nach dem Markus-Evangelium," *ZNW* (1922) 206–9; W. Gerber, "Die Metamorphose Jesu, Mark 9, 2 f. par.," *TZ* (1967) 385–95. Metamorphosis is, for the author of the Gospel of Mark, the only philosophically acceptable way to describe such a transformative event in the life of Jesus. In the Markan transfiguration there is no glorification and no shining face. Jesus is simply changed – permitted for a brief moment to don a magical invisibility cloak symbolizing his succession to John as prophet-teacher.

[30] Margaret E. Thrall, "Elijah and Moses in Mark's Account of the Transfiguration," *NTS* (1969) 305; emphasis added.

[31] Cf. Mt 17:3: καὶ ἰδοὺ ὤφθη αὐτοῖς Μωϋσῆς καὶ Ἠλίας συλλαλοῦντες μετ' αὐτοῦ and Lk 9:30: καὶ ἰδοὺ ἄνδρες δύο συνελάλουν αὐτῷ, οἵτινες ἦσαν Μωϋσῆς καὶ Ἠλίας, οἱ ὀφθέντες ἐν δόξῃ ἔλεγον τὴν ἔξοδον αὐτοῦ, ἣν ἤμελλεν πληροῦν ἐν Ἰερουσαλήμ, both of which demote Elijah to second position and promote Moses to the subject of the verb as opposed to object of a preposition (σὺν Μωϋσεῖ). The author of Luke-Acts' concern to emphasize Jesus, not John, as Elijah may determine his revision of this sentence. Note the circumlocution οἵτινες ἦσαν Μωϋσῆς καὶ Ἠλίας, οἱ ὀφθέντες ἐν δόξῃ in place of the single verb, ὤφθη.

[32] About Elijah's placement before Moses in 9:4, W. Wink argues, "Mark's reversal of the usual order is surely secondary, since the transfiguration scene has developed as a new 'Sinai' theophany, with Moses in the more prominent place. *Mark must have had strong reasons for the change* (the original order still survives in 9:5)" (*John the Baptist*, 15; emphasis added). Cf.

the endorsement that John's baptism provides for Jesus' agency as healer (the other account in Mark also involving a proclamation by a voice from heaven),[33] John's appearance at the transfiguration endorses Jesus' agency as teacher.

In addition, this interpretation of the Markan transfiguration as a succession narrative has an important and direct parallel.[34] In 1 Kgs 19, the Lord speaks to Elijah on Mount Horeb,[35] directing him:

> Go, return on your way to the wilderness of Damascus; when you arrive, you shall anoint Hazael as king over Aram. Also you shall anoint Jehu son of Nimshi as king over Israel; *and you shall anoint Elisha son of Shaphat of Abelmeholah as prophet in your place"* (1 Kgs 19:15–16; NRSV).

In the narrative of 1 Kgs 19, succession is passed from Elijah to Elisha on a mountaintop with frequent allusions to Moses (e.g., 19:8/Ex 34:27–28; 19:9/Ex 33:17–23).[36] Similarly, in Mk 9:2–8, succession is passed from John (Elijah) to Jesus (cf. also Mk 1:14) also with allusions to Moses. In the transfiguration,

---

Rev 11:3–12 in which the "two witnesses," probably Moses and Elijah (by some understood as Jesus/John), are eschatological prophets, martyred by the beast.

[33] Morton Enslin regards Jesus' baptism and transfiguration as "the two vital turning points in his [Mark's] narrative," commenting that both events reflect "Markan creation" ("The Artistry of Mark," 397). Also, in the last footnote to his article, Enslin adds, "That the descriptions of the scenes of the transfiguration and baptism are definitely and not accidentally parallel and clearly and deliberately related would seem to me too obvious for argument" (399 n. 26). The author of Matthew furthers his association of the two events by importing from Mk 1:11/Mt 3:17 to Mt 17:5 the phrase ἐν σοὶ/ᾧ εὐδόκησα. C. E. Carlston corroborates this point: "Like the voice at the baptism, to which it is certainly related in Mark's eyes, it bears witness to who Jesus is" ("Transfiguration and Resurrection," *JBL* 80 [1961] 238). Nb.: at Jesus' baptism in Mark, Jesus has no disciples (cf. Mk 1:9–1 and 16–20). Not until John is arrested by Herod Antipas (Mk 1:14) does he acquire them.

[34] Justin Martyr's explanation (*Dial.* 49) that Elijah gives John part of his spirit on a parallel with Moses and Joshua (Num 27) suggests Justin read Mark 9 as presented here – as a succession narrative. Bringing the passage from Num 27:12–23 (esp. v. 18) to the interpretation of Mk 9:11 par. widens, for Justin, the Moses-John-Jesus, Moses-Jesus, Elijah-John, John-Jesus prophetic/teaching successions already in play with the added Moses-Joshua (and Joshua=Jesus) one – final touches on a defense of Jesus' legitimacy as successor to these illustrious figures from the past. And, who, least of all Justin, could resist the Joshua/Jesus word play? The present author does not, however, see Num 27 behind the tradition as it appears in Mark 9.

[35] Although succession is passed from Elijah to Elisha on Mt. Horeb, the implied location of the transfiguration in the Gospel of Mark is probably not Mt. Horeb. Although it is a "high mountain," Mt. Horeb is implausibly far away. Most likely the author merges the traditions of Elijah on both the mountains of Horeb and Carmel for his location on an unspecified "high mountain" (Mk 9:2). See below n. 43. Jesus' secret knowledge of which mountain to climb to find John may be compared to how Elisha keeps secret the information regarding the whereabouts of Elijah's corpse (2 Kgs 2:16–18).

[36] This element of the Elijah tradition is reflected in Sir 48:8b (LXX): καὶ προφήτας διαδόχους μετ' αὐτόν. Moses, too, receives his sanction as successor from a divine voice on Mount Horeb (Exod 3). Michael Tilly points out in a note (*Johannes der Täufer*, 153 n. 31): "Das Schülerverhältnis des Elisa gegenüber dem Elija wird allein in der lateinische Rezension des Isidorus Hispalensis erwähnt," citing Theodor Schermann, *Propheten- und Apostel-*

like Elisha in 1 Kgs 19,[37] Jesus receives from his teacher heavenly endorsement as successor. Such a significant cultic shift is witnessed by the prophet/teacher without equal – the one after whom both Elijah's and Jesus' succession accounts are modeled – Moses, but again, receives, in all three, its ultimate sanction from the *bat qôl*.[38] Jesus' white clothing in v. 3 may be compared to Elijah's mantle[39] – a symbol of the prophet's power (cf. 2 Kgs 2:8; 1 Kgs 19:19) – representing succession as in 1 Kgs 19:19–21 (cf. 2 Kgs 2:13–14).[40] In Mark, this legitimation by exalted authorities of the past[41] is provided, not just for the benefit of Jesus, but for his disciples, Peter, James and John (Mk 9:4: "Elijah appeared, with Moses, to *them*") – *and* for Mark's readers – testifying to all that John the Baptist ("Elijah") is risen from the dead.[42] Thus, the Latin title, "*transfiguratio*" misleads about the true emphasis of the passage. Jesus is, after all, transformed in its first verse, whereas "Elijah" appears in the middle of the narrative at its climax. The passage is more appropriately entitled, "*resurrectio*."

---

legenden, nebst Jüngerkatalogen des Dorotheus und verwandter Texte (Leipzig: J. C. Hinrichs, 1907) 113.

[37] Elisha's heavenly endorsement is the Lord's message to Elijah to anoint Elisha successor (1 Kgs 19:16).

[38] As Brenda Shaver correctly points out, however, the influence of Moses legends on Elijah stories could have gone the other way: "It is by no means clear, however, that all of the Moses legends are earlier than the Elijah stories that resemble them. ... Certain aspects of the Elijah legends may have played a part in shaping the Moses legends" ("The Prophet Elijah in the Literature of the Second Temple Period," 59).

[39] An outer garment made of sheep's skin: ἡ μηλωτή in 1 Kgs 19:19; 2 Kgs 1:8, 13, 14 (LXX). Cf. discussion of Jesus' garb (111).

[40] Jesus' metamorphosis also represents a surge of inspiration and enthusiasm on experience of John's exaltation. Cf. Philo, *On the Virtues* 217; Plut., *Rom.* 28; Acts 1–2.

[41] Cf. Akhmimic *Apoc. Zeph.* 9.1–5 in which righteous figures from the past Abraham, Isaac, Jacob, Enoch, Elijah and David appear to the visionary. The visionary also learns from the angel that his name is written in the book of the living.

[42] Cf. Mt 11:13–15; 17:11–13; Lk 1:17. The author's use of cryptic language here is supported, not only by his understanding of his work as a μυστήριον (Mk 4:11), the theme of secrecy, the parabolic teachings (e.g., 4:1–34), and the parallel in Mk 9:13 where Elijah unmistakably refers to John the Baptist, but in specific passages, such as Mk 13:14, in which the author inserts a parenthetical comment indicating that a veiled message is contained in what is written. Furthermore, of eight allusions to Elijah in Mark (6:15; 9:4, 5, 11, 12, 13; 15:35, 36), none contradict the present argument. Finally, background for the link between Elijah and resurrection is found in two Second Temple texts. Sir 48:11 (even if not the view of Sirach) connects Elijah to the idea of resurrection and 4Q521 makes Elijah resurrection's agent. Interpreting Sir 48:11, É. Puech argues that only those who respond to Elijah's call of repentance (that is, who see Elijah when he returns) are guaranteed afterlife ("Ben Sira 48:11 et la Résurrection," in *Of Scribes and Scrolls. Studies on the Hebrew Bible, Intertestamental Judaism, and Christian Origins*, eds. H. W. Attridge, J. J. Collins and T. H. Tobin [Lanham, MD: The College Theology Society University Press of America, 1990] 81–90). See Brenda J. Shaver, "The Prophet Elijah in the Literature of the Second Temple Period," 9, 153, 160. Also, the "saints" raised at the moment of Jesus' death – coming out of their tombs and appearing to many (πολλὰ σώματα τῶν κεκοιμημένων ἁγίων ἠγέρθησαν [Mt 27:52]) – reflect a belief in appearances of dead people other than Jesus among early followers of John and Jesus.

If this interpretation is correct, then the meeting that takes place on the wilderness summit involves an apparition of John (Elijah), an apparition of Moses, and Jesus who, while alive, also appears as a kind of ghost-like specter (καὶ τὰ ἱμάτια αὐτοῦ ἐγένετο στίλβοντα λευκὰ λίαν οἷα γναφεὺς ἐπὶ τῆς γῆς οὐ δύναται οὕτως λευκᾶναι). The wilderness locale (9:2; cf. Mk 6:31, 32) is ideal, not only as a place to expect appearances in general, but to expect appearances of Moses (Exod 15:22–40; and par. in Num), Elijah (cf. 1 Kgs 19:8–18), *and John according to the Gospel of Mark.*[43] As many scholars, most recently James A. Kelhoffer, have observed, in Mark, John's setting in the wilderness is, at least in part, a construct of the author based on the model of Elijah. This redactional observation suggests the likelihood that *John's* appearance at the transfiguration is intentional. Indeed, John's appearance can be seen as (1) foretold in Mk 1:2 when John the Baptist is designated the "messenger" (τὸν ἄγγελον) of Mal 3:1 – popularly understood as Elijah on the basis of an eisegetical connection between Mal 3:1 and Mal 4:5;[44] (2) set up by his diet and clothing in Mk 1:6 (cf. 2 Kgs 1:8, LXX); (3) emphasized by his message of divine judgment by fire in Mk 1:8 (cf. 1 Kgs 18:20–40 [victory over priests of Baal]; 2 Kgs 1:10, 12 [reproving Ahaziah]);[45] (4) furthered by the association between Herod/Herodias

---

[43] The reference in both Mark and Matthew, but not Luke, to "six days" (Mk 9:2/Mt 17:1; cf. Ex 24:16) is crucial to this interpretation. See B. D. Chilton, "The Transfiguration: Dominical Assurance and Apostolic Vision," 115–24. With regard to the location of the transfiguration, the present author interprets κατ᾽ ἰδίαν in Mk 9:2 in light of Mk 6:31–32 as a desert location. It is possible, using this same type of literary comparison, to interpret κατ᾽ ἰδίαν in light of Mk 13:3 arriving at a location on the Mount of Olives which is also the location in Mark's Gospel of Jesus' entry into Jerusalem (Mk 11:1). In the Gospel of Luke and Acts the Mount of Olives is the location of Jesus' ascension into heaven (Lk 24:50; Acts 1:9–12). In this case the wilderness connection with Moses and Elijah would be broken as nowhere is the Mount of Olives referred to as "wilderness." In the secondary literature on the transfiguration, however, the Mount of Olives also never arises as a plausible location for Jesus' metamorphosis probably because it was neither "high," nor "apart" (cf. Mk 9:2). The most common proposals include Mt. Tabor (not, however, "high"), Mt. Carmel (just west of the region of Galilee in Phoenicia) and Mt. Hermon (Caesarea Philippi is at the foot of this mountain). In favor of the Mt. Carmel location are connections with the Elijah-Elisha cycles in 1 Kgs 18 and 2 Kgs 2:25, 4:25. The Carmelite monastic movement takes its name from this mountain. With regard to the origins of monasticism, Jerome refers, in his prologue to the *Life of Saint Paul*, to the theory that both Elijah and John the Baptist were the initiators of this movement. Both Jerome and Cassian note a desire on the part of monks to follow not only the Baptist's eating habits, but his clothing habits as well, including both camel hair coat and *cingulum* (monastic belt); see E. Lupieri, "John the Baptist: The First Monk," 17.

[44] 4Q76 demonstrates Elijah appendix was present in the text of Malachi by the time of John the Baptist. See R. E. Fuller, *DJD XV*, 221–32, pls. XL–XLII.

[45] Cf. Elijah's role in judgment in *Liv. Pro.* 21 "Elijah." Although "fire" is absent in Mark's version (cf. Q 3:16b par.), baptism by "the Holy Spirit" possesses this connotation. "Fire" in the other versions is, thus, explanatory; cf. Isa 29:6; 30:27 ff.; Ezek 1:4; Joel 2:28–32 and 1QS 4:13, 21. Cf. Sir 48:3; Lk 9:54. In addition, the Lukan *Sondergut* passage on Jesus' rejection by the Samaritans summarizes the differences between the two characterizations (Lk 9:54–56). According to v. 53, Jesus sent messengers ahead to a Samaritan village, apparently requesting

(Ahab/Jezebel; 1 Kgs 19:1–3; 21:1–16) in Mark 6; and (5) brought to a climax at the apex of Mark's narrative in this theophanic appearance. John's function as Elijah *redivivus* is even clarified in this gospel in *contradistinction* to Jesus who, the author is careful to note, is only *mistakenly* apprehended in this role: Mk 8:27–28: "And Jesus and his disciples went to the villages of Caesarea Philippi; and on the way he asked his disciples, 'Who do the people consider me to be?' And they answered him, 'John the Baptist; and others, Elijah; and others, one of the prophets.' He asked them, '*Rather* who do you consider me to be?'"[46] Furthermore, we know that expectations of John's rising and appearing were routine. This position may even have represented the official stance of Rome: "But when Herod heard it, he said, 'John, whom I beheaded, has been raised from the dead (ἀκούσας δὲ ὁ Ἡρῴδης ἔλεγεν, Ὃν ἐγὼ ἀπεκεφάλισα Ἰωάννην, οὗτος ἠγέρθη)'" (Mk 6:16).

---

they prepare to welcome the teacher, but the Samaritans refuse. In response to this rejection by the Samaritans, James and John ask whether Jesus wishes them to "command fire to come down from heaven and consume them." The reference to "fire" is derived from 1 Kgs 18:20–40 and 2 Kgs 1:10, 12 when Elijah destroys his enemies with fire from heaven. (On Elijah's use of fire, see Brenda Shaver, "The Prophet Elijah in the Literature of the Second Temple Period," 45–48.) Such a proposal by the disciples is incompatible with Jesus' saving work and is thus met by the Lukan Jesus with extreme disapproval: "But he turned and rebuked them" (9:55). Other ancient, textual authorities emphasize Jesus' rebuke with the following interpolation: "…[he] rebuked them, and said, 'You do not know what spirit you are of, for the Son of man has not come to destroy the lives of human beings but to save them'" (NRSV). The disciples' proposal is, however, consistent with the Baptist's message of the mightier one's destruction ("baptism") of the unrepentant by the Holy Spirit and unquenchable fire (Q 3:16b–17). This section in Luke also contains a second reference to Elijah. To mark the beginning of Jesus' journey to Jerusalem (travel narrative), v. 51 records, "When the days drew near for him to be taken up (ἀναλήμψεως), he set his face to go to Jerusalem." The same verb is used to express Elijah's translation in 4 Kgdms 2:11 (LXX) (καὶ ἀνελήμφθη Ηλιου ἐν συσσεισμῷ ὡς εἰς τὸν οὐρανόν). The emphasis on Jesus' ascension may suggest a belief (hope?) Jesus would not die in Jerusalem, but be translated. Verse 51 reflects Luke's portrait of *Jesus*, not John, as Elijah. In v. 54 the disciples reproduce not Jesus', but John's teaching. In v. 55, John's teaching is corrected/rejected by Jesus.

[46] The insertion, εἰ θέλετε δέξασθαι to Q at Mt 11:14 probably indicates resistance to the interpretation of John the Baptist as Elijah. At least in its Matthean context, the assertion in Mt 11:14 that John "is Elijah who is about to come (αὐτός ἐστιν Ἠλίας ὁ μέλλων ἔρχεσθαι)," may pick up on the question from John in prison, "Are you the one who is to come?" to which Jesus replies, "No, you are!" Cf. Josef Ernst, *Johannes der Täufer*, 6: "Markus illustriert am Beispiel des Johannes erzählend das Dogma des Elias redivivus" (cf. also 9). See below: 192–95. According to John J. Collins, the description of the "one to come" in Q 7:18–19, 22–23, with the insertion of the raising of the dead in Isa 61, may reflect a view of Jesus as Elijah (*The Scepter and the Star*, 121). Indeed Jesus' raising of the dead confused his overall portrait as Davidic king. The prophet, Elijah is the figure with whom expectations of raising the dead are associated (1 Kgs 17:17–24; also, Elisha: 2 Kgs 4:8–37; cf. Sir 48:11). Perhaps for this reason the author of the Third Gospel relaxes (over and against his Markan source) connections between John the Baptist and Elijah, highlighting, rather *Jesus'* connections to this prophet. See John J. Collins, *The Scepter and the Star*, 205. On Luke's rejection of a single all-pervasive ideal, in favor of a wide variety of Jewish and Graeco-Roman model paradigms for the construction of his portrait of Jesus, see: Clare K. Rothschild, *Luke-Acts and the Rhetoric of History*, 99–141.

On the basis of the numerous references to John as Elijah in the preceding chapters, it is possible the reference to Elijah in Mk 15:34–37 also connotes John. At his death, Jesus cries out, "*Eloi, Eloi*" and the bystanders, according to the author, imagine Jesus is summoning Elijah.[47] A person running to offer Jesus sour wine on a "reed"[48] urges the crowd to observe closely whether Elijah appears to rescue him (Mk 15:36). This highly enigmatic passage may signal a tradition maintaining that Jesus cried out on the cross for his teacher, John who was martyred, perhaps, only a matter of months (even weeks or days?) before him. To contain Jesus' awkward misgiving over his master from the cross ("Why have you forsaken me?"), the author of Mark revises the Elijah tradition by means of Ps 22:1. In so doing, however, he transfers Jesus' uncertainty about John to a, perhaps, even less likely (or, at least, theologically more challenging?) alternative: God.

4.3 History of the Debate

The history of the debate of the Markan transfiguration provides all of the necessary background for assessing the cogency of the present hypothesis. Although, as noted above, no clear consensus of interpretation exists for the Markan transfiguration, the greatest proportion of scholars, including certain formidable scholars in the field spanning more than one hundred years of research, concludes, on the basis of much and varied evidence, that the transfiguration is a misplaced resurrection narrative.[49] Arguing against this *consensus opinio*, however, is Robert Stein. Stein claims that because Jesus is very much alive in the account, it is not a resurrection account at all. Rather, the original narrative took place, as Mark records, during Jesus' lifetime. Although the present thesis ultimately rejects Stein's conclusions (much of his case is driven by a literalistic interpretation), elements of his argument are enumerated next for their helpful exposition of a key assumption concerning this passage, namely that any mention of resurrection in Mark's gospel necessarily refers to Jesus (e.g., Mk 8:31; 9:31; 10:34; 16:6).

---

[47] Cf. Mt 27:49: "Leave him alone! Let us see whether *Elijah* will *come* to save him (Ἄφες ἴδωμεν εἰ ἔρχεται Ἡλίας σώσων αὐτόν)."

[48] Cf. the reference to the Baptist as κάλαμος ("reed") in Q 7:24 (Mt 11:7) and, perhaps, in Mt 12:20. There are only two other Synoptic occurrences of this word: Mk 15:19/Mt 27:29 and Mk 15:36/Mt 27:48. Mk 15:36a/Mt 27:48 employs this word in between the two verses on Elijah. Reeds suggest water; see 211 n. 30. On reeds as a feature of the Jordan valley, see 76 n. 149.

[49] C. H. Dodd adduces, as a parallel for understanding the transfiguration, the episode of Jesus' walking on water. See Dodd's "The Appearances of the Risen Christ: An Essay in Form-Criticism of the Gospels," 23–24. Charles E. Carlston agrees that Jesus' walking on water is "probably related to the transfiguration story if either or both are misplaced resurrection appearances" ("Transfiguration and Resurrection," 233–34). Lk 5:1–11/Jn 21:3–11 provides a precedent for the "misplaced" resurrection account argument.

In his argument against the transfiguration as a resurrection account, Stein first notes that not Jesus, but Elijah, "appears" in Mk 9:4.[50] Indeed this argument is the primary difficulty encountered by interpretations of Jesus' transfiguration as a resurrection account. As noted above,[51] the aorist passive form of ὁράω, a *terminus technicus* for resurrection appearances, is not, in this instance, applied to Jesus, but to Elijah: ὤφθη αὐτοῖς Ἠλίας σὺν Μωϋσεῖ.[52]

To this well-known objection, Stein adds:

> We encounter the difficulty that the term occurs too late in the pericope to refer to an appearance of the risen Lord, for Jesus has been present all along and has already been transfigured. Mark would not only have had to change the subject of *ophthe* but also the location of the term.[53]

According to the present argument, however, that *Jesus* does not "appear" in the transfiguration, is no sound basis on which to judge whether the account qualifies as a resurrection narrative. Rather, taking "Elijah" as the one to appear, *as the text specifies*, the aorist passive form of the verb, ὁράω *may retain its technical sense in this passage*. A resurrection *is* here depicted: the resurrection of John.

Stein's second point concerns the cloud (νεφέλη) in 9:7. Against Theodore Weeden and others who hold that the cloud in the transfiguration scene is a kind of resurrection-ascension cloud,[54] Stein argues that because the cloud lands, not on Jesus, but "them (αὐτοῖς)," that is, Elijah, Moses and Jesus, and, unlike other resurrection accounts (e.g., Acts 1:9) does not transport Jesus away, but leaves him behind, the cloud does not prove the account was originally a resurrection.[55] In favor of the argument of this chapter, however, is that the cloud lands on "Elijah" (with Moses) and transports them away, again emphasizing the very unusual meaning that "Elijah" – although *translated* to heaven in 2 Kgs 2 – is here resurrected from the dead.[56] George H. Boobyer provides literary background

---

[50] Others have commented that John is not "resurrected" (ἀναστάσις), but "raised" (ἐγήγερται) in Mk 6:14. This objection is, however, irrelevant. The same might be said of Jesus in Mk 16:6 (ἐγέρθη). See W. Wink, *John the Baptist*, 10.

[51] See above: n. 28.

[52] R. H. Stein, "Is the Transfiguration (Mark 9:2–8) a Misplaced Resurrection Account?" 80–81.

[53] R. H. Stein, "Is the Transfiguration (Mark 9:2–8) a Misplaced Resurrection Account?" 80.

[54] T. Weeden, *Mark – Traditions in Conflict*, 120.

[55] R. H. Stein, "Is the Transfiguration (Mark 9:2–8) a Misplaced Resurrection Account?" 81.

[56] "As they continued walking and talking, a chariot of fire and horses of fire separated the two of them, and Elijah ascended in a whirlwind into heaven" (2 Kgs 2:11) (NRSV). See the excursus on Elijah's assumption in Brenda Shaver, "The Prophet Elijah in the Literature of the Second Temple Period," 52–54. As Shaver points out in a note, לקח, applied to Elijah in 2 Kgs 2:3, 5, 9 and 10, is regarded as a *terminus technicus* for translation from earth to the afterlife (p. 53). See also Shaver's comparison of Elijah with Baal, the "Rider of the Clouds," 47–48. In addition, see C. Houtman, "Elijah," *DDD*, 282–85 and M. Öhler, *Elia im Neuen Testament*

for this point by his observation that clouds were not the exclusive transport of any one figure in Jewish or Christian literature. In the *Apoc. Pet.* 6, after the Son of Man descends on a cloud, *all* the people are caught up in "clouds" and transported away (Mk 13:26).[57]

Further disregarding the blatant form-critical similarities between the transfiguration and resurrection accounts, Stein makes the following categorical statement regarding Jesus' transfiguration and Jesus' baptism: "…the similarities between the baptism and the transfiguration are far closer than those between the transfiguration and any resurrection-account."[58] Happily the present argument both endorses Stein's point about similarities with Jesus' baptism *and* favors similarities he denies with the resurrection accounts. The claim here is that *both* Jesus' baptism *and* the canonical resurrection accounts provide parallels for understanding the transfiguration.[59] Connections between the transfiguration and the baptism are taken up momentarily.

In the final section of Stein's argument against the transfiguration as an account of the resurrection of Jesus, Stein summons the work of Charles E. Carlston.[60] Carlston argues that if the transfiguration happened in Jesus' lifetime, the subsequent behavior of his disciples would be inexplicable; thus, the account must originally have taken place after his death.[61] However, Carlston's objection is, as Stein points out, not cogent. The same argument can be made of Jesus'

(BZNW 88; Berlin: de Gruyter, 1997). The Gospel of John may simply deny eschatological traditions regarding Elijah or may intimate knowledge of "Elijah" as referring to John the Baptist, by denying "Elijah's" translation (Jn 3:13; 8:52–53) and John's qualification as Elijah (1:21). For J. L. Martyn, Elijah's traits are, not the Baptist's, but Jesus' in the Gospel of John. All six Synoptic references to the Baptist as Elijah are missing from the Fourth Gospel. Rather, in this Gospel, Martyn argues, Elijah's and Elisha's miracles provide a model on which to build a portrait of a miracle-working Jesus ("We Have Found Elijah," 181–219). Martyn's thesis understands Jesus' Elijah (and Elisha) characteristics as a competitive element in the Johannine program against the Baptist. Presumably thinking of Mal 3:1, 2 and 4:5 – and citing R. Brown ("Three Quotations from John the Baptist in the Gospel of John," *CBQ* [1960] 292–98), Martyn states that John's "coming one" may be a technical term for "the eschatological Elijah"; cf. Mt 11:14. Raymond Brown argues that Jn 1:30: ὀπίσω μου ἔρχεται ἀνὴρ ὃς ἔμπροσθέν μου γέγονεν, ὅτι πρῶτός μου ἦν is a reference by John the Baptist to Elijah. Brown writes: "Of no other figure in the OT could John the Baptist have said that as truly as of Elias, who had existed nine hundred years before him, and yet was expected to come as a messenger before God's final judgment" ("Three Quotations from John the Baptist in the Gospel of John," 298).

[57] Cf. 1 Thess 4:17.

[58] R. H. Stein, "Is the Transfiguration (Mark 9:2–8) a Misplaced Resurrection Account?" 84.

[59] The question can be posed, but not answered as to which came first: baptism, transfiguration or resurrection accounts. E. Meyer argues the transfiguration is the root to which the others can be traced: "Aus der Verklärung sind die Auferstehung und die Erscheinungen des Auferstandenen erwachsen, sie ist die letzte Wurzel des Christentums" (*Ursprung und Anfänge des Christentums* [Stuttgart/Berlin: J. C. Cotta, 1924] 1.154).

[60] C. E. Carlston, "Transfiguration and Resurrection," 235.

[61] C. E. Carlston, "Transfiguration and Resurrection," 233.

baptism: the behavior of Jesus' disciples after his baptism in Mark is equally incomprehensible. Apparently, these disciples fail Jesus after the transfiguration, just as they fail him after his baptism because, for the author of Mark, they are thick-headed and unaffected by even the most momentous signs and teachings.[62] Jesus, nevertheless, is deeply affected by the events, as shown by his demonstration of miracles after his baptism and by his invigorated commitment to teaching and resolute march to his glorification in Mk 10:1,[63] immediately following John's revelation of his own glorification in the transfiguration. Precisely to this point, the Lukan version modifies Mark, revealing this intention in the insertion in Lk 9:31:

> v. 30 And behold, two men talked with him [Jesus], they were Moses and Elijah (καὶ ἰδοὺ ἄνδρες δύο συνελάλουν αὐτῷ, οἵτινες ἦσαν Μωϋσῆς καὶ Ἠλίας),
> v. 31 the ones appearing in glory, and spoke of his [Jesus'] departure,[64] *which he [Jesus] was about to accomplish in Jerusalem* (οἳ ὀφθέντες ἐν δόξῃ ἔλεγον τὴν ἔξοδον αὐτοῦ, ἣν ἤμελλεν πληροῦν ἐν Ἰερουσαλήμ).

According to Mark, proof of John's resurrection provided great encouragement to Jesus – a sanguinity perceptible to Peter who responds: "It is good for us to be here (καλόν ἐστιν ἡμᾶς ὧδε εἶναι)" (9:5).

Although most of Stein's paper is negative, deconstructing arguments for the transfiguration as a resurrection narrative, he concludes with a few positive observations, backing his theory of a pre-resurrection, "living" Jesus in the transfiguration account. All four of Stein's additional, *positive* observations also support the present thesis.

First, in the transfiguration account, in Mk 9:5, Peter refers to Jesus as "Rabbi," an unlikely title by which to address a glorified Lord.[65] Second,

---

[62] Although a counterargument might be that at the baptism there was nothing for them to hear or see.

[63] Mk 10:1: "Departing there he arrived in the boundaries of Judea beyond the Jordan (καὶ ἐκεῖθεν ἀναστὰς ἔρχεται εἰς τὰ ὅρια τῆς Ἰουδαίας [καὶ] πέραν τοῦ Ἰορδάνου)." In contrast to Jesus, his reluctant disciples cower behind (10:32).

[64] Cf. 1 Kgs 19, esp. v. 8.

[65] The question arises as to why "rabbi" instead of the Greek διδάσκαλε; cf. Mk 11:21; 14:45. As M. E. Boring notes, "Mark seems to be interested in Jesus as a teacher. *Didaskalos* is by far the most common 'title' given to Jesus by others in the gospel, and it is used by Jesus of himself (14:14). *Didasko* and *didache* are used with reference to Jesus more than they are in either Matthew or Luke, despite Mark's smaller size. Likewise, Mark has an interest in the words of Jesus, as is seen not only in his including over 3000 of them, but also by repeatedly including such statements as 8:32 *kai parresia ton logon elalei* (cf. also 2:2; 4:14ff., 4:33). These considerations would lead one to expect more teaching of Jesus in Mark, and only makes more pressing the question, 'Why so few?'" ("The Paucity of Sayings in Mark: A Hypothesis," in *SBL 1977 Seminar Papers*, ed. Paul J. Achtemeier [Missoula, Montana: Scholars, 1977] 371). Cf. Mt 26:25, 49. The "Special M" teaching of Mt 23:7–10, rejecting the titles, "Rabbi" and "Teacher" for Jesus, is anomalous in the gospels. The title, "rabbi" is used of Jesus frequently (Mk 9:5; 11:21; 14:45; Jn 1:38, 49; 3:2, 26 [of John the Baptist]; 4:31; 6:25; 9:2; 11:8), and even defended for him (Jn 13:13). It is possible the contradictory Matthean *Sondergut* teaching

whereas in resurrection accounts Jesus departs from his disciples, as noted above, here they remain together throughout the entire event. Third, the command, ἀκούετε αὐτοῦ makes more sense if referring to a living Jesus. Stein writes: "What need is there for a voice from heaven telling the disciples to 'hear the risen Lord.' In fact, what need would there be of a voice at all?"[66] Furthermore, "listen" – an allusion to Deut 18:15 (cf. Acts 3:22) – the passage in which Moses predicts the Lord will raise up another prophet like himself – is tantamount to a command to obey Jesus' teaching.[67] Like the reference to Jesus

---

(Mt 23:7–10) is traced to John the Baptist. It resonates with the *Pater Noster* (Mt 23:9) and shares the rejection of family theme with other Baptist traditions as well: "Call no man your father on earth" (Mt 23:9). John the Baptist is referred to as "rabbi" in Jn 3:26. NT references to his disciples also offer proof of this role (Mk 6:29; Jn 1:35).

[66] Cf. Jn 12:28–30. R. H. Stein, "Is the Transfiguration (Mark 9:2–8) a Misplaced Resurrection Account?" 91.

[67] Cf. Ovid, *Fast.* 2.500–9; Livy, 1.16.2–8; Plutarch, *Rom.* 28; *Num.* 11.3; *Thes.* 35.5; Cic., *Rep.* 6, 10. C. E. Carlston, however, argues that "the central feature of the voice is its function: It serves as divine confirmation of Peter's confession (Mark 8:29) and perhaps of Jesus' prediction of his coming passion and resurrection (Mark 8:31)" ("Transfiguration and Resurrection," 238). The idea can be traced at least as far back as Ernst Lohmeyer ("Die Verklärung Jesu nach dem Markus-Evangelium," 185–215; *Das Evangelium des Markus*, 173–81). Originally, E. Lohmeyer argued the transfiguration scene was comprised of two parts, one Jewish, one Hellenistic – vv. 2c–3, a Hellenistic insertion (à la Apuleius, *Metam.* 11) into the Jewish expectation of Moses' and Elijah's reappearance at the end of the age. He later emended his view, however, on the basis of the idea of metamorphosis found in Exod 34:29 and 2 Bar 51:10–12 (*Das Evangelium des Markus*, 174 n. 7). C. G. Montefiore summarizes Lohmeyer's position in *The Synoptic Gospels* (London: Macmillan, 1927) 1.206. R. Bultmann, too, argues the point of the transfiguration as confirmation of Jesus' messiahship, specifically, "heavenly ratification of Peter's confession and as a prophecy of the resurrection in pictorial form (cp. 9:31)" (*History of the Synoptic Tradition*, 260). Bultmann adds that Luke "felt the need to … call particular attention to the prophetic character of the story: Moses and Elijah talk to Jesus about his death in Jerusalem (9:31)" (261). Bultmann's interpretation of Lk 9:31 (numerous subsequent interpreters following Bultmann on this point), however, governs his interpretation of Mk 9:2–8: indeed *Luke* took the Markan transfiguration as confirmation of Jesus' messiahship through ratification of Peter's confession and prediction of the resurrection. Seen on it own terms, however, the Gospel of Mark, does not intimate this purpose at all. Rather, it makes blatant a very different purpose. Curiously, 2 Pet 1:16–18 appeals to the transfiguration as a miraculous display that corroborates certain of the author's theological claims, much in the same way as Paul does sporadically throughout his epistles (2 Cor 12:11–12 [satirical?]; Gal 3:1–5; Rom 15:18–19; 1 Thes 1:5; 1 Cor 2:4–5; and 1 Cor 12:9–10, 28–30). On the latter point, see James A. Kelhoffer, "The Apostle Paul and Justin Martyr on the Miraculous: A Comparison of Appeals to Authority." On interpretations of the transfiguration account in 2 Pet, see A. von Harnack ("Die Verklärungsgeschichte Jesu," *Sitzungsberichte der preussischen Akademie der Wissenschaften* [1922] 62–80). Also, cf. Lk 16:29. As above, the entire section concerning the rich man and Lazarus (Lk 16:29–31) contains numerous elements with connections to Baptist traditions, including a negative disposition toward eating ("feasting"), (v. 19), hunger (v. 21), Abraham (vv. 22, 23), flames (v. 24), warning (v. 28), agony (v. 24)/torment (v. 28), punishment (v. 24), repentance (v. 30) and eternal damnation (v. 26). See 104–5 n. 106. Lk 16:31, however, suggests absence in a belief in the resurrection. Indeed John the Baptist may have rejected such a belief – another point on which he may have disagreed with Jesus. John's rejection of the resurrection from the dead may have resembled his de-emphasis of other miracles. It had no apparent effect

as "Rabbi," *it portrays Jesus in John's former role of instructor.*[68] Nowhere, however, does the Gospel of Mark suggest that the risen Lord or Son of Man will return as a teacher.[69] Finally, in most resurrection accounts Jesus appears in *human form* and addresses the disciples (e.g., Lk 24:13–35, 36–43). Indeed, an insistence on Jesus' *untransformed* human likeness impresses as a central point of many of the appearance vignettes, depicting, for example, Jesus' palpability (Jn 20:26–29; Lk 24:39–40), his eating of fish (Jn 21:9–14), his walking, his talking, and his breaking of bread (Lk 24:13–35). In the transfiguration, in contrast, even though the divine voice commands the disciples to "listen," Jesus, in the form of a ghostly specter, does not consent to speak.[70] Thus, as Stein correctly points out, the transfiguration characterizes Jesus as a living, thriving, teaching rabbi. If momentarily transfigured (compare the ephemeral alighting on Jesus of the spirit "like a dove (ὡς περιστερὰν)" (Mk 1:10), nothing suggests Jesus has yet died let alone risen from the dead.[71]

The alternative view that Jesus' fleshly veil is momentarily drawn back to reveal a pre-existent or future eschatological glorified state, also has many adherents. This interpretation, however, has no basis in the Markan text. With Wilhelm Michaelis, "the purely eschatological orientation of the whole story rule(s) [*sic*] out any possibility of regarding the transfiguration as an emergence of the pre-existent δόξα of Jesus, esp. since ideas of pre-existence do not occur in the Synoptics."[72] Complementing Michaelis' conclusion, is the specific point that the concept of δόξα is absent from the Markan transfiguration narrative, although it is frequently imported there from Luke's version of the same event

---

on the author of the Gospel of Mark's (even Jesus') claim that John, once murdered, rose. If Lk 16:31 suggests a lack of belief in the resurrection and if this belief is attributed to John, then the designation of John in the Pseudo-Clementine literature (*Rec.* 2.23) as a "Hemerobaptist" – a sect that, according to Epiphanius (*Haer.* 1.17), held doctrine in common with the Pharisees *apart from their denial of the resurrection* – may have some historical basis. This sect is also mentioned by Hegesippus (Eus., *Hist. Eccl.* 4.22) and Justin Martyr (*Dial.* 80).

[68] As far as I know, the only ancient text preserving a reference to John the Baptist as "rabbi" is Jn 3:26. John is, according to the Second Gospel, "instructor" on the basis of the reference to his disciples (Mk 2:18). See Knut Backhaus, *Die "Jüngerkreise" des Täufers Johannes: Eine Studie zu den religionsgeschichtlichen Ursprüngen des Christentums* (PTS 19; Paderborn/ München/Wien/Zürich: Ferdinand Schöningh, 1991).

[69] M. Thrall, "The Transfiguration: Elijah and Moses," 310. Lk 24:13–49 may be an exception.

[70] Cf. Plutarch, *Thes.* 35.5 in which the apparition of Thesus is also silent, leaving out any discussion of post-mortem existence.

[71] C. H. Dodd was first to argue that, unlike resurrection accounts, in the transfiguration (1) Jesus remains with his disciples throughout this account (they are not "orphaned"), (2) a voice speaks from heaven, (3) Elijah, not the Christ, is the one to appear and (4) Jesus is clothed ("The Appearances of the Risen Christ: An Essay in Form-Criticism of the Gospels," 25). About them, Dodd concludes, "To set over against these points of difference I cannot find a single point of resemblance" (25).

[72] W. Michaelis, "ὁράω," *TDNT*, X.354.

(Lk 9:31, 32).[73] Michaelis concludes, therefore, citing Johannes Behm, that the transfiguration is rather "the anticipation and guarantee of an eschatological reality," warning, however, that the message of the voice from the cloud does not support this reading.[74] Picking up on this exception, the only interpretation that accounts for both the transfiguration as guarantee of an upcoming "eschatological reality" and the command from the voice in the cloud to "listen" to Jesus is that Jesus' transfiguration anticipates and guarantees the eschatological reality of *his* upcoming resurrection by proof of the resurrection of his teacher, John the Baptist, *while also* providing official sanction of Jesus' succession as *teacher* in his teacher's absence for the interim before his own death and resurrection. This prediction of both Jesus' immediate *and* his eschatological future on the basis of his teachers' is witnessed by a heavenly appearance of the teacher *par excellence*, Moses. It is, however, ultimately authorized by the voice from heaven.

4.4 A New Solution to Past Problems

The Elijah as Baptist in Mk 9:2–8 hypothesis not only makes sense of much past research, it also solves certain vexing problems concerning the Markan transfiguration. For example, many have questioned what to make of the fact that, of the three present on the mountain, according to the biblical texts, only Jesus is resurrected from the dead. Moses simply died and was buried (Deut 34:5–6; cf. also Jd 9) and Elijah was translated (2 Kgs 2:11).[75] Josephus (*Ant.* 4.326)

---

[73] Luke's version is in turn reliant, at least in part, on Exod 34:29–35 about the glowing skin of Moses' face (δεδόξασται). E.g., T. A. Burkill, "St. Mark's Philosophy of History," *NTS* (1956–57) 148. For the glowing affect of God's presence in an individual, parallels can be found for Jeremiah, the priest Hananiah, certain early Christian disciples such as Stephen (Acts 6:15) and, according to *Lev. Rab.* 1:1 (on Judg 2:1), Phinehas. In fact, Jesus' metamorphosis in Mark may be influenced by Moses' shining face in Exod 34:29–35. However, like the burning bush incident of Exod 3, the primary purpose of Moses' shining face is not anticipation of Moses' future glorification, even if Moses does go on to play a very significant role in Jewish history. Rather it is part of an overall program to sanction the cultic shift from the patriarchs to Moses – an element of a succession narrative. The radiance of Moses' face, like Jesus' dazzling robe, is the temporary result of close contact with a deity, in these cases a sign of divine approval of cultic succession. The white clothing is an apocalyptic image (cf. Dan 7:9; 12:3; 2 Esd 7.97; Mt 13:43; Rev 3:5; 4:4; 7:9, 13). This glowing effect is not without parallels in Graeco-Roman literary sources. Examples include the *Homeric Hymns* 2.275–80 (prior to the 7th cent. BCE); Plutarch, *Moralia*, "The Fortune of the Romans" 10 (45–125 CE); *Liv. Pro.* 21 "Elijah," (bef. 70 CE); and Philo, *On the Virtues* 217 (15 BCE – 50 CE). Jesus' transformation is probably not, however, only outward and transitory, as in these history-of-religions parallels. For the author of the Gospel of Mark, the revelation to Jesus on the mountaintop is also inwardly transformative (cf. Rom 12:2; 2 Cor 3:18; 4:17; Phil 3:21), permanently impressing on him a commitment to his call.

[74] W. Michaelis, "ὁράω," *TDNT*, X.354–55, citing J. Behm, "μεταμορφόω," *TDNT* IV.758.

[75] The tradition of Elijah's translation is widespread. It is *the reason* he was expected to be able to provide different forms of deliverance in the first place. Josephus recounts Elijah's

provides roughly contemporary evidence to the Gospel of Mark of the idea that Moses, like Elijah, was translated, (as opposed to dying a normal death and being buried).[76] But even if such a belief circulated about Moses, the question

---

translation in *Ant.* 9.28. In Josephus' accounts of the translations of both Elijah and Moses, the Greek verb, ἀφανίζω is used (cf. *Ant.* 4.326 and 9.28). As H. D. Betz point out with regard to its occurrence in Mt 6:16, this verb often appears in the context of fasting (*Sermon on the Mount*, 421 nn. 642–43). What Betz fails to mention, however, is any application of this context to the interpretation of Mt 6:19–20 where the verb recurs. If the context can be carried over to vv. 19 and 20 and said to apply to the whole section – or better, to link the two sections (6:16–18 and 6:19–21), then the passage on storing up "treasures" on earth or in heaven "for where your treasure is, there your heart will be also," too involves, not just "performing good deeds here on earth, in particular by sharing one's possessions with others" (Mt 19:21) with Betz (*Sermon on the Mount*, 434), but specifically the context of ritual fasting, establishing as word-plays both βρῶσις ("eating" or "rust") and ἀφανίζειν (to "fast" or "cause to vanish/consume") in vv. 19 and 20. Moreover, the theme of fasting may also govern the sections from 6:22–23 ("healthy eyes") and 6:24 (serving God or "wealth"). Not only are these short enigmatic segments sandwiched between the above sections on fasting and the long section on eating/drinking and anxiety arising from the need for life's basic staples in 6:25–34, but connections between the themes of health (6:22–23) and wealth (6:24) and fasting are clear; see Betz, *The Sermon on the Mount*, 429. I would not argue the theme of ritual fasting determines the teaching, but I would wish to include it among the implications of its message. With Betz, the idea is not that poverty itself is virtuous, but that a detachment from physical appetites and needs is necessary to a moral life. The entire section may be further linked by this theme to the request in the *Pater Noster* for "daily" or "tomorrow's bread" (Mt 6:10c). This is not to reject Betz's proposed structure and interpretation of these passages, only to emphasize one component within them. The present interpretation is that Mt 6:21 implies a contrast between collecting one's θησαυρός – any receptable or repository for valuables (BAGD³, 456), in the body it is the stomach, serving as a receptacle for food necessities and the heart, a receptacle for transcendent (heavenly, eschato-logical) necessities (later: "intellect," Lk 12:34 [See: Betz, *The Sermon on the Mount*, 437]). On "eating and drinking" or the "eating of bread" as periphrastic alternatives for fasting, see 90–1 n. 33. On Second Temple Elijah traditions, see the excellent dissertation by Brenda Shaver, "The Prophet Elijah in the Literature of the Second Temple Period," 1–9; Ulrich Kellerman, "Zu den Elia-Motiven in den Himmelfahrtsgeschichten des Lukas," in *Altes Testament Forschung und Wirklung. FS H. G. Reventlow*, ed. Mommer and W. Thiel (Frankfurt: Peter Lang, 1994) 123–37; R. Bauckham, "The Martyrdom of Enoch and Elijah: Jewish or Christian?" *JBL* (1976) 447–58. See also C. E. Carlston, "Transfiguration and Resurrection," 237–38.

[76] Josephus' account is modeled after the passing of Aeneas and Romulus in Dion. Hal. *Ant. Rom.* 1.64.4 and 2.56.2. One question involves a testimony of Yohanan ben Zakkai's in which God tells Moses that he will come with Elijah at the end of time (Strack-Billerbeck, *Kommentar zum NT,* 1.757). The dating of this testimony is, however, uncertain. For traditions in which Jewish historical figures are believed to dwell in a risen state after their deaths, see *T. Benj.* 10; *2 Bar.* 76:2; 2 Macc. 15:13; *4 Ezra* 14:9; 4 Macc. 7:19, 16:25; Mk 12:25–27; Q 13:29, 28. For traditions claiming certain historical figures have already risen, see 2 Esd 6:26; *1 En.* 70:4; Akhmim Frag. 5 ff.; Ethiopic text of the *Apoc. Pet.*; and *Sib. Or.* 2:240–51. See also J. Jeremias, "Μωϋσῆς," *TDNT*, IV.854. The Akhmim. fragment of the *Apoc. Pet.* 4–6 confirms the position of this paper that the appearances at Jesus' transfiguration were fellow faithful now living in a glorified state arriving to encourage those *imminently* facing their own deaths: "And the Lord continued and said, 'Let us go to the mountain and pray.' And we, the twelve disciples, went with him and entreated him to *show to us one of our righteous brethren who had departed from the world that we might see in what form they are, and taking courage might encourage the men who should hear us.* And as we prayed, suddenly there appeared two men, standing

remains what to make of the fact that, whereas Elijah *and* Moses were translated, Jesus is not. If, however, "Elijah," refers not to the historical Elijah, but to John the Baptist, then all three men (with the exception of Josephus' version of Deut 34) – Moses, John and Jesus – as different from the biblical accounts of Elijah and Enoch, died and were buried.[77] As some have argued, Mark's overwhelming dedication to Jesus' passion – to the details of his crucifixion, death, burial and empty tomb – reflects his refutation of claims that Jesus did *not* die, but was translated. However, insofar as the Gospel of Mark insists on the details of Jesus' *death,* as perhaps opposed to *translation,* the Gospel of Mark *also* insists on Jesus' resurrection. G. H. Boobyer makes this explains:

> Of special importance are the three predictions of the passion in 8:31, 9:31, and 10:34. But why are these passages generally called forecasts of the passion? That seems entirely to miss their true nature. They are not just forecasts of the passion, but of the passion *and resurrection.* They look beyond the cross to the subsequent triumph. Then there are 9:9, 10:37, the whole of chapter 13, 14:25–28, 62, and the beginning of Mark's account of the resurrection in 16:1–8. These all anticipate, or speak of the resurrection.... [78]

Thus, with Boobyer, while the author of Mark *emphasizes* Jesus' death, he *insists* on Jesus' subsequent resurrection.

Regarding John the Baptist, Mark's "disproportionate," according to E. Bammel, commitment to John's death parallels his emphasis on Jesus' death.[79] Similarly, this "disproportionate" attention to John's death may, as in the case of Jesus' above, have been intended to refute claims that John did not die, but was translated. The emphasis on John's death in Mark, however, is generally regarded as lacking any parallel insistence on John's resurrection. Indeed the voluminous secondary literature, not only on John the Baptist and the Gospel of Mark, but on Jesus, on the four gospels, on the New Testament, on almost the entire corpus of early Christian literature is silent on any resurrection of the Baptist. The present view is, however, that this silence is merely the result of a scholarly unwillingness to look beyond Christological interpretations of the transfiguration. The present hypothesis is that the author's point about the transfiguration is that, *in the same way as John,* Jesus will suffer, die, be buried

---

before the Lord, on whom we were not able to look (emphasis added)" (*NTApo* 633–34; ET: C. Detlef G. Müller).

[77] For John's burial see Mk 6:29: καὶ ἀκούσαντες οἱ μαθηταὶ αὐτοῦ ἦλθον καὶ ἦραν τὸ πτῶμα αὐτοῦ καὶ ἔθηκαν αὐτὸ ἐν μνημείῳ.

[78] "St. Mark and the Transfiguration," *JTS* (1940) 124; emphasis original.

[79] E. Bammel writes, "There is a short report on the appearance of John at the Jordan, with a surprisingly keen interest in his outward description – comprising fifty-two or sixty-seven words in all – and an account of his execution which extends to 249 words" ("The Baptist in Early Christian Tradition," 98). To what extent the narration of John's death in Mk 6:14–29 functions as a literary flashback is unclear. Achtemeier argues that its rarity as a flashback suggests it importance. The present author's view is that its position in setting up the transfiguration overrides its value as a literary flashback ("Mark, Gospel of," *ABD* 4.548–49).

(Mk 6:29) *and rise from the dead.*[80] One might object that Jesus' rising is not narrated in any depth in Mark 16. However, here the present interpretation of the transfiguration helps again. The simple remark by the young man dressed in a white robe at the tomb: "He has been raised; he is not here (ἠγέρθη, οὐκ ἔστιν ὧδε)" (Mk 16:5–6) is sufficient, *on the basis of the earlier narrative of the transfiguration*, to imply this meaning.[81] Indeed numerous scholars accept this implication of Mk 16:5–6, without the present interpretation of the transfiguration, but on the basis of specious arguments of the transfiguration as a misplaced resurrection narrative of Jesus. Consistent with Mark's well-known rejection of theophanic religion, only one appearance is necessary, not Jesus' for whom the author flatly refuses the notion (perhaps as angelic and therefore too lowly for his concept of the Christ), but John's – to illustrate the author's point that *both* leaders go before himself and his fellow congregants in the resurrection of the dead.[82] Although Paul may *not* have agreed, for the author of Mark, it seems, *together* John *and* Jesus are the "first-fruits of those who have died" (ἀπαρχὴ τῶν κεκοιμημένων [1 Cor 15:20]) – the produce from among the season's earliest harvest already dedicated to God (cf. τὰς ἀπαρχὰς τῶν πρωτογενημάτων τῆς γῆς [Exod 23:19 LXX]).

Other perplexing questions for which this thesis proposes solutions emerge in the course of Margaret Thrall's defense of the similarities between the transfiguration scene and the resurrection account in Mark 16.[83] For example, as Thrall correctly shows, the Gospel of Mark emphasizes that Jesus' resurrection takes place on the Sabbath (Mk 15:42; 16:1).[84] Similarly, the opening phrase of the transfiguration, μετὰ ἡμέρας ἕξ suggests that the transfiguration took place "on the seventh day," implying, with Thrall, the event was a resurrection.[85] Indeed Mark 16 is the only other place in the Second Gospel where the date of an event is specified. Thrall enumerates five other such similarities between the Markan transfiguration (Mk 9:2–8) and the Markan resurrection (Mk 16:1–8). They are: (1) Jesus' clothes become shining white in the transfiguration and a divine messenger wears a white robe at the resurrection (Mk 9:3/16:5); (2) Peter is promi-

---

[80] For Mark, neither John's nor Jesus' risings were reincarnations, but heavenly ascensions. For the author of Mark, Jairus' daughter, raised back to life, never died (Mk 5:42–43).

[81] Cf. *T. Job* 39:8–40:4 in which both failure to find the corpses of Job's dead children and a vision of the children taken up to heaven are combined into one account.

[82] This thesis sides with the argument, not that Mark did not know/had no access to appearance traditions, but that he rejected them on the basis of a philosophical/theological objection to any corporeal manifestation of a person either post-death and/or post-resurrection.

[83] M. Thrall, "Elijah and Moses in Mark's Account of the Transfiguration," 305–17.

[84] M. Thrall, "Elijah and Moses in Mark's Account of the Transfiguration," 311.

[85] On this point, C. E. Carlston argues that "a strikingly high percentage of the very infrequent explicit datings in the Synoptics have to do with the Resurrection," citing Mk 8:31; 9:31; 10:34 and parallels, as well as Mt 27:63; 28:1; Lk 24:1; Jn 20:1, 6 and 1 Cor 15 ("Transfiguration and Resurrection," 236; citations in n. 18).

nent in both accounts;[86] (3) a verbal similarity exists between Mk 9:5 (καλόν ἐστιν ἡμᾶς ὧδε εἶναι) and Mk 16:6 (ἠγέρθη, οὐκ ἔστιν ὧδε);[87] (4) the theme of Galilee is present in both narratives (Mk 16:7);[88] and, (5) the fear of those present is evident in both accounts (Mk 9:6/16:8).[89] Thus even without the technical term, ὤφθη, denoting resurrection, Mk 9:2–8 is, without doubt, intended to be read as a resurrection. The present hypothesis, therefore, endorses Thrall's position that similarities between the transfiguration and resurrection accounts in Mark suggest the two events are meant to be interpreted in light of each other.[90] It is not, however, Jesus' *transfiguration* that interprets Jesus' *resurrection*, but *John's resurrection*, that interprets *Jesus' resurrection*. With this important qualification, Thrall's asseveration can be considered correct that "Mark … presents the Transfiguration as the prefigurement of the Resurrection."[91]

---

[86] R. Bultmann argues that originally Peter may have been alone in this account, the other two disciples added later as in Mk 1:29 and 14:33 (*History of the Synoptic Tradition*, 260). C. G. Montefiore also expounds this view in *The Synoptic Gospels*, 1.205. Furthermore, regarding Peter's suggestion to build tents, the first consideration is whether vv. 5–6 were interpolated. Once added, they may be related to Peter's confession in 8:29. The tents represent places of habitation at the end. In both cases Peter is seen to be acting in haste, assuming somehow that salvation is already upon them. Peter may think that John's resurrection implies Jesus will not (as in 8:31–32) have to die. This view is likely if the identification of the Son of Man in 8:31 was at all ambiguous to Peter. The tents also suggest a cultic directive, typical of appearance narratives; cf. Herodotus, *Hist.* 4.14–15. Also, in the context of the narrative, on the revelation of John's rising, Peter may believe that the prediction of Mk 8:31 is fulfilled. On Mk 9:5, see E. Lohmeyer, "Die Verklärung Jesu nach dem Markus-Evangelium," 191; cf. also G. H. Boobyer, "St. Mark and the Transfiguration," 134.

[87] About this similarity M. Thrall asks, "Is it possible that Mark is hinting that the reality of what the empty tomb points to is to be found in the scene on the mountain?" ("Elijah and Moses in Mark's Account of the Transfiguration," 311).

[88] For her point that the mountain of transfiguration was in the region of Galilee, Thrall refers to R. H. Lightfoot's *Locality and Doctrine in the Gospels* (New York: Harper, 1938). Cf. also C. E. Carlston: "… a definite geographical location in Galilee or the region of Caesarea Philippi is quite beside the point. If we *must* locate the mountain specifically, we should probably, with Bultmann, locate it in Matt 28:16" ("Transfiguration and Resurrection," 237; emphasis original). E. Lohmeyer argues that locating the transfiguration on a mountaintop in Galilee demonstrates opposition to Jerusalem as the place of eschatological fulfillment (*Das Evangelium des Markus*, 174, 180).

[89] M. Thrall, "Elijah and Moses in Mark's Account of the Transfiguration," 310–11.

[90] M. Thrall, "Elijah and Moses in Mark's Account of the Transfiguration," 311.

[91] M. Thrall, "Elijah and Moses in Mark's Account of the Transfiguration," 311. Finally, as an account of John's resurrection, the various enthronement motifs of the transfiguration may have provided proof of John's Messiahship to some – an idea, according to the NT, with currency at the time (e.g., Lk 3:15). Of course, such an allegation could have provided an impetus – as his condemnation of divorce (6:18) and/or Herodias' mother's whim probably could not (6:24) – for Herod Antipas to demand John's incarceration/execution, the event narrated next in this gospel. On the ending and, in particular, the Longer Ending of the Gospel of Mark, see James A. Kelhoffer, *Miracle and Mission: The Authentication of Missionaries and Their Message in the Longer Ending of Mark* (WUNT II/112; Tübingen: Mohr Siebeck, 2000).

Finally, are John and Jesus the only two people in the Gospel of Mark raised from the dead? The story about Jairus' daughter in Mark 5 immediately comes to mind. In Mk 5:35 people arrive from Jairus' house to report that his daughter is dead. In Mk 5:41–42 Jesus commands the young girl to "rise" (ἔγειρε; imperative) and she is said to get up (ἀνέστη; second aorist), thus raised from the dead.[92] In Mk 5:39, however, the author inserts a qualifying interpolation about the girl's condition that she is, in fact, "*not* dead, but sleeps" – a kind of pun in that the Greek verb, καθεύδω was often used as a euphemism for someone who had died (Ps 87:6; Dan 12:2; [LXX] 1 Thess 5:10). This pun is intended, while simultaneously clinging to the original meaning of the tradition as a resurrection, to qualify the present "rising" in terms of other risings *following deaths*. A "rising" following a certified death, such as an empty tomb (16:6) or decapitated head (6:28) would never, according to this author, result in the resumption of normal life on the part of the dead person. Mark 12:25 ensures this point. To the question from some Sadducees regarding marriage and the resurrection, Jesus replies: "For when they rise from the dead, they neither marry nor are given in marriage, but are as angels in the heavens (ὅταν γὰρ ἐκ νεκρῶν ἀναστῶσιν οὔτε γαμοῦσιν οὔτε γαμίζονται, ἀλλ᾽ εἰσὶν ὡς ἄγγελοι ἐν τοῖς οὐρανοῖς)." Jairus' daughter is raised back to life as she knew it *only because, in Mark, she never actually dies*.[93] Appearing is for angels (e.g., Mk 1:13) and dead heroes from the past.[94] Such a lower state of glorification was beneath the Markan Christ, but not beneath his "baptizer."[95]

In sum, the view that the transfiguration represents a misplaced resurrection account of Jesus derives from an assumption, imported from, perhaps Paul (e.g., 1 Cor 15:21) and elsewhere, that Jesus is the person expected to rise. When this assumption is suspended, it becomes clear that the Markan transfiguration is surely not a misplaced resurrection *of Jesus*, but a resurrection nonetheless. It is an account of the resurrection of the recently murdered Baptist. According to

---

[92] Mk 5:41: καὶ κρατήσας τῆς χειρὸς τοῦ παιδίου λέγει αὐτῇ, Ταλιθα κουμ, ὅ ἐστιν μεθερμηνευόμενον Τὸ κοράσιον, σοὶ λέγω, ἔγειρε. καὶ εὐθὺς ἀνέστη τὸ κοράσιον καὶ περιεπάτει· ἦν γὰρ ἐτῶν δώδεκα. καὶ ἐξέστησαν [εὐθὺς] ἐκστάσει μεγάλῃ.

[93] Also implying that this healing was originally a resurrection miracle or, at least, as important as one, is that, *similar to the transfiguration but different from all other miracles in Mark*, for the healing of Jairus' daughter Jesus calls Peter, James and John apart (Mk 5:37; cf. 14:33). In Mk 1:23–28, 1:29–31, and perhaps even 1:32–34, Peter, James and John are not explicitly separated by Jesus from the other disciples. Here also we acknowledge the role of anticipation played by the Jairus' daughter narrative, preparing readers for John's upcoming death and resurrection in chapters 6 and 9.

[94] Cf. also Mk 1:2 in which ἄγγελος (from Mal 3:1 LXX) is used to refer to John the Baptist.

[95] To appear momentarily as a dazzling white angel, though living, (Mk 9:3) is referred to as "metamorphosis" by the author of Mark. Appearances by angels (16:5) are also acceptable to this author. Appearances by Jesus after his death are, however, beneath Jesus' role and stature and are, therefore, unacceptable to this author.

current cosmologies, the apex of a mountain was, after all, the nearest one could come to heaven[96] – an ideal place to greet the newly risen.[97] Such a tradition of John's rising could have emerged in the same early Christian circles that either improvised or preserved the tradition of Jesus' baptism by John – followers who sought, at some level, to either forge or maintain a connection between John and Jesus.[98] This position was, according to Mark 6:16,[99] endorsed by Herod – and thus perhaps not solely a theological, but political strategy on the part of the author – a response to the politically charged, even dangerous, environment of the 70s (cf. Mk 13:14).[100]

4.4.1 Vita Sinuthii and History of the Invention of the Head of Saint John the Baptist

This interpretation of the transfiguration is not unknown in the history of inter-pretation. Early monastic communities in which John the Baptist functioned as ascetic model *par excellence*[101] – even to the point of producing doubt regarding their commitment to Jesus – produced two separate accounts, *Vita Sinuthii* (ca. 348–466 C. E.) and Dionysius Exiguus' (6th c. C.E. Syriac monk and scientist), *History of the Invention of the Head of Saint John the Baptist,* that express clear dependence on Synoptic accounts of the transfiguration yet involve John the Baptist.[102]

Briefly, *Vita Sinuthii*, one of the oldest *Vitae Sanctorum*, about the first Egyptian monks, describes a night on which three figures dressed in white clothing

---

[96] M. Eliade, *The Myth of the Eternal Return or, Cosmos and History*, trans. Willard R. Trask (Princeton: Princeton University, repr. 1991); orig. publ. as *Le Mythe de l'éternel retour: archétypes et repetition* (Paris: Librairie Gallimard, 1949) 12–17.

[97] R. H. Lightfoot's *Locality and Doctrine in the Gospels*. Joseph B. Bernardin argues the transfiguration actually occurred in the garden of Gethsemane the night before Jesus died (e.g., Mk 14:32–42). According to Bernardin, in both accounts, Peter, James and John are alone with Jesus on a hillside; Jesus prays while they sleep or wish to sleep ("The Transfiguration," 187).

[98] For Bultmann, the transfiguration is a narrative tradition – specifically a legend. It was inserted in Mk 9 between vv. 1 and 11. Originally v. 7 followed v. 4. Also, originally, two *uni-dentified* heavenly beings, either angels or holy ones, met Jesus and his disciples. This accounts for the inconsistency in naming Elijah first in v. 4, but Moses first in v. 5. The figures were later identified: "By Mark?" Bultmann asks (*History of the Synoptic Tradition*, 259–61).

[99] Contrast the view of A. Y. Collins who writes, with regard to Mk 6:16, "The identification of Jesus with John suggests that Jesus will meet a similar fate at the hands of the authorities. But the mention of resurrection implies, *ironically*, that Jesus, not John, will be raised from the dead" (*The Beginning of the Gospel*, 62; emphasis added).

[100] Although any connection between Baptists and this later group is unproven, Hemerobap-tists did not accept resurrection from the dead.

[101] On the importance of John the Baptist in the development of monasticism and other ascetic movements, see above, Ch. 2.

[102] E. F. Lupieri, "John the Baptist: The First Monk," 14, 18–19.

visit their monastery. After conversing with Shenute they disappear. The figures are identified as John the Baptist, Elijah and Elisha.[103]

A summary of the narrative of *History of the Invention of the Head of Saint John the Baptist* is provided by E. F. Lupieri:[104]

Two monks, visiting the Holy Land, went to Jerusalem and there, inspired by a dream, dug in the ruins of the castle of Herod and found the head of St. John in a rough sack ... [e. g., camel hair]. With their precious bundle they elatedly began their journey back to the monastery. But during their trip a potter from Emesa, financially ruined, caught up with them. John the Baptist appeared to the potter in another dream and told him that he would like to rest in Emesa: the potter immediately stole the head and went back to Emesa, where he put the head of John the Baptist in a vase [a *hydria*] and started a new life, protected by the blessing of St. John. The precious relic remained in the same family for generations, until a certain Eustatius, a pseudo-monk and heretical priest, received it in inheritance and buried the vase in a cave where he lived. But the Catholics forced him to flee in a great hurry and the cave came to be inhabited by holy monks. One day some of them had strange dreams: *John the Baptist appeared in a white tunic, between two other men dressed in white.* ... Finally a star ... guided the monks to the place where the head was buried and they discovered the vase. Then they summoned the bishop, who rushed there with a procession of priests. One of these priests, a certain Malcus, did not believe that it was the real head of John the Baptist and put his hand into the vase. A mysterious power made his hand adhere to the holy head and he was able to withdraw his arm only after the intense prayers of those present. His hand however remained paralyzed. The bishop immediately commenced the construction of a church to shelter the relic, which was transported there in a magnificent procession some months afterwards. During the procession, Malcus, following the instructions received in a dream by John the Baptist himself, touched the head of the saint a second time with his paralyzed hand and recovered his health.

Both examples demonstrate that certain Christian monks making John the Baptist their chief model of imitation utilized the transfiguration as an interpretive tool.[105]

---

[103] *Sinuthii Vita*, 117–18 (CSCO 129; Script. Copt. 16; ed. and trans. H. Wiesman [Paris: Typographeo reipublica, 1906]).

[104] E. F. Lupieri, "John the Baptist: The First Monk," 18–20; ed., J. Migne, *PL* 67: 417D–432. Speculations about John's head derive from the account of his beheading in Mk 6:14–29// Mt 14:3–12. Cf. Lk 3:19–20.

[105] In terms of the relevance of patristic witnesses for this aspect of my thesis as well as the broader claims of the entire project, I would make the following comments. First, I commend Margaret M. Mitchell's approach to John Chrysostom on Paul ("The Archetypal Image: John Chrysostom's Portraits of Paul," *JR* 75 [1995] 15–43), describing the interpretive mode as a "love hermeneutic" (20–21, 25) and demonstrating unassailably how, in his exegetical work on Paul's letters, Chrysostom utilizes literary portraits of a variety of types, including epithets (miniature portraits), to summon Paul's presence for his direct exhortation of Chrysostom's fourth century audiences. In terms of the present project, the question arises as to whether an analogous claim can be made with regard to the canonical gospels: if Paul's mediating presence is brought to bear on John Chrysostom's fourth-century audiences, is Jesus' mediating presence evident in Paul's letters or Jesus'/John's mediating presences in the canonical gospels? See also Paul A. Holloway, "Left Behind: Jesus' Consolation of His Disciples in John 13,31–17,26,"

4.5 Correlations between Baptist Traditions and Q in Mark 6–13

My argument shifts now to connections between above-described Baptist features of the Gospel of Mark and Markan Q parallels.[106] Q parallels in Mark are

---

ZNW 96 (2005) 1–34. Also, I agree with Mitchell that NT scholarship must reject "simplistic
appeals to patristic exegetes" and that patristic witnesses should not be used "piece-meal" as
evidence for a certain position on the NT texts. However, I have yet to see a description of
method for incorporating insights gleaned from patristic witnesses into NT interpretation, taking into account the different rhetorical situations of the early Christian and Patristic periods.
See review by M. M. Mitchell of A. Malherbe, *The Letters to the Thessalonians: A New Translation with Introduction and Commentary* (Anchor Bible 32B; New York: Doubleday, 2000)
in *RBL* (09/2004); eadem, *The Heavenly Trumpet: John Chrysostom and the Art of Pauline
Interpretation* (HUT 40; Tübingen: Mohr Siebeck, 2000; Louisville: Westminster John Knox,
2002); eadem, "Reading Rhetoric with Patristic Exegetes: John Chrysostom on Galatians," in
*Antiquity and Humanity: Essays on Ancient Religion and Philosophy Presented to Hans Dieter
Betz on His 70th Birthday*, ed. A. Y. Collins and M. M. Mitchell (Tübingen: Mohr Siebeck,
2001) 333–55. Finally, that patristic interpreters' failure to doubt a NT literary or historical-
critical point does not constitute positive evidence that that point is moot. Countless examples
can be identified.

[106] As a point of clarification, here "parallel" suggests sayings of closely related content,
irrespective of verbatim agreement. I will not discuss the nature or degree of dependence of
Mark on Q, although these issues are crucial to a deeper understanding of the relationship
between these two entities. The topic of Mark and Q is not in fashion today. M. E. Boring summarizes the issue at hand: "The dilemma is clear: If Mark did not know Q, then how account
for the numerous places where he seems not only to overlap Q or Q-like materials, but to be
excerpting from them? If he *did* know Q, given his interest in the words of Jesus, how account
for his using so little of it, and for his selection? ... The more compelling case has been that
Mark did know Q or a Q-like collection of sayings of Jesus. The chief argument against this
has been, in fact, the lack of a satisfactory explanation as to why, if Mark knew Q, he used it so
sparingly. (Moffatt, Streeter, Throckmorton, Montefiore, Redlich, Harnack.) Source criticism
per se has not been able to present such an explanation" ("The Paucity of Sayings in Mark: A
Hypothesis," 372). Boring also summarizes the four different types of explanations for this dilemma: "(1) Mark presupposes the existence of Q or a similar collection [e.g., J. Weiss, the early
Streeter, the early Rawlinson, B. W. Bacon, F. C. Grant, James Price]. (2) Mark *historicizes* his
material, relating them to the story of the pre-Easter Jesus [e.g., F. C. Burkitt]. (3) Mark *selects*
his material to correspond to his emphasis on the cross-resurrection kerygma [e.g., Morton S.
Enslin, R. H. Lightfoot]. (4) Mark *opposes* some kind or kinds of Christianity represented to
some extent by speech materials [e.g., M. Dibelius, E. Schweizer, E. Trocmé]" (374; emphasis
added). Boring's explanation is: "Mark has so few sayings of Jesus because he is suspicious of
Christian prophecy as it is present in his community and expressed in the sayings tradition. He
creates a new prophetic form intended as an alternative" (374). The present approach picks up
on Boring's fourth category, represented by Schweizer and Trocmé, that Mark is opposed to
this kind of material, not, however because he is opposed to sayings, nor that he is opposed to
Christianities emphasizing sayings, but because he knows these sayings did not originate with
Jesus. Important studies include: Ernest Best, "An Early Sayings Collection," *NovT* (1976)
1–16; M. Eugene Boring, "The Paucity of Sayings in Mark: A Hypothesis"; Michel Devisch,
"La relation entre l'évangile de Marc et le document Q," in *L'évangile selon Marc. Tradition et
rédaction*, ed. M. Sabbe (BETL 34; Leuven: Gembloux, 1974) 59–91; J. Lambrecht, "Q-Influ-
ence on Mark 8,34–9,1"; Rudolf Laufen, "Doppelüberlieferungen," *ETL* 57 (1981) 181–83;
F. Neirynck, "Studies on Q since 1972," *ETL* 56 (1980) 409–13; W. Schenk, "Der Einfluss der
Logienquelle auf das Markusevangelium," *ZNW* 70 (1979) 141–65; B. H. Streeter, "St. Mark's

primarily of two types: (1) narrative about the Baptist (Mk 1:2–6; 1:2; 1:7–8; 1:9–11) and (2) sayings occurring in the latter half of the gospel – specifically, after the narration of John's death (6:14–29) and the transfiguration account (9:2–8) and through the apocalyptic discourse in Mark 13, roughly Chs. 8–13.

4.5.1 Distribution of Teaching Materials and Q Parallels in the Second Gospel

According to M. Eugene Boring, the Gospel of Mark contains seventy-seven possible sayings-units that could have circulated independently.[107] According to the "Index Locorum" in John Kloppenborg's *Q Parallels*,[108] the Gospel of Mark contains a total of forty-six possible Q parallels.[109] Of these forty-six, however, only twenty-nine bear close resemblance to "Q sayings". The others (17) appear in the *Index* for the sake of general comparison.[110] Of those twenty-nine,

---

Knowledge and Use of Q," in *Studies in the Synoptic Problem*, ed. W. Sanday (Oxford: Clarendon, 1911) 165–83; idem, *The Four Gospels*; Petros Vassiliadis, "The Function of John the Baptist in Q and Mark: A Hypothesis," *Theologica* (1975) 405–13. Vassiliadis argues Q reflects pro-Baptist ("perhaps derived from a Baptist source") materials with Christian commentary on it (e.g., v 28a and 28b) (408). In general I agree with Vassiliadis that in Q John the Baptist has significance on his own. Vassiliadis is also correct that Mark takes seriously John's association with Elijah (409, 412). J. Lambrecht argues Mark used Q "extensively and with much consciousness .... When one realizes the relatively early existence of Q and the comparatively late date of the composition of the Markan gospel, too much astonishment at Mark's knowledge of Q is out of place" ("Q-Influence on Mark 8,34–9,1," 303, 304). Regarding the question of "why Mark then did not incorporate the whole of Q in his gospel" (304), Lambrecht hypothesizes it had something to do with Mark's intention not to replace, but to supplement Q (304). Cf. also Harry T. Fleddermann: "The evidence shows that Mark knew and used Q" (*Mark and Q. A Study of the Overlap Texts* [BETL 122; Leuven: Peeters, 1995] 39). Cf. also the thesis of an "R" source by Ernest Best, "An Early Sayings Collection."

[107] "The Paucity of Sayings in Mark: A Hypothesis," 371.

[108] *Q Parallels,* 247–48. Many technical studies of Q/Mark parallels have been undertaken. For a synopsis of important approaches (e.g., Polag, Morgenthaler) in chart form, see F. Neirynck's review of R. Laufen, *Die Doppelüberlieferungen der Logienquelle und des Markusevangeliums* (Bonner Biblische Beiträge 54; Königstein/Ts.-Bonn: Peter Hanstein, 1980) in *ETL* (1981) 181–83. Neirynck lists twenty-five passages with fourteen others labeled uncertain (182–83). About Mark's inclusion of sayings, E. M. Boring summarizes, "...both absolutely and relatively, and in terms of both number of sayings and number of words, and irrespective of whether 'saying' be defined broadly or narrowly, Mark has significantly less sayings material than either Matthew of Luke. Why this is the case has been perceived as a problem in the literature on Mark for almost 200 years" ("The Paucity of Sayings in Mark: A Hypothesis," 371).

[109] Nowhere claiming his list is definitive, J. Kloppenborg includes: Mk 1:2–6; 1:2; 1:7–8; 1:9–11; 1:12–13; 1:21–22; 3:7; 3:13; 3:13–15; 3:22–26; 3:27; 3:28–30; 3:31–35; 4:21; 4:22; 4:24–25; 4:25; 4:30–32; 4:35; 6:6b–7; 6:8–13; 6:34; 7:1–2; 7:5–6a; 8:11–12; 8:14–15; 8:34–35; 8:38; 9:13; 9:28–29; 9:37; 9:40; 9:42; 9:49–50; 10:11–12; 10:28–30; 10:29–30; 10:31; 10:38b; 11:22–23; 12:37b–40; 13:9–11; 13:15–16; 13:21–23; 13:34 and 13:35 (*Q Parallels*, 247–48).

[110] Examples of general reference citations are Mk 1:21–22/Q 7:1–10; Mk 3:7/Q 6:20a; Mk 3:13–15/Q 10:2–12; Mk 3:31–35/Q 11:27–28; Mk 6:6b–7/Q 10:2–12; Mk 6:34/Q 10:2–12, etc. My emended list is Mk 1:2; 1:7–8; 1:9–11; 1:12–13; 3:22–26; 3:27; 3:28–30; 4:21; 4:22;

eighteen (62%) occur between Mk 6:6b–13:35. No Q parallel occurs after Mk 13:35. Before Mk 6:6b, four of eleven Q parallels concern John the Baptist. The other eight are concentrated in two teachings: the Beelzebul Controversy in Mk 3:22–30[111] and the parabolic teaching in Mk 4:21–32 (e.g., Mk 4:21/Q 11:33–35, 36; Mk 4:22/Q 12:2–3; Mk 4:24–25/Q 6:37–38; Mk 4:30–32/Q 13:18–19). Thus, with the exception of the Beelzebul controversy and the parabolic teaching in Mk 4:21–32, the Gospel of Mark utilizes most Q-like materials either with regard to John the Baptist or in chapters 6–13.

Coordination of Baptist traditions with Q parallels in Mark begins in the opening of the Second Gospel. Mark 1 contains four important Baptist traditions: (1) allusion to Mal 3:1, with Isa 40:3 and Exod 23:20; (2) John's clothing and diet;[112] (3) John's proclamation regarding the "coming one"; and, (4) Jesus' baptism by John. Of these four traditions, three have Q parallels: the allusion to Mal 3:1 occurs in Q 7:27; the reference to "the coming one" occurs in Q 3:16b; and Jesus' baptism by John occurs in Q 3:21–22.[113]

In terms of parallel *sayings* between Q and Mark, as above, most are concentrated after the time of John's death (Mk 6:14–29) and the transfiguration (Mk 9:2–8). The first such parallel is found in Mk 6:6b–13 ("the mission of the twelve"). This passage immediately precedes the narration of John's death. With certain discrepancies between the two passages, such as the instructions regarding sandals, this Markan passage contains many of the essential points of Q 10:4, 10–12. Compare, for example, Mk 6:11: "Whatever place neither welcomes nor listens to you, leaving there, *shake the dust beneath your feet* (ἐκτινάξατε τὸν χοῦν τὸν ὑποκάτω τῶν ποδῶν ὑμῶν) as a witness to them" with Q 10:10–11: "But in whatever town you enter and they do not accept you, going out from that town, *shake the dust from your feet.*"[114]

As part of the narration of the death of John the Baptist, Mk 6:18: "It is not permissible for you to have your brother's wife (οὐκ ἔξεστίν σοι ἔχειν τὴν γυναῖκα τοῦ ἀδελφοῦ σου)" has a parallel not only in Mk 10:11–12 (ὃς ἂν ἀπολύσῃ τὴν γυναῖκα αὐτοῦ καὶ γαμήσῃ ἄλλην μοιχᾶται ἐπ᾽ αὐτήν· καὶ

4:24–25; 4:30–32; 6:8–13; 8:11–12; 8:14–15; 8:34–35; 8:38; 9:37; 9:42; 9:49–50; 10:11–12; 10:28–30; 10:31; 10:38b; 11:22–23; 12:37b–40; 13:9–11; 13:21–23; 13:34 and 13:35.

[111] The possibility exists of a connection between "Beelzebul" and Baal-zebub/Elijah (2 Kgs 1). If Baptists associated John (perhaps through Mal 3:1) with Elijah, which there is some reason to believe they did, this passage may reflect Baptist teaching.

[112] The "Satan," "wild beasts," and "angels" Jesus faces in the wilderness in Mark, may function like John's diet of "locusts and wild honey" (1:6) to vivify the author's description of the wilderness. See James A. Kelhoffer, *The Diet of John the Baptist.*

[113] See Jan Lambrecht, "John the Baptist and Jesus in Mark 1.1–15: Markan Redaction of Q?" *NTS* 38 (1992) 357–84.

[114] Compare the two Greek phrases: (1) Mk 6:11b: ἐκτινάξατε τὸν χοῦν τὸν ὑποκάτω τῶν ποδῶν ὑμῶν and (2) Q 10:11: ἐκτινάξατε τὸν κονιορτὸν τῶν ποδῶν ὑμῶν. See *The Critical Edition of Q*, 176, 178.

ἐὰν αὐτὴ ἀπολύσασα τὸν ἄνδρα αὐτῆς γαμήσῃ ἄλλον μοιχᾶται), but in Q 16:18: "Everyone who divorces his wife and marries another commits adultery, and the one who marries a woman divorced from her husband commits adultery (πᾶς ὁ ἀπολύων τὴν γυναῖκα αὐτοῦ καὶ γαμῶν ἑτέραν μοιχεύει, καὶ ὁ ἀπολελυμένην ἀπὸ ἀνδρὸς γαμῶν μοιχεύει)."[115] Although the regulation issued in Mk 10:2–9[116] is more stringent than Mk 10:11–12 (the two verses that follow), the prohibition against divorce with remarriage in Mk 10:11–12 is virtually identical to Q 16:18.

In addition, Mk 9:9–13 on John's coming as Elijah, with the exception of the transfiguration narrative (Mk 9:2–8),[117] is surrounded by Q parallels:[118] Mk 8:12/Q 11:29 (why this generation requests a sign), Mk 8:34/Q 14:27 (taking up cross), Mk 8:35/Q 17:33 (finding/saving life will lose it), Mk 8:38/Q 12:9 (denied before men/angels), Mk 9:35 and 10:31/Q 13:30 (first/last and last/first; cf. also 10:43), Mk 10:11–12/Q 16:18 (as noted above: on divorce/adultery), Mk 10:29–30/Q 12:49–53, 14:26 (leaving house or brothers or sisters or mother or father or children or fields for sake of the gospel) and Mk 11:23/Q 17:6 ("Be taken up and thrown into the sea").[119]

Certain parallels should be dealt with in greater detail. For example, not surprisingly, at least from the perspective of the present thesis, the first words of the first teaching Jesus offers following his official succession of John at the transfiguration event closely resemble John's signature address to crowds in Q 3:7: γεννήματα ἐχιδνῶν ("brood of vipers"). In the account of the healing of a boy with a spirit, when someone from the crowd explains to Jesus that his

---

[115] ET: *The Critical Edition of Q*, 470.

[116] καὶ προσελθόντες Φαρισαῖοι ἐπηρώτων αὐτὸν εἰ ἔξεστιν ἀνδρὶ γυναῖκα ἀπολῦσαι, πειράζοντες αὐτόν. ὁ δὲ ἀποκριθεὶς εἶπεν αὐτοῖς, Τί ὑμῖν ἐνετείλατο Μωϋσῆς; οἱ δὲ εἶπαν, Ἐπέτρεψεν Μωϋσῆς βιβλίον ἀποστασίου γράψαι καὶ ἀπολῦσαι. ὁ δὲ Ἰησοῦς εἶπεν αὐτοῖς, Πρὸς τὴν σκληροκαρδίαν ὑμῶν ἔγραψεν ὑμῖν τὴν ἐντολὴν ταύτην. ἀπὸ δὲ ἀρχῆς κτίσεως ἄρσεν καὶ θῆλυ ἐποίησεν αὐτούς· ἕνεκεν τούτου καταλείψει ἄνθρωπος τὸν πατέρα αὐτοῦ καὶ τὴν μητέρα [καὶ προσκολληθήσεται πρὸς τὴν γυναῖκα αὐτοῦ], καὶ ἔσονται οἱ δύο εἰς σάρκα μίαν· ὥστε οὐκέτι εἰσὶν δύο ἀλλὰ μία σάρξ. ὃ οὖν ὁ θεὸς συνέζευξεν ἄνθρωπος μὴ χωριζέτω.

[117] The only possible link between the transfiguration narrative itself and Q is Jn 12:28–30 which echoes both the language of the transfiguration and the Lord's Prayer (Q 11:2b): "Now my soul is disturbed. And what should I say – 'Father, save me from this hour?' Rather, it is for this purpose that I have come to this hour. 'Father, glorify your name (Πάτερ, δόξασόν σου τὸ ὄνομα).' Then a voice came from heaven, 'I have glorified it and will glorify it again.' Then the crowd standing by heard it and said that it was thunder. Others said, 'An angel has spoken to him.' Jesus answered, 'This voice came not for me, but for you.'" In the Synoptics, Jesus speaks similar words – *in the presence of Peter, James and John* – in Gethsemane (e.g., Mk 14:33–36 par.).

[118] See Jan Lambrecht, "Q-Influence on Mark 8,34–9,1," in *Logia. Les Paroles de Jésus. The Sayings of Jesus. Mémorial Joseph Coppens,* eds. J. Delobel, T. Baarda (Leuven: Peeters, 1982) 277–304.

[119] In addition to these parallels Mk 11:25 is parallel to Mt 6:14.

disciples cannot cast out the demon that causes this boy to foam at the mouth, grind his teeth and become rigid, Jesus responds, "Oh unbelieving generation (ὦ γενεὰ ἄπιστος)! Until when must I be with you? How much longer must I tolerate you?" (Mk 9:19) This expression in Mk 9:19 (Mt 17:17/Lk 9:41: ὦ γενεὰ ἄπιστος καὶ διεστραμμένη) is the only occurrence of this vocative address in the Gospel of Mark. Its application here echoes the formula: epithet + question by the Baptist in Q 3:7 (cf. Mt 12:34, 23:33) and, of course, John's famous castigation, "Generation of vipers!" (Q 3:7) ἡ γενεά occurs in only three other places in Mark's gospel (8:12; 8:38 and 13:30). None are elements of a vocative address.

Jesus' response, however, has a parallel in Deut 32:20 (LXX): ὅτι γενεὰ ἐξεστραμμένη ἐστίν, υἱοί, οἷς οὐκ ἔστιν πίστις ἐν αὐτοῖς. Despite significant thematic and literary correlations, Deut 32:1–43 (LXX), "Moses' valedictory canticle" – a passage self-described as "no trifling matter, *but your very life* (ὅτι οὐχὶ λόγος κενὸς οὗτος ὑμῖν, ὅτι αὕτη ἡ ζωὴ ὑμῶν)" is, generally speaking, ignored as a source of comparison for Baptist traditions. In spite of this neglect, many of John's NT messages could have been constructed on its basis.[120] This song, articulated by Moses *by the Jordan River*, contains references to divine providence in the wilderness, specifying honey (ἐθήλασαν μέλι ἐκ πέτρας) (32:10–14), cosmic destruction of the earth by fire (32:22), destruction of Sodom and Gomorrah (32:32), an imminent day of calamity and judgment (ὅτι ἐγγὺς ἡμέρα ἀπωλείας αὐτῶν, καὶ πάρεστιν ἕτοιμα ὑμῖν) (32:35), the Lord's upcoming cleansing of the land (32:43), and, as above, "a crooked and perverse generation (γενεὰ σκολιὰ καὶ διεστραμμένη)," (32:5; cf. 32:20) and "the anger of serpents, the incurable anger of asps (θυμὸς δρακόντων ... καὶ θυμὸς ἀσπίδων ἀνίατος)" (32: 33; cf. 32:24).[121] As above, the numerous connections between Q and Deuteronomy are persuasively demonstrated by Arland Jacobson.[122]

In addition, the great millstone teaching in Mark begins in 9:42: καὶ ὃς ἂν σκανδαλίσῃ ἕνα τῶν μικρῶν τούτων τῶν πιστευόντων [εἰς ἐμέ], καλόν ἐστιν αὐτῷ μᾶλλον εἰ περίκειται μύλος ὀνικὸς περὶ τὸν τράχηλον αὐτοῦ καὶ βέβληται εἰς τὴν θάλασσαν. In Luke, this teaching appears in 17:1–2 a passage, together with 17:3–4 and 6, found in Q.[123] The Greek expression for millstone, μύλος/μυλικός occurring in the above citation of Mk 9:42 has only two other

---

[120] As a recent example, this chapter of Deuteronomy is not mentioned by Joan E. Taylor in *The Immerser*. James Dunn, however, does note connections between Deut 27–30 and Baptist traditions ("John the Baptist's Use of Scripture," 49). Also, see above: 84–85 n. 10.

[121] This list excludes the following other minor Baptist themes: reference to God as "father" (32:6; *ex hypothesi*); drinking of wine (Lk 7:33/Deut 32:32–33); role of demons (Lk 7:33/Deut 32:17); and the part played by the nations (Lk 3:8/Deut 32:21).

[122] "The Literary Unity of Q," 365–89. See above: 85.

[123] Furthermore, Lk 17:6 shares verbatim agreement with Mk 11:23, another passage in this Markan section.

occurrences in the NT: Rev 18:21–22 and Mt 24:41. The latter occurrence (Mt 24:41) may derive from Q (17:35), although its Lukan counterpart, and thus *The Critical Edition of Q,* omit the phrase ἐν τῷ μύλῳ from their reconstruction.

Furthermore, following the millstone saying, Mk 9:43–48 not only mentions γέενα three times (a word with a Q association in Q 12:5), but spells out twice, εἰς τὴν γέενναν, εἰς τὸ πῦρ τὸ ἄσβεστον (v. 44; cf. also v. 48), a specification clearly evoking the ministry of the Baptist.[124] For example, the Baptist's speech on the "coming one" in Q 3:17 employs the same expression: τὸ δὲ ἄχυρον κατακαύσει πυρὶ ἀσβέστῳ.[125]

The passage concluding this section (Mk 9:49–50) too possesses obvious connections to Q: on salt in Q 14:34–35 (cf. also Mt 5:13) and on the greeting of peace in Q 10:50, as well as the connection to the Q statement on divorce (Q 16:18/Mk 10:11–12), noted above.

In Mark 11 the following literary connections are evident. Mk 11:23 ("Be taken up and hurled into the sea" [Ἄρθητι καὶ βλήθητι εἰς τὴν θάλασσαν]) closely resembles Q 17:6 (Mt 13:29) ("Be uprooted and planted in the sea" [ἐκριζώθητι καὶ φυτεύθητι ἐν τῇ θαλάσσῃ]).[126] Mk 11:25 ("Whenever you stand praying forgive, if you have anything against anyone; so that your Father in heaven may also forgive you your trespasses [καὶ ὅταν στήκετε προσευχόμενοι, ἀφίετε εἴ τι ἔχετε κατά τινος, ἵνα καὶ ὁ πατὴρ ὑμῶν ὁ ἐν τοῖς οὐρανοῖς ἀφῇ ὑμῖν τὰ παραπτώματα ὑμῶν]"), as scholars have observed, shares much in common with Mt 6:14–15 ("For if you forgive the people their trespasses, your heavenly Father will also forgive you; but if you do not forgive the people, neither will your Father forgive your trespasses [ἐὰν γὰρ ἀφῆτε τοῖς ἀνθρώποις τὰ παραπτώματα αὐτῶν, ἀφήσει καὶ ὑμῖν ὁ πατὴρ ὑμῶν ὁ οὐράνιος· ἐὰν δὲ μὴ ἀφῆτε τοῖς ἀνθρώποις, οὐδὲ ὁ πατὴρ ὑμῶν ἀφήσει τὰ παραπτώματα ὑμῶν]") – a passage evidently excluded from Q, although thoroughly integrated into the Q material of the Sermon on the Mount.

On the basis of persuasive arguments defending a tradition history independent of the rest of this gospel, Mark 13 is frequently considered to be separate from Mk 8–12.[127] These arguments notwithstanding, Baptist and/or Q connec-

---

[124] Cf. Mt 5:22, 29, 30; 18:8, 9. "Hell" or "Gehenna" was first a place for burnt human sacrifices (Jer 19:4–6), later for burning rubbish. The enduring quality associated with the location is simply conflagratory; a trait with clear connections to the Baptist with whom the reference may have originated. Cf. Rev. 9:1–2; 21:8.

[125] Cf. also Q 3:9.

[126] Cf. Mt 15:13. The only other NT occurrence of the verb ἐκριζοῦν is Jd 12. Although not as evident in the Markan version (Mk 11:12–14, 20–25), the Matthean version of Jesus' cursing of the fig tree may suggest Baptist connections. The cursing of a tree for failing to "bear fruit" (Mt 21:19) recalls John's message that in the coming judgment those failing to bear fruit will be consumed in an eternal fire (Q 3:9).

[127] See Adela Yarbro Collins, *The Beginning of the Gospel: Probings of Mark in Context* (Minneapolis: Fortress, 1987) 73–91, esp. 90.

tions running through Mk 13 are clear.[128] The following connections are discernible: (1) Mk 13:6, "Many will come in my name saying, 'I am he!' and they will deceive many"/Q 17:20–24; (2) Mk 13:11, "When they lead handing you over, do not worry in advance about what you are to say; but say whatever is given to you in that hour, for you are not the ones speaking, but the Holy Spirit"/Q 12:11–12; (3) Mk 13:12–13, "Brother will hand over brother to death, and a father a child, and children will rise against parents and kill them…"/Q 12:53; 14:26; (4) the woe form of Mk 13:17/Q 10:13; 11:42–52; 17:1; (5) Mk 13:21, "And then if anyone says to you, 'Look, the Christ is here! Look, there!' Do not believe it"/Q 17:20–21, 23–24; (6) Mk 13:29, the nearness of the eschatological judgment/Q 10:9; 11:20; (7) Mk 13:30, reference to "this generation"/Q 3:7; (8) Mk 13:34–35 – parable of a master departing on a journey and the need for watchfulness/Q 19:12–13; 12:39–40.[129]

Mark 13 also possesses an important echo of the transfiguration. In v. 26 the "Son of Man" is described as ἐρχόμενον ἐν νεφέλαις μετὰ δυνάμεως πολλῆς καὶ δόξης ("coming in clouds with much power and glory"). Like John earlier, Jesus, (here on the basis of Dan 7:13–14), as the Son of Man will be transported by clouds.

Although at this point the more general question of the relationship between Mark and Q arises, the present chapter selects not to contest the conclusions of the International Q Project regarding Q's contents. It seeks only to call attention to connections between Mark and Q – some closer literary agreements and other looser, thematic correspondences – for the separate and specific point of the meaning and role of John the Baptist in the Gospel of Mark.

4.5.2 *Thematic Links between Q and Mark 8–13*

In addition to the above-mentioned closer literary associations, a host of more general, thematic links with Q teachings occurs in Mark 8–13. The kingdom of God sayings, for example, recall Q's profound collection (6:20b; 7:28b; 10:9; 11:2b; 11:20; 11:52; 12:31; 13:18–19; 13:20–21; 13:29, 28; and 16:16), especially, Mk 9:47, 10:14–16 and 10:24–25. Also, insistence on strict adherence to the Law and its commandments (10:2–9, 19–20) recalls Q 16:17. Even the theme of financial management in 10:23–27 and the curious cooptation of "baptism" to refer to Jesus' death in 10:38–39 are redolent of Q, specifically, John the Baptist in Q. In addition, three sayings near the end of Mark 10:

(1) It is not so among you; but whoever wishes to become great among you must be your servant (10:43);[130]

---

[128] See B. H. Streeter, "St. Mark's Knowledge and Use of Q," 179–83.
[129] Cf. also Lk 1:78.
[130] Cf. Lk 1:15 in which John is called "great (μέγας)."

(2) And whoever wishes to be first among you must be a slave of all (10:44); and

(3) For the Son of Man did not come to be served but to serve, and to give his life as a ransom for many (10:45),

echo a saying in Mk 9:35 ("If anyone wishes to be first he must be last of all and servant of all") and offer rough equivalence to Q 13:30 ("The last will be first and the first, last"). And, as above, reference to the "faithless generation (γενεὰ ἄπιστος)" in Mk 9:19 suggests John's booming condemnation of his kinsmen in Q (3:7): "Generation of vipers (γεννήματα ἐχιδνῶν)!"[131]

Jesus' teaching in Mk 10:28–31 also illustrates thematic connections with Q. The themes of leaving urban centers and family: "house or brothers or sisters or mother or father or children or fields" (Mk 10:29–30) recall, not urban life, spent primarily in cities among family and friends, but wilderness-dwelling. Q captures this theme at least twice in 12:49–53 and 14:26.

Mark 12 perpetuates these thematic connections. Joan Taylor interprets the parable of the wicked tenants (Mk 12:1–12/Mt 21:33–46/Lk 20:9–19) as a reference to the competition between the ministries of Jesus and John: "The chief priests, scribes, and elders are accused of killing John in the Parable of the Wicked Tenants."[132] In the Gospel of Matthew, the parable occurs just after the Parable of the Two Sons, the referents of which are explicitly John and Jesus (Mt 21:32). Indeed Mt 21:32: "For John came to you in a way of righteousness and you did not believe him, but the tax collectors and the prostitutes believed him; but you seeing him yourselves did not change your minds to believe him"

---

[131] This expression occurs only four times in Mark, all concentrated in this section: 8:12, 38; 9:19 (above); and 13:30. See discussion above: Chapter 3.

[132] Among those arguing for the interpretation of "son" as John the Baptist are: A. Gray, "The Parable of the Wicked Husbandmen," *HibJ* 19 (1920/21) 42–52; esp. 48; Hans-Josef Klauck, *Allegorie und Allegorese in synoptischen Gleichnistexten* (Münster: Aschendorff, 1978); Pierson Parker, "Jesus, John the Baptist, and the Herods," 4–11, esp. 10; Thomas Schmeller, "Jesus im Umland Galiläas: Zu den markinischen Berichten vom Aufenthalt Jesu in den Gebieten von Tyros, Caesarea Philippi und der Dekapolis," *BZ* (1993–94) 44–66. Klauck notes, "Überhaupt ist die innere Nähe dieser Konzeption zur Theologie der Logienquelle mit Händen zu greifen. Nicht nur der Sohnestitel ist davon betroffen, sondern auch die Prophetenmordtradition, die Israelpolemik und die Parusieerwartung. Das Verhältnis der Q-Tradition zu den Mk-Stoffen ist noch ungeklärt. Wir müssen uns mit der Feststellung dieser auffälligen Berührungspunkte begnügen" (310). See J. Taylor, *The Immerser*, 173; the point is repeated on 192; cf. also 250–53. Taylor also cites Malcolm Lowe who also argues that – setting aside the assumption that the "son" of the parable refers to Jesus – "one would be almost compelled to regard all this as a continuation of the question about the Baptist" ("From the Parable of the Vineyard to a Pre-Synoptic Source," *NTS* [1982] 258). Another question concerning the "son" referent is whether the prodigal son story makes an association between John the Baptist as the elder and Jesus as the younger son. Note the younger son *eats and drinks* squandering all he was given, before supplicating himself to the Father for forgiveness (Lk 15:11–32). The link in the Gospel of Luke to the previous story about joy in heaven over the repentance of a single lost sheep or coin (Lk 15:3–10) suggests the prodigal son was first a sheep before departing the fold for a life of profligacy.

is sandwiched between the two parables suggesting its applicability to both.[133] In addition, Mt 21:43 contains the important kingdom saying with the Baptist theme of fruit-bearing: "The kingdom of God will be taken from you and given to a people bearing its fruits" (cf. Q 3:8, 9).

Malcolm Lowe proposes all three of the parables in Mt 21:23–22:14 be regarded as a Baptist sequence. On Lowe's argument, not only do the Parable of the Wicked Tenants (Mt 21:33–45) and the Parable of the Two Sons (Mt 21:28–32) refer to John the Baptist, but – unmistakable in its Lukan version (Lk 14:15) – the Parable of the Great Banquet (Mt 22:1–14) does also:[134]

> Now in *Luke's version* of this parable it is *also* clearly applicable to the Baptist (Lk. 14.15–24): a man sends out a servant (just one) to invite various prominent people to a banquet, all of whom politely decline; he then sends out this same servant to bring in the poor and the maimed, to scour the highways and the hedges, and vows that the original guests shall not taste of his banquet. The master and servant are God and the Baptist, while the point of the story is identical with that of the Parable of the Two Sons (which, as was noted, is explicitly about the Baptist).[135]

Lowe reconstructs the unknown proto-Matthean source in the following manner:

> When Jesus, having cleansed the temple and begun teaching there daily, was challenged by the chief priests and other leading personalities, who asked with what authority he did such things, his response was as follows: first he posed the unanswerable question about John, then he told three parables in succession about the Baptist and against the authorities (and perhaps against the vendors too: the Two Sons, the Great Banquet and the Vineyard), and finally he capped all this with the stone-saying, informing the representatives of authority that they were all going to be "broken to pieces" and "crushed."[136]

---

[133] Cf. the telling replacement in the Gospel of Luke of this parable of the two sons by the following summary: "All the people heard and the tax collectors justified God, having been baptized with the baptism of John; but the Pharisees and the lawyers rejected God's will for themselves, not having been baptized by him" (Lk 7:29–30).

[134] Any efforts by M. Lowe to debunk the theory of Markan priority "in all its forms" by his hypothesis are here dismissed ("From the Parable of the Vineyard to a Pre-Synoptic Source," 261). See the similar, much earlier argument of Arthur Gray, "The Parable of the Wicked Husbandmen," 42–52. Lowe does not acknowledge Gray's article.

[135] M. Lowe, "From the Parable of the Vineyard to a Pre-Synoptic Source," 259; emphases original.

[136] I have deliberately excluded Lowe's argument regarding the Temple cleansing incident. Also, Lowe considers the sequence of these parables in *Gos. Thom.* § 64–66 ("From the Parable of the Vineyard to a Pre-Synoptic Source," 259). Interestingly, M. Thrall attempts to illuminate the meaning of the word "son" in Mk 9:7 by means of the Parable of the Wicked Tenants/Vineyard; see "Elijah and Moses in Mark's Account of the Transfiguration," 312–13. Also of interest is the Parable of the Vineyard in Matthew (20:1–16) which commences with a kingdom saying ("For the kingdom of heaven is like a landlord who went out first thing in the morning to hire workers for his vineyard….") and concludes with a Q saying: "The last will be first, and the first last" (Q 13:30/Mt 20:16) which may represent anti-Baptist polemic: Jesus, "the last" will be first, whereas John "the first" will be last. This parable also offers a fitting life application for the Baptist's teachings in Lk 3:10–14 regarding ethical management of finances.

About this hypothetical source Lowe concludes, "Something like this was bound to happen to the Baptist sequence, especially as the careers of John and Jesus were so similar."[137]

The stone saying is itself an interesting detail. As J. Taylor and J. P. Meier have argued, if Jesus cited Ps 118 in Hebrew, the word play between בֵּן, (son) and אֶבֶן, (stone), would have been evident.[138] If, however, according to Lowe, *John* is the son (Mt 21:39), then he too is the stone (Mt 21:42).[139] Interestingly, Q proffers that John himself shared this exact sense of humor in Q 3:8b: "God is able from these stones to raise up children to Abraham (δύναται ὁ θεὸς ἐκ τῶν λίθων τούτων ἐγεῖραι τέκνα τῷ Ἀβραάμ)."[140] That John, according to Q 3:8b, draws this same connection, points to a flaw in Lowe's argument – namely, his assumption that the relevant parables (the Parable of the Two Sons, the parable of the Great Banquet, and the Parable of the Vineyard) originated *with Jesus* or his followers *about John*. Just as likely, the relevant parables originated *with John* or *his* followers.

Whether or not Lowe's proposal of a hypothetical 'Baptist' source persuades,[141] his argument about the connection between Baptist traditions and these parables begs attention. The fact that the entire sequence occurs in the Gospel of Matthew recalls H. D. Betz's argument regarding the Sermon on the Mount: the SM, like Lowe's hypothetical Baptist source, integrates Q, "Special M," and Markan elements *while* strongly suggesting pre-arrangement/composition prior to inclusion in the Gospel of Matthew.[142] As noted above, that the author of Luke-Acts made significant cuts from his Markan source, suggests "Special M" may contain more Q material than typically admitted. Of the proposed elements in Lowe's

---

[137] M. Lowe, "From the Parable of the Vineyard to a Pre-Synoptic Source," 259.

[138] J. Taylor, *The Immerser*, 253; J. P. Meier, *A Marginal Jew*, 2.75 n. 51.

[139] The reference to the "son" as ἀγαπητός in Mk 12:6 recalls the divine voice at the transfiguration (Mk 9:7) and baptism (Mk 1:11). Meier's conclusion from the LXX (Gen 22:2, 12, 16), that it suggests a beloved child destined to die (also noted above), applies to both Jesus and John in Mark (*A Marginal Jew*, 2.188–89).

[140] Cf. esp. "Special L" saying in Lk 19:40: "I tell you, if these ones [Jesus' disciples] were silent, the stones would cry out"; also, Lk 19:44; 20:17, 18; 21:5–6. For an excellent treatment of the words πέτρα and λίθος in the NT, see Oscar J. F. Seitz, "Upon This Rock: A Critical Re-Examination of Matt 16:17–19," *JBL* (1950) 329–40.

[141] M. Lowe writes, "The other possibility is suggested by the fact that the whole of the Baptist-sequence does, after all, occur in Matthew's Gospel, even though there has been some rearrangement and quite a lot of rewriting. This suggests that the sequence could simply have occurred originally in a Proto-Matthew, upon which Mark, Luke and Thomas drew, and of which the extant Matthew is a revision. The revision would seem to have been influenced by Mark in two respects: the Matthean formulation of the stone saying (which conflates the versions of Luke and Mark) and the inclusion of the Cursing of the Fig Tree" ("From the Parable of the Vineyard to a Pre-Synoptic Source," 260). The arguments Lowe summons in support of his proto-Matthew alternative falter, for one, on their neglect of the possibility that more belonged to Q. On this point, the abundance of Q/Mk parallels is suggestive.

[142] See H. D. Betz, *The Sermon on the Mount*, 33–44.

unknown Baptist source, two occur in Mark (questioning of Jesus' authority and Parable of Wicked Tenants with stone saying),[143] one in Matthean *Sondergut* (the Parable of the Two Sons), and one in Q (Parable of the Banquet). If all are connected by Baptist themes,[144] as Lowe argues, it is possible that Lowe's unknown Baptist source was simply Q, a well-known repository of Baptist traditions (as above, at least three of five narrative segments in Q concern John). Important themes of these parables are also Q's themes, including fruit (Mk 12:2/Mt 21:43; cf. Q 3:9b), harvest time (Mk 12:2/Mt 21:34 and 41; cf. e.g., Q 3:17), punishment (Mk 12:3–5; Mt 22:6; cf. e.g., Q 3:9, 17), and, as above, sons/stones (Mk 12:6, 10/Mt 21:28–31, 37–38, 42, 44; Lk 20:18; cf. e.g., Q 3:8).[145]

The last thematic connection between Mk 8–13 and Q is Mk 12:38–40, the denouncing of scribes for "long prayers." To this can be compared the brevity of the *Pater Noster* (attributed to the Baptist in Lk 11:1; Q 11:2b–4) and the recommendation in Mt 6:7–8 ("When you pray, do not rattle on as the Gentiles…"). Finally, the topic of subsistence in the narrative of the widow's offering (Mk 12:41–44) also recalls the Lord's prayer (esp. Q 11:3) and Q's parables about giving all one has for the sake of the kingdom (Q 13:18–21).

4.5.3 Q Traditions and Mark's Depiction of the Baptist

Summarizing its findings, the present argument now turns from the question of the specific distribution of Q parallels (both literary allusions and themes) to that of the relationship of teaching materials in general in the Second Gospel to the author's depiction of the Baptist.

At least in comparison to other gospels, the Gospel of Mark offers less focus on (and, indeed, fewer of) Jesus' sayings. As John Kloppenborg has observed, "Mark's relationship to prior oral tradition is highly ambivalent. He is extraordinarily sparing in placing sayings on Jesus' lips."[146] In contrast, the Gospel of Mark emphasizes Jesus' role as quiet healer and exorcist (e.g., 1:25, 31, 41; 2:11; 3:5; 5:41). The account involving Simon's mother-in-law is exemplary: "Now Simon's mother-in-law was in bed with a fever, and they told him about her at once. He came and took her by the hand and lifted her up" (1:30–31). Note that in order to accomplish the healing, Jesus *says/teaches* nothing.

---

[143] With or without a connection to Q, at the very least, for the Parable of the Wicked Tenants, Baptist themes and concerns are evident.

[144] As above, see Petros Vassiliadis, "The Nature and Extent of the Q Document," 49–73 in which Vassiliadis argues that *Sondergut* passages can be admitted to Q on the basis of, among other things, theological and stylistic agreement with the rest of Q. See 101 n. 89.

[145] M. Lowe, "From the Parable of the Vineyard to a Pre-Synoptic Source," 260.

[146] *Excavating Q*, 355. On this point, J. Kloppenborg cites W. Kelber, *The Oral and the Written Gospel*, 196, 207–11.

Nevertheless, some teaching material *is* present in Mark, distributed at irregular intervals throughout the discursive narrative.[147] As shown above, the section of Mark with the greatest concentration of teaching materials is chapters 8–13[148] – a section also containing numerous parallels with Q. In addition to the Q parallels, this section also includes both explicit and implicit references to John the Baptist. The two explicit references to John the Baptist are: (1) Mk 8:28 (regarding who people claim Jesus is – "John the Baptist; and others, Elijah; and others, one of the prophets"),[149] and (2) Mk 11:27–33 (regarding the basis of Jesus' authority: "Was the baptism of John from heaven or from people?" v. 30). Two implicit references to John the Baptist in this section are identified in Mk 9:5 and 9:13. The emphasis on teaching, the Q parallels, the explicit and implicit references to John the Baptist *added to* the interpretation of the transfiguration event offered in the earlier section of this chapter together facilitate the general conclusion about Mark 8–13 that these convergences are deliberate: *Mk 8–13 possesses, not only the greatest concentration of teaching material in Mark, but specifically, the greatest concentration of Markan Q parallels because Mark understood Q as a collection of Baptist teachings.* Viewed in this way, the transfiguration scene provides, not only divine sanction upon Jesus as rightful successor to John's teaching ministry, but the author's defense for attribution of Baptist sayings to Jesus in these chapters *after* John's, and *leading up to* Jesus', death. The following discussion provides an explanatory defense of this claim.

In the Markan transfiguration account John the Baptist ("Elijah") appears to be risen from the dead. Why might such a tradition be included in a Christian gospel? According to Mark, during John's lifetime he predicts the end of the age (Mk 1:7–8: "The one who is more powerful than I is coming after me; I am not worthy to bend down and loosen the thong of his sandals. I baptized you with

---

[147] For example, 2:13–3:6; 3:21–4:32; 6:1–13; 7:1–23; 8:11–21; 8:27–9:1; 9:9–13; 9:33–37; 9:42–45; 11:20–13:37.

[148] Cf. important sayings in 2:18–3:6, parables in 4:1–34, and discourse in Mk 13. A tradition with thematic connections to Baptist traditions in Mk 4 is the parable of the growing seed. Not only does the reference to the kingdom of God point to an origin with the Baptist, (for full argument, see Chapter 6), but the warning that once the grain is ripe the farmer will arrive with his sickle for the harvest (4:29) shares decisive similarities with Baptist traditions, including Q 3:9 and 17; cf. also 10:2. This parable appears only here in the NT. A final, minor curiosity is the frequency in Mark with which Jesus is said to live, work and rest by the sea (i.e., the Sea of Galilee), exclusive of any mention of baptism. The Gospel of Mark contains at least the following nineteen explicit or implicit references to Jesus by the sea: 1:16; 2:13; 3:7; 4:1, 39, 41; 5:1, 13, 21; 6:32, 45, 47, 48, 49, 53; 7:31; 8:13; 9:42; and 11:23. Is it possible the two ministries, by the Jordan and by the Sea of Galilee, were deliberately juxtaposed?

[149] As above, the three responses to Jesus' question from three different groups are the same as those in Mk 6:15–16. Each is a different name for John the Baptist (John the Baptist, Elijah and one of the prophets). Thus, the people have only *one* opinion, stated *twice* by the author: the crowds believe Jesus is John. Moreover, according to Mk 6:16, this represents the official stance of Herod (Rome?).

water; but he will baptize you with the Holy Spirit"). When John is murdered, he and his followers would have probably concluded that this prediction was never fulfilled. Parallel to the problem Jesus' death caused for his corpus of teachings, such a failed prediction would seriously jeopardize John's credibility. From a Christian perspective this failed prediction would leave the problem of Jesus' discipleship by a false prophet. Later Christians could, therefore, restore John's integrity by demonstrating in some way the fulfillment of his prediction. By utilizing the tradition of John's resurrection from the dead, without allowing it to usurp the important theological position in nascent Christianity of Jesus' resurrection, (established, in particular, by the Pauline school), the author of Mark is able to demonstrate the accuracy of John's prediction. While useful, in this way, to Christians, the tradition of John's resurrection probably originated among Baptists, seeking, on the basis of a post-resurrection appearance, (in the case of the transfiguration, on appearance not *of*, but *to*, Jesus), to explain (as also various Christians did of Jesus) the untimely death of their leader.

From a source-critical viewpoint, confirmation of what was, perhaps, John's most seminal prediction (Mk 1:7–8) would also have served as a blanket commendation of any wider corpus of instruction known as Baptist in origin. From the standpoint of the Markan narrative, its proof bolsters the Markan (more human/less divine) Jesus' confidence in his own message and ministry, propelling him toward, not only his work of teaching, but, more importantly, his martyrdom. For the Markan Jesus' teaching ministry, on the basis of the confirmation of succession provided by the account of John's resurrection at the transfiguration, Jesus may now avail himself of John's esteemed corpus of instruction (*Ant.* 18.116–19; Lk 3:18) – that *tour de force* that attracted Jesus and so many others to John in the first place. Therefore, after Mk 9:2–8, because he received the endorsement to do so from the *bat qôl* (God), with Moses and John the Baptist as witnesses, Jesus proceeds to widen his sphere of influence by supplementing his healing ministry with noble and important instruction.

4.5.4 An Additional Proof: μετανοίας εἰς ἄφεσιν ἁμαρτιῶν in the Gospels of Mark and Matthew

A few reflections on the key theme of forgiveness in the Gospel of Mark in comparison with the Gospel of Matthew provides a final piece of evidence that the author of Mark intentionally strove to integrate Baptist with Christian traditions. This integration is evident in the author's reapportioning of the once solely Baptist message of forgiveness to both John and Jesus.[150]

---

[150] Morton Enslin refers to the prepositional phrase, "for remission of sins," in the description of John's baptism of repentance, as "dangerous words" ("Artistry of Mark," 391).

Dispersal of responsibility for the forgiveness of sins to *both* John and Jesus in the Gospel of Mark is brought into sharp relief by its eradication in the Gospel of Matthew. As above, the admonition to repent is issued by both Jesus and John in the Gospel of Mark, the Gospel of Matthew carefully removing the overlap.[151] For a Baptist constituency in Mark's audience, the claim that John was first to announce forgiveness of sins would have been inalterable – any flouting of the tradition threatening to drive them away. For the author of Mark, however, some degree of contradiction must have existed between John's offer of forgiveness through baptism and Jesus' offer through his death and resurrection (Mk 10:45; 14:24). Consistent with the Second Gospel's aim to meet the demands of both groups, such a discrepancy is permitted to remain.

Also relevant to this discussion is the interpolation (Mk 2:5b–10) in the story of Jesus' healing of a paralytic in Mark 2.[152] The key feature of this insertion is, of course, its discussion of the forgiveness of sins.[153] As others have shown,[154] without this insertion, similar to the other accounts of healing in Mark, Jesus restores the paralytic without any mention of forgiveness (cf. Lk 7:29–30). The insertion (Mk 2:5b–10), however, introduces that Jesus declared that the paralytic's sins were forgiven *before* directing him to arise, take up his mat, and return home (v. 11). The insertion also includes a brief dispute with those present ("scribes," v. 6) who charge Jesus with "blasphemy" for offering "forgiveness for sins." As shown by others, this allegation is unfounded in the context of Hellenistic Judaism, reflecting a wooden (uninformed?) application of Exod 34:6–7 and Isa 43:25; 44:22. Although forgiveness of sins is the exclusive prerogative of God and the usurpation of this role, a capital offense, *priests* (recall John's apparent lineage) routinely offered forgiveness of sins on God's behalf.[155] Any purported scribal dismay over Jesus' offer, therefore, can only reflect a reaction to Jesus' antiestablishmentarianism. Scholars thus explain this interpolation as the author's misapprehension of the theological dilemma involved. In light of Mark's overall approach to Baptist traditions, however, it seems the aim of this insertion is to impute to *Jesus,* like John, via a mock dialogue with "scribes," a message of forgiveness.[156] It is clearly not the message of forgiveness Jesus'

---

[151] A call to repentance is a key feature of Elijah traditions in both Mal 3:1, 23–24, and Sir 48:1–11; cf. also 2 Chr 21:12–15 (Brenda J. Shaver, "The Prophet Elijah in the Literature of the Second Temple Period," 8–9, 113).

[152] Mk 2:5b may have belonged to the original story, providing the reason for the interpolation of vv. 6–10. See Hans-Josef Klauck, "Die Frage der Sündenvergebung in der Perikope von der Heilung des Gelähmten (Mk 2,1–12 parr)," in *Gemeinde, Amt, Sakrament: Neutestamentliche Perspektiven* (Würzburg: Echter, 1989) 286–312.

[153] The expression, ἀφιέναι ἁμαρτίας occurs *mutatis mutandis* four times in this interpolation at vv. 5b, 7, 9, and 10.

[154] See E. Sanders, *Jesus and Judaism,* 108–13. Like John, Q insists on repentance.

[155] Although priests offered forgiveness, usually the role was democratized.

[156] Cf. also the curious summary comment in Mk 6:12 that the twelve "going out, proclaimed that they should repent (καὶ ἐξελθόντες ἐκήρυξαν ἵνα μετανοῶσιν)."

death will come to offer later in the book and in forthcoming Christian tradition, but it is an offer that competes nicely with John's offer presented earlier in the narrative in Mk 1:4.

4.6 Summation

This chapter assumes that the author's *a priori* understanding of John the Baptist as Elijah pervades the Gospel of Mark. Although the view is common that an Elijah typology determines Mark's presentation of John in the *beginning* of this gospel,[157] this chapter proposes that this characterization is brought to a climax in the center of the gospel at the transfiguration and even occurs elsewhere (Mk 6:15; 8:28; 9:11). These references to the Baptist as Elijah in the beginning, middle and end (Mk 15:34–37) of Mark function as a sub-structure over which the ministry of Jesus is superimposed.[158] On the one hand, the phase of Jesus' ministry based predominantly on displays of the miraculous (source materials of which remain unknown although cogent theories exist about 2:15–28 and 4:1–34), is inserted between the introduction of John as Elijah in Mark 1 and John's resurrection at the so-called mountain of transfiguration in Mark 9. On the other hand, the phase of Jesus' ministry that is based predominantly on teaching, (sources of which frequently recall Q traditions), is inserted between John's resurrection in Mark 9 and Jesus' resurrection in Mark 16. Thus, John's baptism provides the esteemed imprimatur on Jesus' healing ministry; and John's resurrection provides the same for Jesus' teaching ministry, in particular, Jesus' interpretations of the Law.[159]

Building on this observation is the related one that Q parallels in Mark are primarily of two kinds: (1) narrative explicitly related to the Baptist; and (2)

---

[157] Against those claiming the Gospel of Mark has no beginning, but begins *in medias res*, Morton Enslin argues that Mk 1:1–13 "is to be regarded as a unit and serves a deliberate purpose not unlike that of the more famous Johannine prologue. These verses have the deliberate purpose of letting the reader know, before the story starts, who Jesus is" ("The Artistry of Mark," 393–94). This is also the conclusion of Hans-Josef Klauck in *Vorspiel im Himmel? Erzähltechnik und Theologie im Markusprolog.*

[158] Morton Enslin insists on this evangelist's "creative design" of his composition ("The Artistry of Mark," 388) as over and against the view of "a loosely put together catena of ancient traditions" (399).

[159] The divine voice at the transfiguration (v. 7) alters the second person address of the baptism to the third person. Whereas the message at Jesus' baptism was for Jesus alone, the message at Jesus' transfiguration is now revealed to three future leaders of the movement. Also, a comparison may be made between Jesus' experience of the risen John and Paul's experience of the risen Jesus (Acts 9:1–31; 22:1–21; 26:2–23). In both cases a voice is heard, bright light or whiteness is described with respect to the subject, the subject's physical existence is affected by the revelation, and witnesses present do not comprehend fully what has taken place. Cf. also Gal 1:12, 16.

sayings concentrated after the transfiguration account in Mk 8–12. If, as argued above, current models of Q suggest it was a source of Baptist traditions,[160] and if the author of the Second Gospel knew this, then the concentration of Q parallels in Mark after the transfiguration scene may be deliberate: the risen John descends from heaven with Moses to sanction Jesus as successor, formally inaugurating Jesus' appropriation of John's well-known teachings for his own teaching ministry. One can imagine a *Sitz im Leben* in which Baptist followers of Jesus in Mark's congregation demonstrate their willingness to accept the attribution of John's most famous sayings to Jesus *on the basis of John's authority alone.* Furthermore, it should be no surprise that Jesus' appropriation of John's teachings leads straight to Jesus' death. Repeating the teachings of someone murdered on the basis of his message would be worse than delivering such teachings in the first place not just on account of the utter impetuosity of the second perpetrator, but because their repetition points to the ineffectiveness of the initial punishment in containing the potential insurrection. Luke 10:16 makes this point when it warns: ὁ ἀκούων ὑμῶν ἐμοῦ ἀκούει.[161] The strategic depiction of John as Elijah facilitates for the author of Mark his cooptation of these valuable and important traditions. The concentration of Q teachings *after* the transfiguration is the author's way of cutting a compromise with two groups.

A written source, that is Q, in the hands of the author of the Gospel of Mark is not a necessary correlative of the present hypothesis. Most likely, for Mk 8–13, the author utilized oral traditions at his disposal with known associations to the Baptist. These traditions were shared by the author(s)/compiler(s) of Q (or a Q community).

Finally, the abundance of Q traditions and themes duplicated in Mark suggests that the beginning of the assimilation of Baptist and Christian traditions began, *not* with Q's integration in the compositions of the First and Third Gospels, but with *their* Markan 'forerunner.' Not only did the authors of Matthew and Luke incorporate Q traditions into their accounts of Christian origins, but the author of Mark did too – this author, in fact, initiating the tradition of assimilation. Indeed once Mark had established the precedent, the authors of Matthew and Luke were emboldened to open the floodgates, incorporating as many, *now written*, Q traditions as they considered helpful to a persuasive, accurate and clear depiction of Christian origins.

---

[160] This argument is supported, although does not rely on, the argument of my overall thesis, expounded most fully in Ch. 3 above.

[161] Although this passage is in Q, some question remains as to whether the recurring verb was "hear" (Lk 10:16) or "welcome" (Mt 10:40). The IQP selects the latter from Matthew. See *The Critical Edition of Q*, 188–89. For the arguments, see *Q Parallels*, 76. In either case, Q parallels to the idea of the rejection of the missionaries include 11:49–51; 12:11–12; and 13:34–35. This passage also provides an important witness to the general approach to succession on the part of kingdom movement participants.

The implications of this argument are wide-ranging. They may be summarized by an analogy with Conzelmann's ground-breaking thesis on Lukan eschatology in the 1950's: just as, according to Conzelmann's thesis, Luke shifted Mark's eschatology, the present chapter argues, Mark shifted Jesus'.[162] For Mark's *John* the eschatological judgment is near; John announces a more powerful one "is coming" (Mk 1:7). For Mark's Jesus, however, the end of time is commenced already in the death and resurrection of his teacher. Thus, Mk 1:15: "...the time *is fulfilled* (pf. pass.: πεπλήρωται), and the kingdom of God *has come near* (pf.; ἤγγικεν). The two perfect forms suggest something already completed in the past *of Jesus*.[163]

---

[162] See Jörg Frey, "Die Bedeutung der Qumranfunde für das Verständnis des Neuen Testaments" in *Qumran: Die Schriftrollen vom Toten Meer*, eds. M. Fieger et al. (NTOA 47; Freiburg: Freiburg Schweiz/Göttingen: Vandenhoeck & Ruprecht, 2001) 129–208.

[163] On the "apocalyptic" flavor of the transfiguration, E. Schweizer has written, "Perhaps this is the account of an experience of the three disciples (or even a vision) that ... interpreted the coming of Jesus as the beginning of the end" (*The Good News according to Mark,* 181).

Chapter Five

Baptist Traditions and the Origin of the Son of Man Sayings in Q

5.1 Introduction

Over the past half century, a convention has developed among those addressing the Synoptic Son of Man sayings that any essay on this problem begins with a comment on its utter intractability.[1] Indeed, this convention has become so widespread that it has spawned yet another convention: that of listing past references to the intractability of the problem at the beginning of any essay on the topic.[2] At this point, reflection, not only on the problem of the Synoptic Son of Man sayings themselves, but on these conventions of insisting on the difficulty of this line of research constitutes a valid subject of debate.

These conventions are, of course, the oblique manner in which scholars submit the abject failure of the field to come up with, in this case, a cogent explanation for the derivation and origin of the Greek expression, ὁ υἱὸς τοῦ ἀνθρώπου (literally, "the son of the man").[3] Indeed in the most recent articles

---

[1] See for example Matthew Black, "The Son of Man Problem in Recent Research and Debate," *BJRL* 45 (1963) 305; J. A. Fitzmyer, "The New Testament Title 'Son of Man' Philologically Considered," in *A Wandering Aramean: Collected Aramaic Essays* (SBLMS 25; Missoula: Scholars, 1979) 143; A. J. B. Higgins, "The Son of Man *Forschung* Since 'The Teaching of Jesus,'" in *New Testament Essays: Studies in Memory of Thomas Walter Manson*, ed. A. J. B. Higgins (Manchester: Manchester University, 1959) 119; idem, "Is the Son of Man Problem Insoluble?" *Neotestamentica et Semitica: Studies in Honour of Matthew Black*, ed. E. E. Ellis and M. Wilcox (Edinburgh: T & T Clark, 1969) 70–87; M. Hooker, "Is the Son of Man Problem Really Insoluble?" in *Text and Interpretation: Studies in the New Testament Presented to Matthew Black*, ed. E. Best and R. McL. Wilson (Cambridge: Cambridge University, 1979) 155–68; Walter Wink, *The Human Being: Jesus and the Enigma of the Son of the Man* (Minneapolis: Fortress, 2002) 1.

[2] See for example John R. Donahue, S.J., "Recent Studies on the Origin of 'Son of Man' in the Gospels," *CBQ* 48 (1986) 484–98; William O. Walker, "The Son of Man: Some Recent Developments," *CBQ* 45 (1983) 584; and Adela Yarbro Collins, "The Origin of the Designation of Jesus as 'Son of Man,'" in eadem, *Cosmology and Eschatology in Jewish and Christian Apocalypticism* (Leiden: E. J. Brill, 1996) 139–58; an earlier version of this article appeared in *HTR* 80/4 (1987) 391–407.

[3] In this chapter, when referring to the Greek expression, ὁ υἱὸς τοῦ ἀνθρώπου, I use the almost literal ET, "the Son of Man" to establish continuity between my argument and past discussions of the topic and without any preconceived bias to this translation. For a summary of the lengthy discussions of a Greek derivation from Aramaic as well as the English translation of this expression, see Geza Vermes, "The 'Son of Man' Debate," *JSNT* (1978) 19–32; J. A. Fitzmyer,

on the topic scholars rehearse the important past contributions of R. Bultmann, H. Tödt, P. Vielhauer, N. Perrin, H. Koester, E. Lührmann, H. Schürmann, G. Vermes, J. A. Fitzmyer and others with a tone of resignation. Entire articles weigh the dubious merits, not of cogent new arguments, but of only marginally persuasive past ones.[4]

Given this particularly daunting *status quaestionis*, the thought arises as to whether the origin of the designation of *Jesus* as "Son of Man" has been pressed beyond capacity. The present chapter proposes a new solution, namely that the pronounced emphasis on John the Baptist in Q,[5] a principal source of Son of Man sayings, has the potential to illuminate this notoriously thorny problem. According to *The Critical Edition of Q*, the following is a list of Q's Son of Man sayings:[6]

Q 6:22   Blessed are you when they revile and persecute you, and say every evil against you on account of the Son of Man.

Q 7:34   The Son of Man came eating and drinking and you say: Behold, a glutton and drunkard, a friend of tax collectors and sinners.

Q 9:58   The foxes have holes and the birds of heaven, nests, but the Son of Man does not have anywhere he may lay his head.

Q 11:30   For just as Jonah became a sign to the Ninevites, so also the Son of Man will be to this generation.

Q 12:8   Whoever acknowledges me before people, the Son of Man will acknowledge him before the angels.

"The New Testament Title 'Son of Man' Philologically Considered," 143–60; Adela Yarbro Collins, "The Origin of the Designation of Jesus as 'Son of Man,'" 157.

[4] For example, John R. Donahue, S.J., "Recent Studies on the Origin of 'Son of Man' in the Gospels" and Paul Hoffmann, "QR und der Menschensohn. Eine vorläufige Skizze," in Frans Van Segbroeck, eds., C. M. Tuckett, G.Van Belle, and J. Verheyden, *The Four Gospels 1992: Festschrift Frans Neirynck*, 3 vols. (BETL 100; Louvain: Peeters; Louvain University Press, 1992) 421–56; ET, "The Redaction of Q and the Son of Man: A Preliminary Sketch," in ed., R. A. Piper, *The Gospel Behind the Gospels: Current Studies on Q* (NovTSupp 75; Leiden: Brill, 1994) 159–98. Matthew Black assesses Tödt's conclusions in "The 'Son of Man' Passion Sayings in the Gospel Tradition," *ZNW* (1969) 1–8. The literature on this topic is vast. In addition to those articles already mentioned, surveys include: C. Colpe, "Der Begriff 'Menschensohn' und die Methode der Erforschung messianischer Prototypen," *Kairos* 11 (1969) 241–63; 12 (1970) 81–112; 13 (1971) 1–17; 14 (1972) 241–57; R. Marlow, "The Son of Man in Recent Journal Literature," *CBQ* 28 (1966) 20–30; I. H. Marshall, "The Synoptic Son of Man Sayings in Recent Discussion," *NTS* 12 (1966) 327–51; idem, "The Son of Man in Contemporary Debate," *EvQ* 42 (1970) 67–87; and R. Maddox, "The Quest for Valid Methods in 'Son of Man' Research," *Australian Biblical Review* 19 (1971) 35–51.

[5] For example: Christopher Tuckett, *Q and the History of Early Christianity: Studies on Q*, 108–9. See 7–8 n. 11.

[6] Cf. list of twelve, including Q/Matt 10:23 and Q 22:28, in John S. Kloppenborg, *Q Parallels,* 238. In both cases "Son of Man" appears in the Gospel of Matthew only. List of nine (omitting Lk 17:30) in Leif Vaage, "The Son of Man Sayings in Q: Stratigraphical Location and Significance," *Semeia* 55 (1992) 103.

Q 12:10   And whoever says a word against the Son of Man, it will be forgiven him,
           but whoever speaks against the Holy Spirit, it will not be forgiven him.

Q 12:40   You also must be prepared because the Son of Man will come in an hour you
           do not expect.

Q 17:24   For as the lightning comes out of the east ("sunrise") and appears as far as
           the west ("sunset"), so also the Son of Man will be on his day.

Q 17:26   Just as it happened in the days of Noah, so also will it be on the day of the
           Son of Man.

Q 17:27, 30 For in those days they were eating and drinking, marrying and giving in
           marriage, up until the day Noah entered into the ark and the flood came and
           took all, in this way also will the day the Son of Man is revealed be.

This chapter attempts to demonstrate that the Son of Man expression was originally John the Baptist's reference to an authoritative mediator in the imminent
eschatological events of judgment. We begin with an overview of the history of
research on the Son of Man sayings in Q as background to this line of pursuit.

5.2 History of Research

The history of research on the Son of Man sayings in the NT may be subdivided
into four categories based on four different questions: (1) possible connotations
of NT occurrences of "the Son of Man"; (2) correlation of the NT concept with
pre- or extra-Synoptic sources such as Daniel, 1 Enoch, and 4 Ezra; (3) classification of NT occurrences; and (4) possible derivation of NT occurrences of this
expression in the historical Jesus. A fifth, additional group debates the philological question of a possible Aramaic equivalent of this Greek term.

The third group, classification of all NT occurrences is of particular interest
to the investigation of Q's sayings. Taken as a group, the Synoptic sayings are
frequently subdivided into three categories: (1) those referring to the Son of Man
in the *future*; (2) those referring to the Son of Man in the *present*; and, (3) those
referring to the Son of Man's *suffering*.[7] Most scholars have accepted the authenticity of the *future* sayings since R. Bultmann first suggested it.[8] Because Q
contains at least six with *future* orientation, Q's sayings are largely accepted as
authentic. Heinz Eduard Tödt agreed that many of Q's sayings were authentic,
if some reflect kerygmatic developments within early Christianity.[9]

---

[7] R. Bultmann, *Theology of the New Testament*, 1.30. Also, A. J. B. Higgins, *Jesus and the
Son of Man* (London: Lutterworth, 1964).

[8] R. Bultmann, *The Theology of the New Testament*, 1.30.

[9] *Der Menschensohn in der synoptischen Überlieferung* (Gütersloher Verlagshaus, 1963);
ET: *The Son of Man in the Synoptic Tradition*, trans. D. M. Barton (London: SCM, 1965) 64–67.
As authentic sayings of Jesus, Tödt specifies Q 11:30; 12:8; 12:40; 17:24, 26. Tödt questions

Philip Vielhauer, however, questioned Tödt's and others' assumption of the authenticity of the future sayings.[10] Vielhauer charged that mere identification of the Son of Man as one distinct from Jesus (and arriving in the future) is an insufficient basis upon which to argue authenticity and concluded the early church did not *expand*, but *originated* all of its Son of Man sayings. Generally in agreement with Vielhauer, Norman Perrin specified the Son of Man sayings as early Christian *pesher* exegesis of passages from the Hebrew Scriptures.[11]

In response to these hypotheses about Q's Son of Man sayings, Q scholarship offered a solution of its own.[12] Echoing Vielhauer and Perrin in rejection of their authenticity, Q scholars have argued Q's Son of Man sayings are traceable to a redactional layer of Q subsequent to, for example, Q's Kingdom of God sayings.[13] H. Schürmann places the Son of Man sayings after an earlier stage of individual sayings in Q's redaction, as "Kommentarworte" on the original sayings (if before the final redaction).[14] Other Q scholars today consider the

---

the legitimacy of Q 6:22; 7:34; 9:58; 12:10; 17:27, 30, as well as two sayings not considered by the IQP to have originated in Q: Mt 10:23 and 19:28 (64–7, 114–25).

[10] "Gottesreich und Menschensohn," *Festschrift für Günther Dehn*, ed. W. Schneemelcher (Neukirchen: Verlag der Buchhandlung des Erziehungsvereins Neukirchen, 1957) 51–79.

[11] *Rediscovering the Teaching of Jesus* (The New Testament Library; London: SCM, 1967) 164–99.

[12] See Helmut Koester, "GNOMAI DIAPHOROI: The Origin and Nature of Diversification in the History of Early Christianity," in James M. Robinson and Helmut Koester, *Trajectories through Early Christianity* (Philadelphia: Fortress, 1971) 114–57 and "One Jesus and Four Primitive Gospels," in *Trajectories*, 158–204; also, idem, *Ancient Christian Gospels: Their History and Development* (London: SCM/Philadelphia: TPI, 1990); Paul Hoffmann, "The Redaction of Q and the Son of Man: A Preliminary Sketch"; Arland Jacobson, "The Literary Unity of Q"; idem, *The First Gospel. An Introduction to Q* (Sonoma: Polebridge, 1992); D. Lührmann, *Die Redaktion der Logienquelle* (WMANT 33; Neukirchen-Vluyn: Neukirchener, 1969); Leif Vaage, "The Son of Man Sayings in Q: Stratigraphical Location and Significance." About Koester's position, C. Tuckett rightly summarizes, "The fact that there are no eschatological SM sayings in GTh, despite the large number of other parallels between GTh and Q, is a key factor for Koester in arguing that the eschatological SM sayings in Q must be secondary accretions to Q" (*Q and the History of Early Christianity*, 241).

[13] See Werner Georg Kümmel, *Einleitung in das Neue Testament* (17. Aufl.; Heidelberg: Quelle & Meyer, 1973); ET: *Introduction to the New Testament*, rev. ed., trans. Howard C. Kee (Nashville: Abingdon, 1975) 73; Heinz Eduard Tödt, *Der Menschensohn in der synoptischen Überlieferung*. The Son of Man sayings also played a key role in attempts to discern a Christology of Q. The question of, for example, whether resurrection theology is an assumption of Q relies on interpretations of these sayings. Tödt argues Q was the first to identify Jesus with the Son of Man – a figure Jesus himself expected. According to Tödt, "Son of Man Christology and Q belong together both in their concepts and in their history of tradition" (*Son of Man*, 269). Another point of clarification: although Q's Son of Man sayings are considered a later redactional layer, they are "later" only in the sense of their addition to Q. For scholars such as Kloppenborg, redactional stratigraphy is not translatable on tradition-historical terms.

[14] "Beobachtungen zum Menschensohn-Titel in der Redequelle," in *Jesus und der Menschensohn* (FS A. Vögtle; Freiburg; Herder, 1975) 124–47; cf. also J. Klopppenborg, "Symbolic Eschatology and the Apocalypticism of Q"; L. E. Vaage, "The Son of Man Sayings in Q"; M. Sato, *Q und Prophetie* (WUNT 2.29; Tübingen: Mohr Siebeck, 1988) 28–47.

Son of Man sayings part of an eschatological layer of Q deemed later than its sapiential layer.[15] With regard to these developments in Q research John Kloppenborg summarizes:

Independently of each other, and using strikingly different methods, Helmut Koester and Heinz Schürmann both concluded that Son of Man sayings did not belong to the earliest strata of Q. Schürmann, in addition, argued that the Son of Man sayings were not added as late as the final assembling of Q. Hence, these sayings characterize neither the formative layers of Q nor the perspective of the final redaction. This conclusion effectively overturned Heinz E. Tödt's assertion that "Son of Man Christology and Q belong together both in their concepts and in their history of tradition."[16]

In his recent book, *The Human Being: Jesus and the Enigma of the Son of Man*, Walter Wink states that the Son of Man expression is not a "pre-Christian title."[17] While Wink is probably correct that the expression is not a title, the present chapter puts forth that, depending upon where John the Baptist is placed in the history of "Christian" tradition, the expression may be "pre-Christian." Wink also argues that the pre-Christian Son of Man was neither "a messianic deliverer," nor "the Suffering Servant of Isa 53," nor "a heaven-appointed judge who would preside over the last judgment."[18] To be sure, these elements are not traceable to "pre-Christian" traditions such as Ezekiel, Daniel or the Similitudes of Enoch. They may, however, be "pre-Christian" if they are somehow associated with John the Baptist.

Thus, against Wink, the present thesis argues that this expression originated either with John the Baptist or his followers and that Q's Son of Man sayings are an important indicator of this claim. Unlike John Meier who prioritizes Q sayings in his historical analysis,[19] Wink pays only lip service to Q as a source of Son of Man sayings, otherwise ignoring it and the relationships of the Son of Man sayings within it.

Wink does, however, make the important observation that the church is more likely to have supplemented, than originated, an authentic corpus of sayings.

I find it inconceivable that churches that made no use of the son-of-the-man figure in other contexts would have invented some eighty-four references to it, spread about evenly among all four Gospels, all of them (with one exception) with definite articles. At the time the Evangelists wrote the Gospels, the more exalted Christological titles (Messiah/Christ, Lord, High Priest, Son of God, God) were already fully deployed and served as the basis both for christological reflection and liturgical celebration. So why would the church create so many son-of-the-man sayings at a time when no one, so far as we know, was using

---

[15] See Leif Vaage, "The Son of Man Sayings in Q," 124.

[16] John Kloppenborg, "Symbolic Eschatology and the Apocalypticism of Q," 291, citing Tödt, *The Son of Man in the Synoptic Tradition*, 269.

[17] W. Wink, *The Human Being*, 22, 61. Cf. also Douglas R. A. Hare who argues that "Son of Man" was a nickname (*The Son of Man Tradition*, 181–82).

[18] W. Wink, *The Human Being*, 21.

[19] J. P. Meier, *A Marginal Jew*, 2.28, 42–43.

that expression of Jesus? There must have been a critical mass of authentic sayings with the potency to trigger creative additions to the fund of existing sayings. Had the church invented all of the son-of-the-man sayings, would not the preference have been to use *no* articles in order to create a proof from prophecy that pointed directly to the anarthrous (lacking definite articles) phrase in Ezekiel and Dan. 7:13?[20]

Accepting this argument, the present thesis considers whether Wink's "critical mass" of authentic Son of Man sayings among early Christian traditions was Q's, hypothesizing that confusion arose, as with other traditions concerning John, when sayings *of* John were being appropriated and propagated *about* John and *about* Jesus.

5.3 Collins' "The Origin of the Designation of Jesus as 'Son of Man'"

Against the great tide of relegation of the Synoptic Son of Man sayings to later tradition, Adela Yarbro Collins argues that some of the Synoptic Son of Man sayings are plausibly traced to the historical Jesus. In her article, "The Origin of the Designation of Jesus as 'Son of Man,'" Collins makes the case that Jesus himself originates his designation as the Son of Man.[21] Against many important earlier interpreters,[22] Collins proposes:

---

[20] W. Wink, *The Human Being*, 21; emphasis original.

[21] Adela Yarbro Collins, "The Origin of the Designation of Jesus as 'Son of Man,'" 156.

[22] The quantity of secondary literature on the Son of Man traditions in the Synoptics is vast. Important examples include Eugene Boring, *Sayings of the Risen Jesus: Christian Prophecy in the Synoptic Tradition* (SNTSMS; Cambridge: Cambridge University, 1982) 244–45; F. H. Borsch, *The Son of Man in Myth and History* (Philadelphia: Westminster, 1967); John Bowker, "The Son of Man," *JTS* 28 (1977) 19–48; Chrys C. Caragounis, *The Son of Man* (WUNT 2/38; Tübingen: Mohr Siebeck, 1986); Maurice Casey, *Son of Man: The Interpretation and Influence of Daniel 7* (London: SPCK, 1979) 224–40; idem, "The Use of the Term 'Son of Man' in the Similitudes of Enoch," *JSJ* 7 (1976) 11–29; Carsten Colpe, "υἱὸς τοῦ ἀνθρώπου," *TDNT* 8 (1972) 400–77; John R. Donahue, S.J., "Recent Studies on the Origin of 'Son of Man' in the Gospels"; Joseph A. Fitzmyer, S.J., "Another View of the 'Son of Man' Debate," *JSNT* 4 (1979) 58–68; A. J. B. Higgins, *The Son of Man in the Teaching of Jesus* (SNTSMS; Cambridge: Cambridge University, 1980); Joachim Jeremias, "Die älteste Schicht der Menschensohn-Logien," *ZNW* 58 (1967); Ragnar Leivestad, "Der apokalyptische Menschensohn: Ein theologisches Phantom," *ASTI* 6 (1968) 49–105; Rudolf Otto, *Reich Gottes und Menschensohn*, (1934; 2nd ed.; München: Beck, 1940); ET, *The Kingdom of God and the Son of Man* (2nd ed.; London: Lutterworth, 1943); Norman Perrin, "Mark XIV. 62: The End Product of a Christian Pesher Tradition?" *NTS* 12 (1965–66) 150–55; idem, "The Son of Man in Ancient Judaism and Primitive Christianity: A Suggestion," *BR* 11 (1966) 17–28; idem, "The Creative Use of the Son of Man Traditions by Mark," *USQR* 23 (1967–68) 357–65; idem, "The Son of Man in the Synoptic Tradition," *BR* 13 (1968) 3–25; 1968 (repr. 1974a: 57–83); Heinz Eduard Tödt, *Der Menschensohn in der synoptischen Überlieferung*; Philip Vielhauer, "Gottesreich und Menschensohn in der Verkündigung Jesu"; idem, "Jesus und der Menschensohn: Zur Diskussion mit

The conclusion seems warranted then that the ultimate origin of the designation of Jesus as "Son of Man" is in the teaching of Jesus himself. Jesus closely associated, but probably did not identify, himself with that heavenly being. The proximate origin of the designation is thus in the reflection of some of Jesus's followers upon his death who were convinced of his vindication.[23]

In her search for the origin of the Son of Man sayings in the Synoptic tradition, against Bultmann and Vermes, Collins offers her own categorization of all seventy-four Son of Man sayings in the Synoptic tradition[24] – thirty-seven distinct sayings when all variants of a single saying are grouped together. Different from Bultmann who, according to Collins, bases his categorization of the sayings on "subjective exegesis," Collins bases her categorization on "form and function."[25] Of the thirty-seven distinct sayings, the ten "I-sayings" originated, Collins maintains, in post-Easter situations.[26] Three sayings that provide a secondary interpretation of a similitude or parable (Mt 13:37, 41; Lk 18:8b) and four that are parts of so-called "legendary narratives," (Mt 16:13; Mt 26:64/Mk 14:62/Lk 22:69; Lk 22:48; and Lk 24:7), also, according to Collins, reflect post-Easter circumstances.[27] None of these seventeen sayings, therefore, provides a reliable basis for investigations of the origin of the Son of Man idiom. Collins groups the remaining twenty sayings under three headings: (1) "legal sayings or church rules" (two sayings); (2) "wisdom sayings" (two sayings); and (3) "prophetic and apocalyptic sayings" (sixteen sayings).

In the first category, "legal sayings or church rules," Collins places two sayings: Mk 2:10 par. and Mt 12:32/Lk 12:10. With regard to the first saying (Mk 2:10 par.), although the insertion of ὁ υἱὸς τοῦ ἀνθρώπου was probably secondary (a part of the insertion of vv. 5b–10 between v. 5a and v. 11) and not

---

Heinz Eduard Tödt und Eduard Schweizer," *ZThK* 60 (1963) 133–77, repr. in idem, *Aufsätze zum Neuen Testament*. On the Son of Man traditions in Q specifically, see Arland D. Jacobson, "Apocalyptic and the Synoptic Sayings Source Q," in *The Four Gospels 1992: Festschrift Frans Neirynck*, eds. Frans Van Segbroeck et al., 403–19; C. M. Tuckett, *Q and the History of Early Christianity,* 239–82; idem, "Q 12, 8: Once again 'Son of Man' or 'I,'" in *From Quest to Q: Festschrift James M. Robinson*, eds., Jon Ma. Asgeirsson, Kristin De Troyer, and Marvin W. Meyer (Leuven: Peeters; Leuven University Press, 2000) 171–88.

[23] Adela Yarbro Collins, "Origin of the Designation," 156.

[24] Here A. Y. Collins includes the "clearly relevant saying" in *Gos. Thom.* § 86 ("The Origin of the Designation of Jesus as 'Son of Man,'" 145). Cf. different enumerations of total sayings by Günther Schwarz, *Jesus "der Menschensohn": aramaistische Untersuchungen zu den synoptischen Menschensohnworten Jesu* (BWANT 6/19; Stuttgart: Kohlhammer, 1986) 11–12; W. Wink, *The Human Being: Jesus and the Enigma of the Son of the Man*, 17.

[25] A. Y. Collins, "Origin of the Designation," 144–45.

[26] A. Y. Collins offers this list of examples: "Mt 11:18–19/Lk 7:33–34; Mt 17:9/Mk 9:9; Mt 17:12/Mk 9:12; Mt 17:22/Mk 9:31/Lk 9:44; Lk 19:10; Mt 20:18/Mk 10:33/Lk 18:31; Mt 20:28/Mk 10:45 (cf. Luke 22:27); Mt 26:2; Mt 26:45/Mk 14:41; and Mk 8:31/Lk 9:22" ("Origin of the Designation," 145 n. 22).

[27] A. Y. Collins, "Origin of the Designation," 145.

a *verbum domini* in this context, it is plausible, Collins argues, that Jesus used this expression in his activity of forgiving sins/healing.[28]

With regard to the second saying (Mt 12:32/Lk 12:10; cf. Mk 3:28–29), despite its inexplicable shift from referring to human beings in general to referring to Jesus, Collins argues Jesus also may have spoken this saying. For my argument it is significant that *this second saying is,* on most readings, *traceable to Q.*[29]

Collins next evaluates two sayings she classifies as "wisdom saying, proverb, or aphorism."[30] The two Son of Man sayings of the "wisdom saying" type (Mk 2:27–28; Mt 8:21/Lk 9:58), she argues, can *both* be traced to the historical Jesus. The first saying, "The sabbath was made on account of man and not man, on account of the sabbath; so also ὁ υἱὸς τοῦ ἀνθρώπου is lord even of the sabbath"[31] (from Mark [cf. Mt 12:8/Lk 6:5]), although part of a controversy dialogue which was probably composed in some post-Easter situation, could, in Collins' estimation, "be early, even a saying of Jesus."[32] For the second, "The foxes have holes and the birds of heaven, nests, but ὁ υἱὸς τοῦ ἀνθρώπου does not have anywhere he may lay his head," (Mt 8:21/Lk 9:58) Collins argues that, although probably referring to human beings in general, it too may go back to the historical Jesus.[33]

Interestingly, in the latter saying Jesus is depicted as, in Collins' words, "a particular individual who is without an abode."[34] A point Collins does not make here, however, is that this characterization contradicts the majority of Jesus' traditions (Markan) in which Jesus has ample places to lodge.[35] Continuity of this saying is rather observable with traditions regarding John the Baptist who is depicted as itinerant. If, therefore, this saying traces back to the historical Jesus, it was probably not self-referential (and thus not about human beings in general), rather referring to *a Son of Man other than himself.*[36]

---

[28] A. Y. Collins, "Origin of the Designation," 147.

[29] See J. Kloppenborg, *Q Parallels,* 124. Collins' neglect of this point may be intentional: deliberately rejecting the popular assumption (since Bultmann) of the authenticity of Q's sayings, and rather subjecting them, like other Synoptic sayings, to renewed historical-critical scrutiny.

[30] A. Y. Collins, "Origin of the Designation," 148.

[31] A. Y. Collins, "Origin of the Designation," 149.

[32] A. Y. Collins, "Origin of the Designation," 149.

[33] Three out of four sayings concerning "birds" in the NT Gospels originated in Q: 9:58; 12:24; 13:19. The other example is the parable of the sower (Mk 4:1–9 par.). Of those in Q, one is a Son of Man saying (Q 9:58) and another is a Kingdom of God saying (Q 13:19; cf. also 12:31).

[34] A. Y. Collins, "Origin of the Designation," 150–51.

[35] E.g., Mk 1:29, 32–33; 2:1, 15; 3:19b; 7:17; 9:28, *et al.*

[36] The present tense of the verbs in this saying do not imply Jesus is speaking about himself. They do not necessarily even imply Jesus speaks of a Son of Man contemporary to himself. In its context in this type of wisdom saying, the present tense here simply suggests timeless truth.

Collins' final category of "prophetic and apocalyptic" contains sixteen distinct Son of Man sayings. Four appear to Collins as redactional additions to the gospels in which they occur (Mt 16:28; 24:30a; 25:31; Lk 17:22). Another four may predate the gospels, but are still considered post-Easter (Mt 10:23; Mk 14:21 par.; Lk 6:22; 21:36). To sort out the remaining eight sayings, Collins summons the arguments of Bultmann and Vielhauer. First, Collins acknowledges Bultmann's argument that those Son of Man sayings qualifying a *distinction* between Jesus and the Son of Man, such as Mk 8:38 par. and Lk 12:8–9, predate those that *identify* the two figures, concluding that Jesus spoke about a Son of Man (in the third person), but never identified himself with that figure.[37] With regard to Lk 12:8–9 ("Whoever acknowledges me before the people, ὁ υἱὸς τοῦ ἀνθρώπου will also acknowledge him before the angels of God"), Collins agrees, (building on Bultmann, Otto and Tödt), that no post-Easter followers of Jesus would have formulated a saying that "distinguished between these two figures."[38] Whether or not such a claim can be sustained, Collins does not specify Lk 12:8–9 as a passage from Q.[39]

Collins then notes three final Son of Man sayings which, she claims, "could well express his [Jesus'] prophetic message concerning an apocalyptic heavenly figure who was to have a role in the imminent eschatological events."[40] They are: Mt 24:44 par., Mt 24:37–39 par., and Mt 24:27 par.[41] Once again it is significant for the present study that *all three of these passages are traceable to Q* at 12:40, 17:26 and 17:24 respectively.[42]

In sum, of thirty-seven Son of Man sayings in the Synoptic tradition, according to Collins, only twenty have real value in discussions of the earliest recoverable origins of this idiom. Dividing these twenty sayings into three categories, of the two in the first category, "legal sayings or church rules," Collins reconstructs plausible settings in the teaching of the historical Jesus for both the one from Mark and the one from Q. Of the two sayings in the second category, "wisdom sayings," Collins, too, traces both the one from Q and the one from Mark to the historical Jesus. Of the sixteen in the third category, "prophetic and apocalyptic sayings," on Collins' argument, eight are not traceable to Jesus, and

---

[37] A. Y. Collins, "Origin of the Designation" 151.

[38] A. Y. Collins, "Origin of the Designation," 151–52; R. Bultmann, *The History of the Synoptic Tradition,* 122, 128, 151–52; Rudolf Otto, *Reich Gottes und Menschensohn,* 131; Tödt, *Der Menschensohn in der synoptischen Überlieferung,* 52–53. Vielhauer disagreed, arguing a social situation for this saying in which followers were required to make legal statements regarding their allegiance to Jesus ("Gottesreich und Menschensohn," 76–79).

[39] The inclusion of this passage in Q is the consensus of "most authors"; see J. Kloppenborg, *Q Parallels,* 122–23.

[40] A. Y. Collins, "Origin of the Designation," 152.

[41] A. Y. Collins, "Origin of the Designation," 152.

[42] On scholarly consensus regarding the inclusion of these passages in Q, see J. Kloppenborg, *Q Parallels*: Q 12:40, "most authors" (138–39); Q 17:26, 24, "most authors" (190–93).

eight are ambiguous. Of this final ambiguous eight, on Collins' assessment, the four from Q are all traceable to the historical Jesus.[43] Thus, of the twenty Son of Man sayings valuable for discussions of origins, on Collins' critical analysis, only twelve retain this value. This chapter argues that it is not coincidental that of those twelve, *all seven from Q qualify* (Q 12:10; 9:58; 12:8–9; 12:40; 17:26, 30; 17:24).[44] Most modern reconstructions of Q proffer a total of only ten Son

---

[43] As Collins points out, Bultmann argued that five prophetic and apocalyptic Son of Man sayings can be traced to the historical Jesus: Lk 12:8–9; Mk 8:38 par.; Mt 24:27 par.; Mt 24:37–39 par. and Mt 24:44 par. ("Origin of the Designation," 151). Neither Bultmann, nor Collins, however acknowledges that four of these sayings come from Q: Lk 12:8–9 = Q 12:8–9; Mt 24:27 par. = Q 17:24; Mt 24:37–39 = 17:26; and Mt 24:44 par. = Q 12:40 (Bultmann, *History of the Synoptic Tradition*, 122, 128, 151–52). Furthermore, with regard to Mk 8:38 par., the present author wishes to point out that this saying has a parallel in Q 12:8–9 (cf. also Lk 9:26). Because Q 12:8–9 clearly distinguishes between the Son of Man and Jesus, against Vielhauer, many consider a post-Easter origination implausible. See R. Otto, *Reich Gottes und Menschensohn*, 131; H. E. Tödt, *Der Menschensohn in der synoptischen Über-lieferung*, 52–53; P. Vielhauer, "Gottesreich und Menschensohn," 74, 79; and idem, "Jesus und der Menschensohn," 101.

[44] In a later article, Adela Y. Collins addresses the Son of Man sayings in Q. Her argument comprises three parts. First, she critiques Robinson's well-known *logoi sophon* generic categorization of Q, arguing that this category wholly overlooks prophetic and apocalyptic traditions that give wise leaders dual roles of teacher and prophet/visionary ("The Son of Man Sayings in the Sayings Source," in *To Touch the Text: Biblical and Related Studies in Honor of Joseph A. Fitzmyer*, S.J., eds. Maurya Horgan and Paul J. Kobelski [New York: Crossroad, 1989] 389). See also J. R. Robinson, "ΛΟΓΟΙ ΣΟΦΩΝ: Zur Gattung der Spruchquelle Q," in *Zeit und Geschichte: Dankesgabe an Rudolf Bultmann*, ed. Erich Dinkler (Tübingen: Mohr Siebeck, 1964) 77–96; ET (enlarged by author): "LOGOI SOPHON: On the Gattung of Q," in *Trajectories through Early Christianity*, James M. Robinson and Helmut Koester (Philadelphia: Fortress, 1971). Cf. also "Jewish Wisdom Literature and the Gattung LOGOI SOPHON," in *The Shape of Q Signal Essays on the Sayings Gospel*, 51–58.

Second, she argues that the Son of Man sayings in Q "play an important role" at *every* (apparent) stage of Q's redaction ("The Son of Man Sayings in the Sayings Source," 389). C. M. Tuckett draws the same conclusion in his *Studies on Q*, 252. According to Collins, although Tödt may not have been correct that the Son of Man sayings in Q represent a "Christology," they may nevertheless be intimately tied to Q in both "concept" and "history of tradition." Collins argues the latter view persuasively, pointing to the overall weakness within Q studies of assuming traditions, layers of redactions and glosses without, prior attempts to discern continuity. As Collins writes in her review of John Kloppenborg, *The Formation of Q*: "The conclusion that Q had at least two major stages of composition is really a premise; the alternative is never considered" (*CBQ* 50 [1988] 722). On Q's Son of Man sayings as second strata additions to Q's "formative stratum," see Leif Vaage, "The Son of Man Sayings in Q: Stratigraphical Location and Significance." The impulse to stratify this sayings source is, in the history of Q research, traced to theological motivations. As far back as Adolf von Harnack, a majority of those interested in Q have fought, wittingly and unwittingly, to protect Q as the *ipsissima verba* of Jesus. This desire compelled a variety of ingenious methods of ridding the original Q of undesirable sayings. Different literary, historical, and theological stratification systems have served this end. Stratification has, for example, enabled scholars to trace Christology and resurrection theology in Q, to alleviate Jesus of errant apocalyptic tendencies, and, more recently, to observe the development of a non-Pauline kerygma, predating Paul, in an otherwise unknown Jewish branch of the Jesus movement in Galilee.

of Man sayings. On Collins' argument, therefore, only three Q sayings would be relegated to later tradition: Q 6:22, 7:34 and 11:30. In other words, independent of Tödt's claim that, unlike the present and suffering Son of Man sayings, Q's Son of Man sayings are authentic, Collins' appraisal of *all* Synoptic Son of Man sayings leads to a similar conclusion: the origin of the Son of Man sayings in Q is the teaching of Jesus who closely associated himself with this figure.

Before advancing to a discussion of the relevance of Collins' conclusions for a discussion of Q's Son of Man sayings in relation to Q's prominent Baptist *Tendenz*, brief treatment of the origins of the three Q sayings relegated to later tradition (6:22, 7:34 and 11:30) is essential.

5.4 Q 6:22, 7:34 and 11:30

Taking them in their order of appearance in the Gospel of Luke, the first saying, Q 6:22 ("Blessed are you when they revile and persecute you, and say every evil against you on account of the Son of Man") arises in Collins' disputation of Bultmann's categorization of the Son of Man sayings. Collins describes this saying as a beatitude of "Christians being ostracized on account of the Son of Man."[45] Although her point here is that this saying does not fit neatly into any of Bultmann's three categories, her assumption is, nevertheless, that persecution was a post-Easter, "Christian" phenomenon. As Bultmann argues regarding the Q saying about taking up one's cross (Q 14:27), however, persecution was the harsh reality of Zealots and other sectarian groups predating, contemporary with and post-dating the followers of Jesus *and John*.[46] Whether this Zealot

---

Although certain convincing arguments about Q have been made on the basis of stratification, in general, the method is overused. The rampant pace at which a verse or saying in Q is "plausibly assigned to" or "distinguished as" a certain editorial stage (including "preredactional" stages) of transmission (even "the final stage of redaction"), either predating or postdating the plausible assignments of other verses or sayings, is, in part, responsible for the insularity of Q research within the larger field of NT studies. The predicament is, however, that often approaches assuming only a single layer of redaction are even cruder than approaches exploiting stratification. In the face of daunting perplexity, what seems clear is that this niche of NT studies demands new and fresh appraisals.

Third, Collins dismisses Koester's assertion that the Son of Man sayings come from a late stage of Q's redaction on the basis of the *Gospel of Thomas*. All three of Collins' arguments in this article unite for the single purpose of rejecting facile explanations of the relationship between wisdom and apocalyptic with respect to Q or any related text (e.g., Daniel, *Testaments of the Twelve Patriarchs, Coptic Gnostic Apocalypse of Adam, Ethiopic Enoch, Gospel of Thomas, Dialogue of the Savior*, 1 Cor 1–4, 4 Ezra). Conversely, Collins insists on complex and sophisticated formulations of the relationship between the prophetic and sapiential in interpretations of these traditions. See also John J. Collins, *Seers, Sibyls and Sages in Hellenistic-Roman Judaism*, 385–404.

[45] A. Y. Collins, "Origin of the Designation," 144.

[46] One tradition preserves that Jesus had a Zealot among his followers (Lk 6:15/Acts 1:13), although these lists differ from those in Mark (3:18) and Matthew (Mt 10:4) which record,

thesis is slightly anachronistic or not,[47] no convincing reason exists why this and other such persecution sayings could not be traceable to the public ministries of *both* Jesus and John. In her article dedicated to the Son of Man sayings in Q, Collins treats this saying in terms of Schürmann's hypothesis, arguing against Schürmann, that no valid reason exists for categorizing the saying as "Kommentarwort" on another or perhaps the previous three sayings.[48] After all, as Collins points out, the saying shares the "rather prominent" Q theme of the maltreatment of prophets (cf. Q 11:47, 49 and 13:34).[49] Thus, with the future Son of man sayings, Q 6:22 should not be excluded from the group of sayings plausibly traced to the historical Jesus.

Ascertaining a plausible *Sitz im Leben* for the second saying (Q 7:34: "The Son of Man came eating and drinking and you say: Behold, a glutton and drunkard, a friend of tax collectors and sinners") is, however, more difficult. Even its inclusion in Q is disputable because its apparent consideration of the relationship between the ministries of John *and* Jesus appears later than, *even reflective upon,* other Q materials.[50] As a brief comment on the two ministries of John the Baptist and ὁ υἱὸς τοῦ ἀνθρώπου, Q 7:33–34 may be an interpolation in the saying 7:31–32, 35. The passage is further complicated by its suggestion (v. 33) that John fasts or that his diet is distinctive in some way (μὴ ἐσθίων ἄρτον μήτε πίνων οἶνον), (cf. Mk 2:18 par.), whereas ὁ υἱὸς τοῦ ἀνθρώπου does not, or, at least, his diet consists of (more or regular?) eating and drinking (ἐσθίων καὶ πίνων).[51] In light of the many Q passages in which Jesus exhorts fasting (cf. Q 4:2; 6:21a; 11:3; 12:22b–24, 29, 45–46), this saying better reflects other sayings outside of and contradicting those in Q in which Jesus is said to feast,[52] if indeed ὁ υἱὸς τοῦ ἀνθρώπου in this passage refers to Jesus. In other words, in addition to other features of this passage which make it seem later than other sayings in Q, the reference to the eating and drinking of the Son of Man does not comport well with Q's overall depiction of Jesus as one exhorting others to fast.[53]

Adela Y. Collins discusses Q 7:34 with respect to Schürmann's contention that this saying too represents "Kommentarwort."[54] The saying, according to

---

instead of "Simon, the Zealot," "Simon, the Cananean. As above, for Bultmann, the idiom of taking up one's cross is a "traditional figure for suffering and sacrifice" (*History of the Synoptic Tradition,* 161 n. 1).

[47] See 92–93 n. 41.

[48] A. Y. Collins, "The Son of Man in the Sayings Source," 376–77.

[49] A. Y. Collins, "The Son of Man in the Sayings Source," 377.

[50] According to J. Kloppenborg, *Q Parallels,* "most authors" include 7:31–35 in Q (60–61).

[51] For a basis in the Hebrew scriptures for using the idiom "not eating" as a periphrastic alternative for fasting, see 93 n. 33.

[52] E.g., Mk 2:15–17 par.; 2:18–22 par.; Mt 11:19; Lk 15:2; and, Jn 2:1–11.

[53] For the full argument, see Ch. 3.

[54] A. Y. Collins, "The Son of Man in the Sayings Source," 376.

Collins, provides the "only case" that Schürmann's thesis is valid.[55] Q 7:34 may have been added, she argues, as an interpretation of the similitude about children in the marketplace. If ὁ υἱὸς τοῦ ἀνθρώπου here refers to Jesus, then, with Bultmann and Collins, the present author agrees the interpolation is probably post-Easter, postdating other Son of Man sayings in Q and posing an exception to the overall thesis of this chapter.

The third saying, Q 11:30 ("For just as Jonah became a sign to the Ninevites, so also the Son of Man will be to this generation"), is not addressed in Collins' article. Perhaps it was excluded because its Matthean parallel clearly reflects an interpretation of Jesus' death and resurrection using the story of Jonah: "For just as Jonah was in the belly of the whale, three days and three nights, so also the Son of Man will be in the heart of the earth three days and three nights" (Mt 12:40). Luke's version, however, retains only: "For as Jonah became a sign to the Ninevites, so also the Son of Man will be to this generation" (Lk 11:30). According to Bultmann,

The meaning of the saying .... seems to me to be: Just as Jonah came to the Ninevites from a distant country, so will the Son of Man come to this generation from heaven.[56]

In its Lukan version, the saying describes only the preaching of repentance that precedes an act of judgment turned grace by God (e.g., Jonah 3:10). Because, according to many of the Markan narratives, Jesus did not preach repentance,[57] some conclude that the saying must reflect a later addition by the church. According to the Synoptic tradition (Mark, in particular), however, a message of repentance *was* demanded at an even earlier stage of the tradition than Jesus. The message of John the Baptist (Mk 1:4) is overlooked in the discussion.

Collins deals with this saying in her article on the Son of Man sayings in Q[58] in terms of the arguments of both Schürmann and Lührmann who disagree with each other on its interpretation.[59] Lührmann argues that the saying comparing Jonah and the Son of Man (Q 11:30) was composed in order to link the saying about the request for a sign (Q 11:29) to the warning of condemnation by the queen of the South and the Ninevites in the judgment (Q 11:31–32).[60] In contrast, Schürmann argues that these two different pieces (Q 11:31–32 and Q 11:30) are incongruous. In Q 11:31–32 Jesus is a preacher, reflecting on the importance of his message of repentance for the judgment (present), whereas in Q 11:30, as Son of Man, Jesus announces his role as judge in a coming judgment (future).

---

[55] A. Y. Collins, "The Son of Man in the Sayings Source," 376.

[56] R. Bultmann, *History of the Synoptic Tradition*, 118.

[57] Mk 1:15 notwithstanding; see E. Sanders, *Jesus and Judaism* (Philadelphia, PA: Fortress, 1985) 108–13. Arguing in favor of such a divergence of opinion by John and Jesus on the issue of forgiveness is M. Goguel, *Jean-Baptiste*, 257–71. See discussion above: Ch. 3.

[58] See n. 44.

[59] A. Y. Collins, "The Son of Man in the Sayings Source," 377–79.

[60] D. Lührmann, *Redaktion*, 41–42.

In other words, v. 30 could not have been used by an editor of Q to join v. 29 to vv. 31–32, because vv. 29–30 and vv. 31–32 are wholly incommensurate. The latter verses refer to Jesus' earthly ministry of preaching ("something more" than Solomon and Jonah is here), the former, to Jesus' future role in an eschatological judgment (what the Son of Man will be to this generation).

Schürmann argues that v. 30 was added, not to link two individual sayings (v. 29 and vv. 31–32), but to clarify, for the entire subset of vv. 29, 31–32, that *Jesus* is the one referred to in v. 32 as "more than Jonah." Collins points out, however, something Schürmann fails to notice, that vv. 31–32 possess the neuter, *something* greater (πλεῖον), as opposed to the masculine, *someone* greater (πλείων). It is therefore possible, Collins argues, that in vv. 31–32 Jesus announces not his own presence, but that of the Holy Spirit or the proclamation of the early church, leaving open the possibility that v. 30 was added by a redactor of Q.[61]

Another possibility, passed over by these three interpreters, is that the verse representing "Kommentarwort" is actually v. 32, which appears to have been composed as a parallel to v. 31, but with the thematic ideals of vv. 29–30.[62] Lührmann and Schürmann neglect the following two observations. First, v. 30 is integrally linked to v. 29 by no fewer than three catchwords: "Jonah," "sign" and "generation." If v. 29 was originally a separate saying, v. 30 was created, at least in part, to manage or elicit a particular meaning from v. 29. Second, vv. 31 and 32 are parallel: v. 31 about wisdom, v. 32, about an eschatological judgment.[63] Verse 31 emphasizes that "something,"[64] present now – probably a certain teaching – is better than the best wisdom of the past (Solomon), whereas verse 32 stresses that that "something" is also better than some of the most bold repentance preaching of the past (Jonah). Thus the present view is that the two sets (vv. 29–30 and vv. 31–32) were probably brought together in Q through some kind of topical literary grouping based on the motifs of preaching: (1) against this generation and (2) by Jonah to the Ninevites. Both themes have many connections to other Q passages, integrating the segment nicely in the collection overall. On this reading, Q 11:29–32 as likely represents foundational Q as it does a layer or layers of redaction or gloss. Matthew's version (Mt 12:40), reinterpreting the "sign of Jonah" as this prophet's time in the belly of a big fish, is clearly secondary and probably reflects the author's struggle (vis-à-vis Baptist traditions) to explain

---

[61] A. Y. Collins, "The Son of Man in the Sayings Source," 377–78.

[62] Cf. A. Jacobson who argues that both vv. 31–32 are the product of the Q community (*First Gospel*, 71).

[63] The two halves are reversed in Mt 12:41–42 (Jonah-Solomon instead of Solomon-Jonah) probably so that the two references to Jonah are positioned together. Arland D. Jacobson writes: "One should note here a phenomenon attested elsewhere in the redaction of Q, namely the close association of Wisdom and prophetic preaching (e.g., Q 11:49!)…" ("The Literary Unity of Q," 382).

[64] A. Y. Collins, "The Son of Man Sayings in the Sayings Source," 378.

Jesus as a great prophet of repentance like Jonah. Thus the original saying can probably be traced to the earliest layers of tradition.

One final observation also absent from interpretations of this passage is that, according to many NT traditions, Jesus neither polemicized against public display of signs, rather performing them frequently, nor preached a message of repentance, rather welcoming individuals into the kingdom *without requiring* demonstrations of contrition/restitution. Indeed, a majority of Jesus traditions depict a teacher, who did not issue caustic vituperation against – but embraced, rescued, and restored – this generation.[65] In contrast, Baptist traditions convey that John performed few if any signs and preached repentance. Therefore, Q 11:29–32 also shares Q's pronounced Baptist *Tendenz*.

In conclusion, of the three sayings in Q not traced by Collins to Jesus, on the present argument, only Q 7:34 warrants exclusion from the discussion of the origin of the "the Son of Man" designation.

5.5 Son of Man Sayings in Q and Baptist Traditions

The assignation by Adela Y. Collins of a handful of the Son of Man sayings (the majority of which are from Q) to the historical Jesus represents, at the very least, their allocation to the movement's earliest layers of tradition. The remainder of this chapter accepts this more general allocation, only contesting Jesus as its origination point. Specifically, the upcoming analysis examines affinities between Q's Son of Man sayings and NT Baptist traditions.

In order to effectively negotiate the meaning and import of the relationship between Q's Son of Man sayings and NT Baptist traditions, it is helpful to recollect two general points about Q. First, Q's Son of Man sayings, in fact, virtually *all* of Q's sayings, are unattributed.[66] In contrast to the *Gospel of Thomas,* in which the quotation formula, "Jesus said..." is rarely *excluded* from a saying, such a formula appears only one time in Q (9:58).[67]

Second, the sayings themselves (οἱ λογοί), as forms irrespective of content, demonstrate greater affinity with traditions associated with John the Baptist in both the NT and Josephus (*Ant.* 18.116–19) than with Jesus. In the oldest Synoptic traditions (e.g., Gospel of Mark), Jesus says notoriously little – a problem

---

[65] In addition, the beatitudes are concerned with *eschatological* reversals of fortune whereas Jesus reverses fortune in the present.

[66] See 126 n. 184.

[67] Q 7:9 is a part of the centurion narrative. Q 9:58 is a quotation formula for which the verbs of speaking (the second of only three components of these formulae) are different in Matthew (λέγει) and Luke (εἶπεν), casting some doubt on the solidity of the formula. As above, against a dubious maximum of seven for Jesus, John's name occurs a total of eight times in Q. See 97 n. 64.

the authors of both Matthew and Luke sought to rectify with the addition of materials from Q and elsewhere. According to Josephus, however, John *"exhorted the Jews to lead righteous lives,"* "aroused [crowds] to the highest degree by his *sermons"* and possessed an *"eloquence* that had so great an effect on mankind" (*Ant.* 18.118).[68] The word Feldman translates as "sermons" here is λογοί, which, following Robinson, could be taken to indicate an explicit connection between John the Baptist and sapiential forms and traditions.[69] As noted above, Lk 3:18 too substantiates this point about John's reputation for speech-giving: "So, *with many other exhortations*, he [John] preached good news to the people (πολλὰ μὲν οὖν καὶ ἕτερα παρακαλῶν εὐηγγελίζετο τὸν λαόν)." From these passages one may infer John's strength was exhortation. In contrast, at least according to many Markan traditions, Jesus' chief strength was healing. With these features of Q in mind, the purpose of the next section is to demonstrate connections between Q's Son of Man sayings and Baptist traditions through literary analysis.

---

[68] ET: Louis H. Feldman (LCL); emphasis added.

[69] J. R. Robinson, "LOGOI SOPHON: On the Gattung of Q"; see also "Jewish Wisdom Literature and the Gattung LOGOI SOPHON," 51–58. Robinson's category, *logoi sophon*, however, overlooks the incipits attributing *logoi* to named patriarchs in literature not strictly sapiential (e.g., Amos 1:1; LXX 2 Esd 11:1; *TDan* 1.2; *1 Enoch*; *Jub* 21:10; *Ben Sira* and *Pirke Avot*). C. E. Carlston makes the argument that Q "belongs in a tradition (not *Gattung*) of 'wise sayings'" ("Wisdom and Eschatology," 111–12). On the hybrid nature of sapiential and prophetic in Q, Arland D. Jacobson writes, "The peculiarity of the role of Wisdom in Q – its association with prophets and prophetic material – derives from the identification of Wisdom and Torah (cf. Sirach 24; Bar 3:9–4:1; *1 Enoch* 42). When Torah is Wisdom and the prophets are seen primarily as calling people to return to Yahweh and hence to Torah, the prophets can be regarded as the 'wise' and Wisdom as the sender of the prophets" ("The Literary Unity of Q," 387). Cf. also the comments of C. E. Carlston on how sapiential traditions can still be considered reliable within an apocalyptic worldview: "...the assumption [in Q] seems to be that a life under conditions of urgency is under pretty much the same moral constraints as the life encouraged by the wisdom-tradition as a whole. ... What we need to explain, in other words, is the curious – some would say, inconsistent – failure of the community behind Q to conclude that the imminence of Judgment seriously qualified all the old rules. ... In other words, if one starts not with modern concerns about the continuity of history but with the ancient questions of ethics and theodicy, it is quite evident that for many, even in a fallen world, soon to be destroyed, the divine will for humankind remains unchanged. But the time for the awarding of appropriate rewards and punishments has been shifted from this life to the next. Hence God's justice cannot be disconfirmed by the ambiguities of temporal experience" ("Wisdom and Eschatology," 113–16). Finally, H. Conzelmann writes, "It is certain that Jesus was himself a teacher of wisdom. Were this not the case, the volume of wisdom in the Christian tradition would be inexplicable" ("Wisdom in the NT," in *Supplement* to *The Interpreter's Dictionary of the Bible* [Nashville: Abingdon, 1976] 958). In terms of Conzelmann's statement, however, the present author can only agree: "It is certain that" *the teacher of Q* "was himself a teacher of wisdom." The volume of wisdom in the Christian tradition is explained (*ex hypothesi*) by the post-Temple conflation of Christian traditions (healing, realized eschatology, rewards) with Baptist traditions (wisdom sayings, repentance, baptism, imminent eschatology, punishment).

5.6 Analysis

Four important connections between Q's Son of Man sayings and Baptist traditions are taken up in this section. First, Jesus refers to John as the Son of Man in Mk 9:12[70], attesting a literary association between John and this expression. Second, six of the ten references to the Son of Man in Q, depict a figure (not necessarily heavenly) in judgment: Q 12:8, 10, 40; 17:24, 26, 30. This description of the Son of Man contrasts with the description of the Isaianic "coming one" in Q 7:22, but corresponds to both John's prediction of "one to come" in Q 3:16b–17 and the predominant NT portrayal of John's life.[71] Third, Q's Son of Man sayings reflect significant stylistic similarities with NT teachings attributed to John. And, fourth, Q's Son of Man sayings possess a variety of individual thematic links to Baptist traditions.

5.6.1 John the Baptist as the Son of Man in Mark

First, Jesus refers to John as the Son of Man in Mk 9:12 marking an explicit association between John and this expression. The "Son" expression in Mk 9:7 as well as the "Son of Man" expressions in Mk 9:9 and 12, whether referring to John or Jesus, possess eschatological connotations in line with other uses in Mark (e.g., 12:6; 15:39).[72] Nevertheless, as many scholars acknowledge, the reference to the "Son of Man" in Mk 9:12 as one who endures many sufferings and is treated with contempt is, at least on the interpretation offered by Jesus in the next verse (v. 13), a reference to the Baptist.[73] On this basis, we may posit

---

[70] Eberhard W. Güting argues that Mk 1:2–3 and 9:12b represent glosses to the transmitted text ("The Relevance of Literary Criticism for the Text of the New Testament: A Study of Mark's Traditions on John the Baptist," in *Studies in the Early Text of the Gospels and Acts: The Papers of the First Birmingham Colloquium on the Textual Criticism of the New Testament*, ed., D. G. K. Taylor [Text-critical Studies 1; Atlanta: Society of Biblical Literature, 1999] 142–67).

[71] Leif Vaage notes the contradiction: "It may seem strange that in 7:34 the son of man is described as a licentious person, only to be followed immediately in 9:58 by a reference to the same person's austere sleeping habits. Is this not a contradiction in terms, to imagine someone who was simultaneously both a noted carouser and an apparent ascetic?" Subsequently, however, Vaage dismisses the contradiction, referring to Diogenes the Cynic as a "comparable case" ("The Son of Man Sayings in Q," 125).

[72] M. Thrall, "Elijah and Moses in Mark's Account of the Transfiguration," 313. Douglas R. A. Hare argues that because Jesus exhorts others to keep his messiahship a secret in Mark, but refers to himself as the Son of Man an early as 2:10 and 2:28, the "Son of Man" expression possessed no messianic connotations in Mark (*The Son of Man Tradition* [Minneapolis: Fortress, 1990] 181–82).

[73] Rev 11:3–13 and the Coptic *Apoc. El.* provide support for Mark's application of Elijah/ John as a figure of suffering. The *Apoc. El.* also preserves fascinating post-Christian interest in fasting as traced to the figure of Elijah (*Apoc. El.* 1:15–22). However, in its expectation of Elijah's future arrival/martyrdom, Rev 11 contradicts the portraits of John and/or Jesus as Elijah in the NT Gospels. On Jesus' response to John's violent death, see H. Boers in *Theology out of the Ghetto*, 45–47.

a link between the expression, ὁ υἱὸς τοῦ ἀνθρώπου *and John* in neighboring passages as well.[74] For example, once such a connection is made, an association between John's and Jesus' two statements in 8:38:

Whoever is ashamed of me and my words in this adulterous and sinful generation, the Son of Man will also be ashamed of him when he comes in the glory of his Father with the holy angels

and 9:1:

There are some standing here who will by no means taste death until they see the kingdom of God having come with power

surfaces.[75] To clarify, if the Son of Man expression in 9:12 refers to John, this reference may also apply to 8:38. In this case, the Markan Jesus compares his own ministry with John's: "Whoever is ashamed of me [Jesus] and my words in this adulterous and sinful generation, the Son of Man [John] will also be ashamed of him when he comes in the glory...,"[76] an event to take place in the next few verses at the transfiguration (see Ch. 4). The subsequent verse specifying that "some standing here [εἰσίν τινες ὧδε τῶν ἑστηκότων]" will "see the kingdom of God having come with power," bolsters the account of John's appearance at the transfiguration, by forecasting exactly what Peter, James, John *and Jesus* will observe momentarily: the prediction of the kingdom of God, first heralded by John,[77] is substantiated by the witnessing of his resurrection from the dead. John's appearance will testify that on his death he entered the kingdom he first announced (e.g., Mt 3:2).[78]

Thus, what was probably originally John's prediction of a coming Son of Man is customized by Jesus[79] for his disciples in 8:38 *about* John's imminent return, immediately before it is witnessed by the disciples and, more importantly, by

---

[74] As noted above in Ch. 4, one point on which most interpreters agree is that the transfiguration was intended to clarify or somehow respond to Jesus' open rebuke of Peter and his prediction of his own (the Son of Man's) great suffering, rejection, death and resurrection first disclosed in Mk 8:29–31. See, for example, C. E. Carlston, "Transfiguration and Resurrection," 233, 238, and 240. A factor ignored in this equation is, however, that the "Son of Man" reference in 9:12 – also speaking of undergoing "many sufferings" and being "treated with contempt" – may apply, not to Jesus, but to John.

[75] The famous interpretation of 9:1, at least as old as Origen (*Comm. Matt.* 12:31), is that the reference is to Christ's *parousia* glory revealed to them (the prediction thus fulfilled) at the transfiguration.

[76] Here the future tense implies the immediate future.

[77] For the argument that the "kingdom of God" expression was first John's, see Ch. 6.

[78] Cf. Knox Chamblin, "John the Baptist and the Kingdom of God," *Tyndale Bulletin* 15 (1964) 10–16. On John's announcement of the "kingdom of God," see below: Ch. 6.

[79] Here we add to the muddle created by predictions *by* John appropriated by later Baptist and Christian followers as predictions *about* John and *about* Jesus, Jesus' own role: Jesus, it seems, commenced this custom of appropriating sayings *by* John *about* John.

Jesus about which the accurate prediction is made: "will by no means taste death until they see the kingdom of God having come with power."

Some qualification is, however, necessary regarding Mark's use of the Son of Man to refer to John. The present interpretation of the Son of Man in Mk 8:38 offers little clarification for the Son of Man reference in 9:9. In this case, the "Son of Man" expression probably refers to Jesus.[80] However, it may *also* refer, as it does in 9:12, to John. If the latter is true, the disciples' complete loss to explain (v. 10) Jesus' command to "recount to no one what they saw until the Son of Man had risen from the dead" (9:9) would stem from their assumption that they had just witnessed the Son of Man's (John's) rising. For what, they wondered, are we still waiting?

The author's alternating usage of the Son of Man expression to refer to *both* John and Jesus corresponds to his widely-accepted aim of corrective Christology: neither the followers of John, nor those of Jesus, the author argues, possess exclusive rights to this idiom. Such an interpretation suggests, with others in this project, that an important goal of the Second Gospel was integration, even harmonization, of the two ministries of John and Jesus.[81] By using one expression to refer to both John and Jesus, Mark fuses the lives, history and traditions of these *two* crucially important agents of eschatological salvation in a *single*, unifying story of origins. A plausible *Sitz im Leben* of such an account would be an audience incorporating followers of both leaders.

---

[80] See argument below in which "son" is used to refer to John in various parables in the Gospel of Matthew. If "son" alternately refers to John and Jesus in the Synoptics, it is possible that even in Mk 9:7 the divine voice acknowledges the apparition of John, not Jesus, as "Son" and "beloved." Thus, the point of the passage would be that Jesus receives confirmation that John's kingdom message, which Jesus will continue to promote after John's death, is accurate. John has risen and remains God's "son" and "beloved" through/after death. Such a verification, from the standpoint of the narrative, infuses Jesus with the necessary courage to persist in his own kingdom calling. Contrast the view of F. R. McCurley: "There [Gen 22] in verses 2, 12, and 16 occur the only instance in the entire OT where *agapetos* defines someone's *huios*. Isaac is described to Abraham as *ton huion sou ton agapeton* (vs. 2; gen, in vss. 12, 16). Isaac, of course, is the promised son, the only begotten son of Abraham, on whom the further promises to Abraham depend (descendants, land, and blessing) ... It is not difficult to imagine that the author and hearers of the Transfiguration announcement *huios mou ho agapetos* recalled Isaac, the only other *huios agapetos*, in the story about the patriarch's sacrifice and deliverance. .... Thus, the Transfiguration announcement seems to identify Jesus as the promised son who will be sacrificed and then delivered" ("'And After Six Days' [Mark 9.2]: A Semitic Literary Device," 78). Mc-Curley's article is excellent, however, his conclusion that Mark, "who was not concerned with epiphanies and perhaps opposed to epiphany theology, transformed the story [transfiguration] by additions and modifications to address a Christological problem" (81) neglects why Mark wouldn't simply have omitted altogether such a difficult and potentially offensive or otherwise disagreeable story. As above, John Meier also notes that the word "beloved" connotes one destined to die (*A Marginal Jew*, 2.188–89). Cf. also J. Taylor, *The Immerser*, 270.

[81] Similarly integrated depictions of Jesus, Peter, and Paul in Acts provide a parallel. See my earlier work on historical recurrence in Luke-Acts: *Luke-Acts and the Rhetoric of History*, 99–141.

5.6.2 The Son of Man and The Coming One in Q

Second, of the ten references to the Son of Man in Q, six convey a figure (not necessarily heavenly) in the judgment: Q 12:8, 10, 40; 17:24, 26 and 30. This description of the Son of Man (esp. Q 17:24, 26, 30) contrasts with Jesus' description of the Isaianic "coming one" in Q 7:22 ("And replying he said to them: Go report to John what you hear and you see: Blind see, lame walk, lepers are cleansed and deaf hear, dead are raised, poor are evangelized"), but corresponds with John's prediction of "one to come" in Q 3:16b–17.[82] Recall Q 3:7, 16b–17:

> Generation of vipers! Who informed you to flee from the coming wrath? … the axe already lies before the root of the trees. … I baptize you with water, but the one coming after me is more powerful than I. I am not worthy to untie his sandals. He will baptize you with a holy spirit and fire. The pitchfork is in his hand to clear his threshing floor and to gather the wheat in his barn, but the chaff he will burn with an unquenchable fire.

In this passage John predicts one who is powerful, if not Yahweh himself,[83] whose arrival is imminent, and whose work will include vindication of the righteous and condemnation of the unrighteous in a cosmic-scale judgment.[84] The description of the Son of Man in Q bears a striking resemblance to John's "coming one." In Q, the Son of Man will also be powerful, if not Yahweh himself (12:10), arrive unexpectedly (12:40; 17:24, 26, 30), and intercede on behalf of the righteous (12:8).[85]

On a side note, Q 7:22 is notoriously problematic within Synoptic studies for its claim that, although John is apparently the most prominent and authoritative

---

[82] Dieter Zeller comments, "Since ὁ ἐρχόμενος is not a usual messianic title, a redactional reference back to Q 3:16 [//Mat 3:11] is proposed" ("Redactional Processes and Changing Settings," in *The Shape of Q: Signal Essays on the Sayings Gospel,* ed. John Kloppenborg [Minneapolis: Fortress, 1994] 123), citing P. Hoffman, *Studien zur Theologie der Logienquelle* (NTABH NF 8; Münster: Verlag Aschendorff, 1972) 199. Although one of two (3:16b; 7:19) "coming one" sayings in Q makes sense in terms of Q's Son of Man sayings, Q's Son of God sayings are unrelated. Q 3:22, from Jesus' baptism, was probably not original to Q; see J. Kloppenborg, *Q Parallels,* 16. Q 10:22 mentions a son and father without the expression, "Son of God." On the correspondence between Jesus' response and the program of second Isaiah as opposed to Malachi, see J. Reumann, "The Quest for the Historical Baptist," 191.

[83] On the figure expected by John, see Ch. 2. Also: John H. Hughes, "John the Baptist: Forerunner of God"; R. L. Webb, *John the Baptizer and Prophet: A Socio-Historical Study,* 221–27, 259, 283. John may have compared himself with Yahweh and referred to his untying of Yahweh's sandals, but he probably would not have inquired of Jesus in earnest whether Jesus was "the one to come" (Q 7:19), if he was expecting Yahweh. Cf. also Q 13:35. See 192–95.

[84] Cf. 4 Ezra 13:10 in which a stream of fire sent forth from the mouth of the "figure of a man" recollects John's description of the "coming one's" baptism by fire (Q 3:16b).

[85] Cf. also Mk 8:38/Lk 9:26/Mt 16:27; Mt 25:31. J. Fitzmyer argues ὁ ἐρχόμενος in Lk 7:19 should not be considered a messianic title. Rather, in light of Lk 3:7–9, 15–17, Fitzmyer proposes that John's reference implies "'the messenger of Yahweh,' *Elias redivivus*'" which Jesus roundly rejects (*The Gospel according to Luke I–IX,* 666).

witness to Jesus' role in the presently unfolding eschatological events, he must ask his disciples to inquire of Jesus whether or not Jesus is "the one to come."[86] The most popular explanation of this tricky passage is that Jesus' response to John's question in 7:22 suggests Jesus thinks John's expectation must be redefined. Jesus replies that, by his displays of the miraculous (healing the blind, the lame, the lepers, and the deaf; raising the dead; and evangelizing the poor, [if denying to prisoners their freedom, cf. Isa 61:1c]),[87] he demonstrates, on a new definition, that he himself is "the coming one," a plausible implication of the next verse (7:23): "Blessed is whoever is not scandalized/offended *by me*." That either identification of Jesus as "the coming one" and/or the performance of miracles is perceived as a source of offense to John suggests what, most take to be, already known: that John's expectation of the coming one was at variance with Jesus'. On this reading, Q 7:22 poses an exception to this thesis, by more closely resembling non-Q traditions about Jesus than John.[88]

This passage (Q 7:18–23) is, however, more enigmatic than the above description betrays. The initial and most obvious problem is why John, characterized by the NT gospels as the most important witness to Jesus' role in the eschaton, expresses doubts about Jesus by his question, σὺ εἶ ὁ ἐρχόμενος ἢ ἄλλον προσδοκῶμεν; (Q 7:18) The traditional criterion of embarrassment to Christians favors the authenticity of the passage: the Baptist's uncertainty regarding Jesus' identification as the "coming one" contradicts the trend of the early church. Attempts, thus, to explain the difficulty vary from *pretense,* (John possesses no real doubt; he only asks the question to test whether his disciples can correctly identify Jesus) to "failing faith," (the passage reflects a very old tradition of John's genuine surprise that Jesus is not the kind of "coming one" John expects).[89] A third option, however, has been overlooked.

---

[86] Jn 1:29, 36 proffer that John acknowledged the purportedly related role of "lamb of God" for Jesus, but the Gospel of John also omits John's question from prison.

[87] The question might be asked why the "liberty to the captives" segment of Isa 61:2 (LXX; cf. also Isa 26:19; 29:18; 35:5–6; 42:18) is omitted from Q 7:22. According to Q, was John in prison? While John was there, did Jesus neglect his obligation as loyal disciple to bargain for his freedom? Cf. Plato, *Cri.* 4.45. From John's/John's followers perspective, Jesus could not be the Isaianic figure proclaimed in Isa 61 because that passage declares that captives will be made free (61:1), whereas John remained in prison until his execution. If in prison, John would in fact be offended (Q 7:23) by the association of the coming one (Q 7:19) with the person described in Isa 61, and, that much more, by citations of Isa 61, such as the one in Q, omitting this element of a coming deliverer's activities (Q 7:22).

[88] In the Gospel of Luke, the passage echoes Lk 4:18–19 (cf. Isa 61:1–2; 58:6): Πνεῦμα κυρίου ἐπ᾽ ἐμὲ οὗ εἵνεκεν ἔχρισέν με εὐαγγελίσασθαι πτωχοῖς, ἀπέσταλκέν με, κηρύξαι αἰχμαλώτοις ἄφεσιν καὶ τυφλοῖς ἀνάβλεψιν, ἀποστεῖλαι τεθραυσμένους ἐν ἀφέσει, κηρύξαι ἐνιαυτὸν κυρίου δεκτόν.

[89] See summary with other views in J. Fitzmyer, *The Gospel according to Luke I–IX*, 664–65.

We begin by looking at Jesus' reply. Virtually all interpreters of this passage infer that Jesus' answer,

καὶ ἀποκριθεὶς εἶπεν αὐτοῖς, πορευθέντες ἀπαγγείλατε Ἰωάννῃ ἃ εἴδετε καὶ ἠκούσατε· τυφλοὶ ἀναβλέπουσιν, χωλοὶ περιπατοῦσιν, λεπροὶ καθαρίζονται καὶ κωφοὶ ἀκούουσιν, νεκροὶ ἐγείρονται, πτωχοὶ εὐαγγελίζονται

is affirmative, that is,

And answering he said to them, "[*Yes,*] go report to John what you hear and you see: blind see, lame walk, lepers are cleansed and deaf hear, dead are raised, poor are evangelized,"

redefining for John the concept of "the coming one." Jesus' reply is, however, as likely negative. In other words, when asked if he is "the coming one," Jesus replies, "No, I am not the one to come. Any eyewitness to my ministry could attest that I merely work wonders, restoring sight to the blind, enabling the lame to walk, cleansing the lepers, enabling the deaf to hear, raising the dead and evangelizing the poor. I do not baptize with fire and/or the Holy Spirit." On this reading, John's question is both genuine and intended for Jesus. John inquires of Jesus disciple: "On account of your God-given ability to perform miracles, have you rejected my teaching concerning 'the coming one?'" To which Jesus replies with appropriate deference, "No I have not rejected your teaching. With humility I simply uphold my commitment to good works pledged at my baptism by your hand. Indeed I have not mistakenly conflated *human* charisma as an identifying characteristic of 'the one to come.'"

Thus, John's question is, as above, a test. What is more, it *is* a pretext upon which John verifies his disciples' apprehension of Jesus' role. However, the test is not intended for anonymous disciples of John, but for his most well-known and respected disciple, Jesus. And, the test is as much a clarification of Jesus' role as a confirmation of the accuracy of John's teaching. A test Jesus, as disciple *par excellence*, passes! In other words, John's question is, like the many other sayings in Q, instruction – in this case (and, as I argue, the rest of Q), *John's instruction*. Its form as query resembles many other passages in Q in which a teaching is expressed as an interrogative statement – the first and most important: Q 3:7, a saying of John the Baptist (cf. also Q 6:32, 34, 39, 41, 42, 46; 7:24, 25, 26, 31; 10:15; 11:11, 12, 18, 19; 12:6, 23, 24, 25, 26, 29, 51, 56; 13:18, 20; 15:4, 8).[90] This interpretation also matches Q's overall de-emphasis of miracles – a problem posed by this verse that is otherwise difficult for Q scholarship. The new interpretation makes more sense of how John could have asked such a question, more sense of this passage's place in Q,[91] and can easily be conceptualized in

---

[90] Some questions are rhetorical others are not.
[91] J. Kloppenborg, *Q Parallels*, 52.

terms of other traditions, such as Jesus' baptism and transfiguration, concerning Jesus' relationship as disciple to John.

The concluding verse of this passage: καὶ μακάριός ἐστιν ὃς ἐὰν μὴ σκαν δαλισθῇ ἐν ἐμοί (Q 7:23) is also of interest. As a macarism, it is a form common to Q that may possess associations with baptism. It also shares in common with Q 17:1b, 2 the idea of "scandalizing" or "giving offense." In its assumption that displays of the miraculous, such as those described in Isaiah (LXX), scandalize or offend,[92] it completes Jesus' response to his teacher, summarizing its message: "Blessed is the one for whom such miracles pose no stumbling block." From John's point of view, the disciple who correctly interprets healing and other miracles as evidence that the kingdom is near, but no more, will be "blessed," that is, receive eschatological vindication. Damned in the judgment, however, is the disciple who perceives such signs as the onset of the kingdom and/or presence of "the coming one." This saying may even represent a macarism Jesus learned or overheard in the environs of the Jordan River – thus, a student concluding his examination by obsequiously *citing* his teacher *to* his teacher.

John may have considered *himself* the reconciling Elijah-figure described in Malachi, but, according to the remaining evidence, his message and manner were harsher than the description in Malachi's final postscript (4:5–6) and his close association with water contrasts with Elijah's predominant association with fire.[93] However he viewed his own role, in all likelihood John did not consider Jesus the Son of Man or "coming one" expected to arrive in judgment of this generation (Mal 3:2–3; 4:1), on the basis of performances of the miraculous or otherwise. Most likely John died denying any human, or even specific, identification of this figure. For John, the "Son of Man" was a deliberately ambiguous prophetic expression for a messiah, synonymous with his deliberately ambiguous reference to a "coming one."[94] In Q the two figures bear important resemblances. Both are less *titles* than deliberately ambiguous *roles* prompting John's followers, including Jesus, to adopt and reinterpret them to meet the demands of new historical exigencies.

---

[92] As noted in Ch. 3, Acts attests, (e.g., 8:9–24; 16:16–18), that miracles were performed regularly by religious charlatans, magicians, even demons. Cf. also Lucian, *Alex.*

[93] J. A. T. Robinson argues John the Baptist awaits Elijah: "…if John saw anyone as Elijah, it was *not* himself but the one coming *after* him." John's comment, ὁ ὀπίσω μου ἐρχόμενος ἔμπροσθέν μου γέγονεν, ὅτι πρῶτός μου ἦν, according to Robinson, indicates "in a deliberately cryptic manner, that the man (i.30) for whose appearing John was waiting was one who had already been before him namely Elijah" ("Elijah, John and Jesus: An Essay in Detection," 264–65; emphasis original).

[94] Cf. John Meier's comment, "Whether this stronger one is God, Michael, Melchizedek, 'one like a son of man,' Elijah, Moses, a prophet like either of them, a royal messiah, a priestly messiah, or a final prophet is unclear to us perhaps because it was unclear to John" (*A Marginal Jew*, 2.40). Whether it was unclear to John, or not, as a self-respecting prophet, all his predictions should be characterized by ambiguity.

5.6.3 Stylistic Similarities between Q's Son of Man Sayings and Baptist Traditions

Third, Q's Son of Man sayings demonstrate significant stylistic similarities with John's teaching. Background for this argument is provided by Richard A. Edwards who once observed stylistic similarities among Q's Son of Man sayings.[95] Although he overstated his case, Edwards accurately noted stylistic links between Q 11:30, 17:24, 26 and 30. He categorized their similarity as an "eschatological correlative" or a "just as this, so also that" form.[96]

Furthermore, this group of Q's Son of Man sayings (11:30; 17:24, 26 and 30) coheres on other levels. As Leif Vaage has shown, similarities include both "use of biblical tradition and metaphors of violence":[97]

In both 11:30 and 17:26–30, well known persons and their different histories are used to threaten judgment and destruction. Just as the story of Noah (17:26–27) was one of global doom and the figure of Jonah (11:30) heralded Nineveh's demise, so will the arrival of the son of man spell deep distress.[98]

Vaage also notes that, although 12:39–40 and 17:24 do not share explicit references to biblical tradition, they possess a similar sense of "violence and destruction."[99] While Vaage acknowledges that this type of condemnatory invective is common in Q citing Q 3:8 as an example, he fails to note that in Q 3:8 where "calling Abraham one's father is rejected as an adequate defense in the face of the impending wrath,"[100] the speaker is not Jesus, but John the Baptist. John, according to Q and the entire NT, originates this type of invective speech.

Q 6:22, 12:8–9 and 10, according to Vaage, comprise a second coherent group of Q Son of Man sayings. This group possesses the distinctive theme of the implications of one's relationship to the Son of Man. Vaage explains:

Like the preceding group, these sayings do not indicate who the son of man is. Rather, what is discussed are the consequences of association/dissociation with him. A situation of social conflict is apparent, at whose center stands this person. Thus, in 6:22–23 oppression suffered "on account of the son of man" is promised a great reward in heaven. In 12:8–9

---

[95] "The Eschatological Correlative as *Gattung* in the New Testament," *ZNW* 60 (1969) 9–20; idem, *The Sign of Jonah in the Theology of the Evangelists and Q* (SBT 2/18; London: SCM, 1971) 47–58.

[96] "The Eschatological Correlative as *Gattung* in the New Testament," 9–20. Nb. Edwards' observation that the "eschatological correlative" only occurs one time in the Synoptics outside of Q: Mt 13:40. In Mt 13:40, however, as Edwards points out, the Son of Man appears in the subsequent verse: 13:41 as opposed to the apodosis of the correlative (13). See my argument regarding intersections between Baptist traditions and this Matthean passage in Ch. 6.

[97] As R. A. Edwards points out, utilizing a similar form, Paul too correlates Jesus with a figure (Adam) from the Hebrew Scriptures (e.g., Rom 5:19; 1 Cor 15:22, 49) ("The Eschatological Correlative as *Gattung* in the New Testament," 15–16).

[98] L. Vaage, "The Son of Man Sayings in Q," 121.

[99] L. Vaage, "The Son of Man Sayings in Q," 122.

[100] L. Vaage, "The Son of Man Sayings in Q," 122.

acknowledgement versus denial of "me" directly determines what the son of man will do for you above.[101]

Vaage also identifies this theme of association/dissociation with the Son of Man in 12:10, noting here, however, that one's relationship with the Son of Man is inferior to one's relationship with the Holy Spirit. This Spirit component makes 12:10, according Vaage, "anomalous" within the group.

Here again, however, Vaage fails to recognize that the only other place in the NT where an explicit connection between one's relationship to the future mediator figure at the eschatological judgment and one's relationship to the Holy Spirit are linked is Q 3:16: "I baptize you with water, but the one coming after me is more powerful than I. I am not worthy to untie his sandals. *He* will baptize *you* with a *holy spirit* and fire." This statement is, of course, also John the Baptist's.

Finally, with regard to the second set of sayings, Vaage observes that the Son of Man is "active in heaven":

Behavior by human beings here on earth is noteworthy because of the reciprocal response above. This contrasts with the son of man's arena of efficacy in the first group of sayings (11:30; 12:40; 17:24, 26–30). There the son of man's significance was felt on earth after his arrival from heaven.[102]

Here again Baptist traditions provide a parallel example of behavior by human beings on earth eliciting a reciprocal heavenly response. In Q 3:8–9, John exclaims: "For I tell you that God is able to raise up children to Abraham from these stones. The axe already lies before the root of the trees; every tree, then, that does not bear good fruit is chopped down and thrown into the fire."

And, Vaage calls attention to a final similarity of the sayings in this second group:

The son of man is not alone at the secondary stage of Q, but rather one of a coterie of quasi-abstract, larger-than-life figures…Besides the son of man, there is as well "this generation," Wisdom and "her children," "the prophets," "the son," and "he who is coming."[103]

The remarkable point here is that *four out of five of Vaage's "larger-than-life" figures are traced in a direct or indirect way to John the Baptist*: "this genera-tion," (Q 3:7); "Wisdom and 'her children,'" (Q 7:31–35); "the prophets," (Q 7:26); and, the "one who is coming," (Q 3:16b).

Although the two groups of Q Son of Man sayings admit differences, Vaage concludes they are not contradictory, but complementary.

The judgment of this generation and the earth that comes with the son of man will also mean for those whose relationship with him was one of acknowledgment and persever-

---

[101] L. Vaage, "The Son of Man Sayings in Q," 122.

[102] L. Vaage, "The Son of Man Sayings in Q," 122.

[103] L. Vaage, "The Son of Man Sayings in Q," 123.

ance a great reward and their own recognition in heaven. Together, the two groups of sayings betray an apocalyptic sensibility grappling with its social world's (imagined) downfall and hoping not to fail with it.[104]

While Vaage *does* demonstrate important connections among Q's Son of Man sayings, he does not recognize the specificity of these crucial links. Q's Son of Man sayings are related stylistically, not simply to each other and other Q traditions, but to each other *and to Q's Baptist traditions.*

5.6.4 Thematic Connections between the Son of Man and the Baptist

Fourth, thematic ties exist between Q's Son of Man sayings and Baptist traditions. Q 6:22, 9:58 and 11:30 demonstrate this continuity.

As noted above, with regard to Q 6:22 ("Blessed are you when they revile and persecute you, and say every evil against you on account of the Son of Man"), given John's eventual imprisonment and death by Herod Antipas and Jesus' crucifixion also at the hand of the Romans, any saying about how to behave under circumstances of persecution fits the life settings of both men. That this saying may be, not a macarism itself, but a kind of commentary, summation, or contemporary application of other beatitudes does not preclude that it originated in the primitive setting of either John's or Jesus' ministry.[105] If Betz is correct, however, that the *Sitz im Leben* of beatitudes is one of baptism, then, although Betz has in mind the baptismal activity of the early church, given the outright rejection of Jesus as baptizer in the Synoptics (cf. Jn 3:22–23; 4:1–2), from the perspective of the authors of the Synoptics at least, beatitudes align more closely with traditions concerning John than Jesus.[106] There is, quite obviously, no shortage of examples of how the Synoptic authors impute to Jesus many of their own contemporary beliefs and teachings. Mt 16:18 comes to mind as a 'red herring.' In the case of baptizing and fasting, however, the Synoptic authors impute to Jesus practices that, while presumably their own habit, *they themselves trace to John the Baptist.* And, not only do they trace these practices to John, but they trace to Jesus differences with John on these very points, in fact, in more than one case, *rejection* by Jesus of these practices. This observation, from both a literary and historical point of view, demands explanation.

Taking Betz's proposal seriously that macarisms, although doctrinal in their present literary context, may have arisen in the socio-historical context of cultic performance of baptism,[107] the possibilities are three-fold: (1) the early church

---

[104] L. Vaage, "The Son of Man Sayings in Q," 122–23.

[105] H. D. Betz, *The Sermon on the Mount*, 147–51.

[106] H. D. Betz, *The Sermon on the Mount*, 92–105. See argument above: 118.

[107] Betz maintains that the question "cannot be answered with any certainty" (*The Sermon on the Mount*, 95). See above: 113–14.

imitated *John's* practice of proclaiming macarisms as a part of John's rite of baptism; (2) the early church imitated Jesus' practice of proclaiming macarisms as a part of *Jesus'* rite of baptism; or, (3) the early church unites *Jesus'* practice of proclaiming macarisms with *John's* rite of baptism. If Jesus baptized others, adopting the practice from John *and* perpetuated instructional traditions originating with John, then the three options are not mutually exclusive. Although the *first* and *third* options are strained by the silence of the Synoptic evangelists on Jesus' baptizing and the *second* option is strained by attribution in the Synoptics of macarisms to Jesus, the overall picture, *if* ritual baptism is a plausible *Sitz im Leben* of macarisms, is that the traditions form a composite, descending from Baptist circles together. Jesus' baptism itself (Mk 1:11 par.) is also linked to this composite ritual by the verb, εὐδοκέω, a word that actively confers divine sanction on the event ("God is well pleased"), resulting in a state of μακάριος or ὄλβιος ("happiness"/"blessing") of the human being (cf. also Mt 17:5).[108]

Furthermore, although Q 9:58 ("The foxes have holes and the birds of heaven, nests; but the Son of Man does not have [οὐκ ἔχει] anywhere he may lay his head") utilizes the present tense form ἔχει, this saying should not be relegated to later tradition on this basis alone. As an aphorism that, as Collins argues, probably originated in the wider Hellenistic context, the present tense of the verb ἔχω is best understood gnomically, implying that the statement is valid about the Son of Man *generally*, whenever he should appear.[109] Here again H. D. Betz's comments on the SM's collection of macarisms are valuable. Betz makes the argument that such an alternation in tenses among beatitudes in the Sermon on the Mount is deliberate:

The change from the factual present tense in v. 3b to what is evidently an eschatological future tense in v. 4b reveals an intricate relationship between present and future in view of the kingdom of the heavens.[110]

On this logic, Q 9:58 can be integrated with other Son of Man sayings in Q, including 11:30;[111] 12:8, 10, 40, and 17:24, 26 and 30, that make a future arrival of this figure plain.[112] Also, as above, that the Son of Man has nowhere to lay his

---

[108] ἐν ᾧ εὐδόκησα is peculiar to Matthew. Cf. Mk 9:7/Lk 9:35. As noted above, Betz describes the declaration at Jesus' baptism in Mt 3:17 as "close to a beatitude, but the literary form is different" (95). See above: 113 n. 136.

[109] A parallel for understanding this use of the present tense is provided by alternate use of the present and future tenses in macarisms to express eschatological promises (cf. Mt 5:3 and 5:10b with 5:4b, 5b, 6b, 7b, 8b, 9b).

[110] H. D. Betz, *The Sermon on the Mount*, 123–24.

[111] On this point, see, for example, P. Vielhauer, "Jesus und der Menschensohn," 112.

[112] J. Kloppenborg acknowledges that Q 17:24 and 17:26–27 do not specifically identify Jesus with the Son of Man (*Excavating Q*, 376 n. 29). Cf. Christopher Tuckett's comment, "But it would be foolish to try to deny that, for Q, the 'earthly SM [Son of Man]' is not also the same as the figure described in the eschatological SM sayings and that the common use of the same phrase to refer to Jesus makes it meaningful to consider the SM sayings together" (*Studies on*

head shares a connection, not to Jesus who enjoyed an array of possibilities for the resting of his head (see examples listed above), but to John, whose lifestyle was, according to most remaining sources, rigorously and, without exception, itinerant (e.g., Mk 1:4–5/Lk 3:2–3/Mt 3:1, 5–6; Lk 1:80; 7:24–26; Jn 3:23).[113] In short, this Son of Man trait is more easily comprehensible in terms of traditions about John than those about Jesus.

The saying in Q 11:30 that the Son of Man will be like Jonah preaching repentance is likewise distant from Jesus' ministry by its healing and reconciliation *without requisite repentance* (e.g., Mk 1:31, 34, 39, 41–42; 2:5, 11; 3:5 [and all par.] etc.), while aligned with these demands of John's message.[114] Also, the claim in this saying that the Son of Man will be a "sign" (σημεῖον) to "this *generation*"[115] (ἡ γενεὰ αὕτη) evokes John's castigations against this "brood" or "*generation* of vipers" (γεννήματα ἐχιδνῶν). *Indeed there is no explicit connection in Q between Jesus and announcements of judgment against this generation.* Rather, in Q, this condemnation is ascribed to John (Q 3:7). What is more, current models of Q honor John's denunciation against "this generation" with pride of place as the first words spoken by John or anyone in this source:

He [John] said to the crowds coming to be baptized: "*Generation* of vipers! Who informed you to flee from the coming wrath?"[116]

5.7 Summation

The present chapter treats Q's difficult Son of Man sayings in terms of the overall hypothesis of this book. It takes as a convenient *point-d'appui* Adela Yarbro Collins' essay on this topic. Against scholarly claims that all Synoptic Son of Man sayings were created by the church, Collins' traces certain Synoptic Son of Man sayings to the teaching of the historical Jesus. There is no necessary reason, Collins argues, to relegate these sayings to later tradition. Although Collins

---

Q, 244). Tuckett makes the argument that the necessary background for understanding the Son of Man in Q comes from the idea of a persecuted righteous sufferer who "will be vindicated in the future and will himself exercise a key role in judging others" from texts such as Dan 7, Wis 2–5, *1 En.* 62, 4 Ezra, and Isa 53 (*Studies on Q*, 276). While interesting, none of the Son of Man sayings in Q evince, in any apparent way, Tuckett's meaning.

[113] Cf. *1 En.* 42.1.

[114] Mk 2:5b–10 is an insertion in that healing story. As an exception, (to which the Matthean author took obvious offense), in Mk 1:15, Jesus' first proclamation of the kingdom of God includes an exhortation to repent.

[115] C. M. Tuckett rightly points out that too little attention is paid in the vigorous scholarly debate on the meaning of this pericope to the question of the nature of the "sign" here requested (*Studies on Q*, 257).

[116] The only possible exception (breaking with the standard of Lukan versification) is Q 3:0 (!): "… Ἰησου…" (*The Critical Edition of Q*, 2–3).

does not acknowledge it in her article, a majority of the sayings she traces to the historical Jesus originate in Q. The present examination makes this conclusion a basis from which to explore possible connections between these difficult sayings and Baptist traditions.

Four important connections between the Son of Man sayings and Baptist traditions make the case that these sayings originated among Baptists. First, Jesus refers to John as the Son of Man in Mk 9:12 attesting to an ancient association between John and this expression. Second, six of the ten references to the Son of Man in Q, depict a figure (not necessarily heavenly) in the judgment: Q 12:8, 10, 40; 17:24, 26, 30. This description of the Son of Man contrasts with the description of the Isaianic "coming one" in Q 7:22, but corresponds with John's prediction of "one to come" in Q 3:16b–17. Third, Q's Son of Man sayings demonstrate significant stylistic similarities with Baptist traditions. And, fourth, the Son of Man in Q shares more in common with the predominant NT characterization of John than the predominant NT picture of Jesus. Jesus' life and beliefs even at times contradict Q's portrayal of the Son of Man.

One hypothetical literary-historical trajectory of traditions looks like this: John predicts the imminent arrival of a coming Son of Man. Jesus indicates a connection between John and this figure (Mk 9:12) and adds a suffering component to the figure, (perhaps influenced by the Suffering Servant of Isa 53), based on his personal witness of John's suffering and death and his apprehension of his own probable execution. Jesus' followers, on the basis of their view of Jesus' ministry as the only legitimate successor to John's (there were, after all, rival messianic movements) *and* on the basis of the betrayals of John, Jesus, and other leaders and participants in the movement multiply sayings of both the suffering and present types. Some "future sayings" about the Son of Man's *coming* are also, at this stage, reinterpreted as Jesus' *return*.[117]

In conclusion, this chapter argues that the origin of the expression, Son of Man, and the best explanation for its presence in the earliest layers of early Christian tradition is as a reference by John and/or Baptists to an authoritative mediator in the imminent eschatological events of judgment about which John taught.[118] This figure would, according to Baptists, arrive unexpectedly, testify on behalf of the faithful, and separate them from the unfaithful as grain from chaff, burning the chaff in an unquenchable, cosmic-scale fire. Q's Son of Man figure is not integrated or connected in any way to a Christ figure and offers,

---

[117] Cf. Tödt's progression is: from references by Jesus to someone other than himself in Q (Tödt only acknowledges six of Q's sayings as authentic), to an association between Jesus and the Son of Man, to Mark's adaptation of the form for his theme of suffering (*The Son of Man in the Synoptic Tradition*, 144–221).

[118] According to Walter Wink, the Son of Man figure in Ezekiel, Daniel and the Similitudes of Enoch 37–71 (three different expressions in 46:2, 3, 4; 48:2; 60:10; 62:5, 7, 9, 14; 63:11; 69:27, 29 [2x]; 70:1; 71:14, 17) is a human being acting as mediator between God and Israel (*The Human Being*, 61).

therefore, no evidence of Q's "Christology." Features of Q's Son of Man figure resemble those of John the Baptist in Q and elsewhere. Although the Gospel of Mark also associates the Son of Man, with Jesus, conflating this expression with others, such as Son of God and Christ, this author-activity is separate from Q traditions in which ὁ υἱὸς τοῦ ἀνθρώπου is never (with the possible exception of Q 7:34) explicitly connected to Jesus. In Q, the Son of Man reference is deliberately ambiguous, implying a human or human-like mediator, perhaps a priest or a king.[119] The *Gospel of Thomas*, although repeating many of Q's apocalyptic sayings, avoids those about a coming Son of Man, in this way, like Q, refusing any association with Jesus.[120] This omission might be traced to the expression's legacy, evident in Q, of connoting a figure not yet arrived, rather expected in the future.

Finally, the character traits, such as itinerancy that Q's Son of Man shares with John the Baptist are comprehensible in terms of John's understanding of his own role and that of his disciples as *preparatory or even pivotal* for the Son of Man's arrival. The crucial role of the Teacher of Righteousness to the life of his community prior to the arrival of the eschaton provides an analogy.[121] On the Teacher of Righteousness, John Collins comments:

The historical Teacher evidently anticipated to some degree the roles of his eschatological counterpart. He is explicitly said to have been a priest, and he also had some prophetic characteristics (his words were from the mouth of God). He was, in a sense, a new Moses. If our analysis is correct, however, he was not himself regarded as the fulfillment of the eschatological expectation, either as the 'prophet like Moses' or as the 'messiah of Aaron,' and he did not write a law for the end of days. There was yet a more definitive Teacher to come, and this, perhaps, is a reason why the historical Teacher remains such a shadowy figure in the Dead Sea Scrolls.

The analogy to John's role in the NT gospels is striking.

---

[119] For the view that expectations of Elijah and a Messiah were often merged, see 48–49 n. 44. On the identification of "One like a Human Being" in Dan 7:13, including its relevance to NT "Son of Man" expectations, see John J. Collins, *Daniel* (Minneapolis: Fortress, 1993) 304–10.

[120] *Gos. Thom.* has only one Son of Man saying (§ 86); cf. Q 9:57–58. Helmut Koester argues that the *Gos. Thom.*'s single saying shows that Q's Son of Man sayings represent later redaction. See H. Koester, "The Synoptic Sayings Source and the Gospel of Thomas," repr. in J. Kloppenborg, *The Shape of Q*, 38–39.

[121] *The Scepter and the Star*, 115; emphasis added. Cf. also 125 and idem, *Apocalypticism in the Dead Sea Scrolls*, 90. The title "Teacher of Righteousness" is applied to figures of both the past and the future in the scrolls, suggesting persistence, if in a restored state, of present institutions in the future (i.e., 1QpHab 1:13; 2:2; 5:10; 7:4; 8:3; 9:9–10; 11:5; 4QpPss^a 1–10 iii 15, 19; iv 8, 27; 4QpPss^b 1:4; 2:2 (past) and 1QpHab 2:5–6; 9:6; 4QpIsa^a 2–6 ii 26; 7–10 iii 22; 4QpIsa^b 2:1; 4QpIsa^c 6–7 ii 14; 13:4; 23 ii 10; 4QpNah 3–4 ii 2; 3–4 iii 3; 4QpMic 6:2 (future) (*The Scepter and the Star*, 111–12).

Chapter Six

Baptist Traditions and the Origin of the Kingdom of God Sayings in Q

6.1 Introduction

Underlying much of the concentrated scholarly interest in the expression "kingdom of God"[1] over the past century is the conviction, expressed here by Dennis Duling, that: "it stands at the very center of the message of the historical Jesus."[2]

---

[1] In this chapter, when referring to the Greek expression, ἡ βασιλεία τοῦ θεοῦ I use the almost literal ET "the kingdom of God" to establish continuity between my argument and past discussions of the topic and without any preconceived bias as to whether βασιλεία signifies reign, realm or a hybrid version of the two. With regard to the variant, kingdom of heaven(s) the present author understands it as "circumlocution," avoiding the writing of the divine name. See G. Dalman, *The Words of Jesus*, trans. D. M. Kay (Edinburgh: T. & T. Clark, 1902).

[2] "Kingdom of God, Kingdom of Heaven," *ABD* 4.49–69. Norman Perrin claims: "the whole message of Jesus focuses upon the Kingdom of God" (*Jesus and the Language of the Kingdom* [Philadelphia: Fortress, 1976] 1). R. Bultmann opens *Theology of the New Testament* with a similar statement: "The dominant concept of Jesus' message is the Reign of God (*Basileia tou Theou*)" (4). The history of research on this topic is extensive. Works consulted for this chapter include: G. R. Beasley-Murray, *Jesus and the Kingdom of God* (Grand Rapids: Eerdmans, 1986); H. D. Betz, *Essays on the Sermon on the Mount* (Philadelphia: Fortress, 1985); idem, *The Sermon on the Mount*; R. Bultmann, *The History of the Synoptic Tradition*; idem, *Jesus and the Word*, trans. L. Smith and E. H. Lantero (New York, Charles Scribner's Sons, 1934); B. Chilton, ed., *The Kingdom of God* (Philadelphia: Fortress, 1984); Odo Componovo, *Königtum, Königsherrschaft und Reich Gottes in den frühjüdischen Schriften* (OBO 58; Göttingen: Vandenhoeck & Ruprecht, 1984); G. Dalman, *The Words of Jesus*; John J. Collins, "The Kingdom of God in the Apocrypha and Pseudepigrapha," in *The Kingdom of God in 20th-Century Interpretation*, W. Willis, ed. (Peabody, MA: Hendrickson, 1987) 81–95; H. Conzelmann, *The Theology of St. Luke*; O. Cullman, *Christus und die Zeit: Die urchristliche Zeit- und Geschichtsauffassung* (Zollikon-Zürich: Evangelischer, 1946; ET: *Christ and Time: The Primitive Christian Conception of Time and History* [Philadelphia: Westminster, 1950]); Gerhard Dautzenberg, *Studien zur Theologie der Jesustradition* (Stuttgarter Biblische Aufsatzbände 19; Stuttgart: Verlag Katholisches Bibelwerk, 1995) (primarily on the sayings in Mark); C. H. Dodd, *The Parables of the Kingdom*; D. Duling, "Norman Perrin and the Kingdom of God: Review and Response," *JR* 64 (1984) 468–83; Martin Ebner, *Jesus – Ein Weisheitslehrer? Synoptische Weisheitslogien im Traditionsprozess* (HBS 15; Freiburg: Herder, 1998); E. Ferguson, "The Kingdom of God in Early Patristic Literature," in *The Kingdom of God in 20th-Century Interpretation*, 191–208; E. R. Goodenough, "The Political Philosophy of Hellenistic Kingship," *Yale Classical Series* (1928) 1:55–102; R. H. Hiers, *The Kingdom of God in the Synoptic Tradition* (Gainesville, FL: University of Florida, 1970); G. Klein, "'Reich Gottes' als biblischer Zentralbegriff," *EvT* 30 (1970) 642–70; K. Koch, "Offenbaren wird sich das Reich Gottes," *NTS* 25 (1978) 158–65; H. Koester, "One Jesus and Four Primitive Gospels," in *Trajectories,* 158–204; W. G. Kümmel,

Q is a principal source of kingdom of God sayings, yet Q's collection of sayings has attracted relatively little individual attention.[3] The present chapter seeks to trace the origin of the kingdom of God sayings through an exegetical investigation of this Q subset.

As above, Q is also a principal source of Son of Man sayings. Argued in Chapter 5 of the present study, Q's Son of Man sayings share much in common with Baptist traditions. In her consideration of occurrences of the expression, 'kingdom of God' in the *Targum Pseudo-Jonathan, Mekilta Exod* 17:14, *Assumption of Moses* 10:1 and *Alenu* prayer, Joan Taylor arrives at the conclusion that John's message included the kingdom:

All this suggests strongly that if the Aramaic traditions of the Targum were known at the time of John, he may very well himself have announced, "The kingdom of God is revealed

---

Verheissung und Erfüllung: Untersuchungen zur eschatologischen Verkündigung Jesu (ATANT 6; Basel, 1945; 2nd ed., Zürich: Zwingli Verlag, 1953; 3rd ed., 1956; ET: *Promise and Fulfilment: The Eschatological Message of Jesus*, trans. D. M. Baron from the 3rd German ed., 1956 [SBT 23; London: SCM, 1957]); G. E. Ladd, "The Kingdom of God – Reign or Realm?" *JBL* 81 (1962) 230–38; G. W. H. Lampe, "Some Notes on the Significance of *Basileia tou Theou, Basileia Christou* in the Greek Fathers," *JTS* 49 (1948) 58–73; M. Lattke, "On the Jewish Background of the Synoptic Concept 'The Kingdom of God,'" 72–91, in *The Kingdom of God,* ed., B. Chilton (Philadelphia: Fortress, 1984); G. Lündstrom, *The Kingdom of God in the Teaching of Jesus,* trans. J. Bulman (Edinburgh: T. & T. Clark, 1963); B. Mack, "The Kingdom Sayings in Mark," *Forum* 3 (1987) 1:3–47; H. Merklein, *Jesu Botschaft von der Gottesherrschaft,* 2nd ed. (Stuttgart: Verlag Katholisches Bibelwerk, 1984); Rudolph Otto, *The Kingdom of God and the Son of Man: A Study in the History of Religion;* M. Pamment, "The Kingdom of Heaven According to the First Gospel," *NTS* 27 (1981) 211–32; D. Patrick, "The Kingdom of God in the Old Testament," in *The Kingdom of God in 20th-Century Interpretation,* 67–79; N. Perrin, *Jesus and the Language of the Kingdom: Symbol and Metaphor in New Testament Interpretation* (Philadelphia: Fortress, 1976); idem, *The Kingdom of God in the Teaching of Jesus* (New Testament Library; London: SCM; Philadelphia: Westminster, 1963) esp. Ch. 5 on the kingdom concept as both present and future; Karl Ludwig Schmidt, "βασιλεύς, βασιλεία, βασίλισσα, βασιλεύω, συμβασιλεύω, βασίλειος, βασιλικός," *TDNT,* ed. Gerhard Kittel, trans. Geoffrey W. Bromiley (Grand Rapids, MI: Eerdmans, 1964) 1.564–93; R. Schnackenburg, *God's Rule and Kingdom,* trans. John Murray (New York: Herder and Herder, 1963); A. Schweitzer, *The Mystery of the Kingdom of God* (1901; repr. New York: Schocken Books, 1964); and, idem, *The Quest of the Historical Jesus;* B. Viviano, "The Kingdom of God in the Qumran Literature," in *The Kingdom of God in 20th-Century Interpretation,* 97–107; idem, *The Kingdom of God in History* (GNS 27; Wilmington, DE: M. Glazier, 1988); J. Weiss, *Jesus' Proclamation of the Kingdom of God,* trans. R. H. Hiers and D. L. Holland (1892; repr. Philadelphia: Fortress, 1971); A. Wilder, *Eschatology and Ethics in the Teaching of Jesus,* rev. ed. (New York: Harper & Row, 1950 [1939]); W. Willis, ed., *The Kingdom of God in 20th-Century Interpretation.*

[3] The topic has been treated. In addition to chapters in books and monographs, the present author is aware of the following two papers: Walter Grundmann, "Weisheit im Horizont des Reiches Gottes. Eine Studie zur Verkündigung Jesu nach der Spruchüberlieferung Q,' in *Die Kirche des Anfangs, FS Heinz Schürmann* (Leipzig: St. Benno, 1977) 175–200 and Leif Vaage, "The Kingdom of God in Q," unpublished paper distributed to the Jesus Seminar, Notre Dame, 1986. However, attempts to obtain the latter have, to date, failed. Vaage does, however, note in his article on the Son of Man sayings in Q that whereas the Son of Man sayings "are a feature of Q's secondary redaction, its formative stratum by contrast is the privileged domain of almost every reference in Q to the kingdom of God" ("The Son of Man Sayings in Q," 124).

[or: upon you]" as part of his eschatological message to the people who came to him. While Luke has John telling the good news (εὐηγγελίζετο, Luke 3:18), Matthew has John specifically state, "The kingdom of heaven is at hand" (Matt. 3:2; cf. 4:17).[4]

The present chapter aims to supplement the hypothesis of the origin of Q's Son of Man sayings among Baptist traditions with another concerning Q's kingdom of God sayings; namely that, like the Son of Man sayings, Q's kingdom of God sayings resemble not Jesus' "most original proclamation," but John's.[5]

6.2 History of Research

For more than a century, assumptions that the entire group of kingdom sayings in the NT was chronologically and/or theologically unified drove the field's best and brightest to inconsistent solutions concerning the historical background and origin of these traditions. After the insistence by Johannes Weiss and Albert Schweitzer that the kingdom of God in Jesus' teaching was an imminent eschatological entity, (and its reactions by Rudolf Bultmann and C. H. Dodd), had subsided, the majority of interpreters accepted that the kingdom of God had to have been, for Jesus and his followers, somehow *both* instantiated in the present *and* awaited in the future.[6] This convolution led scholars, such as Norman Perrin (following Amos Wilder), either trained in or influenced by semiotic theory, to devise wildly complex hypotheses regarding the expression's meaning. In an effort to ascertain a single, central point from at least two clearly divergent kingdom of God messages in the NT gospels (let alone the entire NT), Perrin and others applied concepts from literary criticism. This trend attracted much scholarly attention during the 1950s and 60s. The discussions are one modern source of the concept "realized eschatology" – a notion applied too hastily to the NT and other related early Christian texts. B. B. Scott's explanation of the difficulty of determining the meaning of the kingdom message by this means provides an example:

---

[4] Joan Taylor, *The Immerser*, 138. See also Knox Chamblin, "John the Baptist and the Kingdom of God," 10–16.

[5] Albert Schweitzer comments, "About the year 28, at the time when Pontius Pilate was governor of Judaea under the Emperor Tiberius and Herod Antipas was ruling Galilee as king, the hermit John came forward with a message of the Kingdom of God that was something *completely new*" (*The Kingdom of God and Primitive Christianity*, trans. L. A. Garrard [New York: Seabury, 1968] 74; emphasis added). Helmut Koester refers to the kingdom sayings in the *Gospel of Thomas* as "an interpretation and elaboration of Jesus' most original proclamation" ("One Jesus and Four Primitive Gospels," in *Trajectories through Early Christianity*, 172). John H. Hughes, however, agrees, "It was John who had first announced the coming Kingdom" ("John the Baptist: The Forerunner of God," 210).

[6] Background for this claim is traceable to concurrent trends in philosophy, in particular existentialist discussions such as can be found in Søren Kierkegaard, *Either/Or*, Howard V. Hong and Edna H. Hong, ed. and trans. (Princeton, N.J.: Princeton University, repr. 1987 [1843]).

In Jesus' language an analysis of the symbol Kingdom of God is complicated because (1) it is a vehicle for an unexpressed tenor, and (2) it is an expressed tenor for the vehicle parable. Further, the various forms of Jesus' language are metaphoric, or better, tensive, frequently compounded tensive language creating intensive semantic plenitude. This is precisely why it is difficult, perhaps even impossible, to state what Jesus meant.[7]

The sheer opacity of these readings ultimately gave way to simplification. Many recognized that, from the viewpoint of historical scholarship at least, the sayings were incomprehensible as a collective unity, and not just on the basis of their varying future and present orientations.[8] In order to obtain clearer and more historically plausible interpretations, scholars conceded that the sayings, or at least the different sources in which they appear, had to be dealt with on a case-by-case (source-by-source) basis. Exemplifying this trend is the collection of essays edited by Wendell Willis entitled, *The Kingdom of God in Twentieth-Century Interpretation*. The titles of the articles alone suggest the point: "The Kingdom of God in the Old Testament" (Dale Patrick), "The Kingdom of God in the Apocrypha and Pseudepigrapha" (John J. Collins), "The Kingdom of God in the Qumran Literature" (B. T. Viviano), "The Kingdom of God and the Historical Jesus" (J. Ramsey Michaels), "The Kingdom of God in the Gospel of Matthew" (Ron Farmer), "The Kingdom of God in Mark" (M. Eugene Boring), "The Kingdom of God in Luke-Acts" (Robert O'Toole), "The Kingdom of God in the School of St. John" (Robert Hodgson, Jr.), "The Kingdom of God in Paul" (Karl Paul Donfried), and even "The Kingdom of God in Early Patristic Literature (Everett Ferguson)."[9] Notably – and despite the fact that Q, like Mark, utilizes the kingdom of God expression almost exclusively avoiding popular variants such as "my kingdom" and "the kingdom of Christ"[10] – *no article in this collection is dedicated to Q.*

---

[7] *Jesus, Symbol-Maker for the Kingdom* (Philadelphia: Fortress, 1981) 170–71.

[8] On past vs. present realization of the kingdom by Jesus, see H. Boers in *Theology out of the Ghetto*, 48–54.

[9] *The Kingdom of God in 20th-Century Interpretation.* Also epitomizing this trend is Dennis Duling's article, "Kingdom of God, Kingdom of Heaven." Walter Wink's book, *John the Baptist* and E. F. Lupieri's article, "John the Baptist in New Testament Traditions and History" (*ANRW* 2/26/1 [1993] 430–61) also utilize this organizational scheme, not just to address "kingdom of God/heaven" sayings, but all depictions of John the Baptist in the NT and Josephus. Wink comments, "If the methodological impasse in the study of John the Baptist has resulted from the failure to take seriously the original intention of the creators of the Gospel accounts, then the logical procedure would be to examine the manner in which each Evangelist has used the traditions about John in proclaiming the good news of Jesus Christ" (*John the Baptist*, xi–xii). The current methodological impasse results from making too much of "original intentions"; see Ch. 2. Although Lupieri neglects Q, Wink does not fail to dedicate a section of his study to this source. Wink's assessment of Q as a source of Baptist traditions is, however, different from the present one. Wink values Q as the "*ipsissima verba* of Jesus," "the cumulative effect" of which is "to throw into sharp relief John's significance for the eschatological crisis created by the presence of Jesus" (*John the Baptist*, 18).

[10] Q 11:2b offers a slight exception: "Your kingdom (ἡ βασιλεία σου)," in its immediate context is "the kingdom of the father."

For the most part, the trend of treating the kingdom sayings in the Hebrew Bible, the Apocrypha and Pseudepigrapha, Qumran literature, and New Testament traditions by source or author persists today. Conclusions about earlier texts provide hypothetical background for later texts. Influence is avoided as an explanation for connections. Parallels are put forth with caution.[11]

6.3 History of Q Research

In terms of Q research, similar to its Son of Man sayings, Q's kingdom of God sayings are usually interpreted along the lines of different stratification theories. The sayings are allocated to one or another stratum of tradition often in juxtaposition to the Son of Man sayings. Phillip Vielhauer, for example, argues that the Son of Man sayings are later than the kingdom sayings.[12] H. Schürmann argues that the Son of Man sayings act as "Kommentarworte" on earlier sayings, such as those about the kingdom.[13] Others divide the different kingdom sayings and distribute them among the various strata according to selected themes and cues.[14] For example, a saying about the coming kingdom may be considered earlier than a saying about the instantiation of the kingdom in some present form.

In contrast to these approaches, in his discussion of the literary unity of Q, Arland Jacobson makes an important observation about Q's presentation of kingdom sayings:

> The basic difference is that in Q attention is focused on the kingdom *rather than on Jesus.* Exorcism is linked directly to the kingdom (Q 11:20). But the context does not permit this saying to refer exclusively to Jesus' exorcisms. Rather, the coming of the kingdom is the presupposition for all exorcisms. ... In Q ... the issue is the kingdom, not Jesus himself.[15]

Jacobson's astute detection that Q demonstrates interest *in the kingdom as over and against Jesus* coheres well with other features of Q that play down Jesus' presence and significance, such as Q's near complete neglect of quotation formulas ("Jesus said…"), indeed Q's almost complete lack of explicit

---

[11] See, for example, Adela Y. Collins on Dan 7 as the possible background for certain Son of Man sayings ("The Origin of the Designation of Jesus as 'Son of Man,'" 142 n. 8.)

[12] "Gottesreich und Menschensohn in der Verkündigung Jesu," 55–91; also idem, "Jesus und der Menschensohn," 92–140.

[13] H. Schürmann, "Beobachtungen zum menschensohn-Titel in der Redequelle," 124–47. Cf. also the work of Schürmann's student Joachim Wanke, *"Bezugs- und Kommentarworte" in den synoptischen Evangelien: Beobachtungen zur Interpretationsgeschichte der Herrenworte in der Vorevangelischen Überlieferung* (EFS 44; Leipzig: St. Benno-Verlag GMBH, 1981).

[14] See, for example, H. Schürmann, "Das Zeugnis der Redequelle für die Basileia-Verkündigung Jesu," in *Logia: Les paroles de Jésus – The Sayings of Jesus: Mémorial Joseph Coppens,* ed. Jöel Delobel (BETL 59; Leuven: Peeters and University, 1982) 121–200.

[15] Arland D. Jacobson, "The Literary Unity of Q," 381; emphasis added.

acknowledgment of Jesus at all.[16] Given the general prominence of the Baptist in Q, Jacobson's observation recommends an investigation of a possible origination point for Q's kingdom sayings among Baptist traditions.[17]

Such a proposition is argued here by means of a series of literary and thematic connections between Baptist traditions and Q's kingdom sayings. The argument proceeds without any initial bias as to a saying's status in a hypothetical primary, secondary, or final redaction layer of Q. The argument addresses Q's kingdom sayings, in order of their appearance in Q/Luke. The sayings are also listed and numbered below in order of their appearance in Luke. For the sake of clarity, these numbers appear wherever the saying is cited in the course of the argument. Ties between Q's Son of Man and kingdom of God sayings are addressed in the chapter's conclusion.

6.4 Analysis

The Critical Edition of Q includes the following twelve kingdom of God, or variation kingdom, sayings in Q:[18]

(1) Q 6:20b: "Blessed are the poor, for yours is the kingdom of God."
(2) Q 7:28b: "Yet the least in the kingdom of God is greater than he (John)."
(3) Q 10:9: "...and cure the sick in that place and say, 'The kingdom of God has come near to you.'"
(4) Q 11:2b: "When you pray, say: 'Father, let your name be treated as holy; let your kingdom come!'"

---

[16] As above, apart from the baptism and temptation, Jesus' name occurs only twice in Q: Q 7:9; 9:58; John's name occurs a total of eight times: 3:2b; 7:18, 22, 24, 28, 29, 33; 16:16. See 97 n. 64.

[17] C. H. Scobie argues John must have preached a coming kingdom (*John the Baptist*, 62). K. Chamblin argues that Lk 7:29 demonstrates that a favorable response to John was a requirement of entry into the kingdom ("John the Baptist and the Kingdom of God," 12). On the basis of parallels in Daniel and the Sibylline Oracles, E. Stauffer points out that no incompatibility exists between the announcement of some version of an apocalyptic conflagration and a coming kingdom (*New Testament Theology*, trans. John Marsh [London: SCM, 1961] 23).

[18] With good reason, most reconstructions of Q omit references to a "kingdom" or "kingdom of God" in Lk 4:5, 9:60 and 62. ET's of the following passages are my own. Primary work consulted: *The Critical Edition of Q*, eds. James M. Robinson, Paul Hoffmann, John S. Kloppenborg. The emphasis in my translations on the kingdom's "nearness," as opposed to its arrival is defended below; this position is *pace* Norman Perrin (*The Kingdom of God in the Teaching of Jesus*, 58–78) and *contra* C. H. Dodd. Cf. also the conclusions of Reginald Horace Fuller that every NT occurrence of the verb, ἐγγίζειν, with a time reference (excluding Mk 1:15), refers to "events which have not yet occurred, but which lie in the proximate future" (*Mission and Achievement of Jesus: An Examination of the Presuppositions of New Testament Theology* [Chicago: A. R. Allenson, 1954] 21–25). Cf. also Werner Georg Kümmel, "Eschatological Expectation in the Proclamation of Jesus," in *The Kingdom of God*, ed., Bruce Chilton (Philadelphia: Fortress, 1984) 36–51.

(5) Q 11:20: "But if, by the finger of God I cast out the demons, then the kingdom of God has come before you."

(6) Q 11:52: "Woe to you, scribes, for you bar the kingdom [of God] from people; you did not enter and you hinder those trying to enter."

(7) Q 12:31: "But seek his kingdom, and these things will be added to you."

(8) Q 13:18–19: "What is the kingdom of God like, and to what will I liken it? It is like a seed of mustard that a person took and threw in his garden. And it grew and became a tree, and the birds of heaven dwelled in its branches."

(9) Q 13:20–21: "And again: To what will I liken the kingdom of God? It is like yeast, which a woman took and hid in three measures of flour until all of it was leavened."

(10) Q 13:29, 28: "And many from east and west will come and recline with Abraham and Isaac and Jacob in the kingdom of God, but you will be thrown into the outer darkness. In that place will be the weeping and gnashing of teeth."

(11) Q 16:16: "The law and the prophets were until John. From then, the kingdom of God is violated and violent ones seize it."

(12) Q 17:20–21: "Asked, however, when the kingdom of God will come, he replied to them and said: 'The kingdom of God will not come with close observation. [Nor will one say:] Behold, here! Or, [there!] For behold, the kingdom of God is among you!'"[19]

Q 6:20b

A preliminary indication of the importance of Baptist traditions to the origin of kingdom sayings is Q 6:20b (1). If, as noted more than once above, H. D. Betz is correct in his proposal that the *Sitz im Leben* of macarisms was one of multiple baptisms,[20] then, the kingdom saying of Q 6:20b (1) fits more naturally with traditions regarding John, known to baptize, than Jesus about whom the practice of baptizing was disputed as early as the Gospel of John (cf. Jn 3:22; 4:2).[21]

---

[19] Cf. Q 17:23–24 for the context of this translation. Also, R. H. Hiers, *The Kingdom of God in the Synoptic Tradition*, 24–25, 28–29.

[20] See above: 113 n. 136.

[21] H. D. Betz, *The Sermon on the Mount*, 92–105. Curiously, Betz's contention is supported by a saying of the 5th century Palestinian ascetic, Hyperechius in his acrostic list: "Like Jordan's stream, tears are a cleansing from sin. For Christ said, 'Blessed are those who weep, for they will laugh'" (log. 115; cf. Lk 6:21/Mt 5:4). For a recent translation/interpretation of Hyperechius, see James Vaughan Smith, "Resurrecting the Blessed Hyperechius," Ph.D. Diss., Loyola University Chicago, 2003. Also interesting is Lk 14:15: "Blessed is whoever will eat bread in the kingdom of God" – a "Special L" saying that combines three possible Baptist links: macarism + theme of fasting in the present + kingdom of God. Additionally, this macarism shares features of the *Pater Noster*, a prayer perhaps attributed to John in Lk 11:1. Indeed a study of all kingdom of God sayings in Luke offers the following observation: of the eighteen sayings in Luke not adopted from Mark: five represent obvious redactional insertions (4:43; 8:1; 9:2, 11; 19:11); seven are from Q (6:20; 7:28; [9:60]; 13:28, 29; 16:16; 17:20, 21), and the remaining six ("Special L") demonstrate strong connections to Baptist traditions (9:62; 14:15; 18:29; 22:16, 18). On Lk 9:62 see above (n. 18). Lk 14:15 is described earlier in this note. Lk 18:29 is from Mark, apart from the kingdom of God expression. Lk 22:18 is closely related to Mk 14:25/Mt 26:29. The "Special L" verse Lk 22:16, however, perpetuates Baptist hallmarks

Q 7:28b

Q 7:28b (2) arises as part of one of Q's so-called "Baptist Blocks," a narrative section of Q dedicated to an explanation of John's role. Although most of this section (7:24–28) holds John in highest regard, the single verse that includes the kingdom of God expression threatens to discredit the others: "Yet the least (μιϰρότερος) in the kingdom of God is greater than (μείζων) he (John)." John Meier argues that the meaning of this phrase *is* consistent with the rest of the passage. According to Meier, the Baptist is still here greatest; others in the kingdom are simply being promoted through the use of "dialectical negation."[22]

A possibility omitted by Meier and others in the research on this saying is, however, that the saying originated with John. Logically, the saying makes best sense if uttered by John in the first person: "Yet the least in the kingdom of God is greater than I [John]."[23] The saying only encounters difficulties in a context in which Jesus is claimed to have said it, while retaining the reference to John whom Jesus implicitly acknowledges as greater than himself in the preceding half of the verse (Q 7:28a).[24] A reconstruction based on this interpretation might read: "I tell you: Among offspring of women there has not arisen [one] who is greater than John. Yet, [as John said], 'the least in the kingdom of God is greater than I.'"

The possibility also exists that μιϰρότερος in its original context connoted not "lesser," but "younger."[25] In this case, John would be arguing that those

---

of refusing food and drink. When the author of Luke-Acts resumes with his Markan text in the next verse (Lk 22:19–20), however, Jesus eats and drinks with his disciples. The passage about not *drinking* is included in Mark (14:25) and Matthew (26:29) *after* Jesus eats and drinks for the last time. The "Special L" verse, Lk 22:16 may suggest an origin of the *Eucharistiam instituit* with John or his followers.

[22] J. P. Meier, *A Marginal Jew*, 2.142–43. Cf. also J. Becker, *Johannes der Täufer und Jesus von Nazareth*, 75; D. R. Catchpole, "The Beginning of Q: A Proposal," 210–13; M. Dibelius, *Die urchristliche Überlieferung*, 8–15, 121 n. 1; J. Ernst, *Johannes der Täufer*, 62–63; P. Hoffmann, *Studien zur Theologie der Logienquelle*, 220–24; J. Meier, "John the Baptist in Matthew's Gospel," 394–95; J. Taylor, *The Immerser*, 301–3.

[23] Cf. Mt 12:6; Mt 12:5–7 is a "Special M" passage citing Hos 6:6, also inserted at Mt 9:13, that, if coming from John, possibly refers to his rejection of current cultic practices. Cf. Lk 7:28: λέγω ὑμῖν, μείζων ἐν γεννητοῖς γυναιϰῶν Ἰωάννου οὐδείς ἐστιν· ὁ δὲ μιϰρότερος ἐν τῇ βασιλείᾳ τοῦ θεοῦ μείζων αὐτοῦ ἐστιν and Mt 12:6: λέγω δὲ ὑμῖν ὅτι τοῦ ἱεροῦ μεῖζόν ἐστιν ὧδε. Cf. also the use of the expression οἱ μιϰροί ("little ones") in the Gospel of Matthew (e.g., 10:42; 18:6, 10, 14). As John's saying about himself the message of this saying exemplifies another: Q 14:11 declaring that whoever humbles himself will be exalted.

[24] Thanks to James A. Kelhoffer for his assistance on this argument.

[25] See Franz Dibelius, "Zwei Worte Jesu," *ZNW* 11 (1910) 190–92; O. Cullmann, *The Christology of the New Testament*, 24, 32; idem, "Ὁ ὀπίσω μου ἐρχόμενος," 180. Joseph A. Fitzmyer summarizes: "Since the time of Tertullian (*Adversus Marcionem* 4.18,8; CC, 1.591) and John Chrysostom (*Hom. xxxvii in Matt.* 11; PG, 57.421) *ho mikroteros* has been taken as a real comparative and understood to mean Jesus himself .... Jesus would be 'less' than John either as 'younger' (in age) or because he has just asserted that John is the greatest of those born of a woman. In this interpretation 'in the kingdom of God' is less closely associated to

younger than he, presumably his students, are greater than he – a statement best interpreted on Meier's model of dialectical negation. It is not difficult to imagine that such a saying of John's might have been appropriated by the followers of Jesus who inferred that John himself was pointing to Jesus as his superior, possibly even leading to adaptations of the saying such as Jn 3:30. The confusion of the meaning of this saying is, in all likelihood, the result of a few stages in its evolution: its origination as John's saying, its appropriation as John's saying about Jesus, and its appropriation as Jesus' saying.[26]

As above, also, the Greek word in the first half of the verse γεννητοί, of the expression γεννητοὶ γυναικῶν, is not only an Aramaism,[27] but a NT *hapax legomenon* from Q (Lk 7:28 (2)/Mt 11:11) with close semantic connections to another *hapax legomenon* from Q – the Greek word γεννήματα from the expression γεννήματα ἐχιδνῶν ("brood of vipers"). The latter, of course, first appears in the NT as an expression of John's (Q 3:7).[28] A close semantic relationship also exists between the word γεννήματα from the expression, γεννήματα ἐχιδνῶν and the numerous castigations in Q against ἡ γενεά or this "generation" (e.g., Q 7:31; 11:29, 30, 31, 32, 50, 51).[29]

Not only does the single verse (7:28a and b) make more sense as a saying of John, but the entire block from 7:24–28 does too. Note its themes of wilderness, reeds (suggesting water),[30] prophets and polemic against soft robes (7:25).[31] As John's, the passage might read:

What did you come out to the wilderness to observe? A reed shaken by the wind? If not, what did you come out to see? A person clothed[32] in fine robes? Behold, those wearing the fine clothing are in the houses of kings. If not, what did you come out to see? A prophet? Yes, I tell you, even more than a prophet. "Behold, I send my messenger before you who will prepare your way before you." I tell you: Among offspring of women there has not arisen [one] who is greater than I. Yet the least in the kingdom of God is greater than I.

The allusion to Mal 3:1: "Behold, I send my messenger before you who will prepare your way before you (ἰδοὺ ἀποστέλλω τὸν ἄγγελόν μου πρὸ προσώπου

---

[26] Cf. Mt 5:19; 18:4.

[27] Cf. Sir 10:18.

[28] Cf. Mt 12:34 and 23:33 in which John's expression is applied to Jesus. See 98 n. 68.

[29] Cf. also εἰς γενεὰς καὶ γενεὰς in the Magnificat attributed to Elizabeth in certain ancient manuscripts (Lk 1:50); see 16 n. 39. D. Lührmann argues "this generation" is one of Q's hallmark expressions (*Die Redaktion der Logienquelle*, 24–28). See also 85.

the comparison, and it would imply that John too is part of it" (*The Gospel According to Luke [I–IX]*, 675). Cf. also Mk 10:41–45 par.

[30] See François Bovon, *Luke 1: A Commentary on the Gospel of Luke 1:1–9:50* (Hermeneia; Minneapolis: Fortress, 2002 [1989]) 283 n. 40.

[31] Contrast John's garment of "camel's hair" (Mk 1:6/Mt 3:4).

[32] Other than its par. at Mt 11:8, the verb in Q 7:25 "to be clothed (ἀμφιέννυμι)" has only one related NT occurrence: Q 12:28: εἰ δὲ ἐν ἀγρῷ τὸν χόρτον ὄντα σήμερον καὶ αὔριον εἰς κλίβανον βαλλόμενον ὁ θεὸς οὕτως ἀμφιέζει, πόσῳ μᾶλλον ὑμᾶς, ὀλιγόπιστοι (cf. Mt 6:30: ἀμφιέννυσιν).

σου, ὃς κατασκευάσει τὴν ὁδόν σου ἔμπροσθέν σου)" describes John earlier in the Gospel of Luke at Lk 1:76.[33] It also apparently describes John in Mk 1:2. Here, however, the citation appears as John's *self*-description as messenger preparing the imminent appearance of Yahweh.

If this saying is John's, it has stylistic parallels in the first chapters of the Gospel of John where, as Ernst Bammel points out, John apparently speaks of Jesus' superiority, "by speaking of himself" – and, not just speaking of himself, but, as Bammel adds, "by emphasizing his own inferiority" (e.g., Jn 1:15, 19–34; 3:30).[34] This is true even of perhaps the most famous and well-attested of John's sayings, Q 3:16b: "I baptize you with water, but the one coming after me is more powerful than I. I am not worthy to untie his sandals." In other words, passages such as Q 3:16b and those in the Gospel of John suggest self-deprecation is a hallmark of Baptist sayings – a rhetorical mode of speech associated with Baptist circles. The teaching of Q 14:11: πᾶς ὁ ὑψῶν ἑαυτὸν ταπεινωθήσεται, καὶ ὁ ταπεινῶν ἑαυτὸν ὑψωθήσεται ("Everyone exalting himself will be humbled, and everyone humbling himself will be exalted)" summarizes the tactic. Q 7:24–28 meets this stylistic criterion well. Consider it again: "I tell you: Among offspring of women there has not arisen [one] who is greater than I. Yet, 'Least in the kingdom of God is greater than I.'" In Baptist-Christian dialogues such as the one behind the Fourth Gospel, one can only imagine the temptation to exploit such self-deprecating sayings as elements of Christian apology.

In conclusion, what makes Q 7:28b (2) odd is an original setting in which Jesus is considered the speaker. Setting this assumption aside, Meier's argument for "dialectical negation" becomes extraneous. Whether or not the present interpretation that the saying was John's persuades, the fundamental value of the passage for this argument is the explicit link in this passage between, not Jesus, whose name is absent from the section, but *John* and *the kingdom*.[35]

---

[33] Mal 3:1 is first cited in Lk 1:76 as part of John's father, Zechariah's prophecy about his son: "And you child, will be called a prophet of the Most High; for you will go before the Lord to prepare his ways." Isa 40:3 is first cited in Lk 3:4b with regard to the Baptist's ministry: "A voice of one crying out in the wilderness: 'Prepare the way of the Lord, make straight his paths."

[34] E. Bammel, "John Did No Miracle," 199.

[35] On the basis of Matthean parallels, K. Chamblin argues that the Gospel of Matthew incorporates John into the time during which the kingdom βιάζεται, interpreting ἀπὸ from Lk 16:16 inclusively (ὁ νόμος καὶ οἱ προφῆται μέχρι Ἰωάννου· ἀπὸ τότε ἡ βασιλεία τοῦ θεοῦ εὐαγγελίζεται καὶ πᾶς εἰς αὐτὴν βιάζεται) ("John the Baptist and the Kingdom of God," 10–16). Cf. also, the context of 7:28 in the Gospel of Luke which includes the comment that rejecting John's mission is tantamount to rejecting God's will: "And all the people having heard, and the tax collectors, justified God, having been baptized with the baptism of John. But the Pharisees and the scribes *rejected God's will* for themselves, not having been baptized by him" (Lk 7:29–30; emphasis added). W. Wink writes, "Even though John's manner of serving God was in so many ways opposite that of Jesus, John was as completely within God's will" (*John the Baptist*, 19).

Q 10:9

Q 10:9 (3) offers an additional example that the continuity between Q themes and Baptist traditions is pertinent to understanding Q's kingdom sayings. This verse arises as the culmination of the section beginning with Q 10:4:

Carry neither [purse,] nor knapsack, nor sandals, nor stick, and greet no one on the road. Into whatever house you enter, [first] say, "Peace [to this house]."[36] And if a son of peace is there, let your peace be upon him, but if not, let your peace return upon you. Remain in that house eating and drinking the things before you. For the worker is worthy of his wage. Do not move from house to house. And whatever town you enter and they welcome you, eat those things placed before you and heal the sick there and say [to them]: the kingdom of God has come near to you.

This passage constitutes advice to itinerant (mendicant?) missionaries on proper host-guest relations. The most ancient and acclaimed literary precedent for such advice is *Odyssey* 8.544–86, in which Odysseus, as honored stranger, dines with the Phaeacians *before* being asked to recount his background and adventures to them.[37]

An assumption of such an instruction is, of course, its audience's need of it, that is, lack of full knowledge/experience about how to behave while traveling, lodging and dining as a guest. Such instruction would, of course, be moot for individuals accustomed to urban life.[38] This advice implies, therefore, an audience distant or otherwise detached from first-century Palestinian metropolitan standards. According to most non-Q early Christian sources (the Gospel of John in particular; e.g., Jn 2:3, 12; 7:3–5; 19:25–27), Jesus remained with his family and friends throughout his life and ministry with the sole exception of a forty-day sojourn to the wilderness immediately prior to the segment of his ministry resulting in his death.[39] The Gospel of Mark, too, depicts Jesus in close filial connections, not only with biological family, but with his disciples whom

---

[36] Lk 10:5 alone has πρῶτον. Lk 10:5 has τῷ οἴκῳ τούτῳ and Mt 10:12 has εἰς τὴν οἰκίαν ἀσπάσασθε αὐτήν. Other variations occur in this passage. See *The Critical Edition of Q*, 164–75.

[37] This passage describes the goal of hospitality as the merriment of hosts and guests alike (*Od.* 8.542–43).

[38] Q 14:16–18, 19–20? 21, 23 offers another example of the same point. It is the highly implausible, even comic, scene of a dinner party the guests of which decline their invitations and are thereby replaced by complete strangers! Both Matthean and Lukan redaction of the parable reveal a discomfort with the account, although neither is willing to expunge it. The saying clearly emanated from a circle, seeking to reverse the strictures of formal social gatherings. In Lk 14:7 the author demonstrates, through redaction, an aim to place Jesus and this saying in an urban context: "He told to the guests a parable, noticing how they chose the 'first couches' (ἔλεγεν δὲ πρὸς τοὺς κεκλημένους παραβολήν, ἐπέχων πῶς τὰς πρωτοκλισίας ἐξελέγοντο)."

[39] Thanks to Rebecca Waltenberger for a fruitful conversation sharing her research on this topic.

he reconstitutes as "family" (Mk 3:35).[40] John the Baptist, however, according to these same witnesses, deliberately spends his days away from cities. He is removed from urban life, according to Lk 1:80 at least, from a tender young age. Thus, although customs certainly varied from city to city (e.g., Galilee to Judea), these host-guest instructions make best sense in the context of wilderness-dwellers – fasting and practicing detachment from worldly goods (anticipating rewards in a world yet to come) – but preparing to enter city centers and receive urban hospitality and wondering how to do so while maintaining sincere kingdom commitments to dependence on God for sustenance.

Q 11:2b

Also indicating an origin of kingdom sayings among Baptist traditions is Q 11:2b (4). As noted above, Eduard Meyer and others since have argued that the enigmatic request by one of Jesus' disciples preceding the Q version of the Lord's prayer in Luke: "Lord, teach us to pray, *just as, also, John taught his disciples* (Κύριε, δίδαξον ἡμᾶς προσεύχεσθαι, καθὼς καὶ Ἰωάννης ἐδίδαξεν τοὺς μαθητὰς αὐτοῦ)," (Lk 11:1) indicates this prayer was originally composed by John.[41] If in Lk 11:1 the author implies that the *Pater Noster* was first used, if not first composed, by John or Baptists, then the kingdom of God expression in this important tradition (Q 11:2b) is traced to them. This argument may also apply to references to God as "father."[42]

If a Baptist origination of the *Pater Noster* could be proven conclusively, the case for Baptist origination of other Synoptic kingdom of God sayings would be strong. Baptist authorship of the *Pater Noster*, however, cannot be proven conclusively. The weight of such a claim overburdens Lk 11:1, indeed the interpretation of its single conjunction, καθώς. In order, therefore, to defend the present claim that this expression originated, in Baptist circles, additional evidentiary support is necessary. Fortunately, such support is ample.

Q 11:52

Furthermore, as noted in Chapter 3, a mood of judgment and sense of crisis pervades Q.[43] Often Q's acrimony takes the form of woes. Although Jesus can

---

[40] Overlooked in scholarship is the tension in the Gospel of Mark between the depiction of Jesus in connection with "family" and the persistent theme of secrecy. Were secrets kept from "family?"

[41] The Greek word, καθώς is ambiguous. See Eduard Meyer, *Ursprung und Anfänge des Christentums*, 1.90–91). See argument above: 86 n. 17.

[42] According to H. D. Betz, pride of place given to the Lord's Prayer in the Sermon on the Mount suggests its authority and antiquity; see *The Sermon on the Mount*, 373. The Greek word πατήρ, referring to God, occurs with relative frequency in Q. Cf. 6:35c, 6:36; 10:21 (2x); 10:22 (3x); 11:2b; 11:13; 12:6; and 12:30. Cf. also Mt 5:45.

[43] Many have observed a ubiquitous sense of imminent disaster in Q. See T. W. Manson,

become indignant with his disciples in the Gospel of Mark (e.g., 8:8:17–21, 33), Mark's Gospel attributes only two formal woes to Jesus (Mk 13:17; 14:21). In the Gospel of Mark, not only is Jesus less inclined to broadcast woes of warning on his generation, on the contrary, often he attempts to assuage his audiences with the gentle insistence that affliction, not moral high ground, is the key to his form of discipleship (e.g., 10:43–45). Woes, however, occur frequently in Q (10:13; 11:42–52; 17:1; 21:23; 22:22). Likewise, suffering in the Gospel of Mark is not an ultimatum targeted at the damned, but an invitation offered to the faithful. Enduring *persecution*, not (eschatological) *prosecution* is Mark's emphasis. Thus, Q's characterization of Jesus as a Jewish prophet issuing woes, contradicts Jesus' depiction in Mark. The pronouncement of woes is, however, consistent with depictions of John the Baptist in all four gospels. The kingdom woe of Q 11:52 (6), "Woe to you, scribes, for you bar the kingdom [of God] from people; you did not enter and you hinder those trying to enter" fits best in a Baptist context.

Q 12:31

A similar line of reasoning applies to the kingdom saying of Q 12:31 (7). Like Q 10:9, this verse provides the culmination of a short Q section. It sums up the passage on embracing the rigors of a more primitive, wilderness lifestyle by resisting anxiety (μὴ μεριμνᾶτε [12:22b]) over life's essentials – food, drink, clothing and shelter:

Therefore I tell you, "Do not be anxious about your life what you will eat or about your body with what you will be clothed. Is not life more than food and the body [more] than clothes? ... Therefore do not be anxious saying, 'What will we eat? Or, what will we drink? Or, with what will we be clothed?' ... But seek his kingdom, and all will be added to you." (Q 12:22b, 29, 31)

In contrast to the traditions regarding the rigorous lifestyle led by John, multiple lines of tradition about Jesus record time spent in homes, at banquets, at feasts, and in other places enjoying leisure, food and fellowship.[44] Even the variety of traditions of the Eucharistic meal perpetuates the motif of Jesus' dining – in this case, the meal is his last – a celebration of betrayal – shared with friends and followers.

Although one can be reliant on God for daily sustenance in urban environments, the sole reliance on God for daily sustenance recommended by this ex-

---

The Sayings of Jesus, 16; W. D. Davies, *The Setting of the Sermon on the Mount,* 382–86; and Howard Clark Kee, *Jesus in History: An Approach to the Study of the Gospels,* 84–117.

[44] The strongest emphasis is observable in the Gospel of Luke. See Josef Ernst, "Gastmahl-gespräche: Lk 14, 1–24," in *Die Kirche des Anfangs, FS Heinz Schürmann* (Leipzig: St. Benno, 1977) 57–78.

hortation resonates best with traditions concerning the Baptist – his diet, clothing and wilderness lifestyle.[45]

Q 13:18–19 and 20–21

Q 13:18–19 (8) and 20–21 (9) are both so-called "growth" parables: the first about a mustard seed planted in a garden and the second about yeast hidden in three measures of dough.[46] Neither, however, suggests growth in the manner in which the concept is usually understood, that is, as an increase in the total population of adherents to the kingdom movement. Although correct that a tree acts as a metaphor for a kingdom, among history-of-religions parallels, no such connection exists between a loaf of bread and a kingdom.[47] The question, therefore, arises whether the two similitudes were intended to be understood on the same or different terms.[48] Given that both parables contain the same referent (the kingdom) and occur together in Q, Luke, and Matthew (13:31–32, 33), an initial attempt should be made to interpret them as parallel. If one reads both in light of a third parable in Mk 4:26–29 (Parable of Growing Seed), as well as the saying in Jn 12:24 ("Amen, amen, I tell you, unless the kernel of wheat falls into the earth and dies, it remains itself alone; but if it dies, it produces much fruit"), the theme of persecution presents itself. This interpretation is corroborated by the additional "Special M" parables of Mt 13:44–46 (Twin Parables: Parable of the Hidden Treasure and Parable of the Merchant in Search of Fine Pearls), occurring in the same section in Matthew. In these two parables the "kingdom of heaven" is likened to something *worth risking all one has*. This theme of personal jeopardy matches well Synoptic traditions regarding John's wilderness existence.

As above, the general conclusion in scholarship about passages referring to persecution is that they reflect post-Easter, "Christian" traditions. As Bultmann points out, however, with respect to the Q saying about taking up one's cross (Q 14:27) persecution may have been the reality of Zealots and other sectarian groups predating, contemporary with, and including the Baptist and Jesus.[49] This and other persecution sayings, therefore, may plausibly be traced to the public ministries of either Christians *or* Baptists.

---

[45] This argument allows some latitude in the interpretations of Baptist traditions. The argument remains plausible even if, for example, Mark's depiction of John's diet of locusts and wild honey (Mk 1:6/Mt 3:4) was less literal than symbolic. See James A. Kelhoffer, *The Diet of John the Baptist*.

[46] Cf. also Mk 4:30–32.

[47] Cf. Dan 4:20–21 (LXX) and Dan 4:20–21 (Theod).

[48] Although some studies conjecture that both parables contain references to a Gentile mission, no persuasive argument for this interpretation exists.

[49] *History of the Synoptic Tradition*, 161 n. 1. The interpretation may be too early for the Zealots. Some unknown line of tradition between the Maccabees and the Zealots is, however, possible. See 92–93 n. 41.

Another possible context for these parables is baptism: in undergoing the rite of baptism, followers experience a metaphorical death, symbolized after the rite by abstention from present material benefits with an eye toward rewards in a world yet to come. This interpretation resembles the "baptism" described in Mk 10:38–39. It is, however, most likely distinctive of Rom 6 and as such, unacceptable for interpreting either Mk 10:38–39 or these two kingdom sayings.[50]

Most strongly suggestive of an origination among Baptists for these two sayings, however, is their context in the Gospel of Matthew. In Matthew 13, these two parables are the second and third in a list of seven focused on risking all for the sake of the kingdom.[51] This so-called "Parable Discourse" section of the First Gospel is organized as follows (the probable source of each section is given in brackets following the description of the passage):

Mt 13:1–9	Parable (1) of the Sower (Mk 4:1–9)
Mt 13:10–17	*Explanation of the Purpose of Parables* (Mk 4:10–12, 25)
Mt 13:18–23	*Explanation of the Parable of the Sower* (Mk 4:13–20)
Mt 13:24–30	Parable (2) of the Weeds among the Wheat ("Special M")
Mt 13:31–32	Parable (3) of the Mustard Seed (Q/Lk 13:18–19; cf. also Mk 4:30–32)
Mt 13:33	Parable (4) of the Yeast (Q; cf. Lk 13:20–21)
Mt 13:34–35	*Explanation of the Purpose of Parables* (Mk 4:33–34)
Mt 13:36–43	*Explanation of the Parable of the Weeds* ("Special M")
Mt 13:44	Parable (5) of the Treasure ("Special M")
Mt 13:45	Parable (6) of the Pearl ("Special M")
Mt 13:47–50	Parable (7) of the Net Thrown into the Sea ("Special M").

Interestingly, in addition to the theme of forgoing material wealth in parables three through six, the second parable, concerning weeds, and the seventh, concerning a net thrown into the sea, share other important literary and thematic connections with Baptist traditions. Each is dealt with in turn.

The second parable about the wheat and the tares contains an allusion to John's description of the coming one in Q 3:17:

Συλλέξατε πρῶτον τὰ ζιζάνια καὶ δήσατε αὐτὰ εἰς δέσμας πρὸς τὸ κατακαῦσαι αὐτά, τὸν δὲ σῖτον συναγάγετε εἰς τὴν ἀποθήκην μου.

First gather the weeds and bind them in bunches in order to burn them, but collect the wheat into my barn. (Mt 13:30b)

οὗ τὸ πτύον ἐν τῇ χειρὶ αὐτοῦ διακαθᾶραι τὴν ἅλωνα αὐτοῦ καὶ συναγαγεῖν τὸν σῖτον εἰς τὴν ἀποθήκην αὐτοῦ, τὸ δὲ ἄχυρον κατακαύσει πυρὶ ἀσβέστῳ.

---

[50] Although not the common understanding of Mk 10:38–39 ("baptism" is taken to imply Jesus' death on the cross), metaphorical interpretation might be evident here. Most likely, Jesus' death on the cross is implied in Romans 6.

[51] For recent scholarship on the Matthean parables, see Christian Münch, *Die Gleichnisse Jesu im Matthäusevangelium: Eine Studie zu ihrer Form und Funktion* (WMANT 104; Neukirchen-Vluyn: Neukirchener, 2004).

The pitchfork is in his hand to clear his threshing floor and to gather the wheat in his barn, but the chaff he will burn with an unquenchable fire. (Q 3:17)

The similarity between these two passages is also born out in the explanation of the parable in Mt 13:36–43: the one who sows the seed is the Son of Man,[52] the field represents the world; the good seed, "the sons[53] of the kingdom"; the weeds, "the sons of the evil one";[54] the one who sows weeds among wheat, "the devil (ὁ διάβολος)"; the harvest, "the end of the age";[55] and the reapers, "angels" (vv. 37–39). On the day of reckoning, the Son of Man will send angels to collect πάντα τὰ σκάνδαλα καὶ τοὺς ποιοῦντας τὴν ἀνομίαν to be thrown into "the furnace of fire (εἰς τὴν κάμινον τοῦ πυρός)" (vv. 41–42), whereas the righteous "will shine like the sun in the kingdom of their Father (οἱ δίκαιοι ἐκλάμψουσιν ὡς ὁ ἥλιος ἐν τῇ βασιλείᾳ τοῦ πατρὸς αὐτῶν)" (cf. Dan 12:12). A point of interest is the word, ἀποθήκη, occurring in only two other locations in the NT: once in Q 12:24 (Mt 6:26) and once in the "Special L" passage, Lk 12:18. The passage from Q (12:24, 27, 28), too, reflects the description by John the Baptist (e.g., Q 3:17) of the circumstances at the end of the age: "Consider the ravens: They neither sow nor reap nor gather into *barns* (οὐδὲ συνάγουσιν εἰς ἀποθήκας), yet God feeds them. … Learn from the lilies how they grow … But if God, in this way, clothes the grass of the field living today and thrown into the oven tomorrow …" Unlike other passages where the kingdom concept is the object of esoteric preaching (e.g., Mt 4:23; 9:35; Lk 4:43) or the basis of a moral exhortation to suffering (e.g., Mk 9:47; 10:15, 23, 24, 25), the kingdom in these passages represents the positive outcome of a great eschatological judgment – a feature of John's message in the Synoptics. The occurrence in

---

[52] In Ch. 5 I defend a closer proximity between John's prediction of the "coming one" and descriptions of the Son of Man in Q than between John's prediction of the "coming one" and Jesus' understanding of the same. Q 7:22–23 may or may not support this point. See 192–95.

[53] Nb., as above, the prevalent Q theme of children (τὰ τέκνα, Q 3:8 [pl.]; 7:35; 11:13; 13:34; cf. also τὸ παιδίον, Q 7:32 and ὁ νήπιος, Q 10:21) *is first traced to John the Baptist in Q*: Q 3:8.

[54] Cf. the phrase in the Matthean version of the Lord's Prayer (Mt 6:13): ἀπὸ τοῦ πον‑ ηροῦ.

[55] Harvest/harvesting (θερισμός/θερίζειν) is a common image for the eschatological judg‑ ment. It occurs in Q 10:2; 12:24; 19:21, 22. Other Synoptic occurrences may be linked to John the Baptist, such as Mt 13:30, 39 (here) and Mk 4:29. The only other NT references to harvesting are found in the Fourth Gospel: "Do you not say, 'Four more months and the *harvest* comes?' Behold, I tell you, lift up your eyes, and observe the fields are white already before a *harvest*. The reaper receives wages and collects fruit for eternal life, so that the sower may rejoice together with the reaper. For about this the saying is true, 'One sows and another reaps.' I sent you to reap that for which you yourselves did not toil. Others have labored, and you have entered into their labor" (Jn 4:35–38). J. A. T. Robinson argues that "others" in v. 38 refers to John the Baptist ("The 'Others' of John 4.38: A Test of Exegetical Method," in *Twelve New Testament Studies*, 61–66; repr. from *SE* [1959] 510–15). Taking Robinson's argument a step further, the present author interprets all three verses as a description of the relationship between Jesus and John. Cf. Rev 14:14–20.

this passage of both expressions "kingdom" (v. 31) and "father" (v. 30)[56] also suggests a link to Q's *Pater Noster* (Q 11:2b), and thus again, through Lk 11:1, to John the Baptist.[57]

The seventh and last of the parables in Matthew's so-called "Parable Discourse" also associates the kingdom concept with one of judgment (Mt 13:47–50). This similitude draws a relationship between the kingdom and a fishing net cast into the sea:

Again, the kingdom of heaven is like a net that was cast into the sea and collected every kind of fish (ἐκ παντὸς γένους); when it was full, they brought it up on the lake shore, sat, and put the good into a container, but threw out the rotten. So it will be at the end of the age. The angels will come out and separate the evil ones from among the righteous and throw them into the furnace of fire. There will be the weeping and gnashing of teeth.

According to this teaching, when the net is full and pulled out of the water, the fish are sorted: good fish are placed into some kind of container for saving whereas rotten fish are thrown out (13:48). The passage compares fishing with the end of the age when, as in the parable of the weeds among wheat, bad and good, evil and righteous will be separated, and evil, destroyed (13:49–50).

Close literary and thematic connections between the four "Special M" parables in the Matthew's "Parable Discourse" and the two kingdom of God sayings from Q (13:18–19 and 13:20–21) offer no definitive proof of connection to Baptist circles. They are not, however, merely suggestive. The message of judgment and condemnation associated by the Synoptic authors with John the Baptist nothing short of contradicts the emphasis on healing and mercy linked by the Synoptic authors with Jesus. Compare the conclusion of A. W. D. Hui in his article on the question of spirit-baptism by John:

But this prophecy of cleansing and judgment stands in considerable tension with Jesus' earthly ministry of salvation and blessing. What John envisages (Q 3:7–9, 15–17) was much more consistent with Jesus' parables of eschatological judgment which speak of a final separation of the wheat from the tares (Matt. 13:24–30, 36–43, cf. *Gos. Thom.* 57), the good fish from the bad fish (13:47–50), and the sheep from the goats (25:31–46). Not surprisingly, there were considerable doubts in John's mind concerning Jesus and the style of his ministry (Q 7:18–23, cf. 7:31–35).[58]

The parables and their explanations within Matthew's great "Parable Discourse" demonstrate literary allusions to teachings attributed to the Baptist that challenge messages by Jesus in non-Q traditions. To be sure, the Synoptic portrait of Jesus'

---

[56] Cf. Q 12:30: "…your Father knows that you need them." Q 12:31: "Seek his kingdom and these things will be added to you."

[57] In his article, "The Eschatological Correlative as *Gattung* in the New Testament," *ZNW* 60 (1969) 9–20, Richard A. Edwards' observes that the "eschatological correlative" occurs only one time outside of Q in Mt 13:40. For a response to Edwards, see Ch. 5.

[58] "John the Baptist and Spirit-Baptism," *EvQ* 71/2 (1999) 99–115.

urban life of feasting among friends openly rebuffs any message of a kingdom worth trading all in the present for entrance and participation at the end of the age.

Q 13:29, 28

The claim in Q 13:29, 28 (10), that those reclining with Abraham, Isaac and Jacob in the kingdom of God will have come "from east and west," demonstrates a thematic connection to John's statement in Q 3:8 that God can produce children of Abraham from rocks.[59] God's ability to make children of Abraham from rocks ("God is able to raise up children to Abraham out of these rocks") is simply here restated positively as welcoming many "from east and west" to recline with Abraham, Isaac and Jacob in the kingdom. Both declarations offer nothing to Gentiles, rather insisting that Jewish parentage (e.g., Abraham) – without the production of good "fruit" and, perhaps, John's baptism – is no guarantee of entrance into God's kingdom. Only Jewish heritage, *with the bearing of good fruit and John's baptism*, provides such assurance.[60] The emphasis in this passage on destruction and punishment, without any mention, let alone guarantee, of vindication/salvation for the righteous ("…but you will be thrown into the outer darkness. There will be the weeping and gnashing of teeth"), matches better Q and Baptist than Christian traditions (e.g., Lk 2:11; 4:21; 5:26; 19:9; 23:43).

Q 11:20 and Q 17:20–21

Two of the final Q kingdom sayings, Q 11:20 (5) and Q 17:20–21 (12), are undoubtedly related. Linked also with Q 10:9, they proclaim the kingdom's nearness. As noted above, Q 10:9 claims that displays of the miraculous (in particular, healing) ensure instantiation of the kingdom *in the near future*: "…heal the sick there and say [to them]: the kingdom of God has come near to you.'"[61] Accordingly, Q 11:20 refutes accusations that displays of the miraculous reflect the work of Beelzebul. In the argument of this rebuttal, miracles testify not to the direct hand of Satan, but to the power (finger or Spirit) of God. As R. H. Hiers notes:

…the controversy between Jesus and his opponents does not center upon the question whether the Kingdom of God was present or future. The issue is whether Jesus' exorcisms are authorized by Beelzebul, the prince of demons, or by the Spirit of God. But when asserting that the latter was the case, Jesus adds, as a warning to his opponents, "then" or

---

[59] Neither Q passage (13:29, 28; 3:8) necessarily implies a Gentile mission. *Contra* J. Kloppenborg, *The Formation of Q*, 119. Kloppenborg also apprehends evidence of a Gentile mission in 7:9; 10:13–15; 11:31–32; 13:29, 28; 14:16–24.

[60] Cf. Q 6:34.

[61] This saying, if John's, implies he expected his disciples to heal as a part of their kingdom ministry.

"in this case" (*ara*) the Kingdom of God *ephthasen eph' humas* ("has come upon you"). It is not likely that he was telling them that the Kingdom of God was "within" them, "in their hearts," any more here than in Luke 17:20 f. The saying appears rather as a solemn promise or threat, like the terrible sayings in Mark 3:29 and par. about those who commit blasphemy against the Holy Spirit. This sense of threatening catastrophe is precisely the meaning Kenneth Clark has found *phthanein* to have in various early Jewish writings – e.g., Judges 20:42 (LXX) – "to press close." The idea is that of "pursuit and *imminent* contact."[62]

Consistent with the other passages about the kingdom in Q, Q 11:20 acknowledges no arrival of the kingdom in the present. In both passages, the kingdom's advent/appearance only speeds stealthily nearer.[63]

Q 17:20–21 enhances claims concerning the kingdom's nearness, *not arrival*, with the advice that its advent will be patently obvious. In the history of research, meanings of the prepositional phrase, ἐντὸς ὑμῶν range from the existential, "the kingdom of God is in your heart(s)," to the communal, "the kingdom of God is amidst" or "among you (pl.)." R. H. Hiers summarizes the arguments:

The decisive question ... becomes whether Jesus meant that the Kingdom was already in the midst of his hearers or that at some future point it would be in their midst. The fact that *estin* ("is") is in the present tense is not decisive, since, as Kümmel notes, "it is usual in Aramaic for the copula to be missing." Furthermore, in Aramaic the present and future forms are indistinguishable. In many of Jesus' sayings about the Kingdom of God or the resurrection the present tense is used when a future time is clearly implied by the context or meaning. Neither *entos humon* nor *estin* explains the meaning of the half verse in question.[64]

Examining the context of this verse, Hiers further argues that the tenses of the verbs immediately preceding and following this verse are determinative for its interpretation:

The present tense is used to point to the future coming of the Kingdom of God in the verse containing the Pharisees' question that introduces the pericope, and appears similarly in Jesus' response, which actually is the first part of the sentence that carries through v. 21. Furthermore, the future is clearly intended

---

[62] *The Kingdom of God in the Synoptic Tradition*, 31; emphasis added. Hiers' interpretation recollects Q 7:23 in which healing is a source of offense at least in terms of any association between the miracle-worker and the expected messianic figure; see 203–6. Historically-speaking, John probably performed some miracles, but insisted on their correct interpretation.

[63] The Beelzebul controversy (Q 11:14–15, 17–20) may reflect tension and factions within the *basileia* movement in its discussion of the fate of a kingdom "divided against itself." In its Matthean version (Mt 12:22–32), the account immediately follows the pronouncement from Isa 42:1–4 (Mt 12:18–21 = a loose rendering) of Jesus as God's chosen servant, "beloved" (12:18), pleasing to God (12:18), and possessing God's Spirit (12:18). There it also includes that Jesus will "not break a bruised reed" or "quench a dimly burning wick" (12:20), perhaps referring to John the Baptist. Cf. references to John as a "reed" in Q 7:24/Mt 11:7. For references to John the Baptist as a light, see Lk 1:76, 79; Jn 5:35 (cf. 1:8).

[64] *The Kingdom of God in the Synoptic Tradition*, 23–24.

and the future tense is used in v. 21a and in the description of events with which the saying closes (17:22–37).[65]

Of greatest importance to Hiers' argument, however, is his observation of the repetition of the ideas in Lk 17:20–21 in 17:23–24 with reference to the future arrival of the Son of Man. He reasons:

> V. 24 explains that the disciples are not to follow those who will mistakenly say "Lo, there!" or "Here!" *for* when the Son of man or the day of the Son of man really comes, it will be just as evident as when the lightning flashes from one side of the sky to the other (cf. Mark 13:24–26). Similarly, our *crux interpretationis*, v. 21b, follows v. 21a to explain why, when the Kingdom of God really comes (or while it is coming), the bystanders will *not* say, "Lo, here!" or "There!," the reason being (*gar*) that then the Kingdom of God will be visibly and dramatically in their midst. When the Kingdom of God comes, one will neither have to look for any special sign to identify it or need a guide to find it somewhere.[66]

And, Hiers concludes,

> The parallelism suggests what is generally evident elsewhere in the synoptic tradition (despite Vielhauer), that Jesus associated the coming of the Kingdom of God with the coming of the Son of Man,

emphasizing that,

> it is clear that these decisive events are to take place in the future.[67]

---

[65] *The Kingdom of God in the Synoptic Tradition*, 24.

[66] *The Kingdom of God in the Synoptic Tradition*, 27–28; emphasis original.

[67] *The Kingdom of God in the Synoptic Tradition*, 25, 28. M. Pamment argues that the author of the Gospel of Matthew wished to draw a distinction between the kingdom of heaven and the kingdom of God, emphasizing the future reality of the kingdom of heaven, as opposed to the present reality the kingdom of God in the Gospel of Matthew ("The Kingdom of Heaven According to the First Gospel," 211–32). *Contra* Pamment, the present opinion is the author knew the two expressions originated in two different settings/schools. One may compare also the viewpoint of Rudolph Otto who argues that John proclaimed the Day of Yahweh, whereas Jesus arrived with the (new) message of the kingdom of God (*The Kingdom of God and the Son of Man: A Study in the History of Religion*, 67). Certain patristic interpreters too questioned, (Isid. Pel., *E* 3.206 (M. 78.889A0), and even denied, (Max., *Cap. Theol.* 90 [M. 90.1168c]), identification of the kingdom of heaven with the kingdom of God. For a study of patristic use of kingdom expressions, see G. W. H. Lampe, "Some Notes on the Significance of *Basileia tou Theou, Basileia Christou* in the Greek Fathers," *JTS* 49 (1948) 58–73. Benedict T. Viviano also covers the patristic materials in addition to the meaning of "kingdom of God" in the "High Middle Ages," "Early Modern Period," and "Twentieth-Century Thought" (*The Kingdom of God in History* [GNS 27; Wilmington, DE: M. Glazier, 1988]). It is fascinating that of the only four (or five, if Mt 6:10 is included) occurrences of kingdom of God in Matthew, two are traced to Q (12:28 and 6:33 [not in all mss]) and two are not (Mt 21:31 and 21:43). In the latter two, non-Q "Special M" phrases, however, the ties to John the Baptist are irrefutable. The first example: "Amen, I tell you, the tax collectors and the harlots go before you into the kingdom of God (Ἀμὴν λέγω ὑμῖν ὅτι οἱ τελῶναι καὶ αἱ πόρναι προάγουσιν ὑμᾶς εἰς τὴν βασιλείαν τοῦ θεοῦ)" is explicitly linked to the next verse (21:32) by the phrase "tax collectors and harlots" about John: "For John came to you in a way of righteousness, and you did not believe him, but the tax collectors and the harlots believed him. You watched, but did not later repent and believe him (ἦλθεν γὰρ Ἰωάννης

Although Hiers' argument is based solely on the Lukan context, his conclusions concerning the futurity of Lk 17:21b pertain to the interpretation of Q 10:9, 11:20 and 17:21b, which also, like traditions about John, but different from those about Jesus, indicate a future (if ominously near) orientation of the kingdom.

Perhaps coincidentally, in the final paragraph of his interpretation of Lk 17:21b Hiers alludes to Isa 40. Such a reference is remarkable considering the NT association between this passage and the Baptist. Hiers claims:

> When Luke 17:21b is taken in its context, the meaning emerges clearly enough: when the Kingdom of God comes, everyone will know it; there will be no need for authenticating clues or signs. Such also was the OT expectation – "the glory of the Lord shall be revealed, and all flesh shall see it together" (Isa 40:5).[68]

In summary, Q 17:21b teaches (corrects/redefines?) that the arrival of the kingdom has not yet commenced. Disciples of the movement, such as Jesus, may produce miraculous displays, only, however, because such displays *portend this impending reign*. Q consistently resolves that the kingdom, with the arrival of the Son of Man, will be an unmistakable, visible reality at some time in the near future. Strong rhetorical insistence on the kingdom's imminence may even be polemical, refuting attempts to extend the meaning of the kingdom to imply a transcendental or any other kind of spiritual or philosophical reality in the present.

Important for the present thesis is simply the recognition that such an insistence on judgment over reward, and future over present, more closely characterizes Baptist-, declaiming a wrathful God prepared to execute imminent judgment than Christian-, emphasizing God's mercy and patience in seeking and saving the lost, traditions.[69] Future orientation itself better typifies Baptists holding

---

πρὸς ὑμᾶς ἐν ὁδῷ δικαιοσύνης, καὶ οὐκ ἐπιστεύσατε αὐτῷ, οἱ δὲ τελῶναι καὶ αἱ πόρναι ἐπίστευσαν αὐτῷ· ὑμεῖς δὲ ἰδόντες οὐδὲ μετεμελήθητε ὕστερον τοῦ πιστεῦσαι αὐτῷ)." And, the second example (Mt 21:43), too, provides a link to Baptist traditions not only with its insistence on the bearing of fruit (cf. Q 3:9): "Therefore I tell you, the kingdom of God will be taken from you and given to a nation producing its fruit (διὰ τοῦτο λέγω ὑμῖν ὅτι ἀρθήσεται ἀφ᾽ ὑμῶν ἡ βασιλεία τοῦ θεοῦ καὶ δοθήσεται ἔθνει ποιοῦντι τοὺς καρποὺς αὐτῆς)," but also with its reference to John's death. Based on an article by M. Lowe ("From the Parable of the Vineyard to a Pre-Synoptic Source," 258), Joan Taylor assumes the entire parable of the wicked tenants refers to the ministries of Jesus and John (*The Immerser*, 173, 192, 250–55). Moreover, Mt 21:43 is a part of the short pericope, Mt 21: 43–45, the latter half of which is reproduced in Lk 20:18. Although many scholars regard this passage as an interpolation in Mt 21:44 from Lk 20:18, Bruce Metzger's committee (*A Textual Commentary on the Greek New Testament*, 47) observes that the wording of each passage is not identical, not to mention that the verse would have been more appropriately inserted after v. 42 ("its omission can perhaps be accounted for when the eye of the copyist passed from αὐτῆς [verse 43] to αὐτόν"). Thus, Metzger retains the passage in square brackets. This argument leaves open the possibility, therefore, that this entire phrase may have originated in Q, partially expunged in its version in Luke.

[68] *The Kingdom of God in the Synoptic Tradition*, 28–29.

[69] Without supporting argumentation, H. Koester proposes that: "John speaks solely about

forth John's work as *preparatory* for an imminent day of judgment. Christian traditions, in contrast, defend Jesus' work as *annunciatory*, proclaiming the arrival of a day of consolation and good news of deliverance.[70] Indeed the verb, ἐγγίζειν in Mk 1:15: "The time is fulfilled, and the kingdom of God has *come near* (ἤγγικεν); repent, and believe in the good news" – applied in the Gospel of Matthew first to John the Baptist (Mt 3:2) and second to Jesus (Mt 4:17) – is the same verb in the instructions to itinerant kingdom missionaries on what to tell those among whom the travelers eat and cure the sick (Q 10:9; cf. Mt 10:7). As noted above, in Mt 3:2 and 4:17, the author of Matthew opts for versions that are different from Mark's verses, but identical to each other.[71] Joan Taylor notes that the phrase in Mt 3:2 likely originated in Q about the Baptist, being applied by the author of Matthew to the ministry of Jesus as well, but avoided by the author of Luke, who sought on many occasions to separate the ministries of the two men with greater exactitude.[72] Although the verb, ἐγγίζειν is not present in the Q kingdom sayings at either 11:20 or 17:20–21, Q 10:9 and Mk 1:15 (adapted as Mt 3:2/4:17) are the only two NT kingdom sayings in which this verb occurs. Mk 1:15 is significant because, in this case, the author's redactional aims are plain. The author avoids any connection between the kingdom and the Baptist by denying mention of the kingdom *until the narration of John's imprisonment* (1:14).[73] Mark's total cooptation of John's kingdom for Jesus brings to mind the second half of Q 16:16 in which God's kingdom is somehow violated and hastily

---

the coming judgment of God – as Jesus speaks solely of the coming rule of God" (*Introduction to the New Testament*, 2.72).

[70] E.g., Lk 4:21. Different from certain passages in Luke, Mark's Gospel also insists on the kingdom's nearness. Enigmatic passages in Mark, such as Mk 1:7 (Q 3:16b), Mk 8:12 (Q 11:29), Mk 13:14–31 (Mk 13:21/Q 17:21, 23), Mk 13:17 (one of only two "woes" in Mark; also 14:21; cf. numerous woes in Q: 10:13; 11:42–52; 17:1; 21:23; 22:22) and others, appear literarily and thematically close to Q. *Ex hypothesi*: this may suggest infiltration of Baptist traditions into Mark's narrative. On the contradiction between the prediction of Mk 13:4, 14 and the refusal to provide signs (Mk 8:12), see Adela Y. Collins, "Mark 13: An Apocalyptic Discourse," in *The Beginning of the Gospel*, 88–90.

[71] For the sake of comparison, the Gospel of Luke follows Mark in the first instance with regard to the Baptist (Lk 3:3; cf. Mk 1:4), but devises his own summary for the second – Lk 4:15 (cf. Mk 1:15; Mt 4:17) recording: καὶ αὐτὸς ἐδίδασκεν ἐν ταῖς συναγωγαῖς αὐτῶν δοξαζόμενος ὑπὸ πάντων.

[72] See Joan Taylor, *The Immerser*, 138. The author of the Gospel of Luke utilizes an Elijah typology for Jesus as opposed to John. He further ensures a separation between their ministries in his presentation of John's imprisonment by Herod before the narration of Jesus' baptism which, then, takes place not by John, but "the Holy Spirit" (cf. Lk 3:20, 22).

[73] On this point, Walter Wink comments, "Here again the historical fact that John was killed before he had opportunity to enter fully into the events of Jesus' ministry is rendered as a theological judgement over him. Unwilling to suppress Jesus' high regard for John ... the church simply hedged Jesus' enthusiasm with qualifications which made clear their perception of the fundamental distinction between still awaiting a coming one and accepting Jesus as the Messiah. The apologetical/polemical implications of the passage are obvious" (*John the Baptist*, 25).

snatched away.[74] Interestingly, the Markan position also pointedly contradicts the first half of Q 16:16, in which, as we will see next, John is accredited with the inauguration of the kingdom. Unlike Mark and probably influenced by Q's position, the Gospel of Matthew exposes the origin of message of the kingdom as John's.

Q 16:16

The final kingdom saying Q 16:16 (11) about the violation and seizure of the kingdom of God represents, according to Walter Wink, "a very primitive tradition, already unintelligible by the time of the Evangelists."[75] Werner G. Kümmel's interpretation of the verse suggests real violence and thievery against the kingdom.[76] Frederick Danker understands a context of Pharisees complaining, with regard to Jesus, that ever since John the Baptist, not just the righteous, but tax collectors and sinners ("the violent") have been barging into the kingdom.[77] Wink, however, emphasizes what the passage reveals not about Jesus, but about John:

> Behind both versions [Luke's and Matthew's] lies the notion that *John has somehow been the instrument of God in inaugurating the kingdom of God*, and this by virtue of his indiscriminate offer of baptism to all who would repent, even tax collectors and harlots. It is unlikely that the church, engaged as it was in asserting Jesus' superiority over John, would have created a passage which credits John with the decisive act in the shift of the aeons, or that it would portray Jesus as merely John's successor.[78]

This passage (like Q 7:28b), therefore, more than indicates a connection between the concept and message of the kingdom and John's ministry. As Wink points out, it definitively credits, not Jesus, but John with the concept's ultimate derivation.[79]

---

[74] Reading ἁρπάζω in Mt 11:12. For another occurrence of this verb in the context of rivalry between the movement's led by Jesus and John, compare Jn 10:28: "And I give them eternal life and they will not perish to eternity and no one will snatch (ἁρπάσει) them from my hand." On this reading of Jn 10:22–42, see J. A. T. Robinson, "The 'Others' of John 4.38," 61–66.

[75] W. Wink, *John the Baptist,* 20.

[76] W. G. Kümmel, *Promise and Fulfillment,* 123.

[77] F. Danker, "Luke 16, 16 – An Opposition Logion," *JBL* (1958) 231–43.

[78] *John the Baptist,* 21–22; emphasis added.

[79] Cf. also the following comments by Wink: "There is no 'preparatory period,' no 'between time'; John's preaching of repentance is already a part of the kingdom of God .... It is with John, according to Q, that the decisive radicalism of the kingdom preaching begins .... He [John] is more than a prophet': *he is the herald of the kingdom of God* (Matt. 11:9). Even John's negativism participates in the good news, *for with John the doors of the kingdom are thrown wide open* to all who will submit to the judgement of God and enter" (*John the Baptist,* 19–23; emphasis added). In the final paragraph to his chapter on John the Baptist in Q, Wink concludes, "John was the agent through whom Jesus perceived the approach of the kingdom of heaven" (*John the Baptist,* 26).

6.5 The Kingdom of God in Paul

The relative insignificance of the expression and concept of the kingdom of God in the Pauline and deutero-Pauline corpus vis-à-vis the canonical gospels may also point to an origin other than Jesus.[80] Paul may have deliberately downplayed the expression because he recognized it as predominant among, or even a hallmark concept of, Baptists[81] with whom he had discrepancies of opinion (cf. 1 Cor 1:14–17; 12:12–13; Rom 6:3–4; Gal 3:27–28; Acts 19:1–7).[82] Interestingly, one of the few kingdom sayings in the Pauline corpus in Rom 14:17 concerns eating and drinking: "For the kingdom of God is not food and drink but righteousness and peace and joy in a Holy Spirit (οὐ γάρ ἐστιν ἡ βασιλεία τοῦ θεοῦ βρῶσις καὶ πόσις ἀλλὰ δικαιοσύνη καὶ εἰρήνη καὶ χαρὰ ἐν πνεύματι ἁγίῳ)." While this saying finds an obvious place in Paul's discussions of the value of Jewish dietary law (e.g., 1 Cor 8:1–13), it is easily imagined as part of purported discussions between Paul and the followers of John, such as the dialogue in Ephesus as reported in Acts 19:1–7. Consistent with Baptist traditions, the concern of John's followers would have been the reflection of righteousness in practices of eating and drinking.[83] In contrast, Paul's message (like that of the Markan Jesus [Mk 7:17–22]) denies the importance of dietary customs, emphasizing rather a righteousness facilitated by the Holy Spirit and reflected in relationships of healing, reconciliation, joy, and celebration. The presence of the kingdom concept in the Pauline corpus may reflect modification of John's concept by Jesus, circles of Jesus' followers influential on Paul or Paul himself.

Furthermore, Paul's relative de-emphasis of the kingdom concept may have been known to the author of Luke-Acts, influencing the concept's less frequent occurrences in Acts (1:3; 8:12; 14:22; 19:8; [20:25]; 28:23, 31). Moreover, when

---

[80] Cf. 1 Cor 4:20; 6:9–10; 15:50; Gal 5:21; 1 Thess 2:12. See K. Donfried, "The Kingdom of God in Paul," in *The Kingdom of God in 20th-Century Interpretation*, 175–90; G. Haufe, "Reich Gottes bei Paulus und in der Jesus Tradition," *NTS* 31 (1985) 467–72; G. Johnson, "'Kingdom of God'" Sayings in Paul's Letters," 143–56, in *From Jesus to Paul: Studies in Honour of Francis Wright Beare*, eds., Peter Richardson and John C. Hurd (Waterloo, Ontario: Wilfrid Laurier University, 1984).

[81] Possibly Apollos; see: Acts 18:25.

[82] Paul too excluded almost all references to Jesus' teaching in his letters. See 128.

[83] On John's diet/practice of fasting as suggesting his Jewish *halakhah*, see E. Lupieri, "'The Law and the Prophets Were until John': John the Baptist between Jewish Halakhot and Christian History of Salvation," 50–51. Also, if as argued here, the teaching in Lk 3:10–14 is John's and reflects, with Mt 6:2–6, his interest in responsible use of finances including almsgiving, this too would represent a particular emphasis by Baptists on this expression of righteousness. Similarly, the long parable in Q 19:12–13, 15–24, 26 reflects an interest in able management of finances as evidence of righteousness. As H. D. Betz points out, emphasis on almsgiving may have been connected to "increasing criticism of some forms of the sacrificial cult" (*The Sermon on the Mount*, 354). The argument is grist for the mill of those wishing to view John as rejecting his own priestly lineage.

the kingdom of God expression does occur in Acts, as for example in 1:3 and 8:12, the reference is to Jesus' or another disciple's message not Paul's. The appearance in 19:8 does concern the apostle Paul. This verse is remarkable, however, in its report of Paul's preaching in Ephesus *to followers of John the Baptist* (19:1–7).[84] Too much should not be made of this observation, however, given the complex relationship between the Pauline corpus and Acts.

6.6 Summation

This chapter attempts to demonstrate that Q's kingdom of God sayings, like Q's Son of Man sayings, reveal significant literary and other thematic ties to Baptist traditions. To summarize, of a total of twelve sayings, one of Q's kingdom sayings is attributed to John the Baptist by the author of Luke-Acts (Q 11:1–2b). Two other Q kingdom sayings (Q 7:28b; 16:16) reference John explicitly, the latter boldly attributing to John, not Jesus, the inauguration of the kingdom. One of the sayings (Q 6:20b) is a macarism – a plausible *Sitz im Leben* of which is baptism – a plausible context for the emergence of sayings by Baptists. Two sayings (Q 10:9; 12:31) occur in contexts espousing fasting and itinerant lifestyles. Two (Q 11:52; 13:29, 28) reflect vitriolic condemnation of their audience. Two (Q 13:18–19, 20–21) reflect persecution (or possibly baptism). And, a final two (Q 11:20; 17:20–21) insist on a *proximity* to, but not instantiation of the kingdom in the present time. In each case, links to Baptist-, over Christian traditions are stronger. Contrary to the time-honored scholarly consensus on the topic, the present investigation, therefore, concludes that the kingdom of God expression and concept originated *not* as the center of Jesus' message, nor among communities formed around the figure of Jesus, but among communities formed around the figure of John, perhaps even at the center of John's message.

---

[84] Although Acts ends with the note that Paul is preaching the "kingdom of God" in Rome "unhindered" (κηρύσσων τὴν βασιλείαν τοῦ θεοῦ καὶ διδάσκων τὰ περὶ τοῦ κυρίου Ἰησοῦ Χριστοῦ μετὰ πάσης παρρησίας ἀκωλύτως)" (28:31; cf. also v. 23), this line functions primarily as a literary *inclusio* with 1:3, also linking the Book of Acts to Jesus' message of the kingdom in the first *logos* (Lk 4:43). It is, as such, unlikely to reflect any message of the historical Paul in Rome. Baptism, too, is not only reinvented, but generally deemphasized in both the authentic Pauline corpus and the deutero-Pauline letters. References to baptism in the Pauline corpus are found in Gal 3:27; 1 Cor 1:13–17; 10:2; 12:3; 15:29; and Rom 6:3. Although water is sometimes present, baptism in Acts emphasizes the receiving of the Holy Spirit (e.g., 2:38, 41; 8:12–13, 16, 36, 38; 10:47–8; 16:15, 33; 18:8; 19:1–6; 22:16). Paul does not baptize with water in Acts, although other disciples, such as Philip, may do so. Repentance, too, while important to the Lukan Paul (who is built, in part, on models of John the Baptist; cf. Acts 17:30; 20:21), figures infrequently in Paul's letters and, when present, functions as an admonition to those within Christian communities to behave ethically. See J. Ramsey Michaels, "Paul and John the Baptist: An Odd Couple?" *TynBul* 42 (1991) 254–55.

Precisely what the kingdom of God may have meant to John and his followers is, however, unclear. Most scholars since Gustaf Dalman have sought formulations of a kingdom concept rigidly emphasizing a *present* (socio-political interpretation), *future* (eschatological) or *existential* (both present and future) orientation.[85] For Norman Perrin, who advocated a *both* present *and* future orientation of the kingdom, the three most central sayings were Luke 11:20, 17:20–21 and Mt 11:12.[86] Although Perrin does not acknowledge it, for the present thesis, it is interesting that all three of these sayings originated in Q.[87] Contrary to Perrin's conclusion, however, according to the present argument, Q's sayings advocate no *present* instantiation of the kingdom. Rather, Q advocates a *coming* (albeit very near) eschatological rule. Not yet in view, the kingdom in Q is anticipated like "the dawn before the sunrise,"[88] (a description of the Baptist in Lk 1:78 [cf. Mt 4:16 and Mk 13:35]), wherever repentance from sin and obedience to the Law can be found. For the Baptist, God's intervention in history is commenced only in the sense that it is on the horizon.[89] Disciples of the message glimpse it in the distance and implore, "Your kingdom come (ἐλθέτω ἡ βασιλεία σου)!" (Q 11:2b)

If, as argued elsewhere, the Son of Man sayings and the kingdom of God sayings in Q are both connected to Baptist traditions, they may, in turn, be connected to each other. In a footnote to one of her articles on the Son of Man sayings, Adela Y. Collins makes the following observation regarding a connection between the Son of Man and kingdom of God traditions in Dan 7:

---

[85] G. Dalman, *The Words of Jesus*. Throughout his article, Dennis Duling consistently uses apocalyptic to refer to what is eschatological or future, ignoring the many other qualifications necessary for any text or context to be labeled apocalyptic ("Norman Perrin and the Kingdom of God: Review and Response"). Rabbinic passages upon which Gustav Dalman relied for his interpretation of the kingdom as partially realized and earlier Jewish passages upon which Weiss and Schweitzer relied for their apocalyptic view of the kingdom urged a redefinition of the NT concept as a hybrid. See G. Dalman, *Words of Jesus*; D. Duling, "Norman Perrin and the Kingdom of God: Review and Response"; N. Perrin, *Jesus and the Language of the Kingdom*; idem, *The Kingdom of God in the Teaching of Jesus*, esp. Ch. 5 on the kingdom concept as both present and future; A. Schweitzer, *The Mystery of the Kingdom of God*; and, idem, *The Quest of the Historical Jesus*; J. Weiss, *Jesus' Proclamation of the Kingdom of God*.

[86] *The Kingdom of God in the Teaching of Jesus*, 171–78. Earl Breech comments on Perrin's concentration on these three sayings: "His [Perrin's] selection of these three sayings begs an important methodological question, since there are at least three other authentic sayings which use Kingdom language. … Perrin offers no criteria for isolating these three sayings from the others that use Kingdom language" ("Kingdom of God and the Parables of Jesus," *Semeia* 12 [1978] 17).

[87] N. Perrin, *Jesus and the Language of the Kingdom*, 40–56. Indeed Perrin's conclusion about these sayings, that Jesus' kingdom language evoked a myth of God's acts of sovereignty over his people throughout history, may hold true, even if the origin of this language was among Baptists.

[88] G. E. Ladd, "The Kingdom of God," 237.

[89] The context in Q suggests, not only a connection to the Son of Man traditions, but a future understanding of this phrase.

In Daniel 7 the dominion of the one like a Son of Man is closely associated with the kingdom of the people of the holy ones of the Most High (vss 13–14, 27). The context suggests that both the dominion of the one like a son of man and the kingdom of the people result from the decree of the Most High, i.e., they are manifestations of the kingdom of God.[90]

Although a background of Dan 7 is not explicit for either the Son of Man or kingdom of God traditions in Q, if the connection between both sets of sayings and Baptist traditions is plausible, then the connection between both groups of sayings to each other becomes more likely, increasing the importance of a proof-text such as Dan 7 in which the concepts appear together and in relationship to each other.[91] Like Dan 7, together Q 17:20 and 17:21 draw a connection between the Son of Man and the kingdom of God. If an association between these two passages was provable, an increased level of clarity in the interpretation of both groups might be attained. Together they might offer the single picture of a future eschatological kingdom – reign *and* probably realm – including a judgment in which the Son of Man would play a decisive role.[92] Parallels with Hellenistic wisdom sayings incorporating both sapiential *and* eschatological features provide the necessary precedent for apprehending complete integration of the two sets of sayings.[93]

Finally, John's execution by Herod Antipas suggests John made claims, if not to his own messiahship (such a presumption apparently existed; cf. Jn 1:20 [also Jn 1:8]),[94] at least from a Roman military perspective, to some sort of insurrectionist ideology. According to Josephus,[95] Antipas felt threatened by the crowds aroused by John's eloquence. Also, Josephus' account, like Mark's, reflects the opinion that Herod should not have punished John, whether by imprisonment

---

[90] A. Y. Collins, "The Origin of the Designation of Jesus as 'Son of Man,'" 142 n. 8.

[91] Cf. Book of Similitudes (*1 En.* 37–71, esp. 61:8; 62:5), although the expression "kingdom of God" is not explicit, only implied (e.g., *1 En.* 63:2–4).

[92] On the future arrival of the Son of Man in Q, see Ch. 5. Relevant here is also John J. Collins' comment: "...the motif of the kingdom of God was a complex one in Judaism in the period 200 B.C.E. – 100 C.E. The basic underlying idea of all conceptions of the kingdom was that God is king of the universe, past, present, and future. In some contexts the kingdom could be understood in an oral or spiritual way, especially in the Hellenistic Diaspora. In the great majority of cases, however, especially in the land of Israel, in the first centuries B.C.E. and C.E., it was expected that the 'kingship' of God would be manifested in an eschatological kingdom" ("The Kingdom of God in the Apocrypha and Pseudepigrapha," 95).

[93] See Martin Ebner, *Jesus – Ein Weisheitslehrer?* See also E. R. Goodenough, "The Political Philosophy of Hellenistic Kingship"; B. Mack, "The Kingdom Sayings in Mark," 11–17. Mack's insistence on the sapiential qualities of the kingdom sayings in Mark is correct. To the extent that his insistence excludes any eschatological dimension, however, (relegating it to Markan redaction), the thesis is rejected.

[94] Cf. also *Ps.-Clem.* Rec. 1.54.

[95] The present author takes Josephus' omission of the eschatological dimension of Judaism in general and in John's ministry, in particular, as deliberate. Josephus also avoids any reference to a messianic character of John's ministry or message because such a sentiment was blatantly anti-Roman. Josephus includes miracles as evidence of fraud on the part of messianic claimants (e.g., *Ant.* 20.97–98; 20.169–72).

in Machaerus (Jos., *Ant.* 18.119) or beheading at the whim of his brother's wife (Mk 6:14–29).[96] Josephus concludes that Aretas' defeat of Herod's army constituted just retribution on Herod for his faulty treatment of the Baptist, but the question is left open as to why, in the words of Maurice Goguel,

a simple message of virtue and piety should enkindle among the people such a spirit of excitement that the political authorities considered it to be dangerous.[97]

Mark's explanation that John attacked Herod's right to marry his brother's wife fails to provide a necessary pretext for Herod's action [Mk 6:18]. Origination and espousal of the imminent inbreaking of a "kingdom of God" by John, however, has the potential to explain why Antipas went after the Baptist with urgency and determination. If John advocated an eschatological kingdom, Herod would unquestionably have perceived such a message as a sign of sedition. John J. Collins summarizes the point:

The common denominator of all eschatological formulations of the kingdom, however, in addition to the postulate of divine sovereignty, was rejection of foreign rule. *The implementation of the kingdom of God, whether by a messiah or a direct heavenly intervention, implied the destruction of the kings and the mighty of this world.*[98]

Thus a kingdom message provides a sound basis upon which to arrest, imprison and execute the Baptist.[99]

---

[96] On John's death, see Michael Hartmann, *Der Tod Johannes des Taüfers: Eine Exegetische und rezeptionsgeschichtliche Studie auf dem Hintergrund narrativer, intertextueller und kulturanthropologischer Zugänge* (SBB 45; Stuttgart: Katholisches Bibelwerk, 2001). Cf. the beheading of Theudas (*Ant.* 20.97–98).

[97] *The Life of Jesus*, 266.

[98] "The Kingdom of God in the Apocrypha and Pseudepigrapha," 95; emphasis added. Cf. also the comment by Morton Enslin: "Their emphasis upon the coming kingdom could not fail to seem to entail a king" ("John and Jesus," 14).

[99] Comments on the derivation of non-Q kingdom sayings such as those from the Gospels of Mark and John (the Gospel of John preserves only two such sayings [Jn 3:3, 5]) cannot be entertained at any length here except to advise against the hasty attribution of these traditions, particularly regarding the kingdom's instantiation in the present, to the church.

Chapter Seven

Conclusion

> That there should be a Baptist gospel at the end of the century is
> far from improbable; the movement somewhat antedated that of
> Jesus, which had possessed written transcripts of the gospel for at
> least thirty or forty years when Luke wrote.[1]

7.1 Epilogue

This investigation began with the rather narrow question of the NT traditions
concerning John the Baptist. What set my investigation apart from others, I
thought, was a Bultmannian insistence on the history of these fragments as
'traditions' as opposed to literary evidence of the historical Baptist. As the work
developed, however, I found profit in reevaluating not just Baptist traditions,
but other Gospel traditions as well, through the lens of what might be called a
Baptist hermeneutic. I also considered, contrary to my every instinct, the historical Baptist, not because I consider such a goal attainable, but as a test of certain
flawed presuppositions of his quest.

In the end, the results were somewhat surprising at least to me. The conclusions of Chapter 4 on the transfiguration in Mark 9 have, in particular, prompted
me to think about possible implications. I do not imagine the last word has been
said on this and other issues contained in this study.

By and large, Chapters 3, 5 and 6 provide literary comparisons. I openly
acknowledge variation in the probability of arguments levied, as well as some
overlap. To this end, I reiterate what is stated in Chapter 3, namely, that in my
experience, many good arguments are cumulative: although not every point is
equally convincing, the sum total persuades. In his article on the historical Jesus
and John, Morton Enslin discussed the hypothetical nature of his own conclusions. His comment reflects my thoughts about my own thesis:

> Nevertheless my hypotheses attempt to face the problem fairly and to be not without plau-
> sibility. Not all of the arguments contained in this study are equally persuasive; hopefully,
> however, their cumulative force will not be denied.[2]

---

[1] Clayton R. Bowen, "John the Baptist and the New Testament," 58. Cf. also J. C. Todd,
"Logia of John," 173–75.

[2] Morton S. Enslin, "John and Jesus," 14.

The purpose of this final chapter is to summarize the central conclusions of each chapter and to suggest areas of further research.

7.2 Summation

Chapter One introduces the topic of Baptist traditions and Q. It notes that most scholarly attention devoted to John the Baptist focuses on the historical Baptist – his baptizing and maintaining a 'wilderness' and/or 'ascetic' lifestyle – neglecting to consider the literary evidence as fragments of tradition with a relationship to the body of teaching attributed to Jesus in the NT and related documents, in particular, Q. This chapter, thus, describes the *scope* of the present project as bringing together two branches of NT studies typically considered separate: Baptist traditions and Q. It qualifies the project's aim as an in-depth analysis of why current models of Q both prominently and favorably feature traditions concerning John the Baptist.

Chapter Two notes how literature on the historical John has failed to acknowledge the special role played by Q, as well as how Q research has neglected the importance of the Baptist *Tendenz* for both reconstruction and interpretation. This chapter also discusses important methodological issues of the quest for the historical John. The central point argued is that the use/abuse of redaction criticism over and against other critical methods in Baptist research, in particular, the flawed assumption that the Baptist is systematically subjugated to the Christ in every case in the four NT gospels, has severely limited appreciation of these ancient historical traditions. This chapter proposes that historical-critical methods are more effective when used together than separately.

Chapter Three lays out evidence in support of the argument that at some point in the undoubtedly complex pre-history of its redactions Q existed as a source of Baptist traditions exclusively. A study is made of (1) the double attribution to John and Jesus of Q sayings in the NT; (2) Q sayings that contradict other Jesus traditions, (e.g., fasting/feasting, afamilial/familial, itinerant/urban, didactic/charismatic); and (3) significant thematic continuities between Baptist traditions and Q sayings.

Chapter Four presents arguments for viewing the so-called Markan 'transfiguration' as a succession narrative. In particular, John's identification as Elijah throughout this Gospel suggests that, in Mk 9:4, where Elijah is said to have "appeared," John has been resurrected from the dead. References to the Baptist as Elijah in the beginning, middle and end of this gospel function as an outline for organizing the ministry of Jesus in this gospel. The more charismatic phase of Jesus' ministry – most of the sources of which are unknown – is inserted between John's baptism of Jesus in Mark 1 and John's resurrection on the mountain of transfiguration in Mark 9, whereas the more didactic phase of Jesus' ministry

– the unknown source(s) of which shares material in common with Q – is inserted between the transfiguration/*John's resurrection* in Mark 9 and Jesus' resurrection in Mark 16. The disproportionate quantity of Markan Q parallels *after* the transfiguration/succession narrative in Mk 8–13 suggest what Chapter 3 of the present study also attempts to show: that Q was, at one time, a collection of Baptist traditions. The author of the Second Gospel does not, therefore, deploy these traditions until Jesus has received official sanction by God (and Moses, teacher *par excellence*) as John's successor. John's baptism, backed by the message of a voice from heaven, provides the divine imprimatur on Jesus' healing ministry; John's resurrection, also backed by the message from heaven, offers official sanction of Jesus' teaching ministry as John's successor.

Chapters Five and Six argue that a careful evaluation of the canonical gospels suggests that the origin and derivation of both the 'Son of Man' and 'Kingdom of God' NT expressions is the proclamation of the Baptist. *Chapter Five* describes as discouraging past research on the derivation and origin of the Greek expression ὁ υἱὸς τοῦ ἀνθρώπου with Jesus. Building on the observation that Q is a principal source of "Son of Man" sayings, this chapter proposes the new solution that the pronounced emphasis on John the Baptist in Q suggests this expression originated with John or among his followers. Literary comparisons between Q's Son of Man sayings and Baptist traditions in- and outside of Q make this case.

The expression, 'kingdom of God' is often thought to reside at the very heart of the message of the historical Jesus. Q is a principal source of kingdom of God sayings, and yet Q's group of sayings has attracted little specific attention. Through an exegetical investigation of the sayings in Q, like Chapter 5 on the 'Son of Man' sayings, *Chapter Six* traces an origin of the kingdom of God sayings to Baptist traditions.

7.3 Questions for Further Research

Questions for further research are three-fold. First, with regard to *method*, overuse of redaction criticism is at an all-time high in our guild, showing few signs of abating. Form criticism is now regarded as old-fashioned: a pipe dream of the founders of the *Religionsgeschichtliche Schule*, who were struggling to take seriously the radical skepticism of scholars such as Franz Overbeck while still salvaging something of history from both the Hebrew and Christian scriptures. This view, as I have attempted to show, sells Baptist traditions short, neglecting plausible interpretations of the fragments in pre-Synoptic *and pre-Johannine* contexts that, at the very least, broaden our perspective of the possibilities for understanding these sundry materials. Form criticism cannot prove various unrelated Baptist fragments originated with the historical Baptist or even within Baptist communities. Neither, however, can redaction criticism prove any evangelist operated with a consistent and comprehensive program for his work. Up-to-date research on the authentic Pauline corpus seriously advises against the latter conclusion in particular. Modern critical scholarship must avail itself of an ever widening array of methodological techniques. Historical-critical and literary approaches benefit from the careful incorporation of socio-historical insights, provided the literary nature of the NT traditions is never inadvertently superseded.[3]

Second, with regard to the *content* of the present study's conclusions, areas for further research are numerous. This investigation concentrates myopically on the texts of the NT. Non-canonical early Christian texts as well as later patristic interpretations, while avoiding Baptist traditions, do not completely neglect them. Although such texts are often supplied in this project in the notes (with a few exceptions), they merit examination on their own grounds. References to the Baptist in the Pseudo-Clementine literature comes immediately to mind as an important example of this need.

Finally, the seemingly immediate early 'Christian' resumption of baptism and fasting (prayer and almsgiving?) challenges NT traditions that insist on Jesus' suspension of such practices. How what we now know as Baptist traditions became the models for these most seminal and widespread of early Christian practices is an anomaly that would be well served by a fresh look at NT Baptist traditions.

In conclusion, the amount of primary material occupying the focus of this study is vast. Because Baptist traditions are scattered throughout each of the four gospels and Q, the scope is broad and the task, difficult. Also, because such a study involves both Baptist traditions and Q, the quantity of relevant secondary literature is enormous. Q studies, the Gospel of Mark, the 'Son of Man' and 'Kingdom of God' sayings, not to mention historical John research, have each, for more than a century, commanded their own area of investigation. Every one of these trajectories of interpretation informs the present argument. Admittedly, I do not possess prolonged or meaningful expertise in any one of these important fields. I am, however, convinced that Baptist traditions have a new and valid perspective to lend to each of these important areas of research and have tried to make this case to my readers. It was neither possible, nor appropriate, however, to do justice to each of these topics on its own terms in the space of a single monograph focusing on Baptist traditions. Over time I hope that the most convincing ideas presented here will attract the more exacting work they deserve.

A final point concerns the religious implications of this project within a broader cultural framework. Against Bultmann's projected *Sitz im Leben*, in the period of the early church, of competition between the disciples of Jesus

---

[3] James A. Kelhoffer discusses this problem in a section entitled, "Method and Eclecticism." See *The Diet of John the Baptist*, 200–1.

and John, the present thesis attempts to demonstrate that the authors of the four gospels knowingly incorporated Baptist sayings in early Christian tradition in a spirit of conversation and compromise. A recurring question for this proposal, then, regards the value of this, heretofore unacknowledged, model of integration, not just for understanding the earliest layers of Christian tradition, but for pre-Christian traditions of the New Testament as well as roughly contemporary non-canonical Jewish, Christian and Gnostic texts. Such work might even inform contemporary discussions of religious ecumenism.

Appendix

NT Logia of John the Baptist

1. Exhortation to Repentance (Mt 3:2)

Mt 3:2: "Repent, for the kingdom of heaven has come near."
Μετανοεῖτε· ἤγγικεν γὰρ ἡ βασιλεία τῶν οὐρανῶν.

2. Announcement of Judgment (Lk 3:7–9 [Q])

Q: 3:7–9: "Generation of vipers! Who informed you to flee from the coming wrath? Bear fruit worthy of repentance, and do not begin to say to yourselves: We have Abraham as father! For I tell you: God is able to raise up children to Abraham out of these rocks! And the ax already lies in front of the root of the trees. Then every tree not bearing good fruit will be chopped down and thrown into a fire."
Γεννήματα ἐχιδνῶν, τίς ὑπέδειξεν ὑμῖν φυγεῖν ἀπὸ τῆς μελλούσης ὀργῆς; ποιήσατε οὖν καρποὺς ἀξίους τῆς μετανοίας καὶ μὴ ἄρξησθε λέγειν ἐν ἑαυτοῖς, Πατέρα ἔχομεν τὸν Ἀβραάμ. λέγω γὰρ ὑμῖν ὅτι δύναται ὁ θεὸς ἐκ τῶν λίθων τούτων ἐγεῖραι τέκνα τῷ Ἀβραάμ. ἤδη δὲ καὶ ἡ ἀξίνη πρὸς τὴν ῥίζαν τῶν δένδρων κεῖται· πᾶν οὖν δένδρον μὴ ποιοῦν καρπὸν καλὸν ἐκκόπτεται καὶ εἰς πῦρ βάλλεται.

3. Prediction of the Coming One (Q 3:16b–17; Mk 1:7–8; Jn 1:26–27)

Q 3:16b–17 "I baptize you with water, but the one coming after me is more powerful than I. I am not worthy to untie the thong of his sandals. He will baptize you with a Holy Spirit and fire. His pitchfork is in his hand to clear his threshing floor and gather the wheat in his barn, but the chaff he will burn with unquenchable fire."
Ἐγὼ μὲν ὕδατι βαπτίζω ὑμᾶς· ἔρχεται δὲ ὁ ἰσχυρότερός μου, οὗ οὐκ εἰμὶ ἱκανὸς λῦσαι τὸν ἱμάντα τῶν ὑποδημάτων αὐτοῦ· αὐτὸς ὑμᾶς βαπτίσει ἐν πνεύματι ἁγίῳ καὶ πυρί· οὗ τὸ πτύον ἐν τῇ χειρὶ αὐτοῦ διακαθᾶραι τὴν ἅλωνα αὐτοῦ καὶ συναγαγεῖν τὸν σῖτον εἰς τὴν ἀποθήκην αὐτοῦ, τὸ δὲ ἄχυρον κατακαύσει πυρὶ ἀσβέστῳ.

Mk 1:7–8: "The one who is more powerful than I is coming after me. I am not worthy to stoop down and untie the thong of his sandals. I have baptized you with water; but he will baptize you with a Holy Spirit."
Ἔρχεται ὁ ἰσχυρότερός μου ὀπίσω μου, οὗ οὐκ εἰμὶ ἱκανὸς κύψας λῦσαι τὸν ἱμάντα τῶν ὑποδημάτων αὐτοῦ. ἐγὼ ἐβάπτισα ὑμᾶς ὕδατι, αὐτὸς δὲ βαπτίσει ὑμᾶς ἐν πνεύματι ἁγίῳ.

Jn 1:26–27: "I baptize with water. Among you stands one whom you do not know, the one coming after me. I am not worthy to untie the thong of his sandal."
Ἐγὼ βαπτίζω ἐν ὕδατι· μέσος ὑμῶν ἕστηκεν ὃν ὑμεῖς οὐκ οἴδατε, ὁ ὀπίσω μου ἐρχόμενος, οὗ οὐκ εἰμὶ [ἐγὼ] ἄξιος ἵνα λύσω αὐτοῦ τὸν ἱμάντα τοῦ ὑποδήματος.

Acts 13:25: "Who do you consider me to be? I am not he. But, behold, one is coming after me. I am not worthy to untie the thong of the sandals of his feet."

Τί ἐμὲ ὑπονοεῖτε εἶναι; οὐκ εἰμὶ ἐγώ· ἀλλ᾽ ἰδοὺ ἔρχεται μετ᾽ ἐμὲ οὗ οὐκ εἰμὶ ἄξιος τὸ ὑπόδημα τῶν ποδῶν λῦσαι.

4. Lamb of God Proclamations (Jn 1:29–34, 36)

Jn 1:29–34: "Behold, the Lamb of God who takes away the sin of the world! This is the one of whom I said, 'After me comes a man who became before me because he was before me.' I did not know him; but in order that he might be revealed to Israel, for this reason, I came baptizing with water." [And John testified,] "I observed the Spirit descending like a dove from heaven and it remained on him. I did not know him, but the one who sent me to baptize with water said to me, 'The one on whom you see the Spirit descend and remain on him, this is the one baptizing with a Holy Spirit.' And I have seen and testified that this is the Son of God."

Ἴδε ὁ ἀμνὸς τοῦ θεοῦ ὁ αἴρων τὴν ἁμαρτίαν τοῦ κόσμου. οὗτός ἐστιν ὑπὲρ οὗ ἐγὼ εἶπον, Ὀπίσω μου ἔρχεται ἀνὴρ ὃς ἔμπροσθέν μου γέγονεν, ὅτι πρῶτός μου ἦν. κἀγὼ οὐκ ᾔδειν αὐτόν, ἀλλ᾽ ἵνα φανερωθῇ τῷ Ἰσραὴλ διὰ τοῦτο ἦλθον ἐγὼ ἐν ὕδατι βαπτίζων. [Καὶ ἐμαρτύρησεν Ἰωάννης λέγων ὅτι] Τεθέαμαι τὸ πνεῦμα καταβαῖνον ὡς περιστερὰν ἐξ οὐρανοῦ καὶ ἔμεινεν ἐπ᾽ αὐτόν. κἀγὼ οὐκ ᾔδειν αὐτόν, ἀλλ᾽ ὁ πέμψας με βαπτίζειν ἐν ὕδατι ἐκεῖνός μοι εἶπεν, Ἐφ᾽ ὃν ἂν ἴδῃς τὸ πνεῦμα καταβαῖνον καὶ μένον ἐπ᾽ αὐτόν, οὗτός ἐστιν ὁ βαπτίζων ἐν πνεύματι ἁγίῳ. κἀγὼ ἑώρακα, καὶ μεμαρτύρηκα ὅτι οὗτός ἐστιν ὁ υἱὸς τοῦ θεοῦ.

Jn 1:36: "Look! Here is the Lamb of God!"

Ἴδε ὁ ἀμνὸς τοῦ θεοῦ.

5. Protestation against Jesus' Baptism (Mt 3:14)

Mt 3:14: "I myself need to be baptized by you; and do you come to me?"

Ἐγὼ χρείαν ἔχω ὑπὸ σοῦ βαπτισθῆναι, καὶ σὺ ἔρχῃ πρός με;

6. John's Relationship to the Coming One (Jn 1:15)

Jn 1:15: "This was he of whom I said, 'The one coming after me became before me, because he was before me.'"

Οὗτος ἦν ὃν εἶπον, Ὁ ὀπίσω μου ἐρχόμενος ἔμπροσθέν μου γέγονεν, ὅτι πρῶτός μου ἦν.

7. Ethical Teaching ("Special L": Lk 3:11, 13, 14)

Lk 3:11: "Whoever has two coats must share with anyone who has none; and whoever has food must do likewise."

Ὁ ἔχων δύο χιτῶνας μεταδότω τῷ μὴ ἔχοντι, καὶ ὁ ἔχων βρώματα ὁμοίως ποιείτω.

Lk 3:13: "Exact no more than what has been commanded you."

Μηδὲν πλέον παρὰ τὸ διατεταγμένον ὑμῖν πράσσετε.

Lk 3:14: "Neither blackmail nor accuse falsely; and let your wages be sufficient."

Μηδένα διασείσητε μηδὲ συκοφαντήσητε καὶ ἀρκεῖσθε τοῖς ὀψωνίοις ὑμῶν.

8. Confession about Himself (Jn 1:20, 21, 23)

Jn 1:20: "I am not the Christ."
Εγὼ οὐκ εἰμὶ ὁ Χριστός.

Jn 1:21: "[Are you Elijah?] I am not."
Οὐκ εἰμί.

"[Are you the prophet?] No."[1]
Οὔ.

Jn 1:23: "I am a voice crying in the wilderness, 'Make straight the way of the Lord.'"
Ἐγὼ φωνὴ βοῶντος ἐν τῇ ἐρήμῳ, Εὐθύνατε τὴν ὁδὸν κυρίου.

9. Johns Answers Questions about Jesus (Jn 3:27–30)

Jn 3:27–30: "A person is not able to receive anything except what has been given to him from the heaven. You yourselves are our witnesses that I said, 'I myself am not the Christ, but I am the one who has been sent before him.' He who has the bride is the bridegroom. The friend of the bridegroom, standing and listening to him, rejoices with joy on account of the bridegroom's voice. Because of this, then, my joy has been fulfilled: that one must increase, but I must decrease."

Οὐ δύναται ἄνθρωπος λαμβάνειν οὐδὲ ἓν ἐὰν μὴ ᾖ δεδομένον αὐτῷ ἐκ τοῦ οὐρανοῦ. αὐτοὶ ὑμεῖς μοι μαρτυρεῖτε ὅτι εἶπον [ὅτι] Οὐκ εἰμὶ ἐγὼ ὁ Χριστός, ἀλλ᾽ ὅτι Ἀπεσταλμένος εἰμὶ ἔμπροσθεν ἐκείνου. ὁ ἔχων τὴν νύμφην νυμφίος ἐστίν· ὁ δὲ φίλος τοῦ νυμφίου ὁ ἑστηκὼς καὶ ἀκούων αὐτοῦ χαρᾷ χαίρει διὰ τὴν φωνὴν τοῦ νυμφίου. αὕτη οὖν ἡ χαρὰ ἡ ἐμὴ πεπλήρωται. ἐκεῖνον δεῖ αὐξάνειν, ἐμὲ δὲ ἐλαττοῦσθαι.

10. John's Question from Prison (Q 7:19)

Q 7:19: "Are you the coming one or are we to expect another?"
Σὺ εἶ ὁ ἐρχόμενος ἢ ἄλλον προσδοκῶμεν;

11. On Divorce (Mk 6:18)

"It is not lawful for you to have your brother's wife."
Οὐκ ἔξεστίν σοι ἔχειν τὴν γυναῖκα τοῦ ἀδελφοῦ σου.

12. John's Prayer (Q 11:2b–4)[2]

Q 11:2b–4: "Whenever you pray, say: Father, let your name be kept holy. Let your king-dom come. Give us today our daily bread and forgive us our debts for also we ourselves forgive all our debtors. And lead us not into temptation."

Ὅταν προσεύχησθε λέγετε, Πάτερ, ἁγιασθήτω τὸ ὄνομά σου· ἐλθέτω ἡ βασιλεία σου· τὸν ἄρτον ἡμῶν τὸν ἐπιούσιον δίδου ἡμῖν τὸ καθ᾽ ἡμέραν· καὶ ἄφες ἡμῖν τὰς ἁμαρτίας ἡμῶν, καὶ γὰρ αὐτοὶ ἀφίομεν παντὶ ὀφείλοντι ἡμῖν· καὶ μὴ εἰσενέγκῃς ἡμᾶς εἰς πειρασμόν.

---

[1] Cf. Acts 13:25
[2] Whether this prayer was John's or Jesus' is unclear in NT traditions.

Bibliography

Texts and Translations

–. *Nicene and Post-Nicene Fathers of the Christian Church*. First Series. 14 vols. New York: Christian Literature Publishing Company, 1886–1890.

–. *Nicene and Post-Nicene Fathers of the Christian Church*. Second Series. 14 vols. New York: Christian Literature Publishing Company, 1890–1900.

Aland, K., et al rev. and ed. *Novum Testamentum Graece*. 27th ed. Stuttgart: Deutsche Bibelstiftung, 1993.

Archambault, Georges, ed. *Justin, Dialogue avec Tryphon*. Textes et documents pour l'étude historique du Christianisme 8, 11. Paris: A. Picard, 1909.

Baehrens, Emil, ed. *Poetae Latini Minores*. Leipzig: B. G. Teubner, 1927.

Basore, J. W., trans. *Seneca: Moral Essays*. 3 vols. LCL. Cambridge: Harvard University, 1928–35.

Betz, Hans Dieter, ed. *The Greek Magical Papyri in Translation: Including the Demotic Spells*. Chicago; London; University of Chicago, ²1992.

Brownson, Carleton L. and John Dillery. *Xenophon, Anabasis*. LCL. Cambridge, MA: Harvard University, ²1998.

Brunt, P. A., ed. and trans. *Arrian. Anabasis Alexandri et Indica*. 2 vols. LCL. Cambridge, MA: Harvard University, 1983.

Butler, H. E., ed. and trans. *Quintilian*. 4 vols. LCL. Cambridge: Harvard University Press, 1920–1922.

Butterworth, G. W., trans. *Clement of Alexandria*. LCL. New York: Putnam's Sons, 1919.

Caplan, H. et alii, trans. [Cicero]. *Ad C. Herennium De Ratione Dicendi (Rhetorica ad Herennium)*. LCL. Cambridge, MA: Harvard University, 1954.

Cary, E., trans. *Dio Cassius: Roman History*. 9 vols. LCL. Cambridge, MA: Harvard University, 1914–27.

–. *Dionysius of Halicarnassus: Roman Antiquities*. 7 vols. LCL. Cambridge, MA: Harvard University, 1937–50.

Chadwick, Henry. *Saint Augustine, Confessions*. Oxford: Oxford University, 1991.

Charlesworth, James H. *The Old Testament Pseudepigrapha*. 2 vols. New York: Doubleday; London: Darton, Longman & Todd, 1983.

Cohoon, J. W. and H. L. Crosby, trans. *Dio Chrysostom*. 5 vols. LCL. Cambridge: Harvard University, 1932–51.

Colson, F. H., G. H. Whitaker, et al. *Philo*. 12 vols. LCL. Cambridge, MA: Harvard University, 1929–53.

Conybeare, F. C. ed. and trans., *Philostratus, The Life of Apollonius*. 2 vols. LCL. Cambridge: Harvard, 1912–50.

Cooke, H. P. and H. Tredennick, et al. *Aristotle*. 23 vols. LCL. Cambridge, MA: Harvard, 1938–60.

Copenhaver, Brian P. *Hermetica: The Greek Corpus Hermeticum and the Latin Asclepius in A New English Translation with Notes and Introduction.* Cambridge: Cambridge University, 1992.

Corcoran, T. H., trans. *Seneca. Naturales Quaestiones*. 2 vols. LCL. Cambridge: Harvard, 1971.

Datema, Cornelis. "Another Unedited Homily of Ps. Chrysostom on the Birth of John the Baptist (BHG 847i)." *Byzantion* 53 (1983): 478–93.

Deferrari, Roy J. *Saint Basil, The Letters*. LCL. London: Heinemann, 1926–34.

Dewing, H. B., trans. *Procopius*. 7 vols. LCL. Cambridge, MA: Harvard University, 1914–40.

Diels, Hermann and Walther Kranz, eds. *Die Fragmente der Vorsokratiker* (Berlin: Weidmann, 1956).

Dillon, John and Jackson Hershbell. *Iamblichus, On the Pythagorean Way of Life: Text and Translation and Notes*. Text and Translations 29, Graeco-Roman Series 11. Hans Dieter Betz and Edward N. O'Neill, ed. Atlanta: Scholars Press, 1991.

Dindorf, Wilhelm. *Historici Graeci minores*. Teubner, Leipzig: Teubner, 1870–71.

Dübner, F. *Theophrasti Characteres; Marci Antonini Commentarii; Epicteti Dissertationes ab Arriano literis mandatae fragmenta et Enchiridion cum commentario Simplicii; Cebetis Tabula; Maximi Tyrii Dissertationes: Graece et Latine cum indicibus; Theophrasti Characteres XV et Maximum Tyrium et antiquissimis codicibus accurate excursis*. Paris: A. Firmin-Didot, 1877.

Elliger, K. ed. and W. Rudolph, et al. *Biblia Hebraica Stuttgartensia*. Stuttgart Deutsche Bibelgesellschaft, 1983.

Elliott, James K. *The Apocryphal New Testament: A Collection of Apocryphal Christian Literature in an English Translation*. Oxford: Clarendon, 1993.

Fagles, Robert, trans. *Homer: The Odyssey*. New York: Viking Penguin, 1996.

Fairbanks, Arthur. *Philostratus, Imagines; Callistratus, Descriptions*. LCL. London: W. Heinemann, Ltd.; New York: G. P. Putnam's Sons, 1931.

Fairclough, H. Rushton, ed. *Virgil*. LCL. Cambridge, MA: Harvard University, [2]1969–74.

Falls, Thomas B. Saint Justin Martyr. FC 6. New York: Christian Heritage, 1948.

Fisher, C. D., ed. *Tacitus. Cornelii Taciti Annalium*. OCT. Oxford: The Clarendon Press, 1906.

Foster, B. A. et al., trans. *Livy*. LCL. 14 vols. Cambridge, MA: Harvard University 1948–53.

Fowler, H. N., W. R. M. Lamb, et al. *Plato*. 12 vols. LCL. Cambridge, MA: Harvard University, 1914–35.

Freese, John Henry, ed. and trans. *Aristotle. The Art of Rhetoric*. LCL. Cambridge: Harvard University, 1926.

Fyfe, W. H., trans. '*Longinus,' On the Sublime*. in Aristotle vol. 23, *The Poetics*. Cambridge, MA: Harvard University, 1927.

García Martínez, Florentino and Eibert J. C. Tigchelaar, eds. *The Dead Sea Scrolls: Study Edition*. Leiden: Brill//Grand Rapids: Eerdmans, 2000.

Gaselee, S., trans. *Achilles Tatius*. LCL. Cambridge: Harvard; London: W. Heinemann, 1969.

Geffcken, Johannes. *Die Oracula Sibyllina*. Leipzig: J. C. Hinrichs, 1902.

Gifford, E. H., trans. *Eusebii Pamphili praeparatio evangelica*. 4 vols. Oxford: Academy, 1903.

Godley, A. D., trans. *Herodotus*. 4 vols. LCL. Cambridge, MA: Harvard University, 1921–25.

Hanson, J. Arthur, trans. *Apuleius, Metamorphoses*. LCL. Cambridge: Harvard University, 1989.

Harmon, A. M. and M. D. MacLeod, trans. *Lucian*. 8 vols. LCL. Cambridge, MA: Harvard University, 1921–61.

Hendrickson, G. L., H. M. Hubbell, et al. *Cicero*. 28 vols. Cambridge, MA: Harvard University, 1912–72.

Henry, René. *Photius Bibliothèque*. Paris: Société d'Édition; Les Belles Lettres, 1960.

Hett, W. S. *[Aristotle/Ps. Aristotle,] Minor Works*. LCL. Cambridge, MA: Harvard University/London: Heinemann, 1963 (1936).

Hicks, R. D., trans. *Diogenes Laertius: Lives of Eminent Philosophers*. 2 vols. LCL. Cambridge, MA: Harvard University, 1925.

Holl, Karl, ed. *Epiphanius*. GCS 25. Leipzig: Hinrichs, 1915.

Holladay. E. R., ed. *Fragments from Hellenistic Jewish Author. Vol. 1: Historians*. Texts and Translations 20. Pseudepigrapha 10. Chico, CA: Scholars Press, 1983.

Inwood, Brad and L. P. Gerson. *The Epicurus Reader: Selected Writings and Testimonia*. Indianapolis: Hackett, 1994.

Jacoby, F., ed. *Die Fragmente der griechischen Historiker*. Berlin: Weidmann: 1923–43.

James, M. R. *The Apocryphal New Testament*. Oxford: Clarendon, 1924.

–. *The Biblical Antiquities of Philo*. 2nd ed. with an introduction by Louis H. Feldman. The Library of Biblical Studies. New York: Ktav Publishing House, Inc., 1971.

Jones, Horace L. *The Geography of Strabo*. LCL. Cambridge, MA: Harvard University, 1982 (1917).

Kirk, G. S., J. E. Raven and M. Schofield. *The Presocratic Philosophers*. Cambridge University Press, ²1983.

Kelburn, K., ed. and trans. *Lucian. The Works of Lucian*. Vol. 6. LCL. Cambridge: Harvard University, 1959.

Kock, Theodor, ed. *Comicorum Atticorum fragmenta*. Leipzig: Teubner, 1880–88.

Kühn, C. G. *Galen. Opera Omnia*. 20 vols. Leipzig: Cnoblochi, 1821–33.

Lake, Kirsopp. *The Apostolic Fathers*. 2 vols. LCL. Repr., Cambridge, MA: Harvard University Press; London: William Heinemann LTD, 1980.

Lake, Kirsopp and J. E. L. Oulton. *Eusebius. Ecclesiastical History*. 2 vols. LCL. New York: Putnam's Sons; Cambridge, MA; Harvard University, 1926–32.

Lipsius, Richard Adelbert, Maximilianus Bonnet and Heinz Kraft, ed. *Acta Apostolorum Apocrypha post Constantinum Tischendorf.* 2 vols. Darmstadt: Wissenschaftliche Buchgesellschaft, 1959; repr., Hildesheim: G. Olms, 1972.

Lucas, D. W., ed. *Aristotle: Poetics*. Oxford: Clarendon, 1968.

MacDonald, Dennis R. *The Acts of Andrew and the Acts of Andrew and Matthias in the City of the Cannibals*. Texts and Translations 33: Christian Apocrypha 1. Atlanta: Scholars Press, 1990.

Macleod, Matthew D. *Luciani opera*. Scriptorum Classicorum Bibliotheca Oxoniensis. Oxford: Oxford University Press, 1980.

Mason, Steve, ed. *Life of Josephus: Translation and Commentary*. Flavius Josephus: Translation and Commentary 9. Leiden: Brill, 2001.

Malherbe, A. J., ed. *The Cynic Epistles.* SBLSBS 12. Missoula, MT: Scholars Press, 1977.

Meyer, Marvin W. and Richard Smith, ed. *Ancient Christian Magic: Coptic Texts of Ritual Power.* New York: HarperCollins, 1994.

Migne, Jacques-Paul, ed. *Patrologiae cursus completes ... Series Graeca ... (Patrologia graeca).* 161 Vols. Paris: 1857–66 = Turnholt: Brepols, 1960.

–. *Patrologiae cursus completes ...Series Latina, ... (Patrologia Latina).* 221 Vols. Paris: 1844–64.

Mingana, Alphonse. "A New Life of John the Baptist." In: *Woodbrooke Studies; Christian Documents in Syriac, Arabic, and Garshuni.* J. Rendel Harris. ed. Cambridge: W. Heffer & Sons, 1927. 1.234–87.

Moore, C. H. and J. Jackson. *Tacitus: Histories and Annals.* 4 vols. LCL. Cambridge, MA: Harvard University, 1925–37.

Mullach, F. W. A., ed. *Fragmenta Philosophorum Graecorum.* 3 vols. Paris: Didot, 1881–83.

Müller, C., ed. *Fragmenta Historicorum Graecorum.* 5 vols. Paris: Didot, 1841–70.

Murray, A. T., trans. Homer, *The Iliad.* 2 vols. LCL. Cambridge, MA: Harvard University, 1946 (1924–25).

–. Homer, *The Odyssey.* 2 vols. LCL. Cambridge, MA: Harvard University, 1963–64 (1919).

Musurillo, Herbert, ed. *The Acts of the Christian Martyrs: Introduction, Texts and Translations.* Oxford: Oxford University, 1972.

Neusner, Jacob. *The Mishnah: A New Translation.* New Haven: Yale University, 1988.

Noblot, Henri, ed. *[Seneca (Y),] Lettres à Lucilius.* Paris: Les Belles Lettres, 1957–64.

Norlin, G. and L. Van Hook, trans. *Isocrates.* 3 vols. LCL. Cambridge, MA: Harvard University, 1928–45.

O'Donnell, James J., ed. *Augustine, Confessions.* Clarendon/Oxford: Oxford University, 1992.

Oden Thomas E., and Christopher A. Hall, eds. *Mark.* Ancient Christian Commentary on Scripture: NT 2. Downers Grove, IL: Intervarsity, 1998.

Oldfather, C. H., C. L. Sherman, et al, trans. *Diodorus Siculus.* 12 vols. LCL. New York: Putnam's Sons; Cambridge, MA: Harvard, 1933–67.

Oldfather, W. A. *Epictetus.* 2 vols. Cambridge, MA: Harvard, 1925–28.

Paton, W. R., trans. *Polybius. The Histories.* 6 vols. LCL. Cambridge, MA: Harvard University, 1922–27.

Perrin, Bernadotte, trans. *Plutarch's Lives.* 11 vols. LCL. Cambridge, MA: Harvard University, 1949.

Peter, Hermann. *Historicorum Romanorum Reliquiae.* Vol. 1^2. Leipzig: Teubner, 1914.

Preisendanz, Karl and Albert Henrichs, eds. *Papyri graecae magicae: Die griechischen Zauberpapyri.* 2 vols. Stuttgart: B. G. Teubner, ^{2}1973–74.

Rackham, H., [Aristotle]. *Rhetorica ad Alexandrum.* LCL. Vol. with *Aristotle. Problems II.* Cambridge, MA: Harvard University, 1937.

Rackham, Harris, ed. *[Plin. (E),] Natural History.* LCL. Cambridge, MA: Harvard University, 1938–63.

Radice, B. *Pliny: Letters, Panegyricus.* 2 vols. LCL. Cambridge, MA: Harvard University, 1969.

Radt, Stefan, ed. *Tragicorum Graecorum fragmenta.* Göttingen: Vandenhoeck & Ruprecht, 1971–77.

Rahlfs, A., ed. *Septuaginta*. Stuttgart: Deutsche Bibelgesellschaft, 1935.

Riese, Alexander, ed. *Anthologia Latina*. Teubner. Leipzig: Teubner, 1868–1930.

Roberts, Alexander and James Donaldson, eds. *Ante-Nicene Fathers: The Writings of the Fathers Down to A.D. 325*. Buffalo: Christian Literature Publishing Company, 1885–1896 = Peabody, MA: Hendrickson, 1994.

–. *Nicene and Post-Nicene Fathers of the Christian Church*. First Series. 14 vols. New York: Christian Literature Publishing Company, 1890–1900 = Peabody, MA: Hendrickson, 1994.

–. *Nicene and Post-Nicene Fathers of the Christian Church*. Second Series. 14 vols. New York: Christian Literature Publishing Company, 1890–1900 = Peabody, MA: Hendrickson, 1994.

Roberts, W. L., trans. *Demetrius. On Style*. LCL. in Aristotle vol. 23, *The Poetics*. Cambridge, MA: Harvard University, 1927.

Robinson, James M., gen. ed. *The Nag Hammadi Library in English*. Revised Edition. San Francisco: Harper, 1990.

Rocha-Pereira, Maria Helena. *Pausanias. Description of Greece*. 3 vols. Leipzig: B.G. Teubner Verlagsgesellschaft, 1981.

Rolfe, J. C. *Suetonius. Lives of the Caesars*. 2 vols. LCL. Cambridge, MA: Harvard University, 1912–13 (Vol. 1 revised 1951).

–. *Sallust*. LCL. Cambridge, MA: Harvard University, 1921; rev. ed. 1931.

Schneemelcher, Wilhelm and Edgar Hennecke, ed. *New Testament Apocrypha*. Revised Edition. 2 vols. R. McL. Wilson, translation ed. Cambridge: J. Clarke; Philadelphia: Knox, 1991–92.

Sparks, Hedley Frederick Davis, ed. *The Apocryphal Old Testament*. Oxford: Clarendon, 1985.

Spengel, L., ed. *Rhetores Graeci*. 3 vols. BT. Leipzig: Teubner, 1854–56.

Stählin, Otto, Ludwig Früchtel and Ursula Treu, eds. *Clemens Alexandrinus*. Vols. 2–3. GCS. Berlin: Akademie Verlag, 1985, 1970.

Stearns, Wallace Nelson. *Fragments from Graeco-Jewish Writers*. Chicago: The University of Chicago Press, 1908.

Sudhaus, Siegfried, ed. *Philodemi Volumina Rhetorica*. 2 vols. and suppl. Leipzig: B. G. Teubner, 1892–96.

Thackeray, H. S. J. *Josephus, The Jewish War*. LCL. Cambridge, MA: Harvard University, 1997 (1926).

Thackeray, H. S. J. and Ralph Marcus. *Josephus, Jewish Antiquities*. LCL. Cambridge, MA: Harvard University, 1998 (1926).

Vince, J. H. and C.A. Vince, A.T. Murray. *Demosthenes*. LCL. Cambridge: Harvard University, 1964–89.

Von Tischendorf, Constantin, R. A. Lipsius and M. Bonnet, eds. *Acta Apostolorum Apocrypha post Constantinum Tischendorf*. 2 vols. Hildesheim: G. Olms, 1959 (1891–1903).

Walz, C., ed. *Rhetores Graeci*. 9 vols. Stuttgart/Tübingen: Cotta, 1832–36.

White, H. *Appian: Roman History*. LCL. New York: Macmillan, 1912–28.

White, Nicholas. *Epictetus, The Handbook (The Encheiridion)*. Indianapolis/ Cambridge: Hackett Publishing Company, 1983.

Williamson, G. A. *Eusebius. The History of the Church from Christ to Constantine*. New York: Penguin, 1989.

Secondary Literature

Achtemeier, Paul. "Mark, Gospel of." Art. *ABD*, 4.548.

–. *Invitation to Mark: A Commentary*. Doubleday NT Commentary Series. Garden City, NY: Image Books, 1978.

Ahearne-Kroll, Stephen P. "'Who Are My Mother and My Brothers?' Family Relations and Family Language in the Gospel of Mark." *JR* (2001): 1–25.

Albright, W. F. and C. S. Mann. *Matthew: Introduction, Translation, and Notes*. AB 26. Garden City, NY: Doubleday, 1971.

Allegro, John M. *The Dead Sea Scrolls*. London: Penguin Books, ²1958 (1956).

Allison, Dale C. Jr. Review of H. D. Betz. *The Sermon on the Mount*. Minneapolis: Fortress, 1995. In: *JBL* 117 (1998): 136–38.

–. *The Jesus Tradition in Q*. Harrisburg, PA: TPI, 1997.

–. "Critical Note on Faierstein's 'Elijah Must Come First.'" *JBL* (1984): 256–58.

Anderson, Hugh. *The Gospel of Mark*. New Century Bible. Greenwood SC: Attic, 1976 = Grand Rapids: Eerdmans, 1981.

Aune, David. "The Use of ΠΡΟΦΗΤΗΣ in Josephus." *JBL* 101 (1982): 419–21.

Backhaus, Knut. *Die "Jüngerkreise" des Täufers Johannes: Eine Studie zu den religionsgeschichtlichen Ursprüngen des Christentums*. Paderborner Theologische Studien 19. Paderborn: F. Schöningh, 1991.

Badke, William B. "Was Jesus a Disciple of John?" *EvQ* 62 (1990): 195–204.

Balch, David L. "Philodemus, 'On Wealth' and 'On Household Management': Naturally Wealthy Epicureans against Poor Cynics." In *Philodemus and the New Testament World*. John T. Fitzgerald, Dirk Obbink, Glenn S. Holland, eds. NTSupp 111. Leiden: Brill, 2004. 177–96.

Baldensberger, W. *Der Prolog des vierten Evangeliums. Sein polemisch-apologetischer Zweck*. Freiburg: J. C. B. Mohr (Paul Siebeck), 1898.

Baltensweiler, H. *Die Verklärung Jesu*. Zürich: Zwingli, 1959.

Bammel, Ernst. "The Baptist in Early Christian Tradition." *NTS* 18 (1971–72): 95–128.

–. "John Did No Miracle." In: *Miracles: Cambridge Studies in Their Philosophy and History*. C. F. D. Moule, ed. London: A. R. Mowbray, 1965. 179–202.

–. "Christian Origins in Jewish Tradition." *NTS* 13 (1966–67): 317–35.

Barton, John. "Prophecy (Postexilic Hebrew)." Art. *ABD*, 5.495.

Bauckham, Richard. "The Martyrdom of Enoch and Elijah: Jewish or Christian?" *JBL* (1976): 447–58.

Beasley-Murray, G. R. *Jesus and the Kingdom of God*. Grand Rapids: Eerdmans, 1986.

Becker, Eve-Marie. "'Kamelhaare … und wilder Honig': Der historische Wert und die theologische Bedeutung der biographischen Täufer-Notiz (Mk 1,6)" In: *Die bleibende Gegenwart des Evangeliums*. FS Otto Merk. Roland Gebauer and Martin Meiser, eds. Marburger Theologische Studien 76. Marburg: Elwert, 2003. 13–28.

Becker, Jürgen. "War Jesus ein Schüler Johannes' des Täufers?" *Vom Urchristentum zu Jesus*. FS Joachim Gnilka. Hubert Frankenmölle and Karl Kertelge, eds. Freiburg/Basel/Vienna: Herder, 1989. 13–33.

–. *Johannes der Täufer und Jesus von Nazareth*. Neukirchen-Vluyn: Neukirchener, 1972.

Behm, J. "μεταμορφόω." Art. *TNDT*, 4.755–59.

Benko, Stephen. "The Magnificat, a History of the Controversy." *JBL* 86 (1967): 263–75.

Benoit, P. "L'Enfance de Jean-Baptiste selon Luc I." *NTS* 3 (1956–57): 169–94.

Bergemann, Thomas. *Q auf dem Prüfstand: Die Zuordnung des Mt/Lk-Stoffes zu Q am Beispiel der Bergpredigt.* Göttingen: Vandenhoeck & Ruprecht, 1993.

Bernardin, J. B. "The Transfiguration." *JBL* (1933): 181–89.

Best, Ernest. "An Early Sayings Collection." *NovT* (1976): 1–16.

Betz, H. D. "On the Problem of the Religio-Historical Understanding of Apocalypticism." *Journal for Theology and the Church* 6 (1969): 146–54.

–. *Essays on the Sermon on the Mount.* Philadelphia: Fortress, 1985.

–. "The Problem of Christology in the Sermon on the Mount." In: *Text and Logos: The Humanistic Interpretation of the New Testament.* FS Hendrikus W. Boers. Theodore W. Jennings Jr., ed. Atlanta: Scholars, 1990. 191–209. Reprinted in: idem, *Synoptische Studien.* 230–48.

–. "Jesus as Divine Man." In: *Synoptische Studien.* 18–34.

–. *Synoptische Studien. Gesammelte Aufsätze 2.* Tübingen: Mohr Siebeck, 1992.

–. *The Sermon on the Mount.* Minneapolis: Fortress, 1995.

Bickerman, E. "La Chaîne de la tradition pharisienne." *RB* 59 (1952): 44–54. Reprinted in: *Studies in Jewish and Christian History Part II.* AGJU 9. Leiden: Brill, 1980. 256–69.

Black, Matthew. "The Son of Man Problem in Recent Research and Debate." *BJRL* 45 (1963): 305–18.

–. "The 'Son of Man' Passion Sayings in the Gospel Tradition." *ZNW* (1969): 1–8.

Blinzler, J. *Die neutestamentlichen Berichte über die Verklärung Jesu.* Münster: Aschendorff, 1937.

Böcher, Otto. "Ass Johannes der Täufer kein Brot (Luk. vii. 33)?" *NTS* 18 (1971–72): 90–2.

Boers, H. *Theology out of the Ghetto: A New Testament Exegetical Study concerning Religious Exclusiveness.* Leiden: Brill, 1971.

Böhlemann, Peter. *Jesus und der Täufer: Schlüssel zur Theologie und Ethik des Lukas.* SNTSMS 99. Cambridge: Cambridge University, 1997.

Boobyer, G. H. "St. Mark and the Transfiguration." *JTS* (1940): 119–40.

–. *Saint Mark and the Transfiguration Story.* Edinburgh: T. & T. Clark, 1942.

Boring, M. Eugene. "The Paucity of Sayings in Mark: A Hypothesis." In: *SBL 1977 Seminar Papers.* Paul J. Achtemeier, ed. Missoula, Montana: Scholars, 1977. 371–77.

–. *Sayings of the Risen Jesus: Christian Prophecy in the Synoptic Tradition.* SNTSMS. Cambridge: Cambridge University, 1982.

Bornkamm, G. *Jesus of Nazareth.* Irene and Fraser McLuskey with James M. Robinson, trans. London: Hodder and Stoughton, 1960.

Borsch, F. H. *The Son of Man in Myth and History.* Philadelphia: Westminster, 1967.

Bovon, François. *Luke 1: A Commentary on the Gospel of Luke 1:1–9:50.* Hermeneia. Minneapolis: Fortress, 2002 (1989).

Bowen, Clayton R. "Prolegomena to A New Study of John the Baptist." In: *Studies in the New Testament: Collected Papers of Dr. Clayton R. Bowen.* Robert J. Hutcheon, ed. Chicago, IL: University of Chicago, 1936. 30–48.

–. "John the Baptist in the New Testament." In: *Studies in the New Testament: Collected Papers of Dr. Clayton R. Bowen.* Robert J. Hutcheon, ed. Chicago, IL: University of Chicago, 1936. 49–76.

Bowker, John. "The Son of Man." *JTS* 28 (1977): 19–48.

Bowman, John. *The Gospel of Mark: The New Christian Jewish Passover Haggadah.* Leiden: Brill, 1965.

Brandt Wilhelm. *Die jüdischen Baptismen, oder das religiöse Waschen und Baden im Judentum mit Einschluß des Judenchristentums. Beihefte zur ZATW* 18. Giessen: Alfred Töpelmann, 1910.

Breech, Earl. "Kingdom of God and the Parables of Jesus." *Semeia* 12 (1978): 15–40.

Bretscher, P. G. "'Whose Sandals?' (Matt. 3:11)." *JBL* (1967): 81–87.

Broadhead, Edwin K. *Mark. Readings: A New Biblical Commentary.* Sheffield: Sheffield Academic, 2001.

Brodie, T. L. "The Accusing and Stoning of Naboth (1 Kgs 21:8–13) as One Component of the Stephen Text (Acts 6:9–14; 7:58a)." *CBQ* 45 (1983): 417–32.

–. "Luke 7,36–50 as an Internalization of 2 Kings 4,1–37: A Study in Luke's Use of Rhetorical Imitation." *Bib* 64 (1983): 457–85.

–. "Towards Unraveling the Rhetorical Imitation of Sources in Acts: 2 Kings 5 as One Component of Acts 8:9–40." *Biblica* 67 (1986): 41–67.

–. "Towards Unraveling Luke's Use of the Old Testament: Luke 7.11–17 as an *Imitatio* of 1 Kings 17.17–24." *NTS* 32 (1986): 247–67.

–. "The Departure for Jerusalem (Luke 9:51–56) as a Rhetorical Imitation of Elijah's Departure for the Jordan (2 Kgs 1, 1–2, 6)." *Bib* 70 (1989): 96–109.

–. *The Crucial Bridge: The Elijah-Elisha Narrative as an Interpretive Synthesis of Genesis-Kings and a Literary Model for the Gospels.* Collegeville, MN: Liturgical Press, 2000.

Brown, Colin. "What Was John the Baptist Doing?" *BBR* (1997): 37–49.

Brown, Raymond E. "Three Quotations from John the Baptist in the Gospel of John." *CBQ* (1960): 292–98.

Brownlee, W. H. "John the Baptist in the New Light of Ancient Scrolls." In: *The Scrolls and the New Testament.* Krister Stendahl, ed. New York: Harper, 1957. 33–53.

Bultmann, Rudolf K. *Jesus and the Word.* L. Smith and E. H. Lantero, trans. New York, Charles Scribner's Sons, 1934.

–. *Theology of the New Testament* (trans. K. Grobel, 2 vols. [New York: Charles Scribner's Sons, 1951–55.

–. *The History of the Synoptic Tradition.* Oxford: Blackwell, ²1968 (²1931).

–. *The Gospel of John.* G. R. Beasley-Murray, R. W. N. Hoare, and J. K. Riches. trans. Philadelphia: Westminster, 1971. German edition: *Das Evangelium des Johannes.* Göttingen: Vandenhoeck & Ruprecht, 1978 (1941).

–. "What the Saying Source Reveals about the Early Church." In: J. S. Kloppenborg, ed. *The Shape of Q.* 23–34. Originally published as "Was lässt die Spruchquelle über die Urgemeinde erkennen?" *Oldenburgische Kirchenblatt* 19 (1913) 35–37, 41–44.

Burkes, Shannon. "Wisdom and Apocalypticism in the Wisdom of Solomon." *HTR* 95 (2002): 21–44.

Burkill, T. A. "St. Mark's Philosophy of History." *NTS* (1956–57): 142–48.

Burkitt, F. C. "Who Spoke the Magnificat?" *JTS* (1905–6): 220–7.

Cancik, Hubert, ed. *Markus-Philologie. Historische, literargeschichtliche und stilistische Untersuchungen zum zweiten Evangelium.* WUNT 33. Tübingen: Mohr Siebeck, 1984.

Caragounis, Chrys C. *The Son of Man.* WUNT 2/38. Tübingen: Mohr Siebeck, 1986.

Carlston, Charles Edwin "Wisdom and Eschatology." In: *Logia: Les Paroles de Jésus – The Sayings of Jesus. Memorial Joseph Coppens*. Joël Delobel, ed. Leuven: University Press, 1982. 111–12.

–. "Transfiguration and Resurrection." *JBL* 80 (1961): 233–40.

Carlston, Charles E. and Dennis Norlin. "Once More – Statistics and Q." *HTR* 64 (1971): 59–78.

Casey, Maurice. *An Aramaic Approach to Q: Sources for the Gospels of Matthew and Luke*. SNTSMS 122. Cambridge: Cambridge University, 2002.

–. "The Use of the Term 'Son of Man' in the Similitudes of Enoch." *JSJ* 7 (1976): 11–29.

–. *Son of Man: The Interpretation and Influence of Daniel 7*. London: SPCK, 1979. 224–40.

Catchpole, David R. *The Quest for Q*. Edinburgh: T. & T. Clark, 1993.

–. "The Beginning of Q: A Proposal." *NTS* 38 (1992): 205–21.

Chamblin, Knox. "Gospel and Judgement in the Preaching of John the Baptist." *TynBul* 13 (1963): 7–15.

–. "John the Baptist and the Kingdom of God." *TynBul* 15 (1964): 10–16.

Charlesworth, James H. "John the Baptizer and Qumran Barriers in Light of the *Rule of the Community*." In: *The Provo International Conference on the Dead Sea Scrolls*. STDJ 30. D. W. Parry and E. Ulrich, eds. Leiden: Brill, 1999. 353–75.

Chilton, Bruce. "Transfiguration." Art. *ABD*, 6.641.

–. "The Transfiguration: Dominical Assurance and Apostolic Vision." *NTS* 27 (1980): 115–24.

Chilton, Bruce, ed. *The Kingdom of God*. Philadelphia: Fortress, 1984.

Cleary, Michael. "The Baptist of History and Kerygma." *ITQ* 54 (1988): 211–27.

Cole, R. Alan. *The Gospel according to Mark: An Introduction and Commentary*. TNTC 2. Grand Rapids: Eerdmans, [2]1989 (1961).

Collins, John J. *Seers, Sibyls and Sages in Hellenistic-Roman Judaism*. Boston/Leiden: Brill, 2001 (1997).

–. *Apocalypticism in the Dead Sea Scrolls*. New York: Routledge, 1997.

–. *The Scepter and the Star: The Messiahs of the Dead Sea Scrolls and Other Ancient Literature*. ABRL. New York: Doubleday, 1995.

–. *Daniel*. Minneapolis: Fortress, 1993.

–. "Wisdom, Apocalypticism, and Compatibility." In: *In Search of Wisdom: Essays in Memory of John G. Gammie*. Leo G. Perdue, Bernard B. Scott and William J. Wiseman, eds. Louisville: Westminster John Knox, 1993.

–. "The Kingdom of God in the Apocrypha and Pseudepigrapha." In: *The Kingdom of God in 20th-Century Interpretation*. W. Willis, ed. Peabody, MA: Hendrickson, 1987. 81–95.

–. "Cosmos and Salvation: Jewish Wisdom and Apocalyptic in the Hellenistic Age." *History of Religions* 17 (1977): 121–42.

Colpe, Carsten. "υἱὸς τοῦ ἀνθρώπου." Art. *TDNT*, 8.400–77.

–. "Der Begriff 'Menschensohn' und die Methode der Erforschung messianischer Prototypen." *Kairos* 11 (1969): 241–63; 12 (1970): 81–112; 13 (1971): 1–17; 14 (1972): 241–57.

Componovo, Odo. *Königtum, Königsherrschaft und Reich Gottes in den frühjüdischen Schriften*. OBO 58. Göttingen: Vandenhoeck & Ruprecht, 1984.

Conzelmann, Hans. *Die Mitte der Zeit*. Tübingen: Mohr/Siebeck, ²1957 (1953). ET: *The Theology of St. Luke*. New York: Harper & Row, 1960.

–. "Luke's Place in the Development of Early Christianity." In: *Studies in Luke-Acts*. Leander E. Keck and J. Louis Martyn, eds. London: SPCK, 1968. 298–316.

–. *History of Primitive Christianity*. John E. Steely, trans. Nashville: Abingdon Press, 1973. German: *Geschichte des Urchristentums*. Göttingen: Vandenhoeck & Ruprecht, 1969.

–. "Wisdom in the NT." In: *Supplement* to *The Interpreter's Dictionary of the Bible*. Nashville: Abingdon, 1976. 956–60.

Coppens, J. *La relève apocalyptique du messianisme royal: III. Le Fils de l'homme néotestamentaire*. BETL 55. Leuven: Peeters, 1981.

Cranfield, C. E. B. *The Gospel according to St. Mark*. CGTC. Cambridge: Cambridge University, 1959.

Crossan, J. D. *In Fragments: The Aphorisms of Jesus*. San Francisco: Harper and Row, 1983.

Cullman, Oscar. *The Christology of the New Testament*. London: SCM, 1959.

–. "Ὁ ὀπίσω μου ἐρχόμενος." In: *The Early Church*: *Studies in Early Christian History and Theology*. A. J. B. Higgins. ed. Philadelphia, Westminister, 1956. 177–82.

–. *Christus und die Zeit: Die urchristliche Zeit- und Geschichtsauffassung*. Zollikon-Zürich: Evangelischer, 1946; ET: *Christ and Time: The Primitive Christian Conception of Time and History* Philadelphia: Westminster, 1950.

Dabeck, P. "Siehe, es erschienen Moses und Elias." *Biblica* (1942): 175–89.

Dahl, Nils Alstrup. *Das Volk Gottes: Eine Untersuchung zum Kirchenbewusstsein des Urchristentums*. Oslo: J. Dybwad, 1941 (1963).

Dalman, G. *The Words of Jesus Considered in the Light of Post-Biblical Jewish Writings and the Aramaic Language*. D. M. Kay, trans. Edinburgh: T. & T. Clark, 1902.

Daniélou, Jean. *The Work of John the Baptist*. Baltimore: Helicon, 1966.

Danker, Frederick W. *Jesus and the New Age: A Commentary on St. Luke's Gospel*. Rev. ed. Philadelphia: Fortress, 1988.

–. "Luke 16, 16 – An Opposition Logion." *JBL* (1958): 231–43.

Daube, David. *NT and Rabbinic Judaism*. New York: Arno, 1973 (1956).

–. "Typology in Josephus." *JJS* 31 (1980): 18–36.

Dautzenberg, Gerhard. *Studien zur Theologie der Jesustradition*. Stuttgarter Biblische Aufsatzbände 19. Stuttgart: Verlag Katholisches Bibelwerk, 1995.

Davies, W.D. *The Setting of the Sermon on the Mount*. Cambridge: Cambridge University, 1966.

Davies, W. D. and Dale C. Allison, Jr. *A Critical and Exegetical Commentary on the Gospel according to Saint Matthew*. ICC. Edinburgh: T. & T. Clark, 1988.

Deane, Anthony C. "The Ministry of John the Baptist." *The Expositor* 13 (1917): 420–31.

Devisch, Michel. "La relation entre l'évangile de Marc et le document Q." In: *L'évangile selon Marc. Tradition et redaction*. M. Sabbe, ed. BETL 34. Leuven: Gembloux, 1974. 59–91.

Dibelius, Franz. "Zwei Worte Jesu." *ZNW* 11 (1910): 190–92.

Dibelius, Martin. *Die Formgeschichte des Evangeliums*. Tübingen: Mohr (Siebeck) ²1933 (1919). ET: *From Tradition to Gospel*. SL 124. B. L. Woolf, trans. New York: Scribner, 1965.

–. *Die urchristliche Überlieferung von Johannes dem Täufer.* FRLANT 15. Göttingen: Vandenhoeck & Ruprecht, 1911.

–. "Style Criticism of the Book of Acts." In: *Studies in the Acts of the Apostles.* Heinrich Greeven, ed. Mary Ling, trans. London: SCM, ¹1956. Mifflintown, PA: Sigler, 1999. German: *Aufsätze zur Apostelgeschichte.* Göttingen: Vandenhoeck & Ruprecht, 1951.

Dodd, Charles. H. *The Parables of the Kingdom.* Rev. ed. New York: Charles Scribner's Sons, 1961.

–. "The Appearances of the Risen Christ: An Essay in Form-Criticism of the Gospels." In: *Studies in the Gospels.* G. H. Boobyer and R. H. Stein, eds. Oxford: Blackwell, 1955. 9–35.

Donahue, John R. "Recent Studies on the Origin of 'Son of Man' in the Gospels." In: *A Wise and Discerning Heart: Studies Presented to Joseph A. Fizmyer In Celebration of His Sixty-Fifth Birthday. CBQ* 48 (1986): 484–98.

Donahue, John R. and Daniel J. Harrington. *The Gospel of Mark.* SP 2. Collegeville, MN: Liturgical Press, 2002.

Donfried, K. "The Kingdom of God in Paul." In: *The Kingdom of God in 20ᵗʰ-Century Interpretation.* W. Willis, ed. Peabody, MA: Hendrickson, 1987. 175–90.

Dubois, J.-D. "La figure d'Elie dans la perspective lucanienne." *RHPR* 53 (1973): 155–76.

Duling, Dennis. "Kingdom of God, Kingdom of Heaven." Art. *ABD* 4.49–69.

–. "Norman Perrin and the Kingdom of God: Review and Response." *JR* 64 (1984): 468–83.

Dunn, James D. G. "John the Baptist's Use of Scripture." In: *The Gospels and the Scriptures of Israel.* C. A. Evans and W. R. Stegner, eds. JSNTSup 104. Sheffield: Sheffield Academic, 1994. 42–54.

Ebner, Martin. *Jesus – Ein Weisheitslehrer? Synoptische Weisheitslogien im Traditionsprozess* HBS 15. Freiburg: Herder, 1998.

Edwards, James R. *The Gospel according to Mark.* Pillar New Testament Commentary. Leicester; Apollos/Grand Rapids: Eerdmans, 2002.

Edwards, Richard A. *The Sign of Jonah in the Theology of the Evangelists and Q.* SBT 2/18. London: SCM, 1971.

–. "The Eschatological Correlative as *Gattung* in the New Testament." *ZNW* 60 (1969): 9–20.

Eisler, Robert. *The Messiah Jesus and John the Baptist according to Flavius Josephus' Recently Rediscovered 'Capture of Jerusalem' and Other Jewish and Christian Sources.* New York: L. MacVeagh, 1931 (1929–30).

Eliade, M. *The Myth of the Eternal Return or, Cosmos and History.* Willard R. Trask, trans. Princeton: Princeton University Press, repr. 1991. Orig. publ. as *Le Mythe de l'éternel retour: archétypes et repetition.* Paris: Librairie Gallimard, 1949. 12–17.

Elliott, John K. Review of Joan Taylor. *The Immerser: John the Baptist within Second Temple Judaism.* Grand Rapids: Eerdmans, 1997 in *NovT* (1999): 198–99.

–. "Did the Lord's Prayer Originate with John the Baptist?" *ThZ* 29 (1973): 215.

Eliot, T. S. *The Four Quartets.* New York: Harcourt, Brace and Company, 1943.

Ellis, E. Earle. *The Gospel of Luke.* Rev. ed. NCB. London: Oliphants, 1974.

Enslin, Morton S. "John and Jesus." *ZNW* 66 (1975): 1–18.

–. "The Artistry of Mark." *JBL* (1947): 385–99.

Ernst, Josef. "Gastmahlgespräche: Lk 14, 1–24." In: *Die Kirche des Anfangs.* FS Heinz Schürmann. Leipzig: St. Benno, 1977. 57–78.

–. *Johannes der Täufer: Interpretation, Geschichte, Wirkungsgeschichte.* BZNW 53; Berlin: de Gruyter, 1989.

Evans, Craig F. *Saint Luke.* TPINTC. London: SCM/Philadelphia: TPI, 1990.

–. "The Central Section of St. Luke's Gospel." In: *Studies in the Gospels: Essays in Memory of R. H. Lightfoot.* D. E. Nineham, ed. Oxford: Blackwell, 1955. 37–53.

Farmer, W. R. "John the Baptist." *Interpreter's Dictionary of the Bible* 2. New York: Abingdon, 1962. 956.

Faure, A. "Die alttestamentliche Zitate im 4. Evangelium u.d. Quellenscheidungshypothese." *ZNW* (1922): 99–121.

Faierstein, Morris M. "Why do the Scribes Say that Elijah Must Come First?" *JBL* (1981): 75–86.

Feldman, Louis H. *Josephus' Interpretation of the Bible.* Berkeley: University of California, 1998.

–. *Studies in Josephus' Rewritten Bible.* Leiden: Brill, 1998.

–. "Josephus." Art. *ABD*, 3.981–98.

Feldman, Louis H. and Gohei Hata. *Josephus, Judaism and Christianity.* Detroit, Wayne State University, 1987.

Ferguson, E. "The Kingdom of God in Early Patristic Literature." In: *The Kingdom of God in 20th-Century Interpretation.* W. Willis, ed. Peabody, MA: Hendrickson, 1987. 191–208.

Ferris, S. *The Hymns of Luke's Infancy Narratives: Their Origin, Meaning and Significance* Sheffield: JSOT Press, 1985.

Finkelstein, Louis. "Introductory Study to Pirke Aboth." *JBL* 57 (1938): 13–50; repr. in *Pharisaism in the Making.* New York: KTAV, 1972. 121–58.

Fishbane, Michael. *Biblical Interpretation in Ancient Israel.* Oxford: Clarendon, 1985.

Fitzmyer, Joseph A. *The Gospel according to Luke (X – XXIV).* AB 28A. Garden City: Doubleday, 1985.

–. *The Gospel according to Luke (I – IX).* AB 28. Garden City: Doubleday, 1981.

–. "The New Testament Title 'Son of Man' Philologically Considered." In: *A Wandering Aramean: Collected Aramaic Essays.* SBLMS 25; Missoula: Scholars, 1979. 143–60.

–. "Another View of the 'Son of Man' Debate." *JSNT* 4 (1979): 58–68.

Fleddermann, Harry. *Mark and Q. A Study of the Overlap Texts.* BETL 122. Leuven: Peeters, 1995.

–. "The End of Q." In: *SBL 1990 Seminar Papers.* David J. Lull, ed. Atlanta: Scholars, 1990. 1–10.

–. "John and the Coming One (Matt. 3:11–12//Luke 3:16–17)." In: *SBL 1984 Seminar Papers.* Kent Harold Richards, ed. Chico: Scholars, 1984. 377–84.

Foakes-Jackson, F. J., and K. Lake, ed. *The Beginnings of Christianity.* 5 vols. London: Macmillan, 1920–33. Grand Rapids: Baker Book House, 1979.

Fortna, Robert. *The Gospel of Signs: A Reconstruction of the Narrative Source Underlying the Fourth Gospel.* SNTSMS 11. London: Cambridge U.P., 1970.

France, R. T. *The Gospel of Mark: A Commentary on the Greek Text.* NIGTC. Carlisle, U.K.: Paternoster/Grand Rapids: Eerdmans, 2002.

–. *The Gospel of Mark.* Doubleday Bible Commentary. New York: Doubleday 1998.

–. *The Gospel according to Matthew: An Introduction and Commentary.* Grand Rapids: Eerdmans, 1986.

Frey, Jörg. "Die Bedeutung der Qumranfunde für das Verständnis des Neuen Testaments." In: *Qumran: Die Schriftrollen vom Toten Meer*. M. Fieger et al, eds. NTOA 47. Freiburg: Freiburg Schweiz/Göttingen: Vandenhoeck & Ruprecht, 2001. 129–208.

Fuller, Reginald Horace. *Mission and Achievement of Jesus: An Examination of the Presuppositions of New Testament Theology*. Chicago: A. R. Allenson, 1954.

Fuchs, Ernst. *Zur Frage nach dem historischen Jesus*. Tübingen: J. C. B. Mohr, 1960.

Gammie, J. G. "Spatial and Ethical Dualism in Jewish Wisdom and Apocalyptic Literature." *JBL* 93 (1974): 356–85.

Georgi, Dieter. *The Opponents of Paul in Second Corinthians*. Philadelphia: Fortress, 1986.

Gerber, W. "Die Metamorphose Jesu, Mark 9, 2 f. par." *TZ* (1967): 385–95.

Geyser, A. S. "The Youth of John the Baptist: A Deduction from the Break in the Parallel Account of the Lucan Infancy Story." *NovT* 1 (1956): 70–75.

Gibson, Shimon. *The Cave of John the Baptist: The Stunning Archaelogical Discovery that Has Redefined Christian History*. New York: Doubleday, 2004.

Gnilka, Joachim. *Jesus von Nazaret: Botschaft und Geschichte*. HTKNT. Freiburg: Herder, 1993.

–. *Das Evangelium nach Markus*. EKKNT 2/1–2. Zurich: Benziger/Neukirchen-Vluyn: Neukirchener, [3]1989.

Goetz, K. G. *Petrüs als Grunder und Oberhaupt der Kirche und Schauer von Gesichten nach den altchristlichen Berichten und Legenden: eine exegetisch-geschichtlich Untersuchung*. Leipzig: Hinrichs, 1927.

Goff, Matthew J. "Reading Wisdom at Qumran: 4QInstruction and the Hodayot." *DSD*: 11/3 (2004) 263–88.

–. "The Mystery of Creation in QInstruction." *DSD* 10/2 (2003): 163–86.

–. *The Worldly and Heavenly Wisdom of 4Q Instruction: Studies on the Texts of the Desert of Judah*. Leiden: Brill, 2003.

Goguel, M. *Jesus and the Origins of Christianity*. New York: Harper Torchbooks, 1960.

–. *The Life of Jesus*. Olive Wyon, trans. New York: Macmillan, 1944.

–. *Au seuil de l'évangile: Jean-Baptiste*. Paris: Payot, 1928.

Goodenough, E. R. *Jewish Symbols in the Greco-Roman Period*. New York: Pantheon, 1953–68.

–. "The Political Philosophy of Hellenistic Kingship." *Yale Classical Series* (1928) 1:55–102.

Gould, Ezra P. *Critical and Exegetical Commentary on the Gospel according to St. Mark*. ICC. Edinburgh: T. & T. Clark/New York: Scribner's, 1983 (1896).

Gray, A. "The Parable of the Wicked Husbandmen." *HibJ* 19 (1920/21): 42–52.

Grobel, Kendrick. "He That Cometh after Me." *JBL* (1941): 397–401.

Grundmann, Walter. "Weisheit im Horizont des Reiches Gottes. Eine Studie zur Verkündigung Jesu nach der Spruchüberlieferung Q." In: *Die Kirche des Anfangs*. FS Heinz Schürmann. Leipzig: St. Benno, 1977. 175–200.

Guelich, Robert A. *Mark 1–8:26*. WBC 34A. Dallas: Word, 1989.

Gundry, Robert H. *Matthew: A Commentary on His Handbook for a Mixed Church under Persecution*. Grand Rapids: Eerdmans, [2]1994.

–. *Mark: A Commentary on His Apology for the Cross*. Grand Rapids: Eerdmans, 1993.

Gunkel, H. *Elias, Jahve und Baal*. Tübingen: Mohr, 1906.

Güting, Eberhard W. "The Relevance of Literary Criticism for the Text of the New Testament: A Study of Mark's Traditions on John the Baptist." In: *Studies in the Early Text of the Gospels and Acts: The Papers of the First Birmingham Colloquium on the Textual Criticism of the New Testament*. D. G. K. Taylor, ed. Text-critical Studies 1. Atlanta: Society of Biblical Literature, 1999. 142–67.

Hagner, Donald A. *Matthew 1–13*. WBC. Dallas: Word, 1993.

Hare, Douglas R. A. *Mark*. Westminster Bible Companion. Louisville: Westminster John Knox, 1996.

–. *The Son of Man Tradition*. Minneapolis: Fortress, 1990. 181–82

–. *Matthew*. Interpretation. Louisville, John Knox, 1993.

Hamm, Dennis. "Zacchaeus Revisited Once More: A Story of Vindication or Conversion?" *Bib* 72 (1991): 249–52.

Harnack, Adolf von. "Die Verklärungsgeschichte Jesu." *Sitzungsberichte der preussischen Akademie der Wissenschaften* (1922): 62–80.

–. *Sayings of Jesus: The Second Source of St. Matthew and St. Luke*. J. R. Wilkinson, trans. London: Williams & Norgate. New York: G. P. Putnam's Sons, 1908.

Harrington, Daniel J. *The Gospel of Matthew*. SP 1. Collegeville, MN: Liturgical Press, 1991.

Hartmann, Michael. *Der Tod Johannes des Taüfers: Eine Exegetische und rezeptionsgeschichtliche Studie auf dem Hintergrund narrativer, intertextueller und kulturanthropologischer Zugänge*. SBB 45. Stuttgart: Katholisches Bibelwerk, 2001.

Heinemann, I. "Josephus' Method in the Presentation of Jewish Antiquities." *Zion* 5 (1939–40): 180–203.

Hentschel, Georg. *Die Elijaerzählungen: Zum Verhältnis von historischem Geschehen und geschichtlicher Erfahrung*. ETS 33. Leipzig: St. Benno, 1977.

Haufe, G. "Reich Gottes bei Paulus und in der Jesus Tradition." *NTS* 31 (1985): 467–72.

Hiers, R. H. *The Kingdom of God in the Synoptic Tradition*. Gainesville, FL: University of Florida, 1970.

Higgins, A. J. B. "The Son of Man *Forschung* Since 'The Teaching of Jesus.'" In: *New Testament Essays: Studies in Memory of Thomas Walter Manson*. A. J. B. Higgins, ed. Manchester: Manchester University, 1959. 119–35.

–. *Jesus and the Son of Man*. London: Lutterworth, 1964.

– "Is the Son of Man Problem Insoluble?" In: *Neotestamentica et Semitica: Studies in Honour of Matthew Black*. E. E. Ellis and M. Wilcox, eds. Edinburgh: T. & T. Clark, 1969. 70–87.

–. *The Son of Man in the Teaching of Jesus*. SNTSMS. Cambridge: Cambridge University, 1980.

Hill, A. *Malachi*. AB 25D. New York: Doubleday, 1998.

Hill, David. *The Gospel of Matthew*. NCB. London: Oliphants, 1972 = Grand Rapids: Eerdmans, 1981.

Hoffmann, Paul. *Tradition und Situation: Studien zur Jesusüberlieferung in der Logienquelle und den synoptischen Evangelien*. Münster: Aschendorff, 1995.

–. "QR und der Menschensohn. Eine vorläufige Skizze." In: Frans Van Segbroeck, C. M. Tuckett, G. Van Belle, and J. Verheyden, eds. *The Four Gospels 1992:* FS Frans Neirynck. 3 vols. BETL 100. Louvain: Peeters; Louvain University, 1992. 421–56; ET, "The Redaction of Q and the Son of Man: A Preliminary Sketch." In: R. A. Piper, ed. *The Gospel Behind the Gospels: Current Studies on Q*. NovTSupp 75. Leiden: Brill, 1994. 159–98.

–. *Studien zur Theologie der Logienquelle*. NTAbh n.s., 8. Münster: Aschendorff, ³1980 (1972).

Hollenbach, Paul W. "John the Baptist." Art. *ABD*, 3.887–99.

–. "Social Aspects of John the Baptist's Preaching Mission in the Context of Palestinian Judaism." *ANRW*, 2.19.1, 850–75.

–. "The Conversion of Jesus: From Jesus the Baptizer to Jesus the Healer." *ANRW* 2.25.1, 196–219.

Holloway, Paul A. "Left Behind: Jesus' Consolation of His Disciples in John 13,31–17,26." *ZNW* 96 (2005): 1–34.

Hooker, Morna D. *The Gospel according to Saint Mark*. BNTC. London: A & C Black/ Peabody, MA: Hendrickson, 1991.

–. "Is the Son of Man Problem Really Insoluble?" In: *Text and Interpretation: Studies in the New Testament Presented to Matthew Black*. E. Best and R. McL. Wilson, eds. Cambridge: Cambridge University, 1979. 155–68.

Honoré, A. M. "A Statistical Study of the Synoptic Problem." *NovT* 10 (1968): 95–147.

Horsley, Richard A. *Whoever Hears You Hears Me: Prophets, Performance, and Tradition in Q*. Harrisburg, PA: Trinity Press International, 1999.

–. "'Like One of the Prophets of Old'": Two Types of Popular Prophets at the Time of Jesus." *CBQ* (1985) 435–63.

Houtman, C. "Elijah." Art. *DDD*, 282–85.

Hughes, John H. "John the Baptist: The Forerunner of God Himself." *NovT* 14 (1972): 191–218.

Hui, Archie W. D. "John the Baptist and Spirit-Baptism." *EvQ* 71/2 (1999): 99–115.

Hultgren, Arland J. *The Rise of Normative Christianity*. Minneapolis: Fortress, 1994.

Hurtado, Larry W. *Mark*. New International Biblical Commentary. Peabody, MA: Hendrickson, 1989.

–. *Mark*. Good News Commentary. San Francisco: Harper & Row, 1983.

Innitzer, Theodor. *Johannes der Täufer. Nach der Heiligen Schrift und der Tradition dargestellt ... Preisgekrönte Schrift*. Wien: Mayer & Co., 1908.

Jackson-McCabe, Matt A. *Logos and Law in the Letter of James: The Law of Nature, The Law of Moses, and The Law of Freedom*. NovTSup 100. Leiden: Brill, 2001.

Jacobson, Arland D. "Jesus against the Family: The Dissolution of Family Ties in the Gospel Tradition." In: *From Quest to Q: Festschrift James M. Robinson*. Jon Ma. Asgeirsson, Kristin De Troyer, Marvin W. Meyer, eds. Leuven: Leuven University Press, 2000. 189–218.

–. "Divided Families and Christian Origins." In: *The Gospel Behind the Gospels. Current Studies on Q*. R. A. Piper, ed. NTSuppl. 85. Leiden: Brill, 1995. 361–63.

–. *The First Gospel. An Introduction to Q*. Sonoma: Polebridge, 1992.

–. "Apocalyptic and the Synoptic Sayings Source Q." In: *The Four Gospels 1992*. FS Frans Neirynck. Frans Van Segbroeck et al., eds. 403–19.

–. "The Literary Unity of Q." *JBL* 101 (1982): 365–89. Reprinted in: John S. Kloppenborg, *The Shape of Q*. 98–115.

Jeremias, Joachim. *Die Sprache des Lukasevangeliums*. Göttingen: Vandenhoeck & Ruprecht, 1980.

–. *New Testament Theology: The Proclamation of Jesus*. London: SCM, 1971.

–. "Die älteste Schicht der Menschensohn-Logien." *ZNW* 58 (1967): 159–72.

–. "Ἠλ(ε)ίας." Art. *TDNT*, 2.928–41.

–. "Μωϋσῆς." Art. *TDNT*, 4.848–73.

Johnson, Luke Timothy. *The Real Jesus: The Misguided Quest for the Historical Jesus and the Truth of the Traditional Gospels*. San Francisco: HarperSanFrancisco, 1996.

Johnson, G. "'Kingdom of God'" Sayings in Paul's Letters." In: *From Jesus to Paul: Studies in Honour of Francis Wright Beare*. Peter Richardson and John C. Hurd, eds. Waterloo, Ontario: Wilfrid Laurier University, 1984. 143–56.

Johnson, Sherman E. *A Commentary on the Gospel according to St. Mark*. HNTC. New York: Harper, 1960 = Peabody, MA: Hendrickson, 1990.

Johnson, Jr., S. Lewis. "The Message of John the Baptist." *BSac* 113 (1956): 30–6.

Jones, James L. "References to John the Baptist in the Gospel according to St. Matthew." *AThR* 41 (1959): 298–302.

Jonge, M. de. "The Word 'Anointed' in the Time of Jesus." *NovT* (1966): 132–48.

Juel, Donald H. *The Gospel of Mark*. Interpreting Biblical Texts. Nashville: Abingdon, 1999.

Käsemann E. "The Disciples of John the Baptist in Ephesus." In: idem, *Essays on New Testament Themes*. Philadephia: Fortress, 1982. 136–48.

Kee, Howard Clark. *Jesus in History: An Approach to the Study of the Gospels*. New York: Harcourt Brace Jovanovich, ²1977. 84–117.

Keener, Craig S. *A Commentary on the Gospel of Matthew*. Grand Rapids: Eerdmans, 1999.

Kelber, W. *The Oral and the Written Gospel: The Hermeneutics of Speaking and Writing in the Synoptic Tradition, Mark, Paul, and Q*. Philadelphia: Fortress, 1983.

Kelhoffer, James A. *The Diet of John the Baptist: "Locusts and Wild Honey" in Synoptic and Patristic Tradition*. WUNT 176. Tübingen: Mohr Siebeck, 2005.

–. "The Apostle Paul and Justin Martyr on the Miraculous: A Comparison of Appeals to Authority." *GRBS* 42 (2001): 163–84.

–. *Miracle and Mission: The Authentication of Missionaries and Their Message in the Longer Ending of Mark*. WUNT II/112. Tübingen: Mohr Siebeck, 2000.

Kellermann, Ulrich. "Zu den Elia-Motiven in den Himmelfahrtsgeschichten des Lukas." In: *Altes Testament Forschung und Wirklung*. FS Henning Graf Reventlow. Peter Mommer and Winfried Thiel, eds. Frankfurt: Peter Lang, 1994. 123–37.

Kierkegaard, Søren. *Either/Or*. Howard V. Hong and Edna H. Hong, ed. and trans. Princeton, N.J.: Princeton University, repr. 1987 (1843).

Kilpatrick, G. D. "The Disappearance of Q." *JTS* 42 (1941): 182–84.

Kirk, Alan. *The Composition of the Sayings Source. Genre, Synchrony, Wisdom Redaction in Q*. Leiden: Brill, 1998.

–. "Some Compositional Conventions of Hellenistic Wisdom Texts and the Juxtaposition of 4:1–13; 6:20b–49; and 7:1–10 in Q." *JBL* (1997): 235–57.

Kirk, Albert and Robert E. Obach. *A Commentary on the Gospel of Matthew*. New York: Paulist, 1978.

Klauck, Hans-Josef. *The Religious Context of Early Christianity*. Minneapolis: Fortress, 2003.

–. *Apocryphal Gospels: An Introduction*. Edinburgh: T. & T. Clark, 2003 (2002).

–. *Vorspiel im Himmel? Erzähltechnik und Theologie im Markusprolog*. BTS 32. Neukirchen-Vluyn: Neukirchener, 1997.

–. "Die Sakramente und der historische Jesus." In: idem, *Gemeinde, Amt, Sakrament: Neutestamentliche Perspektiven*. Würzberg: Echter, 1989. 274–76.

–. „Die Frage der Sündenvergebung in der Perikope von der Heilung des Gelähmten (Mk 2,1–12 parr)." In: idem, *Gemeinde, Amt, Sakrament: Neutestamentliche Perspektiven*. Würzberg: Echter, 1989. 286–312.

–. *Allegorie und Allegorese in synoptischen Gleichnistexten*. Münster: Aschendorff, 1978.

Klein, G. "'Reich Gottes' als biblischer Zentralbegriff." *EvT* 30 (1970): 642–70.

Kloppenborg (Verbin), John S. *Excavating Q: The History and Setting of the Sayings Gospel* Minneapolis: Fortress; and Edinburgh: T. & T. Clark, 2000.

–. ed. *The Shape of Q: Signal Essays on the Sayings Gospel*. Minneapolis: Fortress, 1994.

–. *Q Parallels: Synopsis, Critical Notes, and Concordance*. Foundations and Facets: New Testament. Sonoma, CA: Polebridge, 1988.

–. *The Formation of Q: Trajectories in Ancient Wisdom Collections*. Philadelphia: Fortress, 1987.

–. "Symbolic Eschatology and the Apocalypticism of Q," *HTR* 80/3 (1987): 287–306.

Klostermann, August. *Das Markusevangelium nach seinem Quellenwerthe für die evangelische Geschichte*. Göttingen: Vandenhoeck & Ruprecht, 1867.

Klostermann, Erich. *Das Markusevangelium*. HNT 3. Tübingen: Mohr (Siebeck), [5]1971 (1919).

Knibb, M. A. "Apocalyptic and Wisdom in 4 Ezra." *Journal for the Study of Judaism in the Persian, Hellenistic and Roman Periods* 13 (1982): 56–74.

Knox, John. "The 'Prophet' in the New Testament Christology." In: *Lux in Lumine: Essays to Honor W. Norman Pittenger*. R. A. Norris, ed. New York: Seabury, 1966. 23–24.

–. *On the Meaning of Christ*. New York: C. Scribner's Sons, 1947.

Koch, K. "Offenbaren wird sich das Reich Gottes." *NTS* 25 (1978): 158–65.

Koester, Helmut. "The Synoptic Sayings Source and the Gospel of Thomas." In: John S. Kloppenborg, ed. *The Shape of Q*. 35–50.

–. *Ancient Christian Gospels: Their History and Development*. London/Philadelphia: SCM/Philadelphia: TPI, 1990.

–. *Introduction to the New Testament*. Vol. 2. "History and Literature of Early Christianity." New York/Berlin: de Gruyter, 1982.

–. "Apocryphal and Canonical Gospels." *HTR* 73 (1980): 105–30.

–. "GNOMAI DIAPHOROI: The Origin and Nature of Diversification in the History of Early Christianity." In: James M. Robinson and Helmut Koester. *Trajectories*. 114–57.

–. "One Jesus and Four Primitive Gospels." In: James M. Robinson and Helmut Koester. *Trajectories*. 158–204.

Koester, Helmut and James M. Robinson, *Trajectories through Early Christianity*. Philadelphia: Fortress, 1971.

Kraeling, Carl H. *John the Baptist*. New York: Scribner, 1951.

Krentz, Edgar. "None Greater among Those Born from Women: John the Baptist in the Gospel of Matthew." *CurTM* 10 (Dec. 1983): 333–38.

Kristen, Peter. *Familie, Kreuz und Leben. Nachfolge Jesu nach Q und Markusevangelium*. Marburg: Elwert, 1995.

Kümmel, Werner Georg. "Eschatological Expectation in the Proclamation of Jesus," in *The Kingdom of God*. Bruce Chilton, ed. Philadelphia: Fortress, 1984. 36–51.

–. *Einleitung in das Neue Testament*. 17.Aufl.; Heidelberg: Quelle & Meyer, 1973. ET: *Introduction to the New Testament*. Rev. ed. Howard C. Kee, ed. Nashville: Abingdon, 1975.

–. *Verheissung und Erfüllung: Untersuchungen zur eschatologischen Verkündigung Jesu*. ATANT 6. Basel, 1945; Zürich: Zwingli Verlag, [2]1953; [3]1956. ET: *Promise and Fulfill-*

ment: The Eschatological Message of Jesus. Dorothea M. Barton, trans. of ³1956. SBT 23. London: SCM, 1957.

Ladd, G. E. "The Kingdom of God – Reign or Realm?" *JBL* 81 (1962): 230–38.

Lagrange, M.-J. *Évangile selon Saint Marc*. ÉBib. Paris: Gabalda, ⁵1929 (1911). Reprinted, 1966.

Lake, Kirsopp and Henry Cadbury. *The Beginnings of Christianity*. Vol. 1: The Acts of the Apostles. Vol. 4: English Translation and Commentary; Vol. 5: Additional Notes to the Commentary. F. J. Foakes Jackson and Kirsopp Lake, eds. London: Macmillan, 1933; Grand Rapids: Baker Book House, 1979.

Lamarche, Paul. *Évangile de Marc: Commentaire*. ÉBib n.s. 33. Paris: Gabalda, 1996.

Lambrecht, Jan. "Q-Influence on Mark 8,34–9,1." In: *Logia. Les Paroles de Jésus. The Sayings of Jesus. Mémorial Joseph Coppens*. J. Delobel, T. Baarda, eds. Leuven: Peeters, 1982. 277–304.

–. "John the Baptist and Jesus in Mark 1.1–15: Markan Redaction of Q?" *NTS* 38 (1992): 357–84.

Lampe, G. W. H. "Some Notes on the Significance of *Basileia tou Theou, Basileia Christou* in the Greek Fathers." *JTS* 49 (1948): 58–73.

Lane, William L. *The Gospel of Mark*. NICNT. Grand Rapids: Eerdmans, 1974.

Lattke, M. "On the Jewish Background of the Synoptic Concept 'The Kingdom of God.'" In: *The Kingdom of God*. B. Chilton, ed. Philadelphia: Fortress, 1984. 72–91.

Laufen, Rudolf. "Doppelüberlieferungen." *ETL* 57 (1981): 181–83.

Laurentin, R. *Structure et théologie de Luc I – II*. Paris, Gabalda, 1957.

LaVerdiere, Eugene. *The Beginning of the Gospel: Introducing the Gospel according to Mark*. Collegeville, MN: Liturgical Press, 1999.

Leivestad, Ragnar. "Der apokalyptische Menschensohn: Ein theologisches Phantom." *ASTI* 6 (1968): 49–105.

Lichtenberger, H. "The Dead Sea Scrolls and John the Baptist: Reflections on Josephus' Account of John the Baptist." In: *The Dead Sea Scrolls: Forty Years of Research*. D. Dimant and U. Rappaport, eds. Leiden: Brill, 1992. 340–46.

–. "Reflections on the History of John the Baptist's Communities." *FolOr* 25 (1988): 45–49.

Lightfoot, R. H. *Locality and Doctrine in the Gospels*. New York: Harper, 1938.

–. *History and Interpretation in the Gospels*. London: Hodder & Stoughton, 1935.

Lindemann, Andreas, ed. *The Sayings Source Q and the Historical Jesus*. BETL 158; Leuven: Leuven University Press and Peeters, 2001.

Lindeskog, Gösta. "Johannes der Täufer: Einige Randbemerkungen zum heutigen Stand der Forschung." *ASTI* 12 (1983): 55–83.

Loane, Marcus L. *John the Baptist as Witness and Martyr*. London: Marshall, Morgan & Scott, 1968.

Lohfink, Gerhard. *Die Himmelfahrt Jesu: Untersuchungen zu den Himmelfahrts- und Erhöhungstexten bei Lukas*. SANT 26. Munich: Kösel, 1971.

Lohmeyer, E. *Das Evangelium des Markus*. Meyer I.2. Göttingen: Vandenhoeck & Ruprecht, ¹⁷1967.

–. "Die Verklärung Jesu nach dem Markus-Evangelium." *ZNW* (1922): 185–215.

–. *Das Urchristentum*. Vol. 1: *Johannes der Täufer*. Göttingen: Vandenhoeck & Ruprecht, 1932.

–. "Zur evangelischen Überlieferung von Johannes dem Täufer." *JBL* 51 (1932): 300–19.

Loisy, Alfred. *L'Évangile selon Marc*. Paris: Émile Nourry, 1912.

–. *The Birth of the Christian Religion*. London: G. Allen & Unwin, 1948.

Lowe, Malcolm. "From the Parable of the Vineyard to a Pre-Synoptic Source." *NTS* (1982): 257–63.

Lührmann, Dieter. *Die Redaktion der Logienquelle*. WMANT 33; Neukirchen-Vluyn: Neukirchener, 1969.

–. *Das Markusevanglium*. HNT 3. Tübingen: Mohr Siebeck, 1987.

–. "Q in the History of Early Christianity." In: J. S. Kloppenborg, ed. *The Shape of Q*. 59–73.

Lündstrom, G. *The Kingdom of God in the Teaching of Jesus*. J. Bulman, trans. Edinburgh: T. & T. Clark, 1963.

Lupieri, Edmondo F. "Johannes der Täufer," *RGG*[4], 514–17.

–. *The Mandaeans: The Last Gnostics*. Grand Rapids: Eerdmans, 2002 (1993).

–. "'The Law and the Prophets Were until John': John the Baptist between Jewish Halakhot and Christian History of Salvation." *Neotestamentica* 35 (2001): 49–56.

–. "John the Baptist in New Testament Traditions and History." *ANRW* 2/26/1 (1993) 430–61.

–. "John the Gnostic: The Figure of the Baptist in Origen and Heterodox Gnosticism." *StPatr* 19 (1989): 322–27.

–. *Giovanni Battista fra Storia e Leggenda*. Brescia: Paideia, 1988.

–. "John the Baptist: The First Monk. A Contribution to the History of the Figure of John the Baptist in the Early Monastic World." In: *Monasticism: A Historical Overview*. Word and Spirit 6. Still River, MA: St. Bede, 1984. 11–23.

Luz, Ulrich. *Matthew: A Commentary*. Hermeneia. Minneapolis: Augsburg Fortress, 1990–2001 (1985).

–. *Matthew 1–7*. Wilhelm C. Linss, trans. Minneapolis: Fortress, 1989. German Edition: *Das Evangelium nach Matthäus*. EKKNT. Zurich/Einsiedeln/Cologne: Benziger and Neukirchen-Vluyn: Neukirchener, 1985.

Macina, Robert. "Jean le Baptist était-il Élie?: Examen de la tradition néotestamentaire." *Proche Orient chrétien* (Jerusalem) 34 (1984): 209–32.

Mack, Burton. "The Kingdom Sayings in Mark." *Forum* 3 (1987): 1:3–47.

–. *The Lost Gospel: The Book of Q and Christian Origins*. San Francisco, CA: HarperSanFrancisco, 1993.

MacNeile, Alan H. *The Gospel according to St. Matthew*. London: Macmillan, 1915 = Grand Rapids: Baker, 1980.

MacNeill, H. L. "The Sitz im Leben of Lk 1.5–2.20." *JBL* (1946): 123–30.

Maddox, R. "The Quest for Valid Methods in 'Son of Man' Research." *Australian Biblical Review* 19 (1971): 35–51.

Mann, C. S. *Mark*. AB 27. Garden City, NY: Doubleday, 1986.

Manson, T. W. "John the Baptist." *BJRL* 36 (1953–54): 395–412.

–. *The Sayings of Jesus*. London: SCM, 1949.

–. *The Teaching of Jesus: Studies of Its Form and Content*. Cambridge University Press, [2]1943.

Marcus, Joel. *Mark 1–8: A New Translation with Introduction and Commentary*. AB 27. New York: Doubleday, 2000.

Marlow, R. "The Son of Man in Recent Journal Literature." *CBQ* 28 (1966): 20–30.

Marshall, I. Howard. *The Gospel of Luke*: *A Commentary on the Greek Text*. NIGTC. Grand Rapids: Eerdmans, 1978.

–. "The Son of Man in Contemporary Debate," *EvQ* 42 (1970) 67–87.

–. "The Synoptic Son of Man Sayings in Recent Discussion." *NTS* 12 (1966): 327–51.

Martin Hogan, Karina. "Theologies in Conflict in 4 Ezra: Wisdom Debate and Apocalyptic Solution." Ph.D. Dissertation, University of Chicago, 2002.

Martyn, J. Louis. "We Have Found Elijah." In: *Jews, Greeks and Christians: Religious Cultures in Late Antiquity. Essays in Honor of William David Davies*. Robert Hamerton-Kelly and Robin Scroggs, eds. Leiden: Brill, 1976. 181–219.

März, C. P. "'Feuer auf die Erde zu werfen, bin ich gekommen …' Zum Verständnis und zur Entstehung von Lk 12, 49." In: *A Cause de l'Evangile*. FS J. Dupont. Paris: Cerf, 1985. 479–511.

Marxsen, Willi. "John The Baptist." In: idem, *Mark the Evangelist: Studies on the Redaction History of the Gospel*. Nashville: Abingdon, 1969 (1956, ²1959). 30–53.

Mason, Steve. *Josephus and the New Testament*. Peabody, MA: Hendrickson, 1992.

–. *Flavius Josephus on the Pharisees: A Composition-Critical Study*. Leiden: Brill, 1991.

Massyngberde Ford, J. "Zealotism and the Lukan Infancy Narratives." *NovT* (1976): 280–92.

–. *Revelation: Introduction, Translation, Commentary*. AB 38. Garden City, NY: Doubleday, 1975.

McCown, C. C. "The Scene of John's Ministry." *JBL* (1940): 113–31.

McCurley, F. R. "And After Six Days" (Mark 9.2): A Semitic Literary Device." *JBL* (1974): 67–81.

Meadors, Edward P. *Jesus the Messianic Herald of Salvation*. WUNT 2/72. Tübingen: Mohr Siebeck, 1995.

Meier, John P. *A Marginal Jew: Rethinking the Historical Jesus. Volume Two: Mentor, Message, and Miracles*. New York: Doubleday, 1994: 19–223.

–. "John the Baptist in Josephus: Philology and Exegesis." *JBL* 111/2 (1992): 225–37.

–. "John the Baptist in Matthew's Gospel." *JBL* 99/3 (1980): 383–405.

Merklein, Helmut. *Jesu Botschaft von der Gottesherrschaft*. Stuttgart: Verlag Katholisches Bibelwerk, ²1984.

–. "Die Umkehrpredigt bei Johannes dem Täufer." *BZ* 25/1 (1981): 29–46.

Metzger, Bruce M. *The Early Version of the New Testament: Their Origin, Transmission, and Limitations*. Oxford: Clarendon, 1977.

Meyer, Eduard. *Ursprung und Anfänge des Christentums*. Stuttgart/Berlin: J. C. Cotta, ⁴,⁵1924.

Michaelis, W. "ὁράω." Art. *TDNT*, 10.315–67.

Michaels, J. Ramsey. "Paul and John the Baptist: An Odd Couple?" *TynBul* 42 (1991): 245–60.

Miller, Robert J. "Elijah, John, and Jesus in the Gospel of Luke." *NTS* 34 (1988): 611–22.

Mitchell, Margaret M. Review of A. Malherbe, *The Letters to the Thessalonians: A New Translation with Introduction and Commentary*. Anchor Bible 32B. New York: Doubleday, 2000. In: *RBL*, 09/2004.

–. *The Heavenly Trumpet: John Chrysostom and the Art of Pauline Interpretation*. HUT 40. Tübingen: Mohr Siebeck, 2000; Louisville: Westminster John Knox, 2002.

–. "Reading Rhetoric with Patristic Exegetes: John Chrysostom on Galatians." In: *Antiquity and Humanity: Essays on Ancient Religion and Philosophy Presented to Hans*

Dieter Betz on His 70ʰ Birthday. A. Y. Collins and M. M. Mitchell, eds. Tübingen: Mohr Siebeck, 2001. 333–55.

–. "The Archetypal Image: John Chrysostom's Portraits of Paul." *JR* 75 (1995): 15–43.

Molin, Georg. "Elijahu: Der Prophet und sein Weiterleben in den Hoffnungen des Judentums und der Christenheit." *Judaica* 8 (1952): 65–94.

Moloney, Francis J. *The Gospel of Mark: A Commentary*. Peabody, MA: Hendrickson, 2002.

Montefiore, C. G. *The Synoptic Gospels*. London: Macmillan, ²1927.

Morris, Leon. *The Gospel according to Matthew*. Grand Rapids: Eerdmans, 1992.

–. *Luke: An Introduction and Commentary*. Grand Rapids: Eerdmans, ²1988 (1974).

Mowinckel, S. *He That Cometh*. G. W. Anderson, trans. New York: Abingdon, 1954.

Muilenburg, J. "Form Criticism and Beyond." *JBL* (1969): 1–18.

Muddiman, John. "Fast, Fasting." *ABD* 2.773–76.

–. "Form Criticism and Theological Exegesis." In: *Encounter with the Text: Form and History in the Hebrew Bible*. Martin J. Buss, ed. Philadelphia: Fortress, 1979. 91–102.

Müller, Christoph Gregor. *Mehr als ein Prophet: Die Charakterzeichnung Johannes des Täufers im lukanischen Erzählwerk*. Herders biblische Studien 31. Freiburg: Herder, 2001.

Müller, Hans-Peter. "Mantische Weisheit und Apokalyptik." In: *Congress Volume: Uppsala, 1971*. VTS 22. Leiden: Brill, 1972.

–. "Die Verklärung Jesu: Eine motivgeschichtliche Studie." *ZNW* (1959): 56–64.

Müller, Ulrich. B. *Johannes der Täufer: Jüdischer Prophet und Wegbereiter Jesu*. Leipzig: Evangelische Verlagsanstalt, 2002.

Münch, Christian. *Die Gleichnisse Jesu im Matthäusevangelium: Eine Studie zu ihrer Form und Funktion*. WMANT 104. Neukirchen-Vluyn: Neukirchener, 2004.

Murphy, Catherine M. *John the Baptist: Prophet of Purity for a New Age*. Collegeville, MN: Liturgical Press, 2003.

Murphy, Frederick J. "Sapiential Elements in the Syriac Apocalypse of Baruch." *Jewish Quarterly Review* 76 (1986): 311–27.

Murphy-O'Connor, Jerome. "John the Baptist and Jesus: History and Hypothesis." *NTS* 36 (1990): 359–74.

Neirynck, Frans. Review of R. Laufen, *Die Doppelüberlieferungen der Logienquelle und des Markusevangeliums*. Bonner Biblische Beiträge 54. Königstein/Ts.-Bonn: Peter Hanstein, 1980. In: *ETL* (1981): 181–83.

–. "Q." *IDBSup* (1976): 715–16.

–. "Studies on Q since 1972." *ETL* 56 (1980): 409–13.

Neusner, Jacob. *Introduction to Rabbinic Literature*. New York: Doubleday, 1994.

–. "Types and Forms of Ancient Jewish Literature: Some Comparisons." *HR* 11 (1971–72): 354–90.

Nickelsburg, George W. E. *1 Enoch 1: A Commentary on the Book of 1 Enoch, Chapters 1–36, 81–108*. Hermeneia. Minneapolis: Fortress, 2001.

–. "Wisdom and Apocalypticism in Early Judaism: Some Points for Discussion." In: *SBLSP 1994*. Atlanta: Scholars, 1994. 715–32.

Nineham, Dennis E. *The Gospel of St. Mark*. Pelican Gospel Commentaries. New York: Seabury, 1968 (1963).

Nock, Arthur Darby. *Conversion. The Old and the New in Religion from Alexander the Great to Augustine of Hippo*. Oxford: Claredon, 1933.

Nodet, Étienne. "Jésus et Jean-Baptiste selon Josephe." *RB* 92 (1985): 321–48.

Nolland, John. *Luke.* WBC 35. Dallas: Word, 1989–93.

Nützel, Johannes M. *Die Verklärungserzählung im Markusevangelium: Eine redaktions-geschichtliche Untersuchung.* Würzberg: Echter Verlag, 1973.

Öhler, Markus. *Elia im Neuen Testament: Untersuchungen zur Bedeutung des alttesta-mentlichen Propheten im frühen Christentum.* BZNW 88. Berlin: de Gruyter, 1997.

Otto, Rudolf. *Reich Gottes und Menschensohn.* München: Beck, [2]1940 (1934); ET: *The Kingdom of God and the Son of Man: A Study in the History of Religion.* Floyd V. Filson and Bertram Lee Woolf, trans. London, and Redhill: Lutterworth, [2]1943.

Pamment, M. "The Kingdom of Heaven According to the First Gospel." *NTS* 27 (1981): 211–32

Parker, Pierson. "Jesus, John the Baptist, and the Herods." *PRS* (1981): 4–11.

Parsons, Ernest W. "The Significance of John the Baptist for the Beginnings of Christian-ity." In: *Environmental Factors in Christian History.* John Thomas McNeill, Matthew Spinka and Harold R. Willoughby, eds. Chicago: IL: University of Chicago, 1939. 1–17.

Patrick, D. "The Kingdom of God in the Old Testament." In: *The Kingdom of God in 20th-Century Interpretation.* W. Willis, ed. Peabody, MA: Hendrickson, 1987. 67–79.

Pellegrini, Silvia. *Elija: Wegbereiter des Gottessohnes: Eine textsemiotische Unter-suchung im Markusevangelium.* HBS 26; Freiburg/New York: Herder, 2000.

Perrin, Norman. *Jesus and the Language of the Kingdom: Symbol and Metaphor in New Testament Interpretation.* Philadelphia: Fortress, 1976.

–. *Christology and a Modern Pilgrimage: A Discussion with Norman Perrin.* Hans Dieter Betz, ed. Missoula, MO: Society of Biblical Literature, 1973.

–. "The Son of Man in the Synoptic Tradition." *BR* 13 (1968): 3–25.

–. "The Creative Use of the Son of Man Traditions by Mark." *USQR* 23 (1967–68): 357–65.

–. *Rediscovering the Teaching of Jesus.* The New Testament Library. London: SCM, 1967.

–. "The Son of Man in Ancient Judaism and Primitive Christianity: A Suggestion." *BR* 11 (1966): 17–28.

–. "Mark XIV. 62: The End Product of a Christian Pesher Tradition?" *NTS* 12 (1965–66): 150–55.

–. *The Kingdom of God in the Teaching of Jesus.* New Testament Library; London: SCM; Philadelphia: Westminster, 1963.

Perry, Ben Edwin. *Studies in the Text History of the Life and Fables of Aesop.* Philological Monographs 7. Haverford, PA: American Philological Association, 1936.

Pesch, Rudolf. *Das Markusevangelium I. Teil: Einleitung und Kommentar zu Kap. 1,1–8,26.* HTKNT 2.1. Freiburg: Herder, [4]1984.

Piper, Ronald A., ed. *The Gospel Behind the Gospels: Current Studies on Q.* NovTSupp 75. Leiden: Brill, 1994.

Plummer, Alfred. *The Gospel According to S. Luke.* ICC. Edinburgh: T. & T. Clark, [5]1901.

–. *The Gospel according to St. Mark.* CGTSC. Cambridge: Cambridge University, 1915.

Polag, Athanasius. *Die Christologie der Logienquelle.* WMANT 45; Neukirchen-Vluyn: Neukirchener, 1979.

Pottgiesser, Alexander. *Johannes der Täufer und Jesus Christus: Eine apologetische Studie: Inaugural-Dissertation zur Erlangung der theologischen Doktorwürde der*

Hochwürdigen katholisch-theologischen Fakultät der Rheinischen Friedrich-Wilhelms-Universität in Bonn. Köln: Druck von J.P. Bachem, 1910.

Powell, Mark A. Review of Joan Taylor. *The Immerser: John the Baptist within Second Temple Judaism*. Grand Rapids: Eerdmans, 1997. In: *CBQ* (1999): 171–72.

Pryor, John W. "John the Baptist and Jesus: Tradition and Text in John 3.25." *JSNT* 66 (1997): 15–26.

Puech, É. "Ben Sira 48:11 et la Résurrection." In: *Of Scribes and Scrolls. Studies on the Hebrew Bible, Intertestamental Judaism, and Christian Origins*. H. W. Attridge, J. J. Collins and T. H. Tobin, eds. Lanham, MD: The College Theology Society University Press of America, 1990. 81–90.

Rajak, Tessa. *Josephus: The Historian and His Society*. London: Duckworth, 1983.

Richter, Georg. "'Bist du Elias?' (Joh. 1,21)." *BZ* n.s. 6 (1962): 79–92, 238–56.

Riesenfeld, H. *Jésus Transfiguré*. Copenhagen: E. Munksgaard, 1947.

Reumann, J. "The Quest for the Historical Baptist." In: *Understanding the Sacred Text: Essays in Honor of Morton S. Enslin on the Hebrew Bible and Christian Beginnings*. J. Reumann, ed. Valley Forge, PA: Judson, 1972. 181–99.

Robinson, James M., ed. *The Sayings of Jesus: The Sayings Gospel Q in English*. Minneapolis: Fortress, 2002.

–. "Jesus – From Easter to Valentinus (or to the Apostles' Creed)." *JBL* 101 (1982): 5–37.

–. "ΛΟΓΟΙ ΣΟΦΩΝ: Zur Gattung der Spruchquelle Q." In: *Zeit und Geschichte: Dankesgabe an Rudolf Bultmann*. Erich Dinkler, ed. Tübingen: Mohr Siebeck, 1964. 77–96; ET (enlarged by author): "LOGOI SOPHON: On the Gattung of Q." In: Robinson, James M. and Helmut Koester, *Trajectories*. 71–113.

–. "Jewish Wisdom Literature and the Gattung LOGOI SOPHON." In: *The Shape of Q Signal Essays on the Sayings Gospel*, 51–58.

Robinson, James M. and Helmut Koester, *Trajectories through Early Christianity*. Philadelphia: Fortress, 1971.

Robinson, James M., John S. Kloppenborg, and Paul Hoffmann, gen eds. *Documenta Q. Reconstructions of Q through Two Centuries of Gospel Research*. Ed. Stanley D. Anderson, Sterling G. Bjorndahl, Shawn Carruth, Robert Derrenbacker, and Christoph Heil. Leuven: Peeters, 1996–.

Robinson, James M., Paul Hoffmann, John S. Kloppenborg, Milton C. Moreland, eds. *The Sayings Gospel Q in Greek and English. With Parallels from the Gospels of Mark and Thomas*. Minneapolis: Fortress Press, 2002.

Robinson, John A. T. "Elijah, John and Jesus: An Essay in Detection." *NTS* (1958): 263–81. Repr. in: *Twelve New Testament Studies*. 28–52.

–. "The Baptism of John and the Qumran Community." *HTR* (1957): 175–91. Repr. in: *Twelve New Testament Studies*. 11–27.

–. "The 'Others' of John 4.38: A Test of Exegetical Method." In: *Twelve New Testament Studies*, 61–66. Repr. from *SE* (1959): 510–15.

–. *Twelve New Testament Studies*. London: SCM, 1962.

Rothschild, Clare K. *Luke-Acts and the Rhetoric of History*. WUNT 2/175; Tübingen: Mohr Siebeck, 2004.

Rudolf, Kurt. *Die Mandäer*. Göttingen: Vandenhoeck & Ruprecht, 1960.

Sahlin, Harald. *Studien zum dritten Kapitel des Lukasevangeliums*. Uppsala: Lundequistska, 1949.

Saldarini, A. "The End of the Rabbinic Chain." *JBL* 93 (1974): 97–106.

Sanders, E. P. *The Historical Figure of Jesus*. London: Penguin, 1993.

–. *Jesus and Judaism*. Philadelphia: Fortress, 1985.

Sandy, D. Brent. "John the Baptist's 'Lamb of God' Affirmation in its Canonical and Apocalyptic Milieu." *JETS* 34 (1991): 447–59.

Sato, M. *Q und Prophetie*. WUNT 2.29. Tübingen: Mohr Siebeck, 1988. 28–47.

Schaberg, Jane. *The Resurrection of Mary Magdalene: Legends, Apocrypha, and the Christian Testament*. New York/London: Continuum, 2003.

Schenk, W. "Der Einfluss der Logienquelle auf das Markusevangelium." *ZNW* 70 (1979): 141–65.

Schermann, Theodor. *Propheten- und Apostellegenden, nebst Jüngerkatalogen des Dorotheus und verwandter Texte*. Leipzig: J. C. Hinrichs, 1907.

Schlatter, Adolf. *Johannes der Täufer*. W. Michaelis, ed. Basel: Verlag Friedrich Reinhardt, 1956.

–. *Der Evangelist Matthäus. Seine Sprache, seine Ziel, seine Selbstständigkeit: ein Kommentar zum ersten Evangelium*. Stuttgart: Calwer Verlag, ³1948.

Schmeller, Thomas. "Jesus im Umland Galiläas: Zu den markinischen Berichten vom Aufenthalt Jesu in den Gebieten von Tyros, Caesarea Philippi und der Dekapolis." *BZ* (1993–94): 44–66.

Schmidt, Karl Ludwig, "βασιλεία, βασίλισσα, βασιλεύω, συμβασιλεύω, βασίλειος, βασιλικός." Art. *TDNT*, 1.564–93.

Schmithals, W. "Der Markusschluß, die Verklärungsgeschichte und die Aussendung der Zwölf." *ZTK* (1972): 379–411.

Schnackenburg, Rudolf. *The Gospel of Matthew*. Grand Rapids: Eerdmans, 2002 (1985–87).

–. *God's Rule and Kingdom*. John Murray, trans. New York: Herder and Herder, 1963.

Schneider, Gerhard. *Das Evangelium nach Lukas*. 2 vols. Ökumenischer Taschenbuch-Kommentar zum Neuen Testament 3.1–2. Würzburg: Gerd Mohn, 1977.

Schnelle, Udo. *The History and Theology of the New Testament Writings*. Minneapolis: Fortress, 1998.

Schüling, Joachim. *Studien zum Verhältnis von Logienquelle und Markusevangelium*. Würzburg: Echter, 1991.

Schulz, Siegfried. "Die Bedeutung des Markus für die Theologiegeschichte des Urchristentums." *Studia Evangelica* 2. Texte und Untersuchungen 87. Berlin: Akademie Verlag, 1964. 135–45.

Schürmann, Heinz. *Traditionsgeschichtliche Untersuchungen zu den synoptischen Evangelien*. Düsseldorf: Patmos Verlag, 1968.

–. *Das Lukasevangelium*. HTKNT 3. Freiburg/Basel/Vienna: Herder, 1969.

–. "Beobachtungen zum Menschensohn-Titel in der Redequelle." In: *Jesus und der Menschensohn*. FS A. Vögtle. Freiburg; Herder, 1975. 124–47.

–. "Das Zeugnis der Redenquelle für die Basileia-Verkündigung Jesu." In: Delobel, Jöel. *Logia: Les paroles de Jésus – The Sayings of Jesus: Mémorial Joseph Coppens*. BETL 59. Leuven: Peeters and University, 1982. 121–200.

Schüssler Fiorenza, Elisabeth. *Jesus and the Politics of Interpretation*. New York/London: Continuum, 2000.

–. *Jesus: Miriam's Child, Sophia's Prophet: Critical Issues in Feminist Christology*. New York: Continuum, 1994.

Schütz, J. *Johannes der Täufer*. ATANT 50. Zürich/Stuttgart: Zwingli, 1967.

Schwarz, Günther. *Jesus "der Menschensohn:" aramaistische Untersuchungen zu den synoptischen Menschensohnworten Jesu.* BWANT 6/19. Stuttgart: Kohlhammer, 1986.

Schweitzer, A. *The Mystery of the Kingdom of God.* New York: Schocken Books, 1964 (1901).

–. *The Quest of the Historical Jesus.* New York: Macmillan, 1968 (1906).

–. *The Kingdom of God and Primitive Christianity.* L. A. Garrard, trans. New York: Seabury, 1968.

Schweizer, Eduard. *The Good News according to Mark.* Richmond, VA: John Knox, 1970 ([12]1968).

–. *The Good News according to Matthew.* Atlanta: John Knox, 1975.

Scobie, C. H. H. *John the Baptist.* London: SCM, 1964.

Scott, B. B. *Jesus, Symbol-Maker for the Kingdom.* Philadelphia: Fortress, 1981.

Scott, R. B. Y. "The Expectation of Elijah." *CJRT* 3 (1926) 1–13.

Segal, Alan. "Heavenly Ascent in Hellenistic Judaism, Early Christianity and their Environment." Art. *ANRW* 2.23.2, 1333–94.

Seeley, David. "Interpretations of Jesus' Death in Q." *Semeia* 55 (1991): 131–46.

Seitz, Oscar J. F. "Upon This Rock: A Critical Re-Examination of Matt 16:17–19." *JBL* (1950): 329–40.

Senior, Donald. *Matthew.* ANTC. Nashville: Abingdon, 1998.

Sevenich-Bax, Elisabeth. *Israels Konfrontation mit den letzten Boten der Weisheit. Form, Funktion und Interdependenz der Weisheitselemente in der Logienquelle.* MTA 21. Altenberge: Oros, 1993.

Shaver, Brenda J. Review of Joan Taylor, *The Immerser.* In: *JR* (2000): 306–7.

–. "The Prophet Elijah in the Literature of the Second Temple Period: The Growth of a Tradition." Ph.D. Dissertation. The University of Chicago, 2001.

Smallwood, E. Mary. *The Jews Under Roman Rule.* Leiden: Brill, 1981.

Smith, Derwood. "Jewish Proselyte Baptism and the Baptism of John." *ResQ* 25 (1982): 13–32.

Smith, James Vaughan. "Resurrecting the Blessed Hyperechius." Ph.D. Dissertation. Loyola University Chicago, 2003.

Smith, Jonathan Z. "Wisdom and Apocalyptic." In: *Religious Syncretism in Antiquity.* B. Pearson, ed. Missoula, MT: Scholars, 1975. 131–56.

Smith, Robert H. *Matthew.* ACNT. Minneapolis: Augsburg, 1989.

Snodgrass, Klyne R. "Streams of Tradition Emerging from Isaiah 40:1–5 and Their Adaptation in the New Testament." *JSNT* (1980): 24–45.

Stauffer, Ethelbert. *New Testament Theology.* John Marsh, trans. New York: Macmillan, 1959.

Stein, Robert H. "Is the Transfiguration (Mark 9:2–8) a Misplaced Resurrection Account?" *JBL* (1976): 79–96.

Steinmann, J. *Saint John the Baptist and the Desert Tradition.* New York: Harper, 1958.

Stone, M. E. "Lists of Revealed Things in the Apocalyptic Literature." In: *Magnalia Dei: The Mighty Acts of God.* F. M. Cross, W. E. Lemke and P. D. Miller, eds. Garden City, NY: Doubleday, 1976. 414–54.

Streeter, B. H. *The Four Gospels: A Study of Origins, Treating of the Manuscript Tradition, Sources, Authorship, and Dates.* London: Macmillan, 1930.

–. "The Literary Evolution of the Gospels." *Oxford Studies in the Synoptic Problem* Oxford: Clarendon, 1911. 209–27.

–. "St. Mark's Knowledge and Use of Q." In: *Studies in the Synoptic Problem*. W. Sanday, ed. Oxford: Clarendon, 1911. 165–83.

Strack, H. L. and P. Billerbeck. *Kommentar zum Neuen Testament aus Talmud und Midrasch*. Munich: Beck, 1922–61.

Swete, H. B. *The Gospel according to St. Mark*. London: Macmillan, [3]1913 (1898) = Grand Rapids: Kregel, 1977.

Tatum, W. B. *John the Baptist and Jesus: A Report of the Jesus Seminar*. Sonoma, CA Polebridge, 1994.

Taylor, Joan. *The Immerser: John the Baptist within Second Temple Judaism*. Grand Rapids: Eerdmans, 1997.

Taylor, R. O. P. *Groundwork of the Gospels*. Oxford: Blackwell, 1946.

Taylor, Vincent. *The Gospel according to Saint Mark*. Grand Rapids: Baker, [2]1966.

Tcherikover, Victor A. *Hellenistic Civilization and the Jews*. S. Applebaum, trans. Philadelphia, PA: Jewish Publication Society of America, 1959.

–. *Corpus Papyrorum Judaicarum*. Victor A. Tcherikover and Alexander Fuks, eds. Cambridge, MA: Harvard University, 1957–64.

Theissen, G. "Wanderradikalismus, Literatursoziologische Aspekte der Überlieferung von Worten Jesu im Urchristentum." In: *Studien zur Soziologie des Urchristentums*. Tübingen: Mohr Siebeck, [2]1983; ET: *The Sociology of Early Palestinian Christianity*. Philadelphia: Fortress, 1978.

Thomas, Joseph. *Le mouvement baptiste en Palestine et Syrie (150 AV. J.-C. – 300 AP. J.-C.)*. Gembloux: Duculot, 1935.

Thrall, Margaret E. "Elijah and Moses in Mark's Account of the Transfiguration." *NTS* (1969): 305–17.

Thyen, Hartwig. "ΒΑΠΤΙΣΜΑ ΜΕΤΑΝΟΙΑΣ ΕΙΣ ΑΦΕΣΙΝ ΑΜΑΡΤΙΩΝ." In: *The Future of Our Religious Past: Essays in Honour of Rudolf Bultmann*. James M. Robinson, trans. Charles E. Carlston and Robert P. Scharlemann. New York: Harper & Row, 1971. 131–68.

Tilly, Michael. *Johannes der Täufer und die Biographie der Propheten: Die synoptische Täuferüberlieferung und das jüdische Prophetenbild zur Zeit des Täufers*. BWANT 7/17. Stuttgart: W. Kohlhammer, 1994.

Todd, J. C. "Logia of John." *ExpTim* (1910): 173–75.

Tödt, Heinz Eduard. *Der Menschensohn in der synoptischen Überlieferung*. Gütersloher Verlagshaus, 1963; ET: *The Son of Man in the Synoptic Tradition*. D. M. Barton, trans. London: SCM, 1965.

Trilling, W. "Die Täufertradition bei Matthäus." *BZ* 3 (1959): 271–89.

Trocmé, Étienne. *L'Évangile selon Saint Marc*. CNT 2. Geneva: Labor et Fides, 2000.

–. *The Formation of the Gospel according to Mark*. Philadelphia: Westminster, 1975 (1963).

Trumbower, Jeffrey A. "The Role of Malachi in the Career of John the Baptist." In: *The Gospels and the Scriptures of Israel*. C. A. Evans and W. R. Stegner, eds. JSNTSup 104. Sheffield: Sheffield Academic, 1994. 28–41.

Tuckett, Christopher M. "Q 12, 8: Once again 'Son of Man' or 'I.'" In: Jon Ma. Asgeirsson, Kristin De Troyer, and Marvin W. Meyer, eds. *From Quest to Q*. FS James M. Robinson. Leuven: Peeters and University, 2000. 171–88.

–. *Q and the History of Early Christianity: Studies on Q*. Edinburgh: T. & T. Clark; and Peabody, MA: Hendrickson, 1996. 108–9.

Uro, Risto. ed. *Symbols and Strata: Essays on the Sayings Gospel Q.* Suomen Eksegeettisen Seuran Julkaisuja. Publications of the Finnish Exegetical Society 65. Helsinki: Finnish Exegetical Society; and Göttingen: Vandenhoeck & Ruprecht, 1996.

–. "John the Baptist and the Jesus Movement: What Does Q Tell Us?" In: R. A. Piper, ed. *The Gospel Behind the Gospels: Current Studies on Q.* NovTSupp 75. Leiden: Brill, 1994. 231–57.

Vaage, Leif. *Galilean Upstarts. Jesus' First Followers according to Q.* Valley Forge, PA: TPI, 1994.

–. "The Son of Man Sayings in Q: Stratigraphical Location and Significance." *Semeia* 55 (1992): 103–29.

VanderKam, James C. "The Prophetic-Sapiential Origins of Apocalyptic Thought." In: *A Word in Season: Essays in Honor of William McKane.* JSOTSS 42. J. D. Martin and P. R. Davies, eds. Sheffield: JSOT Press, 1986. 163–76.

–. *Enoch and the Growth of an Apocalyptic Tradition.* CBQMS 16. Washington, DC: The Catholic Biblical Association of America, 1984.

Vassiliadis, Petros. "The Nature and Extent of the Q Document." *NovT* 20 (1978): 49–73.

–. "The Function of John the Baptist in Q and Mark: A Hypothesis." *Theologica* (1975): 405–13.

Vermes, Geza. "The 'Son of Man' Debate." *JSNT* (1978): 19–32.

Vielhauer, Philip. *Aufsätze zum Neuen Testament.* ThBü 31. Munich: Kaiser, 1965.

–. "Jesus und der Menschensohn: Zur Diskussion mit Heinz Eduard Tödt und Eduard Schweizer." *ZThK* 60 (1963): 133–77.

–. "Gottesreich und Menschensohn in der Verkündigung Jesu." In: *Festschrift für Günther Dehn zum 75. Geburtstag am 18. April dargebracht von der Evangelisch-Theologischen Fakultät der Rheinischen Friedrich Wilhelms-Universität zu Bonn.* Neukirchen: Kreis Moers, 1957. 51–79.

–. "Das Benedictus des Zacharias." *ZThK,* xlix (1952): 255–72.

Viviano, B. *The Kingdom of God in History.* GNS 27. Wilmington, DE: M. Glazier, 1988.

–. "The Kingdom of God in the Qumran Literature." In: *The Kingdom of God in 20th-Century Interpretation.* W. Willis, ed. Peabody, MA: Hendrickson, 1987. 97–107.

Walker, William O. "The Son of Man Question and the Synoptic Problem," *NTS* 28 (1982): 374–88.

–. "The Son of Man: Some Recent Developments." *CBQ* 45 (1983): 584–607.

Walsh, Jerome T. "Elijah (Person)." Art. *ABD,* 2.463–66.

Wanke, Joachim. *"Bezugs- und Kommentarworte" in den synoptischen Evangelien: Beobachtungen zur Interpretationsgeschichte der Herrenworte in der Vorevangelischen Überlieferung.* EFS 44. Leipzig: St. Benno-Verlag GMBH, 1981.

Webb, Robert L. "John the Baptist and his Relationship to Jesus." In: *Studying the Historical Jesus: Evaluations of the Current State of Current Research.* B. D. Chilton and C. A. Evans, eds. Leiden: Brill, 1994. 179–229.

–. *John the Baptizer and Prophet: A Socio-Historical Study.* Sheffield: JSOT Press, 1991.

–. "The Activity of John the Baptist's Expected Figure at the Threshing Floor (Matthew 3.12 – Luke 3.17)." *JSNT* 43 (1991): 103–11.

Weeden, T. J. *Mark – Traditions in Conflict.* Philadelphia: Fortress, 1971.

Weiss, J. *Jesus' Proclamation of the Kingdom of God*. R. H. Hiers and D. L. Holland, trans. Philadelphia: Fortress, 1971 (1892).

Wellhausen, Julius. *Das Evangelium Marci*. Berlin: G. Reimer, ²1909.

–. *Das Evangelium Lucae*. Berlin: Reimer, 1904.

Wernle, Paul. *Die synoptische Frage*. Freiburg i. Br.: Mohr, 1899.

Wilckens, Ulrich. "ὑποϰρίνομαι." Art. *TDNT*, 8.559–71.

Wilder, Amos. *Eschatology and Ethics in the Teaching of Jesus*. Rev. ed. New York: Harper & Row, 1950 (1939).

Williamson, Jr., Lamar. *Mark*. IBC. Atlanta: John Knox, 1983.

Willis, Wendell, ed. *The Kingdom of God in 20ᵗʰ-Century Interpretation*. Peabody, MA: Hendrickson, 1987.

Wills, Lawrence M. *The Quest of the Historical Gospel: Mark, John and the Origins of the Gospel Genre*. London/New York: Routledge, 1997.

Windisch, Hans. "Die Notiz über Tracht und Speise des Täufers Johannes und ihre Entsprechungen in der Jesusüberlieferung." *ZNW* 32 (1933): 65–87.

Wink, Walter. *The Human Being: Jesus and the Enigma of the Son of the Man*. Minneapolis: Fortress, 2002.

–. "Jesus' Reply to John: Matt. 11:2–6/Luke: 7:18–23." *Forum* 5 (1989): 121–28.

–. *John the Baptist in the Gospel Tradition*. Cambridge: Cambridge University, 1968.

Winter, Paul. "Lukanische Miszellen." *ZNW* 49 (1958): 65–77.

–. "The Main Literary Problem of the Lucan Infancy Story." *ATR* 40 (1958): 257–64.

–. "The Proto-Source of Luke 1." *NovT* 1 (1956): 184–99.

–. "*Hoti* 'recitativum' in Lc 1, 25.61; 2,23." *ZNW* 46 (1955): 261–63.

–. "Some Observations on the Language in the Birth and Infancy Stories of the Third Gospel." *NTS* 1 (1954–55): 111–21.

–. "The Cultural Background for the Narratives in Luke I – II." *JQR* 45 (1954): 159–67, 230–42, 287.

–. "Magnificat and Benedictus – Maccabean Hymns?" *BJRL* 38 (1954): 328–47.

Wolter, Michael. "Apollos und die ephesinischen Johannesjünger (Act 18,24–19,7)." *ZNW* (1987): 49–73.

Yamasaki, Gary. *John the Baptist in Life and Death: Audience-Oriented Criticism of Matthew's Narrative*. JSNTSup 167. Sheffield: Sheffield Academic, 1998.

Yarbro Collins, Adela. "The Origin of the Designation of Jesus as 'Son of Man.'" In: eadem, *Cosmology and Eschatology in Jewish and Christian Apocalypticism*. Leiden: Brill, 1996. 139–58; earlier version: *HTR* 80/4 (1987): 391–407.

–. *The Beginning of the Gospel: Probings of Mark in Context*. Minneapolis: Fortress, 1987.

–. Review of John Kloppenborg, *The Formation of Q*. In: *CBQ* 50 (1988): 720–22.

–. "The Origin of Christian Baptism." *StudLit* 19 (1989): 28–46.

–. "The Son of Man Sayings in the Sayings Source." In: *To Touch the Text: Biblical and Related Studies in Honor of Joseph A. Fitzmyer*, S.J. Maurya Horgan and Paul J. Kobelski, eds. New York: Crossroad, 1989. 369–89.

Young, Franklin W. "Jesus the Prophet: A Re-examination." *JBL* (1949): 285–99.

Zahn, Theodor. *Das Evangelium des Matthäus*. Leipzig: A. Deichert, ⁴1922 (1903) = Wuppertal: R. Brockhaus, 1984.

–. *Das Evangelium des Markus*. Leipzig: A. Deichert, 1910.

Zeller, Dieter. "Redactional Processes and Changing Settings." In: *The Shape of Q*. John Kloppenborg, ed. 116–30.

Dictionaries and Standard Reference Works

–. "Instructions for Contributors." *JBL* 117/3 (1998): 555–579.

Aland, Kurt, ed. *Synopsis Quattuor Evangeliorum*. Stuttgart: Deutsche Bibelgesellschaft, 1996.

Alexander, Patrick H. et al., eds. *The SBL Handbook of Style: For Ancient Near Eastern, Biblical, and Early Christian Studies*. Peabody, MA: Hendrickson, 1999.

Baird, William. *History of New Testament Research*. Vol. 1: *From Deism to Tübingen*. Minneapolis, MN: Fortress, 1992. Vol. 2: *From Jonathan Edwards to Rudolf Bultmann*. Minneapolis, MN: Fortress, 2003.

Balz, H. and G. Schneider, eds. *Exegetisches Wörterbuch zum Neuen Testament*. 3 vols. Stuttgart: Kohlhammer, 1980–83.

Bauer, Walter, William Arndt, F. W. Gingrich and F. W. Danker. *A Greek-English Lexicon of the New Testament and Other Early Christian Literature*. Chicago and London: The University of Chicago, [3]2000.

Berkowitz, Luci et al. *Thesaurus Linguae Graecae: Canon of Greek Authors and Works*. New York: Oxford University Press, [3]1990.

Blass, F. and A. Debrunner. *A Greek Grammar of the New Testament and Other Early Christian Literature*. W. F. Arndt, F. W. Gingrich and F. W. Danker, eds. Chicago: The University of Chicago Press, [2]1979.

Brown, Francis et al. *The New Brown-Driver-Briggs-Gesenius Hebrew and English Lexicon with an Appendix Containing the Biblical Aramaic*. Reprinted: Peabody, MA: Hendrickson, 1979.

Cancik, Hubert. ed. *Der neue Pauly: Enzyklopädie der Antike*. Stuttgart: J. B. Metzler, 1996–.

Denis, Albert-Marie. *Concordance Grecque des Pseudépigraphes d'ancien Testament*. Louvian-la-Neuve: Université Catholique de Louvain, 1987.

Di Berardino, Angelo, ed. *Encyclopedia of the Early Church*. 2 Vols. Adrian Walford, trans. New York: Oxford University, 1992.

Freedman, David Noel, ed. *Eerdmans Dictionary of the Bible*. Grand Rapids: Eerdmans, 2000.

Galling, K. von, ed. *Die Religion in Geschichte und Gegenwart*. 7 vols. Tübingen: Mohr Siebeck, 1956–65[3]; H. D. Betz et al, eds. 8 vols. 1998–2005[4].

Hornblower, Simon and Antony Spawforth, eds. *The Oxford Classical Dictionary*. Oxford: Oxford University, [3]1996.

Jannaris, Antonius N. *An Historical Greek Grammar*. London/New York: Macmillan Co., 1897.

Jastrow, Marcus. *A Dictionary of the Targumim, The Talmud Babli and Yerushalmi, and the Midrashic Literature*. New York: Judaica, 1989 (1971).

Johnston, William M., ed. *Encyclopedia of Monasticism*. Chicago: Fitzroy Dearborn, 2000.

Klausner, T., E. Dassmann, et al., eds. *Reallexikon für Antike und Christentum*. 18 vols. Stuttgart: Hiersemann, 1950–.

Kittel, Gerhard and Gerhard Friedrich, eds. *Theological Dictionary of the New Testament*. Grand Rapids: Eerdmans, 1964–76.

Lampe, G. W. *A Patristic Greek Lexicon*. Oxford: Oxford University, 1969.

Liddell, Henry G., Robert Scott and H. S. Jones and Roderick Mckenzie. *A Greek-English Lexicon with a Supplement 1968*. Oxford: Clarendon, [9]1992.

Long, A. A. and D. N. Sedley. *The Hellenistic Philosophers*. 2 vols. New York: Cambridge University, 1995.

Metzger, Bruce M. *A Textual Commentary on the Greek New Testament*. Stuttgart: Deutsche Bibelgesellschaft, [2]1994.

Moulton, W. F. and A. S. Geden. *A Concordance to the Greek New Testament*. I. Howard Marshall, ed. Edinburgh: T. & T. Clark, [6]2002 (1963).

Rengstorf, Karl Heinrich. *A Complete Concordance to Flavius Josephus*. Leiden: Brill, 1973–1983.

Robertson, A. T. *A Grammar of the Greek New Testament in the Light of Historical Research*. Nashville: Broadman Press, [3]1934.

Sophocles, E. A. *Greek Lexicon of the Roman and Byzantine Periods*. Hildesheim: Olms, 1983.

Smyth, H. W. *Greek Grammar*. Cambridge, MA: Harvard University, 1980 (1920).

Stevenson, J. *The New Eusebius: Documents Illustrating the History of the Church to AD 337*. Rev. W. H. C. Frend. Cambridge: Cambridge University, 1995 (1957).

Van der Toorn, Karel et al. *Dictionary of Deities and Demons in the Bible: DDD*. Leiden: Brill/Grand Rapids: Eerdmans, [2]1999.

Wissowa, G., W. Kroll, et al., ed. *Paulys Realencyclopädie der classischen Altertumswissenschaft*. Stuttgart: J. B. Metzler, 1894–1972.

Ziegler, K. and Sontheimer, W. *Der kleine Pauly, Lexikon der Antike*. 5 vols. Stuttgart: Alfred Druckenmüller, 1964–75.

Index of References

1. Hebrew Bible

2. Other Jewish Sources

3. Greco-Roman Sources

4. New Testament

5. Other Christian Literature

Index of Modern Authors

Index of Subjects

Wissenschaftliche Untersuchungen zum Neuen Testament
Alphabetical Index of the First and Second Series

Bøe, Sverre: Gog and Magog. 2001. *Volume II/135.*

Böhlig, Alexander: Gnosis und Synkretismus. Teil 1 1989. *Volume 47* – Teil 2 1989. *Volume 48.*

Böhm, Martina: Samarien und die Samaritai bei Lukas. 1999. *Volume II/111.*

Böttrich, Christfried: Weltweisheit – Menschheitsethik – Urkult. 1992. *Volume II/50.*

Bolyki, János: Jesu Tischgemeinschaften. 1997. *Volume II/96.*

Bosman, Philip: Conscience in Philo and Paul. 2003. *Volume II/166.*

Bovon, François: Studies in Early Christianity. 2003. *Volume 161.*

Brocke, Christoph vom: Thessaloniki – Stadt des Kassander und Gemeinde des Paulus. 2001. *Volume II/125.*

Brunson, Andrew: Psalm 118 in the Gospel of John. 2003. *Volume II/158.*

Büchli, Jörg: Der Poimandres – ein paganisiertes Evangelium. 1987. *Volume II/27.*

Bühner, Jan A.: Der Gesandte und sein Weg im 4. Evangelium. 1977. *Volume II/2.*

Burchard, Christoph: Untersuchungen zu Joseph und Aseneth. 1965. *Volume 8.*

– Studien zur Theologie, Sprache und Umwelt des Neuen Testaments. Ed. von D. Sänger. 1998. *Volume 107.*

Burnett, Richard: Karl Barth's Theological Exegesis. 2001. *Volume II/145.*

Byron, John: Slavery Metaphors in Early Judaism and Pauline Christianity. 2003. *Volume II/162.*

Byrskog, Samuel: Story as History – History as Story. 2000. *Volume 123.*

Cancik, Hubert (Ed.): Markus-Philologie. 1984. *Volume 33.*

Capes, David B.: Old Testament Yaweh Texts in Paul's Christology. 1992. *Volume II/47.*

Caragounis, Chrys C.: The Development of Greek and the New Testament. 2004. *Volume 167.*

– The Son of Man. 1986. *Volume 38.*

– see *Fridrichsen, Anton.*

Carleton Paget, James: The Epistle of Barnabas. 1994. *Volume II/64.*

Carson, D.A., O'Brien, Peter T. and *Mark Seifrid* (Ed.): Justification and Variegated Nomism.
Volume 1: The Complexities of Second Temple Judaism. 2001. *Volume II/140.*
Volume 2: The Paradoxes of Paul. 2004. *Volume II/181.*

Ciampa, Roy E.: The Presence and Function of Scripture in Galatians 1 and 2. 1998. *Volume II/102.*

Classen, Carl Joachim: Rhetorical Criticsm of the New Testament. 2000. *Volume 128.*

Colpe, Carsten: Iranier – Aramäer – Hebräer – Hellenen. 2003. *Volume 154.*

Crump, David: Jesus the Intercessor. 1992. *Volume II/49.*

Dahl, Nils Alstrup: Studies in Ephesians. 2000. *Volume 131.*

Deines, Roland: Die Gerechtigkeit der Tora im Reich des Messias. 2004. *Volume 177.*

– Jüdische Steingefäße und pharisäische Frömmigkeit. 1993. *Volume II/52.*

– Die Pharisäer. 1997. *Volume 101.*

– and *Karl-Wilhelm Niebuhr* (Ed.): Philo und das Neue Testament. 2004. *Volume 172.*

Dettwiler, Andreas and *Jean Zumstein* (Ed.): Kreuzestheologie im Neuen Testament. 2002. *Volume 151.*

Dickson, John P.: Mission-Commitment in Ancient Judaism and in the Pauline Communities. 2003. *Volume II/159.*

Dietzfelbinger, Christian: Der Abschied des Kommenden. 1997. *Volume 95.*

Dimitrov, Ivan Z., James D.G. Dunn, Ulrich Luz and *Karl-Wilhelm Niebuhr* (Ed.): Das Alte Testament als christliche Bibel in orthodoxer und westlicher Sicht. 2004. *Volume 174.*

Dobbeler, Axel von: Glaube als Teilhabe. 1987. *Volume II/22.*

Du Toit, David S.: Theios Anthropos. 1997. *Volume II/91*

Dübbers, Michael: Christologie und Existenz im Kolosserbrief. 2005. *Volume II/191.*

Dunn, James D.G.: The New Perspective on Paul. 2005. *Volume 185.*

Dunn , James D.G. (Ed.): Jews and Christians. 1992. *Volume 66.*

– Paul and the Mosaic Law. 1996. *Volume 89.*

– see *Dimitrov, Ivan Z.*

Dunn, James D.G., Hans Klein, Ulrich Luz and *Vasile Mihoc* (Ed.): Auslegung der Bibel in orthodoxer und westlicher Perspektive. 2000. *Volume 130.*

Ebel, Eva: Die Attraktivität früher christlicher Gemeinden. 2004. *Volume II/178.*

Ebertz, Michael N.: Das Charisma des Gekreuzigten. 1987. *Volume 45.*

Eckstein, Hans-Joachim: Der Begriff Syneidesis bei Paulus. 1983. *Volume II/10.*

– Verheißung und Gesetz. 1996. *Volume 86.*

Ego, Beate: Im Himmel wie auf Erden. 1989. *Volume II/34*

Ego, Beate, Armin Lange and Peter Pilhofer (Ed.): Gemeinde ohne Tempel – Community without Temple. 1999. *Volume 118.*
– *und Helmut Merkel* (Ed.): Religiöses Lernen in der biblischen, frühjüdischen und frühchristlichen Überlieferung. 2005. *Volume 180.*

Eisen, Ute E.: see *Paulsen, Henning.*

Ellis, E. Earle: Prophecy and Hermeneutic in Early Christianity. 1978. *Volume 18.*
– The Old Testament in Early Christianity. 1991. *Volume 54.*

Endo, Masanobu: Creation and Christology. 2002. *Volume 149.*

Ennulat, Andreas: Die 'Minor Agreements'. 1994. *Volume II/62.*

Ensor, Peter W.: Jesus and His 'Works'. 1996. *Volume II/85.*

Eskola, Timo: Messiah and the Throne. 2001. *Volume II/142.*
– Theodicy and Predestination in Pauline Soteriology. 1998. *Volume II/100.*

Fatehi, Mehrdad: The Spirit's Relation to the Risen Lord in Paul. 2000. *Volume II/128.*

Feldmeier, Reinhard: Die Krisis des Gottessohnes. 1987. *Volume II/21.*
– Die Christen als Fremde. 1992. *Volume 64.*

Feldmeier, Reinhard and Ulrich Heckel (Ed.): Die Heiden. 1994. *Volume 70.*

Fletcher-Louis, Crispin H.T.: Luke-Acts: Angels, Christology and Soteriology. 1997. *Volume II/94.*

Förster, Niclas: Marcus Magus. 1999. *Volume 114.*

Forbes, Christopher Brian: Prophecy and Inspired Speech in Early Christianity and its Hellenistic Environment. 1995. *Volume II/75.*

Fornberg, Tord: see *Fridrichsen, Anton.*

Fossum, Jarl E.: The Name of God and the Angel of the Lord. 1985. *Volume 36.*

Foster, Paul: Community, Law and Mission in Matthew's Gospel. *Volume II/177.*

Fotopoulos, John: Food Offered to Idols in Roman Corinth. 2003. *Volume II/151.*

Frenschkowski, Marco: Offenbarung und Epiphanie. Volume 1 1995. *Volume II/79 –* Volume 2 1997. *Volume II/80.*

Frey, Jörg: Eugen Drewermann und die biblische Exegese. 1995. *Volume II/71.*
– Die johanneische Eschatologie. Volume I. 1997. *Volume 96.* – Volume II. 1998. *Volume 110.*
– Volume III. 2000. *Volume 117.*

Frey, Jörg and Udo Schnelle (Ed.): Kontexte des Johannesevangeliums. 2004. *Volume 175.*

– and *Jens Schröter* (Ed.): Deutungen des Todes Jesu im Neuen Testament. 2005. *Volume 181.*

Freyne, Sean: Galilee and Gospel. 2000. *Volume 125.*

Fridrichsen, Anton: Exegetical Writings. Edited by C.C. Caragounis and T. Fornberg. 1994. *Volume 76.*

Gäckle, Volker: Die Starken und die Schwachen in Korinth und in Rom. 2005. *Volume 200.*

Garlington, Don B.: 'The Obedience of Faith'. 1991. *Volume II/38.*
– Faith, Obedience, and Perseverance. 1994. *Volume 79.*

Garnet, Paul: Salvation and Atonement in the Qumran Scrolls. 1977. *Volume II/3.*

Gemünden, Petra von (Ed.): see *Weissenrieder, Annette.*

Gese, Michael: Das Vermächtnis des Apostels. 1997. *Volume II/99.*

Gheorghita, Radu: The Role of the Septuagint in Hebrews. 2003. *Volume II/160.*

Gräbe, Petrus J.: The Power of God in Paul's Letters. 2000. *Volume II/123.*

Gräßer, Erich: Der Alte Bund im Neuen. 1985. *Volume 35.*
– Forschungen zur Apostelgeschichte. 2001. *Volume 137.*

Green, Joel B.: The Death of Jesus. 1988. *Volume II/33.*

Gregory, Andrew: The Reception of Luke and Acts in the Period before Irenaeus. 2003. *Volume II/169.*

Grindheim, Sigurd: The Crux of Election. 2005. *Volume II/202.*

Gundry, Robert H.: The Old is Better. 2005. *Volume 178.*

Gundry Volf, Judith M.: Paul and Perseverance. 1990. *Volume II/37.*

Hafemann, Scott J.: Suffering and the Spirit. 1986. *Volume II/19.*
– Paul, Moses, and the History of Israel. 1995. *Volume 81.*

Hahn, Johannes (Ed.): Zerstörungen des Jerusalemer Tempels. 2002. *Volume 147.*

Hannah, Darrel D.: Michael and Christ. 1999. *Volume II/109.*

Hamid-Khani, Saeed: Relevation and Concealment of Christ. 2000. *Volume II/120.*

Harrison; James R.: Paul's Language of Grace in Its Graeco-Roman Context. 2003. *Volume II/172.*

Hartman, Lars: Text-Centered New Testament Studies. Ed. von D. Hellholm. 1997. *Volume 102.*

Hartog, Paul: Polycarp and the New Testament.
2001. *Volume II/134.*
Heckel, Theo K.: Der Innere Mensch. 1993.
Volume II/53.
– Vom Evangelium des Markus zum viergestal-
tigen Evangelium. 1999. *Volume 120.*
Heckel, Ulrich: Kraft in Schwachheit. 1993.
Volume II/56.
– Der Segen im Neuen Testament. 2002.
Volume 150.
– see *Feldmeier, Reinhard.*
– see *Hengel, Martin.*
Heiligenthal, Roman: Werke als Zeichen. 1983.
Volume II/9.
Hellholm, D.: see *Hartman, Lars.*
Hemer, Colin J.: The Book of Acts in the Setting
of Hellenistic History. 1989. *Volume 49.*
Hengel, Martin: Judentum und Hellenismus.
1969, ³1988. *Volume 10.*
– Die johanneische Frage. 1993. *Volume 67.*
– Judaica et Hellenistica.
Kleine Schriften I. 1996. *Volume 90.*
– Judaica, Hellenistica et Christiana.
Kleine Schriften II. 1999. *Volume 109.*
– Paulus und Jakobus.
Kleine Schriften III. 2002. *Volume 141.*
Hengel, Martin and *Ulrich Heckel* (Ed.): Paulus
und das antike Judentum. 1991. *Volume 58.*
Hengel, Martin and *Hermut Löhr* (Ed.):
Schriftauslegung im antiken Judentum und
im Urchristentum. 1994. *Volume 73.*
Hengel, Martin and *Anna Maria Schwemer:*
Paulus zwischen Damaskus und Antiochien.
1998. *Volume 108.*
– Der messianische Anspruch Jesu und die
Anfänge der Christologie. 2001. *Volume 138.*
Hengel, Martin and *Anna Maria Schwemer*
(Ed.): Königsherrschaft Gottes und himm-
lischer Kult. 1991. *Volume 55.*
– Die Septuaginta. 1994. *Volume 72.*
Hengel, Martin; Siegfried Mittmann and *Anna
Maria Schwemer* (Ed.): La Cité de Dieu /
Die Stadt Gottes. 2000. *Volume 129.*
Herrenbrück, Fritz: Jesus und die Zöllner. 1990.
Volume II/41.
Herzer, Jens: Paulus oder Petrus? 1998.
Volume 103.
Hoegen-Rohls, Christina: Der nachösterliche
Johannes. 1996. *Volume II/84.*
Hoffmann, Matthias Reinhard: The Destroyer
and the Lamb. 2005. *Volume II/203.*
Hofius, Otfried: Katapausis. 1970. *Volume 11.*
– Der Vorhang vor dem Thron Gottes. 1972.
Volume 14.
– Der Christushymnus Philipper 2,6-11. 1976,
²1991. *Volume 17.*

– Paulusstudien. 1989, ²1994. *Volume 51.*
– Neutestamentliche Studien. 2000. *Volume 132.*
– Paulusstudien II. 2002. *Volume 143.*
Hofius, Otfried and *Hans-Christian Kammler:*
Johannesstudien. 1996. *Volume 88.*
Holtz, Traugott: Geschichte und Theologie des
Urchristentums. 1991. *Volume 57.*
Hommel, Hildebrecht: Sebasmata. Volume 1 1983.
Volume 31 – Volume 2 1984. *Volume 32.*
Hvalvik, Reidar: The Struggle for Scripture and
Covenant. 1996. *Volume II/82.*
Jauhiainen, Marko: The Use of Zechariah in
Revelation. 2005. *Volume II/199.*
Johns, Loren L.: The Lamb Christology of the
Apocalypse of John. 2003. *Volume II/167.*
Joubert, Stephan: Paul as Benefactor. 2000.
Volume II/124.
Jungbauer, Harry: „Ehre Vater und Mutter“.
2002. *Volume II/146.*
Kähler, Christoph: Jesu Gleichnisse als Poesie
und Therapie. 1995. *Volume 78.*
Kamlah, Ehrhard: Die Form der katalogischen
Paränese im Neuen Testament. 1964. *Volume 7.*
Kammler, Hans-Christian: Christologie und
Eschatologie. 2000. *Volume 126.*
– Kreuz und Weisheit. 2003. *Volume 159.*
– see *Hofius, Otfried.*
Kelhoffer, James A.: The Diet of John the
Baptist. 2005. *Volume 176.*
– Miracle and Mission. 1999. *Volume II/112.*
Kieffer, René and *Jan Bergman (Ed.):* La Main de
Dieu / Die Hand Gottes. 1997. *Volume 94.*
Kim, Seyoon: The Origin of Paul's Gospel.
1981, ²1984. *Volume II/4.*
– Paul and the New Perspective. 2002.
Volume 140.
– "The 'Son of Man'" as the Son of God.
1983. *Volume 30.*
Klauck, Hans-Josef: Religion und Gesellschaft
im frühen Christentum. 2003. *Volume 152.*
Klein, Hans: see *Dunn, James D.G..*
Kleinknecht, Karl Th.: Der leidende Gerechtfer-
tigte. 1984, ²1988. *Volume II/13.*
Klinghardt, Matthias: Gesetz und Volk Gottes.
1988. *Volume II/32.*
Koch, Michael: Drachenkampf und Sonnenfrau.
2004. *Volume II/184.*
Koch, Stefan: Rechtliche Regelung von
Konflikten im frühen Christentum. 2004.
Volume II/174.
Köhler, Wolf-Dietrich: Rezeption des Matthäus-
evangeliums in der Zeit vor Irenäus. 1987.
Volume II/24.
Köhn, Andreas: Der Neutestamentler Ernst
Lohmeyer. 2004. *Volume II/180.*

Kooten, George H. van: Cosmic Christology in Paul and the Pauline School. 2003. *Volume II/171.*

Korn, Manfred: Die Geschichte Jesu in veränderter Zeit. 1993. *Volume II/51.*

Koskenniemi, Erkki: Apollonios von Tyana in der neutestamentlichen Exegese. 1994. *Volume II/61.*

Kraus, Thomas J.: Sprache, Stil und historischer Ort des zweiten Petrusbriefes. 2001. *Volume II/136.*

Kraus, Wolfgang: Das Volk Gottes. 1996. *Volume 85.*

– and *Karl-Wilhelm Niebuhr* (Ed.): Frühjudentum und Neues Testament im Horizont Biblischer Theologie. 2003. *Volume 162.*

– see *Walter, Nikolaus.*

Kreplin, Matthias: Das Selbstverständnis Jesu. 2001. *Volume II/141.*

Kuhn, Karl G.: Achtzehngebet und Vaterunser und der Reim. 1950. *Volume 1.*

Kvalbein, Hans: see *Ådna, Jostein.*

Kwon, Yon-Gyong: Eschatology in Galatians. 2004. *Volume II/183.*

Laansma, Jon: I Will Give You Rest. 1997. *Volume II/98.*

Labahn, Michael: Offenbarung in Zeichen und Wort. 2000. *Volume II/117.*

Lambers-Petry, Doris: see *Tomson, Peter J.*

Lange, Armin: see *Ego, Beate.*

Lampe, Peter: Die stadtrömischen Christen in den ersten beiden Jahrhunderten. 1987, ²1989. *Volume II/18.*

Landmesser, Christof: Wahrheit als Grundbegriff neutestamentlicher Wissenschaft. 1999. *Volume 113.*

– Jüngerberufung und Zuwendung zu Gott. 2000. *Volume 133.*

Lau, Andrew: Manifest in Flesh. 1996. *Volume II/86.*

Lawrence, Louise: An Ethnography of the Gospel of Matthew. 2003. *Volume II/165.*

Lee, Aquila H.I.: From Messiah to Preexistent Son. 2005. *Volume II/192.*

Lee, Pilchan: The New Jerusalem in the Book of Relevation. 2000. *Volume II/129.*

Lichtenberger, Hermann: see *Avemarie, Friedrich.*

Lichtenberger, Hermann: Das Ich Adams und das Ich der Menschheit. 2004. *Volume 164.*

Lierman, John: The New Testament Moses. 2004. *Volume II/173.*

Lieu, Samuel N.C.: Manichaeism in the Later Roman Empire and Medieval China. ²1992. *Volume 63.*

Lindgård, Fredrik: Paul's Line of Thought in 2 Corinthians 4:16-5:10. 2004. *Volume II/189.*

Loader, William R.G.: Jesus' Attitude Towards the Law. 1997. *Volume II/97.*

Löhr, Gebhard: Verherrlichung Gottes durch Philosophie. 1997. *Volume 97.*

Löhr, Hermut: Studien zum frühchristlichen und frühjüdischen Gebet. 2003. *Volume 160.*

– see *Hengel, Martin.*

Löhr, Winrich Alfried: Basilides und seine Schule. 1995. *Volume 83.*

Luomanen, Petri: Entering the Kingdom of Heaven. 1998. *Volume II/101.*

Luz, Ulrich: see *Dunn, James D.G.*

Mackay, Ian D.: John's Raltionship with Mark. 2004. *Volume II/182.*

Maier, Gerhard: Mensch und freier Wille. 1971. *Volume 12.*

– Die Johannesoffenbarung und die Kirche. 1981. *Volume 25.*

Markschies, Christoph: Valentinus Gnosticus? 1992. *Volume 65.*

Marshall, Peter: Enmity in Corinth: Social Conventions in Paul's Relations with the Corinthians. 1987. *Volume II/23.*

Mayer, Annemarie: Sprache der Einheit im Epheserbrief und in der Ökumene. 2002. *Volume II/150.*

Mayordomo, Moisés: Argumentiert Paulus logisch? 2005. *Volume 188.*

McDonough, Sean M.: YHWH at Patmos: Rev. 1:4 in its Hellenistic and Early Jewish Setting. 1999. *Volume II/107.*

McGlynn, Moyna: Divine Judgement and Divine Benevolence in the Book of Wisdom. 2001. *Volume II/139.*

Meade, David G.: Pseudonymity and Canon. 1986. *Volume 39.*

Meadors, Edward P.: Jesus the Messianic Herald of Salvation. 1995. *Volume II/72.*

Meißner, Stefan: Die Heimholung des Ketzers. 1996. *Volume II/87.*

Mell, Ulrich: Die „anderen" Winzer. 1994. *Volume 77.*

Mengel, Berthold: Studien zum Philipperbrief. 1982. *Volume II/8.*

Merkel, Helmut: Die Widersprüche zwischen den Evangelien. 1971. *Volume 13.*

– see *Ego, Beate.*

Merklein, Helmut: Studien zu Jesus und Paulus. Volume 1 1987. *Volume 43.* – Volume 2 1998. *Volume 105.*

Metzdorf, Christina: Die Tempelaktion Jesu. 2003. *Volume II/168.*

Metzler, Karin: Der griechische Begriff des Verzeihens. 1991. *Volume II/44.*

Metzner, Rainer: Die Rezeption des Matthäus-
evangeliums im 1. Petrusbrief. 1995.
Volume II/74.
– Das Verständnis der Sünde im Johannesevan-
gelium. 2000. *Volume 122.*
Mihoc, Vasile: see *Dunn, James D.G..*
Mineshige, Kiyoshi: Besitzverzicht und
Almosen bei Lukas. 2003. *Volume II/163.*
Mittmann, Siegfried: see *Hengel, Martin.*
Mittmann-Richert, Ulrike: Magnifikat und
Benediktus. *1996. Volume II/90.*
Mournet, Terence C.: Oral Tradition and
Literary Dependency. 2005. *Volume II/195.*
Mußner, Franz: Jesus von Nazareth im Umfeld
Israels und der Urkirche. Ed. von M.
Theobald. 1998. *Volume 111.*
Niebuhr, Karl-Wilhelm: Gesetz und Paränese.
1987. *Volume II/28.*
– Heidenapostel aus Israel. 1992. *Volume 62.*
– see *Deines, Roland*
– see *Dimitrov, Ivan Z.*
– see *Kraus, Wolfgang*
Nielsen, Anders E.: "Until it is Fullfilled". 2000.
Volume II/126.
Nissen, Andreas: Gott und der Nächste im
antiken Judentum. 1974. *Volume 15.*
Noack, Christian: Gottesbewußtsein. 2000.
Volume II/116.
Noormann, Rolf: Irenäus als Paulusinterpret.
1994. *Volume II/66.*
Novakovic, Lidija: Messiah, the Healer of the
Sick. 2003. *Volume II/170.*
Obermann, Andreas: Die christologische
Erfüllung der Schrift im Johannesevangeli-
um. 1996. *Volume II/83.*
Öhler, Markus: Barnabas. 2003. *Volume 156.*
Okure, Teresa: The Johannine Approach to
Mission. 1988. *Volume II/31.*
Onuki, Takashi: Heil und Erlösung. 2004.
Volume 165.
Oropeza, B. J.: Paul and Apostasy. 2000.
Volume II/115.
Ostmeyer, Karl-Heinrich: Taufe und Typos.
2000. *Volume II/118.*
Paulsen, Henning: Studien zur Literatur und
Geschichte des frühen Christentums. Ed. von
Ute E. Eisen. 1997. *Volume 99.*
Pao, David W.: Acts and the Isaianic New
Exodus. 2000. *Volume II/130.*
Park, Eung Chun: The Mission Discourse in
Matthew's Interpretation. 1995.
Volume II/81.
Park, Joseph S.: Conceptions of Afterlife in
Jewish Insriptions. 2000. *Volume II/121.*
Pate, C. Marvin: The Reverse of the Curse.
2000. *Volume II/114.*

Peres, Imre: Griechische Grabinschriften und
neutestamentliche Eschatologie. 2003.
Volume 157.
Philip, Finny: The Originis of Pauline
Pneumatology. *Volume II/194.*
Philonenko, Marc (Ed.): Le Trône de Dieu.
1993. *Volume 69.*
Pilhofer, Peter: Presbyteron Kreitton. 1990.
Volume II/39.
– Philippi. Volume 1 1995. *Volume 87.* –
Volume 2 2000. *Volume 119.*
– Die frühen Christen und ihre Welt. 2002.
Volume 145.
– see *Ego, Beate.*
Pitre, Brant: Jesus, the Tribulation, and the End
of the Exile. 2005. *Volume II/204.*
Plümacher, Eckhard: Geschichte und Geschich-
ten. Aufsätze zur Apostelgeschichte und zu
den Johannesakten. Herausgegeben von Jens
Schröter und Ralph Brucker. 2004.
Volume 170.
Pöhlmann, Wolfgang: Der Verlorene Sohn und
das Haus. 1993. *Volume 68.*
Pokorný, Petr and *Josef B. Souček:* Bibelausle-
gung als Theologie. 1997. *Volume 100.*
Pokorný, Petr and *Jan Roskovec* (Ed.):
Philosophical Hermeneutics and Biblical
Exegesis. 2002. *Volume 153.*
Popkes, Enno Edzard: Die Theologie der Liebe
Gottes in den johanneischen Schriften. 2005.
Volume II/197.
Porter, Stanley E.: The Paul of Acts. 1999.
Volume 115.
Prieur, Alexander: Die Verkündigung der
Gottesherrschaft. 1996. *Volume II/89.*
Probst, Hermann: Paulus und der Brief. 1991.
Volume II/45.
Räisänen, Heikki: Paul and the Law. 1983,
²1987. *Volume 29.*
Rehkopf, Friedrich: Die lukanische Sonderquel-
le. 1959. *Volume 5.*
Rein, Matthias: Die Heilung des Blindgeborenen
(Joh 9). 1995. *Volume II/73.*
Reinmuth, Eckart: Pseudo-Philo und Lukas.
1994. *Volume 74.*
Reiser, Marius: Syntax und Stil des Markus-
evangeliums. 1984. *Volume II/11.*
Rhodes, James N.: The Epistle of Barnabas
and the Deuteronomic Tradition. 2004.
Volume II/188.
Richards, E. Randolph: The Secretary in the
Letters of Paul. 1991. *Volume II/42.*
Riesner, Rainer: Jesus als Lehrer. 1981, ³1988.
Volume II/7.
– Die Frühzeit des Apostels Paulus. 1994.
Volume 71.

Theobald, Michael: Studien zum Römerbrief. 2001. *Volume 136.*

Theobald, Michael: see *Mußner, Franz.*

Thornton, Claus-Jürgen: Der Zeuge des Zeugen. 1991. *Volume 56.*

Thüsing, Wilhelm: Studien zur neutestamentlichen Theologie. Ed. von Thomas Söding. 1995. *Volume 82.*

Thurén, Lauri: Derhetorizing Paul. 2000. *Volume 124.*

Tolmie, D. Francois: Persuading the Galatians. 2005. *Volume II/190.*

Tomson, Peter J. and *Doris Lambers-Petry* (Ed.): The Image of the Judaeo-Christians in Ancient Jewish and Christian Literature. 2003. *Volume 158.*

Trebilco, Paul: The Early Christians in Ephesus from Paul to Ignatius. 2004. *Volume 166.*

Treloar, Geoffrey R.: Lightfoot the Historian. 1998. *Volume II/103.*

Tsuji, Manabu: Glaube zwischen Vollkommenheit und Verweltlichung. 1997. *Volume II/93*

Twelftree, Graham H.: Jesus the Exorcist. 1993. *Volume II/54.*

Urban, Christina: Das Menschenbild nach dem Johannesevangelium. 2001. *Volume II/137.*

Visotzky, Burton L.: Fathers of the World. 1995. *Volume 80.*

Vollenweider, Samuel: Horizonte neutestamentlicher Christologie. 2002. *Volume 144.*

Vos, Johan S.: Die Kunst der Argumentation bei Paulus. 2002. *Volume 149.*

Wagener, Ulrike: Die Ordnung des „Hauses Gottes". 1994. *Volume II/65.*

Wahlen, Clinton: Jesus and the Impurity of Spirits in the Synoptic Gospels. 2004. *Volume II/185.*

Walker, Donald D.: Paul's Offer of Leniency (2 Cor 10:1). 2002. *Volume II/152.*

Walter, Nikolaus: Praeparatio Evangelica. Ed. von Wolfgang Kraus und Florian Wilk. 1997. *Volume 98.*

Wander, Bernd: Gottesfürchtige und Sympathisanten. 1998. *Volume 104.*

Watts, Rikki: Isaiah's New Exodus and Mark. 1997. *Volume II/88.*

Wedderburn, A.J.M.: Baptism and Resurrection. 1987. *Volume 44.*

Wegner, Uwe: Der Hauptmann von Kafarnaum. 1985. *Volume II/14.*

Weissenrieder, Annette: Images of Illness in the Gospel of Luke. 2003. *Volume II/164.*

–, Friederike Wendt and *Petra von Gemünden* (Ed.): Picturing the New Testament. 2005. *Volume II/193.*

Welck, Christian: Erzählte ‚Zeichen'. 1994. *Volume II/69.*

Wendt, Friederike (Ed.): see *Weissenrieder, Annette.*

Wiarda, Timothy: Peter in the Gospels. 2000. *Volume II/127.*

Wifstrand, Albert: Epochs and Styles. 2005. *Band 179.*

Wilk, Florian: see *Walter, Nikolaus.*

Williams, Catrin H.: I am He. 2000. *Volume II/113*

Wilson, Walter T.: Love without Pretense. 1991. *Volume II/46.*

Wischmeyer, Oda: Von Ben Sira zu Paulus. 2004. *Volume 173.*

Wisdom, Jeffrey: Blessing for the Nations and the Curse of the Law. 2001. *Volume II/133.*

Wold, Benjamin G.: Women, Men, and Angels. 2005. *Volume II/201.*

Wright, Archie T.: The Origin of Evil Spirits. 2005. *Volume II/198.*

Wucherpfennig, Ansgar: Heracleon Philologus. 2002. *Volume 142.*

Yeung, Maureen: Faith in Jesus and Paul. 2002. *Volume II/147.*

Zimmermann, Alfred E.: Die urchristlichen Lehrer. ²1988. *Volume II/12.*

Zimmermann, Johannes: Messianische Texte aus Qumran. 1998. *Volume II/104.*

Zimmermann, Ruben: Christologie der Bilder im Johannesevangelium. 2004. *Volume 171.*

  – Geschlechtermetaphorik und Gottesverhältnis. 2001. *Volume II/122.*

Zumstein, Jean: see *Dettwiler, Andreas*

Zwiep, Arie W.: Judas and the Choice of Matthias. 2004. *Volume II/187.*

For a complete catalogue please write to the publisher
Mohr Siebeck • P.O. Box 2030 • D–72010 Tübingen/Germany
Up-to-date information on the internet at www.mohr.de

Rissi, Mathias: Die Theologie des Hebräerbriefs. 1987. *Volume 41.*

Roskovec, Jan: see *Pokorný, Petr.*

Röhser, Günter: Metaphorik und Personifikation der Sünde. 1987. *Volume II/25.*

Rose, Christian: Die Wolke der Zeugen. 1994. *Volume II/60.*

Rothschild, Clare K.: Baptist Traditions and Q. 2005. *Volume 190.*

–: Luke Acts and the Rhetoric of History. 2004. *Volume II/175.*

Rüegger, Hans-Ulrich: Verstehen, was Markus erzählt. 2002. *Volume II/155.*

Rüger, Hans Peter: Die Weisheitsschrift aus der Kairoer Geniza. 1991. *Volume 53.*

Sänger, Dieter: Antikes Judentum und die Mysterien. 1980. *Volume II/5.*

– Die Verkündigung des Gekreuzigten und Israel. 1994. *Volume 75.*

– see *Burchard, Christoph*

Salier, Willis Hedley: The Rhetorical Impact of the Sēmeia in the Gospel of John. 2004. *Volume II/186.*

Salzmann, Jorg Christian: Lehren und Ermahnen. 1994. *Volume II/59.*

Sandnes, Karl Olav: Paul – One of the Prophets? 1991. *Volume II/43.*

Sato, Migaku: Q und Prophetie. 1988. *Volume II/29.*

Schäfer, Ruth: Paulus bis zum Apostelkonzil. 2004. *Volume II/179.*

Schaper, Joachim: Eschatology in the Greek Psalter. 1995. *Volume II/76.*

Schimanowski, Gottfried: Die himmlische Liturgie in der Apokalypse des Johannes. 2002. *Volume II/154.*

– Weisheit und Messias. 1985. *Volume II/17.*

Schlichting, Günter: Ein jüdisches Leben Jesu. 1982. *Volume 24.*

Schnabel, Eckhard J.: Law and Wisdom from Ben Sira to Paul. 1985. *Volume II/16.*

Schnelle, Udo: see *Frey, Jörg.*

Schröter, Jens: see *Frey, Jörg.*

Schutter, William L.: Hermeneutic and Composition in I Peter. 1989. *Volume II/30.*

Schwartz, Daniel R.: Studies in the Jewish Background of Christianity. 1992. *Volume 60.*

Schwemer, Anna Maria: see *Hengel, Martin*

Scott, James M.: Adoption as Sons of God. 1992. *Volume II/48.*

– Paul and the Nations. 1995. *Volume 84.*

Shum, Shiu-Lun: Paul's Use of Isaiah in Romans. 2002. *Volume II/156.*

Siegert, Folker: Drei hellenistisch-jüdische Predigten. Teil I 1980. *Volume 20* – Teil II 1992. *Volume 61.*

– Nag-Hammadi-Register. 1982. *Volume 26.*

– Argumentation bei Paulus. 1985. *Volume 34.*

– Philon von Alexandrien. 1988. *Volume 46.*

Simon, Marcel: Le christianisme antique et son contexte religieux I/II. 1981. *Volume 23.*

Snodgrass, Klyne: The Parable of the Wicked Tenants. 1983. *Volume 27.*

Söding, Thomas: Das Wort vom Kreuz. 1997. *Volume 93.*

– see *Thüsing, Wilhelm.*

Sommer, Urs: Die Passionsgeschichte des Markusevangeliums. 1993. *Volume II/58.*

Souček, Josef B.: see *Pokorný, Petr.*

Spangenberg, Volker: Herrlichkeit des Neuen Bundes. 1993. *Volume II/55.*

Spanje, T.E. van: Inconsistency in Paul? 1999. *Volume II/110.*

Speyer, Wolfgang: Frühes Christentum im antiken Strahlungsfeld. Volume I: 1989. *Volume 50.*

– Volume II: 1999. *Volume 116.*

Stadelmann, Helge: Ben Sira als Schriftgelehrter. 1980. *Volume II/6.*

Stenschke, Christoph W.: Luke's Portrait of Gentiles Prior to Their Coming to Faith. *Volume II/108.*

Sterck-Degueldre, Jean-Pierre: Eine Frau namens Lydia. 2004. *Volume II/176.*

Stettler, Christian: Der Kolosserhymnus. 2000. *Volume II/131.*

Stettler, Hanna: Die Christologie der Pastoralbriefe. 1998. *Volume II/105.*

Stökl Ben Ezra, Daniel: The Impact of Yom Kippur on Early Christianity. 2003. *Volume 163.*

Strobel, August: Die Stunde der Wahrheit. 1980. *Volume 21.*

Stroumsa, Guy G.: Barbarian Philosophy. 1999. *Volume 112.*

Stuckenbruck, Loren T.: Angel Veneration and Christology. 1995. *Volume II/70.*

Stuhlmacher, Peter (Ed.): Das Evangelium und die Evangelien. 1983. *Volume 28.*

– Biblische Theologie und Evangelium. 2002. *Volume 146.*

Sung, Chong-Hyon: Vergebung der Sünden. 1993. *Volume II/57.*

Tajra, Harry W.: The Trial of St. Paul. 1989. *Volume II/35.*

– The Martyrdom of St.Paul. 1994. *Volume II/67.*

Theißen, Gerd: Studien zur Soziologie des Urchristentums. 1979, ³1989. *Volume 19.*